By the same author

Under the pen name Robert Black:

Workers Councils in the Hungarian Revolution, 1966
With L. Trotsky and B. Pearce, *A Moscow Trials Anthology*, 1967
With J. Crawford, *Conflicts in the Bolshevik Party in 1917,* 1967
The Ironies of Isaac Deutscher, 1967
Stalinism in Britain, 1970
The Fight for Bangladesh, 1971
Fascism in Germany 1975

Under his own name:

The Seeds of Evil, 1995
Through Frosted Glass, 2018

The Socialism of Fools

The Rise and Fall of Comrade Corbyn

Part II

By Robin Blick

Published by New Generation Publishing in 2019

Copyright © Robin Blick 2019

First Edition

The author asserts the moral right under the Copyright, Designs and Patents Act 1988 to be identified as the author of this work.

All Rights reserved. No part of this publication may be reproduced, stored in a retrieval system or transmitted, in any form or by any means without the prior consent of the author, nor be otherwise circulated in any form of binding or cover other than that which it is published and without a similar condition being imposed on the subsequent purchaser.

ISBN:
Paperback 978-1-78955-690-2
Hardback 978-1-78955-691-9

www.newgeneration-publishing.com

New Generation Publishing

Contents

21 Orient 1
22 You Must Do It 23
23 Holy Hitmen 35
24 Normal 56
25 Spiked 66
26 Dump It! 76
27 Industry 102
28 Chicken 122
29 Lunacy 145
30 Exodus 150
Afterword 155
Appendices 207
A Are Zionists Nazis? 207
B Traison Des Clercs Encores 221
C Swedish Syndrome 232
D Deutschland Sagt Genug 242
E Spoils of War 255
F 9 or 19? 278
G Under the Ayatollahs 279
H Return of the Caliphate? 301
I A Voice in the Desert 304
J Back Channel to Allah? 307
K Volunteers for Genocide? 312
L Jihad 314
M Anything You Can Do… 326
N Goodbye to All That 327

O When Did You Last Beat Your Wife? 329

P Dutch Cowardice 331

Q Sweated Labour 335

R Dialogue? 337

S For the Attention of Mr K. Livingstone.....................................339

T Labour's Black-Shirts: Jeremy and the Jew-Baiters 343

U The Corbynistas Strike Back 416

V Nightmare in Tunisia (with apologies to Dizzy Gillespie) 419

W Stalin's Final Solution of the Zionist Question........................423

X Money for Old Rope 433

Y Who Dunnit?..439

Z Orwell on the Corbynistas (mutatis mutandis).........................440

21 Orient

Integral to Marx's theory of historical materialism, first codified in his *Communist Manifesto* of 1848, was that the rise and then global dominance of capitalism was the unavoidable and indispensable pre-condition for its last stage, the creation of a classless and stateless society. As he put it a later work, 'new relations of production never replace old ones before the materials conditions for their existence have matured within the framework of the of the old society.' It was consequently the task of the bourgeoisie, not the working class, to create a truly modern world, by making 'barbarian and semi-barbarian countries dependent on the civilised ones, nations of peasants on nations of bourgeois, the East on the West.' This schema was embraced by all those regarding themselves as 'orthodox' Marxists, but rejected by non-Marxist Russian populists, who saw the seeds of an imminent socialist order in the common land ownership of the pre-capitalist village 'mir'. Prior to the revolution of 1917, Lenin's Bolsheviks, like nearly all other Marxists, insisted that in accordance Marx's schema, a quasi-Asiatic Russia had to become properly capitalist, that is to say, industrialised and democratic, before it could become communist, to become a country where, as the *Manifesto* has it, the proletariat constituted the 'overwhelming majority' of the population not, as in the Russia of 1917, and even more so in the countries of the Orient, a tiny minority surrounded by a massive peasant majority.

This was and remained the policy of the much-abused and then persecuted and finally outlawed Mensheviks both before and after the Bolsheviks seized power in November 1917. The Bolshevik coup of that month was predicated on what proved to be the false assumption that its example would trigger similar revolutions in the most advanced capitalist states, whose fraternal communist governments would then provide the economic and technical aid Russia needed to overcome its chronic backwardness. When these hopes faded, a disillusioned Lenin turned his back on what he called 'the counter-revolutionary West' and faced towards what he now saw as 'the revolutionary East', an orientation that like his domestic regime, had to await its consummation in the era of Stalin, with peasant-based revolutions in China, North Korea and Indo-China. And surely they are facts of some significance to the matters under review that these regimes are the ones that have endured, while those installed by Stalin at end of the Second World War in eastern and central Europe that were swept away by popular revolts in 1989 were replaced by governments that took the path of liberal democracy, and that Russia, after a brief liberal interlude, began under Putin a regression to Pan Slavism and Tartar methods of rule.

None of this would have surprised Marx because, like all western socialists of his day, he believed that the threat to civilisation, and therefore for socialism, came from the East and, unlike his epigones of today, made no bones about saying so: 'Europe has one of two choices, either an Asiatic barbarism led by the Muscovites will descend upon us like an avalanche, or it must restore Poland, and in this way, separate itself from Asia.' Since their own survival, let alone continued progress, was at stake, Germany and France had to be prepared to 'wage the war of the West against the East, of civilisation against barbarism', to 'fight the barbarian hordes [sic]'. And while the French and the Germans held the line against Russian despotism, the task of the English lay further afield, uprooting the ancient

1

foundations of its parent Oriental version which, for all its 'idyllic village communities, inoffensive though they may appear', had 'quietly witnessed' the 'perpetuation of unspeakable cruelties'. So Marx posed the question, one that as it pertains to the world of Islam, retains all its force today: 'Can mankind fulfil its destiny without a fundamental revolution in the social state of Asia?' If the answer was, as Marx believed, no, then such a revolution would have to be imposed from the outside, by what the Left today left regards as imperialism. As the leading colonial power, England had a special responsibility, namely, 'to fulfil a double mission in India: one destructive the other regenerating - the annihilation of old Asiatic society and the laying the material foundations of Western society in Asia.'

Yes, this is Marx, not Clive of India. And Marx and his life-long comrade and co-thinker Engels were very far from ploughing a lonely imperialist furrow. The organisation which they helped to found in 1864, the International Workingmen's Association (later known as the First International) approved a resolution drafted by Marx denouncing the oppression of Poland by Russia, 'the dark Asiatic power in the background as a last resource against the rising tide of working-class ascendency'. As far as Marx was concerned, culturally, Russia was not in any sense a European nation but the western outpost of the Oriental despotism whose creature it was, implanted by the Mongol hordes of Genghis Khan and his successors, and from which its modes of thought and action it had thus far never been able to tear itself free. Indeed, following his expulsion of the Tartars from European Russia, Ivan the Fourth, the first 'Tsar of all the Russias', with good reason called the Terrible, in 1564 partially re-Orientalised his kingdom by seizing vast tracks of land from the nobility, many of whom he suspected of treasonous plottings. Ivan's enormously expanded crown estates, the *Oprichnina*, and the ensuring purge of the land's previous owners, the Boyars, created a society partially resembling in its essential features those of the Orient...a despotic monarchy, the emasculation if not total elimination of a propertied ruling class, a vast 'public sector', a captive labour force, and an autocratic state that provided Peter the Great in the early 18th century with the power to implement, like Stalin and the homelands of Islam, with imported western technology and expertise, his grandiose but only partially successful programme of modernisation. Just as Ivan was Stalin's favourite tsar, so Peter, (with his thirteen torture chambers) was Lenin's who, without any sense of embarrassment, avowed that he would emulate and even surpass Russia's most illustrious Tsar in 'not shrinking from adopting dictatorial methods', 'not hesitat[ing] to use barbarous methods in fighting barbarism.' With Ivan and his black-coated *Oprichniki,* forerunner of the Soviet secret police, and Peter, who built his new capital with an army of conscripted serfs, as Bolshevik exemplars, it is no mystery why, although its heartlands were located in Europe, Marx described Russia as 'the dark Asiatic power' and, for as long as it remained such, insisted that the watchword of the west had to remain, 'death to the Mongol rule over modern society'. And let us again be clear. By 'modern society' Marx had in mind exclusively European bourgeois society. How ironic then that with the advent and rise to total power of Bolshevism, the movement which, under the Asiatic despotism of Stalin, served as the instrument for consummating Russia's orientalist regression, became for leftists throughout the western world the model of a revolutionary party.

Starting with Lenin's advocacy, after the failure of the Russian Revolution to evoke similar overturns in the capitalist heartlands, of reliance on a 'revolutionary East' to defeat a 'counter-revolutionary West', the strategy for human progress advanced by Marx and Engels underwent a progressive revision, one anticipated even before the Bolshevik seizure of power in November 1917. Addressing the sixth party congress in the August of that year, Stalin tentatively suggested that 'the possibility is not excluded that Russia will lay the road to socialism…We must discard the antiquated idea [that of Marx and Engels] that only Europe can show us the way.' Thus, was born Bolshevism's 'Eastern Orientation'. In little more than a decade, Russia would regress from what Lenin described after the overthrow of Tsarist regime in March in 1917 as the 'freest country in the world' to under his rule, a one-party state and then one-leader party to under Stalin's, a truly Oriental despotism.

Bolshevik global strategy underwent a no less radical and related transformation. Early in 1923, with hopes fast fading of communist revolution in the west, in one of his last published writings, Lenin not only gave Stalin's cautious proposition of 1917 his endorsement, arguing, *contra* Marx, that Russia possessed 'all that was necessary and sufficient' to 'build a complete[sic] socialist society'. He now went much further: 'In the last analysis, the outcome of the struggle will be determined by the fact Russia, India, China etc., account for the overwhelming population of the globe', an anticipation of Mao's 'The East wind will prevail over the West wind'. The inversion of Marx's schema was now total. The route to global communism lay through the villages, farms and paddy fields of the pre-capitalist East, via what later became known as the Third World, not the First World cities and factories of the capitalist West. (The radical nature and consequences of Lenin's departures from the 'Marxism of Marx' are the subject of my *Seeds of Evil*)

Already by 1920, the first steps had been taken in pursuance of this new strategy, with the convening in the September of that year in Baku, the capital of Muslim Azerbaijan, of a 'Congress of Toilers of the East' (One delegate actually used the phrase 'Eastern orientation') Gathered there were its organisers, leaders of the recently formed and Soviet-dominated Communist International, together with at least nominal communists from the Soviet east and nationalists from the Muslim world, in total around 1,800. In his opening address, Comintern President Grigori Zinoviev set the tone when, anticipating Lenin, he made the highly un-Marxist assertion that the 'peoples of the East', comprising as they did 'the majority of the peoples of the world', were 'alone [sic] in a position finally to settle the dispute between labour and capital' predicting that the 'real [sic] revolution will flare up when we are joined by the 800 million people who live in Asia', even though no such 'dispute' as yet existed in the East save in non-Muslim China, where an embryonic workers movement was stirring in its major cities. And yet China was represented by only one delegate at the Congress. In calling for a 'holy war [sic] against the British and French capitalists', Zinoviev provided a clue has to whom would be the real object of the proposed *Jihad*; not a non-existent oriental native bourgeoisie, but capitalist France and Britain, who had been lending military support to the Bolshevik's enemies in the Russian civil war. Already, Russian state interests were visibly impacting on the strategy and policies of the newly-formed International.

With the congress overwhelmingly dominated by Muslim delegations, Zinoviev's 'holy war' against the West required that Islam be treated with kid gloves, as one speaker explained:

> Everyone knows that the East is utterly different from the West, that its ideas are different - and so a rigid application of the ideas of communism will meet with

resistance there. Accordingly, if we want the four hundred million in the Muslim world to join the Soviet power, we need to apply a special yardstick in their case...Muslims will not abandon the Soviet power, but this is on condition that the peculiarities [sic] of the Eastern peoples be recognised.'

One of these 'peculiarities' was, and remains, Islam's teachings on the status and, consequently, treatment of women. A Turkish delegate, one of only two women to address the congress, put her male communist delegates and today's *dhimmi* feminists, with Lindsey German's 'shibboleths', Laurie Penny's 'horror stories' and Professor Laura Briggs' 'personhood', to shame. Spurning Bolshevik multiculturalism and sensitivity training, she defiantly insisted that

> ...if the women who form half of every community are opposed to the men and do not have the same rights as they have, it is obviously impossible for society to progress: the backwardness of Eastern societies is irrefutable proof of this...The women communists of the East have an even harder battle [than the men] because, in addition [to the fight against the imperialists] they have to fight against the despotism [sic] of their menfolk. If you, men of the East, now as in the past, continue to be indifferent to the fate of women, you can be sure that our country will perish.

She then listed a series of demands that showed no respect whatsoever for Muslim 'peculiarities' and which, in each case, are as remote from realisation in the Islamic world today as they were when issued in Baku a century ago, whereas, in Lenin's 'counter-revolutionary West', they are the norm:

1: Complete equality of rights;
2. Equal access with men to education and vocational training;
3: Abolition of polygamy. Equal rights with men in in marriage;
4: Equal access with men to employment and administrative institutions.

To the end of his life, Trotsky, the thoroughly westernised, indeed cosmopolitan, assimilated Jewish internationalist *par excellence*, as an 'orthodox' Marxist, remained convinced that Russia, let alone the Orient, was 'too backward and uncivilised [sic] a country to be able to build a communist society by itself'. And he said this, not in 1917, but in 1938, after Stalin's first Two Five Year Plans had begun the transformation of the Soviet Union, at horrendous human cost, into an industrialised country, one equipped with imported western technology, but nevertheless resembling in all its essentials an Oriental despotism of the classic type. The final judgement as to who was right in this matter was made in 1991 with the ignominious implosion of the state created by Lenin and enslaved by Stalin. (China's post-Mao adoption of capitalism was a tacit admission of a comparable failure.)

With Stalin's elimination by 1927 of the internationalist Left Opposition headed by four Jews, Trotsky, Radek, Zinoviev and Kamenev (all destined to die at Stalin's hand, together with the rest of Lenin's closest comrades bar none) the Lenin-Stalin proposition became official party policy, known as 'socialism in one country'. One of the more exotic fruits of this 'Eastern Orientation' was a statement issued in 1925 in the name of the Surrealist movement led by André Breton. Intended as a first tentative approach to the French Communist Party, it embraced with the customary zeal of converts and an infantile *épater la bourgeoisie* the new orthodoxy on the iniquities of the West: 'Wherever Western civilisation is dominant, all human contact has disappeared except contact from which money can be made. It is the turn of the Mongols [sic] to bivouac in our squares. We should never for a moment worry that this violence should take us by surprise or get out of hand. As far we are concerned, it could never be enough'.

Now I arrive at my destination. Support for a war to the death by the East against the West, waged, not it is true by 'Mongols'; but a no less oriental Islam, has now become, following in the footsteps of the path charted by Lenin and pioneered by Stalin and Mao, the orthodoxy by which those claiming to be of the genuine left are to be judged. We have reached the point today when the Leninist epigones who dominate the far left and exert a substantial influence on the leadership of the Labour Party and a number of trade unions quite openly support the 'revolutionary East' against the 'counter-revolutionary West' whether it be Putin's Russia or Jihadi Islam, a support in its most extreme manifestations not shrinking even from defending the use of indiscriminate terror against civilian targets such as 9/11 and (Jewish) Israelis, and opposing protests against the Russian carpet bombing of civilian targets in Syria. Bearing in mind that this left is composed partly of tendencies, cliques and individuals who have either belonged to or have been closely associated with the residual fragments of the movement founded by Leon Trotsky in 1938, the Fourth International, it is ironic that their mentor should have been no more beguiled by the lure of the East than were Marx and Engels in their day. His comments on Russian history are replete with references to its 'Asiatic barbarism', 'Asiatic patriarchy' (not sis white) and 'Asiatic cruelty', each being aspects of an inherited 'Asiatic culture which has contrived to remain static despite continual jolts from war and mutiny', a society trapped in a cycle of 'hopeless rotations', as the Arab world still is today.

Yet despite its stagnation, and leaving aside the Moorish conquest of Spain in the name of Islam, for centuries Asia's Mongol-Turkic grip extended deep into what is culturally as well as geographically Europe, beyond Russia and reaching as far west as Poland, the Baltic states and the Balkans, Romania and Hungary, as far south as Greece and Cyprus (where it remains), and as far north as Finland and the Laplanders of Sweden and Norway. As an enduring relic of this conquest, the Sami, Hungarian, Finnish and Estonian languages are not related to the Indo-European family but to the Ugric, originating from far east of the Urals. And how many Russians know that Kremlin is the Tartar word for fortress?

Even Russia's two revolutions in 1917 failed to shake off what Trotsky revealing described as its 'Tartar Yoke', within a little more than decade succumbing to the rule of what one of Stalin's Bolshevik victims, Bukharin, called 'an Asian despot, a tyrant,' a 'Genghis Khan'. Another, Comintern chief Grigory Zinoviev, having combined with Stalin to oust of Trotsky only to then find himself on the receiving end of a similar manoeuvre, too late realised that he had been deceived by a 'bloodthirsty Ossetian [sic] who doesn't know what conscience is'. Rosa Luxemburg, although born in Russian Poland, spent her entire adult life in Germany, where her intellectual brilliance rapidly established her as one of the leading theoreticians of the German Social Democratic Party. From that highly cultured vantage point, she detected even in the early Bolshevism of Lenin an incipient totalitarianism, a 'Tartar-Mongolian savagery' that brooked no opposition:

> A dozen outstanding heads do the leading and an elite of the working class is invited from time to time to meetings, where they are to applaud the speeches of the leaders,

and to approve resolutions unanimously.

It could be Stalin's Russia, but what she was describing was the instrument that created it, the party of Lenin. George Plekhanov, the pioneer of Russian Marxism had, through bitter experience, come to the same conclusions regarding Lenin's authoritarian ways and, what is most significant, like her, looked to the East for an analogy:

> Since a [party] congress is in the offing, the central committee 'liquidates' [sic] the elements with which it is dissatisfied, everywhere seats its own creatures and, filling all the committees with these creatures, without difficulty guarantees itself a fully submissive majority at the congress. The congress constituted of the creatures of the central committee amiably cries 'Hurrah', approves all its successful and unsuccessful actions, and applauds all its plans and initiatives. Then, in reality, there would be in the party neither a majority nor a minority, *because we then would have realised the ideal of the Persian Shah*. (emphasis added)

Or a conference of the Corbynised Labour Party.

Under Lenin's (and Genghis Khan's) heir, such a goal was realised and surpassed far beyond the darkest premonitions of Plekhanov and Luxemburg, though not those of Bukharin. In the manner of the riparian tyrannies of antiquity, to fulfil the Bolshevik Sargon's grandiose Five-Year Plans, canals were dug by millions of slaves with their bare hands and tribute squeezed from re-enserfed starving peasants, while in the mines and factories, the lethal whip of the NKVD cracked over the heads of a helot proletariat. At the summits of power stood a court permanently riven by murderous tribal blood feuds and periodically culled by savage purges, presided over by a despot ascribed the powers of a deity, one who on his death, like a pharaoh, was embalmed and laid to rest in a pyramid-shaped tomb. The subject of countless devotional poems, hymns, statues and paintings (an honour also accorded Corbyn, together with a song of praise, and the fascist Fuehrer Sir Oswald Mosely), even more grandly than his Romanov forerunners, who were merely 'little fathers', Stalin was designated the 'Father of the Peoples', ruling over a vast empire forced into submission by unending terror.

Further east again, the current official Head of State of North Korea or, as Corbyn's Stalinist *confidante,* Andrew Murray respectfully calls it, 'People's Korea', is not Kim Jong Un, but his long-deceased grandfather, the founder of the dynasty, Kim Il Sung. To the south, China's red emperor was officially credited with the healing powers of Jesus, allegedly performing miracles identical to those certified by the Vatican as qualification for sainthood, and whose teen-age disciples recited parables from his *Little Red Book*, the same book that Corbyn's Shadow Chancellor John McDonnell read out from and waved defiantly at his Tory opposite number in the debate on his budget. (The miracles have been documented by G. R Urban in his *Miracles of Chairman Mao.*) A few longitudes further east bring us close to the date-line frontier between East and West, and to a land ruled until 1945 by an emperor worshiped as a god, one for whom, like suicide bombers for Allah, his *Kamikazes* were honoured to die. To the east of that line we encounter the total negation of the cultures that lie its West, the most free and technically advanced nation in the history of the human race, the state that by the same law separates church and state and upholds the right of free speech, and which therefore with good reason Iranian theocrats describe as the 'Great Satan'. I will argue that for a number of compelling reasons, theirs is a religion best understood historically as the bastard offspring of an ancient, eastern, mystically-infused monolithic insect culture, one which, like the Islamic *Ummah*, did not recognise any distinction between state and civil society, between god and Caesar or, as with Mohammed, between prophet, law-giver and warrior.

What we might call the Oriental anticipation of modern totalitarianism (where, not by accident, it still survives and, in China, with certain western adaptations thrives) evolved when, as Kautsky put it, society was at 'the stage that the state reaches finally reaches everywhere in the Orient', where 'there is, under normal circumstances, no material power that could be able to oppose the Sovereign inside his country'. Unlike western slave and feudal societies, they had become stabilised, in effect frozen, at 'the end point of the development of such oriental states.' The despotisms of the East, despite the ruthless and highly systematic exploitation of their work forces, were never seriously threatened, let alone overturned, by the revolts and usurpations which periodically shook and even transformed the classical and feudal West...Rome's risings of the plebs, the agrarian reforms of the Gracchi, the slave rebellion of Spartacus,, the oratory of a Pericles and a Demosthenes, Magna Carta, the communist heresies of the millennial sects, the peasant revolts of England and Germany. In the ancient orient, all economic resources, and therefore political power, were firmly in the hands of the absolutist state, which held them in trust for their owners, the gods, whose trustees, we can be sure, enjoyed their use. (Since for 'orthodox' Leninists the sole criterion for a 'workers' state' is not, as it was for Marx, the freedom, political power and well-being of the proletariat, but the absence of private ownership of the means of production, the Oriental despotisms of Sargon, Ramesses and Nebuchadnezzar would have qualified as a celestial variant of the same genre millennia before the emergence of their modern earth-bound successors. We should also include in the first category the Vatican City, whose property according to cannon law is also held in trust for god, and the North Korea of Kim the Third, ruled by his grandfather from a Stalinist Valhalla.)

The Oriental sanctification of property rights and usage is also a feature of early Islam, with the *Koran's* injunction (Chapter 8, Verse 1): 'The spoils of war belong to Allah and the messenger', the difference being that in this case, the prophet gets to share the proceeds with Allah, and what is shared is largely the result of plunder by a marauding desert army, not the fixed assets and produce of the river-based agrarian oriental states. Yet despite significant differences in their sources of wealth, what they had in common was the absence of a productive property-owning class comparable to the bourgeoise of nascent western capitalism, a lack which necessarily excluded the possibility of a political challenge to the rulers comparable to that mounted by the urban classes of Europe in the early modern era. And in the absence of an intelligentsia separate from and therefore potentially opposed to the governing elite and its clergy, as in ancient Greece and Rome, and the Europe of the Reformation, Renaissance and Enlightenment, cultural stagnation necessarily set in, not only in the Orient where their influence was at best negligible, but also with Islam. Today, 22% of the world's population are Muslims. 50%, mainly women, are illiterate and only three have been awarded Nobel Prizes for science, compared to the 100% literate, work ethic-driven Jews, with their 145 science prizes and 0.2% of the world's population. As I like to say, not bad for 'apes and swine'.

Compared with the slave-based economy of Rome, whose low and declining productivity doomed the empire to conquest by German barbarians, the 'hydraulic' economies of the Orient were a model of efficiency But with bonded labour rigidly regulated by the despotic state bureaucracy, they left no role or space for the trade guilds of the medieval west, forerunners of the trade unions of the capitalist era, or the emergence of the estates of feudal Europe, which acted as a check on the powers of the monarchy and, over time acquired, sometimes violently, legislative functions overriding those of king and clergy. No such evolution occurred in the ancient east. Loyalties, such as were permitted, were not horizontal, formed by class, craft and calling, but vertical, to the elders of the clan or tribe, and above all, to the semi-divine despot.

Oriental despotism provided the one exception to Marx's famous assertion that 'the history of all hitherto existing society is the history of class struggles.' The consequences of this exception were and remain crucial. Islamic regimes in the Middle East, whether they be monarchist, clerical, military or 'presidential', including those that now and in the past have received support from part of the Left, have used a variety of means to prevent the development of class conflicts in any way resembling those of the West, in case they bring with them, as they did in the West, destabilisation and radical political change. The most predominant are political repression, clerical-brainwashing and dead-end distractions in which the frustrated and dissatisfied let off steam or seek glory. In Gaza, instead of bread and circuses, Jeremy's friends provide tunnel digging and promise 72 virgins for suicide bombers; instead of gladiator contests and chariot races, Jew-killing. No less effective, if less apparent, is a policy of social engineering that prevents the emergence a western-style proletariat capable of organising itself and fighting for its own interests, be they economic or political. Instead, there has been fostered a client under-class existing on petro-charity and western-funded United Nations aid programmes (50% unemployment in the Gaza Strip). Like ancient Rome's state-subsidised plebs, it is easily manipulated…witness the Hamas-orchestrated weekly mass-assaults on the border of Israel. Most hard physical work is by preference performed, as it was in Rome and in the hey-day of Islam, by unfree labour imported from Africa and Asia, while the highly skilled are enticed from the West by huge salaries.

In Bahrein, 51% are foreign nationals, Oman, 44%. In Saudi Arabia, 56% of its workers are from overseas, mainly India. In the United Arab Emirates, the proportion is 96%. To build stadia for the World Cup of 2022, Qatar's petro-despots imported two million workers, *twenty times* its own adult male population. Paid one tenth of Qatar's per capita GDP, the highest in the world at $64,000, construction teams worked a ten-hour day in temperatures above 40 degrees centigrade. The death rate though heat exposure and accidents soared into the thousands. There were no strikes, no protests from FIFA, some of whose officials had been bribed by the regime responsible for the deaths. Unlike the imperialist west, and as is the case throughout the Arabian Peninsula and beyond, in Qatar, the notion, let alone the reality of political freedom and workers' rights simply does not exist for its native, let alone its imported work force. With the exception of Israel, the Middle East is a region where, as throughout the Islamic world with rare and transitory exceptions, independent trade unions have banned for decades and leftist parties, as under Saddam Hussein and the Ayatollahs of Iran, persecuted with a savagery equal to that inflected on the left in Nazi Germany.

The task of creating a viable workers movement in the Islamic world is rendered all the more daunting by the cynical indifference of the western left which, instead of lending its support to such a hazardous undertaking, sides with labour's oppressors if they are deemed sufficiently anti-imperialist, as for example in Iran, where workers have been flogged and sentenced to long prison terms for organising strikes without any protests by British trade union or Labour Party leaders. There is also amongst the rural population in particular a deeply ingrained culture of deference to the powers that be that inhibits attempts to create organisations that clearly have a western origin, and are therefore seen as non or even anti-Islamic. Indeed, it is on these very grounds that the Ayatollahs have deemed strikes to be incompatible with the ethos of the Islamic Republic of Iran. Kautsky makes this very point when he contrasts the status and mentality of the lower classes of the ancient East with those of the West. '…we do not find in [classical] Greece that servile obsequiousness that in the Orient the peasant and the craftsman exhibit and feel towards the ruling classes.'

Unlike in the west today, where all but a small and shrinking devout minority of believers pays little if any heed to its clergy, numerous surveys have shown it is a different matter entirely for most Muslims. They are deeply devout, and defer no less willingly to their clergy than did the subjects of the ancient Orient to what they truly believed were their divinely ordained masters. Even Muslim prostration at prayer is an inheritance from the identical act of submission to the god kings, gurus and emperors of the East, in Chinese called *kowtow*, Japanese, *dogeza*, Arabic, *sajud*, Hindi, *dandavat*, Punjabi, *mutha tekna*, and English…grovel. Given the cultural and geographic origins of Islam, is it by chance then that while Greece gave the world the system of self-government of the people now embraced by nearly the entire West, and the name by which it is known, one can visit an Islamic website, one of many with the same message, entitled *Muslims Against Voting*, and read at its head a citation from the *Koran*, 'The right of legislation is for none but Allah.'? (Chapter 12, Verse 14. I refer the reader to Appendix G, where Ayatollah Khomeini explains in some detail why this has to be so.)

These historically crucial divergences were and are in no way due to those of inborn racial characteristics. Along with much else, the East invented script, musical notation, astronomy and mathematics (the Sumerian's base number 60 is the origin of the degrees of a circle and compass, longitude and latitude, and modern time-keeping); it invented coins, built the first cities, and codified the first laws. The Mongol settlement of the Americas culminated many thousands of years later in the no less sophisticated (and also no less stagnant) civilisations of the Aztecs and the Incas. The crucial difference between eastern stagnation and western development lay in climate, topography, geology, between a closed culture bounded by sand and an economy totally dependent on rivers, and an open one boarded by seas and oceans and endowed with a temperate climate, fertile soil and easily accessible coal and minerals, between slave, coerced or corvée labour, throughout history always the least productive, whether it be that of the ancient Orient, classical Rome and Greece or the former Soviet bloc, and free labour, which uniquely evolved in the west after the decline of serfdom. The absence of these factors in the East determined that when, over the centuries and even millennia, political change did occur in the Orient, it was never social or economic, merely dynastic, occasioned by an assassination or conquest by a neighbouring empire organised on an identical foundation…Trotsky's 'hopeless rotations', breeding a profound conservatism and fatalism not only in the ruling caste, but even more so in those they ruled, a mindset resistant to and fearful of change, one that inherited by Islam, endures to this day. That is why Marx believed that the impulse for change in the East would necessarily have to come from the outside, from the capitalist west, precisely that which Islam has since the dawn of the modern era always resisted, and no more so than today, especially in its Salafist and so-called 'fundamentalist' versions, where an implacable hostility towards the liberal democratic west permeates the founding charters and declarations of Corbyn's 'friends' Hamas and Hezbollah, and the propaganda of the Islamic State.

Hence the goal of Salafism and its kindred schools; the return to the undefiled purity of the original Islam of seventh century Arabia, to be achieved by Jihad against a west that it believes is the cause of their faith's adulteration and perversion. Al-Qaeda and ISIS, together with its various affiliates, adhere to this school, and it is also active in the Gaza Strip. An ISIS clone much favoured by the Socialist Workers Party for its 'militant Islam' is Somali-based Al-Shabaab, which translated means 'No Western education', which surely says it all. (Massacres of school children and staff have also proved no impediment to the Taliban's enrolment in the Sharia left's anti-imperialist front.) Other Salafist groups operate throughout the Islamic world, all of them engaging in terrorist activities, either against the West, or Islamic regimes they see as servile to it. In Algeria, the Islamic Salvation Front waged a ten-year war that ended in defeat and costed the lives of at least 200,000 fellow Muslims, a carnage that unlike the far smaller Palestinian casualties arising from the terrorist *Intifadas* against Israel which occurred at the same time, went virtually unreported by the Western media, and unprotested, like the Kremlin's rapes of Afghanistan and Chechnya, by the left. (The US-led war to remove the genocidal regime of Saddam Hussein however brought millions of protestors onto the streets of western capitals.)

This hatred and fear of the west is not unique to Sunni Islam. It is shared by its Shi'a version, and exemplified by the Ayatollah Khomeini's diatribe against all things occidental in Appendix G, a xenophobia whose origins in the same region predate Islam by more than a thousand years. It first manifested itself when East and West first encountered each other in the protracted conflicts between the Greeks, who were planting the first seeds of democracy, and the Oriental despotism of the Persians, the wars that began with the invasions of Darius and Xerxes and ended with conquests of Alexander the Great. Today, in what was once the eastern hinterland of Alexander's empire, what is essentially the same battle has been resumed, with the Ayatollahs of Iran pledging, as their ancient predecessors once did of Athens, with the assistance of their proxy army Hezbollah, the 'Party of Allah', to 'wipe Israel off the map' and bring 'death to America'. And in this undertaking, they have the support, true to its founder's 'Eastern Orientation', of what remains of historic Leninism. There is a profound irony that today's revolutionary left should see in a religion founded by an illiterate seventh century Caesaro-Papist desert war lord a means to undermine a civilisation whose secular intellectual heritage fertilized the teachings of its founders, Marx and Engels, who saw in the East the epitome of barbarism.

And not only they. Trotsky in his last exile revealingly related how 'the late Leonid Krassin, old revolutionist, eminent engineer, brilliant diplomat and above all, intelligent human being, was the first, if I am not mistaken, to call Stalin an "Asiatic"', and how Kamenev, after he broke with Stalin in 1926, prophetically warned him, 'you can except anything from this Asiatic'. Stalin had Kamenev executed in 1936, and Trotsky assassinated in 1940. When party leaders complained of Stalin's intrigues and low morals, Lenin would shrug his shoulders and say, 'what else do you expect? He's an Asiatic', while his wife, Krupskaya, called Stalin 'an Asiatic monster'. To Trotsky she confided that her husband had said Stalin 'lacks the most elementary sense of honour...the most elementary decency'. In time, Trotsky would come to an even more devesting judgement, denouncing his 'Asiatic' nemesis as 'the dirtiest, most criminal and most repulsive figure in history'. (However, in Corbyn's immediate entourage are those who see Stalin and his Chinese counterpart in a very different light. With such exemplars, is it any wonder then that just prior to announcing his resignation on the eve of Labour's 2019 party conference, the last surviving member of Corbyn's original core staff, his Head of Policy Andrew Fisher, accused his leader's team of among other shortcomings, disseminating a 'blizzard of lies and excuses' and, like Stalin, 'lacking human decency'? And, given their exalted social station, could it have been Corbyn's silver-spooned trio Seumas Milne, son of a former Director General of the BBC, Andrew Murray, scion of the ennobled Houses of Stanhope and Beauchamp and Momentum founder and son of a property tycoon James Schneider, all alumni of Winchester and Oxford, whom Fisher accused of waging an *haute en bas* 'class war' against their underlings?)

Being called an 'Asiatic' was for Stalin a compliment, in an exchange with Japanese Foreign Minister Yosuke Matsuoka remarking: 'You are an Asiatic. So, am I', to which Matsuoka replied, 'We all are all Asiatics, let's drink to Asiatics'? On another occasion, he took exception to being called a' European', declaring himself 'no European' but a 'Russified Georgian Asian' So it was not by mere chance that in his rise to total power, Stalin collected around himself followers of a like caste of mind who hailed from his own neck of the woods amidst the semi-Asiatic Caucasus mountains, where the ancient private lore of the clans still prevailed, and of which Stalin's vengeful *modus operandi* was the ultimate consumption. As the chief butt of their crude invective redolent of a 'Tiflis gutter', Trotsky would refer contemptuously to Stalin's cronies as the 'Savage Division' after the name of the Muslim unit that served in the tsarist army during the First World War. Even though in each case, the pejorative use of 'Asian' and its analogues always referred to a cultural type, and not race, such statements as these (and I could have cited many others no less pungent) would today assuredly result in their authors being no-platformed by liberals and the left for the thought crime of cultural imperialism and probably also for racism. Thus far have we travelled from a time when Asia and its various cognates served the revolutionary left as a synonym for the barbarism and wanton savagery of a Genghis Khan or Tamburlaine, and for the amorality in human relationships practised by the Islamic Caliphates

The cultural relativism and its analogue, moral relativism, that is now *de rigueur* in polite society, mutated in part from a school of anthropology that in the first three decades of the twentieth century, quite legitimately stressed the need to analyse all human cultures objectively, not, as the politically correct would say today, 'judgementally'. Over time, this approach acquired a political and moral dimension that its pioneers, in the first-place Ruth Benedict, never intended. Their objective was to understand the workings of cultures encountered and even colonised by the west, not to provide grounds for affording them 'respect' or insulate them from criticism. Counterposed to this scientific approach is that of what is best described as the 'one-way' cultural relativism of the late Palestinian-born but western educated and based academic, Professor Edward Said, which denies to the West the ability to say anything of value about the East, while not ascribing to the East the same incapacity in its evaluation of either itself or, what is equally to the point, the West. It is worth noting in this context that according to an Islamic website, it was Professor Said who introduced to the west the term 'Islamophobia', a word that despite its literal meaning, which is to harbour an irrational fear of Islam, has been very effectively used to silence and even criminalise critical remarks made in public about the religion of peace, and even to have them defined and likewise criminalised as a form of racism.

Said's 'Orientalist' thesis was first propounded in 1978, in his immensely influential but now, in the judgement of some, discredited book *Orientalism,* where he made the ludicrous claim that 'since the time of Homer, every [sic] European in what he could say about the Orient, was a racist, an imperialist, and almost totally ethnocentric'. We have it then on the authority of Professor Said that beginning with the 'time of Homer', believed to be *circa* 1,000 BC and consequently about which we know next to nothing, every westerner over the succeeding millennia who ever concerned themselves with the East, and that as we have seen includes Marx, Lenin and Trotsky, was a racist. This claim raises some intriguing questions. Are all those who write about the East (and today that will often as not mean Islam) attracted to the subject *because* they are racists? Or does its study somehow transform them *into* racists? Is the subject, and of course especially its Islamic aspects, which concerned Said the most, to be 'off limits' for all decent (western) folk, lest studying it transforms them into anti-Muslim bigots? If so, then precisely why and how does studying the Orient always turn a non-racist into a racist?

There is another possibility, which has the double virtue of greatly simplifying matters and best fitting Said's thesis: All westerners, whether they display an interest in the Orient or not, are, for whatever reason or reasons, racists. All that western Orientalists do is reveal this universally shared racism in their chosen field of study. Inverting Said's Orientalism thesis, we can describe his critique of the West as 'Occidentalism', though he would have us believe that in his case it is a mode of thinking that illuminates rather than distorts and obscures. In every sense the reverse of a bigoted 'Orientalism', 'Occidentalism' enables those like Professor Said not only to grasp truths about the East that are closed to racist western minds, but to make judgements about the West that because of its ingrained (or inborn) biases, it cannot or dare not make about itself. What is most extraordinary is that Said's claim to have exposed as incurably biased the academic pretentions of western Oriental scholarship is not, he believes, invalidated by his own remarkably frank admission that he has 'no interest in, much less capacity for showing what the true Orient and Islam really are'. But how can one detect and expose a falsehood if one does know, and is even not concerned with the facts of the matter in dispute? Said evidently subscribes to the fallacious *ad hominem* argument that is sufficient to know who is saying it, rather than what is being said.

In fact, very much in the manner of his post-modernist contemporaries, whom he cites with approval, Said does not seem to think there is such a thing as the truth, or even that that there an objective reality that can even if only hypothetically be knowable. In the work of the Orientalists, 'truth, in short, becomes a function of learned judgement, not of the material itself', this perhaps being akin to the unknowable Kantian 'thing in itself'. Then we learn that even this 'material itself' 'seems to owe its existence to the Orientalists', conjured out of nothing by bigoted minds. Is it not then a cause for wonder that Professor Said was able to see clearly through this fog of post-modernism and the mists of time to discern, without on this occasion the least doubt, that as far back as the time of Homer, the best part of three thousand years distant from today, those who studied the East were racists, down to the last man? This is a world of shadows of shadows. One is left more than a little bemused, and wondering...does the 'Orient' even exist at all, except in the minds of the 'Orientalists'? Said apparently thinks not, because he describes the discipline as 'a form of paranoia, knowledge of another kind, say, from historical knowledge', a 'Western ignorance which becomes more refined, more complex, not some body of positive Western knowledge which increases in size and accuracy'...objectives which Said elsewhere suggests are by their very nature unattainable. And Said himself admits, he too not only lacks this knowledge himself but has no interest in acquiring it! The sole purpose of the exercise, one that as we have seen, has nothing to do with investigating the nature the East, is to slander any scholar in the West who does undertake such a study as merely an academic apologist for and accomplice of western imperialism:

> I doubt that it is controversial, for example, to say that an Englishman in India or Egypt in the late nineteenth century took an interest in those countries that was never far from their status in his mind as British colonies.
>
> To say this may seem quite different from saying that all academic knowledge about India and Egypt is somehow tinged and impressed with, violated by, the gross political fact of imperialism- and yet *that is what I am saying* in this study of Orientalism. (emphasis in original)

'...*all academic knowledge*...' How did this claim ever come to be taken seriously? Surely only academics tormented and utterly disoriented by post-colonial guilt could have so lost their intellectual bearings as to give credence to such nonsense, of which the intended and all too frequently achieved result is western prostration before the wonders of Islam. However, cowing those who have first-hand knowledge of these glories is not so easily achieved. When Kanan Makiya, the leftist Iraqi author of the anti-Saddam *Republic of Fear,* took Said to task for his attribution to the West of all the failings (such as they are) of the Arab world, Said resorted to some decidedly un-professorial language by denouncing him as a 'guinea pig witness' and 'native informant' for the United States, in other words, a traitor to Saddam Hussein...all because he described the Ba'athist regime as it was...a fascist dictatorship. Even Arabs, it seems, can succumb to 'Orientalism' when they make the fatal error of valuing truth above tribal loyalty to a faith and a culture. One can only draw the conclusion that Said's 'Orientalism' is little more than a pseudo-academic device to warn off, or if that fails, discredit with accusations of racism, any western scholar who sets out to examine critically certain aspects of Islamic societies, theology and culture.

What now goes by the name of cultural relativism has its academic origins in a number of disciplines, principally philosophy and certain trends in contemporary anthropology, where they concern themselves with issues of ethics and morals. Perhaps inevitably, because in the background there loomed issues associated with the impact of colonial rule on the cultures being studied, quite early on, anthropology became heavily politicised, and has remained so to this day. A sign of things to come was the academic debates that preceded the adoption, in 1948, of the United Nations Universal Declaration of Human Rights. The American Anthropological Association challenged the very concept of universal human rights on grounds very similar to those advanced by dictatorial regimes in China, North Korea, Cuba and the Islamic states today. In a paper submitted to the UN, it argued that such a declaration must 'do more than phrase respect for the individual as individual'. It also had to 'take into full account the individual as a member of a social group of which he is a part, whose sanctioned modes of life shape his behaviour and with whose fate his own is thus inextricably bound.' Thus in a few specious phrases, the rights of the 'individual as individual', which were central to the UN Declaration, were conjured away. The individual was to be subordinated instead to 'sanctioned [by whom?] modes of behaviour that shape his [and under Islam, even more so, her] life,' to which he is 'inextricably bound', and therefore, over which he has no control or say. As we have seen this argument has been deployed by *dhimmi* western feminists to justify the domination of Muslim women by Islamic patriarchy. And as a definition both of what now goes by the name of 'identify politics' and no less of a totalitarian state, be it secular or theocratic, for its brevity and succinctness, this can hardly be surpassed.

It ignores the fact that the real, living human being, independently and irrespective of any 'culture', has his or her biologically determined material wants, which are common to the entire species...food, shelter etc...and must be met to ensure its thriving and reproduction just as with any other species. The one essential difference is that unlike the environment of other species, mankind's culture over time, through the development of technology and science and their action upon nature, has become more and more a human construct. The inevitable consequence is that such an environment, or as we say in this case, 'culture', that fails to provide these pre-requisites of life or fail to compete with those that do, is doomed to decline and even extinction, and along with it, those that live under its sway, unless they can either escape to one that does (as millions of mainly Muslim migrants from Islam are now doing) or, by their own efforts, through collective action, possibly with outside assistance or intervention (such as that envisaged by Marx), are able to create such a culture for themselves.

But more than this. 'Man doth not live by bread alone'. Evolution has endowed the human species with a brain like no other. To function properly, its needs must be met no less than the rest of the body it serves and controls. The study of the history of the human race, together with a range of scientific disciplines concerned with human behaviour in its various aspects, together combine to prove empirically that the freer the human mind is to investigate the reality we inhabit, to store, expand, transmit and have access to knowledge about this reality, to communicate and collaborate with other brains, to dispute and to differ, the more it benefits not only the material well-being of the individuals concerned, but humanity as whole. The spectacular advances achieved in world health by a tiny number of medical scientists operating in a culture of free intellectual inquiry is just one of many proofs that a culture which, by a process analogous to Darwinian natural selection, succeeds in liberating the human mind from secular and religious dogmas, demonstrably also brings, if allowed to, not only innumerable material benefits but also intangible cultural riches to the human species as whole, proving that liberal democracy is a meme whose time has come. Judged by this secular criterion (and how can there be any other worthy of consideration?) western liberal, pluralist democracy is infinitely superior to the stifling totalitarian culture of Islam, one that punishes innovation and dissent while rewarding slavish, even fanatical conformity. So if we can speak in any sense of the 'natural state' of the human species, it is not passively to accept being, as the American Anthropological Association has it, 'intrinsically bound' by 'fate' to 'modes of life' that 'shape its behaviour' but to be active, choosing and controlling its individual behaviour, obviously within certain historical and natural limits, and by collective action, determining the shape and direction of society as a whole. If humanity did not possess the intrinsic capacity to do this, we would still be living in caves.

Humanity, or rather a certain proportion of it, has learned, at great cost, to create through a series of revolutions and reforms, the methods, institutions and principles of liberal democracy which have made this human progress possible. The liberal democracy of the 'west' is superior to all other cultures, past and present, not because it judges them by its own supposedly subjective criteria, as the cultural relativists claim, but because liberal democracy is itself judged, like all other cultures, by a higher, in fact ultimate objective standard, which in the light of overwhelming evidence, finds that however imperfectly and partially, it affords the most fruitful principles, institutions and conditions yet devised for the prospering and thriving of the human species, both materially and mentally, as it engages in its ever more diverse and complex activities.

Yet although the 'west' has abolished famines, plagues, slavery, the persecution of homosexuals and legal discrimination against women, enfranchised all adults, hugely extended the span of life, invented the telescope and microscope, radio, television and powered flight, has travelled to the moon and back, landed a space ship on Mars and one of the moons of Jupiter, sending back to earth scientific data and clear images of their surfaces, split the atom and harnessed its energy, discovered DNA and unravelled the mechanisms of life...despite all this and so much more, the culture of intellectual freedom that made all this possible is, we are told by the relativists, no better than one that has proved itself incapable of achieving by its own efforts a single one of these advances, and whose main preoccupation is with crushing human freedom and either subjugating or killing those who challenge its dominance or deny its claims.

Over the post-war years, this cultural relativism, again fed by liberal and leftist colonial guilt, bifurcated and gave birth to its analogue, moral relativism. This poisonous doctrine, under whose rubric any moral abomination can be committed so long as it is not by Europeans or North Americans, was neatly summed up by one of its advocates, the anthropologist Alison Dundes Renteln: 'There can be no value judgements that are true, that is, absolute judgements independent of specific cultures'. Unless, that is, they are made by Alison Dundes Renteln. Ernst Krieck, a Nazi ideologist, agreed. Here he is, explaining the meaning of 'race truth', or 'thinking with one's blood':

> Each race in each period must form its life according to its own law and fate, and to this law its own scholarship, with all other spheres of life, is also subject. The idea of humanism, with the teaching of pure human reason and absolute spirit founded upon it, is a philosophical principle of the eighteenth century [that is, of the Enlightenment] caused by the conditions of that time. Is it in no sense binding on us as we live under different conditions...Such a race-bias carries its certainty in itself and not in logical criteria of the truth.

Just as Renteln says, 'there can be no absolute judgments independent of specific cultures'. The question needs to be put to those who argue thus: are there no human practices sanctioned by a culture which renders that culture inferior to another that does not permit it? We can cite the examples of the Aztecs, who conducted human sacrifices on a vast scale to their sun god Inti, the Chinese practice of binding of girls' feet, the extension of African women's necks with hoops, female genital mutilation and child marriage, rife in certain Islamic countries and the Muslim diaspora, the Judaic and Islamic ritualistic circumcision of infant boys, the Indian Hindu custom of *sati* (which still continues), etc. The consistent application of the principle in question requires this answer: that all we can say about these examples, or any others for that matter, is that they exhibit different patterns of behaviour, no better or worse, than cultures that reject and regard such behaviour with abhorrence, since unlike 'difference', 'better' and 'worse' are subjective judgements lacking in objective criteria by which to make them.

Legend has it that following the outlawing of *sati* by the British, an outraged Indian insisted that burning widows alive should continue to be done 'according to our custom', to which an English colonial official replied, 'do it, and we will hang you according to our custom'. The logic of multi-culturalism surely demands that the widow-burners were in the right, and the British guilty of cultural imperialism, since 'there can be no absolute judgements independent of specific cultures'. A comforting thought as the flames begin to lick around the widow's body. If it is just as the Nazi Krieck and the anthropologist Renteln say, that 'there can be no absolute value judgements', then surely the same principle of 'relativism' applies to the moral conduct of individuals as it does to individuals collectively grouped in a culture, that one person's behaviour is no better or worse than anyone else's, only different. Would a cultural relativist, for fear of being 'judgemental' not report the sexual abuse of child? Ironically, those who callously say 'none of my business' and those who high-mindedly say 'I must not be judgemental' will, in such situations, behave in the same way and 'walk on the other side', leading to the same result, the sexual abuse of a child. In their ultimate applications, cultural and moral relativism break down because they would result in a world in which theoretically all can behave as they please, as if, to coin a phrase, 'there is no such thing as society', a world where, sooner rather than later, the strong would rule and possibly, as indeed happened in Nazi Germany with its euthanasia programme, even exterminate the weak. It would be world without any notion or institutions of international law and justice, of being my global brother's keeper, only the law of jungle, a world that for fearing of being judgemental, would not have conducted at Nuremburg the trials of the greatest criminals in human history, declared war on Nazi Germany when Hitler invaded Poland or liberated Kuwait from occupation by Saddam Hussein.

Cultural relativism in its normal application is concerned with cultures that exist in the same time period, for example today's liberal democratic 'west' and the Islamic 'east'. But if its principles are valid, they should also be no less applicable to the same society at different moments in its history, since here too, we are comparing cases of societies founded on contrasting principles, only separated in time rather than space. For example, the cultural relativist would have to assert that no meaningful value judgements can be made regarding the racist culture of a nation which once enslaved its black population and of the culture that 150 years later made possible the election of member of that race as its president not once, but twice; or between the misogynistic culture of a nation which denied women the right to vote, and that a century later, had elected two women as Prime Minister; between one that sent children to work in coal mines and another that sent them to school free of charge. If there are no objective judgements we can make about such differences and the principles that underlie them, then the whole idea of human progress, of our ascent (if indeed ascent it is) from the Old Stone Age to the present has been, as classic conservatism always insisted, nothing but an illusion. All we have is change, often at great cost, but no improvement. It this is true, and the logic of cultural relativism leads inescapably to the conclusion that it is, the west has no rational grounds or moral right to make comparative judgements of any kind about any culture in human history. All we are entitled to say about them is they are different. However, when it comes to the culture of Islam, some, like Prince Charles and guilt-ridden, west-hating leftists and white feminists, make an exception to this rule, insisting it is superior.

A perfect illustration of how cultural relativism and dhimmitude has permeated modern 'progressive' thinking is the BBC's regular practice of describing the greatest products of western culture in ways that deny their universal status and significance. For example, broadcast performances of J.S. Bach's most sublime works, the B Minor Mass and the St. Mathew Passion, are routinely introduced as 'pinnacles of western music', and Wagner's *Tristan und Isolde* as, on one occasion, a 'landmark in western music', thereby leaving the listener to infer that this qualification could mean that there is even greater music to be heard hailing from the east. The objection that the BBC is rightly taking care not to make judgements about something so subjective, abstract and elusive as music is nonsense, because a judgement has already been made...the works in question are deemed to be supreme examples of western music. So, if it is legitimate for the BBC to make such judgements concerning the relative merits of a vast range of western composers of different styles, times and places, why stop there? Why not *all* music? Who, for example, describes Mount Everest as the tallest peak in *Nepal*? Does the BBC do this for fear of giving 'offence'? If so, to whom, precisely? Or does the BBC really believe that Bach's or Wagner's music has to take second place to works created by 'eastern' composers? If so, who are they?

If the BBC feels obliged to resort to geographical criteria when evaluating the music featured on its programmes, why not 'northern' music, since all the recognised giants of the classic genres hail from above the equator? The puzzled listener is left wondering...if Bach is only supreme in the west, as the BBC announcer implies, where can I hear the superior music of the East? And yet 'the east' or, *pace* Professor Said, the Orient, has no such reservations about the relative merits of 'western' concert music. Japan, South Korea, Malaysia, Singapore, and now China are just some of the countries in the East that want to hear and play little else. Instrumentalists and ensembles from the 'east' now feature regularly in 'western' concert halls and broadcasting and recording studios, sweeping the board at national and international competitions, all choosing to perform music that originated far from their native lands, whereas significantly, the reverse does not happen and no one expects it to. They would consider absurd the idea of a system of musical apartheid in which the music of 'east' and 'west' cannot or should not be judged by the same criteria. Where it is free to choose (and this of course excludes most of Islamic world, where western music is either severely frowned upon or banned entirely) the 'east' has made its choice, and, when it is allowed to, it is voting with its pockets, ears, lips and fingers for the music of the 'west'. Music, by its very nature, is a universal medium of expression and communication, and it is no sin to judge one composition or performance superior to another, irrespective of where its creator may hail from.

In the world of the arts, cultural relativism and its attendant 'sensitivities' reign supreme, not least, as one would expect, in in matters Islamic. Following the lead of the Iranian ayatollahs, the film *The 300*, which depicts the Battle of Thermopylae between Sparta and Persia, was judged by some critics to be directed against Islam, even though the conflict took place in BC 480, over a thousand years before its birth and even longer before the imposition of Islam upon the Persians. Thus the film was not judged on its artistic merits, but whether it might give 'offence' to Muslims. Where this kind of thinking can lead is demonstrated by the treatment handed out to the anti-Nazi film *Schindler's List* in a number of Islamic states. Malaysian censors complained that the film depicted Jews as 'intelligent' and 'stout-hearted', which was bad enough. But what was even worse, the Nazis were shown as 'brutal'. Indonesian clerics demanded a ban on the film because it was 'too sympathetic' to the Jews. The film was also banned on similar grounds in Jordan, with its substantial Palestinian population, and in the home of Hezbollah, Lebanon. Director Steven Spielberg had no doubt that the bans were 'certainly an attack on the Jews'. Some today might see them as a blow struck against Zionism.

Islamic censorship has other, more direct ways of ensuring that its sensitivities are respected in infidel nations It can issue death threats, unleash mayhem on the streets, as it did in the Rushdie and Danish cartoon affairs, or take the more direct route of murder, as it did in Paris in the *Charlie Hebdo* massacre and the Japanese translator of *The Satanic Verses*. The Dutch film-maker Theo Van Gogh's, film, *Submission*, depicting the misery of a woman's life under Islam, led to his assassination and attempted decapitation on an Amsterdam street. In court, his killer, Mohammed Bouryeri, justified the murder by claiming that 'the [Sharia] Law compels me [sic] to chop off the head of anyone who insults Allah and his prophet'. This was an obvious, and indisputably appropriate reference to the already quoted Chapter 8, Verse 19 of the *Koran,* where Muslims are instructed by Allah to 'smite them ['those who disbelieve'] above the necks'. It is not a comforting thought for non-Muslims that all surveys show that not only the former Archbishop of Canterbury, but a clear majority of Muslims wish to see Sharia law adopted in the UK, as they do throughout almost all the diaspora.

As the west knows to its cost, murder, bombing and arson rank highly among the favoured methods for securing compliance with the dictates of Sharia cultural criticism. Following the publication of *The Satanic Verses,* bookstores that were attacked for selling the novel included two in Berkeley, California, four in London, and one each in Guildford, Nottingham, Peterborough, York and High Wycombe. Following these attacks, some book chains stopped selling the book, while others hid it under the counter. Islamic terror works. The first book burning in the UK took place in Bolton on December 2, 1988, watched by a mob of 7,000 cheering and chanting Muslims, followed by another in Bradford, and an anti-Rushdie march of Muslims through his Leicester constituency led by Labour MP, close friend of Corbyn, devout Christian and cocaine and prostitute user Keith Vaz. On May 27, 1989, Muslims gathered in Trafalgar Square to watch the burning of Salmand Rushdie in effigy and to demand the banning of his novel. The pop singer Yusuf Islam, aka Cat Stevens, as converts so often feel obliged to do, proved his zeal for his new faith by announcing that if by chance, he should discover Rushdie's whereabouts, 'I might ring somebody who might do more damage to him than he would like. I'd try to phone the Ayatollah Khomeini and tell him exactly where this man is'.

In the east, the Islamic mobilisation was on a much larger and more violent scale. In Turkey, officially a secular state but with a largely Muslim population, the venue of a book fair was burned to the ground by a Muslim mob after its participants refused to hand over for lynching Aziz Nesin, who had announced his intention to translate and publish the novel. 37 died in the blaze. Twelve died and another 40 were wounded in an anti-Rushdie riot in Bombay. Contrary to what is generally believed, and UK politicians and diplomats falsely claim, the Khomeini *fatwa* issued on February 14, 1989, and the financial reward of one million dollars (index linked for inflation) for its execution, still stand. As Iranian officials have explained on more than one occasion, a *fatwa* can only be revoked by the cleric who imposed it. Ayatollah Khomeini died on June 3, 1989. There was at least one positive outcome to this Islamic onslaught on freedom of the press. The clerical cretins who set it in motion could not possibly have understood that whereas banning a book incites Muslims to burn its pages and murder its author, in the civilised world it encourages the curious to read it. So, predictably, sales soared, making the novel a best seller throughout the western world. And there was nothing Allah the all-powerful could do about it.

Self-censorship is without doubt morally the most indefensible of all restrictions on the freedom of expression, firstly because it is voluntary and secondly, as it gathers momentum, spreading like gangrene, it can exert considerable pressure on those who are reluctant to comply with it. Hard though it is to credit, in 2006, Berlin's Deutsche Opera company, presumably anticipating objections and possibly violence from the Islamic offence industry, cancelled its production of Mozart's opera *Idomeneo* because its stage set featured representations of Jesus, Buddha and Mohammed. A small detail...the opera is set in the time of the Trojan wars, 1,500 years or more before the emergence of Islam. But no matter. A shame, because we know how Muslims love their opera, and are always seen in large and enthusiastic numbers at all the big festivals. Motivated by the same considerations, and presumably anticipating the usual high proportion of Muslim art lovers amongst its visitors, shortly after the London transport bombings by four Muslim terrorists on July 7, 2005, the London Tate removed from public view a sculpture inscribed with holy texts, including a selection from the *Koran*. The gallery's Director, Stephen Deuchar, offered the following explanation for his act of supine self-censorship: 'It was a very difficult decision, but we made it due to the exceptional circumstances of this summer and in the light of opinions that we value regarding religious sensitivities.' The murder of 52 civilians and the wounding of 770 no more an 'exceptional circumstance'? The 'sensitivities' of those who shared the religion of its perpetrators are to be valued more than freedom of artistic expression?

Instead of these quite disgusting euphemisms, evasions and downlight lies, why not admit, as others have done in similar circumstances, the real reason; a perfectly justified fear of an Islamic attack on London Tate? There is no shame in admitting this, only in inventing pretexts that no-one takes seriously. Two years on, and the Tate Modern was demonstrating to the those 'whose opinions we value' that the London art world had turned over a new, Islam-friendly leaf, mounting a video exhibit about the world's religions...that is, all bar one...that of peace, fear of a violent reaction by its followers having led to its exclusion. In January 2006, in

Middelkerke, Belgium, the exhibiting of an installation that displayed a fibre glass Saddam Hussein floating in a fish tank was likewise banned lest it offend Muslim 'sensitivities'. Saddam was of course just one of many Muslim leaders renowned for their 'sensitivity', one of his pleasures being the sight of his victims dissolving in a tank of acid.

In the same year, a *posse* of equally sensitive young Muslim art critics wielding iron bars had attacked a Paris café staging an exhibition of cartoons mocking religion. According to a report that appeared in the *Middle East Times*, but not in the UK or US media, the owner of the café 'placed white sheets of paper inscribed with the word "censored" over the cartons that were attacked by the gang'. In 2007, a photograph making a pointed reference to Iran's policy of executing homosexuals, namely of two gay Iranian exiles wearing masks of Mohammed and his nephew Ali, was withdrawn from display in The Hague Municipal Museum because, explained Director W[h]im[p] van Krimpen, 'certain people [sic] in our society might perceive them as offensive'. One is left wondering…who could these 'certain people' possibly be? Surely not Muslims, because Sharia law sanctions the execution of homosexuals and ten Islamic states actually enforce it. When the artist in protest withdrew all her work from the museum and accepted an offer to exhibit at a museum in Gouda, its Director immediately received the usual death threats and had to be placed under police protection. The invitation was then withdrawn.

Offending exhibits need not have even the remotest connection with or allusion to the religion of tolerance to fall foul of self-imposed Sharia censorship. When in 2006 the London Whitechapel Art Gallery found that 'space constraints' prevented the exhibiting of nude dolls by the surrealist artist Hans Bellmer, the Curator later admitted that the real reason was that the nudity of the dolls would offend the large Muslim population living in the area. One can just picture the scene, itself surreal: devotees of a faith that forbids any depiction of nature enthusiastically pouring into the gallery, only to turn tail and flee in horror (or alternatively, stage a riot) at the sight a collection of naked dolls. And yet something like thus did take place when in 2008, a Muslim gang burst into the Berlin Galerie Nord and demanded the removal of a poster entitled 'Stupid Stone' depicting the *Kaaba*, the sacred stone in the Mecca Grand Mosque. The exhibition was temporarily closed pending the upgrading of security. In May 2019, after complaints by Muslims, paintings at an exhibition at the London Saatchi gallery were covered over at the suggestion of the *dhimmi* artist, who described their concealment as 'a respectful solution'. Respectful to whom or what? Obviously not freedom of artistic expression or the right of non-Muslims to look at what they came to see. Respect for the right of Muslims to censor what offends their theological sensitivities? Most certainly, as author Stephen King discovered when, in the same month, his *dhimmi* publisher pulled his novel *The Siege of Tel Aviv* after complaints that its futuristic plot, a five-nation Muslim invasion of Israel, was 'Islamophobic' despite its being warmly recommended by a Muslim, Maajid Nawaz. How can the novel be 'Islamophobic', when the destruction of Israel is the dream of countless millions of Muslims across the Islamic world and beyond, is inscribed in the theologically-inspired Charters of Hamas and Hezbollah, the 'Party of God', and was indeed the goal of the five Muslim nations that attacked Israel at its birth in 1948?

In the world of theatre, Sharia self-censorship led to all references to Islam being removed from performances of the play *Tamburlaine* by Christopher Marlowe. We can be sure that no such redaction has been judged necessary for the same author's

The Jew of Malta and Shakespeare's (or to give the author his proper name and title, Edward de Vere, the 17th Earl of Oxford's) *The Merchant of Venice*. In June 2007, the normally iconoclastic London Royal Court Theatre cancelled an adapted reading of Aristophanes' *Lysistrata* out of fear that its allusions to Islam might cause offence to Muslims. The Royal Court's Director Ramin Gray admitted that playwrights 'feel they can't write openly about what they feel is maybe the most important topic facing our society at the moment'. (days later came the London bombings) This view was shared by Nicholas Hytner of the National Theatre, whose policy was 'not to put on a play attacking Islam unless it was by a Muslim.' As if! Not all directors roll over so easily. In 1994, to mark the 300th anniversary of the birth of the leading spirit of the French Enlightenment, the director Herve Loichemol planned to stage Voltaire's play *Fanaticism, or Mahomet the Prophet* in Geneva. The inevitable Muslim protests, led by the self-styled moderate Tariq Ramadan, forced a cancellation of the project. Nothing daunted, Loichemol revived the staging in 2005, in the small French town of Saint-Genis-Pouilly, on the border with Switzerland. Again, self-appointed Islamic leaders, without having seen it, denounced the production as 'an insult to the entire Muslim community' and demanded its cancellation in order to 'preserve the peace' a scarcely-veiled threat of Muslim violence if the play went ahead. Refusing to yield to religious blackmail, the Mayor of Saint-Genis-Pouilly mobilised the town's police force to protect the theatre from a besieging Muslim mob who were burning cars and garbage cans...*over a play*. Mayor Hubert Bertrand described the situation as 'quasi-insurrectional.' But because he stood firm, he proved that Islamic terror can be defeated and western culture defended.

In November 2015, after protests by Muslims in faraway Nigeria and Saudi Arabia, a Glasgow cinema cancelled a screening of a film entitled *The Message* about the early life of Mohammed. Even though the showing was under the auspices of the Islamic Society of Britain and did not depict the prophet (quite an achievement for a film devoted to him), it was deemed unacceptable because some of the actors playing his companions were not themselves Muslims. In 2013, a baroque painting of the nude goddess Juno was removed from the restaurant of the Swedish Parliament in order to avoid giving offence to Muslims. With the same concern in mind, when President Hassan Rouhani of Iran visited Rome in January 2016 for trade talks, once again, in conformity with Sharia law, which bans the depiction of the human body, naked or otherwise, or any other living or otherwise natural object for that matter, all the nude statues in the city's Capitoline Museum were boarded up for the duration of his stay, a capitulation to Sharia law that was denounced by its critics as 'cultural suicide'. This, in the home of the *Renaissance*? Students of football history will recall an equally obsequious and no less futile gesture. In May 1938, to further Chamberlain's policy of appeasing Hitler, on the orders of the Foreign Office, the English team gave the Nazi salute before their match against Germany in Berlin. Little more than a year later, Britain was at war with Nazi Germany. Less than two months after the boxing of the nudes in Rome, Muslim Jihadis staged their massacre in Brussels.

These are just some of many examples of Muslims enforcing on the west their Sharia censorship of the arts, nearly always with the craven compliance of those whose duty it is to uphold and defend the right of creative artists to complete freedom of expression, and to have the public display, sale, performance or publication of their work protected from religiously-inspired thuggery. Putin's

Russia also exercises clerical censorship, not to protect the sensitivities of Islam, but those of the Russian Orthodox Church. The stage settings of a production of Wagner's *Tannhauser* in Novosibirsk were deemed offensive to Christians after protests by Orthodox zealots were taken up by the church's increasingly influential and ultra-reactionary hierarchy. When the theatre director refused to make any changes to the production, he was sacked, we can safely assume with President Putin's approval, by the Minister of Culture, and future performances of the opera banned. Of Russia, more than any other country, we can surely say, *plus la change, plus c'est la meme chose.*

Even the UK's, and arguably the world's most prestigious academic publishers, Oxford University Press, have been unable to resist the pressures of a Sharia self-censorship, in January 2015 issuing instructions to authors not to use the words 'pigs or sausages, or anything else that could resemble pork'. The same considerations and cowardice led to all the UK's major newsagents submitting to Islam's blasphemy laws by refusing to stock the special post-massacre issue of *Charlie Hebdo,* while the reward for brave independent newsagents who did was to be questioned by police as to the source of their supply *and the identities of those who bought it*. Comedians freely admit that to make jokes about Islam (and if ever there was a sitting target for satire and humour, it is Islam) is, in the words of one well-known comic, equivalent to writing a suicide note. Though the absurdities, rituals, claims and pretensions of Islam and the surreal antics of its devotees are wonderful material for satire, we can be sure that in the foreseeable there will be no Ayatollah Ted or Imaness of Tower Hamlets.

Neither can Islam be depicted as it truly is, 'red in tooth and claw,' on the UK's TV screens. Here, as always, the cravenly *dhimmi* BBC leads the way in its eagerness to comply with Muslim demands that their religion be depicted as one of peace, love and tolerance. To this end, the BBC concocts story lines in its dramas that find Muslims almost always being on the receiving end of any religiously-inspired violence going, as in the 2008 series *Bonekickers*, in a which a Christian fundamentalist is shown beheading a Muslim…as they do. Come the Islamic State, and viewers of YouTube, if they had the stomach for it, could watch exactly the reverse, only this time for real. Another BBC series, the spy drama *Spooks*, had the London Saudi Embassy seized by what at first viewers are led to suppose are Muslim Jihadis, but as the story unfolds, turn out to be not Muslims at all but…guess who? Of course, Jews, operatives of Mossad, the Israeli intelligence agency. There's nothing like plausible realism to lend credibility to a story line, as in one episode of the BBC's long-running hospital drama series, *Casualty.* The original script had a young Muslim blowing himself up at a bus station. However, this this was vetoed, and the Muslim suicide bomber transformed into a *kuffar* animal rights activist. Instances such as these reveal a craven west grovelling on its knees before Islam, a west that would censor its greatest cultural achievements, and prefer not to create new ones rather than risk giving offence to a religion that despises it.

22 You Must Do It

Whatever the relativists might say, there is a very straightforward and time-tested way to compare the merits of cultures, and that is by the movement of peoples between them. In the case of Islam and the west, it is, save for ISIS Jihadis, entirely in one direction...away from areas and countries where it holds sway, and by any means possible, even those that entail considerable risk to life, towards continents and countries where, as yet, it does not. And who can blame them? Some, a minority, are genuine asylum seekers, among them non-Muslims fleeing from Islamic persecution. Others, far more numerous, 70% at the very least, are welfare and economic migrants, seeking escape from the poverty that Islam everywhere either creates or is incapable of overcoming, except for a privileged few. In 2014, 219,000 arrived by sea on the coasts of southern Europe, most of them fleeing from the Jihadi-created chaos of Libya. Another 3,500 drowned en route. In April 2015, 950 drowned after an overloaded dinghy capsized. In one month alone, October 2015, the number of those *officially* registered as refugees reached 218,000, accompanied by more drownings.

A closer look at these new Muslim arrivals quickly dispelled the belief of those welcoming them that they were all asylum seekers fleeing the ravages of Islam's civil wars. These were confined to Syria, Afghanistan, Iraq, Somalia, Libya and Yemen. There were no such wars raging in Albania, Pakistan or Bangladesh or, apart from Libya, in the states of North and Central Africa also supplying a sizable proportion of those demanding the right to settle in Germany and Sweden. If these are fleeing families, why are over 70% of the migrants mostly young men? Where are the old men, the women, the children? Those best suited physically to resisting the despoiling of their homelands were fleeing, deserting those least able to protect themselves from the tender mercies of Jihadi rapists and executioners. Evidently a Muslim man defends his 'honour' when it requires the murder of a raped or disobedient woman, but not when it calls for her protection. And, just as was to be expected, the arrival these young Muslim men coincided in Germany and Scandinavia with a sudden increase in reported sexual assaults, including rapes. In the south west German state of Hesse, the sexual abuse of women and children in refugee facilities became so chronic that a women's rights group, LandesFrauenRat, made the mistake of reporting them on its website. However, within a matter of hours, the politically incorrect error of publicising the rape of Muslim women and children was rectified, and the offending item removed.

In the course of discussing the need for the allocation of quotas of migrants in proportion to each country's ability to absorb them, why did politicians not request that Islamic states take up their fair share of the burden? Surely it would have made more sense to re-locate at least some Arab-speaking Muslims, who made up the majority of migrants, in neighbouring countries where they would have shared the same language and religion as their hosts? It would also have had the advantage of avoiding the perilous crossing of the Mediterranean in overcrowded and unseaworthy vessels, and at least reduced the exploitation of migrants by people-trafficking racketeers. Why did no-one with the authority to do so propose such an eminently sensible policy? Was it for fear of offending the oil rich despotisms of Saudi Arabia and the Gulf? And why did not a single Islamic state offer to exercise the compassion that their holy book commands to be shown to fellow Muslims?

It was not for sure a matter of expense. Having ensured that by denying them sanctuary in his and the other oil rich kingdoms of the Saudi peninsula, all Muslim migrants were absorbed in the strategic heartlands of central and western Europe, King Salman was only too willing to accommodate their spiritual needs in Germany by funding the construction of 200 new Mosques to further his Kingdom's strategy of European Islamisation Here again is the uniqueness of the Muslim diaspora. Unlike other migrated peoples who have made their permanent home in new lands, wherever Muslims take root, the overriding allegiance of the vast majority is to a faith, not their new homeland or even the one they or their forebears have left behind. The vast and still expanding Saudi global programme of mosque building and *madrassah* funding is designed to ensure that there will be no integration into the host society, a strategy greatly facilitated by the lunacies of official multiculturalism. Denying them sanctuary in Islamic states ensured that the millions of Muslims arriving in Europe would either be fed into these already existing self-generated ghettos or be located in areas where they would over time create new ones. The inmates of these new Muslim enclaves, as those in the older ones already are, will be expected to serve as foot soldiers in the global spread and final conquest of Islam.

Amidst all the pious clamour of clerics and publicity-craving celebrities concerning Europe's duty to provide a new home for an unlimited number of migrants (so long as the home was not any of their own) it takes a great deal of civic courage to say publicly that the crisis of the Islamic world is not of Europe's making, any more than Europe is able to provide the remedy. The Muslims of north Africa, the Middle East and Asia have to learn, and quickly, that the flight of millions is not the answer, and for the west to encourage the delusion that it is merely postpones the solution. In doing so, it has also created problems for their hosts that politicians and the mainstream media, for a variety of reasons, are reluctant to acknowdge and address. Research has proved beyond all doubt that among migrants, diaspora Muslims are far and away the group most likely to make the largest claims on the welfare system and engage in anti-social and criminal activities of various kinds, and at the same time, the least likely to pursue gainful employment and therefore to contribute to the funding of the system as workers, tax payers and insurance contributors. A sudden increase in their number will therefore only exacerbate problems that are already beginning to appear intractable. In the UK in the year 2012, 75% of Muslim women of working age were unemployed, the vast majority of them we can be sure being those whose religion has confined them to their traditional role of child (preferably male) bearers and domestic slaves. That this state of affairs has little or nothing to do with racism was born out by a survey conducted by the Muslim reformist and integrationist Quilliam Foundation, which found that only 2% of Muslim women who were genuinely seeking work were unable to find it. It is also refuted by statistics which show that the unemployment rate for non-Muslims with a similar Asian profile, mainly Hindus, Buddhists and Sikhs, is far closer to the national average. Therefore, the causes must lie elsewhere, in Islam's teachings on the status of women.

But while confinement to domestic servitude goes a long way to account for under-employment by Muslim women, it cannot explain however why 50% of Muslim men were also unemployed in the same year, while nationally the unemployment rate was less than one fifth of that figure. The welfare system is being milked in other ways too. In 2002, 26% of Muslim women were claiming disability benefit and 21% of Muslim men, compared to the national average of 7%. Even the most zealous Islamophile would be hard put to see in these vast discrepancies the result of racial or any other prejudice. If anything, it suggests the contrary. A study conducted by University College London in 2013 showed that even though immigrants from the European Economic Area to the UK (the EU plus Norway, Iceland and Lichtenstein) paid 34% more in taxes than they received in benefits (compared with UK nationals' 11%), in the period between 1995 to 2011, all immigrants combined still ran up a *deficit* of £114 billion. In Germany, Muslim welfare dependency is if anything even more chronic. 80% of Turks of working age are unemployed and drawing benefits. In Denmark, Muslims comprise 5% of the total population, but draw 40% of the country's welfare benefits.

With minor variations, the same pattern prevails throughout Western Europe. It is certain to be accentuated as more Muslim refugees, many, especially females, poorly educated if at all, and lacking language and other skills essential for employment, continue to find their way in huge numbers into a continent still struggling to recover from the recession that began in 2008. No welfare system can indefinitely withstand this level of strain, given the demographic projections of Muslim diaspora birth rates and ever rising levels of institutionalised *kuffar*-funded parasitism. And to make it clear to those who see in these judgements evidence of racism, I repeat, this is not a race issue, but one of a clash of cultures. A UK government survey conducted in 2002 showed that Muslims of subcontinental origin were four times more likely to be unemployed than Hindus from the same ethnic background.

At this point, let us remind ourselves once again how reluctant the world was to offer refuge to the tens of thousands of German Jews fleeing from Nazi persecution. What a contrast to today, when Europe, in many cases illegally, has opened its doors to a million and more Muslims, a large proportion of whom, unlike Germany's Jews, and as studies have shown, are not genuine asylum seekers, and moreover ,whose faith teaches them to hate and even murder Jews. And how ironic that it is Germany which is the destination of choice for most of the new arrivals. The estimated annual cost to Germany alone of accommodating the basic needs of its migrants is 11 billion euros. How much wealth these migrants will generate is impossible to predict, but on past form it is certain not to even remotely approach that sum, huge even by German standards. According to Germany's Labour Office, 80% of these new migrants have no skill qualifications whatsoever, with less than 10% likely to find employment of any kind in the first year of their stay. The cost to Germany is not only to be counted in money. Within days of the first migrant arrivals, reports began to appear in the German media not only of rapes and the sexual abuse of children, but also of fighting, often by organised gangs, between Sunni and Shi'a Muslims, between Muslims from Asia and Arabs from the Middle East and north Africa, and Muslims of all persuasions against Kurds, Christians and Yazidis. It was bound to happen. Here is a far from complete (pre-Cologne) list of such incidents:

> Hemer: Ten Algerian Muslims attacked a Christian couple from Eritrea with a glass bottle, because the man was wearing a cross.
> Fresing: A Christian family from Mosul were threatened by Muslims: 'They shouted at my wife and hit my child. They said "We will kill you and drink your blood"'.
> Sept. 13: Calden: 60 injured, including 10 children, in fighting between Pakistani and

Syrian Muslims.

Sept. 27: Calden: 700 Albanians fought a pitched battle with 70 Pakistanis, and then Pakistanis with Syrians. (There were no 'war zones' in either Albania or Pakistan, but one had been created in Calden)

Sept. 29: Engelskirchen: Muslims from Algeria and Mali come to blows.

Sept. 28: Dresden: Fighting between 150 Syrian and Pakistani Muslims.

Aug. 10: Dresden: Fighting between Syrian and Afghan Muslims.

Sept. 24: Leipzig: Fighting between around 100 Syrian and Afghan Muslims

Sept. 2: Heidelberg: Fighting between Tunisian and Algerian Muslims.

Sept. 29: Gerolzhofen: Fighting between rival gangs of Syrian Muslims.

Sept. 1: Tegernsee: Fighting between Somali, Syrian and Albanian Muslims.

These clashes are either religious or ethnic, or sometimes even both. A convert to Christianity fleeing a probable death sentence for apostasy in Iran described his ordeal in a refugee camp in the heart of Europe: 'Muslims wake me before the crack of dawn during Ramadan and say I should eat before sunrise. When I decline, they call be a *kuffar*. They spit at me. They treat me like an animal. They threaten to kill me.' As the head of Germany's police trade union, Rainer Wendt was as well qualified as anyone to describe the mayhem and worse that confronted his members in Germany's refugee centres:

> We have been witnessing this violence for weeks and months. Groups based on ethnicity, religion or clan structures go after each other with knives and homemade weapons. When these groups fight each other at night, all those German citizens who welcomed the migrants with open arms at the Munich train station are fast asleep, but the police remain awake and are left standing in the middle. We can only estimate the true extent of violence because women and children are often afraid to file a complaint, since it is also about sexual abuse and rape. Sunnis are fighting Shiites; there are Salafists from competing groups. They are trying to impose their rules in the shelters. Christians are being massively oppressed and the Sharia is being enforced. Women are forced to cover up. Men are forced to pray.

Another confidential report, by German intelligence, found its way into the columns of *Welt Am Sonntag:*

> The integration of hundreds of thousands of illegal migrants into German society is no longer possible in the light of the number of already existing parallel societies We are importing Islamic extremism, Arab anti-Semitism, national and ethnic conflicts of other peoples, as well as a different understanding of society and law.

Those who might be inclined to dismiss such comments simply because they are made by a policeman or an intelligence officer should perhaps listen to Max Klinberg, Director of the Frankfurt-based International Society for Human Rights:

> We have to dispense with the illusion that all of those coming here are human rights activists. Among those who arriving here now, a substantial number are at least as religiously intense as the Muslim Brotherhood [Obama would say, surely a good thing to be]. We are getting reports of threats of aggression, including threats of beheading [nothing unusual there] by Sunnis against Shiites, but Yazidis and Christians are the most impacted. Those Christian converts who do not hide their faith [this is in Germany!] stand a 100% probability of being attacked and mobbed.

No sooner does Europe, in contravention of its own laws on asylum, open its doors to these mostly young male so-called refugees and asylum seekers than some resume, without the least inhibition or sense of shame, the same savage feuds that, so they claim, are the cause of their flight to the sanctuary of the *kuffar*. Confronted with the evidence that has accumulated, and that already millions of Europeans have already personally experienced, few would deny that the generous, if naive, sentiments that inspired the ecstatic reception given to migrants arriving at Munich train station have been cruelly exploited by those Muslims who then ran amok at camps all over Germany. Yet how could anyone expect that overnight, young men reared in the barbaric misogynistic, homophobic, anti-Semitic culture of Islam, the culture that has given birth to Hamas and the Islamic State, would leave all their ingrained hatreds, violence and primitive attitudes behind them and from the first day in their new home, conduct themselves as civilised Europeans?

Having seen what Merkel's illegal open-door policy had led to, the former mayor of the Berlin district of Neukoln, Heinz Buschkowsky, concluded that 'the bulk of the migrants who are arriving here cannot be integrated'. Aware of the growing backlash against the negative - for ordinary Germans that is - consequences of Merkel's rash pledge that 'we can do it' (more honestly, 'you must do it') her administration did what it could to prevent any information reaching the public that could fuel these discontents. For already by the beginning of October 2015, 51% of Germans polled said they were 'scared' of their country's new Muslim migrants.

But Germany, unlike the homelands of the migrants, has a free press, and so, no doubt much to Merkel's frustration, confidential and classified reports on the anti-social activities of some Muslim migrants leaked their way into Germany's national dailies. *Bild* also revealed that the government had raised its estimate of new migrant arrivals for the year 2015 from 800,000 to 1.5 million. In the whole of 2014, the total number of registered migrant arrivals was 'only' 202,000. Ten months on, the UN estimated that in just one month, October 2015, 218,000 migrants had crossed to Europe by sea. But even if correct, the prediction of 1.5 million is far from the final figure, because under existing asylum laws (and all these migrants claim to be asylum seekers) those who are granted asylum status are entitled to be joined by up to eight close family relatives, thereby raising the projection to something in the region of seven million. This is in addition to the approximately four million mainly Turkish Muslims already resident in Germany before the migrant surge began. On top of these numbers, an estimated 290,000 migrants entered Germany illegally. But not to worry. 'We can do it'. According to Uwe Brandt, President of the Bavarian Association of Municipalities, Germany was on course to become home to '20 million Muslims by 2020'. Given the nature and rate of this increase, it would be certain to have profound social, economic and political repercussions. Brandt continues:

> A four-member refugee family receives up to 1,200 euros per month in transfer payments, plus [free] accommodation and meals. Now go to an unemployed German family man who has worked for 30 years, and now with is family receives only marginally more. These people are asking us whether we politicians really see this as fair and just.

On October 25, 2015, *Die Welt* published a portion of a document emanating from the very highest level of Germany's Intelligence and Security services. One of its conclusions was that the 'integration of hundreds of thousands of illegal immigrants will be impossible given the large numbers involved and the already existing parallel Muslim societies in Germany.' Germany's internal security was also under threat:

> We are importing Islamic extremism, Arab anti-Semitism, national and ethnic conflicts of other peoples, as well as different understanding of society and law...The high influx of people from other parts of the world will lead to the instability of our country. By allowing this mass migration, we are producing extremists. Mainstream society is radicalising because the majority does not want migration, which is being forced by the political elites. In the future, many Germans will turn away from the constitutional state.

It was not long before within her own party, the conservative Christian Democrats (CDU) and her coalition partners, the even more conservative Bavarian Social Union (CSU) and the centre-left Social Democrats (SPD), voices were raised against Chancellor Merkel's open-door policy. CDU Bundestag deputy Michael Stuebgen warned his party leader that his disagreement with her was 'fundamental': 'Our capacities are exhausted and there is concern that the system will explode if we do not regain control of our borders. But the Chancellor disagrees and so the conflict is unsolved.' Hans-Peter Friedrich of the CSU described Merkel's open-door policy as an 'unprecedented political blunder' that would have 'devastating long-term consequences.' It was ' totally irresponsible that tens of thousands of people are flowing into the country uncontrolled and unregistered, and we can only unreliably estimate exactly how many of them are Islamic State fighters or Islamic "sleepers". I am convinced that no other country in the world would be so naive and starry-eye to expose itself to such a risk.' He was wrong.

Vice Chancellor Sigmar Gabriel and Foreign Minister Frank-Walter Steinmeir, the two highest ranking SPD members of Merkel's administration, also broke ranks in a joint statement published by *Der Spiegel* warning 'we cannot indefinitely absorb and integrate more than a million refugees a year', while the CSU's Bavarian Finance Minister, Markus Soeder demanded that 'there must be limits and quotas for immigration, we cannot save the whole world. The refugee influx will not be stopped unless we secure our borders and send a clear signal that not everyone can come to Germany.' But those advocating 'open borders' say they can. In densely-populated North Rhine Westphalia, those limits had already been reached. On October 21, 2015, 200 of the state's mayors signed an open letter to Merkel making it clear they could take no more migrants:

> We are seriously concerned for our country and the cities and towns we represent. The reason: the massive and most uncontrolled flow of migrants to Germany and our cities and towns. All available housing possibilities are exhausted, including tents and shipping containers. Managing the migrant shelters is so time intensive that our personnel can no longer attend to other municipal responsibilities.

The mantra 'we can do it' had indeed become 'you must do it'. In fact, so far as who would be required to sustain the financial costs…and worse…of her illegal invitation, it always had been. Police forces already struggling to cope as a result of Merkel's 'austerity' budget cuts were now being overwhelmed as young male migrants spilled out from their emergency accommodation onto the streets of

Germany's cities. According to Norman Grossmann, Director of Hamburg's Police Inspector's Office, of 55 purses snatched in the city each day, 90% were stolen by males between the ages of 20 and 30 from North Africa and the Balkans. In Stuttgart, gangs of Gambians (Gambia is nearly 6,000 kilometres distant from Syria) had taken control of the city's drug trafficking. In Dresden, the same trade was plied quite openly at the city's main railway station by migrants from Algeria, Morocco and Tunisia, again where there were no civil wars to generate genuine asylum seekers. In Berlin, a classified police report leaked to *Bild* revealed that a dozen or so Arab clans exerted control over the German capital's underworld...the new Muslim Mafia. Another police report leaked to *Der Tagesspiegel* documented evidence that 80% of violent crimes in Berlin were committed by non-Germans. And so it went on. In Duisburg, the most Islamised city in Germany, with 60,000 Muslims out of total population of 500,000, *Der Speigel* described districts where 'immigrant gangs are taking over metro trains for themselves. Native residents and business people are being intimidated and silenced. People taking trams during the evening and night time describe their experiences as "living nightmares".'

The consequences for ordinary Germans of Merkel's grand gesture can in some respects be reduced to simple arithmetic. Germany is ranked 58th in the world for population density, twice of that of France and the highest of continental Europe's larger states. Merkel nevertheless believed that her heavily urbanised and densely populated country was capable of absorbing several million migrants steeped in a totally alien and to a large degree, incompatible culture, speaking totally different languages, reading, when they are literate, totally different scripts, reared in a faith that commands them not to make friends with unbelievers, and divided amongst themselves into hostile clans, nations and Islamic factions, all without any serious adverse impact on Germany's economic, social and political equilibrium, or the everyday lives of its host population.

Calden is a small town in the state of Hesse in central Germany, with a population of 7,500. The powers that be in Berlin decided that Calden must accommodate 1,400 migrants. With typical Germany efficiency, a tent city was erected at a nearby airport. Welcoming locals donated enough clothing to fill four garages. But no sooner were the migrants settled in than trouble began. An argument in a food queue between an Albanian and a Pakistani, neither from countries afflicted by civil war, escalated into a full-scale battle involving 300 migrants between rival gangs armed with metal bars and pepper sprays. It took 500 police all night to restore order, three being injured in the fighting. The same locals who had gone out of their way to welcome and help the migrants now expressed their disillusionment to reporters. But what did they expect? Now to the village of Sumte in Lower Saxony, North West Germany. Sumte has an aging population of just 102 but was ordered to accommodate *10 times* that number of migrants. When the locals objected, their quota was reduced from 1000 to...750. In no time, the village's sewage system became clogged...something unheard of in hygiene-conscious Germany.

As in other European countries, attempts were made in Germany to conceal the extent of migrant criminality and anti-social behaviour by doctoring or suppressing crime statistics and even by changing the names of criminals. (A convicted Muslim rapist from Somalia was identified in the press as 'Joseph T' instead of Ali S.) As it had been the practice in ultra-politically correct Sweden for a decade and more, so it was now in Germany. The head of the Association of Criminal Police, Andre

Schulz, revealed that around 90% of sex crimes committed in 2014 did not appear in the official crime statistics. Based on information that had been kept from the public, Shultz warned that with at least 10% of Germany's migrants already involved in crime, Germany's traditionally low crime rate was set to soar to spectacular levels, which in fact has proved to be the case. Even before the 2015 influx, according to Germany's Federal Police, crimes committed by asylum seekers rose from 32,495 in 2013 to 53,890 in 2014. Violent crimes causing injury rose in the same period from 5,172 to 8,994. With Jews, gays and young women especially in mind, it was not unreasonable to anticipate that not only Germany, but Europe, could be in for a bumpy ride. But fear not. 'We can do it'. When Chancellor Merkel was challenged at a public question and answer event to explain how she intended to combat potential threats to Germany's cultural identity, stability and internal security posed by the arrival of more than one million Muslim migrants, this is, in part, how she responded.

> I think first and foremost that Islamism and Islamic terror, [surely a slip of the tongue] a phenomenon predominately operating in Syria, Libya and northern Iraq, and to which, unfortunately, the European Union has contributed a myriad of fighters as well, and therefore we cannot sit there and say this phenomenon has nothing to do with us, because those are people, sometimes very young people, who grew up in our countries, and this is where we also bear a responsibility.

Jihadism also *Europe's* responsibility? Jihadi Islam is in no sense a creation of the European Union, though it certainly appeases it. It is integral to, and as old as Islam itself, and those Muslims who leave Europe to fight for the Islamic State are sworn enemies of everything modern Europe stands for. Merkel's security services will surely have told her that Germany's Jihadis are reared in Muslim families, brain-washed in mosques, and recruited on Islamic State websites. Merkel continues: 'Secondly, fear has never been a good adviser. Neither in our personal lives not in society.' Easily said, for someone permanently protected by a team of between 15 and 20 bodyguards. A little more than a year later, after a series of sex crimes and murders perpetrated by her guests, she stated in her New Year's message that the main task facing her country was combatting the threat of 'Islamist terrorism'. Merkel continued:

> I see that there are these worries, but I have to say that we all have these chances and all these liberties to practice our own religion as well, in so far as we are practising it and believe in it. We should have the courage as Christians to enter a dialogue [Muslim dialogues with Christians often end with decapitation or crucifixion] and while we are talking about tradition [nobody was], maybe please go to church every once in a while or become a tad more versed in the Bible and maybe be able just to explain a painting in a church or at least be able to explain what the meaning of Pentecost is. So there I just have to say that a lot of people's knowledge about the Christian occident leaves a lot to be desired.

Desired by whom exactly? By degrees, although none too subtly, Merkel had moved the debate from one on cultural friction and threats to security to pastoral hectoring, theological debates, and irate exhortations for more Bible study, appreciation of liturgical art and knowledge of the Christian calendar. But there is more. It seems this public decline of interest in Merkel's own faith had resulted in far too many Germans being put to shame by superior Muslim exegesis: 'But then to come back and complain about how Muslims know much more about the *Koran* than they [i.e., Germans] do about the Bible, I find that very curious.' Merkel did not tell her audience where these complaints come from. I suggest that instead of exhorting Germans to study the Bible, Merkel would have been well-advised to recommend to her fellow Germans that they study the *Koran,* where they will have found all the evidence they need to predict what kind of future faced their country and indeed the rest of Europe if it continued to allow millions of Muslim migrants to pour unchecked through their Chancellor's ever-open door. In the light of her flagrant breach of her own and European Union immigration and asylum regulations, there was no more fitting place for Merkel to begin her own study of the *Koran* than Verse 101 of Chapter Four: 'And who emigrates from his country in the way of Allah will find in the earth an abundant place of refuge and plentifulness'… in the welfare states of Germany, Scandinavia and the United Kingdom.

Finally, when Merkel returned to the question she had been evading for the best part of her reply, it was to play the guilt card. Up to this point, her evasions had been puerile to be sure, eccentric even, but not immoral. But this is exactly what they now became. Those Germans responsible for the crimes of the Third Reich are for the most part long gone; many having spent their last years in the service of Jew-hating Muslim regimes. So unless a Biblical, 'lapsarian' political guilt can be passed down through the generations, that to paraphrase St Paul (Romans 5:2), 'in Hitler all Germans have sinned', Germany today has no more reason to feel guilty about the Holocaust or any other crimes of the Nazi era than the descendants of its victims. This is so obviously true, it should not need be stated. But here we have Merkel saying something rather different:

> But let us not forget how just how rich European history is of dramatic and gruesome conflict and war. We should be really careful when we complain if somewhere else [sic] something bad [sic] is happening. Sure, we have to stand up against that, but we have no ground to stand on, to show haughty arrogance towards others. And I have to say that as Chancellor of Germany.

There we have it, again, the Chomsky principle, adapted by Merkel to apply to Germany's migrant crisis. Even the mildest criticism of Islam, and the deeds of those who subscribe to it, is *verboten.* We Germans have no right to be 'haughty' about the behaviour of some Muslim migrants no matter how 'bad' we may think it is. 'We have no ground to stand on', because seventy years and more ago, Germans committed unspeakable crimes. Therefore, only he who is without ancestral sin can cast the first stone. But as it does with Chomsky, this rule only operates in one direction. Muslims can speak their home truths about the West's decadent, materialist, godless ways. But woe betide any German who has the temerity, or 'haughty arrogance' to reply in kind, because Germans, hereditary sinners that they all are, have 'no ground to stand on', whereas the followers of Islam, which had been waging a holy against the west for the best part of fourteen centuries, and has been guilty of in that time, and was still committing, the most appalling atrocities against not only infidels, including those of Merkel's faith, but those of its own, apparently did. One final thought. If I were one of that rare breed of men, a Jew in Germany, I would be doing what tens of thousands of Jews in France have already done. I would be packing my bags and heading for Israel. In the light of Germany's not so distant past, I would not want to run the risk of having as my neighbours potentially violent young men whose religion commands them to regard Jews, as once did the Nazis, as sub-humans, in this case, to be precise, as 'apes and swine'.

What has already happened to Germany will, even if on a lesser scale, also be the lot of any other country that allows easy or uncontrolled access to new Muslims migrants, as the tragic case of Sweden has already shown. The UK, with its official multicultural encouragement and rewarding of Muslim segregation in the name of 'celebrating diversity' (for example, with un-investigated and un-prosecuted child and forced marriages, bigamy, gang rape, FGM and honour killings), will prove no exception., Why should they be any different from those who are already here, and have had years, decades in many cases, to at least make the effort to integrate, but, as even some Muslim commentators themselves have complained, have quite deliberately chosen not to do so? To put it bluntly, and it is time it was, like the bogus asylum-seekers swarming into Europe amidst a smaller number of genuine refugees, a substantial proportion of the existing Muslim population of the UK sees its welfare state as an Allah-given opportunity for free loading, and there is no reason to suppose that new arrivals will behave differently. The proof is in the figures. It has been calculated that as a direct consequence of this traditional parasitic Islamic life style, the financial cost to the UK economy, excluding the costs of services in kind and Muslim crime, and the loss of income tax revenue and insurance payments through unemployment, and therefore counting only cash payments in the form of various benefits, amounts to a colossal £13 billion per year while European migrants to the UK contribute 30% more than they take out. One can see how some UK Muslims have cynically but with some justice described this subsidy as the modern voluntary version of the Sharia-sanctioned plunder of infidels, a *dhimmi* tax on the host *kuffar*. British Jihadi preacher and benefits parasite Anjem Choudary, who was himself until his conviction and imprisonment in 2016 on terrorist charges a long-standing benefit recipient to the sum of £32,000 per year, has described what is technically called the job seekers allowance as the 'Jihad Seeker's Allowance': 'You *kuffar* work. Give us the money. *Allahu Akhbar* [God is Great] We take the money'. And that is exactly what they do, making the British possibly the first voluntary *dhimmis* in the history of Islam.

Those politicians, from left to right, who speak glibly of the 'enormous contribution' Islam makes to British society, always without being able to provide any examples, would do well to consult the statistics presented above before making such claims. In terms of finance, the 'enormous contribution' is in the opposite direction. But there is more. Wherever they have settled, many Muslims have brought with them a propensity for criminal behaviour, particularly offences related to terrorism, drugs, violence against Jews and the sexual abuse and exploitation of non-Muslim females, far above that of the indigenous population. Even if one allows for discriminatory sentencing, that alone cannot explain the enormous disproportion in the prison population of the UK, where 15% are Muslims, compared with only 5% in the population as a whole, or France, where the Muslim prison population is a staggering 70% compared with ten percent in the country as a whole. In Spain, the proportion is again 70%, compared with only 2.3% in the total population. In Norway, it is 30%, Denmark, 20%, Belgium, 16%, Italy, 13%, in each case, far in excess of the share of Muslims in the total population, and what is equally to the point, *of any similar ethnic minority*. Small wonder then that in every opinion poll conducted on the subject, and what is more, in defiance of what their political representatives say to the contrary, be they left, right or centre, large majorities of respondents, irrespective of their voting preferences, have found Islam to be incompatible with their beliefs and way of life, and want an end to illegal mass Muslim migration into Europe. Are they all Nazis for doing so?

Though it will be denounced as racist, despite the subject being the effect of religion and not genes on human behaviour, one should be free, without fear of prosecution, publicly to ask and seek answers to this question: How does it come about that Islam, whose notion of justice, being divine, is supposedly infinitely superior to any man-made system of ethics and law, rears men who, wherever they settle, prove themselves to be the most depraved and criminal on our planet? Why is it that 26% of prisoners in London are Muslim, but Muslims make up only 12%, of London's population? Why is it that the number of Muslim prisoners in the UK has *doubled* over the last ten years, while the UK's adult male Muslim population has increased by far less, and the total prison population by no more than ten per cent? Let us again discount racial factors. Taking the year 2012, Hindus comprised 1.0% of the UK population aged over 15, but only 0.5% of the prison population. With Sikhs, the percentages were 0.9 and 0.7, again *underrepresented*. Muslims however, who made up 4.0% of the UK's over 15 population, constituted 13.1% of the UK prison population, more than three times over-represented as compared with the UK as a whole, and *six* times more so than the no less 'Asian' Hindus. So what has this to do with race? And do those Muslims and non-Muslims who have advocated the adoption of Sharia law in the UK seriously believe that its introduction would have the effect of reducing the Muslim crime rate? Based exclusively on facts, figures and numerous surveys and studies that are all easily accessible, we can construct a partial, but still informative profile of the UK Muslim adult male. Of course, far from all Muslims conform to it, but nevertheless, when compared to the rest of the UK population as defined by religion, he is statistically more likely, in some cases much more likely to be:

- in prison (Muslims in prisons in England and Wales rose from 5502 in 2002 to 1225 in December 2014);
- a convicted terrorist (as of March 2016, 137 of 147 prisoners serving sentences for terrorism offences were known to be Muslims);
- a supporter of terrorism;
- an anti-semite;
- a believer in (usually Jewish) conspiracies;
- a gang rapist;
- a pimp;
- unemployed;
- receiving disability benefit;
- married to a much younger close relative;
- to have sanctioned the mutilation of his female child or children.

Unelected Muslim 'community' spokesmen and Sharia leftists, and we can be sure not they alone, without being able to disprove the facts upon which this profile rests, will object that this is racist stereotyping, even though it is the profile of those who share not a race, but a belief. Consider the following: It is a proven fact that if those who do not believe smoking is harmful to health act on that belief by smoking, they will on average not live as long as those who act on the belief that it does. Likewise, the medical records of 5,558 Christian Scientists have shown that those who on principle refuse conventional medical treatment of any kind are more likely to die younger than those that do not. And such has also been the experience of medical teams working among African tribes in sometimes futile attempts to combat the pernicious influence of witch doctors. In each example, belief, not genes, leads to certain predictable consequences. In fact, it would strange in the extreme if it did not. And yet when the same is said of the effect of another belief, Islam, for example with respect to terrorist or sexual crimes, the same reasoning is condemned as racist.

Of all the disparate national and religious groups that make up the population of Europe, it is Muslims who are the ones most likely to take, legally or otherwise, and the least likely to give, just as they are the least likely to obey the laws of the land, but the only ones to demand that they be replaced by their own. Unless there is a radical and rapid shift away from this imbalance to the point where Muslims pay their way and respect the laws of their hosts like nearly everybody else, more Muslim immigration could bleed Europe's welfare states white. In fact, as the figures quoted above indicate, it is already in danger of doing so. It will then become a matter of right-wing parties advancing policies of xenophobia and *sauve qui peut* welfare privatisation based upon 'fiscal responsibility'. What is beyond dispute is that Europe's welfare states, from which its peoples have gained such immense benefits, are now at risk from causes that originate, not in any inherent fault in European society, but the crisis of Islam, the consequences of which we have allowed to be imported into our own midst. As a result, Europe now faces the greatest challenge to its social and political stability since the defeat of Nazism and the collapse of the Soviet empire.

23 Holy Hitmen

The history of the last century has furnished ample evidence that for all his insights, Marx was certainly over-optimistic, not only about the prospects for socialism, which thus far have proved to be illusory, but even for the global ascendancy of western bourgeois civilisation, which he predicted and indeed celebrated in the *Communist Manifesto*.. Vast swathes of humanity still endure wretched lives outside its orbit *because* they are outside its orbit. And it is certainly the case that those parts that are in the grip of Islam have been the most resistant to the modernising influences and inroads of western 'bourgeois' civilisation, this being, ironically, one of its several aspects that so enthrals the Sharia left. Contrast Pakistan, an Islamic hell hole masquerading as a country, with Japan, until the rise of post-Maoist China, the economic power house of the Far East, and with South Korea, Singapore, Thailand or even its hated secular and democratic neighbour, India, whose GDP per capita is double that of Pakistan's. The example of Japan is perhaps the most interesting and instructive, because here was a nation whose feudal and masculine militarist culture most closely resembled that of Middle Eastern Islam, with its all-pervading Samurai cult of the warrior, and of its most extreme incarnation, the suicide (flying) bomber, the *kamikaze*. (The only other remotely comparable non-Islamic martyrdom of modern times is that of the 3,000 German student volunteers who on November 10, 1914, were mowed down as, singing their student songs, they marched into a hail of gun fire in the battle of Langemark in Belgium...the so-called '*Kindermord*'.)

Religious fanaticism, the fusion of faith and state in the person of the divine Emperor, a disdain for the pleasures of this world and yet an unshakable belief in Japan's mission to conquer and rule it, hatred and contempt for, combined with fear of the outsider, an extreme misogyny, an indifference to suffering and the rights of the individual, a rejection of democracy but a readiness to harness western technology to fight its creators, a joyous acceptance of the duty to embrace death in pursuit of a transcendent cause and yes, even down to executions by beheading with a sword...we could here be describing the culture produced by the religion of peace.

Yet once Japan, like Germany, learned the hard way that the dream of world conquest is not only just that, but that it brings down upon those who attempt to make it a reality the most terrible retribution, the USA was able, in but a few years, to transplant, literally at gun point, much of its own democratic political system and principles, and later its culture, into the far from receptive soil of a nation steeped in centuries of, if Professor Said will permit, an oriental warrior despotism. True, even today, Japan is nowhere near being a carbon copy of the USA. How could it be? But it does conduct its affairs in accordance with the same basic principles that it shares with the rest of the civilised world. Only a matter of decades ago, its people were among the most fanatically devout on the planet, millions being only too willing to die for their divine emperor if he so wished it, yet in 2012, the Japanese were ranked as the least pious in a survey that asked people in a range of countries (but significantly none of them Islamic) the simple question, 'are your certain god exists'? In Japan, only 4.3% of those asked replied 'yes'. In a survey confined to the UK, 90% of Muslims gave the same answer. We can be reasonably sure that similar results would have been obtained not only in the entire diaspora, but Muslims everywhere. And looking at the chaos and carnage unleashed in the world of Islam today, driving millions of its devotees to seek sanctuary and hopefully a new life in the lands of the despised *kuffar,* we can truthfully say, much good has their credulity done them.

This seemingly unshakable grip of religion on the minds of the world's Muslims, blocking access to all the achievements of modern thought, surely helps us to understand why, in contrast to the US occupation of Japan, the western invasion, conquest and colonisation of Muslim territories, for example the British in Islamic regions of pre-independence India (now Pakistan), the British Palestine mandate and the Sudan, the French in Syria, Lebanon and Saharan Africa, and most recently the joint western invasions of Iraq and Afghanistan, have all utterly failed, where it was attempted, to achieve a similar transplantation to that accomplished in post war Japan and in post-independence India. In the cases of post-occupation Iraq and Afghanistan, as soon as the west's back was turned, tribal-based Islamic Jihadis, like unruly schoolboys when teacher leaves the classroom, unleashed orgies of incredible savagery on each other, while politicians working within the post-occupation pluralist system established by the invaders reverted almost overnight to the corrupt ways and sectarian feuds of their ancestors. Like an organism resisting a life-threatening virus, Islam fights modernity, secularism, individual freedom and liberal democracy with every fibre of its being. Even Turkey, once celebrated in the west as proof of the contrary, is being led back towards a theocratic past Ataturk believed he had laid to rest. So while most of the countries of far and south east Asia either have already adopted, or are in the process of adopting all of the technological and, in widely varying degrees, the cultural and political ingredients of western civilisation, most of the Islamic and especially the Arab world is firmly in the grip of a culture that fears modernity like the plague, and resists it with all the means at its disposal. Islam's ideal lies not in present or the future, but in the desert of seventh century Arabia.

A goodly part of our planet is ruled by three legal systems or their derivatives. Two have pagan origins and have evolved into the wholly-secular Common Law and Code Napoleon. The third is theocratic, Sharia law. Common Law, with its trial by a lay jury of peers, and derived mainly from customs and precedent, is Germanic in origin, brought to England by pagan Anglo-Saxon and Viking invaders and subsequently codified, unified and modified by English Kings, Charters, and Parliaments to be then, in the era of empire, re-exported around the globe, again by conquest and migration, where to this day, long after the English have departed, it still shapes the justice systems of entire continents. An analogous process produced the legal system that dominates the European continent; the wholly statute law and professional jurors of the Code Napoleon. Its origins lie in the laws enacted by the Roman Senate of pagan Rome which were then, like the Anglo Saxon's Common Law, exported by conquest until all of western Europe lived by and under the same laws as the citizens of Rome...hence *Civus Romanus Sum.* The decline and then fragmentation of the Roman empire under the impact of pagan Germanic invasions left in its wake a multitude of states, all nominally under the jurisdiction of what was known as the 'Holy Roman Empire of the German Nation', but in practice free to be governed as their rulers chose. As a consequence, Roman law in some regions of Europe became diluted, resulting in a hybrid of local systems inherited or improvised by rulers both secular and clerical. Out of this debris left by declining Rome eventually emerged two centres of power, that of the Franks, founded in the west by Charlemagne, crowned Holy Roman Emperor by the Pope in 800 AD, and in the centre and south, but centuries later, the Austrian Hapsburgs who, by a variety of means, secured their repeated election to the progressively more titular same office.

After an interval of more than a thousand years following the fall of the (western) Roman empire, in which Europe lacked a single, unifying legal system, Roman law in new guise returned to Europe with the coming of the French Revolution. Drawing their inspiration, as in so many other things, from Republican Rome, and guided by Enlightenment rationalism, France's new rulers sought to give effect, in legal terms, to the revolution's maxims of liberty, equality and fraternity. The end result came to be known, after its chief legislator, as the Code Napoleon, a system of law that was not derived from past customs or religious texts but constructed anew on the foundation of the principle of universal natural rights, and to be codified in statute laws. It was this system of law that Napoleon imposed on all the territories that came under his rule. As with the English re-export of Common Law, it in most cases endured and thrived after Napoleon's armies had departed, having travelled from Rome, via Paris, to Europe and, via Europe's empires, to the world. Also in a similar way, starting in the Hejaz of what is now the kingdom of Saudi Arabia, the conquering armies of Islam imposed their language, Arabic, and system of what is now known as Sharia law. It too has endured. But unlike secular statute and Common law, and the Code Napoleon, since it claims for itself divine origin, Sharia law cannot be questioned, nullified or changed either by legislation. or, as in Common, law, amended by precedent, only interpreted. Being perfect, it is unreformable. To propose to reform or amend Sharia law in any way is therefore to challenge the will and purpose of its creator, Allah, who is all wise in all things, and is therefore to commit the ultimate capital crime of apostasy.

By contrast, Common Law and *Code Napoleon*, being secular, made by man for man, can be adapted to meet new needs, attitudes and situations, and right existing wrongs. Thus, in the 1960s, under a Labour government, Parliament changed or abolished UK laws on homosexuality, divorce, the death penalty and abortion, all in defiance of Biblical teaching and in most cases, in the teeth of clerical opposition. The 57-member Organisation of the Islamic Conference makes no secret of the gulf that separates the Islamic concept of law with that prevailing in civilised countries. In doing so, it is simply applying the axiom which commands that Muslims must defy any man-made law which does not accord with the laws of Allah: '…fear not men but Me; and barter not my signs for a paltry price. And whoso judges not my that which Allah has sent down, these it is who are the disbelievers.' (*Koran*: 5: 45) A saying of the Prophet cited by Buhkari elaborates on this: 'A Muslim has to listen to and obey the order of his ruler whether he likes it or not, as long as orders involve not one in disobedience to Allah. But if an act of disobedience to Allah is imposed, one should not listen to it or obey it.' (Bukhari, Volume 9, Book 89, *Hadith* 258)

Should there then be any surprise that when polled on the subject, almost invariably a majority of diaspora Muslims favour the adoption of Sharia law and, as in the UK, in a variety of cases, prefer to have recourse to Sharia courts? But here too, double standards obtain. Self-appointed 'Muslim community' leaders, in accordance with the sanction afforded by Bukhari, are only too happy to use the parliaments and courts of the *kuffar* to seek privileges and special protection for their faith. This is also the case internationally. As we have seen, Islamic states repeatedly accuse Israel at the UN of violating the same human rights they neither observe nor believe in.

Under the terms of the Cairo Declaration of 1990, rights as defined by Islamic law, 'all men' (not 'all men and women', as specified in the Preamble to the UN Declaration) are held to be equal only 'in terms of basic [sic] human dignity', whatever they may be taken to mean, not their rights. Reading on, we then learn that such rights as the Declaration does grant are circumscribed by Sharia law. Being subordinate, as the *Koran* stipulates, to men, women are given their 'own rights to enjoy [sic]' and 'duties to perform', some of which we have already explored in some detail. Article 10 denies the right of non-Muslims to persuade Muslims to 'convert to another religion or atheism', while naturally not forbidding the reverse. This is because 'Islam is the religion of unspoiled nature'. Article 19 forbids any punishments for crimes other than those specified by Sharia law which, as we should all know by now, include amputation, stoning, crucifixion, flogging, and decapitation and, according to some authorities, burning alive. As one would expect, given the constant clamour of diaspora Muslim pressure groups and their Sharia left stooges for ever tighter curbs on what can be said in public about Islam, free speech gets short shrift in the Declaration. Article 22(b) explains what is meant by the often demanded but rarely defined 'responsible' free speech: 'Everyone shall have the right to advocate what is right, and propagate what is good, and warn against what is wrong and evil according to the norms of Islamic Sharia'. It would have been simpler, and more honest, if this clause read: 'You can say what you like, as long it accords with Sharia law'. Or, as Henry Ford once said of his first mass produced model, 'you can have any colour you like, so long as it is black'. So here we have all the evidence we need as to why Islam not only cannot 'adjust' to the modern world, but does not think even it should, and in an alien, secular setting, why its diaspora finds it so hard, when it is encouraged to do so, to integrate into the host society.

The secular world, which at least pays lip service to free speech, and with its man-made laws, treats women as equals and allows people to change their religion or have none at all, is one that both the majority of existing diaspora Muslims, and even more so, those new millions cascading northward from the 'soft underbelly' of southern Europe, not only reject, but for religious and cultural reasons, simply cannot comprehend. True, more astute 'establishment' Muslims gladly exploit the opportunities the western political system offers them to pursue careers that are often more corrupt than devout. But others far more influential among the young subscribe to a totally segregationist theocracy, a stance neatly captured by a poster displayed in the Sharia Borough of Tower Hamlets in the General Election of May 2015: 'Democracy is a system whereby man violates the right of Allah'.

Millions of Muslims have fled their homelands, some from danger, others simply to seek a better life. Yet no matter what the risks, all headed for the realm of the despised *kuffar*. How come? Could it be that the secret of what attracts them, the west's security and immense material superiority over the world of Islam, resides in what their culture and religion has denied them; the valuing and protecting of individual freedom? In the seven decades since the end of World War II, that portion of humanity which inhabits the civilised West has achieved probably the most radical and rapid political transformation in all human history, and certainly since the Renaissance and the Reformation. Beginning with the Allied defeat of the Axis powers, Europe has progressed, in a series of reforms and revolutions, from a continent dominated by totalitarianism of the left and right to one where liberal democracy prevails in all but its eastern hinterland. The classic authoritarian regimes of central and South America have, with the exception of three supported by Jeremy Corbyn, suffered a similar fate. Excluding China (though even here changes are afoot) the majority of the remaining Asians live under political systems that, to one degree or another embrace or pay lip service to the western model of democracy. Even sub-Saharan Africa has taken steps in the same direction, albeit modest and uncertain. Only where Islam rules is there, with few very partial exceptions for example, ex French Tunisia and ex Dutch Indonesia, no progress. Instead, as proved to be the case with the 'Arab Spring', there is regression, either to theocracy or what still seems its only viable alternatives, authoritarian civilian or military rule.

However, that is only part of the story. It is undeniably the case that the west's material progress has not only been caused, but matched to a large extent by the ascendency of rational thought. Flatearthism, geocentrism, witches, alchemy, ouija boards, numerology, the 'paranormal', ghosts, unicorns, magic, palmistry, phrenology, astrology...these and similar fantasies are the objects of ridicule by any even only half-educated person...or at least they should be, for together with religion, they belong to the intellectual infancy of mankind. Yet anti-Semitism, the creature of the two global monotheisms, not only endures but even thrives in the modern world like no other imbecility, seemingly unaffected by the progress humanity has achieved elsewhere. Almost despairingly, one has to ask, has history taught nothing at all? Surely even the most ill-educated Arab must know that Hitler has gone down in history as the world's most spectacular loser, with his Third Reich in ruins, his dream of world conquest shattered, trapped like a rat in his Berlin bunker still cursing the Jews, then finally blowing out his diseased brain to escape capture and humiliation by the 'Jewish Bolshevik' Red Army coming up the road. Yet this monumental failure is the idol and exemplar of countless Muslims the world over, and most of all of the Arabs; not, obviously, because he lost his war against the rest of the world, but because he won his war against the Jews - or rather nearly, because the completion of what Hitler began, according to Livingstone's 'progressive voice for change', Yusef al-Qaradawi , 'will be all the work of the believers'. And so it goes on.

One would think that anyone concerned with the best interests of the Arab peoples, such as the far-left claims to be, would do their very utmost to loosen the grip of this all-consuming, self-defeating hatred on the Arab and Islamic mind. It should say, clearly, loudly and repeatedly, that Jew- hatred is not only ignorant and morally repugnant, but a dead end, not a cure for anything, but itself a disease that inflicts the most degrading and destructive consequences on those infected by it. It should say that even if Israel were, in the words of the former Iranian President Mahmoud Ahmadinejad, to be 'wiped off the map', and its every last Jewish inhabitant killed or even, as Hezbollah and Hamas desire, every Jew in the world, this would solve not a single one of problems that beset the Islamic and, more specifically, the Arab world. Those problems were and are not caused by either Israel or the Jews; any more than the Jews were responsible for Germany's defeat in the First World War and the failings of the Weimar Republic. They so obviously arise from within Arab society itself, re-enforced by its primitive Islamic culture, But the Sharia left does not say this. Echoing the hate preachers of Jihadism, it says the exact opposite, that Israel is the enemy, and has to be destroyed so that the Arabs may prosper.

The origins of the chronic current crisis of the Arab world not only predate the creation of the state of Israel. They have their roots in a centuries-old, religiously-derived and sustained culture that with incredible tenacity and violence, obstructs progress towards modern, civilised ways of living. This was demonstrated in spectacular fashion by the demise of the so-called Arab Spring. Not accidentally, it followed the same sequence of events that accompanied the overthrow of the Shah in Iran in 1979. Fuelled by a pathological hatred and fear of secular modernity, in its wake swathes of the Middle East have been hurled back decades if not centuries. In Libya, al Qaeda and ISIS drove one third of the country's population into exile, while in Syria and Iraq, religious civil wars triggered by the terror of the ISIS Caliphate generated refugees by the million. After an interlude of theocratic Muslim Brotherhood rule in Egypt, a backlash returned the generals to power, who then in turn became the target for Muslim Brotherhood terrorism. Urged on by the western Sharia left, and with logistical and financial support from Qatar and Iran, terrorist, genocidal Hamas rules the Gaza Strip while, with the full support of western politicians, oil companies and arms dealers, the grip of the feudal monarchies of Saudi Arabia and the Gulf, who promote and fund Jihadi Islam, is as tight as ever. Even once secular Turkey, although not Arab, is also heading towards theocracy.

In so far as the Arab Spring set itself the goal of the democratisation of the Arab world, (and this is itself a moot point) it has failed, and was doomed to fail because, as was the case in Iran after the overthrow of the Shah, despite the initial efforts of brave secular minorities, it succumbed to the numerically superior forces and deeper historical roots of Islamic theocracy. In times of upheaval, the legions of Allah are always in the wings, waiting their moment. The entirely predictable outcome of the Arab Spring, and with it, the resumption of the Islamic version of Trotsky's 'hopeless rotations' between theocratic and semi-secular autocratic rule, surely demonstrates that only way ahead for the Arab peoples is to end their obsession with Israel and the Jews, and to embrace the values and institutions that have served the west so well, and whose rejection has reduced the Arabs to their current pitiable and ever-worsening state. And increasingly, brave voices urging this can be heard in the Middle East, even amongst its Muslim clergy (See Appendix I) Rather than challenge those tendencies which are the most retrogressive, in the first place the lie that Israel and the Jews are the problem and the enemy, not the feudal, business, military, clerical and terrorist elites that exploit, oppress and manipulate the Arab masses, the Sharia left justifies and panders to the very delusions that perpetuate the crisis of the region. In short, the anti-Zionist left has become the promoters of an Islamic version of Bebel's 'socialism of fools', an alchemy that can produce for the Arabs and especially the Palestinians only more attacks on and then defeats at the hands of Israel, which will, as they have in the past, feed yet more intense feelings of hatred, frustration and humiliation.

Those millions duped by Hitler's promise of a Jew-free 'Thousand Year Reich' realised far too late that whatever it might have inflicted on the Jews, his 'socialism of fools' had brought ruin, humiliation and moral disgrace to Germany. Now, in its new version, we have a 'Sharia Socialism', a racial and religious war of Muslims against Jews, the fulcrum of a broader war of east against west, an offensive we have not only witnessed on our streets, TV screens and in the press, but one by deploying more subtle methods, including infiltration of the Labour Party, has gained a foothold in the political mainstream. One of the many ironies of the left's support for Jihadi Islam is the delusion that equipped with what it believes is its greater political sophistication, it will be the left and not its Muslim allies of convenience who will call the political tune, evidently unaware (let us be charitable) they are themselves being used as a convenient but none the less, dispensable ally and cover for the aims of their partners, aims which for sure, as the Hamas Charter make very clear, do not include the creation of a society based on the teachings of an atheist Jew. How great, and indeed pathetic, are the delusions of the Sharia left in this respect can be measured by comparing its alliance with Islam to its historic precedents, when unlike today, its partners were forces in their own right, not bankrupt opportunists in search of a new market for their out-dated wares. History provides numerous examples of the near-certainty that in all such combinations of convenience, when one of its partners has outlived its usefulness, it will be discarded and, if the weaker of the two, possibly worse.

Francis I of France, who reigned from 1515 to1547, was constantly at odds and frequently at war with his great continental rival, the Hapsburg Empire. Realist that he was, he never allowed his formal adherence to the faith he shared with Spain and Austria to preclude a strategic alliance with the Islamic Ottoman empire, concluded in 1535 with Sultan Suleiman I. In the First World War, predominately protestant Imperial Germany, already aligned, like Francis I, with Ottoman Turkey, adopted a similar strategy by attempting to kindle an Islamic holy war against the British Empire amongst the Arabs of the Middle East and the Muslims of India. To this end, Kaiser William II proclaimed himself the protector of the world's Muslims, and authorised the construction of Germany's first Mosque in Berlin. The British Empire replied in kind, sending Lawrence on his successful mission to raise an Arab revolt against Germany's Turkish ally. In the Second World War, Nazi Germany, playing not only the anti-British but the anti-Semitic card sought, and as we have seen, found, willing Muslim allies in the Middle East.

General Franco's victory in the Spanish Civil War relied heavily on the Roman Catholic Church for domestic political and 'spiritual' support, and on external military and logistic assistance from Nazi Germany and Fascist Italy. But in the first days of the conflict, Franco's putsch, lacking poplar support, was barely clinging on to its precarious toehold in the south of mainland Spain. With the navy, unlike most of the army, remaining loyal to the republic, Franco's survival was secured only with the aid of Muslim 'volunteers', eventually 87,000 in total, who were initially flown from Spanish Morocco by German transport planes to the mainland, where they were set loose to commit appalling acts of brutality on republican civilians as well as on poorly armed workers and peasants. Following their conquest of Seville, Franco's Moors paraded through the city holding aloft in triumph on their bayonets as proof of their virility the underwear of the infidel woman they had gang-raped, Cologne and Rotherham fashion, as their 'spoils of war'. Symbolically, they were re-enacting in exactly the same location the invasion of Spain in the early eighth century by the armies of Islam, only now not as conquerors but as the mercenaries of Fascism.

Then, in a leftist variant of the same strategy, we have the atheist and Jewish Comintern chief, Grigory Zinoviev, addressing a 'Congress of Toilers of the East' at Baku in 1920, summoning Muslims to join with the Bolsheviks in a 'holy war' against the imperialist west, the first of a series of attempts to implement Lenin's newly-adopted 'eastern' strategy, in which the Soviet Union would be ranged on the side of the 'Orientally backward countries' against the 'most civilised countries', as we have seen, a total inversion of the progression anticipated by Karl Marx. Here we have the prototype, if not the consciously imitated model, of present-day Sharia leftism. A classic application of Lenin's policy, as historic irony would have it, was the Comintern's support for anti-Jewish riots in British-mandated Palestine in 1929, in which 133 Jews died and another 800 were wounded. An even greater irony, the Bolshevik-backed pogrom was sparked, as we have seen, by the agitation of the fanatical anti-communist and future Hitler collaborator the Grand Mufti of Jerusalem, Haj Amin al-Husseini. But then, at the time of the Gaza war of 2014, did not leftists, and in Germany of all countries, march shoulder to shoulder with Nazis and Muslims, to chants of 'Hamas, Hamas, Jews to the gas'?

In the decades of the Cold War, as in the First and Second, both sides sought and found allies in the Muslim world. The Middle East became a focus of Soviet strategy in the mid-1950s when, with the rise of Arab nationalism, post-Stalin leaders took a number of Arab dictatorships under their wings, notably those of Egypt, Iraq and Syria (each of which brutally repressed their domestic communist parties). Huge sums were spent on supplies of Soviet military hardware, all in the end to no avail, as it piled up in the desert as junk after a succession of Arab defeats at the hands of Israel's far smaller, but qualitatively vastly superior armed forces. Also during the Cold War, the USA and conservative Islamic politicians and clerics arranged several marriages of convenience. The first was consummated in Iran when, in 1953, the Islamic clergy, spearheaded by the fanatical Fada'iyan-e Islam sect, collaborated with a CIA-backed monarchist coup that overthrew the left-nationalist government of Mohammad Mosaddegh, which was in the process of nationalising the country's foreign-owned oil industry. Next came Indonesia in 1965-66, in a very similar operation that removed the communist-backed nationalist regime of President Sukharno. Finally, there was Afghanistan, where the US armed and trained Islamic forces fighting against the Soviet occupation, out of which, with the support of Pakistan, emerged the Taliban.

Ignoring for a while the disapproval of the US, a greatly weakened post-war UK did its best to cling on to its imperial footholds in the Middle East, appeasing Arab monarchies and Islamic sentiment by its often quite brutal attempts to prevent Jewish settlement in what was then still the British Mandate. This strategy suffered a partial defeat with the creation of Israel in 1948, followed by the rise of quasi-secular Arab nationalism in Egypt, Syria and Iraq and the humiliation of the US-imposed withdrawal from Suez in 1956. But despite the ensuing official retreat from 'East of Suez', the UK still pursues an Arabist strategy in a modified form, only now in junior partnership with the USA, in the petro-Islamic despotisms of the Gulf monarchies and Saudi Arabia. Western dependence on Arab oil, and highly lucrative sales of military hardware, ensure that here, protests concerning unspeakable violations of human rights are largely off the agenda.

As Soviet and US influence in the Middle East declined, first as Prime Minister then as President, Jacques Chirac of France attempted a return to the 'third force' policy of De Gaulle. He too played the Arab card by exploiting Arab and Islamic hostility towards Israel, which his ambassador to the UK, Daniel Bernard, once described as a 'shitty little country'. The unspeakably venal Chirac courted Middle Eastern despots Gaddafi of Libya, Syria's Hafaz al Assad and especially Saddam Hussein, for whom he provided substantial technical assistance for the Iraqi dictator's bid to develop a nuclear arsenal specifically intended for use against Israel. Although its demolition in 1981 by an Israeli air attack was condemned by a unanimous vote of the UN General Assembly, the collapse of Chirac's 'third force' strategy came when France found itself obliged to endorse the UN-approved and US-led action to evict Saddam from power in 2003.

For as long as the Cold War continued, there was always the possibility for the west, principally the USA, of Islamic movements and regimes being enticed into common actions or even treaties designed to contain Soviet influence in the Arab world, and China's in the Far East. The US-orchestrated 1955 Baghdad Pact between Turkey, Iran, Iraq and Pakistan is one such example, and the CIA-engineered 1965 anti-communist coup in Indonesia, and US military support for the anti-Soviet resistance in Afghanistan, are two others. Perhaps the very success of these operations convinced their architects, as often as not devout Christians, that since Islam shared their hostility towards atheistic communism, it harboured no such feelings for western institutions and principles. There was no question in those now distant days of US Presidents eulogising Islam as a religion of peace, love and tolerance, any more than there was for the Nazis in World War Two or Lawrence of Arabia in World War One. The more Indonesian or Iraqi commies Muslims killed, the better. According to State Department Intelligence officer of the time, Howard Federspeil, 'No-one cared, as long as they were communists that were being butchered.' Australia's conservative Prime Minister Harold Holt was equally sanguine: 'With 500,000 to one million [Indonesian] communist sympathisers knocked off [sic], I think it is safe to assume a reorientation has taken place'.

There was however a problem that at the time was entirely overlooked. The assumption was that Islam could always be relied on to serve as a 'gun for hire' that could be easily unloaded and safely locked away after the job was done. This proved to be a colossal miscalculation. With 9/11 and the Bali bombings of 2002, and this time not 'communist sympathisers' but 3,000 US officer workers and 88 Australian tourists 'knocked off', and Muslim terrorist attacks in Melbourne and Sydney, both the USA and Australia, together with the entire western world, found themselves confronted with an Islamic 'reorientation' that was once believed to be impossible. And yet towards the end of the cold war there was a clear indication as to what might be coming. Hezbollah's founding Charter of 1985 explained how the Jihadist movement was waging a war on two fronts. Founded 'on the Holy *Koran*, the *sunni*s and the rulings of the *faqih*' (experts in Islamic law), it held that 'both capitalism and communism' were 'incapable of laying the foundations for a just society'. This was surely clear enough. 'Capitalism' by which was meant western democracy, was also the enemy, and with the demise of the Soviet bloc, it necessarily became the only enemy. Hence the alignment with it of the Sharia left.

Yet the possibility that Islam could turn on the west after the collapse of the USSR never seems to have been seriously considered by those charged with formulating western grand strategy. Even Iran's explicitly anti-US 'Islamic Revolution' and the ensuing Rushdie affair failed to compel a serious reappraisal of the west's relationship with Islam, while today, incredibly, as the attacks mount in frequency and severity, the fiction is still officially maintained that the 'real,' but for all that always elusive Islam, means us no harm. Perhaps policy makers are still in the grip of a Cold War era mentality, when Islam was amenable to joint action with the west against what was then seen as the overriding threats of Soviet expansionism and native leftist movements in the East. And yes, it is absolutely the case that Islam cannot but loathe atheistic communism, indeed any leftist doctrine or movement that in fighting for the liberation of the exploited and the oppressed, finds itself obliged to combat the religious prejudices and superstitions which help to uphold the old order of things. To this extent, in the fight against the left, Islam has in the past found a temporary common cause with the most reactionary western interests. But with the collapse of the Kremlin's empire and the absorption of its western provinces into NATO and the EU, the shared fears that forged the US alliance with Islam are no more, even though Obama was unable to grasp this so obvious new reality. For Islam today the West and only the West, is the enemy, and manning the front line is Israel, the country so many in the West love to hate.

However often and loudly we proclaim our respect for Islam as a religion of love and peace, it changes nothing. Respect is not enough. Islam means, and demands, *submission*. The Islamic world has its own agendas, and it has no desire to see itself used by, absorbed into, or 'modernised' by the west. Until we either submit or convert to Islam, the war against the liberal, democratic, secular, infidel west will continue. Already its Jihadis have carried the battle to the world's urban centres...Munich, New York, Buenos Aires, Boston, Ottawa, Dallas, Copenhagen, Bombay, Jakarta, Kabul, Buenos Aires, London, Barcelona, Turku, Jerusalem, Baghdad, Moscow, Chattanooga, Sydney, Istanbul, Moscow St. Petersburg, Beslan, Amsterdam, Nairobi, Mogadishu, Volgograd, Melbourne, Madrid, Brussels, Toulouse, Orlando, Budapest, Berlin, Manchester, Paris... Nowhere is safe anywhere there is Islam. More attacks will follow. Deny it as our statesmen may, the former 'bipolar' world of the cold war is yielding to a new global confrontation, not one of a 'clash of civilisations' as some commentators politely describe it, but of one between civilisation and barbarism.

We have seen how the Sharia left's alliance with Jihadism has been justified on the grounds that Islam is an anti-imperialist force, and that organisations inspired by it, such as Hamas and Hezbollah, are in some way 'resistance' movements, simply fighting back against western, and in particular, Israeli aggression. This is nonsense, in the first place because Hamas and Hezbollah do not even claim to be 'resisting' anyone, least of all Israel, but declare explicitly in their founding charters and subsequent statements that they seek its destruction together with every Jew they can lay their hands on. Secondly, Islam, the faith that inspires not only Hezbollah and Hamas, but every Jihadist movement, be it ISIS, Boko Haram, the Taliban, al Shabaab or al Qaeda, is itself an imperialist doctrine and movement like no other in history. Having set itself the goal of nothing less than world conquest and domination, Jihad will continue until, as the *Koran* says, 'religion is all for Allah' (Chapter 8, Verse 39)

As for the great empires of the west, the sun began to set on their colonial possessions at the end of the Second World War, and, like all their predecessors, have shrunk to little more than zero. Why does Islam still pursue its imperialist agenda when the West, whatever the Sharia left might say, has abandoned its own? And why, unlike its two rival monotheisms, has Islam thus far proved incapable of accommodating itself to liberal democracy, but highly proficient at generating a proliferation of movements, some relatively peaceful, others, violent, dedicated to its destruction? Is there something unique about the world from which Islam sprang that might help to explain why this is so?

While Europe's encounters with the East reach back beyond its recorded history, it was only in the nineteenth century that the Orient became the subject of serious academic study. Those who conducted it quickly became aware that the social structures, culture, economy, politics and religions of the East had evolved along lines that were fundamentally different from those of Europe. Though they were the first to develop the essential elements of urban civilisation...centralised state power, literacy and numeracy, codified laws...from early on, each of these once most advanced civilisations stagnated, and were then overtaken, and in many cases conquered and colonised, by a hitherto more backward Europe.

Following in the footsteps of Adam Smith, Hegel and both the Mills, Marx was convinced by his studies of the East (thereby earning for himself Professor Said's designation as a racist Orientalist) that the distinguishing feature of Oriental Despotism was 'the absence of [private] landed property', itself the result of the unique topography and climate of 'great stretches of desert extending from the Sahara right across Arabia, Persia and India and Tartary to the Asiatic uplands', these territories comprising what coincides to a remarkable and highly significant degree with what today is understood as the world of Islam. Here, 'climate and territorial conditions' had not only made 'artificial irrigation by canals waterworks the basis of Oriental agriculture' but required a despotic central power to regulate them. Centred on great rivers in the midst of deserts, such as the Nile and the Tigris and Euphrates, administered by a literate caste of high priests and personified by its god king (or in Egypt also queen) the state, as the divinely ordained sole owner of all factors of production, extracted and allocated for its own purposes the economic surplus generated by its regulation and distribution of the water supply to the surrounding bonded peasantry, who worked on land likewise owned by the state. It was, in effect, a theocratic communism, which Marx described as a 'general slavery of the Orient'. These and several other important features comprised what Marx designated as the 'Asiatic mode of production', and which set it apart from the stages of historical development which, in respect of Europe, he listed chronologically as primitive tribalism, based on communal ownership, the slave system of classical antiquity, (Greece and Rome) then feudalism and capitalism. Marx was especially intrigued by firstly, the 'Asiatic' mode's uniqueness (which, as the second stage, also evolved out of the first, but unlike Europe, retained its absence of individual private property) and, secondly, by its static character, which he contrasted with societies that although emerging much later in Europe, introduced the private ownership of the productive forces that made possible the subsequent transition from the classical mode via agrarian feudalism to industrial capitalism. As we have seen, up until the Bolshevik seizure of power in 1917, Lenin not only subscribed to Marx's analysis and definition of Oriental society, but followed him in extending it, in certain respects, to tsarist Russia, which both Marx and Engels defined as 'semi-Asiatic' with regard to its despotic political institutions and low level of culture, which were the inheritance from the 'Tartar yoke' imposed by the Mongols in earlier times. Only with the failure of communist-led revolutions in the west did Lenin discard this 'orthodox' stance on the Orient, and in a complete reversal of his previous position, herald the East as the vanguard of world socialism.

The analysis of Orientalism was taken further by the German social scientists Max Weber and then more exhaustively again by Karl Wittfogel, who coined the term 'hydraulic societies' and adopted Marx's 'oriental despotism' to denote respectively their determining economic and political characteristics. All three focused on one essential and, for our purposes, highly relevant feature, the absence of an autonomous civil society and of any concept of the individual as belonging to him or herself, possessing rights as well as owing duties, such as emerged in the pagan civilisations of the West even prior to the birth of Christianity. Christianity, with its emphasis on the individual, took root and then flourished in a Graeco-

Roman culture that had for centuries thrived on a civil society not only separate from but to a degree opposed to the state power, and with which the state eventually had to come to terms. While the oriental despotism out of whose soil (or rather sand) Islam sprang knew no such distinction, both in Athens and pre-imperial Rome, the state was not all, and its gods were mere mortals writ large, flawed and fractious. A free citizen could vote, stand for office, pray to any god he chose and even, like Lucretius, mock those who believed in them, and yet remain a free citizen. Even today, the only freedom Islam recognises is the right to be a Muslim or a *dhimmi*, while a thousand years before its birth, in Athens and Rome in their democratic prime, free citizens chose, challenged and removed their rulers in the city square and the senate, cities where men made their own laws and no sacred text handed down or dictated by a god told them how to behave. Athens and Rome gave us the oratory of Demosthenes and Cicero, the philosophy of Plato and Aristotle, the plays of Euripides and Aristophanes, the poetry of Homer and Virgil, scientists who conceived of the atom and measured the circumference of the earth and proved it went round sun, while a thousand and more years later, Mohammed bequeathed to posterity a book whose author thought the earth was flat and the centre of the universe, and preached terror against those who did not submit to its teachings.

It is not by accident that Rome coined the words republic, liberty, justice, citizen, tribune, senate and forum, and the Greeks, philosophy, logic, drama, music, poetry, geometry, mathematics, politics, science and democracy, while the East gave the world the word *Islam*, the Arabic for submission, and the obligatory act of prostration before a tyrannical and vengeful god. Neither we will find in the ancient East representative institutions analogous to the guilds and estates of the feudal West, which served as the germ cell of modern parliamentary democracy. Nor was it by chance or simply the whim of a power-hungry ruler that in the Orient there were no free citizens equivalent to those of Greece and Rome. The concept did not and, given the centrally regulated conditions of life, could not exist. The economic system that made life possible demanded that all human beings, like all material objects, including the water and the land that it irrigated, were the sole possessions of the state, personified by the god king, and that labour was subject to the needs of what was in effect a planned economy, totally geared to the cycle of the seasons and wholly dependent on the riparian water supply.

Only a despotic central power, such as evolved in Egypt under the pharaohs, in Mesopotamia, and around the great rivers of India and China, was capable of harnessing nature to supply both the essentials of life for its subjects and rulers and generate a surplus sufficient to meet the needs of external defence and conquest. As Marx puts it, 'the despot here appears as father of all the lesser communities, thus realising the common unity of all', which in Islam, evolved into the *Ummah*, the world-wide community of all believers, which Obama mistook for the brotherhood of all mankind.

Once having achieved a certain internal equilibrium (although there was always the threat of conquest by similarly structured neighbouring states) stasis sets in. In Marx's estimation, and he has largely been proved correct, states based on or substantially influenced by the Asiatic mode of production could only be dislodged from their socio-economic and political cul de sacs by the action upon them of societies technologically more advanced, either by conquest and colonisation, as in the case of India, trade, as with Japan and China, or a combination of both, as with Egypt and the Middle East. Marx, who in his life time welcomed this development as the only means of overcoming the orient's economic backwardness and cultural insularity, explains why this was the case: 'The Asiatic form necessarily survives longest and most stubbornly. This is due to the fundamental principle on which it is based, that is that the individual does not become independent of the community, that the circle of production is self-sustaining.' Here there could be no question of the individual citizen with rights as well as duties inscribed in law. As Marx explains, individual freedom does not come either cheaply or quickly, 'man is only individualised through the process of history. He originally appears as a generic being, a tribal being, a herd animal - though by no means a "political animal" in the political sense'...an apt description of the *Ummah's* ideal 'Muslim man'. For analogous reasons, neither was there a role or place for popular representation such as we find in the west in the pre-Christian era, either in Germanic or classic form. The functions of decision making and matters concerning religious rites and doctrine were concentrated in the hands of the literate priestly caste and the supreme ruler and law giver, the oriental god king, a Sargon, Amenhotep, Darius or Hammurabi, just as they were with Islam, beginning with Mohammed and then his successors, the Caliphs.

In the west, a totally different economic system, based on decentralised private ownership, necessarily produced a no less fragmented society, in which classes, factions and parties competed in the attempt to curtail and even supplant the power of the monarchy and the hereditary ruling families. In Rome and Greece, this contest for power began in the early fifth century BC, culminating in the overthrow of monarchy, and its replacement by popular representation and decision making, the Tribune in Rome and the city assembly in Greece. In time, both Greece and Rome succumbed to imperial rule, Greece by conquest and Rome by the populist militarism of the first Caesars. But the old traditions died hard, as the contemporary historian Suetonius records:

> [Caesar] Augustus's speeches in the House Senate] would often be interrupted by such remarks as 'I don't understand you' or 'I'd dispute your point if I got the chance'. And it happened more than once that, exasperated by recriminations which lowered the tone of the debate, he left the house in an angry haste, and was followed by shouts of 'You ought to let Senators say exactly what they think about matters of public importance!' ...Yet Augustus never punished anyone for showing independence of mind on such occasions, or even for behaving insolently.

Of his successor, Tiberius, it was said that he was 'quite unperturbed by abuse, slander or lampoons on himself and his family, and would often say that liberty to speak and think as one pleases is the test of free country', which indeed it is, and one that all states ruled by Sharia law comprehensively fail, two thousand years on. Even in tribal Germany, with its primitive rural peoples divided by dialects, rivers, forests and mountains that only under Bismarck achieved the semblance of a united nation, despotism was an alien institution. Justice was administered by a twelve-man jury and politics by tribal assemblies, the Hundred and the Witan, a system of law and self-government that with the migration to England of the Anglo-Saxons, became the seeds of the parliamentary democracy and legal system that governs the UK and most of its former colonies today. Greece, Rome, Germany...each in their own way gave birth to the foundations of what today the west understands as modern civilisation, and what Islam, with its unreformable Sharia law and 'legislation is not but for Allah', not only sees as alien, but as its enemy.

Consequently, as the successor to the despotic theocracies of the East, Islam, not only at home but in its diasporas, has insulated itself from the dissolving contagions of democracy and individual freedom. Muslims are all born, and shall remain, as the often-cited happy mantra has it, 'slaves of Allah'. Neither in the *Koran* nor the *hadith* is there to be found the least hint that Allah, unlike the ancient Greeks and Romans and indeed the Bible, with its 'render unto Caesar', considers his subjects fit to govern themselves or devise their own laws. In the Asiatic despotisms analysed by Marx and his successors we can indeed recognise the prototype of its bastard offspring, the Islamic 'herd', the *Ummah,* that swallows up, homogenises and thus effectively erases the individual 'in the political sense'. Instead of the self-governing citizen, we have the subject, not even of an unchosen earthly power, but of Allah, out of which in their collectivity as raw human material is moulded the anything but 'vibrant' Muslim community. Frozen in time under an all-seeing and all-knowing deity, the *Ummah* is governed on Allah's behalf by theocracy according to an unchanging because unchangeable system of law which, again like its oriental progenitors, fuses state and faith, where all are 'slaves of Allah'. (See the Ayatollah Khomeini's exposition of this system in Appendix G)

The only essential difference between the theocracy promoted by Islam and that actually operated by the ancient societies of the Middle East is economic, though even here there are also continuities. The system of tribute as it operated in the 'Asiatic mode', in which a proportion of the product of the labouring classes was extracted by the state to support the administrative caste of officials and clergy, has its parallel in the rules governing the sharing out of 'booty', the 'spoils of war', both human and material, accumulated by Mohammed's raiding bands, of which one fifth fell to the prophet, who held (and enjoyed) it in trust, exactly in the manner of the Oriental despots: 'Know that one fifth of all booty you take belongs to Allah, and to the messenger [sic], and for the near relatives of the messenger'. (*Koran,* Chapter 8, Verse 40) But the difference is an important one. While Islam emerged from a desert culture, it was not in the setting of a riparian urban-centred society based upon state ownership of property and the exploitation of settled peasant labour, but a tribal semi-nomadic bandit culture situated in the barren north west of the Arabian Peninsula. Although lacking access to the fertile soils generated by the great rivers to its east and west, the one great asset the Hejaz possessed was its strategic location astride the ancient trade routes linking the three continents of Africa, Asia and Europe. Consequently, when Mohammed and his band of followers left Mecca and headed north to Medina, they were able to sustain themselves by the parasitic practice of raiding caravans and the enslavement of captives. (See Appendix L) Private property was not abolished, it simply changed hands.

Only when a more stable Islamic society evolved in the wake of its conquest of more advanced cultures than its own could land thus conquered become transformed into crown property of the caliph or, again through conquest or grants from rich individuals, become the collective property of the clergy. This represented a similar evolution to that of Church and crown property in the west, but with the difference that with the advent of the Reformation, church lands and property were either simply appropriated by the Protestant landed classes or seized and sold off by the state back into private hands. No such property secularisation has ever been sanctioned in the history of Islam or is it every likely to while the clergy either wields or shares state power, as it does in Iran and Saudi Arabia. Significantly, it was the Shah's so-called White Revolution, which involved the transfer of clerical lands to peasant ownership, that caused the clergy to turn against the monarchy it had served faithfully down the centuries.

Clerical ownership, as for example with the vast holdings of the Catholic Church, since it excludes and crucially also necessarily exploits the laity, is not common ownership in the modern sense. It is not even the sharing of 'all things common' of the Acts of the Apostles. It was a form of collective feudal exploitation by both the Christian and Islamic clergy of those who lived and worked on its lands. We have already noted that there is nothing in the *Koran* that advocates or even alludes to the common ownership of wealth or economic resources. It was a concept completely alien and unknown to the culture of the time and place which gave birth to the religion of Islam. That is why today, Jihadism has nothing to do with 'social justice', but everything to do with purity of faith and the spreading to the ends of the earth of the rule of Allah, however the Sharia left and western commentators might try to portray it as in some sense 'radical' or revolutionary. Under the despotic rule of its absentee plutocrats, capitalist Gaza is one of the most unequal societies on planet earth. While the vast majority, the tunnel diggers and cannon fodder, lives in poverty and with an unemployment rate approaching 50%, Hamas supremo Khaled Mashaal Khaled has 'hamased' a fortune of £2.5 billion, and his Number Two, Musa Abu Marzook, £2.3 billion. These are the 'friends' of Comrade Corbyn, billionaires whose Charter denounces Corbyn's policy of 'for the many, not the few' (which if applied in Gaza, would result in their expropriation) as the work of a world Jewish conspiracy. We will in due course encounter another Muslim billionaire engaged with Corbyn in the same joint enterprise, only far closer to home.

Islamic plunder, conveniently sanctioned as we have seen by the faith's holy texts, certainly shared some of the features of its counterparts in the west, for example the Muslim raiding of desert caravans and the piracy of Tudor freebooters, and the Muslim trans-Saharan and Christian trans-Atlantic slave trades. But the economic results of such plunder helped to produce very different societies. In the west, what Marx described as the process of 'primitive capitalist accumulation', pursued at home, as with England's land clearances and enclosures, and abroad by slavery, plunder and theft, greatly helped generate the capital and financial reserves necessary for what economists call the 'take off' phase of modern capitalism. Even in the colonialist west, outcomes varied, depending on circumstances. Spain's looting of the New Word vastly outstripped that of England's, but the proceeds served mainly to satisfy the voracious appetites of a vast clerical bureaucracy (at the height of the Church's power, something like one quarter of the country's adults were in holy orders), finance its continuous wars and to sustain the life style of a no less parasitic aristocracy. By contrast, a post-feudal England, protected by seas and therefore able to dispense with a standing army, with a Church now subservient to the state and stripped of much of its wealth by Henry's reforms, was ideally placed to harness the fruits of its plunder to economic gain and technological innovation. Islamic plunder, conducted on no less grand a scale, produced no equivalent result.... witness the abject economic state of the Arab and, more broadly, the Islamic world today. Instead of disturbing the equilibrium of the old order, plunder re-enforced it. As in the case of Spain, there was no 'take off', because its proceeds, rather than feeding technological innovation and economic growth, flowed into the hands of the clergy, the royal houses and the funding of yet more military adventures and internal religious wars to sustain the rate of plunder. And unlike the original 'oriental' or 'hydraulic' despotism, which could rely on the labour of a sedentary captive peasant class to provide the essentials of life, the marauding bands of Mohammed and his successors relied entirely on plunder and conquest to furnish them. Only this explains why the *Koran,* unlike the Bible, has nothing to say about work and thrift, but provides rules for the seizure and distribution of the fruits of infidel labour and of the bodies of those who perform it. The need to preserve at all costs such an order of things could not but generate an intense and, with Salafism, fanatical conservatism, a paralytic fear of contamination by the modernising and liberalising west, of anything that might disturb, dissolve and undermine the divinely ordained parasitic dystopia born of the seventh century Hejaz. The distinction also needs to made that whereas the infidel nations of the west, at different times and by different methods, eventually abolished the iniquities of slavery, Islamic law to this day upholds them. True, slavery was abolished, at least officially, in Saudi Arabia in 1962, Oman in 1970 and Mauritania in 2007, but only for it to be restored by UK Muslim pimps, and by Boko Haram and the Islamic State in the sexual enslavement ('that which the right hand possesses') of infidel girls.

Today in the Middle East, the centrally regulated irrigation of river water that was the foundation of the economies and power of the ancient 'hydraulic societies' has been replaced by the extraction of oil. Thanks to infidel technology, long departed oriental despotisms have been reincarnated as petro-monarchies and theocracies. But some things do not change. As in the time of the Asiatic despotisms, eternal and all-encompassing laws still emanate from god. They cannot be made by man. According to Islam, any system of law that is of human origin necessarily lacks all legitimacy and conforming to it in the *kuffar*'s 'house of war' is simply a matter of temporary tactical convenience or necessity until such times as Sharia law rules supreme everywhere.

Islam also inherited another feature of the ancient desert despotisms: the urge, and the necessity, to expand. Egypt, and Sumeria and its successor states - the Hittites, Assyrians, Persians and Babylonians - were rarely at peace with their neighbours, just as Islam has from the very beginning sought to extend its rule, and the tribute that it brings, far beyond the place of its origin. Islam's expansion began in the life-time of its founder in the early seventh century, but at that stage, was confined to the Arabic speaking Hejaz. His successors, though more often than not at war with each other as to the legitimacy of their claims, still found the time and energy to extend Islamic rule in every direction:

> West, through the Levant and Egypt along the south coast of the Mediterranean as far as the Atlantic coast of Africa, and from there into Spain, and then Sicily, Crete, Sardinia and Corsica, (whence 'Corsair', originally a Muslim pirate) Cyprus and southern Italy, at the same time carrying out 'white' slaving raids as far afield as Iceland;
> South, across the Sahara to equatorial Africa as far as what is now modern Nigeria, at the same time engaging in a slave trade on a scale vaster and no less iniquitous than that of the European colonial powers.
> East, beyond the Arabian Peninsula through Iran and Afghanistan to India and western China, and what is now modern Indonesia;
> North east, via the Black Sea to what became, beyond the Urals, the Turkic speaking heartland of the sprawling 14th century Islamic empire of Timur ('the lame'), under whose despotic rule, and as a result of his endless military campaigning, 17 million deaths ensued;

Northwards, into Europe via Asia minor to Byzantium, Greece, the Balkans, Hungary and as far as the 'gates of Vienna'; and at the other end of Europe, from Morocco via Spain into France as far as the River Loire and even briefly reaching the upper Rhone valley in what is now modern-day Switzerland.

This immense, sprawling tri-continental realm of Islam was, it is true never ruled from a single centre, being divided by at least two, sometimes more, competing dynasties and caliphates, the most enduring being that of the 'Moorish' Emirate of Cordoba in the west and the Turkish Ottomans in the centre, both Sunni, while the Shi'a power centre, then as now, revolved in the east around Persia. But the great hope still endures that Islam will, after much bloodletting, end its divisions and, united, restore a single caliphate that will conquer the entire world. Such was the dream and appeal of ISIS, and young men and women, not only in the Middle East, but from prosperous families in Europe, rallied to the call in their thousands. Given this record of the creation by Jihad of the largest empire in all human history, it is hard to understand how western politicians can apologise for Christian resistance to its expansion in the Crusades, while at the same time describing conquering, imperialist Islam as a religion of peace, love and toleration. Is it an ignorance of history? The armies of Allah first invaded mainland Europe, via Spain, in AD 711, 384 years before the launching of the First Crusade in 1095. The attempted Islamic conquest of Europe also continued long after the expulsion of the Crusaders from the Holy Land in 1291, only finally being checked at the 'gates of Vienna' in 1683. In each case, for all its many sins, Christendom was undeniably waging a war of defence, and Islam one of conquest.

In considering the teachings underpinning Islamic imperialism, let us put to one side the often-repeated Jihadi boasts of the approaching day when the 'flag of Islam' will fly over Number Ten Downing Street or the White House (but never, interestingly, despite Moscow's butchery of the Afghans and Chechens, the Kremlin) and examine what the most authoritative Islamic sources have to say on the subject. Let us begin, just as all good Muslims do, with the prophet and his *Koran*. Tradition has it that at the very end of his life, in March 632, Mohammed gave this last message to the faithful: 'I was ordered to fight all men until they say "there is no God but Allah"'. The *Koran* itself says something very similar: 'And fight them on until there is no more tumult and oppression [that is, of Muslims], and there prevail justice and faith in Allah altogether and everywhere'. (Chapter 8, Verse 39) Although this citation refers only to fighting, there were and are two other means by which the goal of the universal rule of Islam can be achieved; firstly, by the voluntary conversion of the monotheist infidel or, secondly, failing this, his or her reduction to the inferior status of a *dhimmi*. Those who refuse either to convert or accept dhimmitude are to be killed. The remainder, polytheists, pagans and today, atheists and agnostics, are only given two choices, convert or be killed.

Even though not everyone will necessarily be a Muslim if or when Islam achieves its final goal of world conquest, it is only Islam and its Sharia law that will rule. Despite their divergences in other matters, all four schools of Sunni law agree with the various factions of Shi'a Islam as to the methods and goal of Jihad. The tenth century Maliki jurist Ibn Abi Zayd ruled that 'Jihad is a precept of divine institution', while Hanbali jurist Ibn Taymiyyah (died 1328) concurred: 'Since lawful warfare is essentially Jihad and since its aim is that the religion is God's entirely and God's word is uppermost, therefore according to all Muslims, those who stand in the way of this aim must be fought.' Shaikh Burhanuddin Ali of Marghinan (died 1196) says on behalf the Hanafi school that 'if the infidels, upon receiving the call [to convert], neither consent to it nor agree to pay [the *dhimmi*] capitation tax, it is then incumbent for Muslims to call upon God for assistance, and to make war upon them'. Next up, we have Al-Mawardi (died 1058) for the Shafi school. Of those who refuse to heed the call to convert, 'war is waged against them and they are treated as those whom the call has reached'. Shi'a Islam authorities say exactly the same. In the Persian manual of Shi'a law, written by al-Amili (died 1622) we read that 'Holy War against followers of other religions, such as Jews, is required unless they convert to Islam or pay the [*dhimmi*] poll tax'.

Other, more familiar names from the history of Islam have also voiced similar sentiments. Saladin the (ironically, in view of decades of persecution by their Muslim brethren) Kurdish scourge of the Crusaders, was not, as he is often portrayed a 'resistance fighter', to use current parlance, but an avowed imperialist: 'I shall cross this sea [the Mediterranean] to their islands to pursue them until there remain no-one on the face of the entire earth who does not acknowledge Allah'. In our own time, we have had the high priest of Iran's 'Islamic Republic', the Ayatollah Khomeini promising, in the manner of a Muslim Trotsky, to 'export our [Islamic] revolution throughout the world until the calls "there is no God but Allah and Mohammed is the messenger of Allah" are echoed all over the world.' Finally, there is founder of al-Qaeda and (though many Muslims celebrate him, others rather ungenerously prefer to attribute his deeds to the Jews or George Bush) the architect of 9/11, Osama bin Laden: 'I was ordered to fight the people until they say there is no God but Allah and his prophet is Mohammed'. It seems so simple...and yet, in its pursuit, one after another, Islamic countries are laid waste as refugees flee and corpses pile up by the million, all being victims not of the Jews or 'western imperialism', but the waging of Jihad for Allah.

In today's world of major league power politics, freelancing by third or lesser parties is a risky business with little or no chance of lasting success. Just like that of his mentor De Gaulle, French President Chirac's bid to construct a global anti-US alliance failed miserably. Similar attempts by national Islamic leaders to construct their own geopolitical alliances independently of both the Islamic bloc and the Arab League and also free of any western entanglements, have thus far also met with failure and even fiasco. Gaddafi's vast oil revenues enabled him, quite apart from orchestrating anti-western terrorism on his own account, to become for a while the benefactor of a motley collection of movements and individuals ranging from Neo-Nazis, UK Trotskyists, Jihadis, Italian, German, Japanese, Basque and Irish terrorists, the African 'diamond war' criminal Charles Taylor, responsible for around a million deaths and the pioneering of 'child armies', the Serbian 'ethnic cleanser' Slobodan Milosevic, the assassins Carlos 'The Jackal' and Abu Nidal, and the Ugandan Muslim genocidist, Hitler admirer and cannibal, Idi Amin, to British trade union leaders, the PLO and all manner of splinter anti-Zionists and even earth mother pacifists. Then, changing tack in his last years, his atrocious crimes, although they still continued at home if not abroad, now forgiven or forgotten, he was embraced by the west as a reformed character, becoming a major contributor to the slush funds of the Italian Mafiosi politician Silvio Berlusconi. and the no less venal French Gaullist Presidents Jacques Chirac and Nicolas Sarkozy, as well as Jorg Haider, the openly anti-Semitic leader of the Austrian Freedom party and of course, Gerry Healy's Workers Revolutionary Party. Having abjured terrorism, save against his own people, world statesmen queued up to play host to Gaddafi, including among them benefactors of his largess. As a special favour, Gaddafi even greeted UK Prime Minister Tony Blair in his tent, doubtless gratified that the UK Prime Minister had in a gesture of goodwill agreed to deliver up to the dictator a number of Gaddafi's exiled opponents. And, of course there was as always, ever ready to embrace a Muslim thug posing as a moderate, the-ever gullible Islamophile President Obama. So many friends. And so powerful too. But when Gaddafi's subjects rose up against him, not a finger was lifted to save him.

Meantime, Iran's ayatollahs pursued their own Shi'a version of an Islamic geopolitics to counter the more substantial Sunni alignment of the Saudis, backing Assad in Syria, Hamas in Gaza and Hezbollah in Lebanon, to no great immediate advantage to themselves or their allies. In Yemen, support for the Shi'a Houthi militia brought Iran to the brink of military conflict with the Saudis, who intervened on the side of the embattled Sunni government forces. However, already well advanced on the road to possessing their own nuclear arsenal and exploiting their kinship with the dominant Shi'a minority in Syria, and no less dominant Shi'a majority in central and southern Iraq, Iran's theocrats intend to supplant the Sunni Saudis as the leading power in the Middle East. Being Persian as well as Shi'a will undoubtedly create difficulties in a region overwhelmingly Arab and largely Sunni. And it remains to see if their great Sunni rivals, the Saudis and the Turks, will allow this to happen. In a bid to achieve a more global reach, Iran also forged fraternal links with the populist demagogue, Venezuelan President Hugo Chavez, who in return for substantial Iranian economic aid, pledged that he would 'stand by Iran at any time and under any condition'. How this would have been be done from distance of nearly 12,000 kilometres was never quite made clear. Iran's other major sally into South America was a terrorist attack in 1994 on the Jewish Community Centre in Buenos Aires. Master-minded by Iran's Cultural (sic) Attaché Mohsen Rabbani; it resulted in the deaths of 85 Jews.

Once a Peronist haven for wanted Nazi war criminals spirited away from their would-be Allied captors by courtesy of the Vatican's well-documented 'Rat Line', Argentina has never properly rid itself of its anti-Semitic undercurrents, and these came into play in the sequel to the 1994 massacre. Top Argentinean politicians were only too aware of who was responsible for the outrage, but rather than put at risk their anti-US credentials by exposing Iran's role in the affair, they chose instead to bloc attempts to bring its perpetrators to justice. But Jewish campaigners refused to let the matter die. Eventually an official investigation headed by Federal Prosecutor Alberto Nisman produced a 289-page report indicting amongst others, anti-Semitic Peronista President Cristina Fernandez Kirchner. (Without doubt fully appraised of his stance on the Falklands, she was one of the first world leaders to congratulate Corbyn on his election as Labour Leader. Corbyn had derided the British military operation to liberate the Falklanders as 'a Tory plot to keep their money-making friend's in business...yet another conspiracy.) The report uncovered a deal concluded after the crime between Argentina and Iran in which, in return for a cover-up of the massacre, Iran would supply oil on favourable terms, and would buy Argentinean wheat and military equipment. Four days after the report was released in January 2015, its author was found dead in his Buenos Aires apartment, shot in the head. President Fernandez blamed his faked 'suicide' on...the Jews.

The other dimension to Iran's foreign policy is of course the theocracy's bid to become yet another nuclear power in the region. Already, to Iran's east, there is

Pakistan's Sunni bomb, and to Pakistan's south, India's Hindu bomb. To the north, there is Russia's Orthodox bomb, a high value card in Putin's poker game of imperial expansion, and. in Israel one suspects and I for one hope, a Jewish bomb. Obama, who set the conciliatory tone and terms for the negotiations with the Ayatollahs over their nuclear enrichment programme, probably saw Iran, as he already did the Saudis, as an ally, albeit in this case, an unofficial one, in the bid to 'contain' (this was Washington's stated objective) but not eliminate, the ISIS Caliphate. Just as with Obama's dealings with the Saudi kingdom, this policy required that a curtain be discreetly drawn around the Iranian regime's brutally repressive domestic policies. Like all US presidential candidates, to be electable in his pious nation, Obama had to be god fearing and for capital punishment. Both qualifications could explain why he had not joined human rights organisations in condemning the well-documented relentless succession of torture, forced confessions, frame-up trials and executions of those that had possessed the courage to oppose the clerical fascists who rule Iran. As the USA edges its way, state by state, towards abolition, in Iran, the pace of judicial murder has been quickening, with Kurds, the Sharia left's 'western pawns', being singled out for special treatment. Just between January 1 and July 15, 2015, the number of executions soared to 694, an average of more than three per day. As the 'nuclear' talks between the west and Iran proceeded in Lausanne, back in Tehran it was business as usual, with 'Death to America' rallies and plenty of work for the hangmen. The Kurd Saman Naseen, arrested in April 2013 when only 17 years old, after being tortured and convicted of 'enmity against god' and 'corruption on earth', was hanged on February 20, 2015. On the same day, two Kurdish brothers suffered the fate. Then, on March 4, no fewer than six Kurds were hanged, accused of the same 'crime'.

Except for those of human rights organisations (and who listens to them?) no voices in the west were raised in protest against this judicial carnage, for who would want to rock the diplomatic boat with the Lausanne negotiations at such a delicate stage? And the holy hangmen of Tehran knew it. What more opportune time to rid themselves of trouble-makers? Mina Ahdi of the International Committee Against Executions made this very point, that during the Lausanne talks, 'there was absolute silence with regards to the high rate of executions and human rights violations in Iran' and that 'because of this silence, this matter has taken a turn for the worse.' In Iran's Karaj Central Prisons alone, 40 prisoners were selected for execution on April 11, 2015, and then hanged in batches. While the rebellious Kurds were the main domestic enemy, on November 2014, Iran's Supreme Leader Ayatollah Ali Khamenei declared that 'barbaric' (sic) Israel had 'no other cure but to be eliminated'. Defence Chief Ayatollah Salehi warned that 'no matter how many weapons are given to Israel, we are going to destroy them [the Jews]. We promise this task will be done.' Ayatollah Khamenei pledged that 'Allah willing, in twenty-five years' time there will be no more Israel'. Thus spoke Corbyn's former employers.

What have the Jews done to Iran to deserve a hated comparable to that of the Nazis when, like every other country, it has been the beneficiary of their unrivalled contributions to the betterment of life? Jews, who comprise but 0.2% of the world's population, have been awarded 22% of all Nobel Prizes...169 at the last count. What would it be but for the Holocaust? Though belonging to far and away the most persecuted people on our planet over a period of nearly two thousand years, a Jew is approximately a thousand times more likely to win a Nobel prize than a non-Jew, contributing to the well-being and advancement of a gentile world that in return has treated Jews with at best indifference and at worst, envy, prejudice and like the rulers of Iran and Muslim Jihadis, murderous hatred. Meanwhile Muslims, whose holy book says Jews are no more human than 'apes and swine', although comprising an immense 20% of the world's population, 100 times that of the Jews, have won a paltry 12 Prizes, less than 7% of the Jewish total. Even their three science prizes were each awarded to academics who conducted their research at infidel institutions, while of the seven Peace Prizes for activities that involved no intellectual achievement of any kind, one was laughably bestowed upon Yasser Arafat, despite the anti-Semitic terrorist's role as instigator of the Black September Munich Olympic massacre of eleven Israeli athletes, And they say that Scandinavians don't have a sense of humour?

By contrast, no fewer than 55 of the Nobel Prizes awarded to Jews were for medicine, advances calculated to have saved two billion lives, among them, we can be sure, countless Muslim ones. These were Jews who dedicated themselves not to the taking of life, but its preservation, enhancement and extension. Based upon the above statistics, a Jew is 1000 times more likely to win a Nobel Prize than a non-Jew, and 5,000 times more likely than a Muslim, perhaps the most compelling proof yet advanced for the existence and efficacy of a world Jewish conspiracy. When asked by Terry Woggan on BBC TV to explain anti-Semitism, Chief Rabbi Jonathan Sacks replied that it was due to people 'disliking Jews more than they have to.' The truth is, nobody likes to be made to look stupid.

24 Normal

France has been repeatedly selected as a target in the Jihadi war against the west, not because of its 'foreign policy, as the *dhimmi* left alleges, but because France is a bulwark of western secularism. On June 26, 2015, the Jihadi assault against France was renewed with a failed attempt to blow up a gas plant near Lyon. The attacker, delivery van driver Yassine Salhi, had first killed and decapitated his employer (as per Chapter 8 Verse 12 of the *Koran*) and then photographed himself with the severed head before displaying it as a trophy on the plant's gates, together with an ISIS flag and written messages of an Islamic nature. Unlike our gutless politicians and the Sharia left, the secular and as likely as not, atheist French are not afraid to tell the world what they think about the religious motivations that drive such atrocities. Whereas Tory Prime Minister Cameron laughably described the murder of Lee Rigby by two Muslim converts as 'a crime against [sic] Islam', the local Socialist National Assembly deputy for Bouche-du-Rhone, Patrick Menucci, in a model of plain speaking, told it as it is: 'France is at war. I know it is not good to say so, but this terrorist attack in Saint-Quentin-Fallavier is the proof. We have on our territory individuals who don't obey the laws of the Republic but *fatwas* of the Islamic State...France is the most threatened county in Europe, notably because it defends secularism.' Exactly. Evidently not a paid-up member of the Sharia left, where in secular France, it has found the soil less fertile. Here in the UK, where there is no such tradition, where we are the subjects, not citizens, of an unelected head of state who is also by right of birth head of our tax-payer subsidised state church, it is a sad comment on our lack of political maturity that non-believing mainstream politicians feel obliged to publicly proclaim their respect for ideas they have privately rejected as nonsense, and who, unless it is to oppose it, dare not so much as mention secularism, let alone support it, lest doing so places their careers in jeopardy.

There is another aspect to the Lyon atrocity of June 26 that that was touched in the Preface, and which has a direct parallel with similar cases in the UK. The arrested terror suspect was a Salafi Muslim with known past connections to Jihadist organisations. Yet his wife, before she was herself arrested displayed, genuinely or otherwise we cannot know, exactly the same disbelief that her husband could have committed such a crime as do the relatives of those who, also supposedly without any warning, have made their way to Syria to serve in the ISIS murder machine: 'I know my husband. We have a normal family life. He goes to work, he comes back. We are normal Muslims. We do Ramadan. We have three children and a normal family life'. Her 'normal' husband was indeed guilty, because he confessed to the crime two days later. So we had a scenario in which one day, a 'normal' member of this 'normal family' decided to change his normal routine and instead cut off a man's head and blow up a gas works. Innocent of his intentions or not, I am inclined to believe her when she said that her family, including her husband, was 'normal', and that includes his Salafism if not his past terrorist associations. According to the *Koran,* for example Chapter 4, Verse 96, unless they have very compelling reasons that prevent them from doing so, 'normal', able bodied Muslim men are *supposed* to wage Jihad against the infidel in his own lands, and to cut off their heads if the opportunity presents itself. That is just what happened here, as with the killings in

Toulouse and Paris. Then we have Mohammed Abdeslam, brother of two members of the team of assassins responsible for the Paris massacres of November 13, 2015, who insisted they were 'normal brothers' from 'an honest family'.

But then, like so much else, normality is in the eye of the beholder. In the time of the Nazi Holocaust, men from 'normal families', German in this case, many of them doubtless Nazi German, also went out to work, only they did not have to change their routine to commit murder because it was, so to speak, their day job. Between them they killed, or helped to kill, not just one man, but between them six million men, women and children. The extermination of the Jews would not have been possible if such men (and some women too) from such normal families had refused to carry out the orders of those who planned it and set it motion. It could be argued, and in fact has been, that Nazi Germany being the kind of state that it was, there was no choice, except for the very brave few, than to be become an accomplice, however unwilling, in Himmler's Holocaust. This is simply not true. Diligent research has established that refusing to serve in the various agencies charged with implementing the final solution rarely, if ever, incurred draconian punishments. Many Germans, 'ordinary Germans' as one researcher, Daniel Goldenhagen, described them, who did serve in punitive units were offered the opportunity by their commanding officers of excusing themselves from duties they found too distressing. Hardly any did so. But let the contrary claim stand, if only to make a contrast with the situation in today's France or any other civilised country afflicted with Islamic terrorism. For here the circumstances in which politically or religiously motivated murder takes place are fundamentally changed. A Muslim living in France is under no legal compulsion to wage Jihad against the country he is living in. In fact, the law forbids it, and severely punishes those who do. This is of course to state the obvious, but in these times the obvious occasionally needs stating. However, instead of obeying the laws of the land he is either born in or has chosen to live in, the Jihadi Muslim kills non-Muslims (preferably Jews) because he chooses instead to obey a command from his god that tells him that as a 'normal', 'ordinary', or 'good' Muslim, it is his sacred duty. As we have seen, the *kuffar*-made laws of the land he lives in count for nothing. Let us not forget that throughout the European Islamic diaspora, millions of Muslims have made it very clear they wish to live under their own Sharia law rather than the laws of the country they were born in or have chosen to make their home.

On the same day of the decapitation at Saint-Quintin Fallavier, Friday, June 26, 2015, the first day of Muslim prayer in the holy month of Ramadan, Jihadism also struck in Tunisia, slaughtering 39, mainly British, tourists and wounding another 36 and, for the first time, in Kuwait, where a Saudi-born ISIS suicide bomber massacred 27 and wounded another 200 fellow Muslims at prayer in a Kuwait City mosque. The Tunisian assassin resembled his French brother in arms not only in being a 'lone wolf' killer, but also a very 'normal' one. Aged 23, management graduate Seifeddine Rezgui was described by a bemused uncle as a typically modern, football-loving and carefree young man:

> We are all shocked when we heard the news and saw his picture, and his mother was devastated. Yes, he went to the mosque and prayed, but just like other men he would then go to the cafe and play football with his friends...The entire family is shocked at the hidden reality of what he was capable of. He used to use hair gel, wear the nicest

clothes and go break dancing. He didn't even have a beard and I've never seen him with anyone with a beard. Now he's shooting people with a Kalashnikov.

In other words, like thousands of other suicide bombers, hijackers, Jihadis and assassins, he was just another normal, well-educated, certainly not poor, very ordinary Muslim man. And like so many other young Muslim men, he also was visiting ISIS websites, undergoing terrorist training, at an ISIS camp in Libya, and posting his own messages, the last one of which, smouldering with loathing for the world he seemed so much at one with, read: 'May God take me out of this unjust world and perish its people and make them suffer. They just remember you when you die.' As for the struggle against western imperialism and poverty…not a word. On June 13, 2015, 17-year-old Talha Asmal became Britain's youngest ever suicide bomber when he drove a car packed with explosives at an Iraqi oil refinery. Friends described him as 'an ordinary Yorkshire lad.' Let us hope not. The same applies to 'Jihadi Jack' Lets, now Abu Mohammed, whose parents appeared in court charged with funding his terrorist activities in Iraq on behalf of the Islamic State. According to his friends he was just a 'typical middle-class kid' yet his conversion to Islam transformed him into a hired murderer, something his parents simply refused to accept.

Another incredulous parent was that of the Orlando, Florida, gay night club assassin, Omar Mateen, whose family hailed originally from Afghanistan. His father, Mir Siddique, described his son as 'a very good boy', though his first wife left him after four months of regular beatings. Mir Siddique initially claimed the atrocity, which left 49 dead and another 53 wounded, had nothing to do with religion, but had been triggered by the sight of two gay men kissing in Miami. Even if that had proved to be true, which it did not, the question still remained: why this murderous hatred for gay men? Where did that come from if not his religion? Only a matter of weeks previous to the Orlando massacre, a UK-born Doctor and Islamic theologian preaching in the city's Husseini Centre had instructed his listeners as to the punishment prescribed by Sharia Law for homosexuality: 'Death is the sentence. We know this. There is nothing to be embarrassed about. We have to have compassion for people. With homosexuals, it's the same. Out of compassion, let's get rid of them now.' Following this sermon, Sheikh Farrokh Sekaleshfar was invited to speak at Stanford University. The day after the Orlando massacre, the Husseini Islamic Centre conducted a prayer session for the 49 gays who been compassionately got rid of. When it was put to the Sheikh that his call for the killing of gays may have contributed to the Orlando killings, he replied that 'such a connection is impossible, because had the shooter listened to my lecture, he would have clearly heard me condemn hate and violence multiple times and endorse compassion towards humankind at all times.' He would also have heard that in, in the case of homosexuals, this 'compassion' required that Muslims had to 'get rid of them now.' Sekaleshfar's no-nonsense method of dealing with homosexuality was shared by the Islamic State, which issued a statement saluting 'one of the Caliphate's soldiers in America' for carrying out 'a security invasion where he was able to enter a crusader gathering at a night club for homosexuals in Orlando, Florida, where he killed and wounded more than a hundred of them before he was killed. 'The killer's father, however believed that his son had, theologically speaking, jumped the gun: 'God himself will punish those involved in homosexuality, this is not for the servants of God.'

Any doubts as to the assassin's motives were resolved when later the same day, NBC reported that Mateen, already known by the police, like so many other young diaspora Muslims, to have Jihadi sympathies, had interrupted his assault to phone emergency services to declare his allegiance to the Islamic State, which like any self-respecting Islamic theocracy, also executes its homosexuals, though not by shooting but by throwing them from the roofs of tall buildings. The very next day, in faraway Qatar, venue for the 2022 World Cup, *kuffars* saw another demonstration of Muslim compassion when a Dutch woman was convicted by an Islamic court of the crime of having sexual relations outside of wedlock when she was drugged and then raped by a Muslim man. For her violation of Sharia law, she received a one-year suspended jail sentence and was ordered to be deported. A court official said the sentence was 'lenient' and that 'had she been Muslim, she would have received at least five years in jail'…for being raped while unconscious. Just as Professor Briggs and Laurie Penny say, Muslim women have it so easy compared to their infidel western sisters.

Another run-of-the-mill Muslim was the convert Elton Simpson, one of two Jihadis who were killed by police before they could attack the free speech 'Draw Mohammed' competition in Garland, Texas. Nonplussed by Simpson's desire to kill and be killed for Allah, his lawyer described him as a 'normal guy'. Again, the same adjective and yet, at least by non-Muslim standards, once again very abnormal behaviour. Then we have Kuwait-born Mohammed Yousef Abdulazeez, aged 24. A former school friend, not himself a Muslim, remembered him as 'honestly one of the funniest guys I ever met. I never saw a violent bone in his body.' But on-line, this 'funny guy' was speculating, not with his bones but his brain, on how to 'separate the inhabitants of paradise from the inhabitants of hell fire.' He found the (inevitably violent) solution on July 16, 2015, when he gunned down five marines in Chattanooga, before being killed himself by police. It was same story yet again when a Muslim husband and wife team armed with assault rifles killed 14 and wounded 21 local government workers at a gathering in Saint Bernardino, California in December 2015. It was the usual scenario. While Obama, predictably speculated and obviously hoped that the killings could be 'work place related' (sic) and their lawyers denied (wrongly as it quickly proved) that the killers had terrorist motives, relatives described the husband, Syed Rizwan Farook, as 'cordial, liberal minded [sic] and well-liked'. It quickly transpired that his wife had proclaimed her allegiance to the Islamic State on Facebook shortly before the assault, and that the couple's home had been converted into a Jihadi arsenal liberally stocked with explosive devices.

Global polling has time and again revealed that the beliefs that drive such actions are not abnormal for young Muslims. According to the results of a poll released in July 2015, 42 million Muslims sympathised with the Islamic State. A survey of 1000 UK Muslims conducted in April the same year indicated that 11% of females and 5% of males identified with the Islamic State, a statistic borne out by the increasing numbers of women making the journey to Syria. However, 39% of UK Muslims blame the British authorities when this happens, and only 29% the relatives of those who make the trip. Naturally, just like Cameron and Obama, no Muslim spokesman could be heard entertaining the thought that it could have anything to do with their religion. 'Profiling' of Muslim terrorists has also proved they do not conform to the stereotype of the downtrodden and oppressed rebel concocted by the *dhimmi* media and Sharia left. They are not typically outsiders, losers, loners, poor, uneducated and unemployed. They are not even obviously and demonstrably anti-western or devout, or anything else other than yes, 'normal'. Neither is the Jihadi, with his readiness, his obligation, even his yearning to die, the victim of a perversion of Islam, as so many politicians, in defiance of all the evidence, fondly imagine. As we have seen, the summons to Jihad is repeatedly proclaimed in Islam's holiest of texts, the *Koran.* and everywhere, 'normal', 'ordinary' young men, fathers and husbands as well as sons, and increasingly women, mothers and wives as well as daughters, answered the call. Even then, some politicians, unlike Patrick Menucci, seemed unable to grasp or, if they did, say in public, what was motivating this onslaught. In the wake of the Tunis, Kuwait and French killings, Cameron yet again confidently assured the public that none of those responsible, even though all were at the time totally unknown to him, had anything to do with Islam. Without being aware of any of the details of the three attacks, or what their perpetrators were thinking at the time they were carried out, he still felt able to say with total certainty that these crimes had not been committed by genuine Muslims, but 'in the name of a twisted and perverted ideology'. If that is so, then let Cameron explain firstly how he came by this knowledge and secondly, the name of the 'ideology' (not, be it noted, 'religion') that had, so he claimed, been 'perverted and twisted', and in what ways. While Cameron was evidently certain he knew all that was needed to be known about the suspect in the French murder to be able to ascertain that his motives were not Islamic, on the day after the attack, Paris Public Prosecutor Francois Molins was quite rightly in no hurry to arrive at such a conclusion. 'Questions remain as to the exact chronology of events, what happened when he [the suspect] arrived, the circumstances of the decapitation, the motivation [sic] and whether there were accomplices.'

Perhaps he should have given the UK Prime Minister a call, because Cameron seemed to be privy to information that at the time was not yet available to the French authorities. He also took the opportunity to yet again demonstrate his expertise in matters Islamic when, three days after the triple assaults, he took the unprecedented step of advising the BBC, whose rules of governance are supposed to protect it from such interference, on how to report atrocities committed by Muslims in the name of the Islamic state: 'I wish the BBC would stop calling it the Islamic State because it is not an Islamic State.' Since its independence was at issue, the BBC response was initially commendably robust, though it was not long before for it complied with Cameron's request, even though BBC Director General, Lord Hall of Birkenhead, initially made it clear that the corporation would continue to 'preserve its impartiality'. A Radio Four programme presenter made the telling point that if, as Cameron preferred, all BBC references to the Islamic State were to be prefixed by the term 'so-called', this practice, to be consistent and neutral, would have to be extended to all states whose official title could questioned, as for example the People's Republic of China, the Democratic Republic of the Congo, the Democratic People's Republic of (north) Korea and the United Kingdom.

Re-enforcing Cameron's successful bid to bring the BBC to heel, the Muslim Tory MP Rahman Chiski drafted a letter to Lord Hall endorsed by over a hundred MPs complaining that calling the Islamic State by its name 'gives legitimacy to a terrorist organisation that is not Islamic'. 'Not Islamic? There are millions of Muslims, many of them living in the UK, who would beg to differ. The Caliph of the Islamic State (without prefix, *pace* Cameron), Ibn 'Awwad al-Husyni al-Qurashi (aka Abu Bakr-al Baghdadi) certainly would. Even his Muslim critics do not deny that he is as well-qualified and versed as any other cleric in matters of Islamic theology and law, and certainly more so than the MPs who signed the letter of protest to the BBC. His message to the world, released on May 14, 2015, entitled 'March Forth Whether Light or Heavy', is a summons to all Muslims to wage jihad, if necessary, to the death, for their faith against its enemies. Unlike the MP's letter, which contains none, the Caliph's message is replete with references to and citations from hallowed Koranic verses that sanctify the necessity of war against the infidel. Those cited include: al-Baqarah 216, An-Nisa 74, al-Tawbah 38-39, al-Ahzab 62, al Imran 140-142, Fatir 43 and Al-Ankahut 6. He also cited a *hadith* of Bukhari, which runs:

> And who ever say 'my prophet is Mohammed', it is incumbent upon him - if he is truthful in his claim - to follow his example. And he is the one who said: 'And by he in whose hand is Mohammed's soul, I would love to fight for the cause of Allah and be killed, and then fight for the cause of Allah and be killed again, and then fight for the cause of Allah and be killed again.'

We get the idea. The Caliph is also better versed than his detractors not only in the theology but also the history of Islam: 'Oh Muslims, Islam was never for a day a religion of peace. Mohammed was ordered to wage war until Allah is worshipped alone.' This is indeed what the *Koran* says, in Chapter 2, Verse 194. No Islamic cleric can deny it, though some will submit the words to 'contextualisation' to empty them of their original meaning and purpose. Going on the evidence of the arguments presented for and against the Islamic State being what it claims to be, Caliph al-Qurashi, who has a Doctorate in Islamic Theology, wins hands down. It is simply no contest. That is why no amount of rhetoric from Islam-ignorant politicians was likely to have any impact on the flow of Muslim volunteer Jihadis flocking to the Caliphate, or the far broader ground swell of sympathy its actions generated both in the Islamic world and the Muslim diaspora. Muslim clerics dared not engage al-Qurashi in genuine debate because doing so would have involved repudiating the universally accepted sources upon which he founded his actions. He was not a fraud, or an 'extremist', and his Muslim critics knew it. He believed every word he said, and what he said is rooted in the very core of Sunni Islam. So all we hear from the voices of so-called moderation is denials, but no refutations. The concept and goal of the Caliphate, the world-wide Islamic state that unites all Muslims in one single community governed by Sharia law, the *Ummah,* lies at the very heart of Sunni Islam. It is not, as Cameron, Corbyn and Obama seem to think, an unislamic aberration, any more than is *Jihad.*

Ever since its abolition in 1924 by Kemal Ataturk, the restoration of the Caliphate has remained the goal of theocratic movements like the Muslim Brotherhood (founded in 1928 for that purpose) and its more recent Jihadi offshoots such as Hamas and al-Qaeda. In the last years before the emergence of the Islamic State in 2014, all around the world, voices could be heard demanding the return of the Caliphate and defining how it should rule. Hamza Tzortzis of the UK-based Islamic Education and Research Academy (sic) made it clear that as Muslims 'reject the idea of freedom of speech and even of the idea of freedom', the restored Caliphate would do the same. The individual as such would no longer exist. As slaves of Allah, subjects of the Caliphate would 'engage with each other in a positive and productive way to produce results.' These 'results' were not enumerated, but we can guess what they might be. Hizb ut-Tahrir is a US-based world-wide Muslim organisation which, like so many others, is dedicated to the goal of re-establishing the Caliphate. And, also like the other definitions already cited, that of Hizb ut-Tahrir's contrasts the principles governing the rule of the Caliphate with those of western democracy, which it seeks to undermine and then destroy. One must acknowledge the frankness and clarity of the contrast that it makes between the two systems of rule and, though it is lost on all our politicians, their utter incompatibility:

> The republican system is based on democracy, where sovereignty is given to the people. Thus, the people have the right of ruling and legislation. They reserve the right to lay down a constitution and enact laws and to abolish, alter or modify both the constitution and the law. This bears no resemblance to the Islamic system, which is based solely on the Islamic faith and the Islamic legislation. Sovereignty is to the legislation of Allah and not the to the *Ummah* [the community of Muslims, i.e. the people]. So the Ummah has no right to legislate nor does the Khaleefah. The sole legislator is Allah, and the Khaleefah has only the right to adopt rulings for the constitution that are derived from the Book of Allah and the Sunnah Prophet Muhammad.

In a word, theocracy, where laws are made in heaven, and enforced on earth by a clerical caste. The Syrian Jihadist, Abu Mohammad al-Jualani described the Caliphate in the same totalitarian terms: 'Being Muslims, we do not believe in political parties or parliamentary elections, but rather an Islamic regime based on the *Shura* [an advisory council staffed by clerics].' Another Syrian Jihadi, Ahmad 'Issa, defined the Caliphate as 'a state of justice and truth. We want people to be ruled by an infallible law - the law of Allah. We do not want people to be ruled by man-made laws.' This is of course precisely the definition of 'human rights' enunciated in 1990 by the Cairo meeting of the Organisation of the Islamic Conference. Not only in Syria, destined to be its birth place, but across the Muslim diaspora from Australia through Europe to the USA, the cry was for the return of the Caliphate and with it, an end to western ideas of freedom, democracy and rule by man-made laws. Having failed to detect the signs of its coming, now that the Islamic State was upon them, politicians tried to persuade themselves and their publics that the Islamic State was not Islamic. When Cameron addressed the Global Security Forum in Bratislava on June 19, 2015, he listed the features of what he defined as the 'extremist Islamist ideology' as being 'one that says the West is bad, that democracy is wrong, that women are inferior, that homosexuality is evil, that religious doctrine trumps the rule of law and Caliphate the nation state, that justifies violence in asserting itself and achieving its aims.'

What Cameron is describing here, quite accurately, is not a mythical 'extremist Islamism', *but Islam itself.* Anyone in the least acquainted with the *Koran* would have known this to be so. Yet the current Pope Francis II, who does claim to be well-informed, as he should be, about a faith that has as its aim the supplanting of his own, shares Cameron's belief in an Islam that never existed, does not exist and, at least according accepted teachings and rulings, cannot exist:

> Faced with disconcerting episodes of violent fundamentalism, our respect for the true followers of Islam should lead us to avoid hateful generalisations, for authentic Islam and the proper [sic] reading of the *Koran* are opposed to *every* [sic] form of violence.

A 'proper reading'? Woe betides any Catholic who takes the same liberties with his or any of his predecessors' edicts. Fortunately, there is another way of reading the *Koran*, and it is just like reading any other text, for example this statement by the Pope. It has been exercised by mankind, with totally beneficial results, since the time writing was invented some six thousand years ago. For a true believer, the meaning of a passage from the *Koran* is not contingent on its 'context' since, being the word of God, it is timeless and not subject to revision or 're-interpretation' by mere mortals. And unlike the Bible, which proceeds chronologically, and in which time and place are integral to the message, much of the *Koran* is in fact contextless, as if its receiver, Mohammed is in a limbo, *sans* place, *sans* time. Consequently, if the passage in question unambiguously commands those that read or hear it to commit acts of violence, as the *Koran* does, over and over again, no amount of 'contextualisation', or 'reading', 'proper' or otherwise, is going to make it say and mean anything else, least of all an absolute commitment to non-violence. Because whatever Mohammed was, he was not a pacifist. I strongly recommend that Pope Francis reads again the following two passages from what I assume is his unexpurgated edition of the *Koran*, and explain how he arrives at the conclusion that it is opposed to 'every [no less!] form of violence', including assumedly that of wife beating or, as here, 'I will instil terror [sic] into the hearts of the unbeliever: smite ye above their necks and smite off all their fingertips.' (8: 12) Pope Francis ought to bear in mind that he is, despite his futile ecumenical strivings, also numbered among the 'unbelievers'. (I wrote this a full year before two Muslims cut the throat of a Catholic priest in his Rouen church.) The next citation should have a familiar ring about it:

> ...those who defy their Lord, for them will be cut out a garment of fire: over their heads will be poured boiling water. With it will be scalded what is within their bodies as well as their skins. In addition, there will be maces of iron to punish them. Every time they wish to get away therefrom, from anguish, they will be forced back therein, and, it will be said, 'Taste ye the Penalty of Burning.' (22: 19-22)

'The penalty of burning'! And we thought the Pope's Church had patented it. And whereas the last burning at the stake by the Spanish Inquisition was in 1826, the ultra-orthodox Islamic State was still doing it two centuries later, though in cages. Perhaps Pope Francis II is, in a not too subtle a fashion, advising us to read the *Koran* as so many Christians (including of course Roman Catholics) do the Bible, that is, cherry picking, skipping over the nasty, ignorant and embarrassing bits, which multiply with the advance of civilisation and the progress of science, and concentrating on an ever-shrinking remainder. What Pope Francis failed to understand is that aside from the word games played by clerics and theologians, the overwhelming majority of Muslims who can read - less than half the total - cannot, in fact dare not, 'read' their holy texts in the same 'proper' that is, selective way.

If the Islamic State is not Islamic, then why, only a matter of hours after Cameron gave this assurance, did reports reach the west that the non-Islamic Islamic State had beheaded two married Muslim couples for allegedly practising sorcery, and crucified five Muslim men for violating Ramadan fasting rules? If the Islamic State was not, as Cameron insisted, Islamic, then why should those who govern it care whether anyone practises sorcery, or eat at the wrong times during Ramadan? With his frequently advertised deep understanding of the workings of

Islamic jurisprudence, Cameron should surely have been more aware than most that these actions are serious crimes under Sharia law, and that the Islamic State punishes them in strict accordance with methods prescribed in the *Koran,* namely crucifixion and beheading. As Cameron, given his expertise, must have known, the *Koran* forbids sorcery in Chapter 2, Verse 102, and Chapter 4, Verse 113. According to Islamic sources, 'punishment for the sorcerer has been authentically reported from three companions of the prophet'. The relevant *fiqh* or legal ruling runs thus: 'The prophet commanded, "Kill every sorcerer, for this is the punishment ordered by Allah"'.

The west's ally in the fight against a nebulous 'extremism', the indisputably orthodox Kingdom of Saudi Arabia, also strictly enforces this same Koranic law, by cutting off heads in public, no differently than the supposedly non-Islamic, 'terrorist' and 'extremist' Islamic State. Why is one Islamic and not the other when they both uphold and enforce in the same way the same Sharia laws? Saudi Arabia also indoctrinates children in anti-Semitism, has banned women from driving, imposes the same dress code as the non-Islamic Islamic State, cuts off heads with a sword, promotes the *Protocols,* executes homosexuals, administers 1,000 lashes to anyone who criticises Saudi society and outlaws all religions except Islam. Could not these policies and actions also be considered 'extreme'? And should we not expect from the same MPs who signed their letter protesting against the BBC's use of the term Islamic State to submit another, requesting that the BBC in future refers to the 'so-called Islamic Republic of Iran' because, like the Islamic State, its clerical rulers also sanction the stoning of women to death and executing gays, the only difference being that whereas the Islamic State hurls them from the roofs of tall buildings, Iran throws them from clifftops? In this respect, Iran is more orthodox than the Caliphate, if only for topographical reasons because, according to a *Hadith* of a descendent of Mohammed, the Sixth Imam, Jafar As-Sadiq, there are three methods of carrying out the death penalty for a homosexual act: 'By tying the arms and feet and throwing from a cliff, by beheading, or being burnt alive.'

This constant pussyfooting by politicians led Haras Rafiq of the reformist Quilliam Foundation to complain that they all follow a policy of 'he who shall not be named, with no-one actually coming out and saying it is an Islamist Ideology. It is totalitarian and fascist; it gets people to do things for God in order to rally them to its cause'. Comments such as this have resulted in the Quilliam Foundation being denounced by mainstream Muslim organisations as apostates and by the Sharia left as stooges of western imperialism. Why is it left to reformist Muslims (and it should be said even braver ex-Muslims) to shame our politicians by being the only ones to have the guts and honesty to call things by their right names? The truth was, whatever western politicians said, millions of Muslims thought the Islamic State was not only an Islamic State, but the *only* Islamic State, and amongst them, thousands who were prepared to kill and die for it.

What this semantic chicanery tells us tells us that politicians and clerics are refusing, for a variety of reasons, to publicly acknowledge what they must know to be true, that a religious war is being waged against the West, one *au fond* of the seventh century against the twenty first, of the culture of the ancient desert against that of the modern western metropolis. And we should not assume, because of the west's vastly superior culture and technology (though as regards the latter, the gap is narrowing, and with the west's assistance) that its victory is assured. There have times in the past when a more primitive culture has overwhelmed one more advanced. Byzantium, the last repository of classical Greek learning, was subjugated by primitive Turkic Muslims swarming out of the depths of Asia, while the civilisation that that was once Rome succumbed to successive waves of Germanic barbarian invasions from the north. To this day, Russia bears the all too visible marks of its subjugation by the Mongols, while the Balkans have still to fully eradicate the legacy of the religious and ethnic hatreds bequeathed by four centuries of Ottoman despotism. There can be regression as well as progression. Our hard-won freedoms are an inheritance that can never be taken for granted. The problem is not only that they are, but their value is being questioned even by those who whose responsilbity it is to defend them.

25 Spiked

When PEN America conferred on the murdered *Charlie Hebdo* staff its annual Freedom of Expression Award, 143 writers signed a letter of protest, describing it as a reward for the magazine's mocking 'a section of the French population that is already marginalised, embattled, and victimised'. This of course is a lie, because *Charlie Hebdo's* satire was directed not against individual Muslims, but against the absurdities of a belief system that Muslims, not just in France but throughout the world, through their own free choice (so at least we are told) subscribe to. For these writers, as is the case with politicians, while they pay lip service to free speech in general, when it comes to Islam, different rules are applied. By setting limits to what can or cannot be subjected to satire, the protest was in effect arguing the case for a system of self-censorship in which the criterion for what can or cannot be satirised is not the idea itself, but who believes in it:

> The magazine seems [sic] to be entirely sincere its anarchic expressions of disdain toward organised religion. But in an unequal society, equal offence does not have an equal effect. Power and prestige are elements that must [sic] be recognised in considering almost any [sic] form of discourse including satire.

Down the ages, from the time of the ancient Greeks to Swift and Voltaire, one of the functions of literature and drama has been to provoke thought, to challenge ideas and beliefs that the writer considers false, even absurd; in Shelley's immortal words, to be 'the unacknowledged legislators of the world'. But no longer. Self-censorship has become the order of the day. Instead of exposing the myths, superstitions and falsehoods that cause and sustain injustice, the writers' duty is to protect them from criticism when they are believed in by the 'marginalised, embattled and victimised', as indeed they need to be if the existing order of society is to be upheld. And this from writers who see themselves as the defenders of the underdog! The rule being proposed runs something like this:

> Just because a belief is absurd, laughably ridiculous, patent nonsense, or even harmful in its effects to believer and unbeliever alike, does not mean that it can be lampooned. First it must be established who believes in it. If it is believed in by those with 'power and prestige', then it is open season. But not if it is the belief of the 'marginalised, embattled and victimised'. Their beliefs [which are often the main cause of their 'marginalisation'] are sacred.

But wait a moment. Excluding Sharia feminists, surely few will deny Muslim men use Islam to 'marginalise' 'their' women. So why not 'punch upwards' at the Islamic patriarchy, and ridicule the arrogant delusions of Muslim misogynists? Or at Muslim homophobia, which not only 'marginalises' gays, but under Islamic law, puts them to death? For the sake of the argument, let us allow, even though it is patently not true, that all diaspora Muslims, even those who comprise its clerical, political and business establishment, are the new underdogs of the western world, a substitute, so the Sharia left seems to think, for an indigenous proletariat that will not do as it is told. This diaspora, concentrated overwhelming in Europe, and to a much smaller degree in the Americas, comprises less than 5% of the total world

Muslim population. Nowhere in this diaspora do Muslims suffer political or religious persecution, as for example Shia's do in Sunni-ruled states and visa-versa. Unlike Muslim women in all and non-Muslims in some Islamic states, they are equal before the law. Though they may well be less prosperous on average than those of the host society (partly at least because Muslim women are often confined to their homes), they enjoy an education, health care and welfare and employment rights vastly superior to that provided by any of the 56 countries where Islam is the state religion.

The real under and top dogs of Islam are in those countries where Muslims make up the overwhelming majority of the population. In no sense can the Muslim rulers of the kingdoms of Morocco and Saudi Arabia, and of Sudan, Yemen, Syria, Pakistan, Iran, Indonesia and the oil Sheikhdoms of the Gulf, just to name a few, be described in any sense as 'marginalised, embattled and victimised', or lacking in 'power and prestige', though their subjects, especially when they dare to think for themselves, certainly can. So why then should the cruel and primitive beliefs of their political masters not be considered fair game? Is it the satirist's fault they are shared by those in a less exalted station whom their rulers have brainwashed almost from birth? Apparently yes. One of the signatories to the protest, the US writer Francine Prose (sic), even detected in the award a racist and imperialist plot at work, which she describes in classic post-modernist babble: 'The narrative [sic] of the *Charlie Hebdo* murders - white Europeans killed in their office by Muslim extremists - is one that feeds neatly ['neatly'...but of course...a conspiracy is afoot] into cultural prejudices that have allowed our government to make so many mistakes in the Middle East'. But 'white Europeans' *were* killed by (non-white) 'Muslims extremists. That is a fact, not a 'narrative'

The actual Paris massacre, with its well-advertised religious motive - 'the prophet is avenged' - has been conveniently supplanted by a fictitious 'narrative' with a racist slant (conducted by whom we are not told) which, in its turn, by exploiting certain 'cultural prejudices', 'feeds neatly' as all conspiracies do, into a plot to further the aims of US foreign policy. We only a step away from the staff of *Charlie Hebdo* being complicit in this plot by offering themselves up as its supposed victims. And why not, since millions, and not all of them Muslims by a long way, believe the hijackers of 9/11 sacrificed themselves for Israel, not Allah. The central issue of press freedom versus Islamic intolerance and terror has thus been spirited away, to be replaced by a crackpot racist-imperialist conspiracy theory. Satire, viewed from this perspective, is not only a means of further oppressing the already oppressed Muslim diaspora of the west. It is also a weapon of the US imperialists directed against the Muslims of the East. And yet the harshest critics of Islam are to be found amongst its apostates, which is of course exactly what one would expect. It should be obvious to all but the most obtuse why it is that most are from those who have endured its barbaric rule the longest – the Arabs, Pakistanis, Afghans, Iranians and North Africans. Surely it is they who deserve, and no less need, the support and solidarity of western writers who enjoy all the freedoms Muslim apostates in many cases risk their lives for. What they actually get from the left is ostracism, slander…and 'no-platforming'.

One of the arguments for 'going easy' on Islam is that it is largely a faith of non-white peoples. But here too we encounter another inconsistency. The prevalence of Christianity amongst black Africans has not proved an obstacle to western critiques, including satire, of their faith. And what a target it is! Up there with Allah's' rules on farting is the Roman Catholic Eucharist. The Pope, who undoubtedly enjoys enormous temporal as well as spiritual power and prestige, and commands untold wealth, believes, and demands that others believe, that in the miracle of transubstantiation, a chunk of bread, when consecrated by a priest, is mysteriously transformed into the body of Christ who, while remaining in heaven with his body intact, is also loaning it out at the same time, again intact, to thousands of other priests performing the identical ritual at the same time. This belief in the physical presence of Christ at the Eucharist, together with the supremacy of the Pope, is without doubt the very bedrock of the Roman rite. As the current Catechism of the Roman Catholic Church has it, 'the other sacraments and indeed all the ecclesiastical ministries and works of the apostolate are bound up with the Eucharist and are oriented towards it'.

How strange then that it took the best part of twelve centuries for transubstantiation to become adopted as official dogma of the Roman church at the fourth Lateran Council of 1215! By the Reformation, some had begun to doubt whether bread could be transformed into god. Others rejected it altogether as superstitious mumbo jumbo or, as the English expression has it, *hocus pocus*, a conjuring trick, from the Latin *hoc est corpus,* here is the body. It was with good reason then that the Catechism adopted by the 'Counter Reformation' Council of Trent (1545-1563), after conceding that 'the exposition of this mystery is most difficult', decreed: 'the faithful are to be admonished that they do not inquire too curiously into the manner in which this change may be made, for it defies our powers of conception, nor have we any example of it in natural changes nor in the creation of things itself.' Just so. Yet even today, in a world that thanks to mankind's irrepressible, religion-defying natural curiosity, (the original sin of Adam), science has generated the knowledge and means that sustains and enhances our lives on this planet, millions of otherwise quite rational, educated people, many if not most with some awareness of the workings of the natural world, some even who are themselves scientists, are not only obliged to believe this mumbo jumbo, but actually do, or at least say they do. Nor is this the end of it. Roman Catholics are obliged to believe that no matter how many times the chunk of bread, or wafer (the species or host) is subdivided, each newly created fraction of the whole wafer contains, or rather actually is, the complete body of Christ, not just a *pro rata* portion of it.

Having ruled as heretical the atomic theories of the Greek philosopher Democritus (*circa* 470-360 BC), and the Roman materialist and sceptic Lucretius (99-55 BC) which correctly presumed that matter is composed of finite indivisible (today we know as sub-atomic) particles, the Catholic Church held matter to be infinitely divisible. It was therefore possible by subdivision repeated *ad infinitum* for the smallest imaginable crumb of consecrated bread to generate an infinite number of bodies of Christ. Today, the Church, no thanks to the Bible, knows better. This process of the subdivision of the host now has its natural limits, theoretically continuing until the original chunk is reduced via millions of individual molecules and billions of atoms down through sub-atomic quarks and the like to god's very own sub sub atomic, aptly named god particle, the Higgs Boson, resulting in trillions of bodies of Christ. This, believe or not, is still to this day, and presumably will be for evermore, the official teaching of the Roman Catholic Church on the miracle and aptly described 'mystery' of the Eucharist. No wonder the Council of Trent advised that 'pastors should also use no less caution in explaining the mysterious manner in which the body of our Lord is contained whole and entire under the least particle of the bread.' Here in the 21st century, we find the current *Catechism* still insisting, as its authors feel they must, that the faithful are required to believe 'Christ is present whole and entire in each of the species and whole entire in each of their [the species'] parts, in such a way [sic] that the breaking of the bread does not divide Christ', and perhaps as both a warning and an aid to doubters, quotes St Thomas Aquinas, to the effect that the body and blood of Christ 'cannot be apprehended by the senses, but only by faith.' What a (literally) god given subject for satire! For example, what happens to Christ after the wafer has been ingested, masticated, digested and then excreted into the sewage system? Can a communicant by pretending to swallow the host, retain Christ in the mouth, take him home, spit him out, and give him pride of place on the mantelpiece between a statue of the virgin Mary and a picture of the Pope? But wait. Not only the all-powerful and prestigious Pope believes this nonsense, along with Jesuit scholars, the carefully selected elite of Opus Dei and high-profile converts such as the former Labour Prime Minister Tony Blair and former Tory Cabinet Ministers Ann Widdecombe and John Gummer. So, in their own way, do hundreds of millions of desperately poor 'marginalised' and 'embattled' Africans, South Americans and Phillippinoes. Are we then to assume that *The Life of Brian* parody of the life of Jesus and Father Ted's and Dave Allen's poking fun at the Roman Catholic Church are to be condemned as complicit in the same imperialist and racist 'narrative' that is said to have been conducted (by whom we are not told) to exploit the murder of the white staff of *Charlie Hebdo*?

The principle at work in the minds of those who protested against the PEN Award, though not stated clearly as such, is that the most important, maybe even the only factor that should determine one's attitude to a belief is not whether it is true or false, but the social, ethnic, religious or racial identity of those who hold it. This condescending, paternalist *ad hominem*, masquerading as radical anti-racism, and which was described to me approvingly as 'only punching upwards', is deeply patronising in its attitude towards those it claims to be protecting from the 'narrative' of the 'powerful and prestigious', since it assumes this can only be achieved by insulating them from the need to confront the falsity of their own beliefs, the very beliefs than help sustain their oppression. On the same grounds of protecting the minds of Muslims from hurt and insult, one can proscribe the teaching of evolution and the Holocaust to Muslim children, and in fact, in the case of the latter, this has indeed been demanded by Muslim parents both in the UK and France, and what is more, granted. It has also been proposed, as we have seen, by a German politician, and is actually in force in *dhimmi* Sweden.

In the pursuit of a spurious social or racial justice, objective truth (if it even exists) counts for nothing. By this reckoning Islam is just as valid as Newton's three laws of motion and, even if it isn't, it should be treated as if it is. If indeed it is so wrong to satirise the beliefs of the poor and the weak, then those who argue thus in the name of anti-racism have created for themselves an insoluble dilemma. In the deep south of the USA, in the so-called 'Bible Belt', there still linger on amongst the less affluent whites the old anti-Black hatreds that once fuelled the birth, rise and crimes of the Ku Klux Klan and sustained Jim Crow. Tea Party 'poor whites' or red necks were certainly not powerful and prestigious, though they were manipulated by those who were. Should we then protect from satire their idiocies and hatreds? There were also racist 'poor whites' a plenty in the Protestant farm lands of late Weimar Germany. Under-investment, cheaper imports and a slump in demand had reduced millions of small holders to near destitution. In desperation, they turned to the Nazis, who offered them a glorious future in Hitler's Jew-free Reich. Yet during the Nazi rise to power, Hitler's doctrines were the target of relentless satire by journalists and cartoonists of the left, among them the communist John Heartfield being the most celebrated. But if the critics of the Pen Award are right, in retrospect, subjecting to satire and ridicule the anti-semitic prejudices shared by the Nazi leaders and their deluded poor and 'marginalised' following was a mistake, the wrong 'narrative'.

Yet there was time when the secular left saw it is their duty to undermine the grip of the rich and powerful on the minds of the poor and weak, what another communist, the Italian Antonio Gramsci, described as the struggle for hegemony, the breaking of the ideological hold of the ruling elites on the masses. Was Gramsci wrong then to combat the reactionary influence of Roman Catholicism on the minds of less enlightened Italian workers and particularly peasants? True, Mussolini thought so, because he had him put away for 20 years to 'stop his brain from functioning'. Did not Marx say that the criticism of religion was the beginning of all criticism? Was Thomas Paine generating a 'narrative' for those with 'power and prestige' with his *Age of Reason* demolishing the myths of the Bible? No. They banned it, as the Nazis burned the writings of Marx.

In their eagerness to condemn Charlie *Hebdo's* satire of Islam, our zealous protesters overlooked the obvious truth that all religions, like their secular ideological counterparts, span all social classes, making it impossible to satirise the religious beliefs of the rich, powerful and prestigious without at the same time also satirising the identical beliefs of the poor, the weak, the marginalised and the victimised. In fact, the Sharia left in the UK has arrived at precisely this conclusion and now, especially on campus, vigorously campaigns to outlaw all critiques of religion, no matter what form they might take. Even in the USA, protected though they are by the First Amendment, still journalists come under enormous and growing pressure, not only from their readers, editors and employers, but politicians and the Muslims lobby, to engage in self-censorship of various kinds when reporting on matters Islamic. At its 2007 convention, the Society of Professional Journalists adopted a set of guidelines to be used when covering stories related to Arabs and Muslims. They included:

> When writing about terrorism, remember to include white supremacist, radical anti-abortionists and other groups with a history of such activity; Do not lump Islamic countries together as in constructions such as 'the fury of the Muslims world'; Avoid using word combinations such as 'Islamic terrorist' or 'Muslims extremists'; Avoid using terms such as "jihad" unless you are certain of their precise meaning. The basic meaning of 'jihad' is to exert oneself for the good of Islam and to be better oneself.

Those who chose to obey these guidelines would have been telling lies, because even the most cursory reading of the *Koran* will alight upon numerous passages which demand that Muslims exert themselves 'for the good of Islam' by waging war on its enemies. This is a betrayal of the journalist's calling, which is to report accurately and objectively what a journalist sees and hears, just as a satirist's has for centuries served as a weapon in the struggle against tyranny, injustice, ignorance, superstition and all the other obstacles to human progress and freedom. Together they have made the world a freer and better place to live in. Now they are both menaced by the Islamic subversion of the west's hard-won right to report and read the truth, its freedom to speak its mind and laugh at what it finds funny and ridiculous. Allah does not like jokes, least of all about himself, any more than did Hitler and Stalin, under whose tyrannies jokes about the great leader carried the death penalty. What price now Voltaire's *Candide,* perhaps the greatest classic of its genre? Once rules are imposed for satire, it loses its true function, which is to use wit and humour to cut down to size the impostor, the arrogant, the fraudster, the charlatan, the pretentious. What more fitting target than Islam, a collection of primitive superstitions that claim to be the summation of all wisdom, a doctrine that sanctifies unspeakable cruelties to millions of its believers, especially, yes, 'marginalised' women and, by terror and thought control, prevents their access to ideas and knowledge that can lead to their emancipation and the enrichment of their lives. It is Islam, not its critics, that has rendered them marginalised, embattled and victimised, inciting its believers to despise and reject every benefit western civilisation has to offer them. If ever there was a legitimate target for satire, it is Islam, as not only the enemy of the west, but even more so, *as the enemy of Muslims.*

Those who enjoy, to greater or lesser extent, the freedom to speak their minds on subjects that are forbidden in Islamic states, owe it to those oppressed by Islam to undermine its hold anyway they can, instead of submitting themselves to a humiliating self-censorship that protects from criticism a creed that draws its strength from ignorance and fear. Surely those in the west who have access to the public should speak freely on such matters, to proclaim loudly and often what millions of those living under the tyranny of Islam think but dare not say. Muslims should be confronted with the proof that their faith has placed those who subscribe to it in the rearguard of human progress as measured by all objective criteria, whatever their theologians might claim to the contrary. A few statistics. Spain, not richly endowed with natural resources and economically not among the first rank of western states, with a population of 47 million, still manages to generate a greater gross domestic product than the entire Arab world, with a population of 370 million. Despised (yet envied) Israel, the Middle Eastern state which lacks the most in natural resources, and with a population of only 8.3 million, generates an annual GDP of $291 billion. Egypt, irrigated by the Nile, and by far the most populous of the Arab states, with a population ten times that of Israel, can only generate a GDP of $272 billion. Israel's economy is thus ten times more efficient than that of Egypt. The contrast with Pakistan, a state saturated with, and founded by, for and on Islam, is even starker. With a population approaching 200 million, 24 times that of Israel's, and despite having since independence received foreign aid from the USA alone totalling approximately $100 billion, its economy generates a paltry annual GDP of $197 billion, making Israel's economy a staggering 35 times more productive. Again, not bad for apes and swine.

The divergence is no less great in the realm of academic achievement, as the Nobel Prize awards show. Just as an example, Israel has around 12,000 research scientists, more than the combined total for the entire Arab world. But, leaving aside the ravings of geocentric flat earth Saudi preachers, perhaps the most fitting and revealing comment on the ravages wrought by Islam in the spheres of intellectual endeavour is the fact that for many years now, the geology department at Cairo University has been closed because the findings of the discipline do not coincide with the descriptions of planet earth found in the *Koran*. Allah has spoken the last word on the subject, as he has on everything else. The matter is closed. Yet any objective observer would be obliged to conclude that all for its claims to a divinely ordained superiority, societies governed by Islam, many of them for more than a thousand years, are a total failure in all but one department: oppression and the policing of the mind. In the interests of objectivity, let the final word on the plight of the Islamic world be left to a Muslim, Dr Farrukh Salem, a Pakistani freelance journalist based in Islamabad. These are some of the comparisons he makes between the realm of Islam and the world of the despised and inferior *kuffar*.

First, economy. Muslims comprise 22% of the world's population, but account for less than 5% of its GDP, a figure that would be even lower but for their dependence on western aid and imported *kuffar* skills and technology, and without which Allah's oil would still be under the sand and his armies fighting each other on horseback and camels with swords and spears What is more, this share in world output is steadily declining over time. The combined annual GDP of the 57 Islamic states in 2009 was under $2 trillion, compared with that of the 'Great Satan', the USA, at $10.4 trillion. So, with less than a quarter of the Islamic states' combined population of 1.4 billion, the USA, with a population of 320 million, generates more than five times their wealth, which renders it 22 times more productive. Such statistics as these must surely make more reflective Muslims wonder whose side is Allah on. In 2009, 15% of the Arab labour force was unemployed, and it is projected to double within a decade, mainly because the growth rate of the Arab economies is around 0.5% per annum, among the slowest in the world, while the Arab population has been growing nearly ten times faster.

Moving onto matters cultural, Dr. Farrukh made a no less devastating and damning comparison between educational facilities and performance in the Islamic world and the west. Leaving aside the quality and breadth of the education offered, the 57 Islamic states between them have less than 600 universities, an average of ten per country, to cater for 1.4 billion people, while the USA, with a population of a little under 320 million, has ten times as many, 5,768. The ratio of scientists to population in the 57 Islamic states is 230 to one million, in the USA it is 4,099 per one million, in Japan, 5,095 per one million. And, of course, we should add that many, if not most, of the Islamic states' best scientists graduate at infidel universities. Finally, perhaps the most damning statistic of all, 800 million of the world's 1.5 billion Muslims, the majority being of course female, are illiterate, compared with near 100% literacy in the west.

The political consequences are obvious. With illiteracy comes ignorance. Ignorance invariably begets prejudice, and prejudice, frustration and finally violence. For the minority that can read, the value of such literacy is, as it has been throughout its history, determined what is available and permissible to read. In the case of those countries dominated by Islam, this amounts to very little aside from the *Koran* and texts extolling the virtues of Islam and hatred of the Jews. Spain *in one year* translates more books into its own language than the Arab world has done *since the time of Mohammed*. Sealed off, as is the intention, from any genuine, objective knowledge of the world beyond their faith, the Islamic masses, as was evident in the 'Arab Spring', are all too easily rendered putty in the hands of those who seek to manipulate them for their own political and financial advantage. The result is what we see.... festering, rampant, raging, impotent hatred (and envy) of the west in general and of the Jews in particular, who serve, as always, as the scapegoat for all Islam's many ills. Fortunately, there is a ready explanation to hand to account for why Muslims states, despite their religion's claim to superiority in all things, are not performing as believers think it should. The answer is to be found in the holy texts, in the Hamas Charter, on Arab TV channels and in the sermons at Friday prayers. It is just as Hitler said...the World Jewish Conspiracy. The remedy is therefore as simple as the cause is obvious, requiring little if any brain power. Eradicate Israel, exterminate the Jews, and all will be well.

This appalling poverty of intellectual and cultural life suffered by those living under the rule of Islam is not only the product of an unquestioning belief in a faith devised, and then frozen for all time, by the minds of ignorant, barbarian, desert-bound semi-nomadic bandits. It is also the sad inheritance of a culture that has to a large degree been able to hermitically isolate itself from the destabilising effects of the world-shaping conquests achieved by western thought, advances brought about by the dearly-bought ascendancy of free inquiry, reason and science over the ignorance and superstition fostered and preserved by religion. The rulers and terrorist movements of the Islamic world have made it very clear that they do not intend to suffer the same fate as their western feudal and clerical counterparts. How else is it possible to explain that a state television channel, in the 21st century, is allowed to condemn as false truths that were known to ancient Greece more than 2000 years ago? There have, however, been exceptions to Islam's self-imposed isolation from the West. Two texts in particular have been accorded the rare honour of Arabic translations and wide distribution; namely Hitler's *Mein Kampf* and that Hamas and Saudi favourite, *The Protocols of the Learned Elders of Zion*. Two editions of the former have been published, the first, in 1937 in Cairo, translated by Al Sadati and the second, also in Cairo in 1963, translated by Luis al Haj, formerly Luis Heiden, a fugitive Nazi war criminal and subsequent convert to Islam. Besides enjoying steady sales in the Middle East, Heiden's Arabic translation of *Mein Kampf* is readily available at a number of bookshops in London's Edgware Road, an area of substantial Muslim settlement.

The *Protocols,* a much shorter text and, unlike *Mein Kampf,* wholly devoted to the so-called 'Jewish Question', was the concoction of a Russian orthodox priest at the beginning of the last century. Given the absurdity of its allegations against the Jews, perhaps it can best be described as the idiots' guide to becoming an anti-Semite. Be that as it may, its anti-Semitic slanders soon won endorsement from clerics at all levels of the Roman Catholic Church, and inevitably from the fascist movements that sprang up all over Europe at the end of the First World War. In the USA, automobile tycoon and Hitler admirer Henry Ford funded the printing of half a million copies, while more recently, they were declared to be true by the American 'young earth' creationist, TV evangelist and then convicted fraudster Kent Honvind. This suggests that if someone can still believe, in the 21st century, that the universe is only six thousand years old, or rather young, then they are ready to believe anything. The ubiquity and persistence of Jew-hatred has ensured that endorsement of the *Protocols* can indeed turn up in the most unlikely of places...for example, as we shall see, in on-line postings by devotees of Labour Party Leader Jeremy Corbyn.

Nowhere however were the *Protocols* more enthusiastically received than in the Middle East, where they have subsequently enjoyed a uniquely prolific life at the hands of Arab translators, publishers and book sellers. Even in countries where illiteracy was and still is rife, demand for the *Protocols* has proved insatiable, because it has been graced with no fewer than nine editions, more even than the number published by the Nazis. Neither have its anti-Semitic fabrications been lacking in official endorsement. President Nasser of Egypt, President Arif of Ba'athist Iraq, King Faisal of Saudi Arabia, WRP benefactor Colonel Gaddafi of Libya, and the Grand Mufti of Jerusalem Sheikh Ekrima Said Sabri, are just some of the prominent Arab Muslims who have publicly declared the *Protocols* to be true. Prince Charles' friends, the rulers of the Saudi Kingdom, are especially taken with the *Protocols*. Prodigious quantities have been churned out and made freely available to all visitors to that benighted kingdom, while possession of a Bible is almost certain to result in arrest and probably worse. The text is used as a study aid for tenth grade school pupils, ensuring that Saudi children grow up hating all Jews, as all good Muslims should. The *Protocols* is not only distributed, often free of charge, in vast quantities throughout the Arab world. Displayed at Arab book fairs, its poison infects not only all Arab states, but the entire Islamic world, as far as Pakistan and even Indonesia.

Its slanders against the Jews are regularly dramatised on Arab TV networks, complete with a graphic depiction of the 'Jewish blood libel', in which a Christian child is kidnapped and its blood drained for mixing with unleven bread for the Feast of the Passover. On May 29, 2015, in one of his twice weekly videoed classes on Islamic theology at the Jerusalem Al-Aqsa Mosque, Palestinian cleric Sheikh Khaled Al-Mughrabi provided a graphic description of how it was done:

> The children of Israel would look for a small child, kidnap and steal him, bring a barrel called the barrel of nails. They would put the small child in the barrel and his body would be pierced by these nails. In the bottom of the barrel they would put a tap and pour the blood.

Retribution for this crime was at hand however: 'In the end, it reached the point when they [the Jews] were burned in Germany, because of these things, because they kidnapped young children.' When circumstances dictate, the Holocaust can, if only momentarily, become very real. On June 9, Sheikh Khaled explored another theme dear to the heart of all right-thinking Muslims: 'The Jews actually intend to conquer the world, and they began with the holy land...whoever reads the *Protocols of the Elders of Zion* will see that the final goal of the Children of Israel is to conquer the world...I mean militarily conquer.' [Surely, he means Islam] On July 31, the learned preacher dwelt on a theme dear to the hearts, if not the brains, of Middle East clerics...the Jewish plot to poison the rest of humanity. But this time the tale had a modern twist:

> The Rothschild family own more than half the world's wealth. They [also] own 95% of the world's pharmaceutical industry. Many diseases were created in labs, viruses that were created by doctors bought, trained and taught by the Rothschild family, the Freemasons, the Zionists or [sic] the Jews to create and spread disease so they will be able to sell medicine for it.

On October 16, 2015, at the height of a Jew-stabbing frenzy in Jerusalem, the PA's resident Neo-Nazi preacher mounted the rostrum once again to deliver another videoed genocidal diatribe. Citing, as Muslim clerics love to do, a *hadith*, one of many the Sharia left and the world's media studiously ignore, namely the one which features in Article Seven of the Hamas Charter, he pledged

We will follow the Jews everywhere They will not be able to escape us. It is a reliable promise from the prophet according to which the tree and the rock will speak and say, 'O Muslim there is a Jew behind me, come and kill him'. The children of Israel will all be exterminated.

These are the not the ravings of a free-lance cleric. The Palestinian Authority assumes full responsibility for the content of all such 'educational' programmes conducted by its clerics. This was made very clear in a statement issued by the PA Ministry of Religious Affairs in the name of its then Minister, Mahmoud Al-Habbash, as reported in the PA daily, *Al-Hayat Al-Jadida* of August 16, 2010:

> The mosques and everything belonging to them belong to the Ministry of Religious Affairs, from the employees - the imam, the speaker, the *Koran* teacher, the librarian, the caretaker and custodians. He notes that the religious lessons, Koranic study and other activities going on in the mosque require prior approval by the Ministry.

And funding by gullible *kuffars*.

26 Dump It!

'Inter-faith dialogue' is an activity that is intended to bring together in mutual respect and understanding, though obviously not complete agreement, the representatives of the various faiths and denominations, some of which not only judge all the others to be guilty of heresy but not so long ago, would have gladly tortured and put each other to death and in some Islamic countries, still do so. How the 'inter-faith' project is viewed by some Muslim clerics was demonstrated in a sermon preached by Imam Hajj Saeed in the Copenhagen Al-Faruq mosque on February 13, 2015: 'The people responsible for interfaith dialogue want to make all religions equal. They want to equate Truth and Falsehood...This is a malignant idea of which we must be aware, in order to avoid falling into the traps of Satan and his followers, who advocate such dialogue.' Then our Imam gave an example from the life of the Prophet as to how believers of other faiths should be treated:

> Our Prophet Muhammed had Jewish neighbours in Al-Madina. Did he call for closer relations, harmony, and dialogue with them...Or did he call them to worship Allah? When they [the Jews] violated their pledge, and did not accept this call - well, you know what he did to them. It appears in his Sira [the 'official' life story of Mohammed]. He waged war against the Jews.

What the prophet 'did', was to massacre the Jewish men, and enslave the women and children. (See Appendix L) This diatribe of inter-faith hate, directed, as is the norm, chiefly against the Jews, was delivered on the evening of February 13, 2015. The very next day, Omar Abdel Hamid el-Hussein transformed the Imam's words into deeds when, after proclaiming on line his loyalty to the ISIS Caliphate, he launched his attack on the Copenhagen Free Speech event at the Krudttonden Cultural Institute, followed by the killing of a Jewish guard outside the Copenhagen central Synagogue.

Saudi Arabia's understanding of the terms on which inter-faith dialogue should be conducted reveals how the same words acquire very different, indeed almost opposite meanings, in different cultures. When the Austrian government threatened to close down the Vienna-based King Abdullah Centre for Interreligious and Intercultural Dialogue after its refusal to condemn the 1000 lashes and ten-year prison sentence imposed in 2014 on human rights activist Raif Badawi for 'insulting Islam', the Saudis responded by threatening to move the Vienna headquarters of OPEC to another location. The reply of Chancellor Werner Faymann was remarkably robust: 'If this centre says it stands for interreligious dialogue, then it must do so. But if it wants to remain only an economic centre with a religious fig leaf, then Austria should no longer be a part of it. In any event, Austria will not allow itself to be threatened or blackmailed.' This tells us all we need to know about the relationship between oil and Islam, and the factors that keep the west's eyes averted from the atrocious human rights abuses perpetrated by the favourite monarchy of the Head Apparent of the Church of England.

A genuine dialogue requires that all participants listen to each other, keep an open mind concerning matters in dispute and, above all, do not resort, as the Saudis did in this case, to threats and blackmail. The *Koran*'s Chapter Five, Verse 52, commanding that 'ye who believe should take not the Jews and Christians as friends', and Chapter 4, Verse 102, which warns Muslims who travel to the lands of the infidel that 'verily, the disbelievers are an open enemy to you' undeniably seems at variance with the spirit and purpose of such an exchange, and certainly does nothing to encourage Muslims to integrate themselves into a predominately non-Islamic society. On the contrary it has contributed, along with state-sponsored 'multiculturalism' and 'celebration' of 'diversity', to 'self-ghettoisation', the creation of Muslims enclaves and 'no-go' areas throughout Europe, establishing what are effectively unofficially tolerated mini-Islamic states within states. In the UK, after a series of scandals involving police and social services cover-ups of and even complicity in an organised Islamic sex crime industry, it is at last being admitted that political correctness and fear of accusations of racism, despite Islam's not being a race (though when it suits its purpose it successfully claims that it is) has led to various public authorities turning blind eyes and deaf ears to a range of anti-social and criminal activities, including:

organised gang rape and pimping,
Sharia law enforcement patrols,
the creation of 'no go' Islamic zones,
electoral fraud,
the Islamisation of state schools,
organised attempts, one of them successful, to remove the Holocaust from history syllabi,
forced marriages,
local authority corruption,
self-ghettoisation,
bogus 'charities' that fund terrorism,
nepotism,
the establishment of Sharia courts,
female genital mutilation (now admitted to be rife),
bigamous marriages,
the rape and beating of wives,
'honour' killing of girls and young women, (the honour in question always being that of the male),
paedophilia and the aborting of female foetuses.

Adding to this in some cases officially sanctioned creeping Islamisation of the UK are the concessions or privileges afforded to Muslims, and the imposition on non-Muslims of Sharia practices, always without consent and often without their knowledge, including:

Muslim-only interest free student loans,
Muslim-only interest free mortgages,
Muslim-only free bank overdrafts,
Muslim-only gender-segregated sessions at swimming baths,
Muslim-only days at cinemas,
Muslim-only prayer time at work,
Muslim prayer rooms in secular buildings and institutions,
Muslim super-market staff excused checking-out *haram* alcohol and pork products,
gender-segregated seating at university meetings and in schools,
undisclosed Halal-only menus at fast food chains, restaurants, schools, hospitals, universities and army canteens,
the closure of roads to non-Muslims on Islamic religious festival days,

the blocking of public highways by Islamic prayer sessions,
illegal prayer sessions in royal parks;
and, as a novelty item, the marketing of a Sharia doll, with no facial features.

The absurdity, as well as the perniciousness, of the Islamic offence industry is perfectly illustrated by the following case. A couple were travelling on a bus in Yorkshire with their 15-month-old autistic daughter. When she began to cry, they sang to her the theme song from a cartoon feature, Peppa Pig. A Muslim woman passenger reacted by reporting the parents to the bus driver, accusing the couple of 'racism'. The worldly and Sharia-wise driver, knowing full-well how this incident could develop, and perhaps fearing for his job if he responded in politically incorrect fashion by politely telling the woman not to be so silly and go back to her seat, stopped the bus and told the couple and their distraught child they had to get off: 'Just get off the bus, it's not worth the hassle'. We know how he must have felt. He explained that if they stayed on the bus, the police could get involved...and who knows where that could lead. So, singing a song quietly to a crying autistic child becomes a racist insult to a Muslim woman because the song contained the word 'pig', demonstrating how easily Islam becomes a race when the opportunity to be offended offers itself. If ever there was an incident certain to incite prejudice against Muslims, this was surely it. It also warrants a few observations on what could be called the Islamic Offence Offensive.

What it seeks at the very least is the same protection to that afforded to Christianity under the now-defunct blasphemy laws of England and Wales. Dating from the 16th century as the product of a god-fearing, ignorant and bigoted age, they were, incredibly, only repealed on a free Parliamentary vote in 2008. Up to that point, according to a ruling by Lord Scarman, quoting from the *Stephen's Digest,* in the Ninth Edition of 1950, all it required for a prosecution to be brought under these laws was the publication of a 'contemptuous, reviling, scurrilous or ludicrous matter relating to God, Jesus Christ or the Bible, or the formularies of the Church of England'. However the law chose then, and still chooses now to describe it, 'offence' is at best a nebulously defined, elusive and entirely subjective mental event, and cannot be subject to any viable external proof or, what is equally to the point, disproof that the claimed offence has in fact been experienced or, for that matter, not deliberately intended to be such by the alleged offender. Uniquely in English law, the burden of proof in blasphemy cases necessarily did not so much rest on the accuser, since the law assumed there was a case to be answered, as on the accused, who had to prove there was not. Consequently, the accused faced the near impossible task of proving that no offence had been taken or outrage intended. A verdict of guilty was always the most likely outcome in such cases, and so it proved in the last case tried under the Blasphemy Laws, brought by TV censorship campaigner Mary Whitehouse against the magazine *Gay News* in 1977.

The Blasphemy Laws in England and Wales have gone, but the crime of giving offence to the religious, classified as 'hate speech' has taken its place, and has proved far easier to invoke. Wider in scope than the laws it has supplanted, they now make it possible to prosecute anyone allegedly causing offence on, amongst others grounds, those of race and religion. The Race and Religious Hatred Act of 2006, although it specifies that as regards religion, it does not seek to 'prohibit discussion, criticism or expressions of antipathy, dislike, ridicule, insult or abuse', many prosecutions brought under this law have done just that, since it is at the court's discretion as to whether the behaviour, speech or writings of the accused have transgressed beyond these ill-defined boundaries. The potential, and one suspects, intended restrictions on free speech are enormous. It presents to the professional whinger, victim or grievance-seeker a golden opportunity to take and yes, to seek 'offence' at any comment or encounter which in the slightest way does not accord with their opinions or the 'respect', usually preferential or deferential treatment, they believe they are entitled to. And, true to form, it is Muslims who have proved themselves to be the most energetic, persistent and resourceful exponents of the art of offence taking, always insisting that the right to free speech (unlike the USA, non-existent in law) must be exercised 'responsibly', meaning that nothing bad can be said about their bad religion.

As already noted, one of the problems inherent in legal restrictions on freedom of speech is the impossibility of either objectively proving or disproving whether in fact 'offence' has been experienced or intended. Attempts have been made to surmount this difficulty by devising supposedly objective criteria as to what constitutes offence, or hate, but these fall at the first hurdle of culturally determined subjectivity. Songs about, or images of pigs do not offend atheists, Christians, Hindus, Sikhs or, so far as I am aware, even observant Jews. But apparently, they can have a positively traumatic effect on Muslims. (What I had taken to be a thoroughly 'modern' Muslim girl student I was privately coaching in economic history became distraught when I mentioned pig iron.) So, should the law accommodate itself in this respect to Muslim sensitivities as it has in others, rendering the UK effectively a Sharia compliant pig, pork, gammon and bacon free zone, perhaps even to the extent of banning the words, as Oxford University Press have done? Why not, since Sharia-compliant *halal* meals are served every day by the million to unsuspecting infidels in schools, hospitals and restaurants, with the expressed approval of the then Prime Minister, David Cameron. This obsession with creating categories of the population as defined by what they or others claim are their beliefs, designating them as victims, and then affording them special protection for those beliefs under the law is, by stealth and intention, creating a two-tier legal system, subverting the principle codified by Magna Carta that there is but one law and all are subject to it.

The Islamic campaign against free speech, aided as always by infidel Islamophiles, took what can only be described as a sinister turn with reports in the UK media on February 10, 2015, of police in both England and Wales demanding from newsagents the identity of customers who had bought copies of the post-massacre special edition of *Charlie Hebdo*, and from where they had been obtained. A spokeswoman for Dyfed-Powys Police Authority explained in word perfect Islamobabble that the operation had been carried out to 'enhance public safety and to provide community reassurance.' Despite repeated attempts at my request by Welsh Assembly members to elicit an explanation from the Police Authority as to who ordered this operation, and why, no answer was forthcoming. We therefore are left to conjecture: So...'public safety' is threatened by the sale of a French satirical magazine in the borderlands of mid Wales! Whose 'safety' exactly? Who or what is threatening it? And exactly who is this 'community' that needs 'reassuring'? Given the 'ethnic' composition of the area, it can only be the Welsh. So how can they, or anyone else for that matter, be 'reassured' by the knowledge that the local police are very interested in who is reading what.

Not I believe by chance, these unprecedented police crackdowns on press freedom, one that has all the hallmarks of an authorised attempt to appease Islamic sensitivities, came only days after a demonstration by several thousand Muslims outside Downing Street against *Charlie Hebdo's* depiction of their prophet. It presented a petition signed by 100,000 Muslims demanding in effect the enforcement of Sharia blasphemy laws in the UK. All it took was one crack of Allah's whip for the police, or rather the Home Office, to spring into action. What was particularly humiliating was the petition's praise for the *dhimmi* UK press in not following the example of their continental counterparts in reprinting images forbidden under Sharia law. If the intention is indeed to totally stamp out any public expression of thinking critical of Islam, then logically it would require, in addition to any domestic restrictions, screening and search procedures at all points of entry into the UK, and the monitoring of the internet, incoming mail and all printed matter, to ensure that texts and images offensive to Islam do not find their way into the homes of UK subjects from countries where freedom of thought and expression still survive.

If, as seems to be the case, our legislators truly seek an offence-free society, then it needs to be understood that it can only be achieved at the cost of abolishing the right to free expression of opinion, potentially any opinion, because in this era of global communication, it must be the case that any viewpoint publicly expressed on any subject runs the near certain risk of offending someone, somewhere, somehow. Such an offence-free world will be a silent world, a textless world, a cultureless and artless world. Then, inevitably this will lead in double quick time to a world in which there will be no beliefs to be offended, and no opinions to offend them...Bradbury's *Fahrenheit 451*. Is that what we really want, as the price of not being offended? In return for all our futile, humiliating and truly pathetic attempts to appease simulated Muslim victimhood, Islam gives the UK nothing, but with every concession, demands more...Sharia geld. So-called (by non-Muslims) 'moderate' Muslim clerics and pressure groups, seconded by *dhimmi* Islamophile zealots like Corbyn, assure us things would go much more smoothly here in the UK if only we infidels made the necessary adjustments to our domestic and foreign policies. Coming from a culture totally alien to the principles of western democracy, they simply cannot comprehend how anyone can object to a handful of self-appointed leaders of 5% of the UK population dictating terms to the remaining 95%. And judging by his reaction to the Danish cartoons and the 7/7 and Manchester terrorist massacres, Corbyn agrees.

We have already listed just some of the many and varied 'contributions' that Islam, as distinct from individual Muslims, makes to this country. In short, not just in the UK, but everywhere it goes, Islam, with more than a little help from those who are unwilling, unable or too afraid to resist, is managing to impose its alien ways upon societies with which it has little, if anything in common, and to create within them, often with the collusion of public authorities, enclaves where only the holy writ of Islam runs. This is no exaggeration, as the following incident, far from unique, shows.

In May 2008, two lay Christian preachers were distributing leaflets in a predominately Muslim area of Birmingham. They were stopped by a 'Community' police officer, who charged them with committing a 'hate crime', which carries a maxim sentence of seven years imprisonment, and warned them that if they continued, they would be arrested. Discovering from their accents that the two preachers were by origin from the USA, he unleashed on them a diatribe against

US foreign policy, perhaps unaware that he was himself helping to enforce Allah's sovereignty over a portion of UK territory. The officer ended the encounter by offering some friendly advice: 'You have been warned. If you come back here and get beaten up, well, you have been warned.' Another triumph for multiculturalism and diversity.

Birmingham, England's 'second city' and the UK's Muslim capital, had also been selected as the prime target for an organised Islamic subversion of its public institutions, with schools as always being the strategic target, the so-called 'Trojan Horse' operation by Muslim school teachers. This strategy has been greatly facilitated by the steady flow of Muslim graduates moving on from universities, where as we have seen, entrenched in their 'safe spaces', they form a cohesive and highly motivated body permeated with Jihadist sympathies, into the teaching profession in cities like Birmingham, with their large and rapidly growing numbers of Muslim children of school age. In 2014, an official inquiry revealed that a concerted attempt was indeed afoot to convert many of the city's schools into what were in effect ideological training camps for young Jihadis. The success of the Islamic take-over was in part facilitated by the then Tory-led coalition's so-called 'Big Society' policy, by which schools, along with other public services, would be removed from the control of elected authorities and, while still remaining funded by the tax-payer, handed over, in many cases to 'faith' groups, to be run by academically unqualified religiously-motivated parents and private organisations as so called 'free schools'.

Everything seemed to be going well until 2014, when, after parental complaints, the faith school 'flag ship', the Park View 'Academy of Mathematics and Science', (sic) was investigated and found to have imposed a hard-line Islamic agenda on its pupils not only in its curriculum, but with classes Sharia-segregated into boys at the front and girls at the back These findings led in turn to a comprehensive investigation into 21 schools in the city, and a final report which found that there had indeed been a 'co-ordinated, deliberate and sustained' operation to subvert the Birmingham educational system. Acting on the report, six schools were subjected to a regime of 'special measures', while 100 Muslim teachers were investigated, and 30 removed from their posts. All faced the prospect of a life-time ban from teaching. The report revealed that staff had not only shown pupils ISIS-style videos, complete with masked Jihadis, but had simulated ISIS executions by forcing pupils to kneel as a punishment for misdemeanours. This is how Muslim graduate teachers repay the UK for providing them with an education and employment opportunities that are, at the very least, hard to come by in any country ruled by their faith. Local Muslims, in all probability including Park View parents, vented their anger at the school's 'de Islamisation' by displaying crucified cats and dogs on the school gates and making death threats to its head teacher. Integration?

The Birmingstahn 'Trojan Horse' school scandal is only the most spectacular example of a nation-wide process of Islamic infiltration and subversion, often with official connivance and even encouragement that is taking place at every level, and in every aspect of UK society. As the report made clear, these events do not take place by chance, randomly, or in isolation. In Birmingham, fifty Muslim teachers were organised into what they called the 'Park View Brotherhood' in order to co-ordinate their drive to subvert the city's entire school system, We can be sure that similar operations are under way elsewhere, as indeed was established in the caliphate of Tower Hamlets, with its 35% Muslim population, where no fewer than six Islamic 'free schools', the Sharia fruit of Cameron's 'Big Society', have also been placed under 'special measures' for their pursing an Islamic agenda.

These and other similar scandals are the inevitable and totally predictable consequence of a long-standing socially divisive government policy of imposing on the educational system a multicultural segregation of children on the basis of the real, presumed or in many cases, pretended religious convictions of their parents. Cameron's 'Big Society' policy not only handed over schools to be run by Jihadists but allowed them to be inspected by a private (naturally) company that agreed with their ethos and objectives. The firm in question, the deceptively very non-Muslim sounding 'Bridge School Inspectorate', naturally found that everything was as it should be in schools that used anti-Semitic textbooks, where a teacher was secretly recorded telling her class, either 'choose the way of the prophet or the way of the *kuffar'*, and another where the sole female school governor was obliged sit in a separate room out of sight of the board's male members during meetings. Ibrahim Hewitt, the founder and Chair of Trustees of one of the schools passed by Bridge with flying colours, the Al-Aqsa [sic] in Leicester, was on record as stating that adulterers should be stoned to death, that a man should take a second wife if the first was not up to scratch, and that gays were no better than paedophiles. Presumably his prophet was excluded from this comparison.

Instead of the government using education to further the process of integration into British society, state-funded Islamic schools were stubbornly resisting it, sometimes with the knowledge and even approval of educational authorities. Despite the Tabitha Jamaat Islamic Institute of Education in Dewsbury pursuing a quite openly segregationist agenda and curriculum, it received a ranking of 'good' when inspected by Ofsted in 2011. The inspectors were particularly impressed by the school's 'outstanding' performance in 'Koranic memorisation', driven by its 'excellent tracking [sic] and assessment system'. Forcing already linguistically handicapped children to learn by heart, in a language that is in all probability not their own, and has no practical use whatsoever in British society, a book that repeatedly instructs them not to make friends with non-Muslims, is child abuse, and should be illegal. But instead, it is praised! Nor is this all. This 'Islamic Institute' had a policy of expelling any pupil who socialised with non-Muslims, while boarders were banned from listening to music, watching television, using cameras and mobile phones, and from any number of other activities that were deemed 'prohibited in Islam' and, equally to the point, might provide a means of contact with the outside, enemy infidel world. To repeat: this Muslim ghetto school was rated 'good'. Another all-Muslim school inspected by Ofsted, (the name of which was kept secret as a matter of policy) in addition to its other Sharia-derived failings, was found to be using religious textbooks that advocated rape, yes, *rape*, and violence against women. Finally, we have the scandal and fiasco of another Tory multicultural 'Free School' flagship, the grandly named Bradford Kings Science Academy. Launched in 2011, Cameron conducted a high-profile visit to the Academy in 212, and posed for the cameras with its head teacher, Sajid Hussain Raza. On August 3, 2016, Raza was convicted of making fraudulent payments into his own bank account from grants provided by the Department of Education for the financing of the Academy. The sum embezzled was in the region of £150,000. His sister and the Academy's Finance Director [sic], Daud Khan, were both convicted on the same charge. Each faced the prospect of custodial sentences for what the Crown Prosecution Service described as 'treating public money as their own'.

Islamisation of schools, at taxpayers' expense, and with government assistance, is only one facet of a much larger segregationist operation now under way. An accelerating programme of Mosque building, largely funded by Arab, and in the first-place Saudi oil money, and the conversion of secular and de-consecrated churches and synagogues into Mosques, is central to the objective of establishing and expanding Muslim enclaves, as in Blackburn, where there is now considerable resistance to any more. And no wonder. With a population of 147,000, 39,000 of whom are Muslims, the city already has 47. Bradford, scene of the 1989 burning of Salman Rushdie's *The Satanic Verses*, has 83, Luton, 35, Leicester 55, Manchester 58, London 371 and Birmingham, well on the road to total Islamisation, 165. All told, as of 2014, there were 1740 registered mosques in the UK, of which 550 excluded women, and an unknown, but substantial number of so-called 'house mosques'.

A mosque in a non-Islamic country does not function like any other place of worship. It is essentially a command centre from which to wage a cultural war of infiltration and eventual conquest. Quite apart from cases where mosques have been responsible for hate preaching and inciting terrorism, studies have shown that their mere presence affects the immediate environment in ways that, for example, a synagogue, Methodist chapel or Catholic church would not do and would not seek to do. The shift is not only demographic. What takes place is a creeping colonisation, in which the mosque serves as the focal point for regulating the life of its congregation in ways that render impossible the proper integration of Muslims into the broader society of the host country. And it is reasonable to assume that this is indeed the intended result. The 2011 UK census provides much accurate data on this process of self-ghettoisation. In one area of Blackburn, the proportion of Muslims has reached 85%, in parts of Bradford and Leicester, 70%, Oldham and Luton, 60%, and Tower Hamlets, an entire borough, 38%. These percentages can only rise. Again, this will be seen by those who, usually from a safe distance, 'celebrate diversity', as proof of the irresistible and desirable march of multi-culturalism. To those Muslims trapped, stifled and humiliated by the Sharia-enforced patriarchy of Islamic enclaves, in the first place their women, gays and young girls, it is a mono-cultural prison that permits of no diversity whatsoever, and one that we have allowed to be created by deference to a culture that has no place in a civilised society in the twenty first century. Those brave young women who try to escape it run the risk of either being 'honour' murdered by their own family or re-Islamised by a forced marriage to a usually much older close family relative in a Muslim country. In one notorious case, a young Swansea-born woman was tricked by her father into visiting him in Saudi Arabia, where he imprisoned her in a cage to cure her of her western ways, and defied all legal attempts made in the UK to secure her release.

Most migrations to our shores have a had a religious dimension if not cause, first of all the persecuted Huguenots, then no less persecuted central and east European Jews. Hunger first drove Irish Catholics to the shores of the British mainland in the 19th century, and Nazi and Stalinist terror the equally devout Catholic Poles in the 20th. Finally, there came migrants from the India sub-continent: Hindus, Sikhs and Muslims seeking not refuge from persecution but a better life. With the exception of Muslims, the integration and in some cases assimilation of these groups has been accompanied by a gradual but relentless generational secularisation. These three processes Islam in the UK, as elsewhere in the diaspora, has so far proved itself unable to accommodate. Little wonder that in a recent opinion poll, 81% of those interviewed defined themselves as Muslims rather than British, and only 7% as British rather than Muslim. And this is after more than half a century of Islamic presence in the UK. For the vast majority, and as we have seen, this applies no less to Muslim politicians, loyalty to the faith overrides all else.

From no other religious or ethnic group from Asia - Hindus, Buddhists and Sikhs, Chinese, Vietnamese, Japanese and the rest, do we hear the same incessant whingeing about 'racism', 'alienation' and 'exclusion', and the invention of a word to facilitate the criminalisation of supposed criticisms of their life-style and religion. It is true that with some ethnic and religious minorities, dress styles do have the effect, intended or otherwise, of distinguishing those that adopt them from the rest of the population, for example nearly all male Sikhs sport turbans but, unlike Islam, there is no dress code for women Sikhs. However, with Muslims, dress codes are effectively imposed with the full force of religious law only on women, and with a severity that has even involved murder of the offender. The author has witnessed an example of this sartorial selectivity. A Muslim couple were shopping. The man casually strolled around in *a la mode* shorts, trainers and a brightly coloured T-shirt, while his wife shuffled behind him covered from head to toe in a black shroud, with only a narrow slit for her eyes. This was not a bazaar in mono-cultural Mecca, but a covered market in multi-cultural Swansea. And I have witnessed exactly the same scene in a Swiss hotel.

Unlike Muslims, other immigrants that have arrived in the UK from the European Union or elsewhere, either temporarily to study, or to settle permanently, do not create pressure groups that constantly harass public authorities to demand special treatment by clamouring for changes in the UK legal system, or its domestic and foreign policy, and for laws to institute a system of censorship that will protect their beliefs from criticism. They do not put at risk their children's futures by going to absurd lengths to ensure that they remain segregated from rather than integrated into the societies of which they are, if only legally, a part. They do not subscribe to a religion that demands that they must not take as friends those who do share it. They do not cry 'racism' or invent terms such as Hinduphopia or Sikhophobia to silence those who criticise or do not share their beliefs. Muslims, and the pressure groups that claim to represent them, do all these things and more. Should they wonder that the majority of the public, when polled, say they have had enough? And yet the whining, offence-mongering and whingeing, the simulated victimhood and the privilege-demanding continue unabated. After the Paris massacres, of November 2015, it even moved up a gear, when common sense would seem to dictate keeping a lower profile, at least for the time being. Instead, Muslims organised a large London demonstration, not to dissociate themselves from the killings, but to demand special laws to protect Islam and its prophet from criticism, as if there were not enough such thought-crime laws already. However, laws to protect the public, including Muslims, from Islamic terrorism are opposed on the ground that they violate the very civil liberties that Islam rejects because they are defined and upheld by man and not Allah.

It would be quite wrong to assume that Muslim-self ghettoisation contradicts claims by Islamic spokesmen that they are in favour of what they call integration. The problem is, the word can be and is given a meaning totally at odds with its usage in infidel society. Just listen to how the Muslim Brotherhood theologian,

Tariq Ramadan, goes about defining the Muslim version of integration. Let us pass over quickly Ramadan's refusal to condemn the stoning of adulterers and move on to what concerns here: 'We [Muslims] are in favour of integration, but it is up to us to decide what that means'. Henry Ford drives again. Any colour, so long as it's black.

Hitherto, integration had always meant integration into another society and to a certain extent at least, another a culture, in the first place by accepting and obeying its laws and accepting, if not necessarily embracing in every aspect, the customs and habits of the host culture. In short, when in Rome... Not so with Ramadan. The 'integration' of Muslims will be on their terms, not those of the host nation, more of an occupation than an assimilation: 'I will abide by the laws, but only insofar as the laws don't force me to do anything against my religion.' In other words, I demand the right of Muslims to create enclaves where Sharia law, and not the law of the land, will prevail. And this is the wish, and even demand, of large percentages of Muslims throughout their diaspora. It is happening right now in urban areas across western and central Europe. In 2004, a Muslim woman was stoned to death *in Marseilles* for refusing to allow herself to be raped by a Muslim man. Those who claim to speak for UK Muslims habitually dismiss public disquiet at their inability or refusal to integrate as manifestations of racism. They could not be more wrong.

Leaving aside the 'Islam as a race' ruse, save for a genuine 'tiny minority', public concern over the rise of Islam in the UK and across continental Europe has nothing do with racism. The prime cause is an all too obvious clash of *cultures*, the growing perception that Islam is fundamentally at odds with way the non-Muslims conduct their public and private lives. If racism is indeed, as Muslims and the Sharia left claim, at the root of this attitude and therefore, by deduction, not religion, then why is it not similarly directed, with a similar level of intensity, at other non 'white' minorities, such as other 'Asians' from the Indian sub-continent; Hindus, Buddhists and Sikhs, as well as Black Afro-Caribbeans, Africans, 'Oriental' Chinese, Vietnamese and Japanese? Whingeing Muslims should ask themselves why Chinese immigrants to the UK have seen no need invent the words 'Taophobia' and Japanese, 'Shintophobia', and those from India, Sikhophobia, Jainophoba, Hinduphopia and Buddhaphobia, or from Iran, Zoroastriaphobia. This inability to accept that the demands, beliefs and conduct of Muslims can be subjected to criticism by non-Muslims just like those of any other category of persons is rooted in an unshakable conviction that Islam is superior to all other belief systems, religious or secular (such as democracy), in a similar way to Hitler's equal certainty that the Germans were a 'master race' superior to all others. By what right, then, so the argument goes, does the inferior presume to criticise the superior, the imperfect, the perfect?

The demand so often voiced by multi-culturalists that nations hosting Muslim minorities must be more 'inclusive', if it is to mean anything at all, presupposes that those who are to be 'included' firstly want to be 'included' and secondly, that they understand and accept that of necessity, they cannot be 'included' into the society of the host nation on their terms, that they will have to make some fundamental adjustments, not in what they believe, but in the way they behave and live. But that is not how it works, or rather is not intended to work, in practice. By UK public authorities failing or fearing to insist on integration (not assimilation) as the essential ingredient of a genuine 'inclusion' of UK Muslims, the predictable and inevitable result has been the exact opposite, ghettoisation on a truly vast and socially divisive scale and not least, a level of political corruption never hitherto experienced in the modern era.

As already stated, the Pickles report confirmed what many with direct experience of it already knew, that voter fraud and intimidation had become routine practises in certain areas with a high density of Muslims. But this corruption and infiltration extends far beyond the political arena. It includes, of course, education and, perhaps most worrying of all, the forces of law and order. One of the consequences of multiculturalism has been the official encouragement of racial and religious separatism in the police force, the one public service which above all others, should be the most intransigently opposed to separatism of any kind within its ranks. We have a National Black Police Officers Association headed, before being convicted and jailed for corruption, by an Iranian Muslim who, judging by his facial appearance, would probably be classified as IC2 by the police's own coding system, but never IC3. We also have a National Christian Police Officers Association, one of whose members was dismissed from the force after distributing homophobic propaganda, and, inevitably, an Association of Muslim Police.

Police in Islamic countries are notorious for their reluctance at best to apply the law when it conflicts with what they consider to be the true will of Allah. In non-Taliban controlled territory, they stand by and watch approvingly when young women are stoned to death and burned alive in the Islamic hell-hole that is Afghanistan. We have the case, still pending at the time of writing, of Pakistan police officer Abubakar Khuda Bakhsh. Bakhsh headed a special unit charged with investigating the 'honour killing' in Pakistan of a British subject, Bradford-born Samia Shahid, by her former husband, Chaudhry Shakeel, who before strangling his victim, raped her. Thousands of 'honour killings' go unpunished in Pakistan each year, but since this case had a British dimension, the authorities evidently felt a proper investigation had to be conducted. Samia Shahid's 'crime' had been to divorce Shakeel, her cousin, whom she had been pressured into marrying, and then compound her sin by marrying a man from a different Shi'a sect, with whom she then went to live with in Dubai. Determined to restore their family's 'honour', her parents lured her back to Pakistan so that she could receive her due punishment. According to the charges made against him, namely those of suppressing evidence and 'obstructing justice', it was at this point that Police Officer Bakhsh proved where his loyalties lay. Instead of investigating the part played by her parents in the rape and murder of their daughter, he advised them to leave Pakistan as quickly as possible to avoid prosecution, a charge which if proved to be true, would suggest that like far too many Muslims, Police Officer Bakhsh does not consider honour rape and honour, killing to be a crime. According to his commanding officer, 'he helped people escape the country who were wanted in the case of Samia. Despite clear instructions, he let them go.' It would be naive in the extreme to assume that Muslim police officers in the UK are immune from the pressures of such divided loyalties, when their consequences have been experienced in so many other areas of British public life.

As for the UK's infidel police, aside from turning a blind eye towards organised Muslim sex crime, FGM, honour killings and forced and child marriages, their attempts to further the politically correct version of integration can verge on the surreal. The prize must surely go to the initiative launched by the UK Association of Chief Police Officers on March 6, 2015, entitled, 'We Stand Together'. The idea behind it was well-intentioned enough, even though, as it proved, naive in the extreme. Despite the name given to the initiative, local police forces were instructed to promote not integration but 'diversity', with events and 'photo opportunities' featuring police and what were presumed to be local representatives of a mainstream Islam. It might be instructive as to the wisdom of this policy to look at its operation in Luton, once famed for its hat-making (hence the nickname of the local football team, the Hatters) but notorious now for its near-conquest by Jihadi Islam and a Muslim Labour councillor who rhapsodised over 'my man Hitler and, not surprisingly, also the home town of Tommy Robinson and the birthplace of the English Defence League

To promote 'diversity' (again, be it noted, not integration) in the town, a local police officer was photographed with Qadeer Baksh, Chairman of the Luton Islamic Centre, perhaps not being aware that the cleric standing next to him, far from being an advocate of 'diversity', quite openly advocated the death penalty for homosexuals, itself a crime under the UK's hate speech laws. (As will be related in more detail below, a Christian preacher in Taunton read out in public a passage from Leviticus saying pretty much the same thing, but instead of a photo opportunity with a policeman, he was arrested by one, charged with 'hate speech', and convicted before a Muslim judge whose religion imposes the death penalty for homosexual acts...again, a case of you couldn't make it up.) We have not finished with Baksh's Islamic version of 'diversity'. His Islamic Centre has a website, entitled 'Call to Islam', which specialises in promoting virulent Nazi-style anti-Semitic propaganda: 'We ask Allah that He grant us the ability to pursue the proper means for gaining victory over the Jews and over the rest of the enemies of Islam'. There are reasonable legal grounds for suspecting that these 'proper means', if successfully 'pursued' personally by Qadeer Baksh, would require his arrest on a charge of multiple murder, possibly by the policeman standing next to him in the photo. Like most Islamic clerics, Baksh has a real problem with Jews, for his website cannot resist introducing its Muslim readers into the secret workings of the World Jewish Conspiracy:

> The Jews strive their utmost to corrupt the beliefs, morals, and manners of the Muslims the Jews scheme and crave after possessing the Muslim lands, as well the lands of others. They have fulfilled some of their plans and continue striving hard to implement the rest of them. Even though they do engage the Muslims in warfare involving strength and arms and have occupied some of their lands, they also fight them by spreading destructive thoughts, beliefs and ideologies, such as Freemasonry, Qadiaanisim, Bahaaism, Teejaanism and others, seeking the support of the Christians and others, in order to fulfil their objectives

The list of those who are to be denied the blessings of 'diversity' is certainly comprehensive, even if the identity of some of those to be excluded might not be familiar to everyone. But we get the idea. Whatever it might mean to the Association of Senior Police Officers, 'diversity' to Qadeer Baksh is Orwellian Shariaspeak for the exclusion of everyone who is not his kind of Muslim. Featured in another group photo with police officers was Ashuk Ahmed, the recipient of a Queen's Honour for his work as a Luton 'community leader'. In this capacity, he served as the 'Equality and Diversity Officer' for the Bedfordshire Police Authority until, early in 2015, he was discreetly asked to resign. It transpired that like his colleague Qadeer Baksh, diversity for Ashuk Ahmed had its limits. And, also like Baksh, and so many other

Muslim clerics, he gave every indication of being an avid reader of *The Protocols of the Learned Elders of Zion*, posting on social media a faked picture of Israeli politicians drinking the blood of Palestinian children, being of the same genre that proliferates on Corbynista websites. According to Ahmed, all of Britain's political parties are in the grip of their 'Zionist paymasters', while the USA has been taken over by 'the Jewish Ashkenazi [sic] tribe'. (The puerile intellectual level of Ahmed's anti-Semitism is neatly captured here by his coupling of the standard Sharia left accusation that the Jews are Nazis with accusations against the Jews that are wholly Nazi in their origin and mendacity.)

It is not known whether, in the light of Ahmed's public slanders against the Jews, the Queen had withdrawn her award for his services to 'Equality and Diversity', but they certainly have not impeded his progress in the political arena. Notwithstanding Ahmed's belief that the Liberal Democrats, like all other UK parties, are in the grip of their 'Zionist paymasters', he had been an active member of this party for twenty years, rising in its ranks high enough to be adopted as its Parliamentary candidate for Luton South in the May 2015 General Election. The seat has a large Muslim population, so the calculation could possibly have been that his well-advertised anti-Semitism could win him more votes that it loses. It is also reasonable to assume, despite his adopted party label of convenience, that following the example of other once aspiring but now disgraced Muslim politicians, his agenda was that of advancing the cause of Islam's literal theocracy, not Britain's liberal democracy. While many of those duped into promoting such charades are doubtless motivated by a genuine desire to make Muslims 'feel at home', the results will inevitably further deepen and widen the already yawning chasm that divides the Muslim diaspora, largely through its own choice, from infidel society. In this respect, undoubtedly Luton, together with Dewsbury probably the most heavily Islamised town in the UK, leads the way. (This story is well told by an infidel native of Luton, Tommy Robinson, in his autobiographical *Enemy of the State.*)

Symptomatic of the dominance of Jihadi Islam in Luton is the sight on YouTube of hundreds of Muslims marching through the town chanting 'death to the Jews' without any fear of arrest for 'hate speech', and the election, at the age 21, of a Labour (sic!) Muslim woman councillor who had previously advertised online her admiration for 'my man Hitler' for his extermination of six million Jews, while the town's Labour MP Gavin Shuker saw as one of his constituency duties the promotion of Islam, holding a celebration of Mohammed's birthday in Parliament, even though he has admitted he knows nothing whatsoever about the prophet's life of murder, rape and plunder. Another contribution of the powers that be in Luton towards Muslim segregation and ascendency came on August 4, 2016, when a public swimming pool announced that it would be holding Sharia law gender-segregated sessions for what it termed 'cultural [i.e. religious] reasons'. Muslim men have been allotted the 50-metre pool, while their womenfolk will have to make do, as befits their lowly status under Islam, with one only 20 metres long. Also, assumedly for 'cultural; reasons', these Muslim-only doubly (by gender as well as faith) segregated swimming sessions are being promoted under the title (this is in Luton, England, remember) *Alhamdulillah Swimming,* in English 'Praise be to Allah Swimming'. I should point out there is no record in the *Koran* nor, as far as I am aware, the *Hadith,* of his messenger taking a dip in a desert oasis, though if the Islamic accounts of his battles are true, he frequently bathed himself in the blood of his enemies, beginning with that of the Jews. (See Addendum to Appendix L)

What those who think up and launch these crazy 'initiatives' do not seem to understand, though the evidence is there for all to see in its sacred texts, is that given Islam's unique take on the meanings of 'diversity' and 'inclusiveness', making Muslims 'feel at home' can only be fully achieved by converting the UK into an Islamic state, which is also as it so happens an objective of Islam as part of its final goal of world domination. As an exercise in putting to the test the consistency or otherwise of the multi-culturalist project, let us reverse the case, and apply the same criteria to British settling abroad, possibly, (though this is admittedly highly unlikely) in an Islamic country. Would the same multi-culturalists who 'celebrate' the 'diversity' that Islam has supposedly brought to the UK approve of British immigrants' demands to be 'included', but on their own terms, in their newly-adopted home? To demand they live under UK laws which, among other activities deemed *haram* under Sharia law, permit the consumption of alcohol and homosexual acts between consenting adults? Same sex marriages? Create UK enclaves and no-go areas? Special schools just for UK immigrants, with their own teachers and special curricula with, for example, the removal from the history syllabus any reference to the Crusades and the UK's colonial past? Pressure groups to change the domestic and foreign policy of their adopted country? Sending their school children back to the UK to stay with relatives in term time, to ensure they remain true Brits and perhaps to finalise a marriage? Would they approve of sending UK immigrant children to Saturday schools where they memorise by rote a useless and hate-filled book in a language neither of their adopted country or their own? The list of non-inclusive demands could be extended at great length, but let it stop there. We can be pretty sure what the answer would be, and in this case, it would be the right one. When in Rome…or rather Mecca…

There is one particular feature that clearly demarcates Muslims from the majority of the rest of the UK's religiously inclined population, and it helps to explain their priorities of allegiance. It is their extreme and unquestioning devotion to their faith. A very recent survey of attitudes to religious belief in the UK revealed that whereas only 33% of Roman Catholics and 16% of mainstream Protestants were sure god existed, 88% of Muslims had no doubts whatsoever. How mistaken then, are those, especially our politicians, who try to convince themselves and us that Islam is a religion just like any other, except in that is especially peaceful. Its grip on the minds of Muslims, even in non-Islamic countries, is of a totally different order to that exerted by any other faith, especially in the west, where decades of secularisation have, except in the case of Islam, so eroded traditional loyalties and beliefs that they no longer play a significant role in the political process or in the lives of those who are nominally counted as believers.

Pursuant to this strategy of creating a parallel Islamic society and state, euphemistically described by multiculturalists as a 'community', increasing numbers of UK Muslims are demanding the right to be governed by Sharia, and not UK law, a demand endorsed by the Islamophile former Archbishop of Canterbury Rowan Willams and, until protests by secularists forced a climb down, by of all institutions, the Law Society. This insistence on Sharia law for Muslims is something entirely new in British history, and no less toxic for our legal system, which since Magna Carta and the reforms of Henry II, has evolved on the basis of the the principle, now common to all civilised states, of one law for all. Sharia law, by contrast, rejects this principle, and, in descending order, enforces one law for Muslim men, another for Muslim women, yet another for the subjugated, non-

Muslim *dhimmis,* and finally, at the very bottom of the pile, laws which apply only to slaves and concubines.

Like many others who have expressed concern about the extent of support for Jihad amongst diaspora Muslims, I have been assured, unsupported by any evidence, that if it exists at all, it is confined to a tiny minority. Even if this were true, which it is not, and we were then talking about, say, one percent of the world's 1.5 billion Muslims, that still gives us around a hundred thousand potential Jihadis within the European diaspora, with all the rest presumably seeking only integration and a quiet life. So it is small comfort to know that it took only 19 Muslims to wreak havoc and mass murder in the USA on 9/11, and even fewer to visit massacre and mayhem on Madrid in March 2004, London on 7/7, twice on Paris in 2015, and in 2016, a Brussels airport and Baghdad market, and just one on the beaches of Tunisia, a Gay club in Orlando Florida, a stadium in Manchester, a park in Lahore and a promenade in Nice. Perhaps it has escaped the notice of those who talk glibly of 'tiny minorities', or a few 'bad apples,' as did Sadiq Khan, before his election as Labour's Mayor of London, that the ratio of victims killed and wounded to Muslim killer is unprecedented in the history of land-based warfare. In the 2016 Bastille Day Nice massacre, one Muslim, without the aid of any explosives or weapons, but simply by driving a lorry at high speed along a crowded promenade, killed at random 84 fellow human beings and wounded another 300, an atrocity that provoked the normally impeccably politically correct President Hollande to declare that 'all of France is under the threat of Islamic terrorism'. Not 'Islamist' or Obama's 'extremist' terrorism, but *Islamic* terrorism. (His Prime Minister, Manuel Valls, quickly corrected this correct statement, making a unsustainable distinction between 'radical Islamism' that 'has nothing [sic] to with Islam' and the genuine article. Why then call it 'radical *Islamism*'?)

Germany's *dhimmi* Chancellor Merkel, as always taking care not to offend Islamic sensitives, spoke in the vaguest possible terms of the need for 'solidarity in the fight against terrorism', her sole contribution having been the illegal admission into her country of Muslims who have then committed acts of terror, including those against her own citizens. EU Council President Donald Tusk if anything surpassed her in Obamaspeak, deploring a nameless 'hatred and violence', while the US President himself, just as he had done after all previous acts of Jihadi terrorism, condemned 'what appears [sic] to be a horrific terrorist attack.' Horrific it certainly was. But as Hollande said, it was also Islamic. What Hollande just for once correctly (and given the religious identity of the perpetrators of the previous two Paris atrocities, somewhat belatedly) defined as Islamic terrorism is indeed, by its very nature, the work of 'tiny minorities'. But it is nurtured by a faith that legitimises their acts of violence, a faith that like no other today, shapes the lives of tens of millions of ghettoised Muslims now scattered in increasing numbers across the globe, and it is from this immense self-segregated diaspora that the majority of the cadres of Islamic terrorism, 'normal', 'ordinary', 'decent', 'gentle' Muslims as their friends and relatives almost invariably describe them after their murderous deed is done, have been and will continue to be recruited.

An opinion poll conducted in 2008 jointly by the *Guardian* and the polling organisation ICM found that 60% of the 500 Muslims interviewed wanted Sharia law, enforced by Sharia courts, introduced into the UK for Muslims. In another poll conducted in May 2016, a similar proportion of Muslims believed that religion (obviously their own) should determine the making of government policy, whereas those of other faiths overwhelmingly believe it should not. Even allowing for the usual cautionary provisos as to accuracy that obtain in all such exercises, such wide support for Sharia law and rejection of secular politics and values amongst Muslims hardly vindicate the picture we are always given of a 'tiny minority' of 'extremists' and a huge, 'moderate' majority that wants to settle down, pay its way, become accustomed to and even perhaps enjoy the British way of life, and is prepared to respect UK laws.

Other polls are no more reassuring...that is, if one is not an advocate of multi-culturalism, and instead believes that the integration of Muslims is a desirable objective for all concerned. Of Muslims in the 16 to 24-year age group, one third wanted the death penalty for leaving Islam enforced *in the UK* under Sharia law, while 37% of all UK Muslims regard Jews as a 'legitimate target'. When questioned on specific issues such as Sharia law, the veil, homosexuality, the Holocaust, Jihadism, Jews etc, young Muslims respond in ways that confirm they are invariably and significantly more devout than their parents and grandparents, and therefore more inclined to actively promote their faith. This is in sharp contrast with other religions, including those with an immigrant dimension, where statistics show the trend has been the exact opposite, away from the devoutness of previous generations and towards indifference, scepticism and, more recently open and total rejection of any kind of religious belief. Islam spectacularly bucks this secular trend; with consequences the west is already only too well aware of. No less alarming is that 35% of all Muslims agreed with attacks on UK civilians. 25% of all those interviewed, not just the young, 'sympathised' with the motives of the suicide bombers responsible for the massacres on London transport on July 7, 2007. 25% of those polled after the Paris massacres of January 2015, sympathised with the assassins of the *Charlie Hebdo* journalists.

True, these are minorities, but hardly 'tiny'. Regarding the Jews, 37% favoured attacks on Jews in the UK, 19% deny the Nazi Holocaust of the Jews, while finally, and this should come as no surprise, 56% of Muslims favoured an Islamic boycott of Holocaust Memorial Day. The tendency for young Muslims to be more devout, and significantly more inclined to approve of (and therefore to participate in) violent promotion of their religion than their elders is not confined to the UK. A Pew Global Attitudes project, conducted in what in retrospect seem the quieter times of 2006, revealed that 35% of UK Muslims between the ages of 18 to 29 approved of suicide bombing compared with 'only' 20% of those over 30. In France, the percentages were 42 and 31, Germany 22 and 10, and Spain, 22 and 10. As one would expect, all surveys on this subject show higher, in some cases, much higher percentages in Islamic countries. Even so, the results for the UK and Europe are truly terrifying and again give the lie to talk of 'tiny minorities'. In fact, a survey conducted as far back as 2006 revealed, according to a report in the *Guardian* of all places, that 'Muslim attitudes in Britain more resemble public opinion in Islamic countries in the Middle East and Asia than anywhere else in Europe.' And yet it is true to say that no country, possibly outside of Sweden, has promoted multiculturalism with as much persistence and vigour as the UK, only to paid back with such meagre results.

An example of how little Muslims have or wish to integrate is the prevalence of a mind-set that, despite the overwhelming evidence, refuses to accept that individual Muslims can be in any way responsible for atrocities carried out in the name of their religion. Believing as so many Muslims do in the world Jewish conspiracy, when polled on this issue, only 17% of UK Muslims accept that 9/11 was carried out by Muslim terrorists. 45% are convinced it was either the work of the Jews, the US government, or both. (Millions of non-Muslims also make this claim, as is well known. Indeed, a Church of England Vicar and friend of Jeremy Corbyn was reprimanded in February 2015, but not sacked, for his on-line allegations that 9/11 was the work of the Jews. Just like the crucifixion.) This fantasy also is also naturally given credence in the Islamic and Arab worlds, even as large percentages also salute those who carried out the mission as martyrs to the cause of Islam! A similar confusion infests the conspiracy-crazed minds of UK Muslims in relation to the London suicide bombings of 7/7. In one poll, 24% approved of the killings, while an equal percentage claimed they were the work of the UK government. Make sense of that if you can. Two polls conducted after the Paris massacres of January 2015 and the 'Jihadi John 'affair revealed the following:

60% blamed at least in part the UK police and MI5 for the flood of young Muslims travelling to Syria to fight for ISIS
25% sympathised with Jihadi John, the Islamic State executioner;
30% said it was not their responsibility to condemn acts of Islamic terrorism;
Contrary to the claim made by self-appointed Muslim mind-reader Corbyn in the House of Commons on November 18, 2015, that 'the two million British Muslims in this country are as appalled as anyone else by the events in Paris last Friday' (how did he know - had he asked them?):
25% sympathised with the two Muslims who carried out the *Charlie Hebdo* massacre;
32% believed that the massacre was bound to have happened;
44% thought it was a family's responsibility to prevent its children joining terrorist groups;
75% believed that Islam was compatible with the values of British society.
64% felt they had done enough to integrate into British society.

The British Council of Muslims somehow managed to convince itself if no one else that these results were proof that 'Muslims feel British and have a strong affinity with our [sic] shared universal values'. So why not 'Council of British Muslims'? 25% of respondents in the other survey identified with an ISIS executioner and the *Charlie Hebdo* assassins, 30% would not report terrorist activities to the police, and a massive 75% evidently assumed that the 'values' of the *Koran,* with its wife beating, marital rape, sexual slavery, killing of apostates, beheadings, crucifixions, amputations, Jew hatred and the rest, are compatible with the laws and values of 21st century Britain. We must assume that the remaining 25% at least had the honesty to admit that they were not. A poll of UK infidels suggested that those 65% of Muslims who believed they have done enough to integrate themselves into British society have not convinced the non-Muslim public that this is the case. Less than 25% of those on the receiving end so to speak thought that Islam was compatible with the British way of life...but who are mere infidels to judge? A global poll of Muslim attitudes conducted by Pew in 2013 produced the following results: Of the world's estimated 1.62 billion Muslims, 1.39 billion believed that a wife must obey her husband, 1.1 billion wished to live under Sharia law, 748 million supported the death penalty for adultery, and 584 million for apostasy from Islam. Yet more 'tiny minorities'. If it is true, as politicians would like us to believe, that the overwhelming majority of British Muslims are what is termed 'moderate' (a version of Islam not provided for in the *Koran* or any *hadith* be it said, any more than there can more than one version of the two times table) then this should be reflected in Muslim attitudes towards the Islamic state which, we are assured, is not Islamic at all.

Well now. A poll of the general public, not just Muslims, conducted by the *Daily Mirror* in July 2014 showed 44% of those polled as having a 'very unfavourable' opinion of the Islamic State, or ISIS as it then called itself. Of the two categories that concern us most, those 'slightly favourable' ranked at 5%, and 'very favourable', 2%. A year on, and with the general public now fully aware of exactly what the Islamic State stood for and did, the 'very unfavourables' had nearly doubled (as one would have hoped and expected) to 80%, while the slightly and very favourables had also increased (presumably not as our Islamophiles would have hoped and expected) to 6 and 3 percent respectively, giving a total of nine per cent. This nine percent represents 1.5 million British adults. Even if we allow, as we always should in such polls, for a certain latitude of error in either direction, and assume that this figure could be less than 1.5 million, what we still have is a huge number of people who, to one degree another, identify with a regime that if its promotional videos are anything to go by, certainly equals if not surpasses the Third Reich in the bestial cruelties it inflicts on its victims and which, unlike the Nazis, goes to considerable lengths to broadcast them to the world. That leaves only one question to be answered: who are these 1.5 million who identify with such a regime? There can be only one answer. By a process of deduction and simple arithmetic, we arrive at the conclusion that they are approximately one half of the UK's supposedly overwhelmingly moderate Muslim population of three million; again, by simple deduction, since all such surveys exclude minors, consisting of most of its adults. Once more, so much for 'tiny minorities.

Given that a child's first experience of religion is almost certain to be that of his or her parents, the so-called incubation of Jihadism begins not on the campuses and in the *madrassahs* and Mosques, but in the 'normal', 'ordinary', 'good Muslim' homes of the much celebrated 'tightly knit', 'vibrant' 'community', the same community whose holy book time and again forbids Muslims to accept their hosts as friends. So is it any wonder then, that over time, the infidel host becomes in the eyes of so many young Muslims the enemy, a legitimate target for Jihad?

There is another conclusion to draw from these findings. Comparing the results of the two polls, the more the theology and the actions of the Islamic State became known to Muslims, the more Muslims identified with it, with some actually leaving the UK to serve in its ranks as assassins and concubines. Meanwhile, as the horrors of the Islamic State became more generally known, the reactions of non-Muslims moved in the opposite direction, with revulsion nearly doubling. What does this tell us about the prospects for Muslim integration into British society? As was to be expected, a Muslim 'leader' attributed this trend, which he did not deny, to the failings of British society, and not to his own Jihad-preaching religion. The Muslim Association of Britain (again, not the 'British Muslim Association') adopted the well-rehearsed Sharia leftist explanation for the rise in Muslim support for the Islamic State. It had nothing to do with religion. it was all about anti-capitalism and anti-imperialism. Let Comrade Omer El Hamdoon explain: '

> One reason may be due to the perception that ISIS [sic] represents an opponent to the west and those who are dissatisfied or disenfranchised with new Tory policies or

further cuts and civil rights strangulation [sic- but it is Muslims like El Hamdoon who call for 'responsible free speech] are using this anonymous [?] platform to express their frustration.

A note of realism was sounded by Labour MP Kalid Mahmood, who acknowledged that 'within the Muslim community [we] need to look within our own ranks to see how this happening...there are people within the community who need to be looked at'. A look at the Jihadist verses in the *Koran* would not go amiss either. If El Hamdoon is right, British Muslim support for the Islamic State has nothing to do with approval for its theology or actions but is in essence a left-wing protest against Tory austerity policies and western imperialism...exactly what the SWP and Russell Brand had claimed. If the motivation is indeed entirely secular as El Hamdoon says, then why choose as its vehicle an embattled terrorist theocracy more than 2,000 miles distant whose only concern is cleansing the world of the enemies of Allah? Is that why entire families are making the one-way trip to Syria, to fight against cuts in the UK welfare budget? A sceptic could well reply: But surely there are more effective ways, means that are readily to hand, of opposing government policies than supporting (and even joining) a regime that rejoices in raping, beheading, burning alive, and crucifying people, not because they are Tories or imperialists, but because they have broken some obscure rule in an ancient book, or have different ideas in their heads from the people who are killing them?

For a start, British Muslims, unlike their co-religionists in Islamic countries, enjoy all the rights of the western liberal democracy far too many of them effect to despise. They are not 'disenfranchised' or, at least, if they are 18 or over and they are, it's their own fault or choice, as every UK subject 18 and over (bar certain categories that have nothing to do with religion) is entitled to vote, in other words, to be 'enfranchised'. If they have the vote and, following Russell Brand's advice, don't use it, then, again, that is their choice, and a stupid one. And there are other legal ways in addition to voting whereby Muslims, just like everybody else, can if they choose make their views known and their weight felt, few if any of them available in a state where Islam rules. Instead of enthusing over or volunteering to fight for a regime that murders lorry drivers simply because they can't give the required answer to a question about praying or, as the Islamic State did in April 2016, executes fifty cement factory workers because they adhere to another version of Islam, they can join trade unions, an opportunity not available to most of the world's Muslim workers. They can also join political parties, as in fact some Muslims have already done, although not always with the best intentions or results...not least for other Muslims. In short, integrate. No one is stopping them except themselves, and their self-appointed leaders are only making this more difficult by inventing excuses for their failure to do so.

The most extreme manifestation of this desire to ascribe entirely secular motives to those who volunteer to kill and be killed for the Islamic State is the explanation offered by Malia Bouattia, the anti-Semite elected in 2016 as the Sharia left President of the UK National Union of Students. Ignoring all the evidence that the vast majority of these Jihadis come from at the very least comfortable and in many cases, prosperous middle-class families, some being themselves professionals, including even doctors, she claimed that young Muslims had 'no choice [really? '*no*' choice?] but to go off to Syria' because they felt 'so disempowered' by 'unemployment' (nearly all the recruits left well-paid jobs) and 'the fact that that education is being privatised and rendered inaccessible'. Again, sheer fantasy. None of the recruits to the Islamic had been denied access to state-funded education, and many had degrees. Far from free education being made 'inaccessible' to young Muslims, Ms Bouattia should surely know, and approve, that Tory Prime Minister David Cameron and his successor, the devout Theresa May, made it their special mission to facilitate the establishment of segregationist Islamic faith schools at taxpayers expense. And the growing influence of Islamic Societies on university campuses, to which we can in part at least attribute Ms. Bouattia's election, is hardly indicative of any bias against Muslims entering higher education. If, for a moment, we allow that Ms. Bouattia is right, does it then follow that despite its name, the Islamic State headed by its Caliph, Comrade Abu Bakr al-Baghdadi, is indeed, as many insist, not in any sense Islamic, but shares the allegedly leftist secular objectives of its UK recruits (for why else would they join it?) and that therefore it is the simply the Middle Eastern equivalent of the UK's Socialist Workers Party? Leaving aside questions of morality, if only because they do not seem to trouble Ms. Bouattia, I put it to those who have elected her, those who like their President no doubt believe themselves to be the cream of what will be tomorrow's intelligentsia, that travelling more than two thousand miles at no little expense and risk in order to cut off infidel heads, burn to death fellow Muslims in a cage, rape Yazidi girls and hurl gays from tall buildings, is not the most effective way of righting wrongs that are on your own doorstep. Picture the scene conjured up for us Ms. Bouattia: A UK Jihadi is about to slice the head off his infidel captive. His intended victim asks, 'Why are you doing this to me?' The Jihadi replies: 'Please don't take it personally...I couldn't get my son into Eaton'.

The evidence we have assembled in this work is indicative of an Islamic mind set in which facts, logic, reasoning and just plain common sense give way, if they are present at all, to a fantasy world in which Muslims believe themselves to be at the same time superior to the infidel and also his victim; when it suits, to be both a religion and a race, to be always prepared to exploit the *kuffar's* liberal values while always despising them; where the hand of the Jews is everywhere but invisible; that there was no Holocaust, and yet the Nazis gave the Jews what they deserved; that the Zionists are Nazis, but Hitler is an Islamic hero; that Muslims can say what they like about the evil ways of the *kuffar,* but unbelievers should have no legal right to reply in kind lest they give 'offence'; that to question whether Islam is a religion of peace is to invite yet threats of, and even actual violence; that Islam is a religion of peace, love and universal values, but instructs believers not to take infidels as friends, whose followers create ghettos yet claim they are being 'marginalised' and 'excluded'. In sum, Islam is not only hopelessly 'out of sync' with the modern world, *it is determined and proud to be so.*

For many young Muslims, the myriad contradictions and inconsistencies which reside at the core of Islam do not repel, any more than did those of its secular fascist analogue in the first decades of the last century. *Au contraire*, we have seen, as in the case of thousands of Jihadis flocking to ISIS from Europe (1,500 from, the UK alone), and a series of trials in the UK of Muslims charged with terrorism offences, that they can exert their strongest attraction upon Muslims in the diaspora. Many are students, some no doubt visitors from overseas, all enjoying facilities and freedoms that simply do not exist in any Islamic state. One might have hoped that the experience of being educated at a liberal western university in an environment of unfettered intellectual inquiry would earn their respect for what the west has to offer to those from other cultures, and that at the very least, it would exert a moderating influence on young men and women who might otherwise be attracted to Islamic 'radicalism', weaning them from the irrationalities that cripple the thinking of so many of their co-religionists. One might...but one would be mistaken. 32% of UK Muslim students interviewed said they personally would kill for Islam...yes, 32%. Not just approve of killing *but do it themselves*. And some of them have, while others have tried and failed, or been caught in time. Some have killed and been killed in Syria, fighting, beheading, raping and the rest for the ISIS Caliphate. So I say again, yes, 32% is a minority but also again, not 'tiny'. And what a minority!

So-called 'Jihadi John', the UK cult executioner videoed beheading ISIS captives, and whom Jeremy Corbyn laughably believed should have been arrested and not killed by a US 'drone' attack, fits this profile exactly. From a prosperous Kuwaiti family, Mohammed Emwazi, before turning Jihadi, graduated in computer science from the University of Westminster, where hard-line Islamic proselytising was endemic. For example, the week that the identity of Jihadi John was revealed, Westminster University's Islamic Society was due to host a speaker, Haitham al-Haddad, Chairman of the 'Muslim Research and Development Foundation' and a Judge for the Islamic Sharia Council, which makes rulings in accordance with the four Sunni schools of law. The event was hurriedly cancelled due to 'increased sensitivity [sic] and security concerns'. Sensitivity? The Foundation modestly claims to possess 'the cure of all humanity's ills', one of these 'cures' being for the disobedience of a man's wife. According to Sharia 'Judge' Haitham-al Haddad, 'a man should not be questioned why he hit his wife, because that is something between them'. Another was the 'cure' for what Muslim men regard as a woman's 'uncleanness', female genital mutilation, which, according to 'the consensus of all scholars', was *'sunnah'* [proper]'. He was no less orthodox when it comes to the Jews: 'I will tell you the truth about the fight between us and the Jews, who are the enemies of God and the descendants of apes and pigs.' Partly due to the relentless campaigning of UK-based, but Saudi or Gulf funded clerics, but no less with the connivance of politically correct university authorities, and the support of Sharia left-dominated Student Unions, these are the kinds of beliefs that are now rife on university campuses throughout the UK, not least at the University of Westminster. Is it any wonder that institutions of learning are now said to be serving as 'recruiting grounds' for the likes of Jihadi John, and that at least 45% of those convicted of terrorism offences between 1999 and 2009 had attended university or other or institutions of higher education? Far from serving to integrate Muslims into UK society, education, when accompanied, as it so often and easily is, by exposure to unchallenged Jihadist incitement and recruitment, often serves as a pathway to Islam terrorism. The answer is, however, not to ban so-called 'hate preachers' from campuses, as some politicians and media demanded in the wake of the exposure of Jihadi John. The last place where free debate should be curtailed is a place of learning. Just as it is wrong to yield to demands from Muslims to permit the adoption of Sharia law alongside UK law, so it would be equally unjust to impose on Muslims restrictions on free speech that do not apply to non-Muslims. So-called 'hate preachers' should not banned, but challenged in free and open debate. The only requirements that should be enforced in such exchanges there should no incitement to acts of violence against named persons, a crime under UK law, and that there be no enforced gender segregation of audiences.

Asim Qureshi, Director of CAGE, a registered charity that officially provides support for Muslims unjustly accused of terrorist offences, but which itself has terrorist connections and sympathies, would have the public believe that Emwazi, if indeed he was Jihadi John, was made a victim of *kuffar* injustice before he became an executioner. The blame lay with UK security officials who, as it turned out, with good reason, questioned him regarding his known links to terrorist organisations. The masked executioner who featured in a series of highly successful ISIS promotional videos Qureshi remembered as 'extremely kind' and 'extremely gentle', the 'humblest young person I have ever known', a 'beautiful man'. a description which perhaps tells us more about the company Qureshi keeps and CAGE represents that it does about the character of Jihadi John. From an early age, he was so prone to violence that he underwent 'anger management' and was later was involved in armed 'territorial' gang warfare, before graduating to association with the four failed London Underground suicide bombers of July 21, 2005.

A closer scrutiny of CAGE's *bona fides* (one that should have been conducted before it was awarded charitable status) as a 'human rights' campaigner, rights that Islam has made very clear it does not believe in, leaves one wondering just why it secured such lavish funding from the Roddick Foundation and the Rowntree Trust, and recognition by the Red Cross and of all people Amnesty International, which devotes a considerable, if not the greater part of its time and resources to defending victims of persecution by Islamic states. CAGE, it turns out, was closely associated with members of organisations which not only regard human rights with contempt, but have devoted a considerable, if not greater part of their time and resources to violating them in the most bestial manner...Boko Haram, al Qaeda and the Taliban to name just some. CAGE founder Moazzam Begg is an open supporter of the Taliban, while Qureshi, despite his attempts to present a 'moderate' face to the public, was himself an advocate of the very same Jihadi Islam put into practice by his protégé Jihadi John, as in a speech to a London anti-US rally in 2006: 'When we see Hezbollah defeat the army of Israel, we know where the solution is, and where the victory lies...It is incumbent upon all of us to support the Jihad of our brothers and sisters in those countries when they are facing the oppression of the west.'

The prevailing official wisdom is that education and the advancement of bright young Muslims into the upper echelons of the middle classes, helped along by the lavish funding, patronage and promotion of supposedly 'moderate' Islamic pressure groups, will in good time undermine the appeal of Islamic 'radicalism'. If that is the case, why are university Islamic Societies aggressively imposing their Sharia agendas on students unions and even university authorities? The belief that an educated and prosperous Muslim will be a 'moderate' Muslim is founded on another false assumption, that Jihadism is the revolt of the oppressed, the poor, the 'excluded' and the persecuted. If this were the case why is it then that the Hamas leadership (nearly all living in luxurious exile) are wealthy university graduates? The 'Caliph' of the 'Islamic State', Abu Bakr al-Baghdadi, though according to Obama not a Muslim, holds a Doctorate in Islamic Studies no less, awarded by Baghdad University. Research has found that the same is true of the *cadre* of all other Islamic terrorist movements, exemplified by the graduate, multi-millionaire, father of 26 children, Arsenal fan, one-time play boy and architect of 9/11, the late leader of the Taliban, Osama Bin Laden. All 19 Muslim perpetrators of 9/11 were western educated graduates, some with PhDs. Every study of this subject has come to the same conclusion: education, privilege and wealth do not co-relate with a so-called moderation, but more often its opposite. Shiraz Maher, Senior Research Fellow at the Kings College, London, International Centre for the Study of Radicalisation, said of 'Jihadi John' that 'he has the rather typical profile of those travelling to Syria - he is middle class, educated and from a relatively affluent background.'

Not only self-appointed government and Saudi-funded 'Muslim community leaders' and their Sharia left echoes, but the entire swathe of respectable political opinion will be turned against anyone who dares to say that everything, yes, everything that that diaspora Muslims complain of about life in the UK is entirely, yes, *entirely*, of their own making, and is in no sense the fault of the host nation, whose public authorities have done all and often more than is necessary and reasonable to accommodate them. I am not alone of saying this:

> As the lethal cycle of British [Muslim] involvement in Jihadism deepens, so the cries of victimhood grow stronger. The families of recruits to the Islamic State's barbaric regime seem desperate to pin the blame for the crisis on anyone or anything - from supposed negligence by the police to brain washing through the internet - rather than accept any real accountability...all too often, we are told the same story by the families of those who run off to Syria: that it is always someone else's fault... too many of them are inclined to play the victim, condemning western foreign policy or "Islamophobia"...[This is Corbyn's speciality]This search for scapegoats has got to stop...Instead of endlessly pointing the finger at others, the Muslim communities should face up to their own responsibilities. For the fact is that in too many parts of Britain, they have allowed a backward-looking, insular, reactionary Islamic culture to develop, which has undermined social integration and promoted sectarianism. There are many Muslim families here in Britain who, despite having potential access to the freedoms and prosperity of our advanced society, have chosen to cut themselves off for fear of contamination of their faith by disbelievers. That wilful separatism is reflected in a host of factors, such as the increasingly prevalence of the full veil or burka in Muslim areas…Tragically, the message of separatism is re-enforced and fuelled by a network of mosques and Islamic centres in Britain which preach a message of insularity dressed up as purity. Bankrolled by Saudi Arabia, many of them are in the grip of the ultra-conservative Wahhabism that took root in the Middle East in the 18th century...What is so disastrous is that this refusal [sic] to integrate with mainstream British society is leaving young Muslims in limbo...Spoon fed on a diet of ant-Western propaganda and disillusioned by the "decadence" of British society, they yearn for an uncompromising alternative - and Islamism, even in the form of the blood-soaked savagery of the Islamic State, seems to provide the answer...This is a Muslim problem, and British Muslims have to address it rather than abdicating their responsibilities.

Brave words. Especially as they are not those of the English Defence League, but Manzoor Moghal, Chairman of the Muslim Forum. Strong meat though it is, Manzoor Mughal's indictment of the self-ghettoisation of his co-religionists was surpassed in its brutal frankness, anger and frustration by the extraordinary broadside unleashed, like his fellow Muslim's auto-critique, in the sometimes-non-PC *Daily Mail*, by Dr Taj Hargey, Director of the Muslim Educational Centre of Oxford and Imam of the Oxford Islamic Congregation. It was occasioned by the publication in December 2016 of a report prepared by senior civil servant Dame Louise Casey and commissioned by Prime Minister Cameron devoted to the problem of Muslim segregation, which ironically had been greatly exacerbated by

Cameron's own obsession with creating state-funded but privately-run Muslim-only 'Free Schools'. To summarise the report's findings, they are as follows:

> Public bodies were guilty of ignoring or condoning 'regressive, divisive and harmful' cultural and religious practices for fear of being branded as racist;
>
> The same institutions have 'swept under the carpet' rather than confront these practices, thereby obstructing opportunities to tackle terrorist sympathisers hate preachers, criminal gangs and paedophiles;
>
> Failure to control Muslim immigration had led to the proliferation of Muslim ghettoes in major cities and towns;
>
> A 'right on', that is to say politically correct attitude towards Muslims had led to the ignoring of 'worrying levels' of segregation and social exclusion;
>
> Deep-seated 'misogyny and patriarchy' had created deep divisions between Muslims and the rest of British society';
>
> Muslim women suffered 'abuse and unequal treatment', with only one in five being able to speak English properly, and had been made into 'disempowered second-class citizens' by the 'abusive and controlling behaviour of men', including a 'common acceptance of polygamy' facilitated by such websites as 'Secondwife.com'.

All in all, a glowing picture of the 'vibrant Muslim community' so beloved of our high priests of multiculturalism and 'diversity'. Despite allegations that the report had been watered down on the advice of civil servants, what it did say predictably outraged the self-appointed spokesmen for the UK's Muslims, proof that nothing hurts more than unwelcome truths. Typical was the reaction of the Ramadan Foundation, which while not disputing any of its findings, condemned the report as 'inflammatory, divisive, pandering to the agenda of the far-Right', which, we must then assume, is one of ending the segregation of the UK's Muslims! However, Taj Hargey faulted the report for not being radical enough. While praising its author for having the gumption to 'warn about the devastating effect of mass immigration on local communities' and for 'highlighting the segregation, division and tensions it causes in society', he felt that her proposals to overcome these problems fell far short of what was required:

> The truth is that we have to abandon our insane fixation with political correctness because it is damaging our communities. Legitimate criticism of anyone, regardless of race or creed, is part and parcel of a healthy society, but we have been too afraid to apply it. Until now, the cultural baggage that has arrived with migrants from Islamic nations has been treated as sacrosanct and inviolable. The time has come for Britain to be firm and say: "Dump that stuff or you can't come in." [Bravo!!!] One of the most obvious ways to do this is to tackle head-on the pernicious propaganda of extreme Islam, such as Wahhabism or Salafism, perpetrated in Saudi Arabia and fuelled throughout the world by the country's petrodollars.

Unlike most western feminists, Dr. Hargey has no time for the patronising claim of western *dhimmi* feminists that wearing the burka or other face-concealing garments 'empowers' Muslim women or alternatively, is a freely-exercised fashion choice: 'They denigrate women, are deeply divisive – and to my mind, should be banned. There is no justification for these monstrous garments. Not in religion, not in law – and certainly not in British custom.'

Dr. Hargey continues:

> I was brought up in South Africa during the Apartheid era, when the races were brutally segregated. My family were forced to live in a separate enclave and I was required to go to a separate school from white people. I detested that vile system with every fibre of my being. Now I live in a wonderfully free country. Yet I sadly see voluntary apartheid taking hold - Muslims deciding that they are better off living among themselves. They are imposing segregation on their own communities and ghetto suburbs - the very things I hated so much under South African apartheid; the very things that Nelson Mandela fought so long to eradicate. Not long ago I spent an afternoon walking around Highfields in Leicester. During my visit, I saw only black and brown faces - not a single white person. If that situation had been imposed by a dictatorship, we would fight against it with all our might. Why should it be acceptable in a modern democracy? This isolationist trend feeds on itself: Muslims, especially women and children, are encouraged [and that is putting it politely] to withdraw from the rest of society, to keep themselves 'unsullied'. [and, we could add while some of their menfolk feel free to sully white girls by gang-raping them.] They are taught that they are 'superior' because they are destined for heaven while the *kuffar*, the unbelievers, are not [this is in fact, as we have seen, exactly what the *Koran* says]. Shut away in their homes, many go day after day without seeing anyone who is not a Muslim. They watch Islamist TV stations and read Islamist websites and so the isolationism is re-enforced.

Hargey believes that tinkering with the problem as proposed by the Casey report will not work. The so-called 'Muslim community' cannot be reformed, it has to be uprooted, starting with its children:

> We have to mix up the population of the schools, so that immigrant groups are never predominant in any classroom. If necessary, we should be bussing people to different schools to ensure this. [This measure would be opposed by a united front of Nazis, white racists, multi-culturalists, 'diversity' zealots, Sharia leftists and Muslim clerics and 'community leaders'.] In some cases, Muslim children who attend state schools make up such a high proportion of the class that they grow up imagining that more than half the country looks and speaks like them. Isolationism and separatism must be attacked and dismantled in every way. We must insist that [Muslim] immigrants get involved in the ordinary life of Britain, for example through sport and other cultural areas to bring the disparate sectors together. [Some UK Muslims have seen sport as simply another opportunity for self-segregation, If Dr. Harvey's proposal is to work, apartheid-style Muslim-only sports teams and leagues will have to be banned.] Above all, we must accept it is not racist to face up to the nightmare of the failure of multi-culturalism. To claim that some immigrants, because of their origins, are exempt from the common duties of integration - that's racist. To say that some people, because of their religion or the colour of their skin, can ignore British values of democracy, respect, patriotism, tolerance and equality - that's racist and irrational. We need to be forthright and robust about this. If immigrants are not prepared to fully integrate into British society, arguing that it means sacrificing their religious identity, they can head to places such as Saudi Arabia, Pakistan, Somalia, Yemen, Afghanistan and Sudan. In other words, if new-comers and other immigrants are not happy in the United Kingdom and do not wish to be an integral part of this vibrant democracy, they should leave.

So much for 'open borders' and 'diversity'. Manzoor Moghul and Dr Hargey, for reasons that should need no elucidation, prefer to talk of a 'Muslim problem', whereas as I, as an atheist infidel, direct my attack against what I believe to be in most cases the root cause of this Muslim problem, namely religion. They sincerely believe that the problem with the kind of Muslim they are criticising is part cultural, and part due to a false interpretation of Islam. As I made clear in my *Preface*, I disagree. Islam itself discourages integration, with the *Koran's* repeatedly instructing Muslims not to take infidels as friends. But what we agree on is far more important, that the behaviour of diaspora Muslim often leaves much to be desired, and that it must change. No doubt Dr Hargey was repaid for his brutal not to say courageous honesty by being denounced by spokesman of mainstream Islam in the UK as, to coin London Mayor Sadiq Khan's unhappy phrase, 'an Uncle Tom Muslim'. But that would have been because they knew that every word he said was true, and that the state of affairs he described was exactly as they wish it to be. The last thing they want is for Muslims to be treated, and to behave like every else. And what they want and demand more than anything is what the Law Society and the former Archbishop of Canterbury Rowan Williams have said they are entitled to and should have; the legal consummation of Muslim apartheid …Sharia law. *Dhimmi* Cambridge Professor Wendy Ayres-Bennet has gone a step further, advocating a reverse integration, what she calls a 'two-way street', with non-Muslims learning to speak Urdu, and not Muslims, English. Why is it that she did not propose the same measure to facilitate the integration of other migrants from the sub-continent; that is, for non-Sikhs to learn Punjabi, non-Guajaratis Guajarati and so on. So, Professor Ayres-Bennett, why only Urdu?

27 Industry

Until the Reformation, the power of the Church in English affairs was such that, with the backing of Rome, it was able to secure immunity for its clergy from prosecution in secular courts, the so-called 'Benefit of Clergy'. Even if the crime were one of murder or rape (which it frequently was) the cleric in question could only be tried in an ecclesiastical court, under Cannon Law, with the inevitable and intended result that acquittals came easy and punishments, when imposed, usually involved only an act of penance. Such church immunity from English laws was, from very early on, rightly seen as a challenge to the power of the crown and other secular interests, and was progressively eroded, beginning with Henry II's 'Constitutions of Clarendon' of 1164 and, after further radical limitations by Henry VIII and Elizabeth I, finally abolished by Parliament in 1827. In a quirk of history, Henry II's first attempt to establish a single, unified system of law 'common' to the entire realm (hence 'Common Law') was challenged by one of Sharia law advocate Rowan Williams' predecessors, Thomas a Becket, who paid for his defence of what was termed the 'criminous clergy' by his so-called (by T.S. Eliot) 'Murder in the Cathedral' in 1170.

By its current policy of protecting the thousands of clergy who, over the centuries, have been routinely raping children of both sexes as well as women, the Roman Catholic Church is still living, or rather trying to, in the Middle Ages, when Benefit of Clergy would indeed have ensured that rapists, whether of children or adults, escaped prosecution in secular courts. That this still happens today is not the fault of the law, but of a church that still tries by every possible means to defy and evade it, and what is more, does so at times with the connivance of the civil powers that should be enforcing it. But even here, a distinction must be made between its 'criminous clergy' and the claims of Islam. Even at the height of its powers and legal immunities, except in the Papal States of central Italy, the Catholic Church never demanded that the Catholic *laity* be subject only to ecclesiastical law and courts. It was applicable only to those in holy orders. So far as offences committed by its laity were concerned the Catholic Church was obliged to 'render unto Caesar'.

The situation of pre-emancipation Jews was obviously very different. Jews living in Christian and Islamic states, and therefore subject to any number of punitive and discriminatory laws, were consequently, unlike the Christian Churches, never in a position to demand special legal privileges for their clergy, even less so for their laity. Yet instead of insisting on the right to be ruled by the laws of Moses, they demanded the right to be treated as equals under the law of the land. This was first achieved in Europe by the French Revolution, (inspired, so the Hamas Charter assures us, by world Zionism) when its National Assembly enacted the Declaration of the Rights of Man and Citizen of August 26, 1789, abolishing as it did so at a stroke all legal restrictions imposed on the Jews by the Catholic Church and the Bourbon Monarchy. This demand of the Jews for equality before the law was effected in two Articles Article 1: 'Men are born free and remain equal in rights', and in Article 10: 'No one shall be disquieted on account of his opinions, including his religious views'. In these few words, a thousand years and more of pitiless legal and clerical persecution and segregation were undone. It is, of course, impossible to legislate out of existence the ingrained prejudices of those reared on such deeply ingrained bigotry, as the Labour Party's anti-Semitic scandal has once again demonstrated. Northern Ireland and the Balkans are also sad testimony of this fact. But the French and American Revolutions proved it is possible to deny them a voice in the laws of the land, enabling the Jews, despite their remaining the accursed of Christianity and Islam, to take their first step along the often-tortuous path of genuine emancipation. Perhaps this helps to explain why Hamas decries the French Revolution as the work of a Zionist conspiracy.

Unlike the majority of diaspora Muslims today, not even the most influential Christian Churches, and certainly not Jews, Hindus, Sikhs, Buddhists, Zoroastrians or followers of any other religion save Islam, have ever demanded, either in the UK or anywhere else where it finds itself in a minority, that not only its clergy, but here is the rub, its *laity*, should be subject only to its own laws, and not those of the host nation, and moreover, has as its ultimate objective the replacement of the existing legal system by its own. Only Islam makes such an outrageous demand and, what is more, one that is treated sympathetically in ways that would never be entertained if made by any other faith, the most notorious instance being that of the former Archbishop of Canterbury, Rowan Willams. He has argued that by incorporating parts of Sharia law into the UK's legal system, a development which he anyway regarded as 'inevitable', it would avoid having to confront Muslims with the 'stark alternatives of cultural loyalty or state loyalty.' But why only Islam? Surely in the interests of 'diversity' and fairness, the UK should incorporate into its legal system those of every religion on our planet.

Insulating itself from what it sees as a hostile infidel world, Islam in the UK, as elsewhere in Europe, does as the Islamic states do on a global scale, erect barriers to ward off the corrosive and seductive evils of modernity and secularisation. In areas where its numbers have achieved a social 'critical mass', as in East London and cities in the Midlands and the north, its policy of self-isolation, described and decried as we have seen by Muslim commentators in terms as strong, if not stronger, than any of mine, is directed chiefly against those most susceptible to the temptations of western ways, the young. Self-appointed or corruptly elected leaders of these 'Muslim communities', though constantly complaining of Muslim 'alienation' from the rest of society, do everything within their considerable powers to create as far as possible self-contained Islamic enclaves, with their parallel and rival networks of private and publicly-funded institutions. These include not only an ever growing number of Mosques, many lavishly funded by Saudi Arabia and other oil-rich Islamic states, Islamic 'community centres', Islamised 'free' and state schools and government approved private Islamic schools, 'academies', *madrassahs* and 'Arabic Centres', where children from mainly Urdu or Bengali speaking families, instead of improving their mastery of the English language better to equip them for life in the UK, chant and try to memorise the *Koran* in an otherwise socially useless tongue, and can be beaten if they fail. From time to time, staff at these institutions are convicted of physically abusing pupils in their charge, but the actual level of such abuse is far higher the number of such prosecutions would suggest. In March 2006, Ghayasuddin Siddiqui, leader of the Muslim Parliament of Great Britain, admitted *madrassahs* were operating 'outside the law', with the result that with 40% of staff beating their pupils, as many as 100,000 children were at risk of physical abuse. The same situation obtains with Sharia courts. Again, though many are publicly funded, they impose (mainly on women) Sharia laws that conflict with UK law, while vigilantes enforce it by threats and actual violence in areas where mosques proliferate, creating Islamic 'no go' territories where in an increasing number of major European cities, not only public employees but armed police fear to tread. Another victory for multiculturalism and diversity.

In the Islamic diaspora, contact with the infidel is reduced to the bare minimum necessary for the internal functioning of the 'tight knit' - a euphemism if ever there was one - Muslim 'community', a strategy greatly and gratuitously facilitated by state-fostered and imposed multi, though in its impact on Muslims, mono-culturalism. This contact, such as it is, is very much a one-way street, with official statistics in a number of European countries, including the UK, revealing a massive and growing draining of resources from the infidel society in the form of crime, welfare services, state benefits, housing, education and the like, while the diaspora contributes as little as possible in the form of tax-paying gainful employment.

This parasitism should surprise no one familiar with the early history of Islam. As we have already seen, it was a creed founded by marauding desert bandits, slavers, rapists and plunderers, origins that are faithfully reflected in the detailed provisions for the distribution of what is called 'booty', human and otherwise, in the *Koran* and numerous *Hadith*. Trade and taxing also loomed large in the early Islamic economy, which is what would one expect from an armed band astride the crossroads between three continents. Fighting, killing, raiding, conquering, enslaving, raping, looting, taxing, buying, selling...anything in fact except actually making something...these were the occupations pursued by the founders of Islam, and they are described and regulated in its founding texts. Productive physical labour and concubinage were reserved for *dhimmis* and slaves, domestic chores and child-bearing for Muslim women.

These features are still to be found, albeit in an attenuated form, in all Islamic states and diaspora enclaves, and go a long way to explaining their chronic backwardness. Historically, the focus of Islamic economic life in its homelands has not been the farm, mine or factory of capitalism, but the bazaar, just as its political centre has been and remains the Mosque and the palace, not the elected assemblies of the west. Since the Islamic world lacks any tradition of the equivalent of a Jewish or Protestant 'work ethic', with its free and not bonded labour force, and a productive, innovative entrepreneurial class akin to a Brunel, Stephenson or Wedgwood as distinct from the merchant who merely buys (or as in Mohammed's case, the caravan raider who steals) and sells what others have made, should we be surprised then that even today, the diaspora parallel Muslim economy still retains some of these essentially unproductive or parasitic features? Unlike the 'host' economy, it is overwhelmingly male and likewise more located in what is defined technically as the tertiary or service sector; at the bottom end, corner shops, restaurants, minicab hire and the like, in the middle, the lucrative *halal* trade and at the top end, property dealing. Some of its revenue-generating activities are not only parasitic on the state and society, but illegal, such as bogus charities, drug dealing, the embezzlement and misuse of public funds, nepotism and large-scale trafficking, grooming and sexual exploitation of under-age non-Muslim girls. Here the 'Muslim community', more precisely its male half, exercises a near total monopoly.

Just how politically sensitive the issue of Muslim gang rape was in the UK became clear when in July 2007, five years before the issue finally burst into the public domain, a planned televised appeal to the public by the police to help apprehend a Muslim suspected of rape was cancelled to avoid what was called a 'racist backlash', precisely the fear that enabled Muslim rapists to continue raping non-Muslim girls by the thousand for three decades until the scale of the scandal could be contained no longer. Before exploring this sordid subject in detail, let us dispose of the Sharia left red herring that it is racist and 'Islamophobic' (whatever that might mean) to associate Muslim men with organised pimping, trafficking and gang-raping of non-Muslim school girls, because the majority of Muslims are innocent of all three, just as they are of acts of terrorism. True...but also irrelevant. What is relevant is that statistical evidence incontestably proves that both sets of crimes are carried out by Muslims to an extent vastly in excess of their proportion of the total UK population, and it is that immense disproportion which requires to be acknowledged, analysed and explained. Based on the known religious identity of those convicted of the trafficking, grooming, pimping and rape of mainly underage girls, the co-relation of those convicted of these crimes with being a Muslim is in the order of 90%. So whatever the Islamophiles might say to the contrary, as both Corbyn and the SWP have done, the one factor common to nearly all, if not all, organised gang rape in the UK is...the religion of peace. One of the first Muslim rape gang operations to be brought to trial plied its trade in Rochdale. In May 2012, at Liverpool Crown Court, nine Muslim men were convicted of a string of sexual offences committed against under-age non-Muslim girls. Sentenced to 19 years in prison, the 59-year-old ringleader of the gang called the presiding judge a 'racist bastard' and claimed, through his defence council, that all the accused had been convicted on account of their 'faith and race'. What had happened to the girls was the fault of 'society', and 'now that failure is being blamed on a weak [sic] minority group.' Poor Muslim rapists.

Nevertheless, this 'weak minority group', represented by nine male adults, for years still managed to groom and then hire out for rape children young enough to be their daughters and even granddaughters. A middle-aged family man is caught gang raping and pimping children, but it's society's fault...a 42-year-old Muslim family man, sentenced to nine years for trafficking, made a girl of thirteen pregnant, his defence being that he thought she loved him. None of those sentenced showed the least remorse. And, why should they? Sharia law permits married men to take concubines, and permits sexual intercourse with girls who have reached puberty. They had simply enjoyed 'what their right hands possessed'. (*Koran,* Chapter 4, Verse 24) Some of the more recent cases were in Oxford, Aylesbury (Buckingham) and Keighley and Halifax in Yorkshire. In Oxford, a rape and pimping gang of seven Muslim men was convicted in March 2015 of sexually abusing at least 370 girls, some as young as eleven, over a period of 16 years, again with the knowledge and even connivance of the very public officials whose responsibility it was to investigate, report and prevent such crimes.

In July 2015, six members of a largely Muslim Aylesbury rape gang were convicted at the Old Bailey of sexually abusing and pimping two vulnerable young girls over a period of seven years, hiring them out at £25 a time as often as six times day from the age of twelve, to scores of mainly Muslim men. The 'spoils of war' can be good business. It was the usual story of at best indifference to the plight of the victims. The children's charity Bernardos became aware of the abuse as far back as 2008, and 'made a referral to the local authority and the relevant agencies'. As in all the other cases of Muslim rape gangs, nothing was done, or, as Michelle Lee-Izu for Bernardos put it rather tactfully, there was 'insufficient action'. Evidently, Bernardos, like the other 'relevant authorities', let the matter rest, because the raping and pimping continued unchecked for another five years. Unusually, David

Johnstone, Director of Buckingham's Children's Services (sic) did not plead political correctness but ignorance of the law as the cause of his department's complicity in the crimes being committed under its very nose: 'We know a great deal more [now] about children's sexual exploitation than we did back then'.

The reader will in all probability immediately recognise this as the identical explanation proffered by the Roman Catholic Church for its complicity in the systematic abuse by its clergy of children in its care, not just over decades, but centuries. Does David Johnstone really expect anyone to believe that after years of training for and service in an agency whose sole responsibility is to protect the welfare of children, none of its staff saw anything wrong 'back then' as he puts it, or illegal in the systematic rape of girls as young as twelve, or if they did, none had the duty and authority to prevent it? I do not believe Johnstone's explanation is the correct one. I suspect he doesn't either. Nor will anyone else credit that he and his staff were, as he implies, unaware that organised child abuse and rape were criminal offences, only to then, when the investigations began in 2013, suddenly one morning realise that they were. One can hardly imagine such a relaxed attitude being adopted had their victims been the children of the social workers in question. (One of the two victims had been on their so-called 'at risk' register from the age of seven!) Whatever the cultural and moral relativists might say to the contrary, since time immemorial, any half-way decent person has known that the rape of children is wrong, and the laws that say so, at least in non-Islamic countries, are just as old. Those who chose to ignore the plight of the rape gang's victims were not in other respects morally deficient, or ignorant of the laws on rape and under-age sex. Indeed, one of their tasks was to see that they were enforced.

The real cause, one that until other similar scandals were uncovered, dared not speak its name, was fear...fear of being branded a racist and an 'Islamophobe' by their friends, work colleagues and superiors, and criminalised by a battery of so-called 'hate speech' laws, especially those of 2005, which were specifically designed to prevent any serious criticism of Islam; and again, fear, especially in difficult economic times, of losing one's job as a result of such branding. How else explain that over a period of more than three decades, of the UK's 1.3 million school teachers and support staff, 100,000 police and as many social workers, *not one* was prepared to blow the whistle on the gang rapists whose victims, in their tens of thousands, were entitled to their protection from their abusers? Avoiding accusations of racism and preserving 'social cohesion' came top of their list of priorities, and the child victims of gang rape, firmly as the bottom. And this is the UK in the twenty-first century! Had the roles been reversed, with twelve-year-old Muslim girls being groomed and hired out to be raped by non-Muslim men, then back in 2006, Buckinghamshire Children's Services, just like their counterparts in Rochdale, Rotherham, Oxford, Keighley and Sheffield and a dozen or more other locations, would have experienced no difficulty in recognising child rape for what it was then, is now, always has been and always will be; an abominable crime.

We can be reasonably sure that more trials of Muslim rape and pimping gangs are in the pipe line, and now that the game is up for those who have been protecting them, that more will be apprehended and convicted. (This prediction has proved to be correct. The backlog of those accused runs into the hundreds.) The final official report on the all-Muslim Oxford rape gang described in some detail the humiliations and sexual tortures inflicted on young girls by men reared from the cradle on the religion of peace and love:

The sexual abuse included vaginal, anal and oral rape, and also involved the use of a variety of objects such as *knives, meat cleavers and baseball bats*. It was accompanied by humiliating and degrading conduct such as biting, scratching, and acts of urinating, being suffocated, and tied up. (emphasis added)

Of the hundreds of girls abused, six were reported missing 500 times from either family or care homes. As in all the other cases, no investigation as to their whereabouts was conducted, though the reason why they were missing was common knowledge amongst those whose job it was to find and protect them. This includes the police. A father who tracked down the whereabouts of his daughter, and found her being sexually abused by Muslim man, after calling the police, was himself arrested. Not just local Muslims, but those from far and wide came to rape the girls, while local girls were ferried around England for the same purposes with total impunity under the noses of P.C. police, brain-dead or brain-washed social workers, corrupt local politicians, un-elected Muslim 'community leaders' and misogynist imams. This highly organised and for its pimps, highly lucrative Muslim rape industry, with its transport network and safe rape houses, operated for at least 16 years in Oxford, unapprehended, by imams, police and various other authorities whose responsibility it was to prevent it. The Keighley rape gang consisted of 12 Muslim men, who in February 2016 were together sentenced to a total of 143 years in prison. One 13-year-old girl, put to work serving the sexual needs of scores of Muslim men, was reported missing by her mother 71 times. The police response was to tell her to keep a dairy of her daughter's movements! The girl in question, whose testimony in court helped to convict the rapists, was known by social services to be subject to sexual abuse, but instead of reporting this to the police, they suggested she use a coil to avoid becoming pregnant. On one occasion, she was raped by five sex savages in succession in a back alley.

Sentencing the convicted paedophiles, Judge Roger Thomas said they had taken 'terrible and heartless sexual advantage' of the girl. Zafar Ali, a Muslim local Councillor, however begged to differ. He claimed that 'it takes two to tango', implying that this was not a case of gang rape, but teenage promiscuity. There was 'some feeling that the girl had her part to play'. This 'feeling' is of course the deeply entrenched Muslim conviction that rape is as much, if not, more, the fault of the victim than the rapist, and when the victim is not a Muslim, that it is not even to be considered rape at all, but simply 'the spoils of war'. Another case resulted in June 2016 in the conviction of no fewer than fifteen Halifax Muslims, who between them received jails terms totalling 168 years for raping, grooming and trafficking, in plain English, pimping, under-age girls, in one case, one of thirteen years.

The focus in the wake of these trials was on the political correctness that led to the abysmal failure of the various agencies whose duty it was to protect the vulnerable girls who were being reduced to sexual slavery as Muslim 'spoils of war', and to prosecute those who were exploiting them. However late in the day, too late in fact, this was of course right. But political correctness had not been totally dispelled, for why else was there no criticism of those who, by virtue of their position and role in the 'Islamic community', must have known, from its very beginning, not only the purpose and scale of these operations, but the identity of their perpetrators and even of many of their customers? How can such an activity, conducted quite openly on such a scale, over so many years, carried out on a daily basis by hundreds, probably thousands of Muslim male adults, many of them family men, living in a closed in, almost hermetically sealed 'community', remain unknown to the one individual who more than any other, is responsible for his community's 'spiritual' and moral welfare? We speak of course of the eyes, the ears, and in theory at least, conscience, for what it is worth, of this 'community'...the imam, always ready to take offence at often imagined slights to his own faith, but wilfully blind to crimes committed by those who profess it. This accusation is not made lightly. We are repeatedly assured that these so-called 'Muslim communities' are, like some quaint old English village, 'warm', 'vibrant' and 'close' or 'tightly knit' - euphemisms for the ugly, oppressive misogynistic reality of a self-generated, segregationist quasi-parasitic ghetto in which, as the Rotherham rape scandal has proved yet again, all manner of primitive, savage, vile and frequently illegal customs and activities flourish, unchecked and even condoned not only, as we now know, by public agencies, but without doubt by those with authority within the 'community' itself.

In the 40...yes, *forty* locations where they have been trials and convictions of Muslim gang rapists, traffickers and pimps, there are all told 739 mosques; 4 in Liverpool, Colchester 2, Coventry 24, Yeovil 1, Dewsbury 31, Manchester 66, Peterborough 8, Barking1, Ipswich 2, Accrington 3, Nelson 14, Preston 17, Huddersfield 15, Sheffield 7, Luton 25, Oldham 30, Blackburn 45, Leeds 26, Skipton 1, Nelson 18, Derby 14, Leicester 73, Accrington 7, Chesham 2, Barking 8, Middlesbrough 7, Bristol 19, Slough 15, Banbury 3, Newcastle 16, Oxford 7, Blackpool 2, Rotherham 7, Birmingham 164, Cardiff 19, Telford 4, Keighley 7, Halifax 10, Rochdale 18 and Buckinghamshire 17. So, we have 739 mosques servicing areas where Muslim rape and pimping gangs had been operating quite openly and with impunity, and on what the Jay report on Rotherham calls an *'industrial scale'*, in some cases, for periods of *thirty years and more*. Assuming that each of these mosques is staffed by its resident clergy, it is surely reasonable to ask, how come that with hundreds of pimps and tens, possibly hundreds of thousands of their rapist customers in their congregations, not one imam out of a potential 739 had an inkling of what was going on? And if, as seems more likely, they did, why did they not report it to the police?

Beginning no later than the early 1980s, year after year, tens of thousands of non-Muslim school girls were being groomed, trafficked and gang-raped on a Sharia assembly line by what must have been hundreds of thousands of utterly depraved Muslim males, the majority of them family men... *and yet not one clerical whistle-blower,* even though they were safe in the knowledge that they could not be accused of Islamophobia or racism. We now, belatedly, demand that Catholic clergy be held to account for their acquiescence in similar crimes ...why not imams? Because we prefer to go hunting a phantom Islamophobia. And where were the feminists? The metooers? Obsessing about the 'white patriarchy' in the columns of the *Guardian.* Why has no mainstream politician asked these so obvious questions?

Yet the already quoted outspoken Dr. Taj Hargey, Imam of the Oxford Islamic Congregation, certainly has, and he provides the answer that that infidels fear to give. In mosques across the country, he says that imams preach a doctrine that 'denigrates all women, but treats whites with particular contempt'. Muslim men are taught that women are

> second-class citizens, little more than chattels or possessions over whom they have absolute authority...The view of some Islamic preachers towards white women can

be appalling They encourage their followers to believe that these women are habitually promiscuous, decadent and sleazy - sins which are made all the worse by the fact that. they are kaffirs or non-believers...According to this mentality, these women deserve to be punished for their behaviour by being exploited and degraded.

Should we be surprised then that when asked in 2013 to read out to their congestions a condemnation of gang rape, less than a third of the UK's Mosques did so, with one dismissing the request as 'a stunt'? Those imams that refused, by their silence stand condemned, morally if not legally, of condoning Islamic gang rape, according to the principle, *qui tacit, consentire videtur.* No less guilty are Corbyn and the Sharia left who, by denying the very existence of organised Muslim paedophiliac gang rape, have helped to perpetuate it. For the Labour Leader, despite the mounting statistical evidence that proves the contrary, gang rape is a general problem, not a Muslim one. 'The problem is the crime that is committed against women in any community. Much crime is committed by white people, crime is committed by people of other communities as well'. True, but again, totally irrelevant, as Corbyn must surely have known, because the issue was not crime in general, such as speeding, drink driving, murder, drug-dealing, shop-lifting, burglary, dropping litter etc etc or even all those of a sexual nature, but specifically *organised, 'industrial scale' grooming and gang rape*, in which Muslim men, as has been proved beyond doubt by a series of trials, exercise an almost total monopoly, being statistically 170 times more likely to commit this particular crime than less spiritual non-Muslims.

If, as Corbyn seems to be saying, 'industrial-scale' grooming, trafficking, pimping and gang rape of children are to be found in equal measure across all 'communities' (again, presumably, as defined by religion) then, according to the 2011 Census, Muslims should account for 4.4% of perpetrators, equal to their 'community's' share of the total UK male population, and likewise Hindus 1.3%, Sikhs 0.7%, Jews 0.4%, Buddhists 0.4%, Christians (and *pro rata* with their various subdivisions, such as Quakers, Methodists etc) 59.5%, those of no religion 27.5% and unstated, 7.2%. Peter McLoughlin, the author of *Easy Meat*, has posted on line a running total of gang rape convictions. Updating this as of February 28, 2019, of 360 convicted of child gang rape, assuming, almost certainly wrongly, that all those with non-Muslim names were not converts to the religion of peace, at least 307 were Muslims, just under 90% and not, as Corbyn would seem to be implying, 4.4%.

White girls are not the only victims of Muslim child rape. Initially, until their menfolk fought back, *and were arrested for doing so*, Sikh girls were the prime target. Under the nose of Corbyn, in his own Parliamentary constituency, imams he surely knew personally have officiated at illegal Sharia marriages between children as young as nine and much older (probably closely related) Muslim men, just as they do in Yemen and other Islamic latrines where the law and example of the paedophile prophet holds its misogynistic sway. In the words of the British imam, Bilal Philips (sic), 'the prophet Mohammed practiced it, it wasn't abuse or exploitation, it was marriage'. And as the prophet did, so can every Muslim male: 'Verily you have in the prophet an excellent model.' (*Koran*, 33:27) By denying what the criminal justice system has proved beyond all doubt, Corbyn is in fact perpetuating the very political correctness that made Rotherham and a score or more similar tragedies across the UK possible. Bearing in mind that Corbyn hopes one day to be Prime Minister, and that nearly all these cases occurred in towns and cities with large and growing Muslim electorates, one has to ask, are there no depths of dishonesty, political irresponsibility and sheer depravity he will not sink to in order to remain in good standing with Labour's Muslim constituency? As the Jay report says, 'in their desire to accommodate a [Muslim] community that would be expected to vote Labour', Labour politicians preferred 'not to rock the boat, to keep a lid on it' hoping 'it would go away'. Exactly. Corbyn's denial of the proven vastly disproportionate Muslim involvement in gang rape was, ironically, in its turn, refuted by Muslims in the findings of the reformist Islam Quilliam Foundation, published in December 20017, which showed that since 2005, 84% of gang grooming rape crimes have been committed by Pakistanis, in other words, by Muslims, who regarded white girls as 'worthless'.

Chief Crown Prosecutor Nazir Afzal did not try to deny the truth of this statistic - how could he when he had personally brought many of these perpetrators to trial while serving in the North West - but he feared that public awareness of the predominance of Muslims in gang grooming and raping would facilitate the growth the far right. If it does, that will surely be the responsibility of politicians on the rest of the political spectrum all of whom have lacked the courage to place the blame for a crime unknown in the UK before the emergence of the 'Muslim community' where it belongs, with the mysongistic attitude of many Muslim men towards women in general, and *kuffar* women in particular. And had it not occurred to him that attempting to conceal a truth that the public is already well aware of, given the publicly that such trials have received in the media, would have exactly that effect? If he wants to keep the lid on such information in future, the only answer is for such trials to held *in camera*.

At least Afzal was honest in acknowledging the religious identity of the preparators. He could hardly not, since had been prosecuting them. The same cannot be said of the Socialist Workers Party, committed as it is to its strategy of Sharia-friendly shibboleth-dumping', in this case, the right of under-age infidel girls not to be gang-raped by Muslim men. The SWP agreed there had indeed been a rape issue in Rotherham, but it was a white one, covered up by white police. The *Socialist Worker's* non-reporting of the Rotherham and other similar rape scandals faithfully applies the principles enunciated by the Sharia feminists Lindsey German and Laurie Penny, namely that white males (unless of course they are converts to Islam) are the worst of all offenders when it comes to the abuse of women. Muslim rape and pimping gangs do not exist. It is white men who are doing the raping and are getting away with it because the (white) police are letting them. It is a case of a race closing ranks, and then putting the blame on Muslims. As proof to support this claim, the SWP's *Socialist Worker* of September 2, 2014, quoted what purported to be an unbiased authority, Shaista Gohir of the Muslim Women's Network UK. She claimed that the problem is not the rape of white girls by Muslim men, but the toleration by the police of the rape of Muslim girls by white men: 'The danger is that when a youngster says they have been exploited by a white man, they won't be a priority.' Gohir was in the same state of denial as the authors of a leaflet published in 2010 jointly by Unite Against Fascism [sic] and the Muslim Council of Britain, which dismissed as 'racist myths' reports of 'Asian men "grooming" white girls.' (Once again, Islam becomes a race)

No-one reading these items, or any others from the same sources devoted to the Muslim rape scandal, would have had the least inkling that as reported by the official Alexis Jay report, in Rotherham alone, with a population of 109,000, 'at least 1,400' young, mainly working class white girls had been subjected to decades of sexual abuse by organised Muslim grooming and pimping gangs, or that in one of many cases of police collusion with the rapists, when officers came across an eleven-year-old girl being gang raped in a derelict house by five Muslim men, in an English version of Sharia law, they promptly arrested the girl, not for adultery, but for being drunk and disorderly. Instead, the cited leaflet purveyed a fable of public authorities in Rotherham and elsewhere who, instead of hunting down white rapists, had preferred to focus on mythical Muslim sex offenders! Everyone now knows that the exact opposite was the case. No white men have been convicted of trafficking, grooming, pimping or raping Muslim school girls.

Consider this. Muslim males comprise 1.5 % of Rotherham's population, a little over 1,500. Of these, roughly half fall into the age group convicted of gang-rape, between the late teens and middle fifties *Over half* of this group have either been convicted of gang rape, or, at the time of writing, are being investigated by the police as suspects for the same crime. Yet Corbyn insists that Muslims are no more likely to commit child gang-rape than members of any other 'community'. Just how toxic the Muslim gang rape sandal had become for the Corbynistas was demonstrated when Labour MP Naz Shah, after denouncing as a Nazi (sic) the *Sun's* Editor Kevin Mackenzie for running a story by Rotherham Labour MP Sarah Champion focusing on the identity of the gang rapists (an accusation made by an MP who was herself suspended by her party for recommending a Nazi-style final solution to the Palestinian question), days later approvingly retweeted in good faith a spoof tweet which read: 'Those abused girls in Rotherham and elsewhere just need to shut their mouths. For the good of diversity.' When in July 2018, a petition was circulated among MP's demanding tougher sentences for gang groomers and rapists, it was signed by only 20 MPs. Shah's petition against the *Sun* was signed by over a hundred. Please read this sentence again, and then consider its implications.

Thorough as it is, the salient weakness of the Jay report is that in one crucial respect, it too suffers from the same wilful myopia that it rightly sees as an integral cause of the rape gang scandal…political correctness. Throughout her report she refers to the perpetrators as being of 'Pakistani heritage', never as Muslims, which in nearly every case, they were. Consequently, when she takes to task public officials and institutions who failed to report or even colluded with their crimes, she invariably attributes this to a fear of being accused of racism and not 'Islamophobia', a term that for all its frequent (and spurious) invocations in other contexts, never occurs in her entire report, because if it had, it would have identified the rapists as Muslims and not just Pakistanis. In depicting the rape gangs as exclusively a product of Pakistani culture, she therefore necessarily excluded their religious dimension. But the Cologne sex assaults of New Year's Eve, 2015, were not perpetrated in the main by men of 'Pakistani heritage' but by Muslims from a wide variety of Islamic countries. French rape gangs are mainly of Algerian origin, in Holland, Moroccan, in Sweden, many are Afghans, in Germany, Middle Eastern. The common denominator is that they are all *Muslims*. Jay also never asks the highly pertinent question; why are these rape gangs composed mainly of men of 'Pakistani heritage' and not also of men from an identical or very similar ethnic background, namely Indian Sikhs, Buddhists and Hindus?

However, while steering well clear of the teachings of Islam on the treatment of women, the Jay report did reveal that Muslims girls had indeed also been horrifically sexually abused, but not by white men, as the *Socialist Worker* implies. Citing the UK Muslim Women's Network study of the sexual abuse of Muslim girls, the Jay report says that contrary to the allegation made by the Network's Shaista Gohir,

> they were most vulnerable to men from their own communities who manipulated cultural norms to prevent them from reporting their abuse [The 'tightly-knit, warm, vibrant Muslim community']. The Network's own report found that 'offending behaviour mostly involved men operating in groups...The victim was being passed around and prostituted amongst many other men...The physical abuse included oral, anal and vaginal rape; role play, insertion of objects into the vagina, severe beatings, burnings with cigarettes, lying down, enacting rape that included ripping clothes off and sexual activity over the webcam.'

And Muslim clerics would lecture the infidel west on its low morals, and the lack of respect shown by its men towards 'their' women? Anyone who doubts the scale of the Muslim rape industry and the degree of complicity of those whose job it was to protect its victims and prosecute the perpetrators, should read the Jay and Casey reports, which are readily available online, as an antidote to the lies of Corbyn and the *Socialist Worker*. Here are just a few samples from the Jay report, which for the first time, lifted the lid on the sexual code of countless male Muslim savages in the UK. We learn that the rape industry in Rotherham, as elsewhere, is closely linked to the mini-cab trade. With a population of 109,000, Rotherham, is serviced by well over a hundred cab firms, and no fewer than 1,300 drivers:

> One of the common threads running through child sexual exploitation across England has been the prominent role of taxi drivers in being directly linked to children who were being abused. This was the case in Rotherham from a very early stage... In the early 2000s, some secondary school heads were reporting that girls were being picked up at lunchtime and being taken way to provide oral sex to men in the lunch break.

Despite repeated requests by various agencies made to the police to take legal action against the companies and drivers involved in drug dealing and various kinds of sex trafficking and abuse, they declined to do so. Need one wonder why? These are just three case reports:

> We read cases where a child was doused in petrol and threatened with being set alight, children who were threatened with guns, children who witnessed brutally violent rapes and were threatened they would be the next victim if they told anyone. Girls as young as eleven [one was only nine] were raped by large numbers of male perpetrators, one after another...In two of the cases we read, fathers tracked down their daughters and tried to remove them from houses where they were being abused, *only to be arrested themselves* when police were called to the scene. In a small number of cases...the victims [sic] were arrested for offences such as breach of the peace or being drunk and disorderly, with no action taken against the perpetrators of rape and sexual assault against children...One child who was prepared to give evidence received a text saying the perpetrator had her younger sister and the choice of what happened next was up to her. She withdrew her statements. At least two other families were terrorised by groups of perpetrators, sitting in cars outside the family home, smashing windows, making abusive and threatening phone calls. On some occasions

child victims went back to perpetrators in the belief that this was the only way their parents and other children in the family would be safe. In the most extreme cases, no one in the family believed the authorities could protect them. (emphasis added)

To which can be added that beginning at the age of thirteen, between 1998 and 2001, just one Rotherham girl was subjected to illegal sexual intercourse by at least a hundred Muslim men, being made pregnant when aged fourteen. Bearing in mind that at least 1,400 girls in the town have been subject to illegal sexual exploitation, it is not beyond the bounds of possibility that most of Rotherham's adult male Muslims had availed themselves of the services provided by its sex industry. Cases such as these prove that for years, in fact, the best part of three decades, Muslim men were free to rape whom they wished, not just under the noses of but protected by the police and social workers, and that everyone in Rotherham knew it, just as they did in other towns and cities where pimping devotees of the religion of love plied their obscene trade. And what was the response of the normally anti-police Sharia left to the exposure of the Rotherham scandal? It was to stage a demonstration in Rotherham, not in defence of working-class girls abused by Muslim rapists, not against police complicity and corruption, but...yes... against 'Islamophobia', just as their German counterparts demonstrated against 'racism' after the night of the Muslim gang rapes in Cologne on New Year's Eve, 2015.

No evidence has come to light in any of the places where Muslim rape gangs have been brought to trial and convicted that similar crimes have been committed by non-Muslims, 'white' or otherwise. How did this Sharia fairy tale come to be taken seriously? Surely even Sharia left credulity (or mendacity) has its limits. Apparently not. Concerned as always to preserve its harmonious working relationship with Muslim pressure groups, the SWP offered its own 'leftist' explanation for what took place in Rotherham: 'Blame cops and the cuts, not "political correctness"'. One is left puzzling: exactly how do cuts in public expenditure turn Muslim men into gang rapists? Maybe it is the same alchemy that we are told transforms them into Islamic State Jihadis.

Much was said, *post facto,* both in official reports, and in the media and by politicians, about the 'failings' of the police and care agencies. Such an explanation would be plausible if confined to one or a few instances in one location. But we are dealing here with highly organised, professional gangs that have operated, supposedly undetected and, so we are now told, even protected, and certainly unhindered, in some cases for more than three decades, in cities and towns all over England. We can be sure that still more await detection and hopefully, prosecution. Official acquiescence in such a multiplicity of identical large-scale operations, spanning such a long period of time, can only be explained by causes that are deeper seated than the 'failings' of individuals. How come that these 'failings' came to be shared by several generations of tens of thousands of public officials from all over England, ranging from social workers, care home staff, school teachers, council officials, civil servants charged with child protection to politicians and high-ranking police officers? Who honestly can say they believe that a series of identical responses to a series of identical criminal activities, occurring regularly over a period of up to thirty years, from Rotherham, Keighley, Rochdale and Sheffield in the north, to Oxford and Aylesbury in the south and Bristol and Cardiff in the west, is to be explained in each case by local individual professional incompetence or, as the SWP would have us believe, by cuts in public spending that only began at the earliest in 2010? What we have here are not 'failings', an explanation that itself fails to explain anything.

Allowing unhindered the operation of the Muslim gang rape industry over decades is the fruit of a consistent *policy*, one not generated independently, locally and 'on the hoof' so to speak by those charged with various public duties. Its nationwide uniformity totally excludes such origins. It can only have come from on high, from central government, specifically the Home Office and departments and agencies responsible for the making and implementing of social policy, and at the bottom of the chain of command, from attitudes and practices instilled into staff which resulted in the toleration of bestial crimes that if committed by any other group than Muslims would, once detected, have led to immediate prosecutions.

Here we have the most damning evidence, coming from the very top of the criminal justice system, that these 'failings' were in fact deliberate government policy. Crown Prosecutor Nazir Afzal told the BBC that in 2008,

> the Home Office sent a circular to all police in the country saying 'as far as these young girls who are being exploited in towns and cities, we believe they have made an *informed choice* about their sexual behaviour and it is therefore not for you police officers to get involved in.'. (emphasis added)

'being exploited', that is, groomed, trafficked and gang-raped, an '*informed choice*'? And 'informed choice' or not, the girls who were presumed to be making it were nearly all under 16 years of age. The Home Office was therefore *instructing* the police force to condone of the most serious crimes on the statute book. And who at the time was Home Secretary? Labour's Jacqui Smith. And yet it was Smith who in the same year, after admitting that she did not feel safe walking the streets of London at night, introduced legislation making it a criminal offence to pay for sex with a prostitute controlled or trafficked by a pimp...evidently, so long as the pimp or trafficker was not a Muslim. Her instructions to the police ensured that whatever Smith feared might await her on the streets of London, far worse would continue to go unprevented and unpunished in the safe rape houses of Rotherham. We shall meet the execrable Smith again, doing more than her bit for Allah. And, one suspects, for Labour's Muslim vote.

So, having eliminated local 'failings', the root causes boil down to three: a central government policy of the appeasement of Islam, involving the sacrificing of under-privileged, non-voting young non-Muslim girls to organised Muslim rape gang of voting age; 'political correctness'; and, on the part of the rape gangs, the teachings of Islam on the Allah-created inferiority of all women, and the even greater inferiority of non-Muslim women in relation to Muslim men. This teaching, inscribed both in the *Koran* and in numerous *Hadith* is sufficient to justify and motivate, but not, on its own, to make possible the kinds of barbarities we have seen inflicted on non-Muslim girls not just in Rotherham, Oxford, Aylesbury and Sheffield, but wherever Muslim men have access to non-Muslim women, as in the ISIS occupied territories of the Middle East, or those controlled by Boko Haram in Nigeria. In order for the wish to become a reality, *those in power have to allow it*.

Where those in power are themselves the rapists, as with the Jihadis of ISIS and Boko Haram, everything goes according to plan. But before Muslim men can have their Sharia way with *kuffar* women in non-Islamic countries, there has to be a special kind of facilitating factor in play that in its absence, would in any civilised country result in their conviction, receiving lengthy jail sentences and in the UK, entry onto the sex offenders register. And the reality is that here in the UK, instead of such judicial actions, the green light for Muslim gang rape had indeed been provided by our public authorities and politicians with results in no way different from those in the Islamic State and north eastern Nigeria. It is those at the very summits of society, irrespective of political party, and beginning in the 1970s, who devised, initiated or approved the intensive indoctrination of public servants in 'cultural sensitivity' and 'community awareness', and authorised intensive compulsory courses of 'diversity training', all under the banner of multi-culturalism, who are responsible for generating the political, ideological and moral climate that allowed these crimes to go unpunished for decades and in doing, so blighting the lives of their victims.

The tragic results of this politically-correct brain-washing, what Mao Tse-tung called 'thought reform', demonstrated how the Nazis were able, in the space of a few years, to inculcate and then exploit a similar indifference by millions of Germans to the fate of the Jews. However, there is a difference in the two situations. Those few Germans who spoke out against (as distinct from declining to take part in) the extermination of the Jews knowingly risked losing their liberty and most likely, their lives in doing so. The worst that whistle-blowers could expect in Rotherham or the other towns and cities where Muslims rape gangs freely operated was the loss of a job, social ostracism and accusations of racism. But, incredibly and shamefully, as the years rolled by and the rapes continued on an ever-expanding scale, there was silence and even collusion. And in situations where those have the power to prevent a wrong, silence conveys assent.

(Inter alia, I cannot at this point resist recalling an episode from my own career in academe, dating back to the mid-1980s, when the onslaught on Enlightenment values was already gathering its current vast momentum. I had been obliged, along with my all lecturer colleagues, to attend a day-long seminar of totalitarian mind bending on the need for 'racial awareness' in education, a state of mind, one would have thought, more fitting for those attending a Nuremburg rally, a Ku Klux Klan convention or a pro-Apartheid demonstration in South Africa. Utterly bored and not a little disgusted with the proceedings, I idly leafed through the booklet that accompanied the event, only to discover, much to my amusement, that I, along with every other white person in the room except the (white) instructor, was a hardened and probably incurable racist, the reason being that the number and varieties of racism listed were so all-encompassing they covered almost every possible thought anyone could have on the subject. Which was of course, and was intended to be, grist to the mill of the then burgeoning 'anti-racist' industry. The version which I, without knowing it, was practising in my lectures was described, perfectly accurately, as the 'colour blind' approach in which the educator does their level best to pay no heed to the skin colour (or the gender for that matter) of who is being taught, and instead focuses on imparting knowledge to their colourless minds. Many years later, I had confirmation of my guilt in an article by a Dr Monnica Williams for *Psychology Today*, that 'treating people as individuals as equally as possible, without regard to race, culture or ethnicity' was indeed 'a form of racism'.

As this publicly funded lunacy (for such it surely was) ground uselessly on, a colleague sitting near me, sensing that my detachment was evidence of my disapproval of the proceedings, turned to me and in a low voice said, 'all this makes me realise how right George Orwell was'. Need one say more? Were he with us today Orwell would have also had confirmed his worst fears about the future of western civilisation by the adoption of newspeak at one of the UK's top educational institutions, the academic madhouse that goes by the name of Goldsmiths College. In April of the year 2015, an event convened by the Students Union to promote 'diversity' did so by banning from attendance all male and non-black women students. The college 'Diversity Officer', a certain Bahar Mustafa, who tweeted the Third Wave feminist war cry, 'kill all men', and who in appearance at least was certainly not 'black', announced in flawless newspeak that 'this meeting is for all self-defining [sic] BLACK and ETHNIC MINORITY women and non-binary [sic] people with gender identities that include "women".' (note the emphases, and the quotation marks around 'women'.) If 'self-defining' is taken to mean what it means, it would seem that skin colour, like gender, is not in the genes, but in the mind, or as post-modernism would have it, is a 'social construct' that can presumably be modified at will, as in the case of Bahar Mustafa, to suit the occasion. It should give us pause for thought not only that lunacies such as this can be indulged at public expense, but that those who promote and take part in them will hold positions of influence and even authority in British society in the not too distant future.)

Returning to the main theme, there is another question that has to be asked, and answered, however much the Islamophiles may dislike what that answer is. Where and how have so many Muslim men (and the combined number of rapists and pimps, we have been informed, runs into the thousands) learned to treat girls and women habitually in ways that not only place them beyond the moral boundaries of civilisation, but the human race? Although the vast majority of these biologically quite normal but culturally sub-human sub-savages were born and raised in the UK, they are now being described as of 'Pakistani heritage', as if that is the explanation for their behaviour rather than their religion, ignoring the fact that some of the convicted perpetrators were Muslims from Albania, Kuwait, Morocco, Sudan, Bangladesh, Somalia, Turkey, Kurdistan, Palestine, Iraq, Iran and Syria. The number of Christian 'Asians' in Pakistan is currently 2.5 million, and of Hindus 3 million. Are they to be tarred with the same racist brush? But of course, even now, when 'political correctness' has at last been blamed for the decades of public authorities' refusal to confront and deal with the issue, nothing is said of the root cause of their behaviour, which is neither one of race nor nation, but the great unmentionable, *religion.*

Not only in Rotherham but in Sheffield, a rape and pimping gang of at least 320 men also operated with impunity, abusing at least 200 young girls. According to an ex-police officer, parents of the victims were silenced by death threats and the victims themselves by holding kettles of boiling water over them. One girl *had her tongue nailed to a table* to deter her from informing on her on her pimps and rapists, and another girl aged 12, had her foetus aborted by a *claw hammer rammed into her vagina.* When the same police officer volunteered to create a special unit to combat the rape gangs, he was told by a senior officer, 'it's not going to happen. Return to your districts.' This was after all official, if not publicised, Home Office policy. A member of the Oxford rape gang branded a girl on the buttocks with the first letter of his name which just happened to be Mohammed. All this and more happened in England, not the Islamic State. Whatever else may be said about the police, by refusing to take any action against these barbarians, it ensured that it could not be accused of Islamophobia.

In Rotherham, and other town and cities not only throughout the UK, but

Scandinavia, decades of multi-culturalism and political correctness have combined with Islamic teachings on the inferiority of women to create an open season for the treatment of young non-Muslim girls as prostitutes and rape fodder or, as the *Koran* has it, 'booty'. The *Koran* is quite explicit concerning the permissibility of what amounts to the possession and rape of non-Islamic women, and no amount of 'contextualisation' can make it say and mean other than what it says and means: 'And all married women are forbidden unto you save those captives whom your right hand possesses '. (Chapter 4, Verse 24) The meaning here is obvious. Other Muslims' wives, being the property of their husbands, you cannot touch. But infidel 'captive' women, including wives, are fair game. It is easy to see how this Koranic teaching came to be applied in a necessarily modified form here in the UK, as in other countries of the Muslim diaspora. In theory, at least, no raping of Muslim women or other Muslim men's wives (raping one's own is of course entirely another matter) but also, in infidel lands, because of the risks involved, not as a rule of non-Muslim wives either. By a process of elimination, that leaves infidel single girls, the younger and the more vulnerable the better. Let the exponents of 'contextualisation' explain away the 'surface' meaning of this Koranic verse sanctifying the treatment of such 'slave girls' as nothing but sexual 'booty: 'Prophet, we have made it lawful to you the wives you have granted dowries and the slave girls whom God has given you as booty'. (Chapter 33, Verse 50) And the prophet, being perfect, is to be emulated in all things by devout Muslims, as we have seen in Rochdale, Rotherham, Keighley, Halifax, Aylesbury, Oxford, and Sheffield and a score or more of other towns and cities across the UK.

As a series of spectacular trials has proven beyond all doubt, over at least the last three decades, tens, probably even hundreds of thousands of *kuffar* girls have been in effect taken 'captive' and treated as 'booty' by Muslim (not 'Asian') rape gangs and reduced to a state of abject sexual servitude. And whatever the Islamophiles might say, the *Koran* permits it. Anthropologists will tell us that most, if not all traditional, essentially tribal-based cultures practised the kidnapping and rape of the women of enemy tribes. And this indeed is the case. As recently as the 1990s, for all the denials of Corbyn, Serbian militiamen murdered the husbands of thousands of Croatian and Muslim Bosnian women, who were then gang raped as the (in this case Christian Orthodox) spoils of war. This ancient but still surviving custom of treating women prisoners as sex slaves is indeed sanctified not only by the *Koran*, but the Old Testament of the Bible, from which much of the *Koran* has been clumsily cribbed. In fact, the Bible not only justifies these practices, but commands them. Deuteronomy Chapter 20 is here quite explicit: '...thou shalt smite every male thereof with the edge of the sword. But the women and the little ones, and the cattle, and all that is in the city, even all the spoil [sic] thereof, shalt thou take unto thyself.' (Verses 13 and 14) Chapter 21 goes into more detail:

> [T]he Lord thy God hath delivered them into thine hands and though hast taken them captive. And seest among the captives a beautiful woman, and hast a desire for her to be thy wife; then thou shall bring her home to thine house...and she shall remain in thine house and bewail her father and mother a full month: and after that thou shall go in unto her [sic!], and be her husband, and she shall be thy wife. (Verses 10-11)

Irrespective of what Obama might say to the contrary, for we can easily imagine him claiming, in response to accusations of Islamic abuse of females, that 'no religion condones the rape of women', this is biblically-sanctioned Boko Haram or ISIS-style abduction and rape, pure and simple. However, whatever their holy book might tell them to do, Jews don't do it now and have not been in a position to do so since the Roman conquest of Palestine in the first century AD, though Christians in the Balkans have as recently as the 1990s. Muslims, whether it is Boko Haram, ISIS, or the rape gangs of Rotherham and forty or more cities and towns across the UK, still do. Those in authority, including police, social workers, school teachers, and politicians, both Muslim and infidel, have found this abuse by Muslim men of young non-Muslim girls, organised in many cases on an industrial scale (1,400 girls in Rotherham alone) and capable of generating an annual income for pimping just one girl of £100,000 and more, quite acceptable, possibly in some cases lucrative, and have ignored or connived at it and even, in the case of Rotherham, participated in the abuse themselves. And when, after decades of denial, it was finally exposed, it was invariably blamed on 'Asians', a racist slur if ever there was one. Taking 'Asian' to mean the peoples of the Indian sub-continent, and not those of the rest of Asia such the 'Orientals' of China, Korea, Japan, the Malayan Peninsula and Indo-China, out of a total of 1.702 billion 'Asians', just over a quarter, 482 million are Muslims, while an even smaller minority of the world's Muslims, totalling in 2017 1.8 billion, are 'Asians'. Such is the respect political correctness pays to facts. Even more to the point, no evidence has been produced that diaspora 'Asian' Hindus, Sikhs, Jainists, Christians and Buddhists are in the same business of gang rape and pimping.

While the names of those who were convicted leave no doubt whatsoever as to their religious identity, the nearest the final report came to properly identifying the Rotherham rape gangs was to describe them as men of 'Pakistani heritage'. This explains and defines nothing, as not all Pakistanis are Muslims, while all the convicted rapists were and what is more, proud to be so, on hearing their sentence, crying out, *Allahu Akbar*, God is Great. One of their number demonstrated his devoutness when, according to evidence given to police and then ignored, he 'raped with a broken bottle' one of his victims, and another, who ordered a girl he had been raping to 'kiss the perpetrator's feet at gun point'. The police took all this in their stride. Nothing out of the ordinary. It was a routine matter. One rape victim was offered the following advice by an officer of the law: 'Don't worry - you aren't the first to be raped by XX and you won't be the last.' The *Oxford Mail* reported how gang rapists...all Muslims… had 'scratched, choked, beaten, gang raped, burnt' their victims and sexually assaulted with '*knives and a baseball bat'*. One described how she had 'turned up at the police station at 2 or 3 AM, blood all over me, soaked through my trousers to the crotch. They dismissed me as being naughty, a nuisance. I was bruised and bloody.' This was the reaction to child rape by an English police officer, not of a tribal elder in the Pakistan or Afghan outback, and in a UK where the same officer had the power to arrest anyone who dared to publicly speak the truth about the religion that makes these crimes possible. Of one thing we can be absolutely sure. Had the roles been reversed, with 'infidel' rape gangs pimping young Muslim girls, as the SWP alleged and Corbyn implied, it would not have taken thirty years before the perpetrators were identified, apprehended, charged, tried, convicted and punished.

Why do Muslim rapists mainly use white English girls for their pleasures? For the Muslim male, young Muslim girls, being the property of their male relatives and destined, unless they are raped by an older male relative, to stay virgins until marriage are, officially at least, off limits. That is why it is generally accepted as being open season so far as non-Muslim girls are concerned. No such latitude however is allowed to Muslim females, again as recent tragic cases have demonstrated. Marriage, or any kind of romantic relationship with a *kuffar,* is taboo. Muslim girls are chattels, to be FMG'd, and then married or even sold off within the clan, sometimes to a much older relative who seeks a new, younger additional wife and is ready to pay the going rate. So, should a Muslim young female choose to ungratefully reject the marital future mapped out for her by family and, worse again, be suspected of forming a genuine romantic attachment to an infidel young male, exemplary retribution is called for, usually carried out by the girl's family. By murdering the errant daughter, the violated honour of the family, in the first place its males, can be restored in the eyes of clan and the 'close knit, vibrant community'.

There is ample evidence that, as in the cases of organised Muslim gang rape and pimping, the customary blind eye has been turned by public authorities towards Islamic 'honour killings'. Whether this is due to a politically correct desire to preserve at all costs harmonious 'community relations', or is motivated by a racist and sexist indifference to the plight of young Muslim females is hard to tell, since both lead to the same result...'none of our business'. What we do know of what is officially called 'honour violence' is believed to be but a glimpse of a much larger and still growing aspect of a young woman's lot in the Islamic 'community'. The scale of this species of Islamic male violence on women can be appreciated by the fact that in 2011 alone, the number of 'honour violence' incidents *recorded* by 37 of the UK's 52 police forces was 2,823. And since then, the number has continued to rise. The religion of peace and love. *Hadith*-sanctioned female genital mutilation (inflicted on as many as 130,000 Muslim girls in the UK with, thus far, only one successful prosecution), *Koran*-sanctioned wife-beating, 'honour killing' and *Koran*-sanctioned marital rape and Hadith approved FGM and child marriage constitute a pattern of life, and of death, for Muslim women that we have knowingly allowed to take root and flourish almost unchecked and, what is worse, in the name of 'tolerance', 'cultural diversity and sensitivity' and good 'community relations'. And those who should be protesting the loudest, the feminists, are silent. Because there is the glass ceiling and the white patriarchy.

The UK is far from being the only country where infidel girls and women have been the preferred victims of rape by Muslim men, only in most cases, they are not of the 'Pakistani heritage' that the Jay report, studiously eschewing a religious cause, wrongly implied explained their behaviour in Rotherham. Sweden, before the onset of mass Muslim immigration, was among the safest, if not the safest, country for women anywhere in the world. Today, it is on the way to becoming one vast Rotherham. Back in 1975, the year in which Sweden, with the very best of intentions, decided to become an official 'multicultural society', the number of recorded rapes was 421. By 2014, it had soared to 6,620, an increase of 1472%. As a result, Sweden now has a rape rate of 53.2 rapes per 100,000 of the population, *second in the world only to Lesotho*, at 91.6. Inevitably, all manner of politically correct explanations were forthcoming to divert attention from the principal cause of this unprecedented surge in rapes, the main one proffered being that more women were now prepared to report it. This of course could account for part of the increase, but only a small fraction, for we are looking at here is a 14-fold increase! One young man interviewed by the Swedish Daily *DN* summed up the attitude of his fellow male Muslims towards rape. He is describing his feelings about Swedish women, but it could just as easily be working class white girls in Rochdale, Halifax, Keighley, Rotherham, Oxford, Sheffield or Aylesbury:

> It's not as wrong to rape a Swedish girl as an Arab girl. The Swedish girl gets a lot of help afterwards, and she's probably been fucked already. But the Arab girl will get problems with her family. For her it is a great shame to be raped. It is important that she retains her virginity when she marries...I do not have much [sic] respect for Swedish girls. You could say they get fucked till they are broken.

Swedish women are treated as rape fodder...barely human, Muslim girls, chattels. Surely no feministic would deny this. The question is, would they publicly deplore it? In seeking an explanation for the soaring rate of rapes, the one factor studiously ignored by most Swedish commentators was that the increase in reported rapes coincided exactly with the parallel surge in Muslim immigration, one that was partly responsible for a 1.5 million increase in Sweden's population from 1975 to 2014. Of Sweden's total population of 9.7 million, today around 500,000 are Muslims, 5%. This percentage is set to increase, as it is in many other European countries, and not only through continued and accelerated immigration. While the net reproduction rate of native Swedes is below 1, with Muslims, it is well above 1. Multiculturalists, confronted with this unprecedented increase in rape might, as a last resort, want to believe that native Swedish men, from being the world's most respectful of a woman's right to say no, have suddenly turned into the world's second worst sexual predators. They might want to, but no-one else is going to believe it.

Though hard to come by in the ultra-politically correct culture of modern Sweden, police rape statistics show that a rapist is ten times more likely to be of foreign extraction than a native Swede, even though native Swedes comprise around 90% of the total population. At least 70% of rapes in Sweden are perpetrated by males belonging to the 5% of the population who are Muslims; a ratio that indicates that when it comes to rape, as with other crimes, Muslim males were performing what is known technically as 'heavy lifting'. (See Appendix C) The same trends in rape statistics, accompanied by similar patterns of Muslim immigration, have also been recorded in Denmark and Norway and more recently, thanks to Merkel, Germany. Again, it must be stressed, we are looking at the impact of a culture and a religion, not the behaviour of a race or races. While UK Muslim rape gangs are described as usually 'of Pakistani heritage', Sweden's Muslim rapists originate from a totally different ethnic background, being either from Africa (mainly Somalia) Afghanistan or the Middle East. So what they each have in common is not 'ethnicity' or a place of origin, but a misogynistic religion that sanctions the rape of non-Muslim females. In its dealings with Muslim immigrants, Sweden has had a rougher ride than most European countries, mainly because of its world-renowned tradition of toleration, pluralism and openness, principles that Muslims despise in their own countries but are only too ready to exploit in everybody else's.

Though reluctant at best to confront Muslim anti-social and criminal behaviour at home, especially rape, in Sweden's external relations with the Muslim world, everything has its limits, as the Saudi Kingdom discovered. The Swedish government, a left-wing coalition, marked International Women's Day of March 8, 2015, by sending its Foreign Minister, the Social Democrat Margot Wallstrom, to a session of the Arab League convened in Cairo. The speech she was due to make on March 9 was never given because, briefed as to its contents, the newly-crowned and western boot-licked King Salman pulled rank and denied her the right to speak. The usual Muslim 'offence' had been taken to the following passage in her censored address: '

> Human rights are a priority in Swedish foreign policy. Freedom of association, assembly, religion and expression are not only fundamental rights and important tools in the creation of vibrant societies. They are indispensable in the fight against extremism and radicalisation. So is a vibrant civil society.

King Salman rightly saw this a barely veiled (no pun intended) attack on his own misogynistic feudal despotism, and also as being totally at odds with the definition of Islamic 'human rights' adopted at the OIC summit in Cairo in 1990. Obviously at his instigation, the Arab League issued a justification of its silencing of the Swedish Minister. Her statement was 'irresponsible' [but to whom?] and unacceptable' (but not it seems, untrue). Obviously and intentionally, Wallstrom had struck a raw nerve; because the statement went on to specifically rebut her implied criticism of the Saudi regime. The kingdom was 'based on the Sharia' (true), 'defended the rights of the people' (which famously did not include the right of a woman to drive a car) and 'safeguarded their blood [frequently shed at public beheadings and floggings], wealth [concentrated in the hands and Swiss bank accounts of the Saudi Royal family] and honour [as in honour killings]'. On March 10, the Swedish government unilaterally terminated its contact to supply arms to Saudi Arabia. The next day, Saudi Kingdom recalled its Ambassador. Petro-Islamic blackmail works, but so does calling its bluff.

28 Chicken

Native Brits are, by and large, a tolerant, easy going lot, the young especially, and more so now than ever before, and this is surely a good thing to be. Certainly, far more so than Muslims who would rather be governed by the laws of a religion that regards unbelievers as inferior than by those of the country in which they have made their home. The trouble is that in the noble exercise of tolerance, the UK's political representatives and institutions, as in other nations of a similar liberal disposition, sometimes permit and even excuse conduct that should not be tolerated. Let us be clear, we are referring to behaviour, not the expression of beliefs and opinions, which should be as much the right of Muslims as anyone else. The toleration by public authorities of abuses both within the 'Muslim community', such as female genital mutilation, bigamous, child and forced marriages and the like, and outside it, with the grooming and gang rape of non-Muslim girls, has multiple causes - political correctness, fear, the courting of the Muslim vote, corruption. Even naivety plays its part, being the mistaken assumption that like everyone who has come to the UK to live, Muslims, despite the inevitable political, cultural, linguistic and religious differences that they bring with them, share essentially the same values, or in time will come to do so, as the host nation. Serious deviations from this norm are therefore ignored or explained away, rather than confronted, which in today's political climate can easily lead to accusations of racism.

We should also bear in mind that until the last twenty years or so, the assumption that integration would proceed naturally over the generations has proved to be a sound one. Successive waves of immigration, going back as far as the persecuted Calvinist French Huguenots in the 16th century, have enriched British society in numerous ways and, over time, the descendants of those who first settled in the UK have integrated and even assimilated into the society of their hosts. Even when retaining certain elements of their native culture, successive generations have not in any sense mounted a challenge to the UK's political and legal institutions. Being in many cases the victims of persecution in their countries of origin, they were only too willing to embrace a political culture that afforded them not only a safe haven, but equality under the law, the opportunity to earn a living and play a part in the democratic process. Tragically for all concerned, the last two decades have provided clear indications that this is not the case with many Muslims. But this was not so initially. The first post-war wave of Islamic immigration into the UK, mainly from Pakistan, was in most ways like those that preceded it. Together with Sikhs and Hindus from India, they found employment, mainly low-paid, in industry and services. The father of Labour's Muslim Mayor, Sadiq Khan, was a bus driver. Many joined trade unions and, obviously in smaller numbers, the Labour Party.

This pioneer generation was as hard working and law abiding as any other migrant group that had made its way to Britain's shores. And while remaining Muslims (though not in the main, excessively devout), and to a large degree (like most newcomers to a strange land) living separate lives from their hosts, there was every reason to assume, based on the history of previous migrations, that if not they, then their children and certainly their grandchildren, would follow the same path of gradual but irreversible integration. However, it was not to be. External events in the Islamic world, primarily the Middle East and Iran, began to exert what has proved to be an irresistible force of attraction acting on young British Muslims, enticing many to follow a path utterly different from earlier generations. 1979 witnessed Iran's 'Islamic revolution', establishing for the first time in the modern era an Islamic theocracy, and one moreover with political ambitions that reached far beyond its borders. But it was Ayatollah Khomeini's *fatwa* of 1989, the death sentence imposed on Salman Rushdie, that brought young Muslims onto the streets in their thousands against a book none had read, but had cheered to see burned, feeling outraged and betrayed by those who defended the author in the name of a freedom of expression that was utterly alien to their religion.

For the first time, young British Muslims were now experiencing the thrill and sense of power that only militant street action and media attention can create. At that moment, the process of integration, so far as the younger generations of Muslims were concerned, came to a halt. Then, in response the invasion of Iraq in 1991 after Saddam's seizure of Kuwait, followed by 9/11 and the ensuing US-led wars in Afghanistan and Iraq, the integration process went into reverse. Egged on and organised by an emerging Sharia left, the increasing mobilisation of young Muslims was dragging much of the older generation in its wake, as represented by organisations such as the Muslim Association of Britain. As advocates and even fighters for theocracy, large numbers of young Muslims, unlike the first generation of Islamic migrants, openly began to denigrate man-made democracy and human rights. Again, unlike their forebears, their religious zeal has led them to opt out of the UK's political system, preferring to take to the streets in demonstrations against Israel, organised by Corbyn's Palestine Solidarity Campaign and, as we have seen, answer the call of the Islamic State either in Syria or as 'lone wolf' assassins in the UK.

It must be said that in this respect, they have not been set the best of examples by those of their elders who claim to speak for the UK Muslim diaspora. Some local Muslim politicians have proved to be out and out gangsters as in the case of Tower Hamlets, and vote riggers, as in Peterborough's council elections of 2004, and by-election of 2019, practices that would not raise an eyebrow in any Islamic state which allows elections but, until the emergence of Muslims onto the political scene, were vitally unknown in the UK. Can it be mere coincidence that all large-scale electoral fraud (tactfully explained by the Electoral Commission as due to a 'lack of understanding of the electoral process') occurs in areas of substantial and long-established Muslim populations? The problem of political corruption is not confined to local politics. As we have seen on several occasions, Muslim politicians at Westminster, when faced with the choice of advancing either their religion or their party, opt for their faith, prompting the suggestion that it would have surely been more honest, and have shown more respect for voters, even if less likely to advance their political careers, if they had stood for office on an Islamic ticket rather than, like the far left, exploit the electoral machine of a mainstream party to which they have no real loyalty.

In politics, as in life generally, there is much wisdom in the old saying that one cannot serve two masters. Come 9/11 and military clashes erupting between Israel and its Arab and Islamic enemies, the stage in the UK was set for the forging of today's anti-Zionist 'popular front'. As we have seen, support for an avowedly anti-Semitic, even genocidal Islamic Jihadism, with its goal of theocracy, became the order of the day, together with hatred for all things western, especially the USA and, of course Israel and the Jews. Here too, as we have also seen, the Sharia left made the necessary adjustments, simply echoing and justifying even the most racist and primitive prejudices of its young Muslim marching companions. But this is not simply a clash of generations, in the sense of a rite of passage in which the son, to prove his manhood, feels obliged to rebel against his father. It of course includes that, but it is so much more. Their revolt is not just against something, but for something, which they truly see as holy, sacred. In Islam, they have found a purpose to both life and death, a cause, a call to action, even to Jihad, not, like their parents and grandparents, as a code to live by and a call to prayer. Azzam Tamimi of the 'moderate' Sharia left partner, the British Council of Muslims, captured this new-found devotion to the cause perfectly when he objected to the description of Jihadis as 'suicide bombers': 'Do not call them suicide bombers. Call them martyrs. We love death. They [the Jews] love life.'

In the holy texts on which their parents and imams have reared them, young Muslims find a message that, for all the protestations, denials and theological gymnastics of clerics and politicians, is really there, and which undeniably does indeed clearly summon the Muslim male to do battle, literally, on behalf of his faith. Only this, and not the spurious motives others proffer, can explain the surge of mainly young British Muslims who made their way, by devious routes, to the ISIS killing deserts of Syria and Iraq. They leave behind them, quite probably for good, in some cases at least, genuinely bewildered parents, who are at total loss as to why their loved ones are choosing to kill and be killed in a faraway desert rather than achieve academic and professional success, settle down and in time provide then with grandchildren. Always, they describe their runaway Jihadi offspring as 'good Muslims', not comprehending for one moment that if they were bad Muslims or not Muslims at all, they would still be safely at home with their parents.

Yet the answer as to why they become assassins is so obvious, so simple, that only a Muslim parent cannot grasp it. Brought up from the cradle to be 'good Muslims', that is, to believe that every word of the *Koran* is true, 'good Muslims' is exactly what they believe they are now proving themselves to be, not by study, then a beginning a career, followed by buying a home and begetting children, in the process becoming more British than their parents but, just as the *Koran* commands, by leaving behind the old, the infirm and the fainthearted, and earning by death in battle the rewards that await the martyr in Paradise. That is what the *Koran* urges and promises and, sure enough, devout young Muslims, not just in the UK, but throughout Europe, answered the call in their tens of thousands. The following small selection of verses from the *Koran* urging Jihad are taken from just Chapters 2 and 3. (a fuller selection, numbering 61 is provided in Appendix L) All told, Koranic scholars have identified a total something in the order of 170, though politicians, US academics and Christian clerics, in the first place the current Pope, have detected none: 'Fighting is ordained for you, though it may be repugnant to you.' (2: 217) 'Those who believe and those who emigrate [sic] and strive hard in the cause of Allah, it is these who hope for Allah's mercy.' (2: 219) 'And fight them until there is no more persecution, and religion is professed only for Allah.' (2: 194) 'Do you suppose that you will enter Heaven while Allah has not yet caused to be distinguished those of you that strive in the way of Allah and has not yet cause to be distinguished as steadfast?' (3: 143) 'We shall cast terror into the hearts of those that have disbelieved.' (3: 152) 'And if you are slain in the cause of Allah or you die surely forgiveness from Allah and mercy are better than what they hoard.' (3: 158) 'Think not of those, who have been slain in the cause of Allah as dead. nay, they are living in the presence of the Lord, and are granted gifts from him.' (3: 170

While there is, in defiance of these and many other similar citations, a public consensus among all sectors of the political and clerical establishment that nothing in the teachings of Islam justifies acts of violence, this does not hold true for the criminal justice system and in its courts of law, where evidence and the truth still matter. We have seen that in a number of cases involving Muslims charged with terrorism offences, evidence presented in court by the prosecution to prove criminal intent has included passages from the *Koran* which defendants had invoked to justify acts of terror against infidels. At least here, evidence, realism and a refusal to defer to political correctness still prevail. The same is however not true of the Prison Service. In July 2016, the BBC reported that after a review of prison libraries conducted in 2015 by a team led by Ian Acheson, a senior Home Office official and former prison governor, five Islamic texts stocked by libraries were identified as 'extremist' for their advocacy of Jihadism.

In nine of the eleven prisons inspected, one or more of these texts had been found in chaplaincy rooms. Acheson first conveyed his concerns to the Ministry of Justice in November 2015, and again in March 2016, but to no effect. The release of his report on his findings was also repeatedly delayed. The order to remove the texts in question was eventually made on June 20, 2016. Perhaps one of the reasons for the delay in publication and action was that one of the texts Acheson believed was responsible for encouraging Jihadism contained numerous citations from the *Koran*. Giving evidence to the House of Commons Select Committee, Acheson expressed both unease and surprise that the Ministry of Justice had taken so long to act on his recommendations: 'I made it clear to the Ministry of Justice last November that my assumption was that urgent action will be taken to remove these materials. Their free access to vulnerable and suggestible prisoners is an obvious security risk.' Could it be that political correctness was taking precedence even over national security?

Among the texts scheduled for removal was *The Way of Jihad* [sic!] by the founder of the theocratic Muslim Brotherhood, Hassan Al-Banna. In his preface, the author asserts that 'Jihad is an obligation from Allah on every Muslim and cannot be ignored or evaded'. In the main body of the work, Al-Banna then cites certain passages from the *Koran* that validate this claim, for example: 'Against them make ready your strength to the utmost of your power, including steeds of war, to strike terror into the hearts of the enemies of Allah and your enemies', (8: 60) and 'Verily Allah has purchased of the believers their lives and their properties; for the price that is theirs shall be the Paradise. They fight in Allah's cause, so they kill others and are killed.' (9: 11) UK tax-paying readers may be interested to learn that this particular verse, one that like so many others from the same source, incites Muslims to kill non-Muslims, is included in the Ministry of Justice-approved manual for Islam courses taught in HM prisons since 2011. (Why such courses are needed is another question.) Given that the *Koran* contains over a hundred similar injunctions to take up arms for Allah, for the ban on Jihadist literature to be truly effective, Islam's holiest text would have to be removed from every prison in the UK.

No less a matter of concern to Acheson was the discovery that of the 244 Muslim chaplains operating within the prison system, no fewer than two thirds were adherents of the Deobandi school of Islam, which also controls around 40% of the UKs registered 1,750 mosques and many of its 2,000 *madrassahs*. Preaching its own version of multi-culturalism, Deobandism advocates the strictest possible segregation of diaspora Muslims from their *kuffar* hosts and, sharing a close association with Wahhabism, promotes Jihad against the infidel West. Particularly influential in Pakistan and Afghanistan, its teachings inspired the founding of the Taliban. One of its private schools, situated in the heavily Islamised former Yorkshire mill town of Dewsbury, was found by a Sky News investigation to be inculcating in its 140 pupils the belief that there existed a Jewish conspiracy to conquer the world, an exercise justified by the school's management as 'spiritual training for the soul'. The school also prepared its pupils for martyrdom in the name of Islam, with teaching materials exhorting Muslims to 'expend even life for Allah's just order'. Is it any wonder then that 1000 or so young UK Muslims, exposed on such a scale to these doctrines, in many cases learned from early childhood by rote at *madrassahs*, turned ISIS Jihadis, comprising possibly the largest contingent, one quarter of the total, from any western country?

What hope integration when so many of a rising generation sees as its role models depraved sadists who video beheadings to cries of god is great? Surely it is time to realise that after the UK has done everything within reason and, in pursuing the follies of 'multi-culturalism', even beyond, to accommodate the followers of Islam, infidels are now seen by many Muslims, and with some justification, as dupes to be milked, and at the same time as enemies of Islam who must be treated as such. To repeat, the *Koran* is quite explicit: 'Surely the vilest of animals in Allah's sight are those who disbelieve.' (Chapter 8, Verse 55) 'Ye who believe take not the Jews and the Christians as friends' (Chapter 5, Verse 52); and 'O ye who believe, take not others than your own people as intimate friends; they will spare no pains to ruin you. They love to see you in trouble. Hatred has already shown itself through the utterances of their mouths and what their breasts hide is greater still.' (Chapter 3, Verse 119) It is difficult, if not impossible, to see how these condemnations and commands can further the process of integration of young Muslims into the broader society in which they or their antecedents have chosen to live, especially when they are also incited by their leaders to do exactly the opposite. In 2008, the then Turkish Prime Minister, and now Islamising President Recep Erdogan addressed a meeting of 20,000 diaspora Turks in Cologne: 'I understand very well that you are against assimilation. One cannot expect you to assimilate. Assimilation is a crime against humanity.'

Faced with this organised resistance to integration, instead, we see the reverse, the public policy of the host society accommodating increasingly to the demands, laws and mores of Islam, one that in Sweden, has resulted in native Swedes effectively being reduced to second class citizens in what was once their own country. (For details, see Appendix C) One of the most frequently rehearsed explanations for the failure of Muslims to integrate is that the young in particular feel 'alienated', as if this was somehow not the inevitable consequence of Islamic teachings and diaspora preferences, but the fault of the host nation. One way to respond to this complaint is to offer the Muslims of the UK an alternative to the status which they, along with all other UK subjects, enjoy at the moment. The deal would go like this. The UK would offer to its resident Muslims its own carbon copy of the same Sharia law that a true Islamic state would imposes on *dhimmi* non-Muslims in its own domain. As a legally Christian country with its own state church, the UK would confront Muslims with three choices, just as Islam does non-Muslim monotheists: convert to Anglicanism, accept the second-class status of Muslim *dhimmis* and pay the tax, or suffer death as Muslim martyrs. (There would also be a fourth option of emigration within in a set time period.) Any Muslim converting to Anglicanism and then reverting back to Islam would be killed as an apostate. By strictly enforcing an inverted carbon-copy of Islamic *dhimmitude,* non-converting Muslims accepting this status, in addition to paying the dhimmi tax, would not be allowed to

1: build any new Mosques in the UK;
2: pray or read out aloud from sacred Muslims texts in any place where this may be heard by Anglicans;
3: reproduce Islamic holy texts, and sell them in public places;
4: Display religious symbols on their houses or places of worship;
5: Use the media in any shape or form to promote their faith;
6: Gather in public for a religious purpose;
7: Not allowed to serve in the armed forces, unless engaged as mercenaries under Anglican command.

If these conditions of servitude were to be enforced on the UK's Muslim population, it would not be too hard to predict the probable reactions. In the UK, there would ensue entirely legitimate Muslim massive protests, joined by many others who shared their outrage at these measures. I would be among them. They could quite easily spill over into violent clashes in several of the UK's largest cities. There would be a world-wide Muslim boycott of all UK goods and services. Ambassadors of Muslim countries would be withdrawn. The UN, which by accepting without protest a religious monopoly of Islam in Saudi Arabia, violates its own Universal Declaration of Human Rights, would convene an emergency session to protest against the UK's violation of Islamic religious freedom, while its Human Rights Council would also call an emergency session to pass scathing resolutions of condemnation and find the UK guilty of umpteen human rights violations.

The Arab League and the Organisation of the Islamic Conference would likewise convene emergency sessions to the same end. Overnight, the UK would become a pariah state in the eyes of not only Muslims but the entire world. Abroad, vast armies of outraged Muslims would storm and reduce to rubble UK embassies in fifty or more Islamic capitals. The mayhem, destruction and carnage would dwarf any that Muslim mobs have unleashed in past responses to a cartoon, a film or novel most had neither seen, read or could have read. And all because the UK had decided to treat Muslims in the same way that Sharia law and the *Koran* require Islamic states to treat those who are not Muslims. And yet there never have been, and probably never will be, analogous resolutions, boycotts and street mobilisations against the very real and mounting persecution of religious minorities imposed in countries governed by Sharia law, under which religious toleration, like so many other aspects of Islam, is a one-way street, demanded as of divine right by Muslims in the lands of the infidel, but denied by Allah to infidels in his own realm: 'Fight them [the unbelievers] until there is no more persecution [of Muslims] and religion is professed only for Allah.' (*Koran*, Chapter 2, Verse 194)

Sometimes, 'Islamisation' has its absurd, even comic aspects, though the following examples also have a deadly serious dimension, since they illustrate the mounting assault being mounted by Islam, with the connivance of a range of public authorities, on the increasingly restricted to right to free speech. That offensive is resulting a series of court rulings and convictions in the UK that are flagrant violations of Article 10 of the European Convention on Human Rights, to which the UK is a signatory, but which in order to appease its Eurosceptics, the Conservative Party is committed to repudiating. Article 10 is defined thus:

> Everyone {sic] has the right to freedom of expression. This right shall include the freedom to hold opinions and to receive and impart information and ideas without interference by public authority and regardless of frontiers. In a commentary on this article arising from case law, the Court has ruled that Article 10 'protects not only the information and ideas that are regarded as inoffensive but also those that shock, offend or disturb, such are the demands of that pluralism, tolerance and broad mindedness without which there is no democratic society.' Opinions expressed in strong or exaggerated language are also protected.

In Article 10 of the European Convention, yes, but not in the courts of the UK where they can be judged as crimes meriting in some cases prison terms of up to seven years. In the May 2014 elections for the EU Parliament, a candidate for the anti-Islam Liberty GB Party was reading out aloud from a book by Winston Churchill while standing on the steps of the Winchester Guildhall. The work in question was Churchill's *River War*, an account of the British campaign against the Sudanese Mahdi, in which Churchill played a prominent role as an army officer. The work, containing views arrived at through first-hand experience of the Islamic faith and its impact on those who adhere to it, would by today's less robust standards, certainly qualify as 'Islamophobic'. And so it proved.

The reading, which was videoed, was brought to an abrupt end following a complaint to the police by a Guildhall official, who almost certainly was unaware of the identity and therefore almost legendary reputation of the Nobel Prize winning author, whose leadership in the Second World resulted in his being voted the 'Greatest Briton' by BBC viewers, and the only British commoner ever to have been awarded a state funeral. No matter. Charged with the offence of 'religious and racial harassment' no less, even though the reading made no reference to race, only Islam, and the complaint had not been made by a 'harassed' Muslim, the offender was arrested, searched (possibly for more incriminating writings by Churchill) and bundled into a van by a *posse* of no fewer than seven policemen. After having his fingerprints taken, providing a DNA sample and spending several hours in a cell, he was released, still facing racial hate speech charges carrying a maximum prison sentence of two years. Naturally, the Thought Police action won approval from Muslims, for whom free speech exists only to propagate Islam and to demand the silencing and punishment of those who dare to criticise it. Mohammed Shafiq of the Ramadan Foundation, whom we earlier encountered demanding of infidels not only respect for but the 'celebration' of his faith, put it thus: 'Of course [sic] there should be freedom of speech, but [there is always a 'but'] with freedom of speech comes responsibility'. How easily 'of course' trips from the tongue.

Translated from an Orwellian Shariaspeak into less opaque and more honest prose, Shafiq was saying that we Muslims do not like criticism of our religion, and so we demand the right to be the judges of what can and cannot be said about it. As Rafiq was well aware, that is exactly how the matter is handled in Islamic countries, where freedom of speech and religion are only conspicuous by their total absence.

The Shafiqs of this world want the same system of censorship to operate in west, in the guise of demanding 'responsible' free speech. Who decides what is 'responsible'? Who enforces it? And 'responsible' to whom? We can guess. The only responsibility that comes with free speech is firstly to defend it, come what may, and to exercise it, irrespective of whom it may offend. Free speech qualified by a 'but', as it so often is, is no longer free speech. In fairness, I should point out that this at best equivocal stance on the right to free expression is shared by many non-Muslims, not least those on the left. When, some twenty or so years ago now, in an article on Lenin that I wrote for the quasi-Trotskyist *New Interventions*, I took the Bolshevik leader to task for reneging on his party's pre-revolution pledge to uphold freedom of the press 'to its last drop of blood', the journal's editor replied in the next issue that 'Yes, we are all for freedom of the press, but Blick does not seem to consider that in some circumstances certain newspapers should be closed down'. George Orwell would have loved that one! In the same breath, 'all for' and 'close down'. What these 'circumstances' might be, and the identity of the 'certain papers', was left unsaid, though the principle and object of the exercise itself were manifestly clear. Should we then be surprised that given this shared denial of the unqualified right to freedom of expression, the Leninoid totalitarian left and theocratic Islam would prove such amicable bed-fellows? To take two examples. Um Ibtihal, in the website *Islamic City*, after noting with concern that some Muslims living under repressive Islamic regimes are attracted to the idea of freedom of speech, made it clear that 'Islam does not allow the adoption and propagation of "Freedom of Speech" as propagated in the West, since this would permit the promotion of such ideas that contradict Islam'. He then invokes the Henry Ford 'black car' principle: 'This is not to say that Islam does not allow the Muslims to express their opinions freely.' However, that is exactly what it does do, as the previous quotation, and what follows, makes clear: 'But [always the 'but'] this opinion must be derived from the *Koran* and *Sunna* [words and deeds] of the prophet Mohammed'. So much for 'freely'...just like the editor of *New Interventions*...any opinion you like, so long as it is Islamic. Our second commentary is to be found in the website '*Brotherhood and Unity*'. And yes, it is indeed the precise theocratic analogue of Lenin's post-revolution dictum that press freedom 'helps the force of the world bourgeoisie'. Freedom of speech, we are informed, is 'a colonial tool', a concept

> derived from the capitalist [sic] ideology that is based on the belief that God and religion should be separated from life's affairs...the right to speak and what are the limits of free speech are therefore all defined by human beings This view completely contradicts Islam. In Islam, it is the creator of all human beings, Allah, who gave the right [surely, in view of the context, faculty] of speech to people and the limits on what is acceptable and unacceptable speech.

Muslims who might be tempted to venture beyond these limits are warned that Allah has installed a celestial Sharia Big Brother audio monitoring system by which 'every word a human being speaks is recorded by the two angels Kiraman [and] Katibeen' so that 'even the speaking of one "bad" word may lead someone to the hellfire.' While being resolutely opposed, like Lenin, to unfettered 'colonialist' and 'capitalist' free speech, and yet always demanding that 'capitalist' infidel laws be used to silence and punish those that fail to display the required respect for their faith, Islamic clerics expect the *kuffar's* police to protect them when they exercise their Allah-given right to applaud acts of terror against this same 'colonial' and 'capitalist' enemy. And of course, our *dhimmi* police duly oblige. The date was September 11, 2002, the location, Labour Leader Jeremy Corbyn's favourite Finsbury Park Mosque, and the event, a celebration of the first anniversary of the killing by Muslims of 3,000 employees at the World Trade Centre in New York. Around 1000 Muslims crowded into the mosque to celebrate mass murder, pray to their warrior god and hear sermons of hate against the west. On this occasion, however, the police were there to protect the exercise of what they evidently regarded as 'responsible' freedom of speech, unlike a Churchill text which belongs to the 'irresponsible' category.

Travelling west from Winchester, we find ourselves at Taunton in Somerset. There, Michael Overd, a Christian lay street preacher, was arrested and charged, under one of our speech crimes laws, with preaching a 'religiously aggravated' sermon, ironically the identical fate that befell the founder of his religion, if the biblical account of his life is anything to go by. It is difficult to see how Overd's guilt could have been in any doubt, in the light of the testimony given by one witness for the prosecution. The preacher had, she claimed, made 'defamatory comments' about Mohammed and, horror of horrors, made 'no mention of any good' in the Islamic faith. So, cuff him. The legal implications of this trial were potentially truly horrendous, that in order to remain within the law, public speakers could be obliged to balance any adverse comments they might dare to make about Islam with an equal number that are favourable, even if it involved inventing them. There is also another aspect of this prosecution that needs to be considered. As we have already noted, the 57 Islamic states of the Organisation of the Islamic Conference have been pressing for years now for the United Nations to make it a criminal offence, binding on and enforceable within all its member countries, to defame Islam and its prophet. The Taunton trial was just that, a blasphemy trial by another name, in which adverse comments made about Islam and Mohammed are regarded as sufficient evidence to warrant criminal proceedings against the person who made them.

As *kismet* would have it, how appropriate that the presiding judge in this trial should be none other than Shamim Qureshi, who in his other legal capacity, plays a leading role as a judge in the UK's publicly financed and gender-biased Sharia court system. All this was bad enough. But what followed was worse again. Before Overd had even begun his sermon, it transpired that a police officer had warned him, 'If I hear one homophobic word out of your mouth here today, I will arrest you'. Quite aside from the contentious issue of how a single word can be 'homophobic', there is the more important matter to consider of a police officer, note book or perhaps recording device in hand, monitoring every single word uttered by a public speaker, and ready to pounce if, in his judgement, just one of those words violates a speech crime law. No less a cause for concern is the same speech police officer's subsequent warning to Overd that though he had a right to free speech, this had to be exercised without offending anyone - precisely the kind of 'responsible free speech' Muslims are seeking to enforce on those who do not share their exalted opinion of Islam. How can anyone, addressing a gathering of people whose beliefs and opinions cannot possibly be known in advance to the speaker be able, with the certainty demanded by this officer, to guarantee that they will not say anything that could offend anyone in the audience? This is impossible. The only way to comply with this instruction is to say nothing, which is exactly the result Muslim offence-takers seek.

But there is yet more. Next, we come to what must be the most alarming feature of the many that comprised this judicial assault on free thought and its free expression. A police officer present in court took time out to speak to the journalists who were covering the trial. He invited them, in words that cannot be construed in any other way, to encourage the public, as they were in Nazi and then Stalinist East Germany, to become informers on their fellow citizens. This, verbatim, is what the officer said: 'I'd advise people that if they are offended to record any incident on their mobile phone and send it to us.' Does this require any comment? In the event, Overd was found guilty of using 'abusive' language and ordered not only to pay the costs of his trial, rated at £1,200, but damages to one of the passers-by whom, it was claimed, he had offended, to the tune of £250. If this is not an incentive to be offended, what is? He rightly chose to appeal against his conviction and elected to stand trial again before a jury.

That the Sharia judge found the preacher guilty is in itself outrageous enough, as was his financial reward to the allegedly offended party for choosing to be offended. But his closing remarks had a sinister ring that those who value what remains of their civil liberties can ill afford to ignore. In the course of his sermon, Overd had quoted from the Old Testament of the Bible, Leviticus, Chapter 20, Verse 13: 'If a man also lie with mankind, as he lieth with a woman, both of them have committed an abomination: they shall be surely be put to death; their blood shall be upon them.' As it was reading out aloud this particular verse that helped secure the preacher's conviction, the Muslim judge told Overd that he should have selected another verse instead. This was indeed rich coming a Judge whose religion, to say the least, has a no less condemnatory attitude towards homosexuality than the Bible's, and to this day punishes it with the same penalty. He also warned Overd that his offence carried the option of a prison sentence...*for reading from the Bible*. So, just as in the Churchill case, the courts can if they choose prosecute and, if they see fit, convict anyone reading aloud in public a passage from a book that is not only in general circulation but, in the case of the Bible is, in its King James version, beyond dispute the prime text in the English language and, in various versions, is still to be found in the UK in millions of homes, thousands of public and academic libraries, schools and hotels, in every Anglican Church, from which are made readings, and in all serious bookshops and, what is more, is still the chief doctrinal authority of the established Church of England, at whose head stands the *Fidei Defensatrix,* Her Majesty the Queen. A Judge, a *Muslim* judge of all people, tells a Christian preacher what can and cannot be read out from his holy book in public. Just imagine the reverse, a Christian judge, or better still, a Jewish one, giving the same instruction to a Muslim preacher! How have we managed to arrive at this state of legally and self-imposed censorship, to the point when a pathological fear of anyone giving or taking offence results in a preacher being arrested and convicted for reading from the Bible?

Now to that religious hot spot, Belfast, where on 18 May 2014, another preacher, Pastor James McConnel, delivered in his church a sermon that he also publicised on line. Its subject was Muslim persecution of Christians, and everything he said about their sufferings was true:

> Allah is a heathen deity. Allah is a cruel deity. Allah is a demon deity. A deity that this foolish government of ours pays homage to and subscribes financial inducements to

curry their favour, while in Muslim lands Christians are persecuted for their faith. Their homes are burned, their churches destroyed, and hundreds [in fact thousands] of them literally have given their lives for Christ in martyrdom. A lovely young Sudanese woman by the name of Miriam, 27 years of age, because she has accepted Christ as her Saviour, will be flogged publicly and hanged publicly...I know the time will come in this land and in this nation when to say such things will be an offence to the law.... Islam is satanic. Islam is a doctrine spawned in hell.

The time he warned of had already arrived, in fact it had come more than decade previously, as the Pastor quickly discovered when, acting on a complaint by the Belfast Islamic Centre, police charged him under a totalitarian thought crime law, dating from 2003, with the offence, which carries a prison term of up to six months, of 'sending, or causing to be sent, by means of a public electronic communication network, a message or other matter that was grossly offensive'. No such proceedings ensued when Channel Four exposed calls by Birmingham imams for the murder of homosexuals and Muslims who did not pray the required number of times per day. Instead it was Channel Four who were the subject of an eight months investigation by the CPS, accused of distorting the message of the preachers' sermons.

Pastor McConnel, unlike many of our higher clerics, was made of sterner stuff than the clerical quislings who turn a deaf ear to cries for help of their Christian brothers and sisters, hunted down and murdered in their thousands for their faith by the zealots of the religion of peace, love and tolerance. Unrepentant for expressing views that are integral to his own chosen faith, he made it clear that the target of his invective was not people, but ideas that he sincerely believed to be both false and wicked: 'I have nothing against Muslims. I have never hated Muslims. But I am against what Muslims believe.' My view exactly. Just as Muslims are against what non-Muslims believe, and are allowed, quite rightly, to say so. He continues: 'They have a right to say what they believe in and I have a right to say what I believe in'. If only this last were true! His prosecution, and others like it, proved that when the subject is Islam, it is not.

Pastor McConnel, rather than accept the option of a lesser punishment, elected to stand trial and was ready to risk a six-month term in prison: 'I am 78 years of age and in ill health but jail has no fear for me. They can lock me up with sex offenders, hoodlums and paramilitaries and I will do my time'. In which event, would Sharia-friendly Amnesty International have adopted him as Prisoner of Conscience? Obviously more concerned to placate Belfast's outraged Muslims than permit freedom of speech and conscience to its Christian preachers, the Prosecution announced that it would be calling no fewer than eight (we can safely assume deeply-offended Muslim) witnesses. This was obviously a test case, and the Belfast Islamic Centre intended to win it. The Centre's Executive Director Raied al-Wazzam told the BBC that the Pastor's sermon had contained 'inflammatory language and it is definitely not acceptable'. Acceptable to whom? Here we have the Islamic veto being exercised yet again, with a Muslim laying down the (Sharia) law as to what can and cannot be said by non-Muslims about Islam, not only in a non-Islamic country, but one that is officially Christian. He and others like him are, with the full support of the law courts, deciding what constitutes 'acceptable' or, as another cleric put, 'responsible' speech, the criteria always being, what is acceptable to Muslims under Sharia law. With each new case, entire branches of UK law are, by stealth and precedent, not only accommodating Sharia law, but becoming extensions of it. Raied al Wazzam had complained of the Pastor's 'inflammatory language'. He should know. Some months later, in January 2015, he gave another interview to the BBC, in which he proclaimed himself to be an admirer of the Islamic State: 'Since the Islamic State took over Mosul, it has been the most peaceful city in the world'.

With such impeccable theological credentials, it was only to be expected that Raied al Wazzam would be chosen by the CPS as its chief witness in the trial of Pastor McConnel. I am pleased to record that on this occasion, Pastor McConnel was found not guilty by a Judge who, by his verdict, obviously placed a higher value on free speech than appeasing professional Muslim offence takers. Even so, the Pastor would have been outraged to learn, if he did not already know it, that as the law on 'hate crime' has thus far been interpreted, it can be a crime for a person to burn in public, without endangering either property or other persons, their own copy of a *Koran*, while the same does not hold true for a copy of the Bible. In November 2010, a 15-year-old Birmingham school girl was arrested and accused of 'inciting religious hatred' after burning a *Koran* in her school's playground. Two months previously, after being 'tracked down by the *Daily Mail* (as the paper proudly reported) six masked Gateshead men were arrested after posting a video of themselves burning a copy of the *Koran* in a protest against 9/11. Commenting on the two cases, Catherine Heseltine, Chief Executive Officer of the Muslim Public Affairs Committee, explained that 'the *Koran* is the most sacred thing to over a billion Muslims worldwide…we will never destroy the Koranic texts'. Nobody was saying they should. As her 'we' clearly refers to Muslims, and Muslims alone, it therefore follows that non-Muslims are in no sense, legally or otherwise, obliged to display the same reverence for the texts of a book that they do not believe in. If someone chooses to burn their own property in the shape of a book in a manner that is totally legal in all other respects, that should be entirely their own affair, as indeed it is in the USA under the First Amendment. It is also allowed in the UK, when the book is *The Satanic Verses* and those burning it in public are Muslims, but not when the book in question is the *Koran,* and those burning it are infidels.

Defending the right to do something, as I do in this instance, is not the same as approval of the said act, a distinction most Muslims and now our courts simply seem incapable of making. Although there was no place in Rousseau's Utopia for a free press, he is justly famed for his retort, when it was one of his own writings, the novel *Emile,* that was consigned to the flames by the Calvinists of Geneva, that 'burning is no answer'. Book burning, historically associated with the Roman Catholic Inquisition and the Nazis, and more recently with Muslim mobs outraged by a book they have not read (and in many cases, could not read) or an image they have probably not seen, is not only stupid, futile and uncivilised, but demonstrates a refusal or inability to engage rationally with ideas with which one disagrees. But that should not be grounds for making it a crime when it is one's own book that is being destroyed without risk to persons or property. Here again in such cases, we see a blatant attempt by UK law officers to use the courts to enforce Sharia blasphemy laws.

Just how crazy and the same time menacing these legal restrictions on free expression have become (all of which, significantly, have a religious dimension) was demonstrated by another extraordinary case that came to court in the UK in March 2015. As we have seen over and again, politicians in the UK, as they do world-wide, insist there is no causal connection between Islam and terrorism, and anyone who makes such a linkage is guilty of defaming the religion of peace. But it seems there can be exceptions to this otherwise universal truth. And, as we might have expected, these exceptions, far from allowing the defaming Islam, work in its favour. To appreciate how, consider the following: Liam Edwards appeared in Manchester Magistrates court, charged with 'racially aggravated criminal damage'. From the wording, one would reasonably infer that Edwards had vandalised, or maliciously damaged in some way, property belonging to a member of an ethnic group other than his own, and that his motive for doing so was that of racial hatred. But one would be wrong. Nothing of the kind occurred. Not remotely. Describing himself as 'animal lover, and like millions of other non-Muslims, though not the *dhimmi* Green Party, Edwards was opposed to the unnecessarily cruel ritual slaughter of animals, having witnessed it in a TV documentary on the subject. Seeking to draw attention to the issue, he entered a Sainsbury supermarket, and affixed stickers to *Halal* products and supermarket trolleys belonging to Sainsbury, which read thus: 'Beware! Halal is barbaric and funds terrorism. Ban Halal'.

The entire case against Edwards rested on these words printed on the stickers, and nothing else that he had said or, apart from affix his stickers, done. Edwards pleaded guilty to criminal damage, as not all the stickers could be removed from the *Halal* products, resulting in a loss to Sainsbury of £16.50 in sales revenue. But he pleaded not guilty to the 'aggravated racial' component of the charge, which was referred to trial by jury at a later date. As his defence council correctly pointed out in support of his not guilty plea, 'he used the word terrorism, but that cannot denote race or indeed religion'. Indeed, it cannot. And are we not told over and again that there is no connection between Islam and terrorism? But even so, and here is the ironic twist to the whole affair, the prosecution case rested on the assumption that there is! The additional objection could have been made that such 'damage' as there was done was to the property of Sainsbury, a company, and not a race, a point that that I will expand on below. First, let us look at the connections, whether they be real or imaginary, between terrorism, Islam and race as they pertain to this extraordinary case. To repeat, have we not been told *ad nauseam* that it is wrong, Islamophobic and even racist to suggest there may be a connection between Islam and terrorism? But once inside a court of law, everything can change as if by magic. When the word terrorism appears on a sticker opposing ritual slaughter, it can only mean, and intend others to infer, that there is a connection between terrorism and Islam. What is more, the inference is taken to be true, for otherwise why did the charge assume the connection without any supporting evidence? And not only that. The specific charge brought against Edwards in this case, '*racially aggravated* criminal damage', carries with it the implication that even without causing criminal damage to another's property, the public display of these words alone could be actionable in a court of law, for otherwise, why was Edwards not simply charged with criminal damage? And why introduce 'race' into the proceedings, when the alleged allusion was to a religion? One suspects that this case has a great deal more to do with protecting the 'sensitivities' of Sainsbury's Muslim customers than the loss of £16.50 to Sainsbury shareholders, a loss that was readily made good by Edwards being required by the court to pay this sum in damages to the company.

The sane amongst us are left puzzling: How does a sticker, one that mentions neither Islam nor a race, but refers disapprovingly to a method of killing animals, and makes the allegation (not surely in and of itself a criminal offence, and for which there are moreover reasonable grounds) that revenues from the *Halal* meat industry are funding terrorism, constitute a *racially* motivated offence? If, in the eyes of law, it does, then which race is being aggravated, so to speak? Bear in mind that the stickers were only attached to chickens and trolleys legally belonging to Sainsbury. So, was Sainsbury claiming not only to have suffered damage to its property (which in the case of the chickens was true and conceded to be such by the defendant) but also to have inflicted 'racially aggravated' damage, rather than just damage *per se,* on its *chickens*? Was Sainsbury, a company, claiming itself, its trolleys or its chickens to be a race? Surely not. Yes, it was their property that was damaged, but precisely who had been 'racially aggravated' remained a mystery. Let us assume for sanity's sake that it was not Sainsbury, or its trolleys or chickens, that had been the victim suffering the 'racially aggravated' component of the charge, but rather that a Muslim customer had made a complaint to the effect that they had been 'racially aggravated' on reading the offending sticker. even though, as we have noted, there was no reference to Islam or even allusion to race in the wording. So, we have damage to Sainsbury property in the form of one or more chickens, but no 'racial aggravation' to the same party; and a presumed 'racial aggravation' to a (possibly hypothetical) Muslim customer of unspecified , and therefore potentially of the same race as the accused, but no damage to the customer's property, since the damaged chicken (s), being unsellable, still belonged to Sainsbury.

What legal chicanery, worthy of a Kafka novel! It leaves one wondering as to the motives of those who decided that this case had to be brought to court, not as one of simple damage to property, which it was, but as one which, we must presume, involved a spurious charge of giving offence to Muslims even though only race was mentioned in the indictment, not religion, let alone Islam. Could it be that the learned minds that shape and administrate our laws had yet again fallen for the oldest trick in the Sharia book, and been duped into believing, or at least into pretending to believe, that a protean Islam, when it suits its purpose, can be simultaneously a race and religion? But even if it can bifurcate itself thus, which race had it in this case become? A racially motivated act has to be directed at a person or persons belonging to a specific race, not at an idea or belief system, such as Islam is. Otherwise, how can it be racist? So again, we must ask, which race was targeted by the wording on the stickers? Edwards was found guilty of both charges, ordered to pay £160.00 in addition to the £16.50 to Sainsbury, and given a one-month curfew from 9.00 PM to 7.00 AM. This verdict could set the precedent of making all protests against Halal ritual slaughter liable to prosecution under existing 'hate crime' laws, violations of which can carry a prison sentence of up to seven years.

In Australia, when snowflake Muslims claimed they were offended by the words 'Non-Halal Certificated' in an Adelaide butcher's shop window, the Adverting Standards Board ruled that it be removed, as it was 'demeaning to people of that faith [i.e., Islam] or are of Muslim ethnicity.[sic]' Again, Islam is simultaneously a faith and a race. The traumatised Muslims claimed the sign, displayed because customers were constantly asking if the shop's products were halal, 'poked fun of [sic] a specific group of people based on religious belief', thereby 'perpetrating a culture of vilification towards religious minorities'. Refusal to remove the sign would result in a fine of $20,000. However, there is no redress in law for those offended by the sight of butchers adverting halal, and neither should there be. Rather, it is ritual slaughter that should be outlawed.

Calling Halal ritual slaughter 'barbaric' was also one of the sins that in February

2019 got student Sebastian Walsh into hot water at the *dhimmi* University of Central Lancashire, along with expressing opposition in a class discussion to the Islamisation of Britain and free health care for non-UK citizens, views which, as he said, 'are held by many people in the public'. But not to be voiced and contested in a place of supposedly higher learning. Instead, like tale-telling infant school children… 'please Miss, Tommy said "bum"', infantilised adult snow flake snitches ran to Sir and had Walsh suspended and required to undergo 'diversity training', which he refused to do. Finally, to take one more no less crazy case, in 2006, schoolgirl Codie Scott found herself in court on a charge of racist 'hate speech', when all she had done was to state a fact. Her crime consisted of saying she found it hard to communicate with Pakistani classmates engaged with her in a joint project because they didn't speak English. No doubt they also found it hard to communicate with her because she didn't speak Urdu. But that was not considered a crime. This happened, not in Pakistan, but England.

That such cases can come court, let alone result in successful criminal prosecutions, while Muslim rape gangs can go unpunished for decades, should be sufficient proof for those who wish to silence criticism of Islam that the UK's formidable battery of hate crime laws is achieving its objective. But when it comes to combating 'Islamophobia', some people are never satisfied, one being the former Labour Party leader Ed Miliband. With Muslim votes possibly holding the balance in what all believed at the time would be a close-run General Election, in an interview with Ahmed Versi, editor of the *Muslim News*, he promised that if elected, a Labour Government would 'change the law on this [Islamophobia] so we make absolutely clear our abhorrence of hate crime and Islamophobia. It will be the first time that police will record Islamophobic attacks right across the country'. (This proposal has since been adopted by Cameron, who in October 2015 announced the introduction of a national police register of convicted Islamophobes akin to the sex offenders' register.)

Nowhere in the interview did Miliband explain what he meant by 'hate crime' and 'Islamophobia', or what constituted an 'attack'. If by 'attack' Miliband meant a physical assault or deliberate damage to property, then no new laws are required, because assault and criminal damage are already offences, and should be punished as the law dictates, whether the victim is a Muslim or not. So, one is left to draw the obvious conclusion that 'attack' can include actions that are not physical assaults or threats of such, but the expression of ideas and opinions, conveyed either verbally, or in written, printed, electronic and pictorial form, that can be construed as evidence of 'Islamophobia', resulting in those responsible being liable to criminal prosecution and entered on a register of convicted Islamophobes. Much therefore hinges on the meaning of the term 'Islamophobia'. The Runnymede Trust first introduced the word in 1991, ten years before 9/11, defining it as an 'unfounded hostility towards Muslims, and therefore fear or dislike of most Muslims.' Who decides what is 'unfounded'? And, as in this definition pertains not to a belief system, Islam, but to those who believe in it, Muslims, actual people, why not 'Muslimphobia'? And why not 'Christianphobia' for those who in various ways display less than the required respect for Christians? No such word exists, and I am confident it never will. The on-line Oxford Dictionary offers the following definition of Islamophobia: 'Dislike [of] or prejudice against Islam or Muslims, especially as a political force'. Here, Islam *is* included together with Muslims, with all manner of implications, not least legal. But adding to the confusion, the same

Oxford dictionary defines 'phobia' as an 'extreme or irrational fear or aversion to something'. So what happened to 'irrational fear' in its definition of 'Islamophobia'? The definition is also, from the standpoint of free speech, dangerous in the extreme, since, as is the case in Canada and several European countries, Islamophobia is classified as a 'hate crime'. And fearing (irrationally or otherwise) or disliking a person or group of persons as defined by their religion does not necessarily mean that they will be treated prejudicially. The phrase, 'especially as a political force' adds nothing to the definition, and in fact confuses the issue further, since Muslims, who though like members of all other faiths, hold a wide variety of political opinions, define themselves only by their religion, as does the law.

Demos, the cross-party 'Think Tank', while avoiding the usual reference to anti-Muslim prejudice, still contrives to get the meaning wrong, defining Islamophobia as the propagation of 'anti-Islamic ideas'. In what sense is the *propagation* of an idea a 'phobia'? And when they provide examples, it is evident that in practice, their definition not only encompasses criticism of Islam, but equates it with blatant racism. The first example of Islamophobia offered is a tweet that runs thus: 'Morocco deletes a whole section of the Koran from school curriculum as it's full of jihad incitement and violence the Religion of peace.' Now the second, also a tweet: 'I hate fucking Pakis'. Is this the best that the combined brains of Demos can produce? Where Islam is concerned, the tank seems to have sprung a large leak. The first is a statement of fact, with a touch of irony added, while the second is directed at a race (though Pakistanis, strictly speaking, do not constitute a unique race) not a religion. What is common to all these definitions of Islamophobia, and any number of others I could have cited, is the strong implication that there is something inherently reprehensible in advertising one's dislike of a faith that sanctifies wife beating, marital rape, decapitating and crucifying unbelievers, amputating limbs for petty crimes and killing apostates, to name what to an infidel such as myself and no doubt millions of others are just some of its more objectionable practices. As I have already asked, why is it that there are no equivalent terms applicable to a similar distaste for the tenets of other faiths, such as 'Christianphobia' or 'Hinduphopia'? But by now you should know the answer.

My *Chambers* dictionary defines 'phobia' as 'a fear, aversion or hatred, especially a morbid or irrational one'. It therefore follows that in its literal sense, and in law, that is where matters should stay, with the word 'Islamophobia' meaning an irrational fear or hatred of Islam. What possible grounds can there be to make it a criminal offence to fear (rationally or otherwise) or for that matter hate an *idea*? As far as the law and medical science are concerned, a phobia is not a crime but an abnormal medical condition, for example agoraphobia. Fear that is not irrational, as I, again along with millions of other non-Muslims, believe fear of Islam is, is a perfectly natural and necessary human (and animal) instinct, one that has evolved through the mechanism of natural selection to protect life from danger. Fear that is irrational is no less spontaneous, not wilful. No-one chooses to be afraid, as distinct from being cautious when we are. Therefore, to attempt to banish or curb fear by punitive legislation is an act of sheer lunacy. So if the term is correctly construed, which it never is, to mean a not a hatred of Muslims, but an irrational fear (or hatred) of what they believe, we are therefore confronted by the absurdity of making it a crime to irrationally fear or hate a system of beliefs. And yet fear, or rather 'terror', of Islam is explicitly what the author of the *Koran* intends to arouse in non-believers, with his threat to 'cast terror into the hearts of those who disbelieve' (8:13) and 'strike terror into the hearts of the enemies of Allah'. (8: 60)

Did Miliband intend to make it a crime to react to these threats in exactly the way Allah intends? Why punish the terrorised and not the terrorist? Even if we substitute hate for fear, we still left with a law that seeks to criminalise hating, rationally or otherwise, *an idea.*, and not the person or persons who subscribe to it. As I have already asked, and I ask again, *if*, hypothetically, the intention is to make hating Islam illegal, then why is the same legal protection not being extended to all other doctrines, be they religious or secular? Why not 'Quakerphobia', 'Naziphobia' and 'anarchophobia'? Using the law to stop people hating an idea is as insane as compelling people to love a piece of music, since, like a number of human emotions, hate is a spontaneous feeling over which we have no control. One cannot choose to hate any more than one can to love. Acting upon it is of course another matter entirely, (thus, so-called 'hate management) and if its manifestations warrant it, such as threats of or actual bodily violence against the object of the hate, are rightly actionable under existing laws. If by 'Islam' in the word 'Islamophobia' is meant Muslim, as its false usage implies, then firstly, the term should be changed so that it not only, at least for some, implies it, but actually says it, Muslimophobia. Now, with this newly minted term, we can start afresh, and see where the proposed new law might take us. Unlike Islamophobia, Muslimphobia does mean an irrational fear or hatred of Muslims. So, we ask again, as this is a medical condition (for why else the term 'phobia'?), should this be a crime? However, deliberately seeking to *cause* fear by making verbal threats, as in the above citation from the *Koran*, or by gestures, is a crime under UK law, Common Assault. And if being afraid of a Muslim or Muslims, rationally or otherwise, were, however absurdly, to be made a crime, it could still quite easily be the case that the Muslims or Muslims that are feared (irrationally or otherwise) are not made aware of the fact. So even within the terms of the proposed law, in what sense has a harm been done and therefore a crime committed? (Some time after I made these observations, I was gratified to read that that Maajid Nawaz of the reformist Quilliam Foundation largely agrees with me: 'To scrutinize and challenge an idea like religion that comes with so much power must surely be the right of every free-thinking individual and formed the very basis of Europe's Enlightenment. That is why the word "Islamophobia" is too blunt. It fails in principle to distinguish between hating Muslims and criticising Islamic doctrine.')

Another case that could arise would involve deliberately conveying in some way to a specific Muslim or group of Muslims that they are feared or hated, irrationally or otherwise. But this is madness. We know that there are Muslims who definitely want to be feared, just as the *Koran* requires. Using the same terminology as Allah, unless we work for the BBC, we call them terrorists. Surely it is they who are breaking the law, not those who fear them. And some would argue that Muslims who carry out or approve of atrocities on the scale of 9/11, 7/7 or the Paris and Madrid massacres should expect to be hated. Is this the hypothetical offence, that of hating Muslim terrorists, the one that Miliband had in mind? Surely not. In lieu of any specific indicators as to Miliband's legal proposals, by a process of elimination, we arrive at the only possible rational conclusion, that his intention must have been not to criminalise fear or even hatred of an idea, Islam, nor fear of Muslims, but only hatred of Muslims, and at that, only as Muslims, because one can surely be entitled to harbour and even express feelings of hatred towards a person or persons for what they have done, for example the gang rape of a child, irrespective of and as distinct from what the rapists claim they believe. Always assuming we can arrive at a satisfactory definition of what hate is (and this will have its difficulties for sure), there then arises the problem of defining its manifestations...verbal, visual, textual etc. And will the law apply only to someone who hates Muslims *per se*, or only to those who hate a specific Muslim, or group of Muslims, such the Caliph of the Islamic State, and/or those UK subjects who have volunteered to fight for him and committed appalling acts of brutality and sadism?

But by now, it should have become obvious that our projected crime of Muslim hatred, which by using the Greek prefix *miso* for hate, as in misogynist, should be designated *misomusiimia*, is already covered by laws relating to the incitement of religious hatred in general, which are so worded to ensure, despite the intentions and efforts of Tony Bair, that such laws do not protect religions, but only persons who believe in them. But even here, there are anomalies. Why is it illegal to 'incite hatred' against a person or persons on account of their religion, but not their politics? Why should it be potentially illegal to say to or about a particular Muslim that I hate him (or her) for the way he or she insults and abuses Jews and gays, praises Hitler or denies the Holocaust, but it be within the law to say exactly the same to or about a secular Nazi? There are also other ways in which existing and projected so-called 'hate speech' laws have created or could create any number of absurdities and anomalies. Could it be a criminal offence, for example, to violate Sharia law by creating and then displaying images of Mohammed where they might be seen by Muslims? When organisers of a free speech event in the Dallas suburb of Garland did precisely that on May 3, 2015, their right to do so was protected by both the First Amendment and armed police, who shot dead two pro-ISIS Muslim gunmen who were intent on providing the world with yet another demonstration of Islam's 'proud tradition of tolerance' by attempting to re-enact the Paris *Charlie Hebdo* massacre of January 7, 2015. The reader is invited to contrast Miliband's thought crime proposals with the statement made by Garland Mayor Douglas Athas after the thwarted attack: 'There was concern, which is why we had heightened security in the area, but we all swear to uphold the Constitution: free speech, free assembly and in this case possibly free religion.' It is reasonable to assume that under Miliband's proposed new laws, if anyone had been brave enough to organise a similar event in the UK it would have been a question who got to them first, armed Muslim assassins, or police armed with arrest warrants.

Miliband's proposals were bad enough in themselves. But their vagueness was even worse, because they would have left the voting public in the dark, in the event of a Labour government being elected, as to what it would be have been possible to say without running the risk of ending up in court and possibly even in prison. All we were told was that Islamophobes were to be punished by toughening up and adding to laws that are currently on the statute book and have already led to a number of successful prosecutions. For example, given his declared intentions, it is reasonable to suppose that it could have become a criminal offence under Miliband's proposed anti-Islamophobia laws for a non-Muslim to say in public, or in print, something about Islam that is demonstrably true, such as the *Koran's* sanctioning of wife beating (Chapter 4, Verse 34) or the amputation of hands and feet for theft (Chapter 5, Verse 39) or that an adult male emulating, with a nine year old girl, Mohammed's consummation of his marriage to his last wife Aisha, as recorded in the relevant *Hadith* (e.g., Sahih Bukhari 4.1.1) would be liable to conviction as a paedophile under existing UK sexual offences laws. And as we shall, see, saying just that led in Austria to prosecution and a conviction upheld on appeal by the European Court of Justice

A law which criminalises saying something that it is demonstrably true, and which does not endanger the security of the state or materially harm any individual, is manifestly and inherently an unjust law. Why then did Miliband propose to add more of the same to those we already have? Both the above statements are true, because there are Islamic texts to prove it, and they would also be endorsed as true by any honest Muslim cleric or scholar. But they would nevertheless run the risk, even under current thought crime laws, of being seen as Islamophobic not only by overly sensitive Muslims but also by zealous politically correct police. Supposing, as is plausible, that the proposed legislation had been so framed that these and other similar statements, all culled from authentic Islamic sources, would only have been actionable if made by non-Muslims, what then would have ensued would have been two sets of laws, one for Muslims, and another for the rest; in fact, the very Sharia law that many Muslims are currently demanding.

This is not so absurd as it might sound. Such a law has been proposed in Canada and demanded at the United Nations by Doudou Diene, the UN's special rapporteur on 'racism, racial discrimination, xenophobia and related intolerance'. In 2007, in response to the drive by the OIC to criminalise Islamophobia, Diene proposed the adoption of a law binding on all UN member states that would define 'quoting from the *Koran* accurately but critically [sic] as an act of bigotry'. Such quotations 'needed to be proscribed'. Diene explained why:

> One may note a number of Islamophobic statements have been falsely claimed to be scientific or scholarly in order to give intellectual clout to arguments that link Islam to violence and terrorism. Furthermore, the manipulation [sic] and selective [sic] quoting of sacred texts, in particular the *Koran,* as a means to deceptively [sic] argue that these texts show the violent nature of Islam has become current practice.

If such a law, applicable only to non-Muslims, were to have been had been enacted in the UK, we would then have found ourselves in the humiliating situation of being the only country in the world that had repealed its blasphemy laws protecting Christianity only to have had them replaced with new blasphemy laws applicable only to non-Muslims and protecting only Islam. If on the other hand such a law had been so framed as to have applied to everyone, then legislation designed ostensibly to protect the Islamic faith would have made it illegal for not only infidels, but for Muslims to cite certain passages from their own holy books! And we have seen already, in the case of the Taunton Preacher, a Muslim magistrate convicting a Christian whose offence consisted of reading out in public a passage from the Bible.

A novel, but also retrogressive, solution has been proposed by one Labour MP, Keith Vaz, to ensure the protection of Islam from criticism. Vaz, a devout Roman Catholic, in March 1989 led a march of several thousand Muslims in his own constituency of Leicester to demand that Salmand Rushdie's novel, *The Satanic Verses,* be banned. Consistent with his support for Sharia censorship, Vaz (a close friend of many years of Jeremy Corbyn), with Islam obviously in mind, has advocated the re-introduction of the Blasphemy Laws, extended to cover all religions rather than just Christianity. Justifying what would constitute an unprecedented clamp down on free speech, he argued at an event convened by the Muslim Council of Britain on November 12, 2015, that 'religions are very special to people' and, we could add, especially so to the Muslim assassins who, the very next day, massacred 131 civilians in Paris to cries of God is Great. But so are other beliefs 'very special' if not to his Muslim friends, for example democracy, secularism, and the right to free speech, yet nobody in their right minds would propose that advocates of Muslim theocracy who attack them should be subject to criminal proceedings. Those who believe in democracy and free speech are perfectly capable of defending their principles without the assistance of the police, and the courts or resorting to terrorist violence. So why not Muslims?

With a view to yet further tightening of laws that curtail what can be said about Islam, the Corbynised Labour Party and, belying their name, the Liberal Democrats, defined Islamophobia as 'a type of racism that targets expressions of Muslimism [sic] or perceived Muslimness [sic!]'. Since they are terms intended to be used in a court of law, what, precisely, are 'Muslimism' and 'Muslimness'? Do they mean a belief in Islam? If not, what do they mean? Even the police and Muslim clerics joined academics and secularists who protested to Home Secretary Sajid Javid that if enacted into law, this definition of Islamophobia, quite apart from inventing words whose meanings are not explained and one that yet again conflates race with religion, would create a blasphemy law drastically inhibiting criticism of Islam. By so doing, it will, contrary to the intentions of those proposing it, fuel the already existing hostility towards a faith that is widely perceived as enjoying privileges neither demanded by nor afforded to any other.

It is not only in the United Nations and the UK that in the name of combating Islamophobia, serious proposals are being made to impose ever tighter restrictions on what can be legally said about Islam. While in the USA, to the palpable chagrin and frustrations of the Social Justice Warrior left, free speech without buts is protected from such assaults on personal freedom by its First Amendment, to the north, in Canada, no such bulwark exists. There, in September 2015, Minister of Justice Stephanie Vallée brought before Quebec's National Assembly Bill 59, whose ostensible purpose was to criminalise the ubiquitous 'hate speech'. However, it became evident that something more specific was in mind when Jacques Fremont, Quebec's Human Rights (sic) Commissioner, revealed that if the Bill were to become law, he would use it to prosecute 'people who would write about the Islamic religion on a website or a Facebook page'. Not criticise, but merely 'write about'! As in the UK with Miliband's proposals, under this law, offenders would be entered onto a hate speech offenders' register and being fined up to $10,000 for 'writing about' Islam. Human Rights in Quebec are clearly in safe hands. In the case of Miliband's proposed, though not defined, new laws, always assuming that they were intended to be implemented, and were not simply a ruse to attract the Muslim vote, only to be quietly laid to rest once the election was over, the proposed legal suppression of 'Islamophobia' would have required not only a wide extension of police powers, but the involvement of border agencies to prevent the importation of printed matter deemed 'Islamophobic', the surveillance and if necessary the blocking of the electronic transmission of offending texts and images such as is currently practised by China, North Korea and a number of Islamic regimes, and more raids on newsagents, as well as on internet cafes, book shops and libraries, and possibly even private homes.

Considerations such as these suggest that Miliband, in his eagerness to court the Muslim vote, either had simply not thought the matter through, or that he really believed that like the Sharia left and the rest of the political establishment, not offending Muslims outweighed the right to free speech and a free press. But worst of all is that enacting legislation empowering the police to 'record Islamophobic attacks right across the country' would have encouraged offence-seeking Muslims, the politically correct and Sharia leftists to act as police informers. While no one in their private capacity as citizen would have been obliged to report to the police an Islamophobic offence, as the law stands, all public officials (whose numbers run into the millions) when acting in that capacity would have had such a duty, as defined by the Criminal Law Act of 1967. This would have created a thought control police on such a vast scale that that a free discussion of Islam could only have been safely pursued in the privacy of one's own home.

Free speech and a free press were obviously not on Miliband's agenda, at least, not when he was being interviewed by the editor of the *Muslim News*. Had it occurred to him that if the beefed-up thought crime laws he was proposing had already been on the statute book, they would for sure have resulted in the prosecution of anyone in the UK re-printing or offering for sale the post-massacre edition of *Charlie Hebdo?* Perhaps Miliband had already forgotten that only three months previously, on the very day of the Paris massacre, he had declared to the House of Commons: 'We stand in solidarity with the people of France against this evil terrorist attack by people [sic] intent on attacking our democratic way of life and freedom of speech'. If we understand Miliband correctly (and that is not easy), the attack on *Charlie Hebdo* constituted 'an attack on freedom of speech', which indeed it most certainly was. But if again we understand Miliband aright, his proposed anti-Islamophobia laws would have also necessitated an 'attack on free speech', outlawing the kind of images that led to the assassinations in Paris. These two positions cannot be reconciled. Trapped as he was between what he saw as the necessity of appeasing incessant Muslim demands for the criminalisation of anything that smacked of criticism of Islam, and the need to reassure the broader public that he upheld 'our democratic way of life and freedom of speech', Miliband found himself defending principles that were totally and obviously incompatible.

The open-ended legislation proposed by Miliband was, at that point in time, the most extreme of a series of attempts by politicians to devise laws that will further curtail freedom of speech. However, flushed with his unexpected outright election victory on May 7, 2015, David Cameron, no longer constrained by his former Liberal Democrat coalition partners, announced his intention to crack down on 'extremism', by which term was meant the Islamic variety. The proposals he had in mind went far beyond even what had been implied by Miliband in his war on Islamophobia. Miliband wanted to change the law but remain within it. Cameron, incredibly and unambiguously, proposed to circumnavigate it: 'For far too long, we have been a passively tolerant society, saying to our citizens, as long as you obey the law, we will leave you alone.' So we should become aggressively intolerant...like some Muslims? This is the same Cameron who in the wake the *Charlie Hebdo* massacre proclaimed to the world from the steps of No. 10 Downing Street his belief in freedom of speech. Hitherto, freedom of expression had been increasingly curtailed by so-called 'hate crime' laws that have been approved by Parliament. Indefensible as they from a free speech standpoint, they were subject to debate and amendment, and in their final wording at least gave an indication of what can and cannot be said in public about certain matters and afforded those so accused the right to defend themselves in a court of law.

What Cameron proposed implied an intention, by methods not at the time specified, but that do not have the force of law, to augment the constraints of already existing or new laws on free speech. That and that alone was the meaning of his warning that certain people are 'not to be left alone' even if they conform to the law. The reasonable assumption that the intended target of this extra-legal attack on what remains of freedom of speech will be 'extremist' Muslims is totally irrelevant. Whoever they might prove to be, they have as much right to free speech as anyone else, little though that now is. Perhaps the time is approaching when those who value their right to free expression will be called upon to act in the spirit, if not strictly the letter, of Voltaire's axiom, 'I despise what you say, but I will defend to the death your right to say it', by defending even those who say, 'I despise what you say, and if I could, I would put you to death for saying it.'

If it was integration that Cameron was seeking, this was hardly the best way to go about it. How fitting that Cameron's proposed assault on the rule of law came only a matter of weeks before the 800th anniversary of the adoption of Magna Carta on June 15, 1215, subsequently condemned by Pope Innocent III as heretical for its placing secular limits on the power of god's' anointed sovereign. Cameron's; proposed measure violated one of the Charter's three articles, number 39, which still remain on the statute book: 'No free man shall be seized or imprisoned, or stripped of his rights or possessions, or outlawed or exiled, or deprived of his standing in any other way, nor will we proceed with force against him, or send others to do so, except by the lawful judgement of his equals or by the law of the land.' The proposed measures also violate what is regarded as the bedrock of all (western) law: *'Nullum crimen, nulla poena sin praevia lege poenali';* No crime can be committed, or punishment inflicted, without a pre-existing criminal law. Cameron's threat became a reality with the proposal, following his election victory in May 2015, to enforce 'Extremist Disruption Orders' to silence Muslims deemed 'extremist', a term reminiscent of Apartheid South Africa's 'Banning Orders'. No longer would obeying the law of the land' be sufficient protection. The days of 'passive tolerance' were over.

Miliband, who as we have noted, is an atheist, would surely insist that his convictions, though entirely secular, are no less sincere and deeply held than those of a religious believer. So why then did he advocate legal protection for one, but not the other? On what grounds does UK law not treat all beliefs equally, as does the constitution of the USA? And if beliefs are not treated equally, as Cameron also proposed, though in an opposite sense to Miliband, then it follows inescapably that neither are those who hold them. Even under current thought crime laws, a Muslim cannot be prosecuted for negative comments about socialism, but a socialist can end up in prison, just as he could in an Islamic country, for negative comments about Islam. So in effect, there are already two systems of law in operation, working to the advantage of Muslims and discriminating against infidels. Cameron's proposals will not remedy this situation, but simply complicate it further. It needs to be said that Miliband, possibly trying to over-compensate for his own lack of faith, had form on this issue, voting in 2006 for Christian zealot Tony Blair's failed attempt to introduce a law that would have criminalised 'insulting religion'. How it is possible to insult an idea? How can it be a criminal offence to insult either the ideas or the person of someone who died thirteen hundred years ago? Under UK law, only the living can be libelled, defamed or slandered. An attempt to change this law was rejected in the House of Commons in 2012. Justice Minister Jonathen Djanogly ruled that 'a case for damage can only be brought by the person who has suffered the injury, loss or, in this case, damage to his or reputation.' To provide for the protection of the reputation of the dead, in the case under our consideration, that of the prophet Mohammed, would therefore constitute one more concession by our legislators to Sharia law. Perhaps as a sign of worse things to come, at a Labour Party pre-election rally in Birmingham on May 2, 2015, the audience was segregated by gender, with a photo clearly showing women sitting to the left as they faced the platform, and men to the right. Yet when the news first broke of university student meetings being similarly segregated by gender if addressed by Muslim speakers, the Labour Party promised that if elected, it would ensure that this practice would be outlawed. Justifying the segregation at its own meeting, a Labour Party spokesman ingenuously claimed that men and women were being treated as equals, because 'everyone was together in the same room'...just as they were at the gender segregated university meetings the Labour Party promised to outlaw. So here we had the Labour Party abiding by Sharia law even before it was elected.

29 Lunacy

As we have already seen, zeal in assuaging what are assumed to be Muslim sensitivities can be carried so far that can they embarrass and, as in this case, bemuse those whom it is intended to protect. The following exercise in what might be described as multi-cultural astronomy was conducted at North Primary School in Southall, West London, an area of dense mixed Asian settlement. On the morning of Friday, March 20, 2015, pupils were eagerly looking forward to viewing a partial eclipse of the sun, due to take place at around 9.30 A.M. Then, at the very last moment, the school's Headmaster announced to the school that all children had to remain indoors. There would be no viewing of the eclipse after all. Puzzled and angry parents obviously wanted to know why. One, Phil Belman, was furious: 'My child went in having spent an hour preparing and making up her pinhole camera. This is an issue about science matters versus religion. I am outraged - is it going to be Darwin next?' Muslim parents were no less perplexed by the ban. One said, 'I am Muslim myself and my religion does not say we can't watch it'. Without wishing to be churlish, would he still allow his child to watch an eclipse if it did? A statement by the school Head, Ivor Johnstone confirmed that there were indeed religious reasons for the ban: 'The school made this decision when we became aware of religious and cultural concerns associated with observing an eclipse directly.' When asked by parents to provide more details as to the reasons for the ban, Johnstone explained that issues relating to 'confidentiality' prevented him from doing so. Again, one asks, could you make this up?

Perhaps Mr Belman had good reason to be concerned. Whatever Islam might have to say about eclipses, there are no doubts as to its attitude towards teaching the Holocaust and evolution. Although, despite attempts by Muslim mayhem and murder to force its observance on non-Muslims, it is still not a criminal offence to reproduce nature in the non-Islamic world, the first unofficial steps in that direction have been taken on at least two occasions, in of all places, Italy, the home of the Renaissance. When the Saudi Crown Prince Mohammed bin Zayed bin Sultan al-Nahyan visited Florence in October 2015, possibly to save his blushes but more likely to avoid jeopardising a trade deal, a cordon was placed around a nude statue by the US artist Jeff Koons. With more trade deals in the offing, following the ending of sanctions on Iran, identical steps were taken to enforce the Sharia when Iranian President Hassan Rouhani visited Rome in January 2016. Wine was removed from the menu at all official functions, and without it even being requested, all nude statues that his eyes might alight upon were covered with large white panels, giving a new twist to a venerable old saying: When Muslim potentates visit Rome, do as Muslims do'. Outraged Italians denounced the submission to Sharia law as 'cultural suicide'.

There are, however concessions to Islam that by virtue of its history, culture and constitution, at least one country is unable to make, however much its leaders might wish to. When President Rouhani's tour of European capitals took him to Paris, he was invited to have lunch with President Hollande at an upmarket restaurant. No French meal is complete without a glass or two of wine, and this one was intended to be no exception. As a strict Muslim, the Iranian President felt obliged to decline the invitation unless wine was removed from the menu, and only halal meat served, not just for himself, but for everyone. If he expected the same deference to Sharia law from his French hosts that he was accorded in Rome, he was rudely disabused. Rather than concede to his demands, Hollande cancelled the invitation. French officials later explained that an 'Iran (sic) friendly' meal violated French republican, in this instance, secular principles. *Vive du Vin, Vive la France!*

Islam, as we seen in the cases we have cited, has proved time and again how, even when playing away from home so to speak, and consequently constrained by laws not of its own making, with a little help from its friends, it has managed to secure for itself a preferential treatment never accorded to any other religion in the UK in modern times. However, on its home ground, Clegg's religion of 'love and peace' is not obliged to wear its mask of what passes for 'moderation'. There, Islam can reveal its true nature. President Obama would have the world believe that 'Islam has a proud tradition of tolerance', so let us see how this plays out, so to speak, in the Islamic cesspit that goes by the name of Pakistan. This wretched and benighted apology for a nation has provided many obscene examples of how its Sunni Muslims prefer to conduct their dealings not only with other faiths but other versions of their own when they have the whip hand. Leaving aside the usually well-reported instances of Christian church burnings and the butchering of non-Sunni Muslims, let us instead focus on a largely unreported feature of how Islamic toleration goes about upholding its 'proud tradition'. Of all the many horrific cases where individuals or single families rather than buildings or congregations have been targeted, among the worst must surely be the burning alive, in a village near Lahore on November 12, 2014, of a Christian couple falsely accused...as always...of desecrating a *Koran*. A 'call to murder' from the local mosque rounded up a raging mob of more than a thousand pious savages. The couple were seized, had their legs broken to prevent their escape and were then hurled into the flames of the kiln where they both worked as indentured labourers, little better than slaves. As the couple burned, the mob, now in a state of religious ecstasy, chanted 'Allah is great' and 'kill the infidel Christians'. Thus was Allah duly avenged. No one was punished.

This is how the religion of peace, toleration and love conducts the charade of inter-faith dialogue in the UK's fellow Commonwealth member and ally Pakistan. Burning alive in Pakistan is not just a punishment reserved for non-Muslims. In the spring of 2016, two young Muslim women were burned alive by fellow villagers after running afoul of the local Islamic court, the *Jirga*. The first occurred in April in the village of Makol where, after a ruling by the court that she had violated her family's, that is, her male relatives' 'honour', with the approval of her mother she was locked in a Suzuki van which was then set alight. The second burning took place on May 31 in the village of Muree. A young female school teacher refused to marry the school's owner, so, again after a ruling by the *Jirga,* a mob, led by the jilted groom, burst into her home, beat up her up, dowsed her with petrol, threw her into a ditch and burned her alive. Such atrocities are routine affairs in the land specially created for the practise of the Religion of Peace and Love. The reader will surely have learned by now that these outrages will not have been the occasion for protests outside the Pakistan High Commission in London by our Sharia feminists. They long ago learned not to pay any heed to what the *Guardian's* Laurie Penny called 'horror stories' of Muslim male abuse of women. Like the good internationalists they are, they understand that the battle is here at home, against the 'white male patriarchy', the glass ceiling in the boardroom and, of course, Islamophobia.

ISIS, then the 'Islamic State', the 'Caliphate', had its own way of conducting debates about the finer points of Islamic theology. The Caliphate's speciality was its staging of videoed mass executions, live burials, burnings alive, beheadings and crucifixions of fellow Muslims, Christians or indeed anyone who they deem to be deviating in any way from the path of Allah. This carnage is of course nothing new in the blood-drenched history of Islam. What is novel is the use of infidel technology to enable the world to witness its latest phase on its television and computer screens and, by so doing, win more admiring Muslim recruits, female as well as male, to its cause. One such production begins with an ISIS road block forcing three trucks to stop. At gun point, the drivers are made to leave their cabs and sit down at the roadside. Suspected of being Alawite Shi'as, they are subjected to a theological quiz. The three truck drivers realise that they are doomed if they give one 'wrong' answer. The questioning continues at gun point until, inevitably, this happens. One of the drivers, asked how many times he should pray at a certain time of the day, gives the 'wrong' reply, even though there is nothing in the *Koran* about the rules for prayer, any more than is about the 'Five Pillars of Islam'. All three are duly condemned as 'polytheists' and shot. And ISIS is not Islamic? Another promotional video displays a Christian on his knees, surrounded by brave armed masked Muslims. He is told if he converts to Islam, his life will be spared. Then follows the 'conversion', again dictated at gun point. Finally, a masked Muslim grabs his head from the rear, and cuts off his head, *Koran*-fashion, 'above the throat' with a long knife, to the obligatory wild cries of 'God is great'. This is how Allah's warriors conduct their dialogue with Christians in the ISIS Caliphate. And again, Christian leaders, with rare exceptions, are silent.

In Kenya, it is the same. Following the success of their massacre, on September 21, 2013, of Christians at the Nairobi Westgate shopping complex, which left 67 dead and 175 wounded, on April 2, 2015, four al Shabaab Jihadis believed they had booked their passage to paradise when, to the obligatory cries of 'God is Great', they staged an identical slaughter at the University of Garissa, freeing Muslim students and then killing in cold blood 148 Christians and wounding another 79. And once again, in its wake politicians were reassuring us that just like all others, this atrocity had nothing to do with Islam. It could only have been by sheer chance that just Christians were murdered and all Muslims escaped unscathed. No one who understands the nature and workings of Islam would expect these atrocious crimes to be sincerely condemned by Islamic clerics in the UK or anywhere else. In the case of the Pakistan murders they had, after all, been organised from a Mosque, and desecrating the *Koran* is undeniably a capital offence.

Legally and by tradition, Britain is still a Christian country. That being so, one would expect its Christian clergy to use all its many resources and ready access to the media to denounce the perpetrators of these terrible crimes. 26 Bishops (unelected of course) sit as of right in the House of Lords...the ideal tribune, one would have thought, from which to denounce the sub-human bestialities of Muslim Christian killers. But no. Like the Sharia left, where the atrocities of Islam are concerned, they prefer to hear nothing, see nothing...and say nothing. Their concerns are far closer to home, namely the preservation of their power, privileges and incomes. When almost daily headlines of atrocities compel clergy to address the problem of how to respond to the onslaught on Christians sweeping through the Islamic world and even beyond, as in Kenya, the best they can do is to offer prayers for its victims, praise their martyrdom and, in the words of Justin Welby,

Archbishop of Canterbury, advise that 'Christians must resist without violence the persecution they suffer'. Not 'should, but, 'must'. Presumably, this injunction, being not a human law but that of God, applies in all such situations where the innocent are being persecuted and murdered by the guilty. This being so, Welby and the rest of his crew of clerical quislings, singing the praises of Christian martyrdom from the comfort of their security- proof palaces and Cathedrals, would presumably have given the same advice to those Jews who, faced with certain death in the gas chambers of the Third Reich, sinned by rising against and killing their SS guards to escape from the Sobibor extermination camp in 1943.

The Christian clergy's response to the Islamic onslaught on their own faith is in all probability derived from the pacifist homily given by Jesus in Mathew: 'Whosoever shall smite thee on thy right cheek, turn to him the other also.' (6: 39) Has it never occurred to Christian clergy that there is no Islamic instruction to the same effect? However, with the Bible being such an arbitrarily assembled concoction of myths, legends and doctrinal contradictions, it is only to be expected that also in Mathew, Chapter Ten Verse 34, we have the response that Jihadis out for the blood of Christians deserve but our gutless politicians and clergy refuse to give: 'Think not that I come to send peace on earth: I come not to send peace, but a sword.' Where is our sword?

Another feature of the Christian clergy's response to Islamic persecution is that in deference to Islamic sensitivities, just as with the UK Muslim rape gangs, the religious identity of the perpetrators is rarely if ever specified. After listing some of the countries where Christians were being killed by Muslims in their thousands for their faith, and offering prayers for their departed souls, neither Welby nor the Pope in their Easter Messages of 2015 dared mention the identity of their murderers. Not even after the slaying of a French Catholic priest at his altar could the Pope bring himself to even allude to the religion of his assassins, preferring instead to speak of his 'pain and horror' at an 'absurd murder' that had been motivated, not by religion, since 'all religions want peace', (especially one that preaches Jihad) but by 'interests, money, resources', though there was no evidence that the two assassins had raided the Church's collection box or purloined any of its artefacts.

The Pope should not have made the mistake of assuming that the motives of Jihadis are the same as those of his own church, which for all its talk of spirituality, owe more to the stock exchange than the Sermon on the Mount. And yet it is so obvious that the sole objective of the killers was religious. Why else target a priest? The best the Pope could offer as an alternative explanation for the Jihadi onslaught on Europe was a tautology in the finest traditions of medieval scholasticism: 'The world is at war because it has lost peace'. He could just as easily have said, and to just as little effect, 'the world has lost peace because it is at war.' These were the pearls of wisdom spoken by god's chosen representative on planet earth. Three days later, Pope Francis visited Auschwitz, where he wrote in the visitors book a plea for god to 'forgive so much cruelty'. Instead of asking his god to forgive his fellow Catholic Hitler and his accomplices (many of them also Catholics, including Himmler) for murdering six million Jews, the Pope would have been better advised to confess that he is the head of a church that far more any other institution is responsible in the first place for the creation and propagation of anti-semitism, without which there could have been no Holocaust of the Jews; secondly for failing to publicly protest against the crimes Pius XII knew were being committed by the

Nazis and, finally, spiriting away in their thousands to South America and the Middle East those who shared responsibility for them.

30 Exodus

In the light of humanity's indebtedness to them for their unparalleled contributions to human progress, if ever a people deserved a break after nearly two thousand years of persecution and worse, it is the Jews. And, until the rise of anti-Israeli Jihadism in the Middle East, it seemed that even if rather grudgingly, they were getting one. The western reaction to the Gaza conflict has, to its shame, proved this assumption to be unduly optimistic. All over the world, public opinion researchers are finding firm evidence that the Jews are once again being depicted and seen in a totally negative light, and on a depressingly large scale. The talk is only of 'Israel's crimes', not of the crimes committed against the Jews by enemies who seek their annihilation. And it is not only attitudes that are changing. After attacks by anti-Semitic mobs, European synagogues are being converted into barricaded fortresses. Some are also under 24-hour armed police and even army protection. Some politicians, instead of showing a little civic courage by denouncing those responsible for these extraordinary measures, find it easier to blame the Jews whom, they claim, have invited such attacks by their supposed sympathies for Israel, while there is understanding and approval for terrorist, anti-Semitic Hamas and Hezbollah and even ISIS.

Who would have believed, on the eve of the outbreak of the Gaza conflict in the summer of 2014, that within months Jews, secular as well as religious, would be quitting Europe in droves to settle in Israel where, in the light of such threats and attacks, they rightly feel they will be more secure? 7,000 French Jews made this decision in 2014 and 10,000 more were expected to migrate in 2015. By the end of 2018, the total leaving since 2000 had reached *55,000*. Who too who have believed that in the wake of the Paris massacres of January 7-8, 2015, the French army would be mobilised on a scale not seen since the Second World War to protect Jewish schools and synagogues from attacks by anti-Semitic Muslims? And this is just France! Why do Jews who for decades have felt secure and settled in their European diaspora now suddenly feel isolated and vulnerable? The gentile generations around them that can remember the Holocaust and the trials of those that perpetrated it are either growing old like myself or dying out, taking with them the memory, and the compassion that it engenders, of the unparalleled sufferings of the European Jews under Nazi rule.

Today, in politics and the media, and among the public as whole, we have generations of whom for many the Holocaust is at best one dimly remembered topic amongst many on a school history syllabus, (unless, as has been the case both in the UK and on the continent, it has been removed after complaints by Muslim parents) or possibly a theme in a film or televised documentary. And as we have seen, for others, usually but not always Muslims, it is an event, possibly exaggerated, invented or even facilitated by Jews and certainly exploited by them to win support for the aims of Zionism. Far more vivid in the public mind are today's images and reports of what many genuinely believe to be Israel's war crimes against the Palestinians. So much so, that for many, and as we have seen, surveys bear this out, the words Holocaust and genocide now no longer describe what the Nazis did to the Jews, but with increasing frequency, as it does for Labour Leader Corbyn and his cultic followers, what the Jews are allegedly doing to the Palestinians. It is not too hard to understand what is feeding this obscene animus against the Jews. For centuries, lacking a country of their own, and until the French Revolution heralded their emancipation, also denied equality under the laws of their hosts, the Jews could be and were persecuted, insulted, plundered, slandered and even killed with impunity. The Jews were always seen as fair game, an alien people who dared not and could not fight back as others did when suffering similar injustices. But no more. With the birth of the state of Israel in 1948, all that changed. Now Jews, if they chose to live in Israel, could enjoy at last the freedoms and security that the world had denied them for so long, and then as a final infamy, had passively witnessed, and in some cases subsequently even denied, the Nazi Holocaust.

As Israel, from the first day of its existence, came under attack from its Arab neighbours, the world saw the emergence of a new kind of Jew, despised no less than the old, but for opposite reasons. The diaspora Jew had been scorned for his alleged cowardice, who went like a lamb to the Holocaust slaughter, a passive, submissive, almost willing victim of genocide. Only those who know nothing of the Warsaw Ghetto uprising of 1943, when its Jews took on the might of the SS and German army, the mass rebellion and escape from the Sobibor death camp later the same year, and the uprising, again in 1943, at the Treblinka death camp, can believe such slanders against an entire people. Even then, in the face of hopeless odds, when not only the Poles, their minds poisoned by centuries of Roman Catholic anti-Semitism, but also the Allies, watched and did nothing, there were Jews who were prepared to fight to the death rather than tamely submit to those who sought their extermination. The Israeli Jew is pilloried today because, having learned the lesson from the Holocaust that he is essentially on his own, he is ready and able to defend himself from his genocidal enemies. He can and does fight back, because at last he has a country that provides him with the means and the will to do so. That is the purpose and the meaning of Zionism, that the Jews should have a state like any other, with rights and obligations like any other. Anyone who says they are not ant-Semitic, but only anti-Zionist, as so many on the Left now do, is also saying that alone among all the peoples of the world, the Jews have no right to a homeland of their own, one in which they have lived for three millennia. The waves of anti-Semitism sweeping through the world today show that for the most part, humanity is not ready to grant this perfectly reasonable request. It is as if the Jews, once persecuted because of their perceived 'otherness', are now, as Israelis, to be condemned for wanting to be like everyone else.

Down the ages, anti-Semitism has been the fool's gold of those who believe that all their own, and maybe even the world's problems, can be solved by persecuting or even eliminating entirely the Jews. Incredibly, in the second decade of the twenty first century, there are millions who still cling to this delusion. Bebel's 'socialism of fools', despite its utter failure throughout history to bring any lasting benefits to those who have succumbed to its seductions, still casts spell. Even the annihilation of Nazi Germany, followed by the repeated failures of vastly larger Arab armies than Israel's, and now Jihadi terrorism, to 'wipe off the map' the Jewish state, seem not to have convinced millions of Muslims that anti-Semitism sooner or later leads to the humiliation and self-destruction of those who embrace and practice it.

With Jews quitting Europe for Israel in their tens of thousands, we are witnessing the most shameful moment in the West's history since Allied politicians refused to lift a finger to save the Jews from the Nazi Holocaust when, deferring to the anti-Semitism of the Arabs, Western leaders denied all but a handful of those fleeing the Nazi terror passage to what was to become Israel, at the same time as government officials dismissed as 'horror stories' (again) and 'sob stuff' put about by 'wailing Jews' a series of authenticated reports of the death agony of European Jewry. Justifying his policy, one designed to appease the anti-Semitism of Arab leaders in the British Mandate, Foreign Secretary Anthony Eden argued 'it would be more merciful [sic] to turn these ships back', which elicited the comment from his private Secretary Oliver Harvey that 'unfortunately A.E. is unmovable on the subject of Palestine. He loves Arabs and hates Jews.' *Plus la change*...More than two years after it had begun, the first British press report of the true scale of the Holocaust appeared, tucked away in the bottom left hand corner of the front page of *The People* of October 17, 1943. Its sixty words, entitled 'Hitler Murdered Three Million Jews in Europe', were allocated less space than an advertisement for the cleaner Mirro on the same page. Though within range of Allied bombers, Allied politicians and military officials repeatedly rejected desperate pleas by Jewish leaders and organisations to bomb the infrastructure of Hitler's extermination industry on the grounds that it would be a diversion of resources from the war effort, even though Auschwitz supplied Jewish slave labour for a nearby Krupp armaments factory, an AEG electricity generating plant and a vast IG Farben synthetic rubber complex, each of which were bombed.

Today, a second, but this time unimpeded exodus is underway, as tens of thousands of Jews quit a Europe whose politicians have done next to nothing to protect them from in some cases, the lethal consequences of Neo-Nazi and Islamic anti-Semitism, while the Corbyns add more fuel to the fire from the left with their lying, obsessional campaigning against the state of Israel. 24-7, day after day, year after year, and now decade after decade, it is Israel, Israel, Israel and only Israel. No other state in the world, whatever it has done in the past or does now, is subjected to the same scrutiny, or attracts remotely the same degree of venom as Israel. No other government, no matter how many crimes it commits, is compared with that of Nazi Germany, only Israel's. And those who do so took to the streets in their thousands to oppose the removal from power of the one regime that more than any other, deserved such a comparison, that of the genocidist Saddam Hussein. No state or political movement, of whatever complexion, demands that any state other than Israel should cease to exist, not even those that have come into existence by the near-extinction of their native populations, such as was the case with all the New World states and those of Australia and New Zealand. For all the mindless anti-Americanism that prevails today, not even the far left demands that the United States should be 'wiped off the map' because it once (like Islam) practised slavery, and to this day is criticised, despite its twice electing a black President, for its vestigial racism, or demanded that apartheid South Africa had no right to exist.

Of all the world's 193 states, scores of them guilty of human rights abuses immeasurably worse than any allegedly committed by Israel, only that of the Jews is repeatedly targeted by these very same states with demands that it be expelled from the United Nations and its various associated agencies. Yet no state or political movement demands this of North Korea or China, or Iran, Saudi Arabia, Yemen, Sudan, or any other of the 56 Islamic hell holes that in Cairo in 1990, publicly repudiated the UN Charter of Universal Hunan Rights. There are currently around 170 territorial disputes in the world, but the media only takes an interest in the one that uniquely does not involve two sovereign states, and where the disputed territories do not belong to anyone. There is no BDS for any of the countries that rule the 17 'Non-Self-Governing Territories' listed by the United Nations. But there is one, the only one, for a country that because it does not claim sovereignty over the West Bank, is not on that list. While Social Justice Warriors demand restitution and even privileges for wrongs committed in centuries past, the Jewish response to a genocide committed in living memory is denounced as a 'colonial enterprise'.

Nobody, not even the Jews, argues that Germany should not exist on account of the Holocaust, or Turkey because of its Islamic genocide of the Christian Armenians, or Russia because of Stalin's deportation of a dozen or more minorities during the Second World War, the slaughter of the Chechen and Afghan Muslims and Putin's annexation of the Crimea, ethnic cleansing in South Ossetia and proxy war against the Ukraine; or Serbia on account of its ethnic cleansing of Bosnian and Kosovo Muslims and Croatian Roman Catholics (denied incidentally by Corbyn in the House of Commons), or questions the legitimacy of the more than a score of states in Africa and the Middle East conjured into existence by boundaries arbitrarily drawn on a map by western colonial powers. No one accuses the millions of descendants of Irish migrants scattered around the world of disloyalty to their host country when they celebrate St Patrick's Day or, in the time of the 'troubles', supported, sometimes quite actively, the violent Republican campaign to evict the British from the Six Counties and in the USA, lobbied politicians to the same end. And when Muslims from all over the world who, unlike the Irish diaspora's links with Ireland, have in most cases no connection whatsoever with Palestinians except a shared religion (and not all Palestinians are Muslims), place their loyalty to the anti-Zionist cause above any to the country of their domicile, this is also regarded, and not just by Muslims, as perfectly understandable, and by the Sharia left as laudable. Certainly, there is no talk of a 'world Islamic conspiracy', even though Islam's aim, despite its being described by the gullible and the mendacious, as a religion of peace, is indeed avowedly world conquest. But in the case of diaspora Jews and despite their far from uniform attitude to Israel, here as in so many other respects, different rules apply, ones that never seem to work in their favour, so deeply is Jew-hatred woven into the fabric of Islamic and western cultures.

There was a time when all Jews were, according to Christian teaching derived from Biblical accounts of the crucifixion, judged to be collectively guilty for the death of Jesus, a guilt that could only be purged, and the persecutions that accompanied it ended, by conversion to Christianity. Herein lies the original source of all western anti-Semitism, including that of the largely atheist Sharia left, even if the guilt of the Jews has now in the West largely assumed a secular guise in the form of Zionism. For once again Jews are being indiscriminately accused of a collective crime, this time for a mythical genocide of the Palestinians. And once again, this sin can only be purged, and the targeting, harassment and even murder that accompanies it ended, by conversion to anti-Zionism, to an acceptance that of all the peoples of the world, only the Jews have no right to nationhood. It is for this reason that anti-Zionism, which rests on this claim, can so easily serve as a vehicle and cover for anti-Semitism, as it indeed does for the likes of Livingstone, Corbyn, Galloway and the organised Sharia left. The theologically rooted anti-Semitic prejudice and discrimination which was once the lot of the diaspora Jew, and which always contained and often exhibited the potential for something far worse, has mutated into an anti-Zionism that criminalises not only the Jews of Israel, but, through 'guilt by Semitic association', Jews everywhere.

To conclude where we began. Bubbling up from the sewers, onto our streets and now permeating and polluting the organised left, the plague is once again amongst us, and spreading fast, especially in circles that were once supposedly immune to infection. The Islamic war against the Jews, and the endorsement it has received in the West, has forged a new anti-semitic popular front. In this war against Israel - for it is a war – Stalinists, feminists, gay liberationists, academics, Greens, liberals, self-proclaimed anti-fascists, *soi-disant* followers of three Jewish atheists, Karl Marx, Rosa Luxemburg and Leon Trotsky, have combined their forces with those of avowed Nazis and Jew-hating, misogynistic, homophobic, arch-reactionary Muslims, all united, whether they admit or not, by a common loathing, not just for Israel and Zionism, but for Jews. All Jews. For reasons that this book has attempted to explore, and I hope least go some way to explaining, Israel today is manning the front line against an assault that is directed not only against the Jews but the entirety of western civilisation. Does the Left want Pastor Niemoeller's admonition to read, 'First they came for the Jews, and the socialists stabbed them in the back'?

Addendum

I referred earlier to a proposal made at the United Nations to criminalise the citing of certain Islamic texts by non-Muslims. In October 2018, the European Court of Human Rights (sic) made a ruling that in effect did just that. In 2011, an Austrian court convicted a woman academic, identified only as E.S., of 'disparaging religious doctrines' for saying in two public seminars in 2009 that Mohammed's last marriage to Aisha when she was six, and consummating the marriage when she was nine, was akin to paedophilia. The Court of Human Rights did not contest the truthfulness of the evidence on which her comments were based, which were derived from universally accepted Islamic sources, but instead chose to uphold the Austrian court's judgment after it has 'carefully balanced her right of freedom of expression with the right of others to have their religious feelings protected.' What this ruling means is that saying something about Islam which is factually true, when weighed against the alleged 'feelings' of Muslims, can constitute a criminal offence, and that based on the precedent of this judgment, all future appeals to the court concerning similar cases by any of the 47 countries subject to its jurisdiction could result in the same ruling. Germany went even further down the road of appeasing Islam when in December 2018 its Supreme Court upheld (for Muslims only) the legality of child marriage, those registered totalling 1,475, of which 361 were to girls under the age of 13. However, Sharia law was first enforced in Germany as long ago as 2007, when a woman judge, Christa Datz-Winter, dismissed a divorce case brought by a Muslim wife on the grounds of wife-beating, (correctly) citing that it is sanctioned by Chapter 4, Verse 34 of the *Koran*.

Afterword

You Are My Sunshine

The election on September 2015 of Jeremy Corbyn as leader of the Labour Party with 59% of first preference votes cast should have come as no surprise to those who are familiar with the ways of the far left. As I have argued in the main body of this work, given a favourable conjuncture of events and forces, and the incompetence and cowardice of its opponents, the far left can exert an influence out of all proportion to its numerical strength. Emulating their Bolshevik exemplars in their capture of the Russian Soviets in 1917, albeit on a far more modest scale and with less disastrous consequences, they have time and again proved themselves past masters in the art of subverting and then manipulating the machinery of organisations and institutions created by others for other purposes. Corbyn, who until the summer of 2015 was deservedly largely unknown to the general public and even to most Labour voters, bumbled onto the political scene not because he possessed any great political acumen or charisma, but because, as much to his own surprise as anyone else's, he found himself serving as the fulcrum of three largely disparate movements with which he had shared an involvement. Of the first two, one is quite recent, comprising largely young anti-austerity activists; the other consisting of residual and recently revived 'Old Labour' leftists. Though generationally distinct, both had been concerned mainly with domestic economic and social issues. The third is the anti-Zionist movement, an amalgam of the Sharia left and Muslim pressure groups, whose emergence and convergence dates back to 9/11 and the Iraq War of 2003. The two entirely distinct policy concerns cannot be easily reconciled. Corbyn's Jihadi 'friends', whose Hamas Charter claims that socialism is an invention of the World Jewish Conspiracy, are no more concerned with the parlous state of the UK's National Health Service than the patients in its under-funded hospitals are in the destruction of the state of Israel.

Corbyn's election and then, a year later, re-election with a larger majority, were all the more remarkable in that none of the many well-publicised revelations concerning his numerous and long-standing associations and joint activities with Muslim Jihadis, Islamic theocrats and despots, Irish terrorists, Latin American *caudillos*, Jewish conspiracy theorists and Holocaust deniers had worked to his disadvantage amongst those who cast their votes for him. If anything, it may have operated in the opposite direction. In the Middle East however, his election received, to put it mildly, a mixed reception. Correctly describing Corbyn as a 'leftist MP who has empathised with Hezbollah and Hamas', the *Israeli Times* reported that 'British Jews were alarmed by his ties to Holocaust deniers, terrorists and some outright anti-Semites'. For exactly these same reasons, the *Al-Risalah* Hamas website hailed the new Labour Leader as 'one of the most prominent British figures who voiced solidarity with the Palestinian cause and declared his rejection of the Gaza war'. (but not the rocket attacks, tunnelling and murder of three Jews that provoked it.) A year later, it was revealed that during the course of Corbyn's campaign for the Labour Party leadership he had been sent a cheque for £10,000 by Friends of Al-Aqsa, an organisation whose leader, Ismail Patel, was known to be in sympathy with Hamas. Corbyn's former Iranian employers, the executioners of

Kurds, gays, feminists, leftists, poets, trade unionists and secularists, were likewise predictably delighted with their useful idiot's election victory, with a regime spokesman laughably describing him, with no apparent intended irony, as a 'lifelong peace and human rights activist'. This from the theocracy that rejects the very concept of human rights and promises to 'wipe Israel off the map', and about a 'peace activist' who counts anti-Semitic terrorists among his 'friends' and devises pretexts for President Putin's bellicose and expansionist foreign policy. Syed Salman Safavi, a political adviser to Iran's Supreme Leader Ayatollah Khamenei, praised Corbyn for his opposition to NATO and his insistence that to 'ensure security [sic] in the Middle East, Hezbollah, Hamas and Iran need to participate in the dialogue [sic] and in the exchange of views.'

Quite aside from his anti-Zionism, it was only to be expected that Corbyn's general anti-western stance should earn him plaudits in Moscow. Putin's Ambassador to the UK, Alexander Yakovenko, praised the newly elected Labour leader for his 'opposition to military interventions of the west [those of the Kremlin are another matter entirely], support for the UK's nuclear disarmament [though not Russia's, with its 7,500 nuclear warheads, the world's largest nuclear arsenal compared with the UK's 215] and conviction [shared by US President Donald Trump] that NATO has outstayed its *raison d'etre.'* (Russia's' military budget expanded by 59% between 2012 and 2015)

Shortly after his election Corbyn attended a state banquet at Buckingham Palace for the visiting Chinese President Xi Jinping where, according to the Guangdong Province-based *South Metropolis Daily,* they had a 'cordial and constructive encounter'. (In 2019, he declined a similar invitation when Trump was the guest, only to then to request a private meeting, which Trump turned down.) This was standard protocol for such meetings and tells us nothing. A little more informative was the comment by an academic at the Shanghai International Studies University, who ventured the thought that the Chinese President's interest in the Labour leader could have been aroused by his belief that 'Corbyn's ideas about socialism and the working class are similar to the ideology of our country's ruling party.' Support for this supposition was leant credibility when, in the debate on his Tory opposite number's Autumn Statement, Corbyn's Shadow Chancellor John McDonnell quoted from Chairman Mao's Little Red Book on how to conduct economic policy. Perhaps McDonnell was unaware that in Mao's 'Great Leap Forward' of 1958, the Great Helmsman ordered his serfs to neglect their farms and instead devote their energies to producing in 'people's communes' what inevitably proved to be useless steel to accelerate, Stalin fashion, China's industrialisation. The result was a Mao-made famine and 45 million deaths by starvation.

It is not only Mao's economic policies that appeal to McDonnell. Corbyn's Shadow Chancellor also revealed he has a hankering after the way the China's despot dealt with his political opponents in his so-called 'Cultural Revolution', when he described a Tory minister as 'a stain on humanity' and asked, 'why aren't we lynching this bastard?' Undoubtedly McDonnell has his own special take on Corbyn's 'kinder politics', at a London Momentum rally, deriding his leader's Parliamentary opponents as 'fucking hopeless', a term he afterwards justified as a 'normal political description'. At the same event, held to celebrate Corbyn's inclusion on the ballot in a new leadership contest, another speaker, perhaps, like McDonnell striving to establish his proletarian *bona fides,* bellowed 'Blair, fuck you', while a third called those MPs who resigned from Corbyn' shadow front bench team 'lying dishonest leaders with no values', begging the obvious question ...why had Corbyn appointed them in the first place?

All in all, Corbyn's inner team projected themselves as a pretty macho crew, an image very much in accord with their predilection for totalitarian methods of governance. Not only McDonnell seemed unable to contain his admiration for China's ultra-Stalinist mass murderer. Back in 2008, when Diane Abbott suggested on a TV political chat show that Mao 'on balance did better than harm', former Tory politician Michael Portillo challenged her to name 'the good things Mao did that made up for the sixty million people he murdered.' Unperturbed by the death tally, which she did not deny, Abbott stuck to her guns. Resorting to the Stalinist 'no omelettes without egg shells', she argued in Mao's defence that 'he led his [sic] country from feudalism, he helped to defeat the Japanese, and he left his [sic] country on the verge of the great economic success they are having now.' (The reader will recall that Noam Chomsky made a similar claim for the 'positive side' of the Pol Pot regime, just as Seumas Milne has for Stalin's and Neo-Nazis for Hitler's.) Ironically, the 'success' that China's new bourgeois elite are now enjoying has been achieved by jettisoning the disastrous policies pursued by Mao and recommended by McDonnell. Informed viewers must have been left wondering why the overcoming of feudalism, a system dominated by a tiny minority of wealthy landlords, the defeat of Japan, which involved the killing of Japanese soldiers not Chinese civilians, and economic growth, necessitated the premature deaths of around ten per cent of China's population.

Guardian journalist and Stalin apologist Seumas Milne was inducted into Corbyn's inner circle with the exalted title of 'Director of Strategy and Communications'. He shares his chief's admiration for Hamas, saluting to cheers at an anti-Israel rally its 'spirit of resistance' that 'will not be broken'. But not only for Hamas. In his own version of 'they had it coming', two days after 9/11, he wrote that al-Qaeda's nearly 3,000 civilian victims were 'reaping a dragon's teeth harvest they themselves [sic] sowed', while London's 7/7 was 'driven by world-wide anger at US-led domination and occupation of Muslim countries', the only surprise being that it was 'so long coming'. Milne did not take the trouble to explain why randomly selected airline passengers, New York office workers and London commuters had to be murdered in order to expiate the guilt of US policy makers. Stop the War Coalitionist Lindsey German whom, the reader will recall, in the interests of placating the homophobia and misogyny of the Sharia left's Muslim comrades, advocated the ditching the 'shibboleths' of gay and women's rights and approved gender segregation at public meetings, had a similar 'take' on the murder of a rabbi and three Jewish school children in Toulouse in March 2012. She began by seeming to agree that 'no one can justify these attacks'; only then to do just that: 'but [there is always a 'but'] the shootings in Toulouse are the terrible and disastrous outcome [not of Islamic anti-Semitism, as one might naively suppose, but] the West's war policies and anti-Muslim racism'. 'Our fault', again. When German delivered on the Coalition's official website this apologia for what was so clearly an atrocity fuelled purely by hatred of the Jews, Corbyn was Chairman of the organisation that published it.

Given Milne's predilection for the indiscriminate murder of civilians, it is no surprise at all that along with Mao, he also has a soft spot for Stalin, even though his death count is at least 20 million, a total Milne has claimed is 'wildly exaggerated' - just like the number of Jews murdered by the Nazis, say his Jihadi comrades. In what amounted to a Bolshevik version of Holocaust revisionism, Milne claimed that Stalin's regime was motivated by 'genuine idealism', and 'for all its brutalities [sic], communism in the USSR delivered rapid industrialisation, mass education and job security[sic]'. Yes, there is always plenty of work for slaves. What Milne calls 'genuine idealism' was responsible for three famines in which at least 15 million died and reduced countless others to cannibalism, and a reign of terror that sent millions to their deaths, either by shooting, or starvation and disease in Siberian and Arctic slave camps. As for 'rapid industrialisation', being geared almost totally to Stalin's military requirements, it reduced living standards for all but the Bolshevik elite to levels lower than they had been under the last of the tsars. Milne's apologia for Stalin is no different to those who used to say (perhaps they still do) that 'Hitler built the *Autobahn*, gave everyone a job, and won Germany back its self-respect.' Needless to say, Milne's estimation of Stalin is not shared by his most steadfast opponent, perceptive critic and illustrious victim. With numerous candidates to choose from, Trotsky described Stalin as 'one of the filthiest figures in history'. It is worthy of note that hack historians in Putin's Russia are currently hard at work rehabilitating Stalin precisely along the lines indicated by Milne. Yet for all his whitewashing of Stalin's crimes, Corbyn has praised Milne as 'a man of immense [sic] intellect and a scholar'. As to his Maoism, one fellow Oxford undergraduate recalls that 'he spent his entire time at Balliol wearing a Mao jacket and talking with a fake Palestinian accent. It was like a performance art, the sort of think Gilbert and George would do. He launched a string of motions in the Junior Common Room attacking Israel.'

Hard-core Corbynistas such as McDonnell, Murray, Livingstone, Milne and Abbott take in their stride indiscriminate terrorism and the deaths of millions for goals that invariably, whatever their claimed intrinsic worth, always require the suppression of democracy and individual freedom, and invariably inflict the greatest harm on those they purportedly are intended to benefit. For example, aside from swelling the bank accounts of arms dealers and providing a jet-set life style for professional Jew-baiters and the representatives of various terrorist movements, what benefits has anti-Zionism brought to the Arabs of the Middle East? But should Israel successfully, and with minimum force, defend itself in response to terrorist attacks, as it did in in the summer of 2014 after being bombarded by Hamas rockets, then the cry will go up of a Zionist genocide of the Palestinians, or, as Milne describes it, 'the killing of civilians by Israel on an industrial scale'. But when in October 2016, Putin intensified his killing of Syrians 'on an industrial scale' by bombing an aid convey trying to reach Aleppo, Milne claimed that condemning such actions 'diverted attention' from western military operations in the region, which of course Corbyn had repeatedly opposed.

When Labour MP Ann Clwyd proposed protest demonstrations outside the Russian embassy, Stop the War Coalition Deputy Chairman Chris Nineham in an interview on BBC Radio Four invoked what should be by now the familiar Chomsky principle: 'Our focus is on what our government is doing. If we demonstrate outside the Russian embassy, it wouldn't make a blind bit of difference to what Putin does, because we are in the west and we are Britain.' And this is called internationalism! Strange, because such geographical considerations have never prevented the Coalition from demonstrating outside the US and Israeli embassies. And for best part of a decade, Grosvenor Square was the scene of a succession of massive protests against the US military involvement in Vietnam. Nineham tortuously tried to explain why his Coalition had not and would not become involved in any anti-Putin protests, nor indeed against the actions, no matter how belligerent, of any non-western state or movement: 'We were set up as a coalition in response to 9/11 [which the SWP, its main initiators, defended] and in response to the Western, British-supported drive to war back in 2001, and that is our focus'. Nineham concluded his interview with a blunt assertion of Leninist defeatism, that to mobilise against the threat of a 'confrontation' between 'Russia and the Western powers, including Britain' means 'opposing the west', that is, to take the side of the west's enemies.

Corbyn, we will recall, was a founder and then Chairman of the avowedly anti-Western, pro-Jihadi Coalition from 2011 until his election as Leader of the Labour Party in September 2015. At no time during his high-profile involvement with the Coalition did he dissent from its founding principle, enunciated in 2006 by its National Officer, John Reece: 'Socialists should unconditionally stand with the oppressed against the oppressor, even if the people who run [sic] the oppressed country are undemocratic, and persecute minorities, *like Saddam Hussein'.*(emphasis added) How George Orwell would have loved that! In the name of 'standing with the oppressed' it is quite in order to support their oppressors, even a fascist dictator who waged a genocidal war to subjugate a rebellious 'minority', the Kurdish 'western pawns'. It is from this anti-western and more specifically, anti-Israeli (and anti-Jewish) political milieu that Corbyn emerged to become Leader of the Labour Party.

Some might be puzzled as to why Corbyn, a 'peace campaigner', had chosen to collaborate over the years with those who wage a war of terror war against Israel, and identify himself with regimes that use violence against not only against their own citizens, as in Syria, Nicaragua, Venezuela and Iran, but against those of other countries, as has Putin. They also might find strange what appears at first sight to be an inconsistency, given what he declares is his unequivocal commitment to world peace and human rights, namely his selection of a top team, prominent among whom are a number of vocal supporters of Islamic Jihadism, endorsers of Putin's expansionist foreign policy, and apologists for Maoist and Stalinist mass murder. And yet there is no mystery here. The already-discussed Chomsky principle, according to which the only legitimate target of protest and political action is one's own government, is self-evidently the one that guides Corbyn's foreign and in certain respects, such as defence, his domestic policies. It goes like this: Putin can bomb and assassinate whom he likes, Assad can massacre whom he likes, Jihadis can murder whom they like, the Ayatollahs can hang whom they like, Maduro can rig elections when he likes, the Islamic State can rape, behead, burn and torture whom it likes…they are not our enemies. Indeed, in as much as they help our struggle to undermine western imperialism, they are our allies, even if it is not opportune for a Leader of the Labour Party to say so openly. The enemy, western imperialism, is here, in London, and in Paris and Berlin, and above all in Washington and Jerusalem.

That is why I call Corbyn's 'peace campaigning' 'selective', because in essence, it is simply a mask for defeatism and in a state of war, potentially treasonous. It has significant antecedents. In the run- up to the Second World British pacifists, aristocrats and fascists called for an 'understanding' with Nazi Germany, while in the Cold War that followed it, Stalinist-controlled 'peace movements' specialised in enlisting naïve and dim-witted 'peace campaigners' of the Corbyn brand, who could then be easily prevailed upon, sometimes after a Potemkin visit to the USSR, and despite Russia having by far the largest military capability in the world, to say nice words about the Kremlin's peaceful intentions, while staging demonstrations at home demanding that the west disarm itself unilaterally. Corbyn, we will recall, has been a member CND since the age of 15, and more recently, served as its vice President and vice Chair. But this too was *deja vue*. Well into the Second World War, the Peace Pledge Union followed an identical policy, undergoing the most incredible contortions in condemning the Allied war against the Axis powers as immoral while at the same time, dismissing out of hand accounts of the horrors of Hitler's Reich as Allied war propaganda. George Orwell summed up the consequences of their stance rather well: 'Since pacifists have more freedom of action in countries where traces of democracy survive, pacifism can act more effectively against democracy than for it. Objectively, the pacifist is pro-Nazi.' And in the era of the Cold War, pro-Soviet and today, pro-Putin.

One of the mobilising forces behind the Corbyn throne is Momentum and its organiser James Schneider. Very free in his condemnation of what he calls 'comfortable elite liberals', Schneider is himself just that. The son of a shady multi-millionaire property tycoon, his irresistible ascent to Oxford, where he studied theology (sic), began with attendance at the elite Oxford Dragon Prep School, followed by spells at two no less exclusive and extremely expensive public, that is to say, private schools, Winchester and St Pauls. (Two other top Corbynista silver spoons, Milne and Murray, followed the same educational path leading from Winchester to Oxford) So much for Schneider's simulated contempt for the 'comfortable elite'. His liberalism (purely nominal, as his reputation for inciting Momentum thuggery suggests) flourished while at Oxford, when he became President of the university's Liberal Democratic Society, during the period when the party was in coalition with the Tories. Schneider voted Liberal Democrat at the 2015 General Election, but then, within a matter of weeks, re-surfaced as a born-again Corbynite, his previous total lack of any identification with left wing politics proving no obstacle to his subsequent meteoric rise as a high priest of the Corbynista cult. Such men are evidently born to rule. In this new persona, the theology graduate could be seen parading in public sporting a red T shirt emblazoned with the moto 'Jeremy Corbyn for Labour Leader', the all too familiar spectacle of a thoroughly spoilt upper class playboy savouring the limelight and notoriety that goes with Momentum's *épater la bourgeoise* style of politics.

Those most zealous in their devotion to (and in some cases, manipulation of) the Corbynista cult, are recruited from a new breed of leftist-posturing, self-righteous, self-promoting gilded youth, ever-ready to jump on any bandwagon that promises to inject the spice of notoriety into their hitherto jaded lives. Such were the highly-born activists of the ephemeral British wing of the US 'Black Lives Matter' campaign, one which had already been hijacked by the anti-Zionist left before it crossed the Atlantic. The main form of protest engaged in (briefly, before they got bored) by its UK chapter was to cause as much disruption as possible to the lives of ordinary people, for example by blocking access to airports in peak holiday periods. Those who tend to find conspiracies lurking around every political corner can on this occasion be forgiven for suspecting that preventing working class families bound for sunnier climes from catching their booked flight was calculated to repel and not attract support for black victims of police violence. But given the protestors social background, should we be surprised at such behaviour? Only those with a profound contempt for the 'masses' they fondly imagine they are destined to liberate could, without any moral qualms, indulge in such conduct. And sure enough, among the all-white black freedom fighters gracing the London magistrates court in September 2016 on charges of Aggravated Trespass at London's City Airport were the tripled-barrelled Natalie Geraldine Twistleton-Wyykeham-Fiennes, at 25, still living at her parents £2 million mansion off Clapham Common (occupation, baby-sitter); Esme Waldron, who describes herself as an 'expert on lesbian culture'; Alex Etchart, (occupation, 'youth empowerment' with a degree in 'ethnomusicology' and director of The Sex Workers' Opera); with only two barrels, Sam Lund-Market (occupation, University Environmental Officer) and Debora Francis-Grayson, at 31, still to complete her PhD in 'Media and Communications'. Such pedigree, in the normal run of things, would consign this parasitic crew to the deepest of the dungeons reserved for those cursed by their 'privilege' But like others of like provenance, they had at least been sufficiently street-wise to avoid this designation by nailing their family escutcheons to the mast of the latest fashionable noble cause. I can write the script. 'You say we are rich and white? True. But in our hearts, we are poor and black. And next week we will all be Muslim women, posing for the cameras in our burkas outside the French embassy.'

There is a profound irony in all this. Readers will no doubt recall that especially in recent years, the left has with some justice derided the Tory party as one dominated by 'toffs. As one might expect, the EU referendum battle was essentially one between two Bullingdon Club Tories, Cameron of Eaton and Oxford and Johnson, of Eaton and Oxford. But Labour's token pro-Remain campaign was effectively sabotaged by two champagne Corbynistas from the same top drawer, Seumas Milne of Winchester and Oxford and James Schneider of… Winchester and Oxford. And what of the credulous crank who is the UK's Prime Minister-in waiting? As befits one who throughout his Parliamentary career has shown himself to be incapable of consistent and serious thought about anything of note, Corbyn's main sources of political inspiration have been highly eclectic, ranging from Stalinism and third world dictators to Islamic theocracy and Jihadism. Earlier in his career, when Soviet-style communism still seemed a going concern, Corbyn began writing for the pro-Moscow *Morning Star*, successor to the Communist Party's *Daily Worker* and, together with Diane Abbott, explored on a motorbike the Kremlin's East German prison as a guest of Brezhnev's puppet jailer Erich Honeker. (This became one of a series of hilarious episodes in *Corbyn the Musical*) Then, with the breeching of the prison's wall and the ensuing spectacular collapse of the entire Soviet bloc, while retaining more than a residual loyalty to post-Soviet Russia, his strongest attachments shifted to any Latin American regime no matter how repressive that displayed the continent's traditional and often well-merited hostility towards the Great Satan in Washington.

Corbyn was not alone. In 2008, 69 MPs, 65 of them Labour, backed a Parliamentary motion which ignored Cuba's appalling human rights record (including torture) and instead applauded the Castro one-party dictatorship for its 'achievements'. Among those signing along with Corbyn were some of the usual suspects, including former Saddam stooge George Galloway of the Sharia 'Respect', and two of Corbyn's most loyal current shadow ministers, John McDonnell and once again, Diane Abbott. Inevitably, Castro's death in November 2016 found Corbyn heaping the usual effusions of praise on Latin America's last surviving dictator, the *Lider Maximo* having not only outlasted the military juntas in Chile, Brazil and Argentina but, like the Kim dynasty which has ruled the slave camp that is North Korea since 1945, ensured that all power remained in his family by abdicating in 2008 in favour of his younger brother Raúl without even the pretence of an election. He inherited a totalitarian regime that held more 200 political prisoners in its jails, allows only one party, permits no free trade unions and ensures that all the media speak with one voice. None of this troubled Comrade Corbyn, any more than it does the dictator-doting clique who comprise his core leadership team.

Hyperbole ran riot: 'Fidel Castro was a massive figure in the history of the whole planet [sic], ever since the revolution of 1959.' Perhaps peace campaigner and CND Vice-President Corbyn was alluding to those days in October 1962 when Castro brought the 'whole planet' to the verge of nuclear war between the USSR and the USA by agreeing to the stationing of Soviet missiles on Cuban territory…an act of sheer madness. And before elevating Castro to the pantheon, perhaps those mourning him needed reminding that his defiance of the USA not only won him the admiration of the left, but of General Franco, who together with the entire Spanish right, yearned to revenge Spain's defeat by the hated Yankees in the Cuban war of 1898 and more generally, for displacing Spain as the major power in Latin America. As for Castro, in his youth, he was an avid reader of the writings of Jose Antonio Primo de Rivera, the founder of Spanish fascism. So, it should hardly be cause for surprise that acting on the principle that the enemy of my enemy is my friend, from the outset, Castro and Franco were on the best of terms. Every January 1, the official anniversary of the seizure of power by the Castro movement, Franco would send a telegram of greetings to his Cuban counterpart, and, incomprehensible though this must seem to those for whom the Stalin-Hitler pact of 1939 is a closed book, Castro would return the compliment. When Castro's ambassador to Spain, Jose Miro Cardona, first presented himself to the *Caudillo,* at the end of the audience, Franco asked 'How is Fidel doing?' and then with some vehemence added, 'Tell Fidel to give hell to the Americans'. In return, the Franco regime defied pressure from Washington to support the US embargo on trade with Cuba and provided the only air link with western Europe, a solidarity that was publicly acknowledged when Castro declared three days of official mourning on the fascist dictator's death in November 1975, and by the Cuban Communist Party's daily paper, *Granma,* which carried on its front page the tragic news that 'Franco is Dead' and a tribute to the butcher who in the Spanish Civil War of 1936 to 1936, secured the aid of the Pope, Hitler and Mussolini to crush the Spanish left and establish a clerical fascist dictatorship. But no matter, because Castro is on record for praising Franco as 'honourable', a man of 'moral and political stature' for whom he had 'a certain admiration'. For his part, Franco described Castro as 'very intelligent' and 'a great strategist' who had brought Cuba 'needed change'.

Just as Franco defied the western boycott of Cuba, so Castro defied the western left's boycott of Franco Spain. Castro's overtly friendly relations with a regime that had marched to power over the corpses of hundreds of thousands of slaughtered leftists did not find favour with the Spanish government-in-exile, any more than it did with the underground leftist resistance in Spain. Neither did the Castro regime look kindly on the campaign to isolate and weaken the Franco regime when leftists advocated the boycott of Spanish tourism, a growing source of revenue for the country's investment-starved economy. Castro's one-time second in command, Che Guevara, evidently considered himself exempt from this policy, because he was caught on camera strolling round Madrid and at a bull fight, always accompanied by a bodyguard provided by Franco's red-hunting security service.

Also captured on camera, socialising with the Cuban Ambassador to the UK at a Cuba Solidarity trade union garden party in 2016, was 'special guest' Jeremy Corbyn, evidently unconcerned that like Franco Spain, there are no free trade unions, press or elections in one-party Cuba. Another 'special guest' in attendance was John McDonnell, currently Corbyn's Shadow Chancellor, one-time Deputy to GLC mayor Ken Livingstone, a former co-editor with Livingstone of the Gadhafi-funded *Labour Herald*, and as such, close associate of the soi-*disant* Trotskyist Gadhafi-funded Workers Revolutionary Party. He surely should have known that following his release from a Mexican jail in 1960 after serving 20 years for the assassination of Leon Trotsky, 'Hero of the Soviet Union' Ramon Mercader served Castro as his special adviser and Inspector-General of Cuba's prisons.

With the semi-retirement and then death of Castro, Corbyn's Latin exemplar became the Peronist-style President of Venezuela and ally of Putin and Iran, Hugo Chavez who, like Mao, in the name of progress specialised in visiting unprecedented poverty and misery on his people; no mean achievement in a country endowed with the world's largest oil reserves. Livingstone shares his long-standing collaborator's admiration for Chavez. In 2006, as Mayor of London, he hosted a special event held in Chavez's honour at the capital's City Hall. On Chavez's death in 2013, the future leader of the Labour Party posted a tribute to the architect of his nation's tragedy on his website: 'Thanks Hugo Chavez for showing that the poor matter and wealth can be shared. He made massive contributions to Venezuela and a very wide world'. His hero, who once famously declared that 'being rich is bad', certainly knew how to 'share the wealth', albeit unevenly. By plundering his regime's oil revenues, just like any other bent 'Third World' politician, he was able to make 'massive contributions' to those closest to him, in the first place his daughter and Ambassador to the United Nations, Maria Gabriela, to the tune of $4.2 billion, all of it of course invested in foreign banks, just in case. Even this immense sum, filched from a people whose poverty is among the worst in South America, was dwarfed by the $11.2 billion stashed away in a Swiss bank account by Chavez's Treasury (sic) Minister Alejandro Andrade. When, in the wake of the Panama tax haven scandal, Corbyn took to task those world figures who had been proven guilty of 'tax avoidance on an industrial scale', someone should have reminded him of what his Venezuelan kleptocratic comrades had been up to in the years of their misrule. At the time of the President's death, the Chavez clan between them owned 17 country estates covering more than 100,0000 acres and liquid assets of $550 million. Sharing the wealth indeed.

Corbyn's top adviser, 'Spin Doctor' Seumas Milne, waxed no less lyrical. Petro-Chavism had 'redistributed wealth [again!] and power, rejected western neo-liberal orthodoxy and challenged imperial domination'. However, even the effusions of Corbyn and Milne for Chavez were surpassed in their obsequiousness by 9/11 conspiracy film maker 'hug a Muslim' (but preferably not one wearing a suicide vest) Michael Moore: 'Hated by the entrenched classes Hugo Chavez will live forever in history. My friend [sic], rest finally in a peace long earned.' Corbyn has remained loyal to the Chavista cause in the years after its founder's death, no less indifferent to his successor's continued violations of human rights. Shortly after Corbyn addressed a London rally in June 2015 praising the Chavista regime for its 'achievements', Amnesty International issued a statement condemning its use of forced labour: 'A new decree establishing that any employee in Venezuela can effectively be made to work in the country's fields as a way to fight the current food crisis is unlawful and effectively amounts to forced labour.' Human Rights Watch issued the following indictment of the human rights abuses perpetrated by Corbyn's Venezuelan comrades:

> Under the leadership of President Hugo Chavez and now President Nicolas Maduro, the accumulation of power in the executive branch and erosion of human rights guarantees have enabled the government to intimidate, censor, and prosecute its critics, leading to increasing levels of self-censorship. Leading opposition politicians have been arbitrarily arrested, prosecuted and convicted, and barred from running for office. Police abuse, poor prison conditions, and impunity for security forces when they commit such abuses as arbitrary arrests, beatings, and denial of basis due process remain serious problems. Other concerns include lack of access to basic medicines and supplies - the result of problematic government policies - and continuous harassment of human rights defenders by government officials.

Another report contained descriptions of tortures that resemble those inflicted on opponents of the far-right regime of General Pinochet in Chile:

> Detainees testified in court they had suffered physical abuse that could amount to torture, including brutal beatings and electric shock and threats of rape [sic] or murder…Some detainees said they were tortured to coerce into confessing to crimes, and that SEBIN [the Bolivarian, i.e., Venezuelan National Intelligence Service] agents tape-recorded their confessions.

Always following to the letter the anti-Western policy of the Stop the War Coalition, which he helped found in 2001 and chaired between 2011 and 2015, Corbyn's support for any regime, however despotic and domestically unpopular, which pursues an anti-US agenda, taken together with his exemplary anti-Zionist track record on Israel, were clear enough evidence for the far left that Labour's new leader was one of their own. Leading the pack, as one would expect, were Corbyn's long-term collaborators in his various anti-Zionist enterprises, the Socialist Workers Party. In an official statement, the Party 'congratulated Jeremy Corbyn on becoming Labour Party leader', and 'looked forward to continue [sic] to work with [him] and his supporters' in the future. The *Guardian* was if anything even more enthusiastic. As one would expect, nothing was said about his anti-Zionist agenda, or the unsavoury company that this obsession has led him to keep as a result of his continuous involvement in Sharia left operations during his years as a back-bencher. One contributor heralded his victory in tones and with prose that were unmistakably messianic: 'There was for more me something profoundly satisfying, not to say moving, in the victory of the man who came from nowhere, the man who was reviled by the powerful, the rich and the mighty. It was almost Biblical: the last became first.' Having found his messiah, and been born again, 'within in an hour of his winning, I joined the party. '

'Reviled by the powerful and the rich'? Robin Hood…or even Jesus? Let us not forget that the object of this quasi-religious devotion, one that was already resembling that of a cult, was a politician who has spent the greater part of his career as an MP in the company of well-heeled Muslims who reviled the Jews, and whose war of extermination against their homeland was financed by powerful, oil rich despotisms. While of all the national dailies, the *Guardian* certainly had been the most sympathetic to the Corbyn cause, there was at least one writer on its staff whose intellectual self-respect prevented him from succumbing to the sycophantic hero-worship that was already emerging around the new Labour leader. Again, the imagery is Biblical, but the picture that emerges is anything but adulatory:

> 'The cult of Jeremy Corbyn is truly astonishing...every utterance, however gnomic, is now thought to contain a greater truth. [Shades of *The Life of Brian*] Corbyn disciples now regard the man who would turn up at a political rally at the drop of a pamphlet as a seer...He has become a blank slate on which believer's project paint their dreams. His story could equally be a Biblical parable about patience or a (far-fetched) political satire'

The Life of Jeremy perhaps? Sometimes fact is stranger than fancy. In April 2016, a new show hit the London stage, entitled *Jeremy Corbyn: The Musical,* followed even more bizarrely, in November by a Corbynista bid to top the Christmas single chart with 'JC for PM for Me', and a riposte from the Musical cast, 'You Needed a Hero - You Got Corbyn). The lyrics of the Corbynista entry capture perfectly the banality of great leader's thought processes and the degree of sophistication of his target audience: 'I'm voting Jeremy C [not Labour be it noted] / I like his ideas / they're fair and they're clear / Jezza and me we agree'.

No doubt as a result of his track record as an indefatigable campaigner for any number of Islamic causes, Corbyn's election as Labour leader aroused hopes in the 'Muslim community' that the party's policies in its areas of special interest were about to change for the better. Two Muslim commentators pictured Corbyn's spectacular eruption onto the political scene in the most elemental terms, ascribing to the new leader almost superhuman qualities. The Vice President of the Muslim Association of Britain and Chairman of Corbyn's local mosque in Finsbury Park saw in Labour's new leader a 'humble and wise man', 'one of very few politicians who recognises that the government must and needs to engage positively with British Muslims'...code for changing its foreign policy. 'Humble and wise'...but also a Titan, one who single-handed 'has shaken the political landscape of Britain'. Writing in the *Morning Star,* the Stalinist daily that has over the years featured articles by Corbyn, Rabbil Sidkar, a young Muslim leftist, saw the newly-elected leader as a cross between a monk and a Nordic god, 'a quiet, humble and hugely impressive giant [?] who has set off [sic] like a thunderstorm in the Labour Party' And 'the rumbles are reverberating around the [Muslim] community'. They certainly reached the eager ears of the Council for Muslims in Britain, the influential publicly-funded Muslim pressure group that like the Muslim Association of Britain, maintains close links with the ultra-conservative and theocratic Muslim Brotherhood while at the same time collaborating closely with the Sharia left in a number of anti-Zionist enterprises. Because no doubt the Council had its reasons for issuing a statement welcoming Corbyn's election as leader of the Labour party.

The Corbynite movement not only resembles a religious cult. In some ways, it also is an exotic offshoot of the new celebrity-obsessed culture, since it palpably serves to satisfy a craving by the young, reared as they have been on a diet of Big Brother, I'm a Celebrity, X Factor, the Apprentice and other similarly inane TV productions, to become identified in some way with a prominent public figure, preferably one that has the aura of anti-establishment notoriety. And as it evolved, the cult did indeed merge with the world of pop with the staging of a series of gigs, promoted as 'Concerts for Corbyn' and not, as some noted, for Labour or even Socialism, a Jeremy anthem, the proliferation and marketing of Corbyn kitsch and memorabilia and even an oil painting of the Dear Leader Himself.

In Corbyn we had a celebrity unlike any other: the image if not the reality of a man of destiny, and yet at the same time simple (to be sure), humble, kindly, honest, sincere, work-a-day, a man who despite his advanced years, has the gift of awakening in the young a sense of adventure, optimism and idealism, a preacher with a dream and a message of hope and deliverance, a visionary who is betrayed, reviled and ridiculed by the Judases within his own party, a latter day Pied Piper, an infallible leader whose policy summersaults, like those of Hitler and Stalin, either pass unnoticed or are swallowed in one gulp, a seer who has a cure for all ills, not least for those who prefer to avoid the irksome task of thinking for themselves by following a messiah who does their thinking for them. And what thinking! In every respect, Corbyn fitted the bill to perfection. And yet, at the time of writing the fates seems to have turned against him. He has lost every election contested under his leadership, whether international, national or local. As of September 2019, in recent months, both his and his party's ratings have sunk to an all-time low, behind not only the Tories, but the Liberal Democrats and the Brexit Party, and with the Greens not far below. His party, divided from his first days in office, is torn apart by its anti-Semitism scandal, for which his obsessive anti-Zionism has been the main catalyst. (see Appendix T) 100,000 members have resigned in less than year. There is open dissent even among his hitherto closet collaborators. All this and more could mean that he may never become Prime Minister, and, in failing to do, possibly ensure Tory dominance for the foreseeable future. But to his devotees, that will hardly matter, because he makes them feel holy and special.

The Corbynistas, a party, or rather church, within a party, except for their overwhelmingly middle-class composition, are heterogonous in the extreme. First there is the Islamic component, Muslim political activists at local and increasingly at national level mobilised by Corbyn's well-publicised track record as a fanatical anti-Zionist. Then there are the re-activated 'Old Believers', akin to the Russian sect of that name who refused to accept the Church reforms of Peter Great and took themselves off into the Siberian wilderness. Hailing from the election-losing era of Michael Foot and Tony Benn, Labour's Old Believers reacted in a similar way to the 'New Labour' reforms of Tony Blair, either dropping out of the party altogether, some for pastures Green, or simply lapsing into inactivity. Corbyn, along with a small group of like-minded MPs and seasoned operators, like the former anti-Semitic Labour MP and London Mayor Ken Livingstone, is very much of this generation, but with the crucial difference that he found his new pastures for the most part in the oases of the Middle East. Next, we have the far left. Some are old-guard Stalinists, but the majority are younger, more aggressive and even thuggish, some again neo-Trotskyist 'entryists', many of them lobotomised by campus political correctness, zealously anti-Zionist to the point of open anti-Semitism, utterly intolerant of any opinion other than their own, and sanctimonious with it. Their aim is to transform the Labour Party into one huge 'safe space' where the only ones commanding the platform will be themselves.

The irony is that these new-wave entryists had looked upon the Blair-era Labour Party as an obstacle on the road to fully blown socialism until Miliband's crazy three-pound membership rule provided them with a golden opportunity to elect as leader a figurehead who could be manipulated to serve their own totalitarian ends. They now provide the cadre of the Corbynista Momentum, whose task it is to take over the local machinery of the Labour Party and de-select non-Corbynista MPs by flooding the constituencies with new and mainly very naive recruits, for whom Corbyn is akin to the guru of a religious cult. Momentum rallies chant his name, cultists hold aloft home-made banners inscribed 'Corbyn [not Labour] in, Tories out', while the saviour's heretical 'Blairite' Labour Party opponents are cast variously in the roles of Judas and Satan, accompanied by audible mutterings of a 'Zionist Plot'. One constituency party secretary described the tensions that had risen as result of the Corbynite influx: 'There are members who have been here for 10, 15, 20 years who think he has to go. Those who have joined in the last year think he walks on water. [Believe it or not, there was an attempt to stage such a miracle at a seaside Labour Party conference, only to be frustrated by incoming waves almost certainly activated by Mossad.] There's an almost religious-like following and if you criticise him you're a blasphemer.' (I have been the recipient of exactly this reaction by someone who was not even a Labour Party member.)

It is indeed as the *Guardian* critic said, all rather Biblical, even explicitly so. In my local paper, one enthusiast breathlessly described her conversion at a gathering conducted in a manner more appropriate to a Billy Graham rally: 'We went to a meeting and Christian [?] songs were sung with placards saying "Support Jeremy" …nothing but 1,000 people meeting together to support Jeremy'. 'Support *Jeremy*'? But not the Labour Party or socialism. And *Christian* songs? Tread carefully, because Jeremy prefers mosques and declaiming his unbounded respect for a religion whose holy book repeatedly (six times in all) instructs its followers not to take Christians as friends. Perhaps the location explains why on this occasion hymns were in order and not a call to (Muslim) prayer. Here was a scene set in the chapel land of South Wales, home of the Revival of 1904-5, not the minarets of Finsbury Park, Rotherham or Peterborough.

Such converts, and they number tens of thousands, believe that at last, after so many betrayals, they have found the infallible leader who will guide them to the promised land of true socialism. Spell bound, his audiences hang on his every banal word, clearly believing that he is capable of performing secular miracles that will painlessly transform Britain almost overnight into a land of plenty for the many, not the few. As a man of peace, Corbyn has made it very clear that he wishes to leave NATO and drastically scale down the UK's military budget by abandoning the upgrading of the UK's Trident nuclear submarine fleet. Perhaps he hopes that this will release the revenue required for the funding of his ambitious domestic programme. Anyone who raises the smallest doubts as to the viability of the Corbyn project is liable to be denounced as 'Blairite scum', heckled and jostled at meetings, besieged at their home or their local Labour party offices, accused of involvement in a Zionist plot, and even threatened with rape and death.

Like all true believers, nothing will shake their faith. All attacks on the object of their devotion simply serve as more proof that he is indeed the chosen one, even though, beginning in the run-up to his election as Labour Leader, irrefutable evidence began to accumulate of the kind of low-life and decidedly non-socialist company Corbyn had been keeping throughout his Parliamentary career. But no one cared. It was either all lies, or alright. His closest comrades rallied to his defence, no one more enthusiastically than fellow anti-Zionist campaigner, East Germany pillion-rider and anti-white bigot Diane Abbott. Unable to refute that her mentor had consorted with known anti-Semites, Jihadis and Holocaust deniers, since the evidence was irrefutable, she offered the following justification for keeping such company:

> Jeremy has been an MP for thirty years. In those thirty years he has done thousands]sic] of meetings, rallies, memorial events …Now if over those thirty years he has been on a platform with someone who is clear is now [sic] an anti-Semite and a Holocaust denier, whatever it is [sic!]…given the chaotic nature of the liberation movement [what kind of 'liberation movement', however chaotic', is represented by anti-Semites and Holocaust deniers?], that will happen. That doesn't make Jeremy a fellow traveller with anti-Semitism.'

Yes, it most certainly does, because it 'happened' not just once or twice in 'thirty years', 'chaotically', by chance, but deliberately, consistently and regularly, as the record of these collaborations, many of them videoed, has established. These were no random encounters, but the fruits of a shared cause, the vilification of Israel and the promotion of Jihadi Islam. Corbyn's leading role over decades in a number of campaigns led him, by his own free choice, to collaborate on the closest terms with those whom Abbott admitted were both anti-Semites and Holocaust deniers *and known to be so at the time*, not subsequently as Abbott implies.

In addition to anti-Semites, high-profile recruits to the Corbynite cause can come in wide variety of shapes and sizes. One who attracted particular media attention was Tom O'Carroll. Like others of his kind, O'Carroll had been politically active for many years, but had only joined the Barrow Constituency branch of the Labour Party after Corbyn's election as Leader in September 2015. In February 2016, Barrow's Labour MP demanded that O'Carroll be expelled from the Labour party, not for his pro-Corbyn views, but for his advocacy of sex with children, having served as Chairman of Paedophile Information Exchange, the pressure group founded in 1974 to campaign for change in the law on under-age sex. In 1981 he was jailed for 'corrupting public morals' and again in 2006 for distributing indecent images of children. Such activities and views do not go down well with the average Labour voter, though given the example set by the Prophet Mohammed with his nine-year-old wife Aisha and bearing in mind the sexual preference of hundreds of convicted paedophiles, in Rotherham, Oxford, Sheffield, Keighley, Aylesbury, Halifax, Rochdale and a score or more other locations, this may not necessarily be the case with all male Muslim voters.

Next, we have four high ranking Corbynistas, of whom three are MPs, who have allegedly run afoul of the standards of public conduct one has a right to expect from a politician. First, Clive Lewis. Standing for the first time as the Labour candidate for Norwich in 2015, he was asked by the *New Statesman* whether he took victory for granted. He replied that he would only lose if he was 'caught with [his] pants down behind a goat with Ed Miliband at the other end'. Once elected, he rapidly proved himself one of Corbyn's loyalist supporters, being one of the 36 MPs who voted for him in the leadership contest in 2015. On becoming an MP, Lewis wasted no time in joining the PLP Labour Friends of Palestine. Could this explain why despite his lack of Parliamentary experience, Lewis was rewarded with a series of placements in Corbyn's shadow cabinet, first in the Energy and Climate Change team, then Defence, and finally Business, Energy and Industrial Strategy? All seemed to be going well until he fell out with Corbyn over the Labour leader's switch to a 'hard' Brexit'. Lewis resigned in February 2017 from the Shadow cabinet, while remaining in most other matters a loyal Corbynista. At the Brighton Labour Party conference of September 2017, Lewis attended a Momentum event, where from the platform, he called out to the actor Sam Swann (not a goat this time) to 'get on your knees, bitch'. A Labour Party spokesperson said the language used was 'completely unacceptable and falls far short of the standard expected of Labour MPs.' Lewis later apologised, and that seemed to be that. But then, two months later, as each day, fresh stories broke about alleged sexual misconduct by male MPs, Lewis was accused of sexually harassing a woman at the same Momentum event, which Lewis denied, saying, 'it's not how I roll'. A Labour Party Spokesperson said the complaint was being investigated.

Then there is the sensational case of the anti-Zionist Jared O'Mara, who shares with Lewis what one might describe as a free-wheeling style in matters sexual. After twice failing to be elected as a councillor, O'Mara was catapulted into Parliament as Labour MP for Sheffield Hallam in the General Election of June 21017. Momentum activists were mobilised from far and wide to get Jeremy's man in, although his very non-PC past was an open secret. His loyalty to the Corbynista cause, already proven by his high-profile campaigning against Israel, was quickly rewarded, his meteoritic ascent continuing when, despite his total lack of political experience, he was appointed by Corbyn to represent the PLP on the House of Commons Women (sic) and Equalities (sic) Select Committee, while still pursuing his commitment, now inside as well as outside the House, to the anti-Zionist cause, being briefed by the Hamas-linked Palestinian Return Centre for this purpose. Those citizens of Sheffield Hallam who believed that an MP's first duty is to represent the interests of their constituents would have been interested to learn that up to the time of his public fall from grace, all three of his questions asked in the House by O'Mara had concerned Israel, and that a matter of days before Corbyn's representative on the Women and Equalities Selected Committee was exposed as flagrant misogynist, homophobe and racist, their MP was featured in a photo standing between two officials of the same terrorist-linked organisation. Among the issues they discussed was how to organise opposition to the commemoration the 100th anniversary of the Balfour Declaration.

In matter anti-Zionist, O'Mara was decidedly 'on message' That is why, one suspects, even though he had known about the charges against O'Mara for a month, Corbyn did all he could to save him, saying it would be a 'shame' if he had to resign from the Select Committee, while Baroness 'whitewash' Chakrabarti, indulgent, as one would expect on her past form, to a wayward Corbynista, told the BBC 'people should be allowed to make mistakes'. All in vain, as the uproar in the media and the House grew to such a pitch that O'Mara jumped before he was - reluctantly - pushed. Two postings capture the MP's idiosyncratic approach to 'equality'. One, in the run-up to a football match between England and Spain, went thus: 'Let's beat the Dagos'; and another, in an on-line riposte to a Dane: 'I might be a "ginge" [O'Mara is indeed ginger-haired] but at least I don't practice bestiality like you Danes! Up yours with brass knobs on, pig shagger.' Decency forbids citing most of his 'sexist' and homophobic 'mistakes', which reveal a mind that would be a gross insult to any decent human waste disposal system to liken to a sewer. Suffice to say, they are hardly the best advertisement for his fitness to serve on the Women and Equality Select Committee. On August 23 2019, reports appeared in the media that O'Mara had been arrested by police in connection with another 'mistake', fraud.

Hot on the heels of the O'Mara scandal came that of Corbyn's Shadow Culture Secretary, Kelvin Hopkins. As Parliament buzzed with reports of sexual misbehaviour by Labour and Tory MPS, it was revealed on November 3, 2017, that the Labour Leader appointed Hopkins to his post despite being aware that serious charges of sexual harassment had been made against him by a party activist. 'Hard Brexiter' Hopkins, MP for that hotbed of Islamic Jihadism, Luton, where a Muslim Nazi can be elected as a Labour councillor, was another one of the 36 MPs whose votes enabled Corbyn to enter the contest for the Labour leadership in 2015, and is, like all good Corbynista Parliamentarians, also a member of the Labour Friends of Palestine, the up-market counterpart to the anti-Semite infested Palestine Solidarity Campaign, more of which anon. A posting by a zealous Corbynista, working on the assumption that the women who made these accusations were liars, speculated on their possible source and motive: 'This is another attack. Probably by the establishment, maybe by the Blairite faction and distantly possibly the work of Mossad (given the Israeli aim to stop JC at all costs).' Thus, the Jewish conspiracy.

In the wake of these three cases, each involving a male MP from the small coterie who can be described as belonging to the Corbyn camp, came that of Corbyn's former speech writer (sic) and then his communications manager to the shadow cabinet, David Prescott, son of Corbyn enthusiast and one-time Labour Deputy Prime Minister John Prescott. He was suspended after an unspecified complaint was made against him. Although not eligible for membership of the PLP Labour Friends of Palestine, given his two job descriptions, I would say that the odds are on his views on Israel coinciding with those of his employer. Poor Jeremy. He really does pick them. Livingstone, Naz(i) Shah, Lewis, O'Mara, Hopkins and Prescott. How many more? As of January 2019, three. Solicitor, Labour Whip and MP for Peterborough Fiona Onasanya, described by Corbyn as 'this wonderful woman', and who reportedly aspired to be the UK's first black woman Prime Minister, was jailed for three months and barred from the legal profession for perverting the course of justice when she lied to police about a speeding offence, falsely claiming a Russian man was the driver who, as luck would have it, happened to be in his homeland at the time. A devout Christian, she compared her conviction to the suffering of Jesus on the cross.

Next, Kate Osamor, MP for Edmonton and Corbyn's Shadow International Development Secretary, She lied in a letter to the Judge presiding in the trial of her 'beautiful son' Ishmael, a 'person of high integrity', a Labour Councillor in Harringay, who was convicted of four charges of possession of illegal drugs with intent to supply. (His other job, on £50,000 per annum, was assistant to his mother.) Interviewed on the doorstep of her £700,000 housing association-funded property by a journalist, she threw a bucket of water over him, told him to 'fuck off' and said 'I should have come down here with a bat and smashed you face in.' Once again, a kinder politics. Kate's mother, Martha, is now Baroness Osamor, selected by Corbyn for one of four appointments to the House of Lords, even though in 1990, she was deselected by the Harringay Labour Party as a councillor, and barred from standing for office ever again, after funding intended for community organisations was subject to 'unexplained withdrawals and expenditures' amounting to more than £100,000, some on items of a personal nature. As one would expect, both mother and daughter have impeccable anti-Zionist credentials. Martha has spoken up in support of members expelled for anti-Semitism, while her daughter is a prominent advocate of the BDS policy of boycotting Israel. Sex pests, racists, drug-dealers, embezzlers, anti-Semites, perjurers, liars... What a wretched crew of chancers! Some would say Corbyn brings it on himself, since a great deal more than a hunger for the good life and a loathing of Israel is required to qualify as a responsible politician.

However, despite these causalities, he can take comfort in that at least one staunchly anti-Zionist replacement is on the way up, namely Nasreen Khan, a prospective candidate for the safe Bradford Council seat of Little Horton. Like her co-religionist in Luton, Councillor Aysegal Gurbuz, Khan has advertised on-line her hatred of the Jews and admiration for Hitler. In one posting, she complained that teachers in her school were 'brainwashing' pupils into 'thinking that the bad guy was Hitler.' 'What good have the Jews done in the world?', she asked, rhetorically. Denying that these opinions made her a Nazi (perhaps because it was the Zionists who were supposed to be the Nazis) Khan revealingly explained 'I am an ordinary[sic] Muslim that had an opinion and put it across. We have worse people than Hitler in the world now... Stop beating a dead horse. The Jews have reaped the reward of playing victim. Enough is enough.' In that hotbed of Islamic Jew-hatred that is today's Bradford, these views, infinitely more suited to membership of a Neo-Nazi party than the pre-Corbyn Labour Party, did not prove an obstacle to her becoming one of two candidates for the Little Horton seat.

Another interesting recruit to the Corbyn cause is David Carter. He describes himself as a 'semi-retired international senior manager with over 15 years of extensive experience throughout the Middle East.' Outraged at what he saw a conspiracy to block the election of Corbyn as leader of the Labour Party, Carter posted a series of comments that left no doubt as to whom he believed was behind it: 'I will continue to speak out on the smears and slurs aimed against Jeremy Corbyn from the pro-Israeli Jews'. Other postings made it clear it was not only 'pro-Israeli Jews" whom he had in mind: 'Jewish power has the unique capacity to stop anyone talking about Jewish power.' And yet here was Carter doing just that! Carter fulminated against the 'pro-Zionist attack on Jeremy Corbyn' while 'washed-up Labour failures [possibly a reference to amongst others, Tony Blair, the only Labour leader to win three successive general elections] snap and bark like a pack of toothless dogs'. Carter claimed that 'organised Jewry' was 'trying to portray Jeremy Corbyn as a kapo at Auschwitz [sic!] in their desperation'. As a Holocaust denier, Carter, amidst this welter of posts exposing the Jewish conspiracy against Corbyn, still found the time to dismiss the Anne Frank dairy as a 'fraud', unlike Corbyn, who was so obviously the real anti-Zionist deal.

Around the same time, yet another Holocaust denier, Mathew Kees, crawled out of the same latrine, announcing as he did so, 'Corbyn is great. Am all for him.' Kees is also another high-flyer, or so he wants the world to think, describing himself as a 'renowned [sic] professional photographer, art teacher and sculptor.' Like Carter, Kees believes he is the victim of Jewish persecution, complaining that 'there's no organisation to protect us from Zionist Supremacists.' For all Corbyn's repeated protestations that he is not an anti-Semite, (and his apologists need to ask themselves why no previous Labour leader has felt obliged to do this) there are many who obviously do not believe him. Some, like Kees and Carter, are themselves anti-Semites, while there are others, both Jew and gentile, including myself, who are not. What is undeniable is that Corbyn attracts the support and adulation of anti-Semites and Neo-Nazis like iron filings to a magnet. Proving the point, we have the intriguing case of Jeremy Corbyn's kid brother, Piers. Whereas his older brother, for all the parental investment in his schooling, turned out to be a dunce, one indeed so dim-witted that as an advocate of homeopathy, believes water possesses (like himself) a selective memory, Piers prospered academically, with a First-Class Honours degree in physics at Imperial College London, and then an MSc. in astrophysics at Queen Mary College London. in 1981.

Unlike most scientists with his background who took an interest in the subject, Corbyn junior became an outspoken and much sought-after opponent of the claim that global warming in part at least is caused by human activity, a judgement on his part no better founded than his brother's belief in the cerebral powers of water. In 1995, Piers founded his own company, Weather Action, specialising in long-term weather forecasting. While his stance on global warming has aligned him with large-scale corporations and politicians of the right, who see proposals to reduce carbon emissions as an anti-capitalist conspiracy, his early political commitment was, like his elder brother's, to the left, but to Trotskyism rather than Stalinism. In his student years, he became an activist for the now defunct 'Pabloite' International Marxist Group before moving on to the Labour Party in the 1980s. He then left the party in 2002, to resurface again in 2016 as a Labour member active in the Brexit campaign to leave the EU, while at the same time giving his endorsement, for what it was worth, to Donald's Trump's bid for the US Presidency. The reader will legitimately object – what has any of this to do with Jeremy Corbyn? The sins of his brother, such as they are, can no more be visited on Jeremy than can those of his forebears. Correct. But what follows can.

In response to the global protests staged to coincide with the inauguration ceremony of Trump as US President, Piers recycled a tweet from 'WhiteKnight0011', who describes himself as a 'White National Socialist': 'They will force Trump in to war. What do you think happened to Hitler? Bilderberg CIA IMF Banker Gangsters'. The tweet endorsed by Piers Corbyn is accompanied by images of two Jews who are alleged to control the world, Lord Jacob Rothschild and Israeli Prime Minister Benjamin Netanyahu. (As we shall see, the Rothschilds and Netanyahu proliferate on Corbynista websites) Although never disowned by his brother, and in fact on occasion defended by him, (he told the *Sun* in 2016 that '*actually we fundamentally agree*') Corbyn junior has form as an anti-Semite. He has tweeted that 9/11 and ISIS are both the work of the Jews. Now we get to it. When in 2016 the Jewish Labour MP Louise Ellman complained of Corbynista anti-Semitic threats, Piers tweeted: 'Absurd! JC [Jeremy Corbyn] and all Corbyns are committed anti-Nazis. [Why then recycle Nazi anti-Semitic tweets?] Zionists can't cope with anyone supporting rights for Palestine'. *To which brother Jeremy tweeted*: 'He's not wrong'. Regarding Piers' Nazi re-tweet, Joe Glasman of the Campaign Against Anti-Semitism commented that 'Jeremy Corbyn's endorsed his brother's views last time he alleged there was a Jewish conspiracy. We don't expect Jeremy will expel him from the party now, after all, re-tweeting Jewish conspiracies is perfectly normal in the Labour Party of today. Maybe he'll give him a peerage.'

In his role of all-purpose useful idiot, among the high-ranking positions Corbyn has held in the past or currently is that of Patron of the Palestine Solidity campaign, which several diligent investigations have revealed to be inundated with anti-Semites and Neo-Nazis. One such in the latter category is Reading PSC activist Tony Gratrex. One of Gratrex's postings claims the Jews caused the first and second world wars, and then framed-up the Nazis at the Nuremberg Trials for a Holocaust that never happened. In another, he promotes *The Protocols of the Learned Elders of Zion*. On the same website he can be seen, on two separate occasions, posing for the camera next to Corbyn, who is smiling and has his right arm around the Neo-Nazi's shoulder.

Perhaps the most revealing and damning recruit to the Corbyn camp was the notorious Jewish conspiracy theorist, former Ku Klux Klan Grand Wizard David Duke, Trump supporter and founder of the white supremacist National Association for the Advancement of White People. In a radio interview conducted by Duke just after Corbyn had been elected as Labour Leader, Jewish conspiracy theorist James Thring, a guest speaker at an anti-Israel meeting hosted by Corbyn at Westminster in 2014, at the beginning of the interview introduced himself as 'a long-standing friend' of the newly-elected Labour Leader, and then described how

> ...people like Jeremy and me are coming together over the Zionist and Jewish power...he doesn't mention Jewish power actually, but you know, it's obviously behind his mind...I think it's quite clear from people like Jeremy and some of the people he's chosen for his[shadow] cabinet, like John McDonnell and people in the [House of] Lords as well [that] they do know who is really running the country and they are itching both for an opportunity to make it known to the public and to do something about it. [Duke responds]:

> We must keep looking for sunshine and I do believe we are going to find sunshine in this world. I think things are opening up.... I know you are a friend of Mr. Corbyn and I knew that you respect his positions on the Middle East. It's a really good kind of evolutionary thing isn't it when people are beginning to recognise Zionist power and ultimately the Jewish establishment power in Britain and in the Western world isn't it?

Further far right endorsement for Corbyn came when, on August 23, 2018, he vowed to challenge 'the stranglehold of elite power and billionaire domination over large parts of our media.' Duke immediately tweeted, 'he's right you know'. The same day, a video emerged of Corbyn making a speech in 2013 in which he claimed British Zionists (sic) 'don't understand English irony, adding, 'they needed two lessons [sic], which we [sic] could perhaps help them with.' In response to this story, Neo-Nazi Nick Griffin, who had previously announced that he would vote Labour because of Corbyn's opposition to UK military action against chemical weapons plants in Syria (President Assad had previously played host to both himself, twice, and Corbyn) tweeted, 'Go Jezza! I wonder how many Labour activists the hysterical Zionist media campaign against Corbyn is repelling?' Corbyn and Griffin also share the same warm feelings towards Hezbollah, the Lebanon-based and Syrian and Iranian-sponsored terror organisation dedicated to the elimination of the state of Israel. Corbyn has described the movement, together with Hamas, as his 'friends' and featured as a speaker at its annual anti-Israel 'Quds Day' rallies in London. For his part, in March 2019, Griffin was a member of a far-right EU Parliamentary delegation which met with Hezbollah leaders in Beirut, endorsing a statement that expressed support for Hezbollah's 'fight against Israel, terrorism [sic] and imperialism.' Of Griffin, Corbyn has said, 'no-one should share a platform with an avowed racist', even though, according to Diane Abbott and his own admission, he has done this on numerous occasions. Platforms aside, as the above citations prove beyond any doubt, there are policies that the Labour Leader does share with the Holocaust-denying Griffin, not least their abiding hostility to Israel and their solidarity with those bent on destroying it.

Another Holocaust denier and Hitler apologist, the historian David Irving, gave his judgement on Corbyn, as quoted in the *Guardian* of January 14, 2017: [He] 'seems a very fine man...I'm impressed by him'. The U.S. Neo-Nazi website, *Daily Stormer* (after the Nazi weekly *Der Sturmer*) and the white supremacist *Occidental Observer* announced that they were backing Corbyn in the general election of June 2017. As *Stormer* publisher Andrew Anglim put it, Corbyn 'is genuinely against Israel' and 'seriously anti-Jew'. Similar sentiments spilled out during the election campaign itself in a giant poster displayed by Momentum in Bristol. On the left was a huge picture of Corbyn, and facing him on the right was an equally large one of Tory PM Theresa May. Hanging from her left ear was a star of David earing and above, in large letters, the word 'Balfour', an obvious reference to the Balfour Declaration of November 1917, which stated;

> His Majesty's Government view with favour the establishment in Palestine of a national home for the Jewish people and will use its best endeavours to facilitate the achievement of this object, it being clearly understood that nothing shall be done which may prejudice the civil and religious rights of existing non-Jewish communities in Palestine, or the rights and political status enjoyed by the Jews in any other country.

The message of the poster was therefore clear. A vote for the Tories was a vote for the Jews and Israel. A vote for Corbyn was vote against the Jews and Israel, and for the Palestinians. And also against the Balfour Declaration itself, as became evident when Corbyn declined an invitation to attend a dinner celebrating its 100th anniversary in November 2017, a clear signal that he does not recognise the legitimacy of the state of Israel, and one that was understood as such by his Hamas friends: 'Corbyn says no to dinner on celebrating the Balfour 100 in UK. UK should apologise and compensate Palestinians.' Two months previously, Corbyn has also turned down the customary invitation to attend the Labour Friends of Israel reception at the Brighton party conference, claiming he was too busy preparing a speech. This proved to be a lie, as he was seen that same evening whooping it up at the *Daily Mirror's* annual conference bash. Never before in living memory had a Labour Leader rejected this invitation.

Anyone conversant with Corbyn's attitude towards Israel and his collaboration with those who seek its destruction and the extermination of its entire Jewish population would surely ask themselves, was it by accident that Corbyn should choose to participate in the launching an 'Islamophobia Awareness Month' in the same week as supporters of Israel were commemorating the 100th anniversary of the Balfour Declaration? And was it also by chance that of the several organisations that campaign in this area, Corbyn should choose to join forces with one which is notorious for its vicious hostility towards Zionism? Sufyan Golam, Executive Officer of the group in question, MEND, (Muslim Engagement and Development) used a sermon in a Manchester mosque to launch into an attack on Tell MAMA, another organisation in the same business of combatting what it regards as Islamophobia: 'We don't want the Government to fob us off with some phoney thing called Tell MAMA, which has got a pretty much pro-Zionist heading it, or in a very senior capacity, and is making comments we might not agree with when it comes to homosexuality, to be recording Islamophobia.' Corbyn's choice seems to imply that he agrees. In addition to deviating from Sharia law in not being homophobic, (the punishment for being gay is death) one of Tell MAMA's besetting sins is that it has sought from and been given advice by the Jewish Community Security Trust…surely the kiss of death. With good reason then, Jennifer Gerber, Director of Labour Friends of Israel told the *Jewish Chronicle* it was 'utterly unacceptable' that Corbyn 'should choose to attend an event organised by a group which has repeatedly peddled myths about the power of the "Israeli lobby" that play into classic anti-Semitic tropes'. This judgment is borne out by an investigation into MEND by the Henry Jackson Society, the cross-partisan 'think tank', which described the group as 'Islamists masquerading as civil libertarians' who 'regularly hosted illiberal, intolerant and extremist Islamist speakers at public events.' Amongst its staff and activists were 'those who have promoted conspiracy theories, anti-Semitism and intolerance of other Muslim minority denominations'. Evidently unconcerned by these unsavoury associations, a former Tory government minister, the Muslim Baroness Warsi and, inevitably, the ubiquitous Jeremy Corbyn, are to be seen in a promotional video on MEND's Twitter page, proving that as on so many similar previous occasions, anti-Zionism can be thicker than party. This is the kind of company Corbyn preferred to keep, rather than with Jews celebrating the realisation of the Zionist dream.

This was not the first time Corbyn had declined to associate himself with an historic Jewish event, only this time one that was monumentally tragic. In 2016, he was invited by his opposite number, the leader of the Israeli Labour Party, Isaac Herzog, to visit the Yad Veshem Holocaust Museum in Jerusalem. Herzog had been 'appalled' by Livingstone's claim that the policy of Hitler in 1932 was 'that the Jews should be moved to Israel'. Following Livingstone's suspension, Herzog issued his invitation to Corbyn 'to witness that the last time Jews were forcibly transported it was not to Israel but to their deaths'. After several weeks' delay, Corbyn declined the invitation, claiming he was too busy, offering to send party General Secretary Ian McNichol or Chairman Tom Watson instead. Too busy? But Corbyn is rarely if ever too busy to front up anti-Zionist rallies alongside his Jihadi 'friends' from Israel's enemies in the Middle East, or take free-bees as a guest of Jew-killing terrorists and anti-Semitic despots. And there is another consideration. Imagine the reaction of these 'friends' if comrade Jeremy was a guest of a Jewish socialist in of all places Jerusalem, bearing witness to a crime that in their estimation, either never happened, or if it did, was a cause for celebration?

During his campaign for the Labour leadership, Corbyn, having said he wanted 'a kinder politics', understandably came under considerable pressure to disavow his long-standing associations with avowed anti-Semites, Jihadis, Iranian theocrats and Holocaust and 9/11 deniers. Despite equivocations and convenient memory lapses, it became obvious that Corbyn was not prepared to do so. Even when he attended, *pro forma,* a 'fringe' meeting of the Labour Friends of Israel at the September 2015 Labour party conference, in a speech lasting eight minutes on the subject of Israeli-Palestinian relations, he could not bring himself to utter even once the word 'Israel', not even when challenged to do so by a member of the audience. Amongst the company Corbyn has kept this last decade and more, Israel is for his Arab Jihadi friends a taboo word, 'Zionist entity' being the standard term for the state that must be destroyed. So, without saying the forbidden word, he still somehow contrived to condemn Israel for its 'siege of Gaza', while having no words of criticism for Hamas's kidnappings, renewed tunnelling and rocket attacks.

For how long Corbyn would be able to continue serving as the Sharia left's useful idiot remained to be seen. Now that he wore Labour's crown, would the former Sharia Prince Hal remain true to his Jihadi John Falstaffs? His pusillanimous response to the Paris massacres of November 13 2015, which earned him the epithet 'fucking disgrace' from a former Labour Minister, suggested that he would, despite continued press revelations of his continued very public association with fanatical anti-Zionists. In March 2016, a report appeared in the *Daily Telegraph* of his close links with Mohammed Kozbar, Chairman of the Finsbury Park Mosque. This jewel in the crown of UK Islam was opened by its Patron Prince Charles in 1994 and its construction funded by King Fahd of Saudi Arabia. It is also notorious for its celebration of the first anniversary of 9/11, and as a breeding ground for 'home grown' recruits to the Islamic State. Kozbar, who is on record as calling for the destruction of Israel and has engaged in fund raising for Hamas, is shown at a mosque function in July 2015 shaking hands with Corbyn in front of the logo of the Muslim Brotherhood-affiliated Muslim Association of Britain, together with a Corbyn tweet which reads: 'With Mohammed Kozbar at the Finsbury Park Mosque Itfar supper and thanked them for being a superb [sic] community.'

Also pointing in the same direction was his appointment of two former associates of the WRP, the Sharia leftists and co-editors of the PLO, Gaddafi and Saddam-subsidised *Labour Herald:* Ken Livingstone, as co-chairman of the Labour Party's defence review, and John McDonnell, back in the 1980s Livingstone's deputy leader of the GLC, as shadow Chancellor of the Exchequer. Within hours of his appointment, Livingstone was advising a critic that he 'might need some psychiatric help', just one of many instances of Corbyn's 'kinder politics'. Then in April 2016 came the bombshell and body blow to Corbyn of the suspension of his closest ally on a charge of anti-Semitism. For Livingstone watchers such as myself, it was hardly a surprise, since he has never disguised his venomous hatred of Israel, whose creation he regards as 'a disaster', and of the ideals that created and sustain it, which he has likened to Nazism. His views on the fate of the Jews in Nazi Germany are likewise coloured by his visceral anti-Zionism, with Livingstone even claiming on Irish state radio in August 1983 that English rule in Ireland had been more destructive than the Holocaust. In the event, the remarks that triggered his suspension were the claim that until his last years, Hitler was a supporter of Zionism, and another made in defence of Muslim Labour MP for Bradford West Naz(i) Shah, adviser to Shadow Chancellor John McDonnell. Shah had proposed as a 'solution [sic] to [the] Israel-Palestine conflict' that all of Israel's six million Jews should be, quote, 'relocated' to the United States, and on another occasion, had advised readers of her website to 'never forget' that 'everything that Hitler did in Germany was legal'.

Against Corbyn's wishes, Labour's National Executive Committee immediately suspended her. We have to assume, given the categorical nature of this statement, that her insistence on Hitler's legality includes the 'relocating' of an earlier generation of the same number of Jews to their deaths in the Nazi version, a final one, of a 'solution' to the 'Jewish Question'. Shah was also defended against charges of anti-Semitism by fellow Muslim MP Rupa Huq, while Corbyn's most senior adviser, Seumas Milne claimed that when Livingstone described Hitler as a supporter of Zionism, he 'had a point'. If we combine what Shah, Milne and Livingstone each say about Hitler, what emerges is a picture of a successful, law-abiding German politician who, until, according to Livingstone, he 'went mad and ended up killing six million Jews' and therefore, being insane, became no longer legally or morally responsible for his actions, went out of his way to help the Jews realise their dream of returning to the Holy Land. Livingstone would be well-advised to check his sources before sounding off about Hitler and the Jews. For example, his assertion that Hitler 'won his [sic] election in 1932' is wrong. Hitler and his party contested not one, but four national elections in 1932, and in each of them failed to win anything like a majority of the votes cast. The first two were for the post of President. In the first round, on March 13, Hitler secured 30.1% of the votes cast. In the run-off on April 10, when he collected extra votes from voters who had backed right wing candidates eliminated after the first round, Hitler's share of the vote was 36.8%. The last two were elections to the Reichstag. On July 31, the Nazi Party's share of the votes was 37.27%, their largest in a free election, and on November 6, 33.09%, less by some margin than the vote for the two left parties, the Communists and the Social Democrats with 37.29%

'Hitler supported Zionism'? Also, wrong. In his *Mein Kampf* (1925) he predicted that a 'Jewish state in Palestine' would serve as a 'central organisation for their international world swindle'. Supported Zionism?

Of the half a million Jews living in Germany at the time of the Nazi take-over, by the outbreak of the war, 252,000, after being stripped of their money and possessions, had been allowed to emigrate. Of that total, only 33,390 finally managed to reach what was at the time the British Mandate. Nearly all the Jews left behind in Germany perished in Hitler's 'Final Solution'. As for going mad, wrong yet again. In an exhaustive survey of all the considerable medical evidence, the Nazi-era specialist Richard Evans has concluded that right up to his suicide in a Berlin bunker on April 30, 1945, Hitler, 'certainly was not mentally ill, not at least in in any sense known to medicine or psychiatry.' But Livingstone, perhaps privy to facts that Evans either had no access to or had overlooked, knows better.

Livingstone, Milne and Shah would no doubt place themselves on the left of the Labour Party. Yet their unorthodox, to say the least, slants on the history of the Third Reich overlap with two historical schools at other end of the same political spectrum, both of which have been attacked, and rightly so, as essentially apologists for Hitler. The first is that established by the post-war German historian Ernst Nolte who, while not as categorical in his claims as Shah, argued that most of Hitler's actions were legal, while those that were not were justified by necessity. Further to the right again we have David Irving. Although usually identified as belonging to the Holocaust denial camp, he has always insisted this designation is false, and in fact brought a libel action, which he famously lost, in an attempt to prove it. What Irving does say is that in so far as the Jews were persecuted, Hitler, pre-occupied with military matters, did his best to protect them, but 'had the wool pulled over his eyes' by his SS chief Heinrich Himmler, who was bent on their destruction. In his own words, Hitler 'was the best friend the Jews ever had', which, assumedly, quoting now Livingstone, would include 'supporting Zionism'.

Returning to Shah, if her assertion that Hitler was indeed innocent of any crime is true, then so too were those Nazis acting under his orders who were condemned at the Nuremberg Trials. It follows in turn that the Holocaust, being 'legal' (that is, if Shah believes it did happen) was not a crime and the Nuremberg Trials, as Neo-Nazis claim though for different reasons, because the Holocaust never happened, were one huge frame-up. As already stated, this is what leading Palestine Solidarity Campaign activist Tony Gratrex and Corbyn photo partner says on the Reading PSC website. Yet Livingstone, though he conceded that Naz(i) Shah's comments were 'over the top', insisted they were not anti-Semitic, only 'offensive'. They were 'a bit of criticism of Israel and Israel supporters.' And he went further, claiming 'in 47 years I have never heard anyone say anything anti-Semitic'. That presumably includes Labour Councillor Aysegal Gurbuz's 'if it wasn't for my man Hitler, these Jews would have wiped Palestine years ago'. Livingstone had the usual explanation for why he had been targeted as an anti-Semite. There had been 'a well-orchestrated campaign by the Israel [for which read 'Jewish'] lobby to smear anyone who criticises Israel as anti-Semitic'. The World Jewish Conspiracy strikes yet again. The Socialist Workers Party naturally rushed to the defence of the two traduced anti-Zionists: 'Shah is not anti-Semitic, and neither is Livingstone.' And if judged by the SWP's somewhat lax standards on this issue, they perhaps had a point. The online *Socialist Worker* of April 29, 2016 explained, as Livingstone himself had done in his own defence, that 'anti-Semitism and anti-Zionism are not the same thing.', and also, again like Livingstone, failed to offer its own a definition of anti-Semitism to establish this distinction. Instead, the reader was presented with one of Zionism that is itself anti-Jewish and, as we shall see, is shared by Corbyn: 'Zionism is based on the idea that Jewish people cannot live peacefully alongside non-Jewish people [for example, like the tsarist Black Hundreds, the anti-Dreyfusards and the Nazis] and that Israel should be an exclusively Jewish state.' The ignoramus who wrote this was, like so many other professional anti-Zionists, either obviously unaware of, or chose to ignore the fact that in the 'exclusively Jewish' state of Israel, 1.7 million Arab citizens live, not 'alongside', but mingle, peacefully, with Israel's six million Jews. It is not Zionism, but Hamas and Hezbollah, the two terrorists, anti-Semitic movements supported by the SWP, that refuse to live peacefully 'alongside' Israel, that reject the 'two-state solution' agreed by Israel and the PLO in Oslo in 1993 and quite openly seek its destruction and the extermination of its Jewish population. And let the SWP produce one single citation from any authoritative Zionist text which expresses in any form the idea that 'Jewish people cannot live alongside non-Jewish people'. The founder of modern Zionism, Theodore Herzl, from the beginning, made it clear, over and again, that the opposite was the case, and that the need for a Jewish state was the response to the fact that the rise across Europe of organised anti-Semitism demonstrated that increasing numbers of gentiles *did not want to live peacefully alongside Jews*, a conclusion tragically vindicated by the Nazi Holocaust of the Jews:

> We have sincerely tried everywhere to merge with the national communities in which we live, seeking only to preserve the faith of our fathers. [Like many Zionist leaders, Herzl was himself an atheist] It is not permitted us. In vain we are loyal patriots [as indeed was Captain Dreyfus] sometimes super loyal…[yet] in our native lands where we have lived for centuries, we are still decried as aliens.

The Jewish state he envisaged in what was still then Ottoman territory would be 'founded on the ideas which are the common product of all civilised nations…It would be immoral if we were to exclude anyone, whatever his origin, whatever his descent…our moto must be now and forever; "Man, you are my brother".' Numerous other texts from the various stages in the evolution of the Zionist movement both before and after the creation of the state of Israel in 1948 each express in different ways the same principle. And there are also texts by anti-

Semites that have asserted the contrary, that non-Jews, be they German Nazis or Arab anti-Zionists, cannot and should not live in peace alongside Jews.

Livingstone's claim that until the last years of the Third Reich, when he supposedly 'went mad' and turned against the Jews, Hitler was a 'supporter of Zionism', can be construed in one of two ways. For some it can, and indeed has been seen as attempt to whitewash Hitler, to depict the pre-Holocaust dictator in a favourable light, as someone who until in his last years when he lost his sanity, was trying to help the Jews rather than exterminate them. Others will see in Livingstone's historical fictions confirmation that the Zionists conspired with the Nazis to create a Jewish state in the homeland of the Palestinians. I have good reasons to believe this was indeed what Livingstone intended. But this interpretation has its own complications for Muslim admirers of Hitler like Luton Labour councillor Gurbuz, who praises 'her man' as the friend, not of the Jews, but of the Palestinians, and his defender Naz(i) Shah, for whom, far from 'going mad', Hitler was to the very end the custodian of legality. When he appeared at his hearing on charges of anti-Semitism, Livingstone should surely have been asked: 'If these and other statements quoted above, *all made by Labour Party members, and widely publicised in the media,* do not in your judgement qualify as anti-Semitic, what does?' Shah's is a particularly interesting example of how Muslim anti-Semitism has eaten into the very heart of the Labour Party. Herself an adviser to Shadow Chancellor John McDonnell, she in turn employed as her Parliamentary aide the anti-Semitic Muslim Bradford Labour Councillor Mohammed Shabbir, who has claimed that Russian Orthodox Jews are involved in 'the sex trafficking trade', and that the Jews of Israel are responsible for 'a Palestinian Holocaust in Gaza'.

Though united its hostility towards Israel and mainstream 'Blairite' Labour, relations within Corbyn's camp have not always been comradely. Displaying the kind of mutual loathing unique to religious and political factions contesting the same ideological turf, sundry neo-Trotskyist cliques have taken time out from cursing Zionist Nazis and Blairite traitors to call each other fascists on websites as they jostle for control over the Corbynite 'Momentum' operation. One faction singled out for special treatment was the Alliance for Workers Liberty, notorious on the far left for its unorthodox stance on Israel, which it believes should be allowed to exist, and in the past, its opposition to the Argentinean junta's invasion of the Falklands and Serbian ethnic cleansing in Bosnia and Croatia. This maverick grouplet of no more than one hundred members, some of whom I know and respect, was described by one Corbyn loyalist as a 'wrecking operation designed to undermine the political Left in Britain'. But behind the AWL stood even more sinister forces: 'There are well-founded rumours that they receive funds from Israeli lobbyists. They have been planted [sic] in the labour movement to disrupt and divide.' The Jewish Conspiracy strikes yet again! The difference with Hitler's version is that while here, assuming a leftist guise, it was seeking to undermine and destroy socialism, Hitler saw it as a Marxist plot to subjugate the Germanic peoples. But whatever guise or aims it might assume, left or right, both are agreed...there is a Jewish conspiracy.

Such is Momentum, a neo-Leninist cuckoo's egg laid, hatched then squawking amidst Labour's already divided brood. Tensions over his foreign policy, for want of a better term, emerged soon after Corbyn's victory. Following a succession of Jihadi atrocities in 2015, beginning with the downing of a Russia passenger jet on October 31, and continuing with the Paris and Beirut massacres of November 13 and a week later, the assault on the Mali Radisson Blu Hotel in Bamako, on November 20, the 15 member United Nations Security Council unanimously adopted a resolution which declared the Islamic State to be 'a global and unprecedented threat to international peace and security' and 'call[ed] upon member states that have the capacity to do so to take all necessary measures on the territory under the control of ISIUL [the Islamic State] in Syria and Iraq'. This was the long overdue blank cheque from the UN for those who could, and wished to, to invade and destroy the Islamic State. If acted upon seriously, as the French, who proposed the motion, appeared to intend, it could have compelled Obama to abandon his disastrous strategy of 'containment'.

Corbyn's opposition to any military action against the Islamic State and, even after the Paris massacre, rejection of armed responses to its assassins in the diaspora, now found him not only in direct conflict with the UN and public opinion, but with many Labour MPs and even within his handpicked Shadow Cabinet. What a humiliating spectacle! Within weeks of his election as Labour's Leader, the first test of his much-vaunted internationalism found him refusing to lift a finger in solidarity with the embattled Socialist government of France. His pretext was that joining with other European nations in the fight back against the Islamic State would put British servicemen 'in harm's way', as if this was somehow outside their job description, while 'the loss of civilian lives' was 'sadly [sic] almost inevitable'. And meantime, as the Islamic State continued to deliberately slaughter civilians by the thousand, Corbyn was advising the USA and France to cease their attacks on the Islamic State and instead 'put their efforts into a peace process'...presumably with this same Islamic State. With his usual impeccable timing, on the same day that Corbyn declared himself favour of a 'back channel' approach to the Islamic State it was reported from the east Syrian city of Deir-ez Zor that ISIS Jihadis had slaughtered in one day at least 800 of its inhabitants and abducted another 400. Not military action, but 'a negotiated settlement' was the course recommended by this later day Sharia Chamberlain to bring such atrocities to an end. A negotiated 'peace process' with the Islamic State? Yes, says Corbyn. 'There has to be some route through somewhere'. But even the gullible and dim-witted Chamberlain realised in the end that appeasement of fascism simply stimulated its appetites.

In respect of his foreign policy, of all Labour Leaders, Corbyn's resembles most closely that of George Lansbury, who became Leader in 1932, in the year after the defection of Prime Minister Ramsey MacDonald to a National Government coalition with the Tories and some Liberals. As a pacifist, he believed that Britain should set an example to the world by divesting itself of its means of defence: 'I would close every recruiting station, disband the army and disarm the Air Force. I would abolish the whole dreadful equipment of war and say to the world, "do your worst"'. Which is exactly what Hitler did six years later. At the Labour Party's annual conference of 1935, held in October on the eve of Mussolini's invasion of Abyssinia, Lansbury made a speech opposing his own Party Executive's support for League of Nations sanctions against Fascist Italy for its unprovoked attack on one of the League's member states. He was decisively rebuffed by the trade union leader and, after 1945 Labour Foreign Secretary Ernest Bevin, who famously derided Lansbury's sanctimonious posturings as 'hawking your conscience from body to body asking to be told what to do with it'. Days afterwards, with the fascist dictators arming themselves for a new world war, Lansbury, his pacifism rejected, resigned, and was replaced by Clement Atlee, who returned Labour to a policy of national defence and opposition to Tory appeasement of Hitler. Lansbury however continued in his Corbynesque quest for a world without war by seeking disarmament agreements with dictators who were busily and quite openly preparing to launch another one. In April 1937, he was granted a private audience with Hitler, followed by another with Mussolini. In October 1938, Lansbury, quite logically from his pacifist standpoint, welcomed the Munich agreement that handed over to Hitler the Czech Sudentland.

If a pacifist, in a purely private capacity, chooses to proffer his cheeks to the first thug that comes along and tries to persuade others to do the same and, in doing so, only puts at risk his own life and liberty, that is his own affair. However, it is an entirely different matter when the same pacifist, but now in a position of political authority, as Lansbury was then, and Corbyn, although he rejects that label, is now, seeks to make the same choice for others by denying to them the means to defend themselves if they wish to do so, as was without doubt the case with the majority of the public in Lansbury's time as Labour Leader. Few, apart from pacifists, Leninists and pro-Jihadi Muslims, will disagree with the proposition that the first duty of any UK government, be it left or right, is to protect the country's territorial integrity, democracy, freedoms and security from attack, whether internally from terrorism, or externally, from conventional military threats. Lansbury did not think so, and rightly paid the political penalty. Neither does Corbyn, but in his case, he has been rewarded by being elected twice to the leadership of the Labour Party, ironically with the assistance of some of the present-day successors to Ernest Bevin.

Let us be clear about Corbyn's stance on the defence of the UK. When asked at a party leadership husting by his opponent Owen Smith whether, if required to do so, he would honour Clause Five of the Washington Treaty, which obligates all NATO member states to come to the assistance of any member that is attacked, Corbyn declined to answer. Instead of giving an honest statement of his position, as Lansbury did in refusing to endorse a similar commitment to League of Nations sanctions against Mussolini, he offered a sanctimonious platitude that could also just as easily come from the lips of Lansbury: 'I don't wish to go to war. What I want to do is achieve a world where we don't need to go to war.' No sane and decent person would *wish* to go to war. But wishing is not the issue. There are occasions, as for example when there is a straight choice between submitting to tyranny and resisting it, a sane and freedom-loving person would accept that that fighting back, or as Corbyn calls, it 'going to war', is the only option. For those who always value 'peace' above all else, even if it is a peace brought about by submission to tyranny, war must be avoided at all costs, including those of democracy and freedom.

Pacifists make much of their belief in the 'sanctity of life' and regale those who are not convinced by their arguments with homilies on 'the futility of war', for example the wars that defeated Hitler, put an end to slavery in the USA, drove the US military out of Vietnam, removed the fascist Saddam regime in Iraq, and repelled the five Arab armies who invaded Israel at its birth in 1948. The reality is that so long as the entire world's population does not share its absolute rejection of violence, pacifism, far from being a means of preserving life, will more resemble a death cult. No-one has demolished the case for pacifism better than Sam Harris:

> While it can seem noble enough when the stakes are low, pacifism is nothing more than a willingness to die, and to let others die, at the pleasure of the world's thugs. It

should be enough to note that a single sociopath, armed with nothing more than a knife, could exterminate a city full of pacifists.

'A willingness to die' is exactly what Gandhi recommended to the Jews of Europe as the Nazis herded them into the gas chambers of the Third Reich. A 'general massacre of the Jews' was not only to be preferred to any active resistance, such as took place at Sobibor and a number of other death camps. Extermination at the hands of the Nazis would be 'a day of thanksgiving and joy that Jehovah had wrought deliverance of the race even at the hands of the tyrant'. It was in the same spirit that after the fall of France in June 1940, and with the UK faced with the threat of a Nazi invasion, Gandhi chose that very moment to call on the British, *but not the Germans*, to lay down their arms, the same policy that Corbyn has advocated consistently throughout his more than four decades of membership of the Campaign for Nuclear Disarmament. His substitute for a defence policy has not impressed voters, not least his laughable attempt to appease trade union leaders whose members' jobs depended on the up-dating of the Trident fleet, by agreeing to spend tax payer's money on the construction of new nuclear submarines on the condition that they carried no nuclear weapons! So why not go the whole pacifist hog and have guns with no bullets, warships and tanks with no means of propulsion and ammunition, and planes with no wings?

Who exactly are the Corbynistas, those dream-world idealists who reject the need and right of their country to defend itself, but in many cases, if their online missives are any guide, support the right of Jihadis to kill Israeli Jews? A 2016 study revealed that of those who evince an interest in politics, the younger the age group, the higher the value that its cohort places on extra-parliamentary activities such as protest meetings, 'flash mobs', demonstrations, publicity seeking-stunts, and interaction via social media and the like, whereas voting rated the lowest. As is all too evident from the chants at meetings and the slogans displayed on banners, posters and even T-shirts, their first loyalty, one that it totally uncritical and akin in its naivety and fervour to religious devotion, is to Saint Jeremy, and not the party founded by British trade unionists to provide a political voice for the working class in Parliament. Parliament, a nest of traitors, is not where the real action is, but on the street, on the smart phone, in a mass meeting or a pop concert addressed by the Supreme Leader where the faithful hang on his every (invariably banal) word as if it were gospel, or at a husting where doubters and dissenters are booed, heckled and insulted, and on-line, where traitor MPs can be anonymously bombarded with anti-Semitic slurs and death and even rape threats.

This preference among the young for 'direct action', and rejection of what is seen as 'establishment' politics has created a fertile source of recruitment by the more seasoned far left. Reared in the elitist tradition of Lenin, popularity with the broad public was always generally a secondary concern, the prime objective being the creation or, by means of an entry operation such as Momentum, the capture of a political machine. This machine, staffed by a cadre of professional political activists, those whom Lenin termed as the 'vanguard', would then, at the appropriate moment, and armed with political insights, strategy and tactics beyond the comprehension of the untutored masses, place itself at the head of movements that could be harnessed for the overthrow of the bourgeois order. Such has been the dream since the Bolshevik coup of November 1917, that what Lenin achieved in

Russia can and one day will be accomplished in the countries of the democratic west.

The classic exponents of the entryist version of this strategy were of course the so-called Militant Tendency, the remnants of which, after a series of splits and expulsions from the Labour Party, remerged in their new guise of the Socialist Party under the leadership of the veteran Trotskyist Peter Taaffe. Replying to entirely justified accusations that Momentum was being manipulated by Trotskyist entryists, Taaffe revealed he had already sounded out Corbyn as to the possibility of lifting of the ban imposed on groups such his own, who could then be accepted as individual members of the Labour Party. Corbyn, said Taaffe, was 'a good bloke. He's principled. He's on the left.' So was Stalin. Taaffe was not the least concerned that the conflict between the Corbynistas and their opponents might lead to a split in the Labour Party: 'The civil war, now it's open, cannot be called off.' He was perfectly sanguine about a Corbynite rump being reduced to as few as 20 MPs. Who needs a majority in Parliament when 'the lava of revolution was still hot'? That is why ousting the Tories by winning a General Election was the least of the far left's concerns, as Momentum Chairman Jon Lansman explained: '"Winning" is the small bit that matters to political elites who want to keep power to themselves'. The 'political elites' in question are those 170 or so anti-Corbyn Labour MP elected by the votes of millions and accountable to their constituents, while the self-selecting elite that owns and controls Momentum directs a party within a party, complete with a constitution, membership subscriptions, offices and full-time staff, all totally contrary to Labour Party rules and with the approval of its leader. Lansman, together with Corbyn's Chief of Staff Simon Fletcher, is one of the two directors of the company that legally owns Momentum, 'Momentum Campaign (Services) Ltd'.

Yet for all the far left's genuine and undisguised scorn for conventional political activity and established democratic institutions, entryists have been elected as councillors, Labour MPs, and even, briefly and disastrously, as in Liverpool, have captured a majority on a Labour Council. For a number of reasons, among them its rich ethnic mix and large and politically active radical middle class, London is especially vulnerable to a leftist take-over, as the Livingstone experience has demonstrated. Half of the Corbynised Labour Party membership lives in London. So it was no surprise when, following hard on the heels of the Corbynite putsch, Sadiq Khan, the Muslim Labour MP for Tooting, South London, was adopted as Labour's candidate for Mayor of London by the Sharia left-dominated London Labour Party. Perhaps the assumption was that as Muslim, he would be amenable to toeing the Sharia leftist line. If so, it would have been a reasonable, though, as it proved to his credit, false one. He became one of Corbyn's harshest critics, not least for his abject failure to curb the surge of anti-Semitism in the Labour Party that followed his selection as Leader. After failing in their bid to prevent him addressing the 2017 Labour Party Conference, Momentum delegates took their revenge by heckling him throughout his speech A kinder politics. He also did himself no favours with his more bigoted fellow Muslims, incurring a death sentence *fatwah* after declaring his support for same-sex marriage, and likewise, also with Corbynistas, by joining the Campaign Against Anti-Semitism, instrumental in launching the EHRC investigation into Labour Party anti-Semitism. In all, as Mayor of London, Sadiq Khan proved himself an exemplar of how Muslims should conduct themselves in public office. True, there had been times in Khan's legal career when as solicitor, he had become involved in cases and causes that had

Jihadist undertones, to say the least. Be that as it may, no doubt acutely aware of the political climate following the rise of the Islamic State and the two massacres in Paris, every effort was made to present Khan as a strictly Labour, and not Muslim candidate. However, just as was the case with Corbyn, once he became a candidate for London Mayor, his past came under close scrutiny. What was revealed was not so much anything detrimental to Khan himself, but a glimpse of the Muslim political underworld that swirled around him.

When Khan was first elected to Parliament in 2010, Nasser Butt, the Liberal candidate was also a Muslim, though as a member of the Amadiyyah sect, not recognised as such by Khan's Sunni Muslim supporters in the constituency. So great was the sectarian hatred directed against the Liberal candidate (though it must be stressed, disowned and condemned by Khan) that for his safety he was advised not to attend a husting (attended by leading Labour anti-Semite Ken Livingstone) at Khan's local mosque, the Tooting Islamic Centre. When Mark Clarke, the part-Asian Conservative candidate, arrived, he was mistaken for the Liberal one and, to save him from a lynching, he had to be locked in a room together with his election agent at the rear of the building. Members of the Tooting Islamic Centre's congregation were instructed not to vote for Nasser Butt, since he was deemed to be an apostate, the punishment for which under Sharia law is death. Not surprisingly then, Tooting was the focal point for a campaign of incitement to murder members of the local Amadiyyah congregation, one which in the very best traditions of Islamic tolerance, included a leaflet in Urdu inviting Sunni Muslims to 'kill a Qadiyani and the doors to heaven will be open to you.' This was in Tooting, London, not Lahore, Pakistan. The Tooting Centre's imam, Shaikh Sulaiman Ghani, notorious for his hatred of the Amadiyyahs, had shared platforms with Khan on no fewer than nine occasions, and had tried, unsuccessfully to organise a Muslim boycott of Amadiyyah shopkeepers. He was also billed to share a platform on April 30, 2016 in Dewsbury with other four Muslim speakers and local Labour MP Paula Sherriff, at a Gaza (that is to say, Hamas) fund raising event. Even though it was made clear on its promotional materials that the meeting would be segregated, and ticket applications had to made separately for men and women, Sherriff only withdrew after protests at her participation in a segregated event.

Why had a Tooting imam agreed to speak with a local Labour MP in support of Hamas in of all places, Dewsbury, a run-down Yorkshire mill town? What possible interest could a Muslim terrorist movement dedicated to annihilating Israel and murdering all its Jews hold for the good citizens of Dewsbury? Let me provide some facts about the town, and then leave it to you, the reader, to decide for yourself what that answer might be. Dewsbury is a small town, population 62,000, but it has, at the latest count, no fewer than 28 mosques, some, including the largest, funded by the Saudi monarchy. The concentration of mainly Sunni Muslims is so dense, in the west of the town more than 50%, that it has been called the Islamic Republic of Dewsbury. In the Savile Town area, the 2011 census revealed that only 4, repeat, four, of its 4033 inhabitants were non-Muslims. So much for 'diversity'. In Dewsbury, the triumph of anti-integrationist multiculturalism had been so complete that even the lady in the Rossi's ice cream van wore a burka to protect herself from being raped by her almost exclusively Muslim schoolboy customers. In recent years, after centuries of obscurity, Dewsbury has repeatedly been in the news, on each occasion for religious reasons. In 2005, the town provided two of the four Muslim suicide bombers who carried out the 7/7 attack on the London transport system. A Dewsbury born and bred Muslim, the 16-year-old Hammad Munshi, brought more fame to the town when he became the UK's youngest convicted terrorist. He was arrested while walking home from school carrying two bags of ball bearings. Dewsbury also holds the record for having reared the UK's youngest ever suicide bomber, Talha Asmil, aged 17, who in June 2015, on an Islamic State mission to murder Shi'a Muslims, blew himself up in Iraq.

Then in March 2016, once sleepy Dewsbury yet again featured in the mainstream media when it was revealed that a local *madrassah*, the Islamic Tarbiyah Academy no less, taught an anti-Semitic, Jihadi curriculum to its 140 Muslim pupils. As in Saudi Arabian schools, amongst its teaching materials were those based on the text so often cited and much revered by the Nazis and Hamas, *The Protocols of the Learned Elders of Zion.* ensuring, for such is the intention, that like millions of other young Muslims, the *madrassah*'s brainwashed pupils will grow up believing that they are the victims of a conspiracy by 0.2% of the world's population to subvert a religion followed by 22%. The founder of the 'Academy', Mufti Zabair Dudha, was no small-town preacher. He was the overseer for around half of the UK's Mosques and *madrassahs*. So, again, I pose the question…why did the Tooting Mosque imam decide it was expedient to speak in of all places, Dewsbury, in support of a genocidal terrorist movement? Shaikh Ghani makes no attempt to conceal his Jihadi convictions, calling publicly on Muslims to establish an Islamic State in the UK, and depicting women as inferior and therefore necessarily 'subservient' to men. He also, again publicly, has denounced attempts by UK security agencies to prevent British Muslims travelling to Syria to fight for the Islamic State. It was no surprise then that when Khan's local imam learned the result of the Labour leadership contest, he posted the following message: 'Congratulations to newly elected leader of the Labour party, Jeremy Corbyn. Brilliant victory. Things can and will change'. And how. A month later, two Muslim youths were arrested after an arson attack on the Tooting Amadiyyah mosque, followed by the murder of Glasgow Amadiyyah shopkeeper by a Sunni Muslim after he tweeted Easter greetings to Christians, and within the Labour Patty, a barrage of anti-semitic comments by Muslim councillors, Momentum activists, a Labour MP and Corbyn's defence adviser and former London Mayor, Ken Livingstone, each representing the key constituent participants in what was to become the Corbynista hijacking of the Labour Party: the old, Benn era left, the student radicals and entryists, and Muslims, with anti-Zionism, in some cases shading into anti-Semitism, as the common denominator.

Just how firm the grip of the Sharia Left on the upper echelons of the Labour Party had rapidly become following the election of Corbyn was highlighted by the way its National Executive Committee handled the case of Gerry Downing. Downing is the leader of the tiny Trotskyist group that goes by the name of Socialist Fight. He shares with many others on the Sharia left and in the Arab world the belief as he put it that 'the Nazis collaborated with the Zionists in transporting Jews to Palestine' and not, as non-Sharia left history tells it, to death and slave camps in Poland. We have already seen how, as an integral part of the Sharia left's obsessional campaigning against Israel, a new, totally inverted history of the Second World War had been concocted over the years by those who rallied to the Corbynite leadership of the Labour Party, in which Jews were depicted as allies of the Nazis, and the Arabs as their victims This Sharia left version of Holocaust denial, as featured in Downing's *Socialist Fight* of October 15, 2014, proved no obstacle to his enrolling in the Labour Party, along with other like-minded anti-Semites, with a view to electing Corbyn as its leader. Nor did his declaration in a TV interview that 9/11 'must never be condemned'. In his case, it took months before the Labour Party's highest body in March 2016 finally enforced its rule that members of rival socialist parties or groups such as Downing's cannot be at the same time also members of the Labour Party. However, the NEC initially saw things differently, and only suspended him from membership, a decision which begged the question, since his allegiance and anti-Semitic views were well known, why was he allowed to join in the first place? What was so special about Downing that required the waving of the party's long-standing regulation, Clause II, 5 A? It reads as follows:

> Political organisations not affiliated or associated under a national agreement with the party, having their own programme, principles and policy, or distinctive and separate propaganda, or possessing branches in the constituencies, or engaged in the promotion of parliamentary or local government candidates, or having allegiance to any political organisation situated abroad [Hamas and Hezbollah evidently do not qualify as such], shall be ineligible for membership of the party.

Socialist Fight competes with the SWP in being the most virulently anti-Zionist group on the far left, so much so that some of its comments became indistinguishable from Nazi anti-Semitism. It evidently attracts those who share its leader's stance on this issue, because a recruit to Socialist Fight, Ian Donovan, had been expelled from the orthodox Leninist Communist Party of Great Britain on a charge of anti-Semitism, specifically for subscribing to a leftist version of the claim, normally only encountered amongst Arabs, other Muslims and Nazis, that there exists a world Jewish conspiracy: 'For without the Zionist project, the Jewish-Zionist bourgeoisie, which is a key component of the vanguard of world capital, would have no unifying ethos to hold it together…Without the Zionist project as a unifying force, it would over time dissolve into the various imperialist bourgeoisies.' It was precisely for holding views such as this that he was encouraged to find a more welcoming home in Socialist Fight. Its leader, Gerry Downing, explains: 'I invited Ian Donovan to join Socialist Fight because I studied the dispute he had with the *Weekly Worker* [the CPGB weekly] …and concluded that Ian was correct…In fact he was taking a very courageous[sic] stand against the liberal Zionism of the soft left in Britain and globally.'

Socialist Fight also runs the SWP close in its support for what the latter calls 'militant Islamism': 'We defend the Islamic State in Syria and Iraq against the bombing of US imperialism'. But what could have endeared him most to his supporters on the Labour Party's NEC was his tweet denouncing the 'glaringly obvious' 'role the Zionists [for which read 'Jews'] have played in the attempted witch hunt against Jeremy Corbyn's leadership campaign.' In addition to smuggling open anti-Semites into the Labour Party, Momentumistas have proved adept at hounding those Labour MP s who do not toe the anti-Zionist line of their leader, especially if the MP happens to be Jewish. Such was the case in the Liverpool Riverside Constituency Labour Party, where a Corbynite claque week after week disrupted normal Party business by demanding that the sitting MP, Louise Ellman, declare her attitude towards the state of Israel. On at least three occasions, these sessions involved open anti-Semitic abuse, one local councillor describing the atmosphere generated by the attacks as 'intimidating and hostile'.

Momentum activist Vicky Kirby, former Parliamentary candidate for Woking and Vice Chairperson of its Constituency Labour Party was suspended (only suspended!) *and then re-admitted* to the party after tweeting: 'Hitler was a Zionist God' (shades of Livingstone). Other offerings included 'What do you know abt Jews? They've got big noses and support the Spurs' and 'I will never forget and I will make sure my kids teach their children how evil Israel is', and yet another, that Jews 'slaughter the oppressed'. When members demanded her expulsion, Corbyn's office came to her rescue, saying that any further action would be taken only on the basis of 'new evidence'. Given that the evidence cited here did not constitute any kind of proof for Corbyn of anti-Semitism, it is difficult to conceive what this 'new evidence' would have to consist of to secure her expulsion. Another prominent Corbynista, Jacqueline Walker, Vice Chairperson of the Momentum National Steering Committee, weighed in with the accusation that the Jews 'were the chief financiers of the sugar and slave trade' and demanded that the Jews should make amends for their 'contribution to the African Holocaust'. But not Christians and Muslims, who were its real perpetrators. Briefly suspended along with scores of others of a like mind, she was then restored to full membership.

No such kid glove treatment was afforded *Sunday Times* journalist Rod Liddle, a Labour Party member of some thirty-seven years standing, who was expelled for having the courage to say what everyone knew to be true, that 'anti-Semitism is visceral for many Muslims'. Yet what he said, or rather wrote on his blog, was no different from what the Shi'a Muslim Mehdi Hasan, the biographer of former Jewish Labour leader Ed Miliband, said in the leftist *New Statesman* three years previously, that anti-Semitism was 'our dirty little secret', 'routine and commonplace'. Following his suspension, (on grounds that were not made public) Liddle remained unrepentant. Speculating on the probable motives for the action, he wrote on his blog: 'Perhaps it is my suggestion that many Muslims are not favourably inclined towards the Jews', a reasonable deduction from the well-established fact that many high-ranking Muslims have quite openly either denied the Holocaust or proclaimed their admiration for Hitler, including elected office holding members of the Labour Party and associates of its current leader. Liddle also thought the same of his no less well-founded prediction that 'if the Palestinians were given Israel', as was indeed proposed by Muslim Labour MP Naz(i) Shah, after the 'relocation' of its six million Jews to the USA, 'they would turn it very quickly into a Somalia" He could have added, just as the PLO did to Lebanon. Such home truths, Liddle believed, had evidently enraged Labour's 'new commissars'. Speculating on his forthcoming Kafkaesque trial on as yet unspecified charges (I suggest 'Excessive zeal and honesty in combatting anti-Semitism') Liddle commented, ironically, 'I see this as an opportunity and also a chance to apologise for having dared to suggest that any Muslim anywhere could ever be accused of anti-Semitism, and to insist that my reference to Somalia was a dreadful mistake, for which I am terribly, grovelling sorry – I meant they could turn it into a Switzerland. I sometimes get countries beginning with 'S' confused.'

Liddle shares my belief, for which there is ample evidence, that anti-Semitism is, as he puts it, 'endemic within two sections of the Labour Party, the perpetually adolescent white middle class lefties and the Muslims – the latter of whom now comprise a significant proportion of Labour activists and voters in parts of London and the dilapidated former mill towns of West Yorkshire and East Lancashire. And Luton. And parts of the Midlands.' Spot on. Cases such as those described above…and there are many others similar…invites the suspicion that the election of the anti-Zionist patriarch Corbyn as Labour leader, and with it, the combined impact of the arrival in the party of several thousand fanatical Sharia leftists, together with its Islamisation in areas of dense Muslim diaspora settlement, have triggered an outpouring of public Jew-hatred not experienced in the UK since the pre-war heyday of Sir Oswald Mosley's Black Shirted British Union of Fascists. Incidentally, his admirers are still in business, with Robert Edwards lending his voice to the anti-Israel chorus of Muslims and Sharia leftists with his accusation of Zionist genocide in issue number 17 of his *European Socialist [sic] Action* of 2008 that 'in Israel's "War of Independence", entire villages of innocent Palestinians were slaughtered without mercy.' Ignoring the fact that it was the combined armies of five Arab countries that had invaded the newly-born state to slaughter its outnumbered and poorly-armed Jews, Edwards described the embattled Jews as 'psychopaths' who had waged 'cold blooded campaigns against the Palestinian people' and, recycling on the far right another charge promoted by the Sharia left, complained that Jews 'to this day use the same moral blackmail of "anti-Semitism" against those who dare criticise this criminal behaviour'.

The toleration within Labour of an often-identical anti-Semitism since the election of the party's new leader can partly be put down to the fact that Corbyn and those closest to him have for years mixed in company where such comments are regarded as perfectly normal and justified. One such is Kahdim Hussain, former Labour Mayor of Bradford and currently a Bradford Labour Councillor, who endorsed a Facebook posting praising Hitler for killing 'six million Zionists', a Holocaust that is distinctly at odds with one popular Muslim version that is also, it would seem, favoured by Downing, the one that has nameless Nazis (not Hitler) killing a far smaller number of non-Zionists Jews and allowing (or in Downing's version, actually 'transporting') the remainder to emigrate to an as yet non-existent Israel. But however wildly the fantasies may vary, the bigotry is constant. Coherence and evidence however were never anti-Semitism's strong point, and so it has also proved with Muslim and Sharia left evaluations of the Islamic State. While the Kensington Labour Councillor and 'Big Brother' contestant, the Muslim Beinazir Lasharie, was suspended (only suspended) in October 2015 for posting a video entitled 'ISIS: 'Israeli Secret Intelligence Service', and adding her own comment that 'many people [also] know who was behind 9/11', John Tummon, formerly of the anti-Zionist 'Socialist Unity' but now a Corbynite Labour Party member, continued to advertise his support for the Islamic State (one with a 'progressive potential') as a necessary factor in achieving an 'overarching settlement in the northern Middle East'. Predictably, the claim, first made by the Palestinian Authority, that Israel Intelligence had mastermind the 2016 Brussels massacre (See Appendix Y) quickly went the rounds on Labour's Corbynite left. Bob Campbell assured fellow party members that Mossad 'runs ISIS and was behind the Brussels bombings', an accusation endorsed by John MacAuliffe, who claimed it was 'a fact' that 'all countries back rebel and terror groups all the time'. Following the Corbynista influx, comments such as these were becoming quite routine on Labour's left. Then there is the case of Luciana Berger, a Jewish Labour MP. Despite being (briefly) a member of Corbyn's shadow cabinet, she was designated as 'hostile' to the Labour leader in a list produced by Corbynite loyalists. Opponents of Corbyn claimed this evaluation was motivated by anti-Semitism. True or not, there was no doubt that such was the case when she received anti-Semitic hate mail, including a photo of herself with the star of David superimposed on her forehead.

In areas where Labour is partly dependent on the Muslim vote to secure the election of its candidates, in some cases the result has been the conversion of the party from a movement performing its original role of representing the interests of working people, irrespective of creed or race, to one that panders to the ambitions and anti-Semitic prejudices of those who claim to speak for 'the Muslim community'. The classic case is Luton, where Jihadi Islam is so deeply rooted inside the local Labour Party that that it secured the election to the town's council of an avowed anti-semite and admirer of Adolf Hitler. Aysegal Gurbuz was a busy young lady. As a student at Warwick University, she served on its Friends of Palestine Society, while back in her home town, and aged only 20, she had already been elected as a Labour councillor for Luton's High Town Ward and appointed a member of the panel that supervises the Bedford Police Authority. Since Islam holds that women are endowed with intellects inferior to those of men, and given not only her gender but her age, one naturally suspects that Gurbuz owed her extraordinary rise to the men who dominate the affairs of Luton's Muslims, and would therefore be beholden to them rather than those she was elected to represent. In the main body of this work, evidence was provided that at least one leading and, by gullible *kuffars*, respected Luton cleric publicly proclaimed his belief in a World Jewish Conspiracy. Councillor Gurbuz went one step further by praising the politician who dedicated his life to combatting it. On her twitter account, she announced to anyone who might have read it that not Mohammed, but 'my man Hitler' was' the greatest man in history', possibly because Hitler killed far more Jews than the founder of her religion. Unlike many of her co-religionists and Sharia leftists, Councillor Gurbuz evidently does not subscribe to the belief that the Nazis were the architects of Israel: 'If it wasn't for my man Hitler, these Jews would have wiped Palestine years ago.' She expressed the hope that Iran would use nuclear weapons to honour its Supreme Leader's pledge to 'wipe Israel off the map' instead. Another posting said, 'Jews can't expect us to sympathise with their history under Hitler'. A tweet before the 2015 General Election seemed to imply that a Tory victory was to be welcomed: 'Ed Miliband is Jewish. He will never become Prime Minister.' A substantial number of her co-religionists must have agreed, because at that election, the Conservatives secured their highest-ever Muslim vote.

Traditional Labour Party members with an awareness of their movement's past must surely be asking themselves: how does in come about that someone selected and then elected to hold office on behalf of the Labour Party reveal herself to be an admirer of the head of a regime that not only exterminated six million Jews, but of one that destroyed the most powerful workers movement in history, and was directly responsible for the imprisonment, torture and murder of countless thousands of its most dedicated and courageous militants? The answer lies in the fact like so many other Muslim Labour Party members, her prime allegiance lies elsewhere than in the secular world. Hers is with a religion. Nobody in her local party or her Arab friends at Warwick University, a hot bed of anti-Zionism, appears to have been troubled by her views on the Jews and the Nazis. Hers was after all a milieu in which such attitudes are a commonplace. It was only when they were detected by the Campaign Against Anti-Semitism and reported to the relevant authorities was any action taken. In April 2016, High Town Ward's Hitler-loving genocidal councillor was suspended from her Labour Party membership...

suspended but not summarily expelled. What then does it take to be expelled? After initially implausibly claiming that the tweets were her sister's, (the *Koran* in Chapter 3, Verse 28, sanctions lying to *kuffars*, this being the tactic of *taqiyya*) she admitted they were hers and resigned. She is now free to join a Nazi party of her choice.

She was very far from being the only Muslim councillor to vent such views. Salim Mulla, Mayor then a councillor of Blackburn, felt compelled to post on Facebook that 'Zionist Jews are disgrace to humanity' and that ISIS was a Jewish creation. Nottingham Councillor Llyas Aziz, in addition to endorsing Shah's call for what should properly be called her 'final solution of the Israeli Question', could not resist adding for good measure that the Jews of Israel were behaving like Nazis in their treatment of the Palestinians. This comment was then in its turn endorsed by yet another Muslim Labour Councillor, Burnley's Khadim Hussain. Former Lord Mayor of Bradford, Hussain claimed that 'your [sic] education system only tells you about Anne Frank and the six million Zionists [sic] that were killed by Hitler, and nothing about the millions killed in Africa'…nor we can be sure about the victims of the Muslim slave trade. Finally, in this small selection of Jew-baiting Labour Muslims (See Appendix T for more), Newport Councillor Miqdad al-Nuaimi, first suspended and then re-instated after he tweeted that the Jews of Israel have 'the same arrogant mentality as the Nazis'. These Muslims quite openly conducted themselves as if they were elected to office to wage a theologically-inspired vendetta against the Jews, and not to represent all their constituents, irrespective of their political and, if any, religious allegiances.

Aside from political correctness, which can licence Muslims to say what infidels must not, maybe a clue as to why expressing such views did not result in automatic expulsion from the Labour Party was provided when, in the same year, 2016, a matter days before council, regional and mayoral elections, potential Labour voters were confronted by the spectacle of the suspended Livingstone trying to persuade TV interviewer Andrew Neil that anti-Semitism was 'not exactly the same thing as racism'. This was a judgement shared by Corbynista MP Naz(i) Shah who, following her suspension for on-line comments on the Jews, confessed she 'didn't get [sic] anti-Semitism as racism'. In her case, understandably, because as one Muslim has publicly admitted, in the 'Islamic community', the 'dirty little secret' of Jew-hatred is the norm.

When Labour's anti-Semitism crisis become compounded by a challenge to Corbyn's leadership by Owen Smith in the summer of 2016, so the more was it attributed by vigilant Corbynistas to the machinations of Zionists. A prominent critic of Corbyn and member of Labour Friends of Israel, MP Margaret Hodge, was accused by the anti-Zionist website *Electronic Intifada* of 'launch[ing] a coup against Labour Party leader Jeremy Corbyn' whom, the item hastened to add, 'supports boycotts of Israel'. What it called 'Labour's fake anti-Semitism crisis' had been 'almost entirely manufactured and was based from the outset on fabricated and exaggerated claims of anti-Semitism that were deliberately aimed at smearing Corbyn, the left, and the Palestinian solidarity movement in general.' Livingstone, perhaps forgetting that it was his claim that 'Hitler supported Zionism' which triggered the affair, implied that the Jewish issue had been manufactured by anti-Corbyn MPs to lose Labour support at the polls: 'You've had smear after smear against Jeremy. The anti-Semitism stuff [sic!] damaged us with the local elections, but not enough to trigger a leadership challenge then.'

With their leader's grip on the party supposedly threatened by Zionist plottings, Corbyn's street army rose to the challenge. As his support amongst Labour MPs shrank, outside Westminster, in Il Piazza Del Parliamento, Corbyn rallied his enraged *squadristas,* some sporting on their red T shirts the snappy logo 'Eradicate the Right-Wing Blairite Vermin'. His audience, partly composed of SWP Brexiteers, demonstrated their loyalty to the beleaguered *Duce* with rhythmic chants of 'Corbyn, Corbyn, Corbyn', interspersed with 'Blairite scum' and 'Blairites out', holding aloft North Korean-style placards bearing portraits of the Dear Leader. Around the UK, constituency party offices were besieged, one having a brick thrown through a window. Rebel MPs were bombarded with death and even rape threats to themselves and their families, with some requiring police protection. The level of intimidation was such that even the party's Corbynista-dominated NEC found it necessary to suspend all local party meetings until the voting for leader had been completed. And of course, anti-Semitism was never far away. Shadow cabinet member Jess Philips revealed in her resignation letter to Corbyn that 'writing or saying anything against you risks my job, the livelihood of family. The threats are rolling in'. Among her other crimes, her letter said, was that of being…yes, but of course, a 'Zionist plotter', bought, she later told a meeting of Labour MPs, by 'Zionist money'. One of Corbyn's most vocal trade union supporters, Len McClusky, claimed in a TV interview that Momentum had nothing to do with such incidents. It was the work of intelligence agents posing as Corbynites: 'Do you believe for one moment that the security forces are not involved in dark practices?... Do you think there's not all kinds of right wingers who are not able to disguise themselves and stir up trouble? I find that amazing if people think that isn't happening.' Whether it was Mossad or MI5, the consensus, akin to that of a Manichean religious cult, was that opposition to Corbyn had to be conspiracy and could not be motivated by genuine and sincere disagreement with his polices and his fitness to lead the party.

Corbyn's campaign for the Labour leadership had been dogged from its first days by a succession of damning (at least for some) revelations concerning his many and long-standing associations with avowed anti-Semites, so it was only to be expected that the 'Jewish question' would loom large in the dramatic events unfolding in his bid for survival. On June 30, 2016, one week after the Brexit referendum, at the meeting where Corbyn launched the Labour Party's report on its internal inquiry into anti-Semitism, copies of a leaflet were circulated claiming the accusations of anti-Semitism within the Labour Party were 'unfounded' and therefore the inquiry and report were 'unnecessary'. Very much in the same spirit, and evidently unable even on such an occasion to resist an opportunity to attack Zionism, in introducing the report, Corbyn drew a direct parallel between Israel and the Islamic State: 'Our Jewish friends [sic…closet anti-Semites habitually boast of having 'Jewish friends'] are no more responsible for the actions of Israel or the Netanyahu government than our Muslim friends are for those of various self-styled Islamic states.' While there are 57 states, if we include the Palestinian Authority, that have Islam as their official religion, there is only one that calls itself the Islamic State. And surely, he could not have been referring to his former employer, the Islamic Republic of Iran.

The fallout following these comments was immediate and for Corbyn, should have been devastating. UK Chief Rabbi Ephraim Mervis said Corbyn's comments 'however they were intended, were themselves offensive', while his predecessor, Jonathan Sacks, was less charitable, describing them as

> a demonization of the highest order, an outrage. That this occurred at the launch of the report into the Labour Party's recent troubles with anti-Semitism shows how deep the sickness is in parts of left-wing British politics today. Israel is a democratic state. The Islamic State is a terrorist entity. In the current political climate, this is all the more shocking.

Two other Rabbis, one ultra-Orthodox, (and also a Labour Party member) and one Liberal, weighed in with similar highly critical comments, the gist being that Corbyn himself was afflicted by the same prejudices that the report was supposedly designed to combat. Avrohom Pinter, the Labour Rabbi pointed out, 'one can disagree with the polices of the Israeli government, but to compare the democratically elected representatives of a sovereign state to a terrorist state which beheads people is totally unacceptable.'

The same fallout struck much closer to home when after only a few hours in office, Corbyn's newly-appointed Jewish Shadow Minister for Europe, Fabian Hammond, resigned, citing his leader's lamentable performance at the report launch. Within minutes of the incident, Corbyn had been reported to Labour's Compliance Unit for a possible breech of his own party's newly-adopted rules on anti-Semitism. The event sunk yet deeper into anti-Semitic slime when the *Guardian* journalist Marc Wadsworth of 'Momentum Black Connexions'(sic), was filmed accosting a Jewish Labour MP, Ruth Smeeth. He refused to hand her a press release calling for the deselection of anti-Corbyn MPs (including Smeeth herself), accused her of involvement a 'media conspiracy' and then ostentatiously made a note of her name, which he presumably already knew. Wadsworth then rounded off his performance by bellowing to his fellow journalists 'how white you all are', a demonstration of 'black truth' exposing 'white privilege'. Smeeth left the meeting in tears. Corbyn saw the incident and not only failed to intervene but was videoed later shaking hands and chatting with his Momentum comrade. The following recorded exchange took place: Wadsworth: 'I outed Smeeth, bloody talking to the Torygraph this morning.' Corbyn: 'I sent you a text about it.' The incident had apparently been pre-arranged. The leaflet in question described the 172 MP's who voted no-confidence in Corbyn as 'traitors' and endorsed Livingstone's call for their de-selection as candidates at the next general election. And yet from all this, Corbyn emerged unscathed not only amongst his faithful, but what is far more alarming, save for the UK's Jews, with the public at large

As for the report, while it spoke vaguely of a 'toxic atmosphere', it deployed the classic device of the straw man, fatuously insisting that the party was not 'overrun by anti-Semitism'. But nobody had claimed it was. Much worse, not only did the report fail to provide a working definition of anti-Semitism, nowhere in its 41 pages did it find to find room to cite so much as a single instance of the many cases of anti-Semitic statements made by Labour Party members, and to reveal the identity of those who made them. Here was an opportunity to show that the Labour Party meant business when it talked of combatting anti-Semitism. But instead, there was total silence on statements and activities that had been the subject of national media comment and criticism from the first weeks of Corbyn leadership bid. One of the reports several toothless recommendations was that those indulging in it could be dealt with by sanctions other than suspension or expulsion! As many expected, given that the guilty parties were either Muslims, supporters of Corbyn, or both, the inquiry had produced a report that was little more than a whitewash. Its failings were summed up by Jonathan Sacerdoti, Communications Officer of the Campaign Against Anti-Semitism:

> It did not examine the disgraceful cases of anti-Semitism in the party [such as, for example, 'Hitler is my man' and 'relocate Israel to the United States' to name but two of many] or even more disgraceful handling by the party leadership, including Jeremy Corbyn, who presides over a regime of the lightest slaps on wrists for the most deliberate and offensive anti-Semites. Inexcusably, the report proposes making it harder to suspend anti-Semites and keeping suspensions secret so as not to affect elections.

In a well-merited thrust at the company kept over the years by Corbyn, Sacerdoti drew attention to the report's rejection of 'any claims of anti-Semitism arising from sharing a platform with anti-Semites', and its suggestion that 'any anti-Semitic incident coming to light after two years should not be considered, a limitation period so short it has no parallel in any other disciplinary regime that we are aware of.' The report read as if Corbyn had drafted it himself, to protect himself. But he did not need to. Having just experienced at first hand a sample of the Momentum Jew-baiting the report was designed to cover up, Ruth Smeeth issued a statement:

> I call on Jeremy Corbyn to resign immediately and make way for somebody with the backbone to confront racism and anti-Semitism in our party and in the country…Until today I had made no public comment about Jeremy's ability to lead our party, but the fact that he failed to intervene is final proof for me that he is unfit to lead, and that a Labour party under his stewardship cannot be a safe place for British Jews.

Hardly an exaggeration, bearing in mind she was targeted by a Corbynista anti-Semite at, of all places, at event convened to promote Labour's opposition to anti-Semitism! Days before the September 2016 Labour Conference, Ruth Smeeth revealed that she had received 25,000 abusive online messages, including death threats. Many were of a blatantly anti-Sematic nature. One accused her of being a 'CIA/MI5/Mossad informant', and three others, 'a Yid cunt', a 'fucking traitor' and a 'dyke'. Abuse on this scale and consistency can only have been planned and co-ordinated, and understandably, Smeeth decided it was necessary for her own safety to attend the Labour Party conference accompanied by a bodyguard. A kinder politics! (It was this that led me to end my 40 years membership of the Labour Party. See Appendix N)

Also on the eve of the conference, more evidence accumulated that Momentum had no intention of reining in their attacks on the party's Jews. A campaign video released on Corbyn's official social media website featured topics that his supporters were tired hearing about. One of those featured was anti-Semitism. The Campaign Against Anti-Semitism (CAA) responded by sending a letter of complaint to Party Deputy Leader Tom Watson, accusing Corbyn of 'committing act that are grossly detrimental to the party' by 'characterising Jewish people as dishonest and dissembling in their reporting of anti-Semitism'. Its letter described how 'Corbyn's personal Facebook and Twitter accounts released a video featuring supporters declaring they were "tired of hearing" about anti-Semitism, characterising the Jewish community's complaints as "rubbish", physically and metaphorically to be tossed to the floor.' Before being withdrawn, the video had attracted *200,000* endorsements. At the same time, police were reported to have interviewed the author of a 1,000-word description of how he would murder Ruth Smeeth. Initially thought to be the work of a Neo-Nazi, in the event, the author proved to be a Corbynista. At the conference itself, more evidence emerged that Smeeth's concerns for her safety were well-founded. A leaflet, wholly Nazi in tone and content, was distributed to delegates demanding the dis-affiliation from the Labour party of the Jewish Labour Movement on the grounds that it was involved in a Zionist conspiracy against Corbyn, and being Jewish, was 'a representative of a foreign power'. (Back in May 1984, together with among other anti-Zionists Ken Livingstone, Corbyn launched a campaign to secure the expulsion of the Jewish Labour Movement from the Labour Party and, for good measure, for the TUC to severe all its fraternal links with the Israeli trade union movement, *Histadrut*. No support from these two was forthcoming for a campaign I was personally involved in at the same time for the TUC to sever its 'fraternal' links with state-run company unions of the Soviet bloc and the Labour Party with Soviet-bloc communist parties.)

No such considerations of national loyalty apply to those Muslims, or any other anti-Zionist members for that matter, who openly proclaim their allegiance to movements that wage a war of terror against this 'foreign power'. The demand to expel the Jewish Labour Movement from the Labour Party was identical in its anti-Semitic motivation to the eviction, with the connivance of security officials, of Jewish trade unionists from the TUC's 2015 Tolpuddle Martyrs commemoration event in Devon by a gang of Pro-Palestinian thugs. Very much in the same spirit, again at the 2016 Labour Party conference, an Israeli journalist reporting a Momentum fringe meeting has his credentials revoked little more than an hour after receiving them, with the transparently spurious excuse there were no more available. How then, did he get them in the first place? Someone not fully up to speed with Corbyn's version of zero tolerance of anti-Semitism had obviously blundered. Conference had not done with its abuse the Jewish Labour Movement. When its Chairman Mike Katz addressed the penultimate session, he was barracked and heckled for saying the lack of Jewish support for Labour made him 'weep' and that the report on anti-Semitism had failed to address the problem properly. Delegates shouted 'rubbish' and 'you don't speak for all Jews'.

On the final day of the conference, the story broke that at a Labour Party training event for combatting (sic) anti-Semitism, Momentum Vice-Chairman Jackie Walker, who earlier in the year had been briefly suspended for such choice comments as 'the Jews were the chief financiers of the sugar and slave trade ' and 'the Jewish Holocaust does not allow Zionists to do what they want', in the same spirit had endorsed a proposal first made by Corbyn in 2011 to in effect 'de-Zionise' Holocaust Memorial Day by renaming it 'Genocide Memorial Day'. It would be 'wonderful [sic!]' said Walker, if Holocaust Day was 'open to all people who experienced Holocaust', starting, we can be sure, with the Palestinians. Among messages posted after her suspension, one read: 'This was no training event. It was an Israeli-sponsored honey trap' and another: 'If Jackie Walker is sacked, I am done with Momentum. I will not betray the victims of Zionism.' Another read: 'Right wing smear tactics from Zionists and the right wing of the Labour Party. Jackie said NOTHING that can be construed as anti-Semitism…I am a member of Momentum and if the [Momentum] Committee expels Jackie then I can guarantee hundreds will stop paying their subscription.' When the question was put to the Momentum Steering Committee, a resolution to remove her from her post as Momentum Vice-Chairperson, but clearing her of all charges of anti-Semitism, and opposing her expulsion from the Labour Party, was carried by seven votes to three. Even though suspended from the Labour Party, she retained her position as a member of the Steering Committee.

The Labour Leader's second in command, Shadow Chancellor John McDonnell, often said quite openly what others of a like mind for tactical reasons chose to discuss only amongst themselves. The Chairman of his own leftist clique, the Labour Representation Committee, claimed, in an online article, that under its pre-Corbyn leadership {the most recent being the Jewish Miliband) the Labour Party had become 'a pawn [sic] of Zionist organisations'. And McDonnell went much further. Following in the footsteps of the *Protocols*, he implied that by subverting the entire party system, Jews were in effect ruling the UK: 'The most senior members of both the main parties and the Liberal Democrats [are] part of the network of Israeli influence.' His detestation of Israel was nothing new. From the early 2000s, McDonnell was featuring on his MP's website items glorifying Palestinian suicide attacks on Israeli civilians, one quoting the father of a suicide bomber who killed 19 mainly teenaged Jews in a Tel Aviv disco as saying, 'When martyrs blow themselves up, the Jews and the Americans listen'. After another suicide bombing that ended in the deaths of two Jews in a Jerusalem supermarket, McDonnell praised the attack as a 'successful heroic operation' that was 'an example to every Palestinian woman'. Unlike many on the left, McDonnell does not even pretend to support the 'two state solution'. 'Even if the Zionist state was the size of a postage stamp, it would have no right to exist'. On being elected Labour Leader, Corbyn chose McDonnell as his shadow chancellor of the exchequer along with another no less fanatical anti-Zionist, Livingstone, as his defence (sic) adviser.

As I have already said, anti-Semitism follows Corbyn and his inner circle around like a bad smell. But what else should we expect after spending most of their political careers in a sewer? Under his leadership, Momentum was still issuing blank cheques for Jew-baiting as if the Chakrabarti report had never happened. Setting an example in this respect, on the following Sunday after the release of the toothless report, and safe in the knowledge that his party's proposed rules on anti-Semitism would him allow to continue as before to associate with his friends from Hamas and Hezbollah, Corbyn was due back in his natural element at the annual London 'al-Quds Day' march sponsored by his Iranian pimps, which as in previous years, ended with a rally outside the Embassy of the Great Satan in Grosvenor Square. On campuses around the UK, 'no platforms' for ex-Muslim feminists, free-speech campaigners and supporters of Israel, but as the report's guidelines recommended, the Labour Party's leader sharing a platform with known anti-Semites was quite in order. The event's organisers, Corbyn's admired and comically-named 'Iranian Human Rights Commission', announced, as surely befitted the UK's highest profile anti-Zionist, that their dupe would be 'leading the march', but already in deep enough water for his anti-Semitic associations, he, or more likely his minders, decided a low profile was the more prudent option. Low profile was not the order the day however for Corbyn's Hezbollah friends who, as on previous marches, held aloft their movement's flag, the displaying of which possibly violated section three of the Terrorist Act of 2000. Asked to comment on the flaunting on the streets of London of the emblem of an anti-Semitic, terrorist movement dedicated to the destruction of Israel, London Mayor Sadiq Khan said that he understood 'the concerns of the Jewish community and the distress these flags cause many Londoners', but the matter was in the hands of the police.

As always, the Quds Day proceedings home and abroad were accompanied by messages of encouragement from Iran, with one cleric of the religion of peace, Hossein Salami, announcing that there were '100,000 missiles' in Lebanon alone, and thousands more around the Islamic world, all ready to 'strike at the heart of the Zionist regime, awaiting the command, so that when the trigger is pulled, the accursed black dot will be wiped off the geopolitical map of the world once and for all.' Strange company for a peace campaigner. Though the military wing of Hezbollah was banned in the UK as a terrorist organisation, its so-called 'political wing', under whose auspices the Quds Day rally was officially conducted, was not. In reply to claims that the distinction between the military (that is to say terrorist) and political wings of the move was fictitious, since they shared the same flag, the Home Office replied 'the context and manner in which the flag is displayed must demonstrate that it is specifically in support of the proscribed elements of the group.' So had Corbyn taken his usual place on the speaker's rostrum festooned by Hezbollah, flags, legally all would have been well. Finally, in February 2019, against Labour protests, a blanket ban was imposed on 'The Party of God'.

On June 4 2016, the day after the Quds Day rally, Corbyn found himself being questioned by his old friend and fellow Islamophile of many years standing, anti-Rushdie campaigner Labour MP Keith Vaz, in his capacity as Chairman the House of Commons Select Committee on Home Affairs The subject was Labour Party anti-Semitism. Even though given an easy ride, his lamentable and at time, distinctly shifty performance, consisting of little more than a succession of diversions, evasions and lies, can be viewed on line, so I leave it to the reader to draw their own conclusions as to whether such a person is fit to hold any public office, let alone that of a leader of a party or, Allah forbid, Prime Minister. At the outset of the proceedings, after being pressed on the matter, Corbyn reluctantly finally conceded that the Labour Party's own inquiry had not been independent since it had been conducted by someone who herself was a Labour Party member. (Having joined when she was given the task, she was on its completion elevated to the House of Lords for what many saw a reward for producing an anodyne report on Labour anti-Semitism,) A number of exchanges captured perfectly just how seriously Corbyn took the issue of anti-Semitism within his own party. Setting the tone for the entire proceedings, at the very outset, he claimed, contrary to other accounts that had put the number nearer to 80, that fewer than twenty members had been suspended (only suspended) after allegations of anti-Semitic conduct of one kind or another, implying, as he and his supporters had done on previous occasions, that the whole affair was a storm in a tea cup. Subsequent revelations as to its actual scale, and not least his own track record on the 'Jewish question', would give the lie to that claim.

Asked by Vaz what should be done with party members who use words like Hitler and 'Zio' to insult Jews, Corbyn replies, 'what will happen is they will be told they should not use them', this being the approach recommended by the party's powder-puff Chakrabarti report. So, a party member calls a Jew a Nazi, and is told not to say it again. And that would be that. Vaz, obviously dissatisfied by Corbyn's laid-back approach, told him that Committee members were concerned that the report described such manifestations of anti-Semitism as merely 'unhappy [sic] incidents'. Corbyn disagreed, defending the report as 'a bold step that we should be commended for', so bold indeed that it recommended that members guilty of anti-Semitic conduct should not be necessarily expelled or suspended, and that it was quite in order for members to appear on the same platform, as Corbyn did regularly, with anti-Semites. Questioned as to why a report devoted to the problem of anti-Semitism within the Labour Party offered no definition of anti-Semitism, Corbyn gave this substitute for an answer: 'I thought it would be very obvious what anti-Semitism is'. But if the offence is never defined, how can anyone be found guilty of it? And we know that within Corbyn's immediate circle there is at least one prominent anti-Zionist who has so defined anti-Semitism, at least to his own satisfaction, as to be able to claim that not once in his more than forty years in the Labour Party has he ever encountered it, and that moreover, anti-Semitism was 'not exactly the same thing as racism'. If so, why the inquiry?

Then there was the question of Israel, and Corbyn's decades of close involvement with campaigns, movements and individuals who, to put not too fine a point on it, do not wish Israel and its Jewish population well. Asked if he thought the state of Israel had a right to exist, Corbyn, seemingly caught off his guard, replies, 'Sorry?' Asked again, he replies with a blatantly evasive *non-sequitur*: 'Yes, the state of Israel exists, of course'. Yes, indeed it does, despite all the bloody endeavours of Comrade Corbyn's Jihadi 'friends'. But that was not the question, so Vaz tries for a third time. 'Yes, of course, our party's policy is for a two-state solution'. And so it is, though it most certainly is not that of his 'friends' Hamas and Hezbollah. But was it Corbyn's? This surely was the nub of the issue. But Vaz chose not to pursue it, perhaps because he already knew the answer, and wanted to save his friend from the dilemma of either of answering it truthfully or telling yet another lie that might put in him bad standing with his jihadi 'friends'. I provide in this work irrefutable evidence of what Corbyn's truthful answer to that question would have been, had Vaz asked it.

Instead, Vaz moved on to the anti-Zionist company Corbyn had kept over the years, highlighted by the meeting he hosted in Parliament in March 2009 for representatives of Hezbollah, of whom he said, together with Hamas, it was a 'pleasure and an honour' to call his 'friends'. When pressed by Vaz to say whether they were still his friends, Corbyn replied that he had used 'inclusive language' to further a 'peace process', but that they were not his friends now, and 'never were'. Readers are of course free to believe him if they wish. Either he was lying then, or lying to the Select Committee. All the evidence points to the latter, that they were his friends, are still his friends, and will remain his friends. As for a 'peace process' (something he has also recommended be pursued with the Islamic State) even the gullible Corbyn, for all his 'inclusive language' during his dealings with his friends in both Hamas and Hezbollah, must have realised that the two terrorist movements were seeking, not a negotiated peace with Israel, but its destruction, along with the murder of its entire Jewish population, because all he had to do to be aware of this was to read their founding charters, and the declarations of their leaders. Corbyn's claim that his involvement with anti-Semitic, genocidal terrorists was purely in the interests of a 'peace process' not only non-existent but impossible was, however, not challenged by Vaz. Neither was Corbyn asked to give evidence of the tangible results, if any, of his peace-making efforts, probably because Vaz knew they amounted to zero.

Perhaps the most extraordinary and damning exchanges occurred in relation to Corbyn's dealings with two notorious anti-Semites. The first was Sultan Raed

Salah, the Hamas preacher who claimed that no Jews went to work in the World Trade Centre on 9/11, and that Jews use murdered children's blood to mix with their Passover unleven bread. The second slander had been the cause of his conviction in an Israeli court. His notorious anti-Semitism also led in 2011 to an attempt by the Home Office to have him deported from the UK when Corbyn invited him to attend an anti-Zionist rally in Leicester and a meeting the next day of the Palestine Solidarity Campaign hosted by Corbyn at Westminster. Salah appeared at the Leicester event, but was arrested in London before the second. He was electronically tagged and, pending the outcome of his appeal against deportation, placed under house arrest where, Corbyn related to the Select Committee, he visited him, even though Corbyn must have been fully aware on what grounds Salah's freedom of movement was being restricted. After a lengthy legal process, an immigration tribunal found that although Salah was, as the Home Office originally claimed, an anti-Semite, his right to free speech entitled him not to be deported. (I agree with this decision. It is a scandal however that Home Office has also denied entry into the UK of a US scholar and a Dutch MP, not for telling lies about the Jews, but the truth about Islam.) The fact that Salah was an avowed anti-Semite of the most extreme kind did not seem to have troubled Corbyn in the least, engaged as the Sheikh undoubtingly was in the noble fight to eliminate the state of Israel. Had not Corbyn praised Salah as an 'honoured citizen' with 'a voice that must be heard', and looked forward to the day that he could take tea him with him on the House of Commons terrace? Vaz reminded Corbyn that he had shared a platform with Salah, 'who was found guilty by a British Judge of using the Blood Libel, the lie that Jews use Christians for rituals. You invited him for tea in the terrace of the House of Commons.' Corbyn saw nothing wrong with this, calmly replying: 'He didn't come', as if that resolved the matter of his involvement with a notorious anti-Semite. Vaz repeats, 'but you invited him'. Corbyn then explains why he couldn't make it:

> He was under house arrest. I met him to discuss the terms of his house arrest. He is an Israeli national and I was quite surprised if he was seen to be such a dangerous figure in Israel that he was allowed to travel. He travelled to this country and I did meet him while he was under house arrest and I had a very long discussion with him about how to bring about an eventual peace process in the Middle East and his concerns about the Palestinian people living within the borders of the state of Israel, and I said to him that I condemned any form of racism.

Let us see exactly what Salah had to say in a notorious speech made in Jerusalem in 2007 about the so-called 'blood libel', and then ask ourselves, how can anyone who wishes well of the Palestinian cause actively bring discredit on that cause not only by associating with someone who promotes such vile slanders against the Jews, but acts as their public champion?

> We have never allowed ourselves to knead the bread for the breaking of the fast during the blessed month of Ramadan with the blood of the children. And if someone wants a wider explanation you should ask what used to happen to some of the children of Europe, whose blood was mixed in the dough of the holy breads. God almighty, is this religion? God will confront you for what you are [sic] doing.

Vaz, palpably perplexed and embarrassed that his friend of many years did not seem in the least perturbed by Salah's particularly virulent anti-Semitism, asked if he would still invite him to tea on the House of Commons terrace. Corbyn replied, 'no, I don't think so' and added, sadly, 'but he is not coming back anyway'. He was then pressed on his no less amicable relations with the Reverend Stephen Sizer, who shared both Sultan Salah's belief that the Jews were responsible for 9/11 and a platform with Corbyn at the 2012 annual Iran-sponsored Quds Day march in London. Vaz put it to him: 'You wrote to defend a friend, Stephen Sizer, a vicar disciplined by the Church of England for anti-Semitism, saying he was under attack by a pro-Israeli smear campaign. Do you regret those comments?' Corbyn again evaded the question, opting instead as he did with Salah to sing, somewhat incoherently, the praises of yet another anti-Semitic brother-in-arms in the anti-Zionist movement: 'I've met Stephen Sizer on many occasions in his role as a vicar [?] and as somebody that does support Palestinian people, who feels with much justification that their human rights are under attack. There are people living in the Palestinian territories, and I was very surprised when that [sic] was done to him'. The inference one could draw is that he had been disciplined for supporting the Palestinians, and not his views about 9/11. Even so, Corbyn believed that Sizer's claims about 9/11 did not constitute anti-Semitism, and consequently, did not deserve the reprimand he received from his church, or indeed believe that his own claim that Israel was behind the affair was false. So Vaz tried again: 'Do you still support what he does, support what he says?' Again, Corbyn evades the question: 'I supported what he was doing in supporting the Palestinian people. The things [sic] that emerged later I was unaware of at the time.' So why then write a letter in Sizer's defence claiming that he had been victimised because he had 'dared to speak out against Zionism'?

When challenged, as he was on this occasion, to justify his many and long-standing associations with notorious anti-Semites, Corbyn's defence has always been that irrespective of their opinions of the Jews, which of course he does not share, his reason for collaborating with such people has been their mutual concern for the cause of the Palestinians. Puerile though it is, one could at least take this excuse seriously if Corbyn's concern for the Palestinians had been extended to the nearly 3,500 Palestinians who had been killed in Syria between 2011 and mid 2016 as a direct consequence of the civil wars being waged in that country. But since they were not victims of a Zionist genocide, their deaths have passed unprotested by world Islam and its Sharia left accomplices. Indeed, in 2011, Corbyn was a guest of the very regime responsible for many of those deaths.

These and other similar exchanges established beyond any doubt that Corbyn was prepared to ignore or deny the existence of the most extreme manifestations of anti-Semitism in those he chose to collaborate with so long as the shared goal was opposition to the policies and, as I firmly believe, existence of the state of Israel. The very next day after the hearing, just what Corbyn's 'bold step' in combating anti-Semitism amounted to became clear when Naz(i) Sha, the suspended Muslim MP for Bradford West, who not only tweeted that the Jews of Israel should be 'relocated' to the USA, but also, in another tweet that had been consistently ignored in her case, that 'never forget that everything that Hitler did in Germany was legal', after a *pro forma* apology that, given the viciously anti-Jewish and pro-Nazi nature her two statements, could not possibly have been sincere, was re-instated to full membership. It was a decision that must have left many non-Corbynite Labour Party members wondering, if advocating the Nazi-style deportation of six million

Jews and claiming that Hitler committed no crimes are not sufficient grounds for expulsion, what is? Could it be mere chance that until her suspension Shah was an 'adviser' to Corbyn's second-in-command and some say, *eminence grise,* the no less obsessively anti-Zionist Shadow Chancellor John McDonnell?

One June 16, 2016, Shadow Foreign Secretary Hilary Benn was sacked by Corbyn after making a number of statements in the Commons on Syria and the Islamic State that were diametrically opposed to the policies of his Leader. Benn's dismissal was followed by the resignation of 63 of Corbyn's shadow front bench team, together with a joint statement by all 20 Labour Euro MPs demanding his resignation. The day before, a no-confidence vote of MPs had been carried by 172 to 40, leaving Corbyn with insufficient loyalist candidates to fill all the shadow vacancies. This inevitable, long anticipated and historically unprecedented revolt had initially been signalled on December 2, 2015, when in a speech in the Commons, Labour's decidedly non-Sharia Shadow Foreign Secretary Hilary Benn defied and outraged his leader by supporting a UN resolution and Parliamentary motion authorising the bombing of the Islamic State, and compounded his sin by listing some of its worst atrocities and describing its regime as fascist. So it was not unexpected when within hours of the referendum result, which many in the party blamed on Corbyn's at best, lukewarm commitment to a remain vote, Benn finally raised the standard of revolt and was then promptly sacked by Corbyn.

For sure. though not by design, Diane Abbott's opaque pronouncement that 'if there is any politician who stands for not-politics-as-usual it's Jeremy Corbyn'. was spot on. No previous Labour Leader had ever been accused of failing to deal with anti-Semitism in his party, let alone been accused of it himself, or associating with representatives of a movement whose declared goal was the elimination of an entire country and the extermination of 80% of its population. By now, even the *Guardian* had reluctantly admitted, prematurely, as it turned out, that 'the Corbyn experiment [sic] is effectively over at Westminster'. But deep in his bunker, with the rumble of the rebels' tanks and guns growing ever louder, the leader, deserted even by some of his most faithful supporters, yet convinced of the rightness of his cause, Corbyn fought on. He promoted untested new officers (who then in their turn began to desert him) disposed of imaginary forces and talked of victory, victory over the traitors within, and the enemies without. As the pressure built up on Corbyn to step down, stories found their way into the media that the strain was beginning to tell. If the front man caved in, all would be lost. At all costs, the show had to be kept on the road. So while projecting to the party and public at large an image of a powerful leader and creative thinker called upon and eminently qualified to set his country on a new path, every effort was made to insulate him from hostile or even friendly advice. To keep the media at bay, in public he was always surrounded by a team of 'minders' headed by the silver spoon Winchester and Oxford duo of Milne and Schneider. Labour MPs were denied access to him, even including the party's Deputy Leader Tom Watson, because he might 'jab his finger at him'. In terms that replicated the 'safe spacism' and 'no platformism' of the campus Thought Police (whence hailed the cadres of Momentum), the request for an audience with the Dear Leader was rejected on the grounds that Corbyn was 'a seventy-year-old man' to whom his minders had 'a duty of care'. A duty of care to protect him from a private conversation with his own party's Deputy Leader? To he who would be *Prime Minister*? A duty of care for someone who according to his minders, needed to be protected from having finger pointed at him, and yet was praised by trade union official Len McClusky of UNITE, as 'a man of steel'? (Could this have been a Freudian slip? This translates into the language of Putin as 'Stalin'.)

As if aware of his fragility, even rebel front bench MP's carefully chose their words in their resignation letters, balancing criticism of his glaring inadequacies with what in many cases seemed an agreed *pro forma* listing of Corbyn's supposedly positive qualities... 'kind and genuinely decent', 'a man of principle'. This is of course standard procedure for someone whose incompetence requires that he be 'let go'. Yet given that his extra-Parliamentary causes and associations were known to all concerned and had been a subject of much public debate and concern from the outset of his leadership bid, it was strange to find not a single MP as much as alluding to them, even though they rendered him far less fit to hold any office in the Labour party than his chronically meagre political and intellectual capacities. Can one be 'kind' and 'genuinely decent' and at the same have as your 'friends' those who seek the extermination of the Jews and recycle the vilest anti-Semitic myths? It has been said in Corbyn's defence, both by himself and his supporters, that he cultivates these friendships in order firstly to enable others to hear what they have to say, and secondly, to persuade them to seek other means than violence to obtaining their ends. Persuading is one thing, regularly sharing platforms and never dissenting in public with those whom you have failed to persuade is another, which is what Corbyn had been doing for two decades and more. Could he then perhaps point to any area of policy where his friends in Hamas and Hezbollah had to the smallest degree deviated in word or deed from their declared aim of destroying the state of Israel by armed struggle? It is obviously in their interests to let their useful idiot believe that that one day, such a shift might occur. But then, that is exactly what another gullible old fool thought in his dealings with Hitler.

After decades in the far-left political wilderness, but now with their noses in the Labour Party trough, when the tide threatened to turn against them, those who pulled the strings of Momentum showed no signs of going quietly. But there is no doubt that the Corbynistas had been caught off balance by the depth of a crisis that over the next three years, would see Corbyn summoned to appear before a House of Common Select Committee hearing on his handling of his party's anti-Semitism, followed by three Parliamentary debates and investigations by the Metropolitan Police, the Equality and Human Rights Commission and BBC Panorama into the same subject, and mass resignations from the party up to the highest levels. All this lay in the future when super-loyalist Diane Abbott, shadow minister for International Development and later Shadow Home Secretary, took the bullet for Corbyn. Notorious for her racist comment about nurses from Finland with blue eyes and blond hair taking jobs in the UK's NHS, she refused in an interview on BBC TV to condemn as anti-Semitic a notorious cartoon that appeared in Livingstone's Gaddafi-financed *Labour Herald* depicting an Israeli Jew in a Nazi uniform giving the Hitler salute and captioned 'The Final Solution'. Her response was to ignore the cartoon and instead claim that 'it is a smear to say that the Labour Party has a problem with anti-Semitism'. And her leader was no less relaxed, insisting that there was 'not a problem' with anti-Semitism, and that talk of a crisis 'comes from those who are nervous of the strength of the party at local level'.

No less sanguine was Len McCluskey, General Secretary of UNITE trade union, who predicted that 'once the mood music [sic!] of anti-Semitism dies down then next week there'll be another subject'. Yes, indeed...the fallout from the EU referendum. However, another official of the same union, the Corbynite Martin

Meyer, who also sat on the Labour |Party's National Executive Committee, begged to differ. The crisis was real enough, and had been instigated by…yes, of course, just as Livingstone claimed, the Jews. In an email entitled 'How Israel manufactured UK Labour Party's anti-Semitism crisis', Meyer claimed that the whole affair, including presumably the scores of anti-Jewish statements made by the likes of Livingstone and Shah, had been the work of the 'Blairite right wing' in cahoots with a 'Zionist lobby'. There was a time when one could have been certain that the views of the Muslims and Sharia leftists quoted above could only have been those of avowed Nazis, a time when advertising such bigotry would have not only have been regarded as incompatible with membership of the Labour Party, or indeed any organisation on the left, but of any party other than the openly Nazi. Under the new Sharia dispensation of Ayatollah Corbyn, this was no longer the case. Hatred of the Jews, always the common coin of the far right, had now become also the lowest common denominator of the far left, where it found shared ground with large swathes of the UK's Muslim diaspora, increasing numbers of whom were acquiring positions of influence both in the Labour Party and as its elected representatives in local and central government. Do not take my word for the truth of this allegation. A (liberal) Muslim himself, this is what Mehdi Hasan wrote in the *New Statesman* on March 23, 2013, in an article entitled, *The sorry truth is that the virus of anti-Semitism has infected the British Muslim Community:*

> It pains me to say this, but anti-Semitism isn't just tolerated in some sections of the British Muslim community, it's routine and commonplace…it's our dirty little secret…I can't keep count of the number of Muslims I have come across from close relatives and friends to perfect strangers for whom wired and wacky anti-Semitic conspiracy theories are the default explanation for a range of national and international events.

As for the Holocaust, his fellow Muslims replied, 'don't be silly. Never happened'. And in a survey published in December 2016 of more than 3,000 UK Muslims, only 4% of those interviewed believed that Al Qaeda was responsible for 9/11. Bear in mind these would have been the opinions in many cases of educated Muslims, some the so-called 'pillars' and 'role models' of a 'community' that the multi-culturalists enthuse about and politicians never tire of praising for its immense and varied contributions to British society, a community which on the commendably honest testimony of one of its members, seethes with hatred against the Jews and lives in a make-believe world of collective denial where Muslims are always the victims of infidel, usually Jewish conspiracies. A survey of UK Muslim attitudes released in April 2016 and featured on Channel Four TV confirmed the personal testimony of Mehdi Hassan. More than a quarter of UK Muslims questioned believed that Jews caused most wars, compared with 6% for the UK as a whole. No less than 40% believed that the Jews, who comprise 0.2% of the world's population compared to 22% for Muslims, exert 'too much control over world affairs', compared to 10% of the whole UK population, clear evidence, if the belief were true, of a world Jewish conspiracy. A third of UK Muslims think the Jews have too much power and exploit the Holocaust to their own advantage, compared to 6% for the UK as a whole. In each of these cases, it is obvious that a sizable proportion of the total percentages holding these opinions is comprised of Muslims, even though they account for less than five percent of the total UK population.

Unfortunately, the opportunity was missed to ask whether, like the Muslim Labour Councillor in Luton, they approved of the Holocaust, or like so many of their co-religionists in the Middle East, believed it never happened. It is this 'dirty little secret', only now no longer either little or secret, and as filthy as it can get, that has been embraced and recast after its own fashion by the Sharia left as the price for its collaboration with the leaders of this 'Muslim community' in their joint campaign of hate against Israel and all things Jewish. Encouraged and protected by the Corbynite ascendency, this anti-Semitic cancer has eaten its way into the very fibre of the Labour movement, and it will take brave as well as decent and honest men and women to resist and defeat it.

At 2016 May Day rally in Trafalgar Square, from a rostrum fronted by a huge hammer and sickle banner and a giant portrait of Stalin, Corbyn repeated yet again the false claim that 'we stand absolutely against anti-Semitism in any form' The next day, the story broke that on his own website, Corbyn, the 'friend' of Jew-killing Jihadis, and associate of Holocaust deniers and Jewish conspiracy theorists, had praised as 'an icon', to be compared with Nelson Mandela no less, a Fatah terrorist, Marwan Barghouti, convicted by an Israeli court in 2004 of plotting the murder of Jewish civilians. This was followed by the revelation that Hamas had sent a message of solidarity to their embattled champion and subsequently, a cheque for £10,000. Their message made it very clear that like its UK supporters, Hamas did not regard waging war on the Jews of Israel as terrorism, any more than it considered Labour Party members' praise of Hitler, belief in a world Jewish conspiracy and demands for the deportation of all Israel's Jews as proof of anti-Semitism:

> We see his [Corbyn's] engagement as a very important statement that is also a very hit [sic] that the Zionist enemy received. Hamas is not and will not be considered a terrorist group and our struggle is reduced [i.e., confined] to the borders of occupied Palestine [that, is Israel] This is a Zionist campaign to define Labour Party leaders as anti-Semitic, a desperate move that reflects the weakness and confusion of the Zionist entity.

Rich, coming from a movement that endorses the *Protocols* and claims to have uncovered a world Zionist conspiracy going as far back as the French Revolution. As Mehdi Hassan says, some Muslims really do have a problem when it comes to the Jews. For this very reason, it would have been be naïve to assume the Muslim source of Labour Party anti-Semitism would have been addressed as it should have, especially in view of that Muslims were crucial both as |party member supporters of Corbyn and as Labour voters in key constituencies. Why else the insertion of 'Islamophobia' into the Chakrabarti inquiry, if not to present Muslims as victims of prejudice in the Labour Party, when they in are fact prominent amongst its perpetrators? Appearing before the House of Commons Home Affairs Select Committee's inquiry into Labour anti-Semitism (not to be confused with the Labour Party's parallel and strictly in-house investigation) Jonathen Arkush, President of the Jewish Board of Deputies got to the heart of the matter when he traced the origins of the surge of anti-Semitism within the Labour Party to the election of Corbyn as its leader:

> The election of a leader who is closely associated with the Palestine Solidarity Campaign [in statement on the campaign's website congratulating Corbyn on his election as Labour leader, he is described as a 'long -time patron of the PSC], with

Stop the War, [of which Corbyn was the chairman until elected Labour Leader] with a very hostile position on Israel, very well-known and very well publicised, and someone who has thought it appropriate to meet here in the democratic mother of parliaments with terrorist organisations whose stated mission in life is to kill as many Jews and Christians as possible [presumably an allusion to Article 7 of the Hamas Charter] has clearly sent the wrong kind of message to some people. With the advent of a more leftward tilt in the leadership of the Labour Party, some people think a space has been opened up for them, or they feel emboldened to say things which previously they felt they could not say in polite society …We are concerned that the impression is being given by the leader of the Labour Party of a certain reluctance to accept these issues.

Arkush told the Committee that he had asked Corbyn to agree that on reflection, his meetings with Hamas and Hezbollah had been 'inappropriate' but that he had refused to do so. To invite their leaders to address meetings in Parliament, to promote their genocidal cause in public rallies, to call these anti-Semites and genocidists one's 'friends'…none of this did the Leader of the Labour Party consider 'inappropriate'. It would also have pertinent to ask Corbyn why, when choosing to associate with and promote movements in the Middle East that claimed to represent the Palestinian cause, he had selected two that are not only avowedly dedicated to the destruction of Israel but the murder of its entire Jewish population, and not Fatah, the PLO, and the Palestinian Authority, which even if only on paper, recognise the state of Israel and are committed to a two-state solution to the Palestine question. A perverse preference, some might say, for someone who is always advertising his devotion to the cause of world peace. And not just for Corbyn. Only a matter of days after Chakraborty's elevation to the Peerage in return for services rendered, more revelations surfaced concerning her patron's anti-Semitic connections. In 2014, Labour MP Grahame Morris, Corbyn's Shadow Communities Spokesman and, not by chance, also Chairman of the anti-Zionist Labour Friends of Palestine, demanded of the then Prime Minister David Cameron that British Jews who had served in the Israeli Defence Force should be treated as terrorists. He had also posted on-line a picture of an Israeli flag with the caption: 'Nazi in my Village: do you see the flag fly?' Following the example set by his leader, Morris hosted events featuring anti-Semitic Muslims. One such gathering was chaired by the UK-based Palestinian journalist Sameh Habeeb who, with a fine sense of timing, chose Holocaust Memorial Day to publish an article in his *Palestinian Telegraph* denying the Holocaust ever occurred. Habeeb is also the originator of the accusation, subsequently recycled by PSC Patron and Liberal Democrat Peeress Baroness Tonge, that while carrying out relief work after the Haiti earthquake of 2010, Israel soldiers harvested the organs of its victims.

The story also broke on the same day, August 8, 2016, of Corbyn's involvement with yet another anti-Semite, the academic and *Guardian* columnist Sama Ramadani, whom the Labour leader once described as a 'fascinating [sic] great friend.' Ramadan had offered a simple and all-too-familiar explanation for his friend's troubles. His academic training led him to the only possible explanation…the Jews. Accusations of anti-Semitism could only have one source, 'backers of Israel' who were seeking to 'undermine Jeremy's support for Palestine' As for the 172 MPs who voted no confidence in his friend's leadership, they too were 'Zionist mouthpieces'. Corbyn's office declined to comment on these revelations, a sure indication that under his leadership the Labour Party would continue to be a Safe Space for anti-Semites.

While not saying so in so many words, the final report of the House of Commons Home Affairs Select Committee investigation into the rise of anti-Semitism within the Labour party under Corbyn's leadership came to pretty much the same conclusion. Corbyn personally was accused of a 'lack of leadership' on the issue, rendering the Labour Party 'a safe space [sic] for those with 'vile attitudes' towards Jews. The failure of the leadership to 'consistently and effectively deal with anti-Semitic incidents in recent years' had left the party open to the charge that 'elements of the Labour movement are institutionally anti-Semitic'. Like many other of its critics, the Select Committee was far from satisfied with the report of the Chakraborty inquiry commissioned (reluctantly) and then praised by Corbyn. One Committee member said it was 'not worth the paper it was written on'. (However, it did earn a peerage for its author) The report had failed to deliver 'a comprehensive set of recommendations, to provide a definition of anti-Semitism, or to suggest ways of dealing with anti-Semitism'. As for Corbyn himself, the Committee found that his failure to deal appropriately with the issue showed that he did not fully appreciate 'the distinct nature of post-war anti-Semitism'…in other words, its assuming the guise of anti-Zionism, which as we have seen, has been one of Corbyn's main preoccupations in his time as an MP.

I have a proposal, made in all seriousness, that will, if strictly enforced, go at least some way to towards combatting and identifying the sources of anti-Semitism within the Labour Party, and certainly further than the whitewash of a report cooked up by the official party enquiry. It follows the excellent example set by the US occupying forces at the end of the Second World War, when they compelled German civilians living close to Nazi concentration camps to witness at first hand, if Naz(i) Shah will permit, the crimes their beloved leader had committed in their names. The US forces also obliged civilians to watch the screening of films specially made by the US army of the horrors revealed by the liberation of Nazi death camps. In one such showing, two teenage girls giggled and laughed at they left the showing, so they were made to watch the whole film again in a private screening. Just to make sure the message got home, civilians were conscripted by the US army to bury the tens of thousands of skeletal and diseased corpses of prisoners starved and worked to death by their tormentors, not nearly enough of whom were either beaten to death by their former captives, or shot on the spot by outraged US GIs.

Following, though of course not in every detail, the excellent example set by the US imperialists in post-Nazi Germany, what I propose is the following: The archive of film material on the Holocaust is now so comprehensive that compiling a representative documentary, say of some two hours' duration, on the practical consequences of anti-Semitism should present no technical difficulties. I suggest that it begins with that part of Hitler's speech to the Reichstag on January 30, 1939, in which he announces to the world the fate he had in store for the Jews and concludes with footage of the various Nazi death camps that were the scene of the Final Solution. All Labour Party members should be required to attend a screening of such a production, at a suitable venue to be chosen by each local Constituency Party. There can be as many showings as are necessary to ensure that all members have the opportunity to attend. Any member who refuses or fails to attend such a screening will be automatically and instantly expelled from the party for life, with no right of appeal. Those who join the party after the screening programme has been completed will be required to view the film at a subsequent showing for new members a year later. Once the screening programme has been completed, any expressions of hostility towards the Jews, for example comparing them with Nazis and accusing them of genocide, calls for the destruction of the state of Israel, denial of the Holocaust and the right of Israel to exist (as distinct from criticism of its policies), and involvement in any activities with organisations or individuals which likewise deny the Holocaust and Israel's right to exist, promote conspiracy theories about the Jews or have the destruction of Israel and the killing of Jews as their objectives (such as Hamas and Hezbollah), will also be met with immediate expulsion for life with no right of appeal. If these proposals were to be adopted, they would in all probability involve some changes of party leadership, as well as representation at Parliamentary and local level. And undoubtedly, they would leave Labour, at least for a while, a smaller party. But it would also be a much cleaner one.

Appendices

A Are Zionists Nazis?

'Zionism is Nazism in a new guise.' *La Documentation Catholique,* July 17, 1949.

'Brooklyn-born [Jewish] settlers are Nazis, racists. They should be shot dead.' Tom Paulin, poet, BBC broadcaster and Lecturer in English at Hertford College, Oxford, interview in the Egyptian weekly *Al Ahram*, cited in the *Guardian*, April 12, 2002.

'The Zionists claiming Palestine speak with the accents of Mussolini claiming an Empire, or Hitler, or Japan in China'. *Daily Worker,* Communist Party of Great Britain daily, August 14, 1937

Are Zionists Nazis? And is Israel a Nazi state? In act of despicable bad taste, Labour MP Jeremy Corbyn chose Holocaust Memorial Day of 2010 to host a meeting in Parliament entitled, 'From Auschwitz to Gaza', the theme of the event being that the Jews of Israel were no less guilty of a genocide of the Palestinians than the Nazis were of one of the Jews. Pursing the same tack, the next year, Corbyn supported a motion in the House of Commons to change the name of Holocaust Memorial Day to Genocide Memorial Day, effectively decoupling it from Hitler's bid to exterminate the Jews of Europe. It received a derisory 23, votes, 21 of them Labour. Equating Zionism with Nazism has become one of the standard ploys of the far left in its obsessional campaign of vilification of the state of Israel, but the tactic in fact dates back to the time of Stalin, when he slandered his opponents on the left as agents of the Nazis, and 'social fascists', only then to sign a pact of friendship with Hitler in August 1939. Today, there are those on the left who go one better than Stalin in duplicity, denouncing Zionists as Nazis while *simultaneously* collaborating with Muslims who advertise their genocidal intentions towards the Jews and their admiration of Hitler.

Let us begin with Noam Chomsky, a professor of linguistics, a discipline that concerns itself with the meanings of words. However, when it comes to the word 'Nazi' we find Professor Chomsky putting his academic skills to one side in using, or rather abusing this term to describe the policies and actions of the Israeli government, so much so that a survey of his writings conducted by Werner Cohn has revealed that in nearly every case, Chomsky uses the word Nazi almost exclusively in this sense, and not in connection with the policies and deeds of the Third Reich. In fact, Professor Chomsky has never evinced the least interest in the Nazi regime except to equate it with Israel. For example, his anti-Zionist diatribe, *The Fateful Triangle,* highly recommended and advertised by the Neo-Nazi Holocaust-denying *Journal of Historical Review*, contains twelve references to Hitler, each one of them likening his policies to those of Zionism. And while by comparing Zionists to Nazis, Chomsky pioneered what has become the fashion on the left today, nowhere in any of his writings on the Middle East has he made any reference to the one political leader in that troubled region who not only openly admired the Nazis, but as we have seen, in 1941, made his way to Berlin to begin more than three years of intimate collaboration with the chief architect the Jewish Holocaust, Adolf Hitler. We speak of course of the Grand Mufti of Jerusalem, Haj Amin al-Husseini.

If there is one policy that in the informed public mind, the Nazis are identified by, it is their fanatical persecution of the Jews, and their near-successful attempt to wipe them off the face of the planet. But as I have demonstrated in the main body of this work, there are those, non-Muslims as well as Muslims, for whom the two questions I have posed are not absurd in the least. It is to the former group, those belonging to what I have termed the Sharia left, that they are primarily addressed. When the Hamas Charter refers in Article 20 to the 'Nazism of the Jews', (not of Israel); when diaspora Muslims chant 'Nazi' at Jews they encounter and even physically assault on university campuses, on anti-Israel demonstrations, picket outside Jewish-owned stores and during attacks on synagogues; when Fatah Central Committee member Jamal Muhaisen says there is 'no [sic] difference between [Israeli Prime Minister Binyamin] Netanyahu and Hitler' while in the West Bank, bookshops stock copies of the Arabic edition of *Mein Kampf;* when Hezbollah, a movement whose leader dreams of completing Hitler's Holocaust of the Jews, stages rallies in London (addressed on more than one occasion by Labour's Jeremy Corbyn), displaying banners and posters likening Israel to of all countries, the Third Reich; in each case, such Muslims not only display their visceral anti-Semitism, but an ignorance of the historical and political nature, meaning and significance of Nazism that is so profound, and is motivated by hatreds which run so deep, that attempts to overcome it by rational argument and the presentation of historical facts will, in nearly every case, prove to be a sheer waste of time.

What can one say possibly to convince a gang of Muslim storm troopers who broke up a meeting of the Kings College London Israel Society to chants of 'two, four, six eight, Israel is fascist state' that it is their own conduct, and the doctrine that feeds it, that are fascist, and that Jews have always been fascism's victims? Then there is the glib comment which has become common coin amongst non-Muslim critics of Israel that its Jews are no better than the Nazis. Only those who know nothing of what the Nazis did to the Jews or are no less badly informed as to the history of Israel, could make such remark, unless it is motivated not by ignorance, but as it is for example with the Labour Party's most notorious Jew-baiter, Ken Livingstone, by anti-Semitic malice. The same applies to those on the right who share the mind set of Paddy Sing, the UKIP Parliamentary candidate for North Wiltshire in the general election of June 2017. Three weeks before the election it emerged that in 2014, he had tweeted that Israelis were 'basically Nazis in mentality', 'Nazi Jews like wild dogs on the rampage'. So by a process of elimination, I address myself to a movement that I was once part of and which, for all its blinds spots and illusions, taught me political and historical lessons I could not have learned elsewhere. I speak, of course, of the far, predominately *Trotskyisant* left

True, by surrendering its principles in its pursuit of an alliance with Jihadi Islam, it has completely lost its political and moral bearings. But this movement has its origins in a tradition in which honesty, facts and rational thinking mattered. For those who claim to subscribe to his teachings, Trotsky's legacy is essentially threefold. First, he was with Lenin, the organiser of the Bolshevik seizure of power, and then, as Commissar for War, of its defence and eventual victory; secondly, from 1923, he headed the opposition to the rise to total power of Stalin, a resistance that led in his years of final exile to the foundation of the Fourth International as a rival to the Third controlled by Stalin; and finally, perhaps his greatest intellectual legacy, there is his analysis of the rise to power of the Nazis. Not only did Trotsky more than any other commentator of the time accurately dissect the forces that brought into being the Nazi movement and propelled its path to power. He also foresaw with uncanny prescience the consequences of Hitler's victory not only for the German worker's movement and Germany, but for Europe, the world...and the Jews.

When the Nazi share of the vote surged from 2.6% in 1928 to 16% in the Reichstag election of September 1930, Trotsky warned communist workers that unless their party leaders abandoned Stalin's policy of denouncing the Social Democrats as 'social fascists', by exploiting the disunity in the ranks of the left, the Nazis would 'ride over your skulls and spines like a terrific tank'. As early as 1931, ten years before the actual event, he predicted that 'a victory of fascism in Germany would signify an inevitable war against the USSR'. Not only after, but before the Munich Agreement of September 30, 1938, with the USSR officially opposed to the appeasement of Hitler (but already engaged in secret exchanges with the Nazis), Trotsky foresaw that Stalin would seek a deal with Berlin. George Orwell wrote in 1944 that so far as he was aware, no one on the left foresaw either the Stalin-Hitler Pact or grasped that 'the Nazis were dangerous even when they were on the verges of seizing power.' He obviously had not had full access to Trotsky's writings of the period. In December 1938, while statesmen pursued their fool's gold of 'peace in our time' with a Third Reich preparing itself for the conquest of Europe, and as the world offered platitudes but denied refuge to Jews fleeing mounting Nazi persecution, there came from Trotsky's final Mexican exile another unheeded warning, not only of impending world war, but of what today we know as the Holocaust of the Jews:

> The numbers of countries that expel the Jews grow without cease. The number of countries able [or willing] to accept them decreases...It is possible to imagine without difficulty what awaits the Jews at the mere outbreak of the future world war. But even without war the next development of reaction signifies with certainty *the physical extermination of the Jews.* [the emphasis is Trotsky's]

Those who claim to be the defenders and continuators of Trotsky's theoretical legacy should surely be obliged to answer the following question: how can their current practice of equating Zionism with Nazism, and of accusing the Jews of Israel of complicity in a crime uniquely associated with the Third Reich, namely the attempt to exterminate an entire race, be reconciled with the assessment of Nazism contained in the writings of their mentor? Are they right when they claim Israel is a Nazi state, and that all Jews who support it are Nazis? Let us begin with Trotsky's definition of Nazism, and the regime that it created, and then see if it can in any way be made to apply to Zionism and the state of Israel as it is today.

Trotsky undertook his first detailed analysis of Hitler's version of fascism when as we have said, the Nazis increased their vote from 2.6% in the Reichstag elections of May 1928 to 16% in September 1930. The distinction between German and Italian fascism is important because Muslims and the Sharia left, if they so wanted, could just as easily call Zionists fascists. But they rarely if ever do, because the intention is to depict Zionists as *racists*, not totalitarians. And it is indeed the case that unlike Italian fascism, which described itself as totalitarian and placed not race but nation and state at the centre of its doctrine, Hitler's ruling obsession, and that of his party and Reich, was anti-Semitic racism, as Trotsky readily acknowledged. Hitler was totally in thrall to the same fantasies of the *Protocols* that so captivate Hamas and the preachers of the West Bank and in the UK, frequenters of Corbynista websites. As Trotsky himself said, for Hitler, anti-Semitism was a 'universal key to all the secrets of life', a 'zoological materialism.' As for Nazi 'socialism', this too reduced itself to a struggle against what the theorists of national socialism called 'international Jewish capital'. 'Bowing down before capitalism as a whole, the [Nazified] petty bourgeoisie declares war against the evil spirit of gain in the guise of the Polish Jew in a long-skirted kaftan and usually without a cent in his pocket'…Bebel's 'socialism of fools'… and of hundreds if not thousands of members of the Corbynised Labour Party.

As a Marxist would do, Trotsky sought the explanation for this sudden rise in the fortunes of the hitherto marginalised Nazi Party in social and economic factors. First of course was the economic crisis that overwhelmed Germany in the wake of the Wall Street crash the previous year. Already burdened by reparations payments, and heavily dependent for its economic survival on massive US loans, when after the crash, markets for German exports began to contract, and US loans to be called in to meet rising debts at home, the German economy plunged into recession faster and more deeply than any other. Already by the winter of 1929, unemployment had reached two million. A year on it stood at three million. On the day of Hitler's appointment as Chancellor on January 30, 1933, it had peaked at six million. Germany's worsening economic plight inevitably had far reaching political consequences, as they did in every country affected by the depression. In the USA, there was a sharp swing to the left, with the election of Roosevelt, a surge in trade union membership, strikes and factory occupations, and the adoption of the interventionist New Deal. In the UK, events followed an opposite course, with the collapse in 1931 of a minority Labour administration and the formation of a Tory-dominated 'National' coalition headed by Ramsey MacDonald committed to *laisser faire* austerity. In less industrialised France, where the depression as a result came later and less severely, there was a gradual but powerful swing to the left, culminating in 1936 in the formation of a 'Popular Front' Socialist-Radical coalition under the Jewish socialist Leon Blum, followed as in the USA by radical reforms and an unprecedented wave of strikes and factory occupations. In the same year, Spain plunged into civil war as the propertied classes and the Catholic Church threw their weight behind General Franco's military rebellion in a bid to reverse the newly-elected centre left government's programme of land reform, regional autonomy and improved conditions for urban workers.

In Germany the onset of the world depression ended the series of centre-left coalitions that with only brief interruptions, had dominated political life since the end of the First World War. As was the case in the UK with the bulk of the Labour Party, the Social Democrats (SPD), under pressure from their Trade Union partners, found it impossible to endorse the austerity policies of their liberal and Catholic Centre Party coalition partners. Hermann Mueller, Weimar's last Social Democratic Chancellor, resigned in March 1930, to be replaced by the Centre Party's Heinrich Bruening. Lacking a majority in the Reichstag, Bruening now governed by presidential decree in accordance with the notorious Article 48 of the Weimar Constitution. As the recession deepened, cuts in wages, unemployment benefit and welfare services progressively eroded the living standards of all but the upper and upper middle classes. The communist party (KPD) began to gain votes at the expense of its larger Social Democratic rival, the SPD, which although now officially in opposition, chose after much agonising to sustain Bruening in office as the 'lesser evil' to a cabinet dominated by the extreme right. On the more moderate right, the conservative big business-oriented People's Party (DVP) and the more liberal Democrat Party (DP) lost votes not only to the Nazis, but also, initially, to the anti-Weimar and mainly agrarian Nationalists (DNVP) and a host of smaller parties representing regional and small business and rural interests. As the crisis deepened, the Nazis emerged as the most dynamic force on the far right, mopping up not only the votes of the sectional parties, but biting deeply into the support of the much larger DNVP. This is the backdrop to Trotsky's writings on Germany between 1930 and 1933.

Unlike Stalin and his servile but still frequently purged retinue, Trotsky was a highly sophisticated thinker, one of, if not the most perspicacious political minds of the 20th century. This enabled him to understand that for all its hostility towards the left, the Nazi movement and what passed for its ideology were neither tame creations or creatures of Germany's ruling classes: the Junker landowners and officer caste, the big industrialists and the bankers. Trotsky regarded National Socialism in every sense as an outgrowth of the diverse social strata ranged immediately below these groups and above Germany's most numerous and well organised class, the urban industrial proletariat:

> Under the impact of the crisis, the petty bourgeoisie swung, not in the direction of the proletarian revolution, but in the direction of the most extreme imperialist reaction...The gigantic growth of National Socialism is an expression of two factors, a deep social crisis, throwing the petty bourgeois masses off balance, and the lack of a revolutionary party that would be regarded by the popular masses as the acknowledged revolutionary leader...fascism, as a mass movement, is the party of counter-revolutionary despair.

Recent historical research into voting trends in the late Weimar period have established that the picture presented here by Trotsky is not the whole story. And of course, he understood that no political party, however obviously it gears its appeal to one or more social interests, only attracts support from those groups, any more that it gains the support from all those who comprise them. Political life is much more complex than that. And, by advertising themselves as both 'national' and 'socialist' the Nazis deliberately challenged, with much success, the traditional lines of demarcation that apart from the denominational and aptly named Catholic Centre Party, defined and separated the established political parties of the Weimar Republic. As the deepening crisis of Weimar exposed the bankruptcy of Germany's traditional ruling class parties, significant numbers of Germany's elite switched their political allegiance, giving the Nazis not only their votes but in some cases, their money and influence. Down below, while the Nazis failed to make any inroads into the left vote, which remained split between the SPD and the KPD, they picked up significant support from what one analyst has called nationalist-minded 'Tory' workers who, repelled by the internationalism of the left parties, had been previously voting for parties of the traditional right, but were now attracted by the Nazi's strident nationalism combined with a promise of a better deal for the neglected 'little man'. However, with these qualifications, Trotsky's depiction of

Nazism as essentially a movement of the urban and rural lower middle classes stands. We must bear this in mind when we come to contrast National Socialism with the movement that pioneered, created, built and for most of its seven decades, ruled the state of Israel...*Labour* Zionism.

Issuing out of Germany's intermediate strata, Trotsky foresaw that the Nazi Party, more specifically its paramilitary formations, the SA and the SS, would, if the opportunity and necessity arose, be used to crush the German workers' movement, just as the Mussolini's Black Shirted private army had been in Italy:

> The period of half-way measures has passed. In order to try to find a way out, the bourgeoisie must absolutely rid itself of the pressure exerted by the workers' organisations; these must be eliminated, destroyed, crushed. At this juncture the historic role of fascism begins. It raises to their feet those classes that are immediately above the proletariat and are ever in dread of being forced into its ranks. It organises and militarises them at the expense of finance capital under the cover of the official government and directs them to the extirpation of proletarian organisations from the most revolutionary to the most conservative

Left, or as it was generally known, Labour Zionism, as distinct from, and to a large degree, opposed to General Zionism, neither in its social composition, circumstances of origin nor principles, bore any resemblance to what Trotsky defines here as the salient features of Nazism. It was in no sense a movement of the Jewish petty bourgeoisie, called upon by the Jewish bourgeoisie, such as it was, to crush the Jewish proletariat. It was itself, if not the only, then certainly the chief movement of the Jewish proletariat both in the heartlands of the Jewish diaspora and in its new home in the Mandate, in the creation and building of Israel. Nazi propaganda was for once not so wide of the mark when it depicted the impoverished Jewish masses of the east as the seedbed and carriers of 'Jewish Bolshevism'. According to one Nazi specialist on the 'Jewish question', Professor Walter Recke, 'the Jewish proletarian is the real solicitor of Bolshevism in Poland'. Of the country's 3,5 million Jews, 'ninety per cent [were] proletarians of the worst kind'.

To return to Trotsky. Does the system he describes here bear any resemblance to modern Israel and, if it does, in which respects?

> The system of fascism is based on the destruction of parliamentarism...At the moment the "normal" police and military resources of the bourgeois dictatorship, together with their parliamentary screens, no longer suffice to hold society in a state of equilibrium - the turn of the fascist regime arrives...finance capital gathers into its hands, as in a vice of steel, directly and immediately, all the organs and institutions of sovereignty, the executive, administrative and educational powers of the state: the entire state apparatus together with the army, the municipalities, the universities, the schools, the press, the trade unions, and the co-operatives.

One can argue that Trotsky erred in his expectation that what he described as 'finance capital' would 'gather into its hands', 'directly' all the levers of state power in the Third Reich. The Nazi leadership made it clear from the very beginning of their rule that they were not the agents or servants of 'finance capital' or anyone else for that matter, that they would share or delegate political power to no-one outside their own ranks. But the point stands that a Nazi regime spelt death not only for the workers' movement, but every last vestige of liberal democracy in every sphere of life, to be replaced by a regime that in its quest for complete domination over society, is usually classified as totalitarian and described by Trotsky as one which necessitates the 'annihilating [of] the worker's organisations' and 'the destruction of parliamentarism'. Do Israel's leftist, in some cases, Trotskyist enemies really believe that Israel is a totalitarian state, governed not by a freely elected parliament based on universal suffrage, with its free press, religious pluralism, leftist and Palestinian parties and free trade unions, but one ruled by a gang of paramilitary thugs on behalf of 'Jewish 'finance capital', where trade unions and strikes are illegal, where the press, academic and cultural life are regulated by the leaders of these same thugs according to the doctrine of the state's one and only party?

If Israel is indeed a Nazi state, and has been, so the story goes, from its very beginning, 'a racist endeavour' then those who created it must have also been Nazis. Who were they, these Jewish Nazis? It is no coincidence that most of the pioneers and early settlers of Israel hailed from eastern Europe. Until the establishment of Israel in 1948, the Jewish diaspora lived in countries whose history and political systems varied enormously, and therefore likewise their attitude towards and treatment of their Jews. While the French Revolution opened up the possibility in the west of emancipation and, especially for more prosperous Jews, assimilation, in the east, well into the twentieth century it was a different story entirely. There a lower level of culture of the host nation prevailed, with its primitive, often murderously violent religiously-inspired anti-Semitism. Tsarist Russia up to 1917 legally confined its five million Jews to the so called 'Pale of Settlement' in the western border regions, where they faced official policies of segregation and discrimination, combined with government-instigated or connived at pogroms by anti-Semitic gangs, the loyalist 'Union of the Russian People', the Black Hundreds. This all-pervading persecution, together with the most terrible economic exploitation and living conditions, convinced large numbers of Jewish workers and the growing Jewish intelligentsia of the necessity to become involved in leftist secular politics. Around the turn of the 19th century, assimilationist intellectuals gravitated towards the Marxist Russian Social Democratic Labour Party, founded in 1898, where after the split of 1903, they comprised the majority of the leadership of the Menshevik faction. Most Jewish workers belonged to the Bund, by far the largest of Russia's labour organisations. Its leaders, while opposed to Zionism, argued in opposition to both Bolsheviks and Mensheviks (who each demanded the Bund dissolve itself and its members individually join the RSDLP) that like the Polish socialists of the Russian Empire, who were allowed to affiliate as a separate party, the Jews were also a nation, and should therefore have the same rights of separate organisation and affiliation.

Both the Bolshevik Russian Lenin and the Menshevik Jew Martov, unlike Trotsky in his last years, vehemently opposed the idea that the Jews constituted a nation, and when the Second Party Congress of 1903 endorsed this position, rather than dissolve itself as required, the Bund withdrew from both the congress and the party, by so doing, providing Lenin's Bolsheviks ('majoritarians') with a narrow lead over Martov's Mensheviks ('minoritarians'). Yet for all its opposition to Zionism, the Bund's insistence on the reality of Jewish nationhood, with its own history, religion, culture, language, literature, aspirations and inner political life, was a harbinger of what was to become Labour Zionism. For what the Jews still lacked was a territory and a state which, like other nations, they could call their own, and where they would be free from persecution and the ever-present threat of pogroms. By 1917, while the membership of Bund stagnated at around 30,000 the movement that would evolve into Labour Zionism counted ten times that number in its ranks.

In the west, where the Jews, at least on paper, had achieved legal equality, the question of a separate organisation for Jewish workers never arose. Just as the more prosperous and better educated Jews assimilated into the liberal bourgeoisie, so Jewish workers and radical intellectuals were absorbed into to the trade unions and parties of the left. True, anti-Semitism was never far away...the Dreyfus Affair, and periodic anti-Jewish riots in London's East End were just the visible tip of the iceberg...but it was anti-Semitism of a different order to that prevalent in the east, rarely violent, never officially instigated or tolerated, and always resisted not only by the Jews, but most of the left and the more enlightened of the middle classes.

As the years passed, apart from the activities of fringe parties and leagues, in the west political anti-Semitism went underground, to ruminate, but not to die. Understandably then, even though the modern Zionist movement was launched in the west by Theodore Herzl in the wake of the conviction in 1894 of the Jewish Captain Dreyfus on a framed-up charge of spying for Germany, it was in east that the appeal of a return to Israel was greatest. And it was this eastern predominance that from the beginning gave Zionism its plebeian, we could even say proletarian character. Not for the comfortable assimilated bourgeois Jew of Paris, Berlin, New York, Vienna, Amsterdam or London the backbreaking slog of turning barren desert into a land of plenty. And so Labour Zionism was born, a Zionism of collective labour and collective ownership in the form of the *kibbutzim,* in which for the first time in over two thousand years, Jews freed from persecution and discrimination, and the ever-present fear of something far worse, could live and work under a government and laws of their own making. The emergence of the principles of Labour Zionism predated by many years its rise to predominance in the Zionist movement of the 1930s. Despite Jews being confined over the centuries by Christian legislation to marginal and despised occupations such as petty trade and money lending, the ideal of collective ownership and labour remained deeply embedded in Jewish culture and re-emerged with the onset of emancipation in the later 19th century.

In 1862, Karl Marx's friend Moses Hess set out his programme for a socialist Jewish state in Israel in his *Rome and Jerusalem: The last National Question.* In this work, he developed for the first time an idea that would recur time and again in writings on the subject of Jewish settlement in Palestine: the Jews must finish with their humiliating semi-parasitic role as marginal petty traders, and return to the soil to engage in honest and honourable productive collective labour. Here already is the germ of the Israeli *kibbutzim* Other writers on the same theme followed, all stressing that Zionism was pre-eminently a movement of and for the marginalised, oppressed and impoverished Jews of Europe and the Middle East, and that the Israel that Zionism created would be a socialist one and in which any Arab minority would have equal rights of citizenship. Though Herzl saw his role as pre-eminently political, drumming up support where he could amongst Jew and gentile alike for his project, his social and economic programme for a Jewish homeland was well to the left of centre by any standards, with proposals for a comprehensive welfare state, public ownership of all-natural resources and co-operative ownership of industry, agriculture and trade.

After the First World war, Labour Zionism in Palestine was initially represented by Poale Zion, which in time split into two parties, the smaller Marxist Mapam, and the larger reformist Mapai. In a speech to the Pale Zion congress held in Jaffa in February 1919, David Ben Gurion, destined to become Israel's first Prime Minister in 1948, defined the guiding principle of what in 1930 was to become Mapai as an 'organic fusion of two worlds, Jewish national redemption and the social liberation of man'. However construed, in no sense can this be represented as in any sense sharing an affinity with the racial exclusiveness of Nazi 'socialism'. To rebut such accusations, I cite at some length from a speech given by Ben Gurion in 1922 to the third convention of the forerunner to Mapai, the United Labour Party, in Hebrew, *Adhut Ha'avoda*:

> For Zionism, the struggle of the working class is daily labour, the organization of the workers as a unified body in control of its class affairs, their organisation in trade unions for offensive and defensive action in the private sector, their struggle for positions of influence in the economy and the national institutions, the setting up of collective farms, increasing the political power of labour in national and civic governmental institutions, the struggle of the Jewish working class for its national rights, the struggle to increase settlement and to direct immigrants toward productive work, socialistic pioneering activities, cultural creativity, and collaboration with the international labour movement. Adhut Ha'avoda considers it the duty of the Jewish worker to take part in all struggles, to impose labour in the life of the people, the land, and the economy. This must be the role of the Jewish worker in creating a socialist society in Israel.

It is irrelevant to the case under consideration whether this goal has been achieved, which it self-evidently has not. The question is, are these goals in any way Nazi? And has the actual result been the creation of a Nazi state or one similar to those of the liberal democratic west? Even Zeev Sternhell, possibly the most trenchant Jewish critic of Labour Zionism, had to concede in his *The Founding Myths of Israel* that 'of all societies that gained independence after the Second World war, Israel was undoubtedly the one in which political liberty, a multi-party system and the supremacy of civilian government were most completely assured'. And, we could add, has remained so to this day, despite being from its birth constantly threatened and periodically attacked by states and movements that have sought its annihilation.

As we have seen, integral to Labour Zionism was its overriding emphasis on the organisation of the Jewish workers in the newly-established British Mandate into a unified trade union movement, a goal that was achieved in 1920 under the auspices of United Labour. The *Histadrut* or General Federation of Jewish Workers, grew in direction proportion to the rate of Jewish settlement in what was to become Israel. In 1948 its membership had reached 330,000, 48% of the adult Jewish population, organising and representing by far the highest share of the work force of any trade union in the world, either then, now or at any other time in history. In the early years of the new Jewish state, the trade unions took on a whole range of functions normally provided by either the public or private sectors, such as banking, insurance, health, publishing and education. These the Federation continues to provide today, while other once-wide ranging economic interests have largely been sold off to the private sector. Initially founded to organise settler Jewish labour, the *Histadrut* now organises all Israeli workers irrespective of religion or ethnic origin, and is affiliated, like the UK.'s Trade Union Congress, to the International Confederation of Free Trade Unions, despite the campaign in the 1980s by Corbyn and Livingstone to bring about their disaffiliation. So to those who claim that Zionists are Nazis, I say, the Nazis destroyed trade unions, the Zionists built them.

The ascendancy of Labour Zionism in the 1930s came as a direct response to the rise to power of the Nazis in Germany, and the re-emergence of anti-Semitic movements right across the rest of Europe. The idea of a safe haven for Jewry was no longer just a dream and a hope, but a matter of urgent practical action. For millions of Jews, neither assimilation nor emigration was the answer to the 'Jewish Question'. While some host nations persecuted their Jews, those who did not refused to accept any more. Discrimination, segregation, deportation, extermination: these were the solutions to the 'Jewish Question' that now forced their way onto the agenda. It was in these times of growing alarm amongst European Jewry that Labour Zionism came to the fore as the most outspoken and militant advocates of action, of the organisation of mass migration to the British mandate as both the only viable means of escape from persecution and worse, and the achievement of the goal of a state, no matter how small, in the ancient homeland of the Jews.

Already by 1933, Mapai, the voice of Labour Zionism, had won 44% of the votes in elections to the Executive at the 18th Zionist Congress in Prague. So great was the danger facing European Jewry that a number of prominent assimilated Jews who had previously declined to endorse the Zionist project now publicly declared their support for the Labour Zionists, most famous among them being Albert Einstein. He felt able to do so because as a socialist and secularist he shared both of the aims of Labour Zionism, the creation of not only a socialist Israel but a secular one. Here too Herzl pointed the way. Like nearly all the founders of Israel, Herzl was an atheist, and would have no truck with any Jew who tried to impose a clerical agenda onto the Zionist enterprise. It was an entirely secular venture. 'Matters of faith' were to be 'once and for all excluded from public influence'. Whether anyone 'sought religious devotion in the synagogue, in the Church, in the Mosque, in the art museum, or in the philharmonic concert, did not concern society. That was his own private affair.'

While denial of the existence of a Jewish nation leads on, naturally, to the denial of the right of Jews to their own nation state, a belief in its existence does not necessarily lead to the opposite conclusion, as in the case of the Jewish Bund, which argued instead for Jewish 'cultural autonomy' within the Russia empire. Interestingly from the standpoint of the matter under review, unlike both the Bolshevik and Menshevik factions, who despite their differences at the Second Congress of the RSDLP in 1903, both denied the existence of a Jewish nation, Trotsky, contrary to his epigones today, in his third and final exile came to recognise both Jewish nationhood and the Jews' right to their own state.

> At one time I thought that the Jews would assimilate into the people and cultures they lived among…But now [this was 1937] it was impossible to say this. Recent history has taught us something about this. The fate of the Jews has been posed as a burning question, particularly in Germany, and the Jews who had forgotten their ancestry were clearly reminded of it…. The Jews…can and should lead their own lives as a people, with their own culture. The territorial question is pertinent because it is easier for a people to carry out an economic and cultural plan when it lives in a compact mass.

Under socialism, that question will arise, and with the consent of those Jews who desire it, there might be a free mass emigration...why shouldn't they be able to do this?

While warning in July 1940, and with good reason, against the dangers of seeking a homeland for the Jews in Palestine at a time when 'further military developments' could 'transform Palestine into a bloody trap for several hundred thousand Jews', which was indeed precisely the objective of the agreement concluded by the Grand Mufti and Hitler in Berlin in November 1941, Trotsky insisted that the Jews had a right to their 'own autonomous republic as the arena for their own culture'. Trotsky therefore did not in principle, unlike the Sharia left, oppose the creation of a Jewish state in Palestine. However, he believed that the Zionist goal of a Jewish state in what was then still the British Mandate was a 'tragic mirage' not least because the British 'were interested in winning the sympathies of the Arabs who are more numerous than the Jews'. This was indeed the case and continued to be so after the war until the creation of Israel in 1948. However, Trotsky's conclusion that Zionism was 'incapable of resolving the Jewish question' because it sought to do so independently of what he still believed was an impending world socialist revolution and was therefore 'utopian and reactionary in character', was wrong. History has passed its own judgement on which of the two paths to Jewish nationhood has proved a utopian mirage

To return to where we began. It is immaterial whether one agrees or not, or to what extent, with Trotsky's definition and appraisal of the role of National Socialism. The question to be answered by Israel's leftist enemies is, does that definition and appraisal apply in any meaningful sense to the nature and policies of the Israeli state, and the political doctrine of Zionism? For Trotsky, fascism was not a term of abuse, as Nazi is today for the Sharia left, to be hurled at anyone with whom one has serious political differences. It was a very specific form of political rule, none of whose essential features exists in the Israel of today. However, for the sake of the argument, let it be granted that all the accusations made against Israel are true: They are as follows:

1) Israel is Nazi or fascist because it occupies (but, save for East Jerusalem, has not annexed) disputed territories beyond its own internationally recognised (but not by all) borders. But nowhere in Trotsky's definition of fascism is there any reference to colonialism or illegally occupied territories. In fact, the Versailles Treaty stripped Germany not only of all its colonies, but national territories in the north, west and east. When the Nazis came to power, Germany had still three years to wait before it regained full sovereignty over the de-militarised zone of the Rhineland, while at the insistence of France, the Saarland remained an 'occupied territory', not of Germany, but of a League of Nations mandate exercised until 1935. If the possession of colonies is the indicator of fascism, then despite its having fought a six-year war against Nazi Germany which possessed none, it would have not been the Third Reich but the United Kingdom which would have been ranked as the world's leading fascist power.

If the illegal or disputed occupation of territories, as distinct from colonial possessions, is a sufficient criterion, then Jordan's illegal annexation of the West Bank in 1948, after the territory had been designated by the United Nations the previous year as part of an independent Palestinian state, would have qualified the kingdom as fascist, as it would for Egypt for its parallel seizure of the Gaza Strip. But since the illegal occupations were the work of Arab Muslims, no-one then or since who claims to support or represent the Palestinian cause has spoken of an illegal occupation of Palestinian territory by Egypt or Jordan, let alone by so doing their becoming fascist states. That only became the order of the day when the occupying (and not annexing) power in 1967 became Jewish. Similar considerations apply to the Soviet invasion and attempted occupation of Afghanistan between 1979 and 1989. Because the occupation was in response to a puppet regime's request, at the instigation of its Soviet masters, for an invasion by the Kremlin to rescue its tottering client, we had a *de facto* rather than technically illegal occupation. But the results were the same. Millions of Afghan Muslims were subjected to a near-genocidal reign of terror that resulted in the deaths of approximately one million civilians. But here too, except on outer fringes of the Maoist far left, no-one described the USSR as a fascist or Nazi state, and those few that did, did so on account of its internal regime, and not its external policies.

2) Israel is a Nazi state because it imposes a racist policy of apartheid on the Palestinians. This is a lie. But even if it were true, following Trotsky, this would not be sufficient grounds to call Israel a Nazi state. Even in the extreme case of South Africa, its apartheid system left intact a whites-only parliament in which, though dominated by the racist Afrikaner National Party, legal opposition of a limited kind was still possible by its three other (white) parties, a luxury not afforded even to pure blooded Aryans by Hitler's one-party Reich. There were also whites-only trade unions, whereas in Nazi Germany there were none. If indeed pre-Mandela South Africa was a Nazi state, it would be unique in history as the first one of its kind to be dismantled peacefully by its own ruling (Nazi) party, release all its political prisoners, conduct free and equal elections and then have its leaders retire either into obscurity or permanent opposition. As the examples of Franco Spain and Mussolini's Italy up to 1938 prove, segregation, whether of race, gender or religion, is not integral to fascism, though it could be pursued by it, as it was in the Jewish ghettos created in Poland by the Third Reich as the prelude to the Holocaust. However, Jews were for centuries also forced by law to live in walled and guarded ghettoes by a 16th century ruling of the Vatican. Did this make the Roman Catholic Church Nazi? Or Tsarist Russia, which enforced a similar servile condition on its Jews? Well into the second half of the twentieth century, blacks in the deep south of the United States were legally as well as socially segregated from whites. Again, one must ask: did this make the USA a Nazi state?

3) Israel is a Nazi state because it is perpetrating the genocide of the Palestinians, just as the Nazis did of the Jews. The first statement is a lie, while many of the Shari left's Muslim friends either deny or celebrate the second. While neither genocide nor anti-Semitism are integral to fascism, in Germany, where its fascism from the outset was obsessively racist, they become its main distinguishing feature. In the case of Italy up to 1938, and Franco Spain, they were not. However, what have been described as genocides by agencies or states that in no sense can be described as fascist...the catastrophic decline in the native populations that followed the conquest and colonisation of the two Americas and Australasia for example...proves the point.

4) Israel is a Nazi state because Zionism subscribes to the belief that the Jews are racially superior to the Arabs. This too is a lie. Nether in law or in ideology are Israeli Palestinians treated or regarded as racially inferior to Jews, and not even the most vehement anti-Zionist has been able to prove they are. While racist parties in Israel are illegal, Israel has on its borders Arab regimes that promote religiously-

inspired race hatred against the Jews as a matter of official state policy. As the *Koran* says, they are 'apes and swine', 'the worst of creatures'. But of course, this in in no sense racism, just theology.

Replicating, albeit in a different context, the lunacy of Stalinist 'social fascism,' these accusations constitute the basis of the claim that Israel is a Nazi state, that Zionism is a racist, Nazi doctrine, and that the vast majority of Jews who live in or support Israel are, *ipso facto,* likewise Nazis. Significantly, all three criteria refer exclusively to Israel's relationship with the Palestinians and not its internal political system, which is a western-type liberal parliamentary democracy, of just the kind which, according to Trotsky, Hitler was bent on destroying in Germany. Since its creation in 1948, Israel has conducted 22 Parliamentary elections on a universal franchise that includes the Arabs it is alleged to be either exterminating, segregating or both. The most recent, in 2019, was contested not by one, as in Nazi Germany, but 13 parties, including two that are explicitly anti-Zionist and attract most Arab voters. Israel's Hamas and Fatah enemies held their most recent election in 2006, since when Israel has held six. Therefore, none of the aspects ascribed, rightly or wrongly, to Israel's political system or policies even remotely resembles those that for Trotsky or, for that matter, any serious analyst of the subject, are integral to a fascist or Nazi regime, namely:

a) The emergence of anti-democratic, chauvinist and, in the case of Germany, also anti-Semitic paramilitary movements of the extreme right, drawn mainly from the lower middle classes;
b) The deployment of these movements by the ruling class, or a faction within it, for the destruction of all labour organisations and institutions of parliamentary democracy,
c) Once in power, the creation by the fascist or Nazi movement of a one-party state that obliterates all political freedoms and democratic practises and institutions, and in quick time, stamps out all ideas opposed to its own doctrine by establishing total control over news reporting and all aspects of political, social, cultural and intellectual life. However, there is a regime, supported by the Sharia left and as I write, the current leader of the British Labour Party, which today closely approximates these three criteria more than any other in the world today. It is the former employer of Livingstone, Galloway and Corbyn, the Islamic Republic of Iran.

Addendum: The Sinking of the *Struma*

That Trotsky predicted correctly when he said the makers of British imperial policy would always side with the Arabs against the claims of the Zionists was nowhere better proven than by the decisions of British officials that led on February 19, 1942, to the sinking in the Black Sea of the *Struma*, a ship carrying more than 750 Jewish refugees fleeing from Romania to what was then the British mandate in Palestine. They were enforcing a policy the diametric opposite to that being pursued today towards Muslims seeking entry into Europe, the majority of whom are not refugees but illegal economic and welfare migrants. By contrast, all on board the *Struma* were Jews fleeing a regime that has already massacred tens of thousands of Romanian Jews, and whose armed forces, acting jointly with the Third Reich in the invasion of the USSR on June 22, 1941, had committed identical atrocities on

Soviet soil. When the ship put in at Istanbul, the Turkish authorities asked the British ambassador whether they should let the vessel continue on its chosen course. If not, it would be refused passage through the straights and its passengers denied asylum in Turkey. The ball was now in the British court.

While making it clear to the Turks that his government 'did not want those people [sic] in Palestine', Hughe Knatchbull-Hugesson, the British ambassador, suggested the Turks let the ship proceed in the hope that on its arrival, its passengers might receive 'humane treatment.' This was not at all what his political masters in London had in mind. E.H. Boyd, a Foreign Office official, condemned Knatchbull-Hugesson for missing a 'heaven sent [sic] opportunity of getting these people [sic] stopped at Istanbul and sent back to [the Romanian port of] Constanta'…and near certain death. An extraordinary pretext for this decision, which in reality was motivated by what Lord Cranborne, the Colonial Secretary, described euphemistically as 'the extremely delicate position in the Middle East' was concocted by his predecessor Lord Moyne who, in a memo to Foreign Secretary Anthony Eden, claimed that 'we have good reason to believe that this traffic [in refugees] is being favoured by the Gestapo, and the [British] Security Services attach the very greatest importance to preventing the influx of Nazi agents under the cloak of refugees'.

So, hidden among the passengers on the *Struma* were Jews, or 'Aryans' posing as Jews, in the employ of the Gestapo. Not a shred of evidence for this claim had been or was later found among all the many thousands of Jewish refugees who arrived, by one means or another, in the British Mandate during the war. Even so, Moyne proposed that the ship be sent back whence it came. On February 19, the Turks ordered the *Struma* to return into the Black Sea, where it struck a mine and sank with the loss of all but one of its passengers and crew. Undeterred by this tragedy, for which the British authorities were wholly responsible, three weeks later, on March 2, 1942, the War Cabinet resolved that 'all practicable steps be taken to discourage illegal [obviously Jewish] immigration into Palestine.' One of the consequences of this decision was the denial by the Colonial Office of asylum to several thousand Bulgarian Jewish children on 'security grounds', since they 'came from a country which we are at war.' Perhaps among them too were child Gestapo agents. (Today, the UK has adopted a more flexible policy, admitting Muslim men posing as children half their age.) To enforce this strategy of bottling up the Jews in Nazi-controlled Europe, where they faced almost certain death, British warships were diverted from the war against the Third Reich to impose a naval blockade against Jewish refugees fleeing the Holocaust, simply to placate the anti-Semitism of Palestinian Muslims, a policy also being pursued by the Nazis, who were playing the same Arab card. Certainly not Churchill's, nor for that matter his deputy Clement Attlee's finest hour.

B Traison Des Clercs Encores

'Give me the liberty to know, to utter, and to argue freely according to conscience, above all liberties.' John Milton, *Areopagitica*

'Freedom is always for the one who thinks differently.' Rosa Luxemburg.

Article 19 of the United Nations Universal Declaration of Human Rights, adopted in 1948: states that

'Everyone has the right to freedom of opinion and expression; this right includes freedom to hold opinions without interference and to seek, receive and impart information and ideas through any media and regardless of frontiers.'

Let us begin with the First Amendment to the US Constitution, ratified in 1791:

> Congress shall make no law restricting an establishment of religion or prohibiting the free the free exercise thereof, or abridging the freedom of speech, of the press; or the right of the people peacefully to assemble, and to petition the government for a redress of grievances.

By instructing the US delegation to the United Nation Human Rights Council to vote, in November 2009, for a resolution criminalising 'racial and religious stereotyping', President Obama opposed the spirit and letter of both of the above resolutions. So did what follows. On December 17, 2015, the following resolution was brought before the United States House of Representatives by 82 Democrat members of Congress. Published on the Congress website, and titled 'Condemning violence, bigotry, and hateful rhetoric towards Muslims in the United States', it read as follows:

> Whereas the victims of Muslim hate crimes and rhetoric have faced physical, verbal and emotional abuse because they were Muslim or believed to be Muslim;
> Whereas the constitutional right to freedom of religious practice is a cherished United States value and violence or hate speech [N.B. See below] towards any United States community based on faith is in contravention of the Nation's founding principles;
> Whereas there are millions of Muslims in the United States, a community made up of many diverse beliefs and cultures, and both immigrants and native-born citizens;
> Whereas this Muslim community is recognized as having made innumerable contributions to the cultural and economic fabric and well-being of United States society;
> Whereas hateful and intolerant acts against Muslims are contrary to the United States values of acceptance, welcoming and fellowship with those of all faiths, beliefs, and cultures;
> Whereas these acts affect not only the individual victims but also their families, communities, and the entire group whose faith or beliefs were the motivation for the act;
> Whereas Muslim women who wear hijabs, headscarves, or other religious articles of

clothing have been disproportionately targeted because of their religious clothing, articles, or observances; and

Whereas the rise of hateful and anti-Muslim speech, violence and cultural ignorance plays into the false narrative spread by terrorist groups of western hatred of Islam, and can encourage certain individuals to react in extreme and violent ways: Now, therefore, be it

Resolved, That the House of Representatives –
1) expresses its condolences for the victims of anti-Muslim hate crimes ['hate crime' being undefined];
2) steadfastly confirms its dedication to the rights and dignity of all its citizens of all faiths and beliefs and cultures;
3) denounces in the strongest terms the increase of hate speech [again], intimidation, violence, vandalism, arson and other hate crimes targeted against mosques, Muslims, or those perceived to be Muslim;
4) recognizes that the United States Muslim community has made countless positive [but as always, unspecified] contributions to United States society;
5) declares that civil rights and civil liberties of all United States citizens, including Muslims in the United States, should be protected and preserved;
6) urges local and Federal law enforcement authorities to work to prevent hate crimes and prosecute to the fullest extent of the law those perpetrators of hate crime; and
7) reaffirms the inalienable right of every free citizen to live without fear and intimidation and to practice their freedom of faith.

If this bill, which sought to suppress criticism of Islam by creating a law banning so-called, but undefined 'hate speech', had been passed by both Houses of Congress, and then assented to by President Obama, it would have conflicted with the First Amendment, which when approved, set no limits on the right to freedom of speech and of the press. The drafter of the proposed law or laws ingenuously conflated speech that supposedly causes upset to Muslims with acts of physical violence against Muslims and Mosques, both of which are already illegal under existing US laws covering crimes of violence against the person and damage to property, irrespective of religion. That part of the proposed law being therefore redundant, the target was obviously the expression of opinion concerning Islam which, under the First Amendment, is not a criminal act. Passages from the *Koran* which both Christians and Jews could find highly offensive were not however covered by this resolution. Here we had again the usual politically correct one-way street, along which Muslims are at the same time entitled to protection afforded to no one else, while being allowed to say what they like about everybody else.

So, while reference was made in the preamble to United States values and traditions of religious freedom and tolerance (but not free speech be it noted) no attempt was made to require or even claim that Muslims share them, only that they should be their beneficiaries. Was the mover of the bill, Donald Beyer Jr. (Democrat, Virginia) aware that Sharia law and the 1990 Cairo Declaration of Human Rights adopted by the Organisation of the Islamic Conference are both incompatible with the spirit and the letter of the US First Amendment? No doubt to the chagrin of the Democratic Party's speech police and, we can reasonably assume, President Obama, on July 18, 2017, the US Supreme Court unanimously ruled that

> restricting speech expressing ideas that may offend...strikes at the heart of the First Amendment. Speech that demeans on the basis of race, ethnicity, gender, religion,

age, disability or any other similar ground is hateful; but the proudest boast of our free speech jurisprudence is that we protect the freedom to express 'the thought that we hate'. [Bravo!]

Nothing deterred, and following the path taken by Corbynista Labour in the UK, the descent into dhimmitude of the increasingly Sharia-leftist Democratic Party continued apace, with the election to Congress in 2018 of two anti-Semitic Muslim women; BDS supporter Rashida Tliab, who made her debut in the Chamber sporting the colours of the Palestinian flag, and Ilhan Omar, the first woman to wear a hijab in Congress, who shortly after her election, claimed that the American-Israel Public Affairs Committee was paying US politicians to back Israel. Her take on 9/11 was 'some people did something'. A subsequent resolution to Congress condemning anti-Semitism proposed by Democrat leaders to placate the party's large Jewish constituency was vetoed by Omar's supporters, and replaced by one that condemned all forms of bigotry. This was followed by a boycott of the annual conference of AIPAC by nine Democratic Party Presidential candidates, and the Democratic majority in the House of Representatives not only inviting an imam to deliver a prayer at the opening of one its sessions, but one, Omar Suleiman, who has called for a third *Intifada* , or 'uprising', against Israel, likened it to Nazi Germany, backs the boycotting of Israel and called Zionists 'the enemies of God'.

Nowhere in West are the Enlightenment's values of the primacy of reason and the inalienable right of free expression more under attack than on its university campuses, institutions once esteemed as their custodians, where leftist academics and their student camp followers see it as an obstacle to the advancement of what they term 'social justice' on behalf of the ever-expanding number of self-proclaimed victims of the ruling sexist, racist, LTGBist, genderist, fatist, ableist and Islamophobic white heteropatriarchy. If SJWers were as genuinely concerned with combating patriarchy as they claim, then their prime target would not be its so-called 'white' manifestations, but the one exerted over Muslim women by Muslim men, not just in the Islamic world, but increasingly in the diaspora. It is a patriarchy which, unlike its supposed 'white' counterpart, is re-enforced by barbaric laws and imposed by male violence. Not only this. The laws which under Islam consign woman to second class status are claimed to be of divine origin, the *sharia*, laws compared with which the so-called 'glass ceiling' fades into insignificance if it exists at all, and which impose often unspeakably brutal sanctions when women are found guilty by all-male 'courts' of violating them. But the Islamic subjugation of white women is necessarily a SJW taboo subject, because Muslim men no less than women comprise an integral component of the 'intersectional' alliance of the oppressed, despite the reality that if they follow the dictates of their faith, Muslim men are not only the vilest oppressors of women but would, if they could, impose draconian punishments, including death, for the life-style and sexual preferences of many of their SJW cohorts. Because Islam, supposedly quintessentially the religion of the oppressed, trumps all, even in matters of race, sexual orientation and gender, a white male convert to Islam should, at least in in theory, be able to beat and rape his black Muslim wife with impunity, simply because his holy book tells him he can. But beneath Muslim men in the SJW pecking order, all is not sweetness and light. A very unsisterly fight has irrupted between feminists and transgenderists over men who claim to be women competing in women's sports events and who are invading women-only facilities and environments.

Another flagrant contradiction in the SJW movement is the demand by its Black Lives Matter contingent to 'resist white capitalism', one akin to the Nazis' equally selective condemnation of 'Jewish interest slavery'. This slogan cannot sit too well with white feminists who complain of their under-representation at the summits of western ('white') big business. (There is no equivalent outrage concerning their even greater under-representation in admittedly substantially less glamourous and remunerative, but infinitely more essential occupations as garbage collection and sewer maintenance.) In view of the inference to be drawn that only 'white capitalism' is to be condemned, it would be an instructive exercise for those who advance this slogan to conduct a comparative global study of the wages, working conditions and trade union rights of workers employed by capitalism's white patriarchal and non-white versions. As for 'patriarchy', there are entire continents, comprising the majority of the world's population, that are ruled by patriarchies of all skin colours other than white and where, in most cases, the status of women would be anything but the envy of their sisters languishing under the rule of its white counterpart. Ignorant though they are of world affairs, given the non-subjects they have opted to qualify in, even SWJers must know this, but who would dare say it?

The contortions and feuding of SJWers over who is most victimised has deservedly been the butt of ridicule by non-believers. However, the goals the movement seeks, and is some way to achieving, are no laughing matter. The totalitarian ideology which fuels this lumpen new campus left has as one of its central goals the denial of the right of dissenters to freedom of speech, the foundation stone of not only America's but the entire West's freedoms and prosperity. It is captured to perfection by Barbara White, (sic) an (oppressed) Women's Studies (sic) Professor (sic) at the University of New Hampshire. Free speech is, it seems, and always has been, the means by which the white (heterosexual) patriarchy maintains its rule:

> Academia has traditionally been dominated by white heterosexual [how does she know this?] men, and the First Amendment and Academic Freedom (I'll call them FAF) have traditionally protected the rights of white heterosexual men. Most of us are silenced by existing social conditions before we get the power to speak out in any way where FAF might protect us. So forgive us if we don't get all dewy-eyed about FAF. Perhaps to you it's as sacrosanct as the flag or the natoinal anthem; to us, strict construction of the First Amendment is just another noose around our necks.

So much for free speech. Another conquest of the Enlightenment, the concept of objective truth and the right and duty to pursue it by unfettered inquiry, fares no better at the elite universities of the USA, where 'mission statements' no longer speak of truth and knowledge but of respecting 'inclusiveness' and welcoming 'diversity', though not to be sure one of ideas, where a mind-numbing conformity prevails, but of race, gender and sexual orientation. An Open Letter, so obviously the fruit of tutorial spoon-feeding, from black students to David Oxtoby, President of Pomona College, protesting against his policy of upholding free speech, not only denounced it as 'a tool appropriated by hegemonic institutions'(sic) which enabled them to 'perpetuate systems of domination'(sic) by providing 'a platform to project their bigotry'. The letter also declared that 'historically, white supremacy has venerated the idea of objectivity' as 'a means of silencing oppressed peoples' and that the idea that there is 'a single truth' is 'a construct of the Euro-west that is deeply entrenched in the Enlightenment'.(sic) The idea of a 'single truth' was 'a myth, and white supremacy, imperialism, colonisation, capitalism and the United States of América are its progeny. The idea that the truth is an entity for which we must search in matters that endanger our ability to exist in open spaces is an attempt to silence oppressed peoples.' Far better, then, to feed non-white students patronising lies. The result one can see on a YouTube video where a black student at a South African university seminar is denouncing the scientific method as 'white' and 'colonialist', and advocating, unchallenged, its replacement by what she calls 'black magic'. This not funny. It is tragic. This, the Nazi doctrine of 'race truth' at a *university?* And what is worse, one where its black majority was not so long ago liberated from the biblically-derived 'race truths' of its white supremacist minority.

In the same spirit, a feminist posing as an academic has given Einstein's epoch-shaping E=MC squared short shrift, denouncing it as a 'sexed equation' that 'privileges' the 'masculine' speed of light over slower feminine speeds no less essential. Newtonian physics fares no better. Since it treats only of the movements of solids, it too is guilty of male privileging. This is attributed to 'men having sex organs that protrude and become rigid', while 'woman have openings that leak menstrual blood and vaginal fluids'. QED. Gravity and the laws of motion, just like everything else we fondly once thought we knew about the universe, are genderist constructs. Such are the fruits of 'different ways of knowing', when two plus 2 can equal anything but 4.

The creators of humanity's most sublime and until 'de-constructed' by post-modernist 'critical theory', universally revered works of philosophy, art, literature and music are likewise found to have white male feet of clay. Introducing criteria of 'identity' of race and gender into the world of the creative arts has led to what one critic of 'third wave' feminism, US scholar Christena Hoff Sommers, described as a situation in academe and beyond where 'the very idea of "genius" is regarded with suspicion as elitist and "masculinist"'. Who needs Bach or Beethoven? Anyone, so long as they have the right genitals and/or skin, can compose a B Minor Mass or Choral Symphony. Plato and Aristotle are now routinely derided as white patriarchs by classicists who are themselves white. The intrusion of the poison of 'identity' politics into the world of classical music has led in the UK to demands by feminazis for concerts to be devoted exclusively to compositions by women composers conducted by women conductors, and for orchestras always to be comprised 50% of women, selected not purely on merit, as is currently the practice, with anonymous auditions from behind screens, but also for their genitals. And at the 2019 Musicians Union conference a motion was carried endorsing this very demand, calling for 'equal representation of female musicians in live music performance and on radio and television'. Indicative of the shape of things to come in the world of music, when interviewed by a white male before the performance of her work on BBC Radio 3, a teenage woman composer was applauded by her audience when she said the purpose of her choral composition was to 'challenge the white male patriarchy'. Racial as well as gender engineering has also been catered for, with the formation of the segregationist Chineke orchestra, which excludes on principle all 'white' musicians, and which, as matter of principle, that of prioritising merit irrespective of race or gender, I will not listen to. Likewise, what goes by the name of 'sexual orientation'. In the USA, which always takes the lead in such innovations, we have had since at least the 1990s the New York Gay Men's Chorus.

How one proves one's eligibility for membership is something best left unexplored.

Contrary to the literal meaning of the word, 'diversity' in practice today means the opposite, segregation and exclusion, always at the expense of equal opportunity, merit and quality. This racist and genderist onslaught on the humanist tradition, rejected for its assertion of the intrinsic unity of mankind, and on science, high culture and more generally, all evidence-based and creative thinking, comes today in the USA not so much from the Christian fundamentalist right as from from the left, in a country where already, half its population still rejects the evidence-based findings of biology, geology and cosmology, fully a third believes aliens have visited earth, and ten percent that Elvis lives. In the land of Yale and Harvard, an increasing number of its academic staff and students have succumbed to post-modernist mumbo-jumbo, resulting in 'learned' journals publishing in good faith spoof articles arguing that gravity and the penis are 'social constructs', the latter perhaps being a parody of 'deconstructionist' guru Jacques Lacan's claim that the penis can be in expressed in a series of equations, climaxing, appropriately, in the square root of minus one.

Far removed from the realm of pure numbers, an SJW activist at Chicago University appeared on Fox TV claiming the right to use violence to prevent a politician he disagreed with speaking on his campus. He was opposed to 'discussing in sanitised [sic] environments' and 'moderated conversations', meaning those conducted according to the traditional rules of debate and discussion, where there is no ever-present threat of the disruptive and intimidatory violence which has become the norm on so many US campuses. As he put it so well, 'it's not about who's right, it's about who has power.' Not the Enlightenment's power of truth, but the totalitarian principle that power defines what is true. This over-privileged (he was a white, male, probably heterosexual student at one of the USA's most expensive universities) barbarian thug unashamedly proclaimed his contempt for the achievements and indeed glories of more than two thousand years of civilisation when he wrote in his college's newspaper that 'deliberation, analysis and "hearing out both sides" is no longer viable...we must take action and dispense with all this sophistry, all these abstract notions of civility'. How would this ignoramus have known that 80 years previously, with his invasion of Poland only days away, Hitler had similarly instructed his military chiefs to cast all scruples aside: 'What matters is not to have right on our side, but simply to win'.

The contempt for logic, evidence and learning, and the free debate and exchange of ideas, first came to fruition in the fascist era, when reason was supplanted, as it is now, by the claimed higher truths of 'feeling' and of an 'identity' then white and hetero-male, and now their inverses. In its new, pseudo-leftist, guise, the same contempt for reason and knowledge dominates most US campuses today. Of America's 4,298 degree-granting colleges and universities, little more than one per cent, 58 as of March 2019, had endorsed Chicago's statement in defence of absolute academic freedom and the right to free speech and peaceful assembly as defined by the First Amendment. Of the ten elite 'Ivy League' Universities, only two had seen fit to support it; Princeton and Columbia. But not Yale and Harvard, Brown and Cornell, Tuck, Dartmouth, Wharton and Pennsylvania; yet more proof that the USA's institutions of higher learning are now in free fall. And there is every indication that the rest of the Anglo-Saxon world is only too eager to follow suit. For example, after engaging the psychologist Dr Jordan Petersen of the University of Toronto to give a series of lectures on the Old Testament Chapter of Exodus,

Cambridge University's Department of Divinity reversed its decision in March 2019 after objections were made by academics and students to his well-advertised rejection, one shared by all biologists worthy of the name, of the claim that gender is purely a 'social construct' and not determined by physiology. What price Genesis 1: 27: 'Male and female He created them'? The university which in better times, when inquiry was unfettered by political correctness, had been the alma mater of some of the world's most illustrious scientists - Darwin, Rutherford, Eddington, Hawking, Crick, Franklin, Maxwell, Chadwick, David Attenborough, Oppenheimer - justified its reversal on the grounds that engaging Dr Petersen would be contrary to its policy of 'inclusiveness', Trigger Police code for *excluding* from campus ideas that students may find upsetting but are incapable of debating and refuting. As on a growing number of US campuses, Cambridge's 'snow flake' divinity students become the arbiters of what can and cannot be said and taught, and by whom. On September 28, 2019, Edinburgh University was the venue for an SJW extravaganza, billed as a Q and A session on the theme 'Resisting Whiteness 2019'. To further this 'resistance to whiteness', white participants were barred from asking questions, and excluded from a 'safe space' reserved for non-whites who felt 'overwhelmed/overstimulated [sic] or uncomfortable', presumably when in too close a proximity to those with a white skin.

In the USA, where SJW lunacy first surfaced, anti-free speech tactics by self-styled 'Social Justice Warriors' are given free rein by college authorities, involving not only the shouting down of speakers whose opinions they disagree with, but mob violence, designed to enforce on all and sundry what Milton described as a 'gross confirming stupidity'. For example, faced with the threat of SJW storm trooper assault, the Jewish libertarian Ben Schapiro had to pay $600,000 out of his own pocket for police protection from SJW mobsters when he spoke at Berkeley University, the home of the 1960s campus Free Speech movement. (With Jewish students subjected to abuse and even violence, their societies in the UK have also been obliged to pay for their own security.) Perhaps the most notorious example of SJW thuggery occurred at Evergreen Washington State College when in May 2017 biology Professor Bret Weinstein refused to comply with demands by SJW activists that white students and staff absent themselves from the campus for one day as an act of atonement for their racist guilt. Acting out, we can be sure unwittingly, since history and its lessons are a closed book to them, the role of Mussolini's 'dynamic minority' and Lenin's 'revolutionary vanguard', student rioters, some armed with baseball bats, stormed the college building, where they sought out and confronted Professor Weinstein as he lectured his class of multi-race students, swearing at and verbally abusing him as a white supremacist. They then besieged and imprisoned in his office, with his consent, the college's Principle, presenting him with a list of demands designed to enforce racial and gender 'equity' (not be it noted, equality), the only one of which he rejected being the summary dismissal of Professor Weinstein. In the following two years enrolments plummeted. Betrayed by most of his academic colleagues, some of who agreed with his stand but, like the majority of the college's students, were afraid to say so, Professor Weinstein resigned later that year, after negotiating a pay-out of $500,000.

This strategy of intimidation, one that replicates the methods used by Nazi students in the early 1930s to subdue their embattled Jewish and democratic opponents, is often not only approved of but even incited by 'progressive' academic staff. If SJW mobsters fail to have a meeting banned by college authorities (who more often than not comply) they attend it not to participate in the question and answer sessions that are always a feature of free speech events, but to drown out the speaker by co-ordinated inane chants and to disrupt it by storming the platform, seizing the microphone, shouting abuse though megaphones, and setting off fire alarms... all with impunity, because they are the good guys, fighting for social justice. The appeal of these tactics is that they require next to no brain power. Like all totalitarian movements, the new campus left, unable by reason, logic and the marshalling of evidence to refute ideas it disagrees with, since all that counts are supposedly wounded 'feelings', instead uses a combination of administrative bans and gangster tactics to silence its opponents and intimidate college officials.

Belying their pretentious name, SJW activists are not driven by compassion but an ego-centric craving to be seen as virtuous. It is a second coming of the 'me' generation, whose spoiled brats they mostly are, only this time round, their self-centredness masquerades as altruism. Their claim on a monopoly of virtue, one that out-Robespierres Robespierre's, has been taken to such ludicrous extremes that it is an article of faith amongst SJWers that non-white people cannot be guilty of racism or any other prejudice, itself a racist proposition. Yet numerous scenes on YouTube show black faces distorted by a murderous loathing chanting racial and sexual obscenities at those cursed for being born with the wrong colour skin and genitals, the SJW version of original sin. Orwell's 'hate week' is no longer a dystopian fiction.

What fuels this movement is indeed pure groupthink fanatical hatred, one of race and of gender. It is now preached in what were once places of learning that all self-respecting women, LGTBs and non-whites must hate all heterosexual white men, while to have any prospect of purging their original sin, straight white men must hate and debase themselves, not necessarily for what they do, *but for what they are*. So much for Martin Luther King's dream of a time when people will be judged, 'not by the colour of their skin, but by the content of their character', and Schiller's hope, immortalised by Beethoven's Choral Symphony, that 'all men shall brothers be'. SJWers subscribe to a contrary doctrine of eternal enmity, that a heterosexual white man's character is defined by the colour of his skin and, for good measure, also the function of his genitals. And yes, out-doing the lynch mentality of the KKK, one popular 'feminist' hash tag demands, 'Kill all White Men', while 'Woman's Studies' 'Professor' Suzanna Walters entitled her *Washington Post* diatribe against patriarchy 'Why can't we hate men?', after objections, subsequently racially re-calibrated to target only white men.

The SJW crusade against the white patriarchy is not merely a matter of verbal abuse. If a white man so much as displays a passing romantic interest in a member of the opposite sex ('opposite'? Careful...that's binary talk, a microaggression) he faces the very real risk of having his life ruined by accusations of attempted rape. Even 'suggestive staring' can lead to disciplinary proceedings against a man who casts a fleeting appreciative glance at an attractive female student. By running tearfully to Sir every time they are triggered and microaggressed, 'social justice' activists demonstrate that they are more wimps than warriors, throwing tantrums more appropriate for a spoilt child in a nursery than an adult in an institution of higher learning. Reared from the cradle to their late teens and even beyond by ludicrously over-protective 'helicopter parents' who have shielded them from what were in saner times regarded as not only the unavoidable but necessary bumps and bruises of the process of growing up, infantilised millennials arrive at university expecting its student body to function as a substitute family, and its staff as surrogate helicopter parents.

Not the pursuit of knowledge but a womb-like 'safety' is what they crave above all and are given, affording them round-the-clock protection from the slings and arrows of outrageous opinions. Consequently, after being cocooned in their racially and gender-segregated safe spaces, they will leave university more ignorant than when they entered, clutching their worthless degrees in race, gender, queer, disability, women's and fat studies. Yes, Fat Studies is now an accredited academic discipline, totally dominated by women 'professors' waging the good fight against yet another man(sic)ifestation of the white patriarchy, namely, 'thin privilege,' with its false claim that obesity is determinantal to a women's mobility, employment prospects, attractiveness and therefore, dare I say it, marriage prospects, longevity, health and happiness. Not only will graduates in this nonsense have been cheated of a once-in-a-lifetime opportunity to enhance their mental powers. It will leave them emotionally and morally retarded, unable to take responsibility for their lives as adults in a world that neither owes them a living nor excuses, scapegoats and alibis for their own shortcomings and failures.

Those academics who have betrayed their calling by promoting ideology instead of pursuing and encouraging in their charges a love of and respect for knowledge are no less despicable than Nazi doctors at Auschwitz, the only difference being they are performing experiments on immature and impressionable minds, not emaciated bodies. They no longer see their role as teaching students how to think critically, but what to think, uncritically, not to revere knowledge for its own sake, but to see it cynically in functional terms, purely as a means to exert or acquire power. Their aim is to replicate themselves not only in the relatively toothless world of academe, but to prepare their charges for entry into those of the media, culture, and above, all politics, where this strategy is already visibly bearing fruit in the increasingly leftist and Sharia-friendly orientation of the Democratic Party. Duly lobotomised and then suitably re-programmed, the long-term goal is for SJW graduates to ascend to the upper echelons of the elite they effect to despise, there to steer the bad ship America onto the path of post-modernist rectitude, a frictionless dystopia where all speak, if not think the same. It is indeed one of the many contradictions within the SJW movement in the USA that it presents itself as 'anti-elitist', or 'anti-establishment', doing battle against various forms of 'privilege', even though its activists are themselves the beneficiaries of an education far too expensive for most children from a working-class background. What passes for the movement's ideology, mainly a meagre repertoire of chants, is anything but the product of a spontaneous movement of the masses, but a greatly simplified version, doled out to captive student audiences, of the latest fashionable trends in 'humanities' academe. As for its policy of enforced political correctness being 'anti-elitist', in the UK, where successive governments have criminalised 'hate speech' while imposing and promoting a segregationist programme of 'multi-culturalism' and 'diversity' at every level of society, often with disastrous consequences as evidenced by the Muslim gang rape scandal, the movement is pushing on a door long since opened wide by 'the establishment'.

If this war on reason and intellectual inquiry currently being waged by the totalitarian left achieves its goal of stamping out free thought, inquiry and expression in the west, as it has in the past and continues to do elsewhere, then our liberal democratic civilisation will be heading, not for what the German philosopher

Oswald Spengler predicted a century ago would be its unavoidable decline, but its suicide, laid low by cowardice and a self-imposed conformity that is the mortal enemy of the creative spirit. And if we in the west submit willingly, that is what we will deserve.

As a first line of defence against this assault on free speech and the right of peaceful assembly in the USA, the wording of the First Amendment is now patently inadequate to the task, and is therefore itself in urgent need of amendment, since it was based on the mistaken but at the time of its adoption, entirely reasonable presumption that no one would ever seek to prevent their exercise by a fellow citizen. How could those who drafted and approved the First Amendment have imagined that two centuries on, American university students, the most privileged generation in the history of the human race would, while righteously proclaiming and wallowing in their ever-expanding categories of simulated victimhood, not only demand, but successfully enforce by illegal riotous assembly their imagined right to silence dissent from their opinions on of all places, a university campus? As the purpose of speech is for it to be heard by those to whom the speech is directed, it logically follows that preventing such speech or rendering it inaudible constitutes a violation of free speech, as it does no less the right of others who have peacefully assembled to hear what is being said. Such an amendment as I propose would therefore stipulate that it is unlawful, either by word of mouth or any other action, to impede the exercise of free speech by another citizen or group of citizens.

Addendum

Always at the cutting edge of progressive groupthink, the *Guardian* coined for its well-heeled readers a new SWJspeak term when, in its online edition of September 15, 2019, it published an editorial which took to task former Tory Leader David Cameron for advertising in his memoirs his 'privileged pain' at the death of his six year old son, afflicted from birth with cerebral palsy. The offending passage read:

> When you watch your tiny baby undergoing multiple blood tests, your heart aches. When they bend him back into the foetal position to remove fluid from the base of his spine with a long, threatening-looking needle, it almost breaks…He could have 20 or 30 seizures a day, lasting for minutes, or sometimes hours, his small frame racked with spams and what look like searing pain. By the end his clothes would be drenched in sweat and his poor body exhausted.

This elicited from the *Guardian* the following obscene response: 'Mr Cameron has known pain and failure in his life but it has always been limited failure and privileged pain'. Former *Daily Mirror* editor Piers Morgan put it well when he asked, 'What kind of mind would write that?' The answer is, that of a privileged, far left *Guardian* journalist. Deleted after a storm of protests from across the political spectrum, a statement admitted that the editorial 'fell far short of our standards'. How so? Surely grief, no less than race and gender, is a 'social construct', not to speak of gravity and the penis. And if so, how was it then that the editorial came to be written, approved for publication and, after publication, until it was removed, not objected to by any of the *Guardian*'s staff? Here we have sample of the Corbynista journal's 'kinder politics', all of a piece with their guru's friendship with Jew killers and 'solidarity' with regimes that murder their opponents. To paraphrase Shylock in the *Merchant of Venice*, to the question, 'cannot a white male Oxbridge Tory not grieve like a white male Oxbridge Guardianista socialist?' will come the reply, 'no, because he is privileged.'

C Swedish Syndrome

Named after the reactions of hostages held captive for six days in a raid on a Stockholm bank in 1973, Wikipedia defines the so-called 'Stockholm Syndrome' as one where 'hostages express sympathy and have positive feelings for their captors.' Today, the hostages are again Swedes, chiefly women, and the reactions are frequently the same. However, their captors are not fellow Swedes, but male Muslim migrants. In 1975, when its Parliament voted to embrace multi-culturalism, Sweden had the lowest incidence of rape in the entire world. Today, it is the second highest, having increased since then by fourteen times. What follows is first, a chronology of incidents in November 2015.

I

November 6: The Gronkulla School in Alvesta closed after reports of a rape at the facility spread on social media. A Somali boy had apparently been sexually harassing a 12-year-old girl for some time. On October 17, he allegedly took his attentions a step further, pulled the girl behind a bush and raped her. The girl's father had been unsuccessful in trying to get the school to address the problem earlier, but even after the reported rape, the school's management did not act. The boy was allowed to continue going to school - just on a schedule different from the girl's. Her distraught parents told the news website *Fria Tide*, 'We are being spat on because we are Swedish'. In protest against the school's management, many parents, viewing the school as having sided with the perpetrators, moved their children to other schools.

November 9: Social commentator and whistle-blower Merit Wager revealed on her blog that administrators of the Immigration Service had all been ordered to 'accept the claim that an applicant is a child, if he does not look as if he is over 40 [sic].' (In the UK, two approximately thirty-year-old migrant 'children' were removed from their schools, but only after protests by parents.) 32,180 'unaccompanied refugee children' arrived during 2015 by December 1. After another 1,130 arrived, the government finally decided to act. Everyone who looks adult is forced to go through a medical age-determination examination. The UK government has refused to adopt this procedure.

November 10: A 28-year-old Iraqi man was prosecuted for raping a woman on a night train between Finland and Sweden. The man had originally planned to seek asylum (illegally) in Finland but had found the living conditions too harsh. He had therefore taken a train back to Sweden. In a couchette (sleeping car where men and women are together) the rapist and two other asylum seekers met one of the many Swedish women whose hearts go out to 'new arrivals'. The woman bought sandwiches for the men; they drank vodka. When two of the men started groping the woman, she told them to stop, yet chose to lie down and go to sleep. Sometime during the night, she was awakened by the Iraqi as he raped her. The woman managed to break free and locate a train assistant. To the attendant's surprise, the woman did not immediately want to press charges. The court documents state: 'The train attendant asked if he should call the police. At first, the woman did not want him to do so, because she did not want to put N.N. [the rapist's initials] an asylum seeker, in a tough spot. She felt sorry for him and was afraid he would be deported back to Iraq.' The man was given a sentence of one year in prison, payment of 85,000 kroner (about $10,000) in damages and deportation - but would be allowed to come back to Sweden after five years.

An Algerian and a Syrian asylum seeker were indicted for raping a Swedish woman in Strangnas. The men, a 39-year-old Algerian and a 31-year-old from Syria, met the woman in a bar one night in August. When the woman left, one of the men followed her, pulled her to the ground, and assaulted her. Afterwards, the woman kept walking, and ran into two other men – the Syrian and another unidentified man - and was raped again. The Syrian reportedly also spat her in the face and said, 'I'm going to fuck you, little Swedish girl.' The men, who live at the same asylum house, denied knowing each other when questioned by police. The verdict was announced on December 1. Rapist number one was sentenced to two and half years in prison, 167,000 kroner in damages, and deportation to Algeria. Rapist number two was convicted of aggravated rape and sentenced to four years in prison. He cannot be deported, however, because 'there are currently hindrances towards enforcing deportations to Syria.' He was also ordered to pay the woman 117,000 kroner in damages.

November 13: A trial began against eight Eritrean men, between the ages of 19 and 26, who according to the District Court, 'crudely [sic] gang-raped' a 45-year-old woman. She had been waiting in a stair well for a friend when the men invited her into an apartment. Inside, she was thrown on the floor, held down, beaten and brutally raped. When questioned by police, she said, 'It felt as if there were hands and fingers everyplace. Fingers penetrated me, vaginally, anally. It hurt very much. I could feel the finger nails.' She said she could also hear the Eritreans laughing and speaking in their own language while they raped her. 'They seemed to be enjoying themselves', she said. When two of the men started fighting over who should rape her next, she tried to flee, but one of the men hit her over the head; she fell unconscious. After coming to, she escaped out of a window and was able to reach a neighbour. The District Court of Falun established that several men had taken part in the attack, but the District Attorney was unable to prove who had done what. Therefore, only one man was convicted of aggravated rape, and sentenced to five years in prison. The others were sentenced to only 10 months in prison for helping to conceal a serious criminal offence. After serving their time, the men will be allowed to stay in Sweden.

November 23: Hassan Mostafa Al-Mandlawi, 32, and Al Amin Sultan, 30, were indicted in the Gothenburg Municipal Court suspected of having travelled to Syria in 2013 and murdering at least two people there…The accused men came to Sweden, one from Iraq, and one from Syria, as children. Both grew up in Sweden and are Swedish citizens. They travelled to Syria in 2013 and joined one of the many Islamist terror groups there. According to the prosecution, they murdered two captured workers in an industrial area of Aleppo by slitting their throats (as per the *Koran,* Chapter 8, Verse 13). The prosecutor wrote that 'Al-Mandlawi and Sultan have both expressed delight at the deeds.' During the trial, films of the executions were shown, but both men still denied having committed the crimes. First the films show a man having his throat slit, the blood gushing before he dies. Then, the other victim's head is severed from the body, and the killer holds up the severed head to loud cheers from the other. The verdict was announced on December 14. Both men were convicted of terrorist crimes and sentenced to life in prison. The verdict will be appealed, defence lawyers said.

November 28: A large mob at an asylum house on Nora tried to break into a room where a woman had barricaded herself along with her son. Some 30 Muslim men apparently thought the woman was in violation of Islamic Sharia law, by being in Sweden unaccompanied by a man. They thought that she should therefore be raped and her teenage son killed. Asylum house staff called the police, who averted the plan

II

Juden Raus

In 1936, the German firm of Günther and Co. marketed a new children's board game. Advertised as 'entertaining, instructive and solidly constructed', it was called 'Juden Raus'. Played with dice, the objective, as the name suggests, was to be the first to round up six Jews and deport them from the Third Reich. I see no reason why, if adapted for use by Sweden's Muslim migrants and those Swedes who see it as their life's duty to indulge their Islamic guests' every appetite, whim and prejudice, it should not enjoy a renewed popularity. Readers will recall that the Sharia leftist Mayor of Malmo justified Muslim migrant assaults on the Jews of his city as warranted by their presumed support for Israel. What follows is a brief survey of similar attempts by Swedes to appease Muslim anti-Semitism.

November 9, 2015: An anti-racist demonstration is held in Umea to commemorate the *Kristallnacht,* the night of crystals or broken glass, when on the night of November 9-10, 1938, urged on by Propaganda Minister Goebbels, Nazi thugs unleashed a pogrom on Germany's Jews, vandalising their property, burning down at least 200 synagogues, murdering more than a hundred Jews and dispatching another 30,000 to concentration camps, to be followed by death in the gas chambers of Hitler's Final Solution. In commemorating what proved to be the prelude to the Holocaust, here was Sweden at its very liberal, tolerant best, one might assume. And indeed, the demonstration had the support of four of Sweden's political parties. But participation in this event was not open to everyone. Incredible as it may seem, Jews, whose persecution was supposedly being commemorated, were barred from attending because, as Jan Hagglund, an organizer, explained, they would perceive the demonstration 'as an unwelcoming or unsafe [sic!] situation for them'…just like Nazi Germany on the night of November 9-10, 1938, or pro-Hamas demonstrations in the summer of 2014. 'Unwelcome and unsafe'? What, one wonders, could possibly give Sweden's Jews that impression? Could it have been because the purpose of the event was not to combat anti-Semitism, but to welcome the arrival of illegal and in many cases, anti-Semitic Muslim migrants in their new home?

January 2009: A pro-Israel demonstration in Malmo was attacked by Arabs chanting 'fucking Jews' and assailing marchers with exploding fireworks, bottles and eggs. Instead of arresting their attackers, police pushed the marchers into a back alley.

2010: Malmo: A series of attacks on the city's synagogue, resulted in a warning by the Simon Wiesenthal Centre in Los Angeles to Jews not to visit Malmo, 'due to harassment of Jewish citizens'. At the most recent count, 30% of Malmo's population was reported to be Muslim, though the actual percentage is probably higher, and certainly rising.

2015: Malmo: In the first six months of 2015, police recorded 30 grenade explosions in the city, parts of which had become Muslim no-go areas for public officials.

October 2015: Malmo: Two members of the Swedish Parliament took part in an anti-Israel demonstration that featured anti-Semitic chants and support for the stabbing attacks on Jews then gathering pace in Jerusalem.

October 2012 The reader will recall that a Bavarian State Minister criticised visits by children of Muslim parents to Holocaust museums. Teaching the history of the Holocaust to Muslim students has also has its opponents in Sweden, just as it does in the West Bank and the Gaza Strip in schools administered by the anti-Semites of UNRWA, the Palestinian Authority and Hamas. Helena Mechlaoui, a High School history teacher, put the case for blotting out the greatest crime in the history of mankind like this: 'If we talk about students from the Middle East, it may be because many of them bear the traumatic experiences that are related to either Israeli or American policies. And the two states are often seen as one'. So? '…the two states are often seen as one'? Then surely it is a history teacher's job to rectify such misapprehensions, not defer to them. But perhaps Mechlaoui shares them. She continues: 'They may [sic] have lost one or more siblings, cousins or peers in an Israeli or American bombing.' Even if true, why does that require excluding the Holocaust, and only the Holocaust, from a history syllabus? The US Eighth Air Force dropped bombs a plenty on Germany in the Second World War, but German schools nevertheless teach the history of the United States.

All states have taken lives, and lost them, in warfare of one kind or another. If applied consistently, this principle would result in the total abolition of all history teaching. But that is not the intention here, which is to abolish only the teaching of the Holocaust to Muslims. Although Mechlaoui's version of the history of the Middle East is, to say the very least, debatable, the main point at issue is that she is prepared to use it to erase or, if you will, trump, the teaching of the true history of the Holocaust. After listing the deprivations that she believes her Muslim pupils may have suffered at the hands of Israel and not, as is so often the case, by fellow Muslims, she concludes: 'In this context [there we have it again: 'context', this time invoked to justify telling lies about history] it is perhaps not desirable to start talking about the Holocaust'. Palestinian Authority President Mahmoud Abbas, David Irving and the Holocaust-denying associates of Jeremy Corbyn would surely agree.

February 2015: Teaching politically correct but factually incorrect history is not only for school children. At an adult education class in Helsingborg, a student questioned whether the Holocaust actually happened. (I leave to the reader to hazard a guess as to the religious affiliation of the student in question.) In reply, the teacher, who being a substitute was evidently not up to speed on the new Sharia history curriculum, outlined the evidence which proved that the Holocaust was a historical fact. The teacher quickly learned that in the new Islam-friendly Sweden, this was not the correct response. Following a complaint by a student (again, guesses as to their religious identity are in order) the teacher was reprimanded by the school administration for defending historical truth: 'What is history for us is not the history of others. When we have students who have studied other history books, there is no point in discussing facts against facts'.

'*Facts against facts*'? *No point*'? The mind boggles. Here we have the leftist, post-modernist and Sharia-correct variant of Trump's 'alterative facts'. Purely in order to appease the ingrained anti-Semitism of Sweden's Muslim migrants, Sweden's educational system is trampling underfoot the conquests of centuries of rational, logical, scientific, empirically-grounded thought and inquiry, reaching back through the Enlightenment to classical Greece. Here we have the fruits of the much celebrated 'cultural sensitivity', 'diversity' and 'inclusivity', and its analogue, cultural relativism; the emergence, in of all places, Sweden, of the Nazi doctrine that there is no objective truth, that each people 'thinks with its blood' and has its own 'race truth', in this instance, Swedes theirs, and Arab Muslims theirs. 'Fact against fact'…as if facts were mere opinions, resting on nothing, one as good or bad as another, with no objective criteria and method by which to judge what is truly fact and what is merely fiction and fancy. Some say the Holocaust happened, while others, Muslim migrants, 'who have studied other books', produced we can guess by whom, say it did not. Who are we to judge between them? There is 'no point' in challenging those who deny the Holocaust. Worse, it causes offence. It's simply a case of 'facts against facts'. It's a 'fact' that it happened, and another that it did not. Who knows? Corbyn's 'friends' could well be right.

But why just the Holocaust? If the principle of epistemological solipsism is valid for history, it surely needs to be extended and applied to every other branch of what we once fondly took to be human knowledge. Some say the earth is a sphere, and goes around the sun, others that it is flat, and some, Saudi Muslim clerics for example, add to this that the sun goes around the earth. Fact against fact. Some say the universe is 13.7 billion years old, while others, Christian 'young earth creationists' as they call themselves in a rare moment of lucidity, say that it is six thousand. Fact against fact. Some say the various species have evolved over a period of four billion years by a process of natural selection, others, Muslims as well as Christians, that they have all been created simultaneously in a matter of hours by an entity called god.

Tens, possibly hundreds of millions of Muslims, and also millions of non-Muslims, believe that the Jews, and/or President George Bush were responsible for 9/11, while others, including many millions of Muslims approvingly and correctly, believe it was the work of 19 Al-Qaeda Muslim martyrs acting on behalf of Allah. Fact against fact. There are Christians today who still say the Jews once used to drain the blood of Christian children to mix with Passover unleven bread, and Muslim preachers, including one praised by Corbyn, who agree with them, while the rest of mankind says it is all lies. Fact against fact. Take your pick. But what about evidence, you may ask. Doesn't it count for *anything*? No longer, especially in Sweden when the subject is the Holocaust and the students are Muslims. In the war against 'Islamophobia', if the first casualty proves to be the truth, as in this instance it surely did, then so be it. As in the Doublethink of Orwell's Oceania, two plus two can equal both four and five.

2015: Complaints are made to Sweden's top television channel, TV4, for featuring in a 'reality' show the rapper Dani M, who specialises in promoting Jewish conspiracy theories in the tradition of *The Protocols of the Learned Elders of Zion*. Putting to one side the related issue of whether anti-Semites should be banned from appearing on television (though for the record, as a believer in free speech, I say no - there is always the off-button or other channels), it is the reply of the show's Executive Producer, Christer Anderson, that interests us here: 'TV4's core values are zero racism and always have been, so long as I can remember, but we cannot cut people off who do not feel the same way. TV4 is a portal through which people with different opinions pass and we must have a broad level of acceptance'. Anti-Semitism and the advocacy of the existence of a world Jewish conspiracy 'a different opinion'? Here we go again. Surely it was possible to defend the channel's right to allow such views to be aired, and at the same express its disagreement with them? When a TV4's employee used the word 'nigger' in a YouTube clip, she was promptly sacked. What happened to the channel's 'broad level of acceptance'? Evidently some racist opinions are more acceptable than others. There are good grounds for suspecting that with the current wave of Islamophilia that is enveloping Sweden, in the unlikely event of even the mildest of critics of Islam appearing on the same show, the complaints would have been far more numerous, and the channel's response cringingly apologetic.

In 2010, the Swedish TV celebrity, Gina Dirawi, who is of Palestinian origin, wrote in her blog that Israel's policies were similar to those of the Nazis, and in 2012, that her fans should read a book which (as neo-Nazis do) denied the Holocaust...both being what one might expect from some Palestinians. These are just two samples of her many anti-Jewish postings. But her well and proudly advertised anti-Semitism has proved no impediment whatsoever to her continued rise to mega-stardom. Today, she hosts a number of shows on SVT, the Swedish public broadcasting network, and although a Muslim, was chosen to host SVT's Christmas show. She was also selected to host the prestigious 2016 Meodfestivalen, one of Sweden's most popular music events of the year.

May 2015: The Swedish think tank Perspektiv Pa Israel released evidence that the director in Sweden of the Swedish government-funded Islamic Relief was disseminating anti-Semitic postings on Facebook. All Sweden's major media companies refused to take the story. One, Nyheter24, explained why: 'Readers are, to say the least, [!!] not interested in this particular issue', the 'particular issue' being Muslim anti-Semitism and its funding by the Swedish taxpayer. But how could Nyheter24 be so sure, since a news blackout of the issue had ensured that the public knew nothing about it? All this and more happened, and is happening now, in of all countries, Sweden. Sweden, the beacon and exemplar of democratic socialism: liberal, cultured, tolerant, relaxed, secular. If it can happen to Sweden, it can happen to any western country that in order to placate Islam, first dilutes, then surrenders and in the end, comes to despise the very values which are the foundation of western civilisation. Be warned.

Malmo, April-May 2016: Under the auspices of the city's ruling Social Democratic and Green Party administration, a number of events were held featuring speakers from the Middle East. One of the participants, specifically invited to attend by the Green Party, was the Saudi imam Salman Al Ouda, referred to in the Swedish media as a 'Salafist megastar'. He was a notorious anti-Semite. He can be seen on YouTube explaining why the Holocaust was a 'myth of tremendous proportions', a 'sacred myth'. The Jews themselves were 'carrying out a Holocaust in Gaza and the occupied land', 'under the pretext of the Holocaust they are trying to substantiate'. 'The role of the Jews is to wreak destruction, to wage war, to practice deception and extortion'. He claimed to have found proof that even today, Jews were 'making matzos with human blood. They eat it, claiming that it brings them closer to their false god Yahweh'. Malmo's Municipal Council has a policy which states that 'racism, discrimination and hate crimes do not belong in open Malmo.' But anti-Semitism does.

Evidently those that determine who can and cannot air their views in Malmo believe like fellow Sharia leftist Ken Livingstone that anti-Semitism is 'not the same thing' as racism. Neither did the policy apply when another invitation was extended to another anti-Semite, the former Grand Mufti of Jerusalem, Sheikh Ekrima Said Sabri, to address the fourteenth 'Palestinians in Europe' event at the prestigious Malmomassan conference centre. Following the precedent set by his most illustrious predecessor, the Nazi collaborator Haj Amin al-Husseini, Sabri had advertised, only now not on a Nazi radio station but democratic Swedish TV, his belief in the authenticity of the *Protocols:* 'Anyone who studies the *Protocols of the Elders of Zion* will discover that one of the goals of these *Protocols* is to cause confusion in the world and to undermine security throughout the world.' When it was pointed out to the event's hosts that Said's anti-Semitism violated Malmo's anti-racist policy, the reply was that 'we do not take positions on the substance of the matter'…that is, unless it is deemed 'Islamophobic'.

Following President Trump's announcement that the USA recognised Jerusalem as the capital of Israel, in Gothenburg, three Muslim asylum seekers were arrested after attempting to stage an Islamic re-enactment of the Nazi Crystal Night by fire-bombing a synagogue, while in Malmo, Muslim storm troopers took the street chanting 'We're going to shoot the Jews'. More than 2,000 Muslim anti-Semites also ran amok in Berlin, burning Israeli flags at the Brandenburg gate. One speaker declared that Israel 'should disappear once and for all.' Berlin police union chief Rainer Wendt blamed such outrages on politicians for 'illegally allowing in more and more foreigners from the most anti-Semitic region in the world and then not even deporting the offenders among them', while at the same time 'proclaim[ing] they are doing everything against anti-Semitism.' Interior Minister Thomas de Maiziere called for the appointment of a Commissioner to combat the recent surge of hatred against Jews and Israel.

III

Bath Time for Muslim Men

Different cultures habituate the people reared by them to do the same things in different ways. We have seen how this plays out when Muslim migrant men encounter the life styles, laws, customs and moral standards of Europeans, and nowhere more so than when it involves relationships between the sexes. Take swimming. Mixed bathing was pioneered by the Swedes (who else?) as long ago as the late nineteenth century, and over time, it has become a norm throughout the western world, the assumption being that increasingly scantily clad women would not have to contend with the unwanted sexual attentions of men. All that changed with the arrival in Sweden of young male Muslim migrants from countries whose Islamic culture had over centuries inculcated the belief that outside her home, a female must be accompanied by a male relative; and no less important, when in public, that her entire body has to be covered up. Swedish women do neither, and therefore, like thousands of other women in other European countries that have played host to Muslim migrants, have found themselves the target of sexual attacks by Muslim men who saw them as fair game for rape. For reasons that should not need stating, the most frequent venue for these attacks has been public swimming baths.

Let us begin in Malmo, now a city with a Muslim population fast approaching a majority. As long ago as 2003, gangs of Muslim youths became so disruptive at the city's indoor water park, Aq-va-kul, that the facility had to be converted into a fortress. It was temporarily closed to install extra security devices and equipment, including taller entrance gates to keep out intruders, a glass security panel around the reception desk to protect staff from attack, surveillance cameras and an Arabic-speaking 'pool host' to deal with the facility's unruly Muslim patrons. Far from solving the problem, the situation rapidly became much worse. These measures were - correctly - seen by young Muslim men as intended to curb their fun, and they reacted as some Muslim men can do when their honour is at stake, with violence. Gangs ambushed staff on their way home, so the pool had to hire security staff to provide escorts. More confrontations ensued when Muslim youth who did use the facility disobeyed hygiene rules, refusing to shower before entering the pool, and swimming in their underclothes. And so the running battle continued until 2013, when a gang of Muslim youths broke into the pool, smashed the protective glass around the reception desk, threw the shards into the water and assaulted swimmers. The pool was again closed, the pool drained and cleaned, and the damage made good. When finally, re-opened, it was closed to the public, and can now only be used by swimming clubs and for competitions.

Muslim trouble in Stockholm's Hushbybadet swimming pool began in 2005, when a 17-year-old girl was raped by a 16-year-old boy. The rapist received a three-month sentence in a juvenile facility. The girl was so traumatised she attempted suicide on several occasions. As more Muslims used the pool, in 2007, city authorities had to build a separate sewage facility to cope with the high levels of nitrogen caused by Muslims swimming in their sweaty dirty underwear and urinating in the pool. With the arrival in Sweden of 163,000 migrants in 2015, the majority being young men, the number of sexual assaults on women swimmers surged dramatically. This was mainly because despite past problems with Muslim males abusing swimming pool facilities, refusing to observe hygiene rules and pestering women swimmers, in their multicultural wisdom, local authorities allowed migrants to use pools free of any charge. Consequently, in the first week of January 2016, Stockholm's national swimming facility, Eriksdalsbadet, introduced gender segregation in its hot tubs after a series of sexual assaults by migrant men on women. This decision proved controversial, as it failed to tackle the cause of the problem, which was sexual aggression by Muslim men. It can also be seen as an accommodation to Sharia law, which enforces segregation of unrelated men and women.

January 15: a local paper reported that two girls had been sexually assaulted in the lift at the Oasen baths in Kungalv. The two perpetrators were described as 'unaccompanied refugee children'. The response of the town's Social Affairs department was to stress the need to 'step up the work concerning issues of equality and interaction [sic] among our new arrivals'. Three days later, the management of the Fyrishov pool in Uppsala belatedly revealed that in the previous year, there had been seven reported cases of child molestation. The suspected offenders were all newly-arrived teenaged migrants.

January 22: local news media carried reports of a sudden increase in sexual assaults at the Aquanova adventure pool in Borlange. While in 2014, there was only one such incident, in 2015, the number jumped to 20. Women had their bikinis ripped off, were groped on the water slide and attacked in the changing rooms.

January 25: press reports of a girl being raped at the Stockholm Eriksdalsbadet pool. Police began regular patrols of the facility.

January 26: reports of sexual assaults at the Storsjobadet pool in Ostersund on two girls and a woman by a group of migrant boys. However, pool staff allowed the boys to remain in the facility.

January 27: Vaxjo municipality announced that it will hire a security guard to patrol its pool after two 11-year-old girls were sexually assaulted by a group of migrant boys.

February 1: local media, again belatedly, reported that over the previous few weeks, five girls and a woman had been sexually assaulted at a pool in Vanersborg.

February 25: another sexual assault is reported at the Eriksdalsbadet pool. A group of girls had been surrounded, Cologne fashion, by ten or so young men, who then started to grope them. A staff member called the police, but there were no arrests.

Given this surge of sexual assaults by migrants at Sweden's pools, it remained for some a mystery why none had been reported at Malmo's recently opened Hylliebadet pool. In the first few days after its opening in August 2015, 27 'incidents' had been reported, but officially at least, none was of a sexual nature. Off the record however, one pool employee confided to a reporter that staff had been instructed not to report certain incidents and never to identify by ethnicity or religion those who had caused trouble at the pool. Another employee, again off the record, was more specific:

> Of course, we have incidents here, particularly involving Afghan men groping girls. Not long ago, a man of Arab descent was caught masturbating in the [mixed] hot tub. But we are not allowed to report things like that. These men understand that it is forbidden when we tell them, but they keep doing it anyway. They just smile and keep doing it.

While Sweden's public officials continue to display their customary indulgence towards Muslim sexual misconduct, when asked to give his opinion of the behaviour of his fellow Afghans, the manager of a large hotel in Kabul adopted a much more enlightened, though politically incorrect, stance:

> What the Afghans [in Swedish pools] are doing is not wrong in Afghanistan, so your rules are completely alien to them. Women stay at home in Afghanistan, and if they need to go out, they are always accompanied by a man. If you want to stop Afghans from molesting Swedish women and girls, you need to be tough with them. Making them take classes on equality and how to treat women is pointless. The first time they behave badly, they should be given a warning, and the second time, you should deport them from Sweden.

Islamophobe…Racist…*Nazi*.

And what of |Muslim women who might want to swim? Those few who do, conform to the Sharia dress code, by covering their entire bodies in an aquatic version of the burka, known as the burkini. For Allah is not only merciful, but resourceful. Responding to news that Marks and Spencer and House of Frazer had launched new lines in Sharia fashions, the staunchly Tory and female reader-oriented *Daily Mail* hailed their burkinis as 'ultimate proof that Britain is truly multicultural.' French feminists, who tend to be made of sterner stuff than the Anglo-Saxon variety, and politicians, defending both their secular constitution and a law which bans the public wearing of the burka, denounced the product. Minister of Families, Children and Women's Rights Lawrence Rossignol went to the heart of the matter:

> What is at stake is social control over the bodies of women. When European brands invest in the lucrative Islamic fashion market, they are shirking their responsibilities and are promoting a situation where women are forced to wear garments that imprison the woman from head to toe…Our role should be to help Muslim women, to support them by putting them in a position to confront radical Islam.

Whereas Sharia feminists hailed the arrival of the burkini as yet another opportunity for Muslim women to celebrate their 'personhood', when interviewed by *Le monde,* the traditional feminist Elisabeth Badinter argued that 'tolerance has been turned against those it was intended to help', with the result that 'the veil has spread among the daughters of our neighbourhoods' due to 'mounting Islamic pressure'. Fashion mogul Pierre Berge was if anything even more blunt:

> Fashion designers have no business being in Islamic fashion. I am outraged. I have always believed that the job of designers is to make women more beautiful, to give them their freedom, not to be an accomplice of this dictatorship which imposes this abomination that hides women and makes them live a hidden life…I do not understand why we are embracing this religion and those manners that are incompatible with the freedoms that are ours in the west. Creators who are taking part in the enslavement of women should ask themselves some questions. All this to make money? Excuse me, but I think that belief should come before money. Give up the money and have some principles. *Vive la France*!

As for Muslim men who cannot keep their groping hands off women in *kuffar* bikinis, as our Afghan Islamophobe proposes, it is high time they took an early bath and were returned pronto to their misogynist homelands.

D Deutschland Sagt Genug

'And whosoever migrates from his country in the way of Allah will find in the earth an abundant place of refuge and plentifulness.' *Koran,* Chapter 4, Verse 101

'We can do it.' German Chancellor Angela Merkel, September 15, 2015

Everything has its limits, even prosperous and liberal Sweden's ability and readiness to accept an ever-growing flow of Muslim migrants. The number of migrants who had arrived since 2012 reached 342,625 at the end of 2015, easily the highest proportion in relation to population of any EU country. And still they kept coming, many attracted by the prospect of an easy but largely unproductive life in Sweden's justly famed welfare state. With entry applications running at 10,000 per week and predictions that another 1.5 million migrants would arrive in Europe in 2016, on January 4, Sweden's coalition of Social Democrats and Greens followed the example of Norway by abandoning their increasingly unpopular policy of an open door for all comers. For the first time in over half a century, all those seeking admission to Sweden by train, boat or bus from Denmark were now required to produce a valid photo ID, such as a passport. Those who failed to do so were turned back. Justifying the *volte face,* the Deputy Prime Minister explained that 'the current situation, with a large number of people entering the country in a short space of time, poses a serious threat to public order and national security.'

Naturally, Denmark, like its northern neighbours also feeling the cultural, social, political and economic stresses of mass Muslim migration, did not want to become a haven for Sweden's rejected migrants, so it too introduced similar controls on its border with Germany. And so the ripple effect worked its way back to where the wave began, with even Merkel, for similar reasons to the Scandinavians, reluctantly considering similar measures to check the flow before Germany, and indeed the European Union as presently constituted, gave way under the strain of importing three million Muslims in two years. The Cologne-based Institute for Economic Research, calculated that the cost to Germany of providing care for migrants in 2016 would be 22 billion euros, rising to 27.6 billion. in 2017. This bill would not have been be footed by those whose decisions have created it, or those who from far, decry those who say enough is enough. The cost measured in increased taxes, strains on services of all kinds, crime, and social tensions would inevitably fall largely on the shoulders of those least able to bear them. As of February 2016, 81% of Germans polled believed Merkel's migrant policy to have been a disaster. By May, only 22% of those polled believed Islam had a place in Germany, a result which gave the lie to the claim that opposition to the religion was confined to the far right. In fact, Muslim migration had become an issue no European leader could afford to ignore. Convened primarily to discuss economic matters, the World Economic Forum at Davos instead found itself exploring emergency measures to prevent the never-ending flow of Muslim migrants from not only undermining the Schengen Treaty on free movement within the EU's borders, but the very existence of the European Union itself.

The Schengen Agreement, first adopted in 1985, then supplemented by

Schengen Convention, and incorporated into EU law in 1990, while allowing for freedom of movement between its signatories, does not in any way modify their pre-existing right to control the movement of people across their external borders. The arrival in 2015 of more than a million migrants in Italy and Greece had put that agreement under severe strain, with the result that in 2016 six countries, Sweden Denmark, Austria Poland, Germany Norway and France, temporarily re-imposed internal border controls. That did not, however, resolve the problem of what to do with those who had already arrived, 70% of whom, according to the United Nations High Commissioner for Refugees, were not refugees, but migrants. Some put the percentage even higher. One Muslim migrant/refugee explained in very candid terms what he saw as the future of his new German home:

> We are multiplying faster and faster. At most you get two children. We are making seven or eight children. And then we take four wives each. Then we have 22 children. So make it Allah, blessed be his name, make it that we conquer you, not with war, here in Germany, but with birth rates, firstly, and secondly, we will marry your daughters, and your daughter will wear a Muslim headscarf. And your daughter will marry a bearded man.

True, it is possible to argue this is the opinion of just one migrant, and therefore not representative of the majority. Those so inclined should listen to what Muslims higher up the Islamic ladder had to say on the same subject. First, and most recently, the Islamising President of Turkey, whose mainly Muslim population of 75 million the Chancellor of Germany would dearly love to enrol as citizens of the European Union, had to say on May 30, 2016: 'I say it clearly; we need to increase the number of our descendants…People talk about birth control, about family planning. No Muslim family can understand and accept that'. Then in a speech mocking rather than marking International Woman's Day earlier the same year, in he asserted that 'a woman is above else a mother'. It was a claim which outraged Turkish feminists, but not the western Sharia variety, since they had more pressing tasks on hand, such as campaigning for a university campus ban on the *Sun* and no 'platforming' ex-Muslim campaigners for women's and gays rights in Islamic countries. Birth control, Erdogan declared in 2014, was 'treason'. This was par for the course for a Muslim politician. Although his geography was a little hazy, the warning former Algerian President Hourari Boumedienne issued in the course of a speech to the United Nations General Assembly in 1974 was deadly serious: 'One day millions of men will go from the southern hemisphere to the northern hemisphere. And they will not go there as friends. Because they will go there to conquer it. And they will conquer it with their sons. The wombs of our women will give us victory.' The late but not lamented, except by the Sharia left and the beneficiaries his largesse, Libyan Dictator Colonel Gaddafi predicted the same future for Europe: 'There are signs that Allah will grant victory to Islam in Europe without swords, without guns, without conquest. We don't need terrorist; we don't need suicide bombers. The 50 million plus Muslims [already] in Europe will turn it into a Muslim continent within a few decades.'

The Hamas Charter, Article 17, defines the role of women as 'the factory of men', pumping out an endless supply of warriors, suicide bombers and, Corbyn's 'friends' hope, one day soon the conquerors of and settlers in a Jew-free greater Palestine. Finally, we have Yasser Arafat, whose specific target for uterine conquest was Israel. He told a closed meeting of Arab diplomats in Stockholm on January 30, 1996, that is, three years after singing the Oslo Accords that committed Israel and the PLO to a 'two state' solution to the Palestine issue, 'we will make life unbearable for the Jews by psychological warfare and *population explosion*. We Palestinians will take over everything, including Jerusalem'. (emphasis added) Barbra Lerner Spectre [sic], a US Jewish high priestess of multiculturalism, embraces this future of a mass Muslim migration (that is for Europe) with open arms and joy in her heart. Unlike Merkel, what she proposes is not an open door just to those claiming to be refugees, but to all migrants, no matter who, why, how many or from where: 'Europe has not yet learned how to be multi-cultural. And I think that we [that, is the Jews] are going to be part of the throes [sic] of that transformation, which must take place. Europe is not going to be the monolithic societies they once were in last century. Jews are going to be at the centre of that.'

Spectre's claim that that Europe is not multicultural is sheer nonsense. In the true sense of the word, it is now, and has been for thousands of years. Quite apart from the recent arrivals of diasporas from other continents and climes, Europe has for centuries, and in many cases for far longer, been the home to a vast kaleidoscopic array of peoples of widely differing cultures, faiths and languages. Just within the European Union, there are 23 officially recognised languages and more than 60 indigenous regional dialects, together with a wide variety of tongues brought to and used in Europe by migrants from other continents. The ethnic variety is also broad. From beyond the Urals came the Finno-Ugric peoples, distant cousins of the native Americans, today comprising the Hungarians, Finns, and Estonians, and in the Arctic the Sami and the Laps. Then there are the Teutonic peoples, in the north, the Scandinavians, and at Europe's core, the Germans, Dutch and Flemish. To the far west, there are the Celts, and to the east, the Slavs, and to south, the Mediterranean Latins and Greeks.

However, for all their diversity…and it is immense…they all share, to varying degrees, a commitment to values, principles and institutions that have come to make Europe what it is today… a beacon and fortress of western civilisation, where 'diversity' has made for mutual enrichment, and not exclusivity and endless friction. This is because the vast majority of Europeans believe in and practice democracy and individual freedom, a secular system of justice and the rule one law for all, the equality of men and women and the rights of children, the toleration of differing opinions, beliefs, life-styles and sexual preferences, the separation of state and faith, freedom of speech, press and artistic expression, the right of labour to organise and the access by all to free public education and welfare. If there was no broad consensus in these matters, the creation and progressive enlargement of the European Union would have been impossible. However, the experience of Muslim migration has proved that these values are not shared by those whose ethos and conduct is determined by slavish adherence to Islam. Far from the passing of time aiding integration, not only the recent emergence of the 'home grown' Jihadi, but numerous surveys have shown that the younger the Muslim, the less favourably disposed he or she is likely to be to the values that underpin the host nation's way of life. No less crucially, unlimited Muslim migration into Europe, quite aside from its inevitable political repercussions, will impose on the continent burdens that simply cannot be sustained without causing possibly irreparable damage to its economic and social infrastructure.

Those celebrities who from within their privileged bubble demand a world with open borders simply have not thought through how it will affect those hundreds of millions of less fortunate Europeans who live outside it. They should ask themselves what the consequences will be of a one-way flow of tens of millions of people from those many countries where the quality of life is substantially lower than the world average, to a much smaller number where it is far higher. As we saw in 2015, this immense migration of peoples will naturally target those relatively few nations which offer the highest standards of living and are most indulgent towards the life styles of new settlers, for example the Scandinavian states and Germany. But as we have also seen, the ability to absorb far less than the numbers of migrants that a permanent open border policy would entail reached its limits in less than a year, along with the tolerance of migrant life styles. Say, for example, that ten million migrants from Africa, the Middle East and South Asia wish to settle in Switzerland, current population, eight million, or Denmark, 5.6 million. Given this opportunity and considering the huge disparities in the quality of life, pitching their number at ten million is conservative in the extreme. And we must bear in mind that the advocates of open borders not only say they must be admitted as of right, regardless of number, but that they must not be treated as second class citizens and should have the right to expect that their everyday needs will be met by the host nation. For otherwise, why migrate in the first place?

Like the planet, the territory and natural resources of a state are finite, and likewise, over the short run, its social and economic infrastructure. To describe, as some do, those who oppose the open border policy on these entirely practical grounds as racist bigots is a slander, though it may salve the consciences of those who claim that all the problems of the poor nations are 'our fault'. It is incredibly naïve, at best, given what we have already witnessed in Europe with 'only' one million plus Muslim migrants arriving in one year, to assume that immigration on such an unprecedentedly colossal scale will have no negative economic and social repercussions upon the host nation's less prosperous classes and its political equilibrium. Then of course there will also be enormous and unprecedented cultural consequences. We are assured by open border advocates that just as in the past, when migrations have resulted over time in the migrants being integrated and, to a lesser or greater extent, assimilated into the host nation (though this is palpably not true of Muslims), this will happen again as a result of the adoption an open border policy. The 'home grown' gang rapists and pimps of Rotherham, Rochdale, Oxford, Keighley, Sheffield Aylesbury and elsewhere all had decades to settle down and assume the ways of their host nation, but they chose instead to behave like barbarians.

References to previous mass migrations also fail to take into account what made them fundamentally different from those that are taking place today, and far more so, from what the advocates of open borders are now demanding. In complete contrast to what is happening with Asian and African Muslim migration, with the exception of a far more protracted flow within Europe from a backward and repressive east to an advanced and liberal west, the great migrations of earlier eras have always been in the opposite direction to today, away from Europe to other continents. Between 1821 and 1932, 32 million Europeans migrated just to the United States. In the same period, nearly seven million migrated to Brazil, over five million to Canada, 3.5 million to Australasia, and from 1856 to 1932, 6.4 million to Argentina. In each case, the movement of peoples was from a continent and countries that were densely populated and becoming more so, to vast territories that in most cases were by comparison sparely settled. In little more than a century, a global European diaspora was generated by 60 million migrants. Such an unprecedented movement of peoples was only possible because in the first place there existed the means to transport them, and once they had arrived, the space to accommodate them, land to feed them and work to employ them. This was the time of the spread of the industrial revolution from Europe to the world, a process that drew in its wake vast armies of migrant labour to build cities and railways, dig canals and coal, and toil on farms and in mills and factories.

Apart from the massive relocation within Europe of so-called 'displaced persons', the last great migration after the Second World War found millions of Asians and Africans, mostly from former or existing colonies, settling in western Europe, initially finding mainly semi or unskilled employment in a continent struggling to rebuild itself with a severely depleted indigenous male labour force. With the exception of Muslims, today, the children and grandchildren of this post war migrant wave have, to a greater or lesser degree, integrated themselves into their host societies. Some have intermarried with the native population, and their children and grandchildren, if not themselves, have become fully assimilated. This development is quite normal and is surely to be welcomed by all concerned. Not of course by racists, but sadly also not by many Muslims. Islam's rules on sexual conduct constitute one of the most effective barriers to Muslim integration. Gang raping a *kuffar* girl is one thing, but marrying one unless she converts, another entirely, and for most Muslim families, strictly *haram,* as is a Muslim woman marrying or taking up with a *kuffar* man, the punishment for which can be so-called 'honour killing'. By in-group marriage, either arranged or forced, to close relatives, sometimes much older than the bride, diaspora Muslims have succeeded in isolating themselves biologically as well as socially and culturally from their host societies, the price for which is the well-documented but rarely acknowledged prevalence of genetically transmitted physical and mental disabilities markedly more widespread and severe than in the non-Muslim host population. The success of self-ghettoisation has led even mainstream European politicians who cannot resist singing the praises of Islam to frankly admit that the integration of Muslims, insofar as it has been seriously attempted, has totally failed. All that unlimited Muslim immigration will do is make a hard task impossible. But then, that is what Spectre appears to be advocating.

Assuming that an open border means exactly what it says, that there are no legal limits to the number of migrants who will be as of right granted legal entry and permanent settlement in the country of their choice, it is surely reasonable to ask that quite apart from the practicalities of providing for the necessities of their life, what could be the cultural consequences of Denmark admitting, as it would be obliged to do, possibly a total of non-European migrant's greater that of its own native population? One result is certain. Denmark as Danes know it today would cease to exist. Barbra Lerner Spectre would doubtless believe this to be a splendid vindication of multiculturalism. And if there is one country more than any other that would be the target of mass migration should the unrestricted opening of borders become a legal obligation on the part of all member states of the United Nations, that country would be Israel. What an Allah-sent opportunity to at last and forever 'wipe off the map' the accursed 'Zionist entity' by flooding it with a sufficient number of Arabs to convert its current 80% Jewish population into a minority that can then be either driven out, exterminated, as proposed by Corbyn's 'friends'

Hamas and Hezbollah, or at best, reduced to the status of second-class *dhimmis* under Sharia law.

Once cold numbers and economic realities are brought to bear on the wishful thinking of champagne internationalists, the whole idea collapses upon itself. Not only that. Quite aside from the impact on the economy, politics and culture of the host nations targeted by unlimited migration, by encouraging and facilitating the draining of failing nations of their most active elements of the population, leaving behind the old, the very young, the mainly female and the infirm, opening borders would condemn these nations to an ever-sinking spiral of demographic distortions, decay, poverty, corruption and lawlessness. Is that what the open doorers want? Let them also consider the following: In 2010, that is, five years before the arrival in 2015 of over a million Muslim migrants and refugees, the continent's Muslims numbered 44 million, six per cent of the total population. Discounting new migrations, this Muslim share of Europe's population, because of various demographic factors, is projected to reach eight per cent by the year 2030, 58 million Muslims. As previously, we can expect that this increase will not be evenly distributed across Europe, or within its individual states, but concentrated in a growing number of large cities in the west, where for some years now, Muslim enclaves have taken root, some of them to the extent that while living off the host society, they are off-limits to its security forces, legal systems and other public agencies.

In every European state where such statistics are available, Muslim unemployment is chronic, in some cases 50% and more, and always greatly in excess of other migrants from a non-European background. In Denmark, Muslims comprise 5% of the population, but draw 40% of its welfare payments, eight times more than the average. According to Germany's former Interior Minister Otto Schily, '70% of newcomer's land on welfare on the day of their arrival'. This applied to migrants arriving *prior* to the current surge of Muslims, all of whom 'land on welfare' and in all probability will, in their vast majority, stay there for the foreseeable future. Given what the statistics tell us about the situation of most Muslims in the Europe of today, we have no reason to suppose that newly-arriving Muslims will be any more successful at integrating themselves into their host nations than those who are already here. And what incentive is there for them to do so, given that current state of affairs works so well in their favour? In 2015, unemployment just in the European Union stood 24 million, 10% of its working population. Since the onset of the recession in 2008, the European economy has struggled to reach let alone sustain a growth rate that matches its annual 2% increase in productivity. Until it exceeds that rate of increase, the jobs market will remain static at best. And the bulk of the new vacancies that are created will be filled by those with high levels of technical, literacy, numeracy and language skills. Are Muslim migrants, at least 60% of whom are functionally illiterate even in their own language, likely to be, assuming that they want to be, first in the queue for jobs in what is an ever-higher tech economy? Leaving to one side welfare payments to jobless migrants, as a direct result of the arrival of well over a million non-contributing potential claimants to its state-of-the-art health service, Germany faced a shortfall in 2017 of one billion euros in its health budget, the balance of which had be made good by raiding the social insurance funds paid in by German workers.

Despite the lenient approach to migrant crime adopted by politically corrected police forces, Muslims, unlike other 'Asians', are still vastly overrepresented in crime statistics and prison populations. 70% of French prisoners are Muslims, while they make up ten per cent of the country's population. 70% of Spain's prisoners are also Muslim, even though they comprise only 2.3% of Spain's total population. And throughout Europe's jails, the trend is for that share to increase. In England and Wales in 2002, 5,502 prisoners said they were Muslims. Twelve years on, and the number had jumped to 12,225. Saxony, which in 2015 received 'only' 45,000 migrants, in the same year experienced a 47% increase in migrant crime, with one migrant in ten being an offender. Included in these offences were 17 murders and five rapes.

Quite apart from the irreconcilable cultural tensions that mass Muslim migration has generated, even Germany, the economic powerhouse of Europe, and the highly organised and prosperous Nordic states have rapidly found themselves unable to withstand the demands placed on their welfare and security infrastructures. So what hope is there for the main recipients of migrants, bankrupt Greece and Italy, and Spain, with 20% unemployment, and the less developed states of the European East? In the radiant, brave new Musli-cultural Europe that so excites the Spectres, will there be any losers? Since according to her, it is the Jews' mission to persuade Europe that it needs to absorb an unlimited number of migrants whose religion demands that they despise Jews, it was not hard to predict who they going to be, and Spectre made no attempt to hide it. In fact, she embraces the prospect, at distance of 3,000 miles: 'It's a huge transformation for Europe to make. They are now going into a multicultural mode and Jews will be resented [sic!] because of our [i.e., Jewish] leading role. But without that transformation and without that transformation, Europe will not survive.' But will the Jews? The surge in Jewish migration to Israel suggests that with their not so disant history in mind, many are not prepared to risk waiting to see.

As if they did not have enough trouble on their hands with Sharia left anti-Zionism, Neo-Nazi and Muslim anti-Semitism and Jihadi terrorism, the Jews of Europe, for some unexplained reason, and at the cost of incurring hostility from fellow Europeans, have to be at the forefront of encouraging the immigration of yet more millions of potential Muslim anti-Semites, a role that in the unlikely event of their being so foolish as to take it on, would indeed ensure the enmity of those many Europeans who see this policy as tantamount to inviting cultural and economic suicide. Thus the Jews would be trapped on both sides in an anti-Semitic vice of their own making. But their sacrifice will not be in vain. The only hope for Europe is more and yet more Muslims, and if this leads to yet more Jews packing their bags and heading for Israel, then so be it. Muslims in, Jews out. And not only Jews. As more Muslims continue arrive, despite nation-wide protests, through Merkel's illegal open door, so more Germans leave. 2 million Muslims arrived in Germany in little more than a year, while 1.5 million Germans have left over the last ten years, 138,000 in 2015 and many more again in 2016. And they were Germans the country could ill-afford to lose. According to *Die Welte,* 'German talent is leaving the country in droves'. However, the official attitude is, good riddance. Those Germans who disagreed with Merkel's immigration policy were advised by Walter Lubcke, President of Kassel, that they were 'free to leave Germany at any time', a sentiment shared by a young Syrian migrant writing in the on-line *Der Freitag*: 'We refugees do not want to live in the same country with you. You can, and I think you should, leave Germany. Germany does not fit you. Why do you live here? Why do you not go to another country? We are sick of you.' Muslims in, Germans out.

French Prime Minister Manuel Valls, whose country had become the prime target for Muslim terrorism, and whose government, unlike Spectre, had understandably shown no great desire to add to its country's six million largely unintegrated Muslims, feared that unless the flow was halted, 'our societies will be totally destabilised. If Europe is not capable of protecting its own borders, it's the very idea of Europe that will be questioned.' In an obvious allusion to Merkel's migrant policy, Valls warned that the message 'come you will be welcome' was producing a major shift in the balance of Europe's population. More than that, Merkel's open-door policy must share part of the blame, together with the people traffickers and the Muslim states that have refused to accept refugees, for the deaths by drowning of those attempting the crossing in overloaded and unseaworthy dinghies from Turkey to Greece, and north Africa to Italy and Spain. Why has Turkey not been instructed to round up its people traffickers and instead allow refugees a safe land route into Europe? Instead, the resulting migrant drownings have been cynically exploited by much of the media and publicity seeking celebrities to urge an ever widening of the EU's door, a policy which will only result in yet more of the drownings they claim to abhor. Madness.

Like all the other European leaders present at Davos, Valls was careful not to directly criticise Merkel's open-door policy, but he did not have to, since its consequences, dramatized by the mass migrant sexual assaults of December 31, 2015, and the participation of Muslim migrants in terrorist attacks in Paris, were all too clear. If the Schengen Treaty does have to be revised, or possibly even torn up, then it will be the German Chancellor who will have to take most of the blame. The Dutch Prime Minister Mark Rutte was no less emphatic. Europe was 'at breaking point, and its leaders need[ed] to get a grip in the issue in the next six to eight weeks'. 'We can't cope with the numbers any longer. We need to get a grip on this.' Yes…but how…and who was going to do it? Germany's Finance Minister Wolfgang Schauble admitted that 'the abilities of the EU countries are not inexhaustible'. My very point. So why then did Merkel conduct her migrant policy as if they were? Schauble claimed that the EU was 'united on the need to reduce the migrant pressure [no longer were they refugees]', ignoring the fact that many EU member states were seeking not a reduction, but an end to this pressure, and even its reversal. Schauble's solution to the migrant crisis could not have appealed to his EU partners, not only because it was totally unrealistic, but would if attempted be both immensely costly and. almost certainly counterproductive: 'We Europeans need to invest billions [sic] in Turkey, Libya [sic!] Jordan and other countries in the region as quickly as possible.' This proposal to bribe corrupt Muslim regimes to stop driving and passing on millions of migrants into Europe…we can call it Allah geld…not surprisingly met with no takers. There is a far cheaper and infinitely more humane and effective alternative, the return of all those except proven genuine asylum seekers who are already in the EU to their countries of origin, and strict enforcement of the EU's asylum rules for all those seeking entry. Faced by the prospect of another 2.6 million migrants arriving in Europe over the next two years, EU leaders at an emergency meeting in Amsterdam on January 25 finally decided, a year late, to stem the tide by agreeing to seal off Greece by closing its border with Macedonia, together with the temporary re-introduction of internal border controls within the EU.

With the percentage of new migrants even claiming Syrian nationality plummeting, and despite adverse weather conditions, 110,00,000 migrants arriving just in January 2016, ten times the number in the same month of the previous year, the Dutch government proposed that all new arrivals should be immediately ferried back to Turkey. NATO announced that it would send three warships to patrol the Turkish coast to deter new migrant arrivals. Meanwhile, Sweden and Finland had already announced they would between them be expelling as many as 100,000 bogus asylum claimants, that is, approaching half of the total number of migrants that arrived in the two countries in 2015. Totally isolated in Europe, and increasingly so in her country, where around half of all Germans were supporting calls for her resignation over her handling of the migrant crisis, to save her own political skin, Merkel announced at the end of January that once it was safe to do so, all refugees would be returned to their countries of origin. Even if the Religion of Peace were to weary of its fratricidal slaughters, the success of Merkel's plan of course depends on whether her guests can be tracked down. By January 2016, as many 600,000 had already disappeared under the radar, many of them men of military age fit enough in some cases to have walked hundreds of miles on their journey from the south of Greece and Italy to Germany, after allowing vastly inferior numbers of fellow Muslims to take over huge areas of their countries almost unopposed, leaving behind their children, womenfolk and the aged to face the consequences. .

Figures released by the BBC on February 18, 2016, revealed the scale of the number of migrants falsely claiming asylum status. We must exclude from any calculations those who are or claim to be Syrians who arrived in Europe in the twelve months between October 2014 and October 2015, 250,000 in all, even though many would, on closer scrutiny than they underwent on arrival, prove to be migrants. Then we have 110,000 Afghans, some of who will have fled locations where the Taliban is engaged in killing fellow Muslims, though how many are from these areas it is impossible to know. Iraqis number 70,000, again, some from areas either occupied or under attack by the Islamic State, or in the throes of inter-Muslim strife between Shi'a and Sunni. Between them, these three countries generated 430,000 asylum claimants, most, let us grant, genuinely so. But the next country on the list is Kosovo, with 80,000, followed by Albania with 60,000 and then Pakistan, with 40,000! Far away Nigeria has contributed 25,000. In the case of Kosovo, this number compromises over 4% of the country's total population! Given that the majority of migrants are young men, the most active and productive sector of the population, this is certain to have negative demographic, social and economic consequences in their homelands on a scale that that will simply encourage yet more migration. Even Ukraine and Serbia have each supplied 20,000 migrants to add to the unchecked flow of bogus refugees wending its illegal way to the rich feeding grounds of western and northern Europe. The extent to which migrants had been posing as asylum seekers was revealed when after the EU concluded an agreement with Turkey to return all those unable to establish their *bona fides,* the number making the crossing to Greece fell by *90%*. As for the impact on Europe, even in politically correct Scandinavia, its Social Democrats, hitherto the most enthusiastic of all parties in the encouragement of a Muslim immigration that had provided them with an ever-growing supply of voting fodder, began to sing a new tune when at last, they woke up to the threat that mass Muslim migration posed to their justly famed welfare states and to their traditional support in the working class. Henrik Sass Larsen, the leader of the Danish Social Democratic Party Parliamentary group, spelled out the new line:

We will do all we can to limit the number of non-European refugees and immigrants to this country. That is why we have gone far, much farther than we ever dreamed of. We do this because we do not want to sacrifice the welfare state in the name of humanism. Because the welfare state is the political project of the Social Democrats. It is a society built on the principle of freedom equality and solidarity. Mass immigration - look at Sweden for example - will undermine the social and economic foundation of the welfare state.

When the full history of this unprecedented episode comes to be written, its prime cause will inevitably be located in a crisis of Islam that set Muslim against Muslim throughout the Middle East, South Asia and North Africa. But such an account, if it is to be true to the facts, will also have apportion considerable blame to European politicians, in the first place Chancellor Merkel, for not only allowing but actually encouraging a mass Muslim migration to Europe that was not only illegal, but, more to the point inhumane in the extreme. The illusion was fostered that Europe, in the first place those countries with the most developed welfare provisions, could absorb unlimited numbers of culturally backward Muslims from the Middle East, Africa and even further afield, on a permanent basis, irrespective of whether they were genuine asylum seekers or simply economic and welfare migrants, and without any serious adverse impact on the economy, security, social stability and politics of the countries foolish enough to accept them on such a basis and scale. It took only a matter of a few months after Merkel announced that Germany's door was open to all comers to demonstrate how wrong this assumption was. Disgusting and for the victims, traumatic though the sexual assaults of New Year's Eve were, they shrink almost to insignificance compared with the drowning of thousands lured on by the promise of a new life in Europe. Their deaths are on Merkel's hands no less than the traffickers who packed them into unseaworthy vessels, and the Turkish authorities who turned a blind eye to this sordid trade in false hope, misery and despair.

Inevitably, the Islamophile lobby, located mainly in countries that have accepted few if any migrants, sanctimoniously depicted any measure taken to stem their flow in the most lurid colours imaginable. When Denmark introduced the long overdue requirement that migrants seeking entry who had the means to do so should contribute towards their upkeep by surrendering valuables (excluding jewellery and items of a sentimental value) or cash in excess of a total value of £1,000, the measure was compared to the Third Reich's pre-war practice of confiscating the property and savings of Jews fleeing Nazi persecution. Firstly, the migrants/refugees in question were not fleeing from Denmark, but to Denmark. Secondly, many had been able to pay extortionate sums to people traffickers to ferry them either from north Africa across the Mediterranean or from the Middle East and even much further afield via Turkey to Italy or Greece, and then the fare to be transported northwards the best part of two thousand miles through either Austria or the Balkans and Germany to Denmark And if they refused to comply, there was always the option of staying in Germany as a guest of Angela Merkel. Ignoring the sanctimonious clamour, several other European countries adopted the same measure.

Here we had yet another case of branding as a Nazi anyone who does not dance to the Sharia leftist tune Only those who are totally ignorant of the history of Nazi Germany, and/or have an agenda that has nothing to do with the welfare of migrants, can possibly make such a comparison between the two situations. Firstly, the Danes had not driven any Muslims out of their homeland, which is what the Nazis did to the Jews. Although it is not politically correct to say so, this has been solely the doing of their Jihadi co-religionists. Secondly, it is the infidel Danes who welcomed some 200,000 Muslim migrants into a country with a total population of only 5.6 million, one migrant for every 28 Danes, with the result that the strain on their tiny nation's resources had reached a level that had become unsustainable without some help from the migrants themselves. The revenues thus raised would be used to help provide for their upkeep, whereas the assets stolen from fleeing German Jews were used to help fund the Nazi war machine and the extermination of the Jews themselves. How can these two situations be compared?

If those, not least publicity seeking celebrities, who parade their concern about the welfare of migrants, regard these regulations as unfair, why have they not demanded of the oil rich despotisms of the Middle East that as they have refused to offer sanctuary to fleeing fellow Muslims, the least they could do would be to contribute towards their upkeep in infidel countries that have, instead of devoting their spare billions to the financing of Jihadi armies, yet more European Mosque building and the distribution of anti-Semitic propaganda? And, crowning irony, it is a reasonable assumption that among those Muslim migrants already safely accommodated in Denmark at the expense of its tolerant and industrious people, there will those who took part in the riots which followed the publication of the so-called Danish cartoons back in 2006. These included attacks on Danish embassies, along with a world-wide Muslim campaign to boycott Danish goods. If the Danes were the vindictive people they are portrayed to be by the critics of their migrant policy, they could have quite easily sought redress by denying any entry to the followers of a faith that sought their destruction for the sake a few cartoons. But they did not. Surely there is a lesson here somewhere.

Rather late in the day…some would say too late…even politicians who not only welcomed the Islamic invasion of Europe, but encouraged it, have now had second thoughts about its consequences, which have been, as those familiar with the ways of Islam have predicted, sexual assaults on women, including gang rape, and attacks on Jews, including their murder. The main accessory to this Muslim crime wave, German Chancellor Merkel, admitted on April 23, 2018, that 'we have a new phenomenon, as we have many refugees among whom for example there are people of Arab origin who bring another form anti-Semitism in the country.' She neglected to point out that this 'form of anti-Semitism', far from being 'new' is in fact as old as Islam Moreover, it is not confined to migrants from Arab countries but can be found everywhere that Islam has spread its poisonous, genocidal message that Jews are not human, but apes and swine.

Seven decades after the Holocaust, Merkel found herself in the humiliating situation of having to announce that she had appointed a government commissioner charged with combatting an anti-Semitism she was responsible for importing illegally and *en masse* into Germany, in an interview on CNN in May 2019, referring to the 'dark forces' not only in Germany but across Europe that were now menacing the continent's Jews, though neglecting to identify who or what they were. In the main body of this work, I predicted that one of the consequences of her decision in the summer of 2015 to illegally open her country's border to uncontrolled Muslim immigration would be a 'bumpy ride' for Germany's Jews, and that is exactly what has happened. Merkel admitted that 'there is not a single synagogue, not single day care centre for Jewish children, not a single school for Jewish children that does not need to guarded by a German policeman'. But again...from whom or what?

The answer came from her own security, agency, the Federal Office for the Protection of the Constitution, which Merkel's migrant policy had violated. (See Addendum) Among the more than a million Muslim migrants that had arrived in Germany since 2015 were activists of anti-Semitic Islamic movements such as the Muslim Brotherhood, Hamas and Hezbollah. According to Germany's Ministry of the Interior, anti-Semitic incidents, had increased in 2019 by 20%, with violent attacks up by 86%. In response to this surge in anti-Jewish crime, Felix Klein, Germany's Anti-Semitism Commissioner' (sic) admitted that he could 'no longer recommend Jews wear a kippa at every place and time in Germany' This was not Hitler's Germany, *circa* 1938, but Merkel's, 2019.

Germany's President, Frank-Walter Steinmeier, had been far less inhibited than his Chancellor in identifying Germany's new Jew-baiters when, in December 2017, he defied the fashionable conventions of multicultural moral relativism by declaring he was 'horrified and ashamed' that Muslims were burning Israeli flags in Berlin in protest against US President Trump's decision to recognise Jerusalem as the capital of Israel. Anti-Semitism was 'showing its face in many evil shapes, including public acts with hate-filled slogans...they do not understand, or do not respect, what it is to be German.' In the light of the Holocaust, Germans more than any other people, he continued, had a special responsibility to oppose anti-Semitism, 'and this responsibility does not recognise caveats for migrant backgrounds and exceptions newcomers. It is non-negotiable for everyone who lives here and wants to live here.'

In secular France, where unlike the UK, a tradition endures that one can speak one's mind publicly about matters religious without the same fear of prosecution, in the wake of the murder of a Holocaust survivor by her Muslim neighbour in April 2018, 300 prominent public figures, mainly from the arts, academe and politics, signed a declaration condemning Muslim (not Arab) attacks on and murder of Jews. Acknowledging the fact that Jews are 25 times more likely than Muslims to be the victims of racist violence, even though Muslims outnumber Jews by a ratio of 10 to one, and with nearly all of it inflicted by Muslims, the declaration made the unprecedented demand, almost unthinkable let alone sayable in the UK, that 'the verses in the *Koran* that call for the death of Jews, Christians and unbelievers must be excised by [Islamic] theological authorities'. Just as in the UK, and in fact any country with a large and growing Muslim population, the unassailable assertion was made that in France too, the lack of concern for the well-being of the Jews arose from the fact that 'the Muslim vote is ten times larger than that of the Jews'. And, we can add, precisely because of this at best indifference, Jews will continue to leave, while the number of Muslims increases, further accentuating their leverage within the political life of not only France, but across the whole of Western Europe. And of course, acting on this cynical calculation, just as in the UK and Sweden, to cite but two examples, is a part of the French left, disguising its war on the Jews as anti-Zionism, and depicting Muslim anti-Semitism as a protest against oppression:

> The anti-Semitism of radical Islam is seen by a part of the French elite [given the context, obviously its left wing is meant here] as purely an expression of social revolt...[Thus] the old anti-Semitism of the extreme right has combined with that of

a part of the radical left, which uses anti-Zionism as an alibi to transform the tormentors of the Jews into victims of society. *Vive la France*!

Addendum

Article 16a of the Constitution of the Federal Republic of Germany, entitled 'Right of Asylum' specifies, in Paragraph 2, that Article 16a 'may not be invoked by a person who enters the federal territory [of Germany] from a member state of the European Communities or from another state in which the application of the Convention relating to the status of refugees and of the Convection for the Protection of Human Rights and Fundamental Freedoms is assured.' It goes on to say that 'measures to terminate an applicant's stay may be implemented without regard to any legal challenge that may have instituted against them'.

Dublin Convention III, like its two previous versions, binding on all member states of the European Union, stipulates that all applications for asylum must be processed by the first country of the applicant's entry into the EU. This law was also flouted by Merkel. In July 2017, the European Court of Justice ruled that despite the unprecedented influx surge of Muslims migrants into Europe, EU member states retained the right to lawfully deport migrants back to their first country of entry into the EU.

E Spoils of War

'The spoils of war are for Allah and the Messenger.' *Koran,* Chapter 88, Verse 2. 111

I

By the Book

Everywhere in Europe where they are available, official government statistics show that inward Muslim migration has been accompanied by a rise, sometimes spectacular, of sex crimes, as in Sweden (by 14 times) and in the case of the UK, by the organised grooming, trafficking and gang rape of several hundred thousand vulnerable non-Muslim girls, some barely in their teens, with the full knowledge and in some cases connivance of the police, public authorities, Islamic clerics, and government and local politicians. In Pakistan, Christian girls are similarly regarded and treated, often with the same impunity, as rape fodder by Muslim men. On January 13, 2016, in Lahore, three Christian girls who resisted the sexual advances of a gang of wealthy Muslim men were pursued in a car and assaulted, one of them later dying of her injuries. During the assault, one of the attackers shouted: 'Christian girls are meant for only one thing, the pleasure of Muslim men.' Local police seemed to agree, because just as in the UK, they showed little interest in pursuing the case. Should we be surprised? As we shall see, however ignorant they may be in matters pertaining to proper conduct in a modern civilisation, Muslim men know their rights under Islamic law when it comes to raping non-Muslim women.

Rape as we understand it today must have been practised before recorded history, despite taboos that sought to regulate relations between the sexes. But it is the sanctioning of rape by religion that concerns us here. And the simple truth is that religion and rape have gone hand in hand over the millennia. We are not talking here about priests raping altar boys in the crypt, but rape explicitly sanctioned by the texts of a faith. But first there is the question of religion and slavery, the latter being in some ways not only morally but physically akin to rape. It is generally known, or at least it should be, that devout Muslims and Christians upheld and practised slavery up until very recent times, Christians well into the 19th century, and Muslims as far into the twentieth…Saudi Arabia and Yemen only abolished slavery, on paper, in 1962. But how many know that the world's two most widely disseminated and influential holy books, the Bible and the *Koran,* both explicitly sanction not only slavery, but the enslavement of women for the purposes of sexual intercourse?

It can have objected that so far as observant Jews and practising Christians are concerned, excluding from consideration religious cults whose gurus practise polygamy, neither today uses holy texts to justify rape, and at this distance in time, it is impossible to know to what extent this occurred when both faiths were young and still all-powerful. Even then, there were laws relating to rape, but only because women were seen as the property of men (in Islam they still are) and since rape necessarily involved the infringement of male property rights, it was punished as such, for example in the code of King Hammurabi of Babylon, dating from BC 1685. The right of a woman not to be raped is a relatively recent legal concept, and a wife by her husband, more recent again. Both these women's rights owe nothing to the so-called Judeo-Christian values that we are told are the foundation of western civilisation.

The original Anglican marriage vow of the bride, dating from 1549, obliged her to 'love, cherish and obey' her husband. More than four centuries later, in 1980 to be precise, in addition to the original vow of 1549, the choice of two more vows was made available in the Alternative Service Book. Option A was the same for bride and groom and therefore omitted 'obey', while option B, though amended as compared with the vow of 1549, still retained the bride's pledge to obey her husband. Then in 2000, yet another version, replacing both that of 1549 and those of 1980, was introduced. It too, like that of 1980, offered two versions, one with obey, and one without. It is difficult to see how the Anglican Church can totally rid itself of the vow to obey without doing violence to the book on which in theory its teachings rest, namely the Bible. Paul, in Ephesians, Chapter 5, Verses 22 and 23, reads: 'Wives, submit yourselves unto your husbands, as unto the Lord. For the husband is the head of the wife, even as Christ is the head of the church'. And in Peter 1, 3,1: '…ye wives, be in subjection to your own husbands…'

Since the Marriage Act of 1949, applicable only in England and Wales, the wording of the civil marriage vows makes no reference to a god, is the same for bride and groom, and does not include a bride's vow to obey. A rare victory for secularism as well as one for gender equality. The ritual of the father 'giving away' what has been, since her birth, 'his' daughter to another man also originates from a time when a woman was either by custom or law, the property of a man. as indeed they still where Sharia law holds sway. Then of course there is the dowry, the payment in money or kind made by the owner or owners of the bride, who is therefore judged to worth less than nothing, a burden, who needs a bribe to persuade another man to assume ownership and upkeep of her. Again, 'giving away' conveys with it the notion that what is being given has no value, hence the need for a bribe.

As one would expect, in the *Koran*, we find the same idea as in Paul, though in this case, it defines the relationship not between husband and wife (or wives) but men and women in general: 'Men are guardians over women because Allah has made some of them excel over others'. (Chapter 4, Verse 34) A Muslim woman's marriage vow reflects this relationship, with its pledge to 'be for you an obedient and faithful wife'. Under Sharia law, there are no restrictions on the age of the wife taking this vow. The founder of Islam is said by all Islamic sources to have married his last wife, Aisha, when she was six, and consummated the marriage when she was nine. True or not, this has become the template for paedophilic Islamic marriage laws and practices, with the predictable result that child and even new-born baby brides, often bought by much older relatives, are a commonplace in a number of Muslim countries, including Yemen and Pakistan. In Pakistan, in January 2016, the ruling Muslim League Party's bid to enforce a law, dating back to British rule in 1929, limiting the minimum age for marriage for women to 16, was decreed to be 'blasphemous' by Pakistan's Council of Islamic Ideology. The Council's Chairman, Mohammad Khan Sheerani, ruled that 'Parliament cannot create legislation that is against the teachings of the Holy *Koran* or Sunnah'. The bill was promptly withdrawn, thereby confirming child rape as lawful in Pakistan. And, as before, our Sharia feminists will continue to rail against 'horror stories' of Muslim misogyny, while they prattle on about the glass ceiling in the boardroom and the 'sexism' of page three of the *Sun*.

In the west, until the advent of laws protecting wives from rape by their husbands, a husband's sexual rights within marriage were usually referred to as conjugal rights, and the wife's as duties. Islam, being perfect and therefore unchangeable, to this day does not recognise rape within marriage (*Koran,* Chapter 2, Verse 223, and Bukhari v.4, b.54 No.460) while English law only ceased doing so in 1991 when not an Act of Parliament, but a ruling by the Appellate Court in the House of Lords made non-consensual sexual intercourse by the husband a crime under Common Law. A survey conducted by the UN in 2006 found that rape within marriage was outlawed in 106 countries, leaving nearly as large a number where it was not. A classic statement on the Islamic denial of the very concept of rape within marriage was made as recently as 2014 by the Lebanese cleric Sheik Ahmad al Kurdi. He complained that criminalising rape within marriage 'could lead to the imprisoning of the man where in reality he is exercising the least [sic] of his marital rights'.

Again, unlike the Muslim world, civilised countries also outlawed, long ago, another ancient right of husbands, namely that of wife-beating. In England, it was called 'the rule of thumb', this being the legal limit under Common Law of the width of the implement used to administer the beating. Wife-beating was outlawed, though of course not eliminated, in the UK by the Aggravated Assaults Act of 1853. The MP Thomas Phinn moved an amendment to stipulate flogging as the punishment for wife beating, but it was defeated by 108 votes to 50. Another attempt to introduce flogging was made in 1856 but was defeated by 135 votes to 97. But such was feeling on this issue, that a third attempt to render the act's enforcement more effective was made in 1860 by Lord Raynham, but it was again defeated, by 221 votes to 81, though not out of any sympathy for the wife-beater who, and I agree with them, was judged to have deserved it, but chiefly on the reasonable grounds that wives would be less likely to report the crime if it led to their husbands being flogged as many believed they deserved. True, no civilised country would or should today contemplate the use of such methods to combat this or any other crime, no matter how barbaric, but one can understand the anger and frustration felt by those who with the best of motives, were ready to resort to flogging as the only means to deter husbands from assaulting their defenceless and more often than not, economically dependent wives. The popular journal *John Bull* captured the mood of the time: 'The brutal bully that maltreats a defenceless woman is, as a rule, a baseless coward, and the dread of retaliation provided for him by the law is the best guard that can be placed on his unruly fists.'

We are now a century and a half on from the time when in England, a women's right not to be beaten by her husband was recognised, if not effectively enforced by law. In the savage, bestial, viciously misogynist world of Islam, wife beating is not only permitted under Sharia law, but in the *Koran,* specifically *recommended*, in Chapter 4, Verse 34. We have encountered it before, but it is worth repeating for the benefit of *dhimmi* feminists:

'And for those [wives] on whose part you fear [only fear, not have committed] disobedience, admonish them and keep away from them in their beds and chastise them. Then if they obey you, seek not a way against them. Surely, Allah is High and Great'. (Some translations use 'beat' instead of 'chastise', which is the correct translation of the Arabic *idrib*'.

There is also a passage in the *Koran* where Allah relates how he commanded Job (in Arabic *Ayyub*) to 'take in your hand a green branch and beat her [his wife] with it'. (38: 41-43) Unlike in the civilised world, where wife beating not punished by the law is a shame and outrage of the distant past, Muslim clerics uphold it today just as it was written in the book of the prophet:

> The *Koran* says 'and beat them'. This verse is of a wondrous [sic...this is not a misprint] nature. There are three types of woman with whom a man cannot live unless he carries a rod on his shoulder. The first type is a girl who was brought up this way...So she becomes accustomed to beatings. We pray Allah will help her husband later. He will only get along with her if he practises wife beating. The second type of woman is the one who is condescending towards her husband and ignores him. With her, too, only a rod will help. The third type is a twisted woman who will not obey her husband unless her oppresses her, beats her, uses force against her, and overpowers her with his voice. (Qatar TV, August 27, 2002. After bribing a sufficient number of FIFA officials, Qatar was selected as the venue for the 2022 World Cup.)

And more recently:

> Islam instructs a man to beat his wife as a last resort before divorce so that she will mend her ways, treat him with kindness [sic] and respect and know that her husband has a higher station than her...A good woman, even if beaten by her husband, puts her hand in his and says: 'I will not rest until you are pleased with me'. This is how the Prophet Mohammed taught his women to be. (Al-Nas TV, Egypt, August 17, 2012)

When we compare the unspeakably vile subjugation of wives under Islam today with their status in marital law in the west, we should take note of the fact that whereas in England, male politicians of the mid-nineteenth century wanted to flog men to enforce a law enacted by men to protect women from male violence, today, in at least two Muslim states, Iran and Saudi Arabia, women are flogged by men for alleged infractions of sex and dress codes devised by men. With the right of a Muslim husband to beat and rape his wife or wives set in stone for eternity by no less an authority than Allah and his prophet, it was inevitable that when the United Nations adopted its Declaration on the Elimination of Violence Against Women in 1993, it would meet with organised and determined opposition by a phalanx of Muslim regimes, some today in the forefront of the heroic struggle to eliminate the state of Israel, where wife beating and marital rape are of course illegal. Typical of this resistance was the objection by Iran's theocratic rulers to a resolution of the UN Commission on the Status of Women calling upon all governments to 'condemn violence against women and refrain from invoking any custom, tradition or religious consideration to avoid their obligation with respect to its elimination'.

If the Ayatollahs were to comply with UN policy in this matter, they would have to forgo, amongst other sub-human abuses of women, the popular (amongst men) spectator participatory sport of stoning to death women accused of violations of Sharia law sex codes. The *Koran* also sanctions, in fact, encourages, the stealing (that is, abduction) of a non-Muslim woman from her previous owner, be he husband, father or brother, and her sexual subjugation by her new one, so becoming what it calls the 'spoils of war'. This is an Islamic euphemism for what is the most vicious, intrusive and hence degrading form of slavery, sexual slavery.

First, as regards slavery *per se,* (though the Bible, in all its versions, prefers the milder and more politically correct, but inaccurate 'servant'), Timothy 1, Chapter 6, Verse 1 says: 'Let as many servants as are under the yoke [sic] count their master's worthy of all honour, that the name of God and his doctrine be not blasphemed'. Honour those who place you 'under the yoke'…such is God's 'doctrine'. And to rebel against the yoke is to blaspheme. And we know what happened to blasphemers. Then we have Paul again, this time to Titus: 'Exhort servants to be obedient unto their own masters, and to please them well in all things; not answering again'. (Chapter 2, Verse 9) In other words, grin and bear it, and suffer in silence. Peter 1, in Chapter 2, Verse 18, if anything goes further, demanding submission to masters cruel no less than kind: 'Servants, be subject to your masters with all fear; not only to the good and gentle, but also to the froward'. Currently available English translations of the *Koran,* unlike those of the Bible, have no problem with retaining the original word slave. Its usage also occurs in those verses that deal with the rules for the sexual enjoyment of captured women, though in this particular verse, selected because here the issue is simply one of slavery *per se,* male slaves are also referred to: 'And marry those among you who are single and those who are fit among your male slaves and your female slaves.' (Chapter 24, Verse 32) A *Hadith* of Bukhari provides an insight not only into the kind of treatment a slave might expect at the hands of his (or her) owner but the nature of the sexual relations between a Muslim man and his wife (or wives). Mohammed is reported as saying: 'It is not wise [sic] of you to lash [sic] his wife like [sic] a slave, for he might sleep with her the same evening'. (6: 60: 466) When it comes to the abduction of women for the purposes of sex, both the Bible and the *Koran* are quite explicit. First Deuteronomy:

> And when the Lord thy God hath delivered it [a captured city] unto thy hands, thou shall smite every male therefore with the edge of the sword: But the women and the little ones and the cattle, and all that is in the city, even all the spoil therefore, shalt thou take under thyself; and thou shalt eat the spoil [sic: like the *Koran*] of thine enemies, which the Lord thy God hath given thee. (Chapter 20, Verses 13 and 14)

The fate of the abducted women is described in Chapter 21, Verses 10-13:

> When thou goest forth to war against thine enemies, and the Lord thy God hath delivered them unto thine hands, and thou hath taken them captive, and several among the captives a beautiful woman, and hast a desire unto her, that thou wouldst have her to be thy wife; then thou shall bring her home to thine house; and she shall shave her head, and pare her nails; and she shall put the raiment of her captivity from off her, and shall remain in thine house, and bewail her father and mother a full month; and after that thou shall go in unto her, and be her husband, and she shall be thy wife.

First comes abduction as spoils of war, then 'going in unto her', that is to say, rape, accompanied by forced marriage. It sounds like the Islamic State, or the Afghan and Pakistan outback but, as every observant Jew and practising Christian should know, it is the Old Testament. Ownership also looms large in

Deuteronomy's rulings on rape within the community, that is, according to whether the victim belongs to her husband or her father. But location also plays its part, as does the behaviour of the victim. In the first case, 'if a man be found lying with a woman married to an husband, then both of them shall die'. (22: 22) Next, 'if a damsel that is a virgin be betrothed unto an husband, and a man find her in the city, and lie with her; then ye shall bring them both out unto the gate of that city and ye shall stone them with stones that they die, the damsel, because she cried not, being in the city'. (22: 23,24) But 'if a man find a betrothed damsel in the field, and the man force her, and lie with her; then the man only that lay with her shall die', obviously because no-one can hear her protests. (22: 25) Finally, there is the case where a man rapes an unbetrothed virgin: 'Then the man that lay with shall give unto the damsel's father fifty shekels of silver, and she shall be his wife; because he hath humbled her, he may not put her away [i.e., divorce her] all his days.' (22: 28,29)

Now the *Koran*: 'Oh prophet! We have made it lawful to thee thy wives to whom thou hast paid their dowers and those whom thy right hand possesses [i.e., slaves] out of the prisoners of war whom Allah has assigned to thee'. (Chapter 30, Verse 50) And: 'O Prophet! We have made it lawful to thee thy wives who thou hast paid their dowries, and those whom thy right hand possesses [i.e., concubines] from among those whom Allah has given thee as gains of war...' (33: 51) The reading here implies a private arrangement between Allah and Mohammed to satisfy the prophet's legendary sexual appetites. The following verse suggests a more general application, one which sanctions the rape of enslaved married women, since they previously belonged to infidel men: '...all married women are forbidden unto you, save those whom you right hand possesses.' (4:24) Then there is Chapter 8, Verse 69: 'But now enjoy what ye took in war, lawful and good.' All told there are four verses which sanction the sexual enslavement of infidel women. That is why Muslim theologians and clerics down the ages have upheld this Allah-sanctioned right to the human spoils of war, not least, captured and enslaved women. They continue to do so to this day. On June 8, 2011 the Egyptian cleric Abu Ishak Al-Heweny expounded to a live and internet audience the finer points of Sharia law as they pertain to this question:

> When I talk about religion, what I say is fixed...according to the rulings of Jihad, if we fight polytheists, the Prophet Mohammed told the military commander he should do three things. This *hadith* appears in the Muslim collection. If you fight polytheist enemies, offer them three options: first call them to join Islam. If they join Islam, let them be...If they refuse to join Islam, they should pay the *jizya* poll tax [that is, become *dhimmis*]. If they refuse to pay the *jizya,* seek the help of Allah and fight them...The basic pre-requisite of Jihad is that your enemy be non-Muslim. If we are the winners, it is only natural [sic] to impose the rules of Islam on the country we invaded. According to the rules of Islam, all the people in that country become booty and prisoners of war: the women [just for once, women come first], the men, the children, the money, the homes, the fields. All these become the property of the Islamic State. [sic] What is the fate of the prisoners of war according to the Sharia? Since they constitute booty, they should be divided between the *mujahidin.* According to the *hadith,* the law states that anyone who did not participate in the raid does not get a share of the booty...Let's say we invaded a country with a population of half a million...Let's say there were some 100,000 *mujahidin.* That's it then. Each *mujahidin* gets five of them...You can take two men, two women, and a child, or the

other way round. You divide them up. Great. {sic] As soon as this system is in place, there has to be a slave market where you can sell slaves, slave girls and children...We are talking about the rulings that are fixed in the *Koran*.

This is not the Saudi desert of the 7th century, the birth place of Islam, or the Islamic State, the Taliban or Boko Haram, but 'moderate' Egypt, in the year 2011. One of the world's leading modern authorities on Islamic law, Majid Khadduri, had this to say on the same subject in his *War and Peace in the law of Islam:*

> The term spoil (*ghanima*) is applied specifically to property acquired by force from non-Muslims. It includes, however, not only property (moveable and non-movable) but also persons, whether in the capacity of *asra* (prisoners of war) or *sabi* (Women and children) ...If the slave were a woman, the master was permitted to have sexual connection [sic] with her as a concubine.

In other words, rape her. Open season? Not quite. It seems that the warriors of the Islamic State, schooled though many are in their holy texts, mistakenly assumed that such verses had given them what amounted to a blank cheque from Allah to seize and rape any non-Muslim women they fancied. *Fatwa* Number 64, issued on January 29, 2015 by the ISIL Committee of Research and *Fatwas,* disabused them of this understandable error. Its preamble reads as follows:

> One of the graces which Allah has bestowed upon the State of the caliphate is the conquest of large surface areas of the country, and one of the inevitable consequences of the jihad of establishment is that women and children of infidels will become captives of Muslims. Consequently, it is necessary to clarify some rules pertaining to captured prisoners to avoid any violations in dealing with them.

As we have seen, Allah has rules for nearly everything, and rape is no exception. Of the 15 rulings on Muslim rape etiquette (and we are not dealing here with Muslim marital rape) perhaps the most revealing is number five:

> If the owner [sic] of a female captive, who has a daughter suitable for sexual intercourse [i.e., rape] has sexual relations with the latter, he is not permitted to have sexual intercourse with [i.e., rape] her mother and she is [therefore] permanently off limits to him. Should he have intercourse with [i.e., rape] her mother, then he is not permitted to have intercourse with [i.e., rape] her daughter and she is to be off limits to him.

The interested reader can access the entire *fatwa* online, so let us close with the fifteenth and final ruling. When trading in or selling on a sex slave, the following rule applies: 'The owner of a female captive should not sell her to an individual whom he knows will treat her badly or do unto her what Allah has forbidden'. Who says Islam treats its women badly?

II

From Rotherham to Cologne

Europe: December 31, 2015. In Germany, in the cities of Cologne, Leipzig, Berlin, Bremen, Bielefeld, Stuttgart, Frankfurt, Dusseldorf and Hamburg, and in 12 of Germany's 16 states, and elsewhere in Europe in Helsinki, Zurich, Malmo, Kalmar, Vienna, Innsbruck and Salzburg, as in other cities and towns across Germany and Europe, the traditional New Year's Eve celebrations get under way. This year, the festivities in these locations were joined by some of the continents recently arrived guests from Muslim lands at the (illegal) invitation of German Chancellor Angela Merkel, all seeking refuge, so we are assured, from the terrors inflicted on them by their co-religionists. According to reports that in a sinister throwback to earlier times, were initially subject to a total news black-out and only made public by the media after a delay of five days, in Hamburg, women reported more than 400 assaults, and in Cologne, 2,000, including not only robbery and sexual assault, but rape, by men whom victims and police described as 'of Arab or North African appearance', in other words, Muslims. In cities across Germany, in all, more than 3,000 women were the victims of premeditated attacks, many sexual and including rape, by Muslim migrants. By July 2016, there had been only four convictions. Two of the four, both Muslims, after being described by the presiding judge as 'animals', walked from the court laughing after receiving *suspended* sentences.

As in other cities subjected to organised Muslim sex attacks, the initial Cologne police report nevertheless said the evening in the city centre had been 'relaxed' with a 'jolly atmosphere'! No less relaxed was the initial reaction the next day of the Minister President of Baden-Wurttemberg, Winfried Kretschmann. In an interview with *Die Welt,* he dismissed as absurd fears of an Islamisation of Germany. 'If you look at the facts, this fear is unfounded. We have a stable democracy and a free society. State and religion are separated. (Not strictly true) How should Muslims, who represent a minority, Islamise our society?' The 'fact' was that the previous evening the centre of one Germany's largest cities had been well and truly 'Islamised', and those responsible for defending Germanys 'stable democracy' and 'free society' had not only done nothing to prevent it but even tried to suppress reports of what had occurred.

However, one local politician, perhaps better appraised of the real state of affairs in Cologne, begged to differ with Kretschmann's assessment of the threat, insisting quite truthfully that the city centre had been turned into a 'no go' zone for German women. Yet as of January 6, police had made no arrests, and admitted that none were likely in the future. This was because on the night of the attacks, they followed the usual practice when dealing with troublesome Muslim migrants of avoiding confrontations, allowing them, many of whom were reportedly drunk, to gather in large numbers at the station prior to launching their assaults. Then, just as they did in Rotherham, the police allowed the sex attacks to proceed without any restraining action on their part, a decision in all probability fuelled by the same fear as in the UK that protecting women from Muslim sex criminals could lead to career-threatening accusations of Islamophobia and racism. Even after the attacks, Cologne police lyingly told inquiring journalists that the night had passed off peacefully. Rather hypocritically, in view of the fact that the Cologne police were simply following guide lines issuing from his own department, Interior Minister Thomas de Maziere complained that 'the police cannot operate like this'.

For at least a decade previous to these attacks, not only the police, but Germany's courts had been following a policy of either ignoring or adjusting to Muslim ways. In 2006, after years of violent abuse, a Moroccan-born woman separated from her Muslim husband and sued for divorce. Forced to leave their marital home, the husband then issued death threats against his estranged wife. Her response was to apply through her lawyer for a speedy divorce, hoping that this would put an end to the threats. In January 2007, the judge handling the case rejected the application on the grounds that the *Koran* permits a husband to discipline his errant spouse, and therefore this was not sufficient cause for a speedy divorce: 'The exercise of the right to castigate [sic] does not fulfil the hardship criteria as defined by paragraph 1565 of German Federal law.'

If Judges were prepared to defer to Muslim cultural practices and indeed Sharia law where women were concerned, why not the police? Just how the police did operate in Cologne, and what they confronted, only became public knowledge when on January 7, the mass circulation tabloid *Bild* published a leaked report by a senior police officer who witnessed the sex assaults in Cologne on the night of December 31. He described in his report how young men involved in the attacks mocked and humiliated police by tearing up their resident permits, one of their number saying as he did so, 'I am Syrian, you have to treat me kindly. Mrs Merkel invited me.' Which of course she did. Another rioter tearing up his permit taunted, 'You can't do anything to me, I can get a new one tomorrow'. Which of course he could. The officer making the report had been in command of a unit of 100 extra police drafted into Cologne's city centre to help cope with what was regarded as an emergency situation, one 'far more serious than previously thought', in which 'there could have been fatalities'. 'Relaxed'? 'Jolly'? The report continues:

> When we arrived, our vehicles were pelted with firecrackers. About a thousand people, mostly males of an immigrant background, were indiscriminately throwing fireworks and bottles into the crowd. Around 10.45 PM, the station forecourt filled with people of an immigrant background. Women literally had to run the gauntlet through a mass of drunken men, in a way you can't imagine. We concluded that the situation threatened chaos or serious injury, if it didn't lead to fatalities...Many women came to officers shocked and crying and reported sexual assaults. Police officers were unable to respond to all the events, assaults and offences. There were just too many at the same time...

It also emerged that the police had prior knowledge of the impending assaults. On December 29, Peter Roemer, the officer in charge of Cologne security, wrote in a report that migrants were planning 'tumultuous [sic] offences and massive thefts' in the city centre, and that 'larger crowds and a larger consumption of alcohol is to be expected with the typical dangers associated with them.' The 'offender clientele [sic]' who were expected to be the cause of the 'tumultuous offences' were described as 'substantially North African repeat offenders'. So not only were the attacks known to be impending, but also the identity of those who were about to carry them out. Yet after they happened, both were initially denied. And to cap it all, no special measures were taken to deal with the attacks until it was too late. In total, 2000 assaults...but on the night, no arrests and, as of March 5, only one conviction...for robbery. So initial police reports were able to claim that as in previous years, everything had passed off peacefully. The police swung into action however when days later, German men vented their anger against the assaults on their wives, sisters, girl-friends and daughters, only to be drenched with water cannons, while *dhimmi* feminists, unmolested by police, protested against... 'racism'.

Some, as we shall see, simply refused to believe migrants/refugees had been responsible the assaults, even though in their aftermath, one police officer revealed that his colleagues had been given 'strict, instructions not to report offences by refugees' (shades of Labour Home Secretary Jacqui Smith), and two local Cologne newspapers, the *Express* and the *Kolner Stadtanzeiger*, both carried the story that an internal police report had identified large numbers of the attackers as recent migrants from Syria, Iraq and Afghanistan. The same 'hands off' policy for migrants was also being applied in Frankfurt, where a senior police officer told *Bild* that 'for offences of criminal suspects who have a foreign nationality, and are reported [to be] in a [refugee] reception centre, we put the case on the desk immediately to the side'- just like in Rotherham and several dozen other towns and cities across England. Based on eyewitness and victim accounts, internal police reports and other leaks, it is beyond any doubt the case that that nearly all, if not all sex and other assaults were carried out by Muslims. That is why the question of their race, or rather, races, is irrelevant. What took place was not the product of so-called ethnicity or skin colour but of a particular religion. Misogyny is not inherited via male genes, as some feminists claim, but from and via a culture, in this case, an Islamic one.

Perhaps because of these and other similar revelations from *bona fide* police sources, the Interior Ministry came clean and revealed that of 31 men suspected of committing assaults of one kind or another in Cologne on New Year's Eve, all but two were foreigners, including 18 asylum seekers. Of the 29, four were Syrians, and one an Iraqi. The other 24 were from countries where there were no war zones: five Iranians, eight Moroccans, nine Algerians, one Serb (!) and one from the USA (!!). Again, the common denominator is not 'ethnic origin', a term much favoured by those who want to avoid using religious descriptions, but Islam. So, in this admittedly small sample, only five were from countries where there were conditions that generate genuine refugees, and no fewer than 24 from countries where no such conditions existed. Why then was this second and much larger group awarded refugee status? If it had not, there would have been at least 24 fewer sexual predators on the loose in Cologne on the night of December 31. After such a spectacular and, for Germany of all countries, humiliating failure to enforce the law on its own streets and protect its women from an army of sexual assailants, a scapegoat had to found. With the storm of criticism of the 'softly softly' method of dealing, or rather not dealing with migrant sex crimes growing louder by the hour, the buck was passed down to Cologne's police chief, Wolfgang Albers who, it was subsequently claimed, had covered up the whole affair because it was 'politically awkward'...just as his counterparts did in Rotherham and a score or more police authorities across England. He was summarily sacked on January 8, as a punishment for implementing what he believed was the official, if never stated policy for handling migrant anti-social behaviour and, possibly on his own initiative, for falsifying reports on the events of December 31. One can indeed sympathise with the predicament that faced Cologne's police chief and his understaffed and politically hamstrung force on the night of December 31, faced as they were with a thousand-strong army of young Muslim men intent on seizing and enjoying their 'spoils of war'. The assaults, aimed exclusively at young women and teenage girls, were conducted with military precision, with groups of thirty so attackers targeting and overpowering their prey, and then subjecting them to sexual assaults, including rape, and robbing them of their possessions. A man described how his partner and 15-year daughter were sexually assaulted outside the station: 'The attackers grabbed her [his daughter's} and my partner's breasts and groped between their legs'.

There is a video on YouTube of a far worse attack, in which a gang of twenty or more migrants surround a young woman and drag her screaming down some steps into what looks like an underpass. Police are nowhere to be seen. What happened next, we can easily imagine. Some women were not only groped, raped and robbed, but had lighted fireworks thrown at them, one being stuffed inside a young English woman's clothes, leaving her, she said, 'scarred for life'. There were no reports of any attacks on German men. True to past form, the Jihadis preferred to attack 'soft' targets.

As outrage at the news spread across Germany, Justice Minister Heiko Mass described the attacks, according to Cologne police pre-arranged and co-ordinated by mobile phones, as 'a completely new dimension of organised crime'. Departing from her mantra that Germany has nothing to fear from the influx of more than one million Muslim migrants, even Merkel found herself obliged to promise that the perpetrators of the 'disgusting assaults' would be brought to book 'without regard to their background or origin'. But then she added the caveat that it was 'completely improper to link a group that appeared [sic] to come from North Africa with [sic] the refugees'. Then why the reference to 'background and origin? The reason why they 'appeared' to come from North Africa, was because they *did* come from North Africa, unless, that is, they were Germans disguised as such with the intention of inciting yet more Islamophobia. And why was it wrong to 'link' them with the refugees'? Surely, they *were* refugees, or at least claimed to be such, and it was Merkel who had invited them in.

Once the German media broke its deplorable self-imposed silence on the events of December 31, the taboo on discussing and challenging Merkel's Muslim migrant policy was dead and buried. It now became possible for mainstream politicians to talk of 'background and origin' without being automatically accused of Islamophobia or, however illogically, of racism. The already-mentioned Justice Minister Heiko Mass, whose Social Democratic Party had hitherto been the most supportive of Merkel's 'open door' policy, had evidently had enough. 'Nobody can tell me this [the Cologne assaults] was not co-ordinated or prepared, when such a horde meets to commit such criminal acts, it looked like it was planned in some form.' The Bavarian Christian Social Union Interior Affairs spokesman Stephan Mayer, whose party is also a member of Merkel's coalition, warned it would be 'fatal' to remain silent when such crimes were being committed by those 'to whom we have granted a generous welcome in our country'. Indeed, especially since it was at Munich's main railway station that his fellow Bavarians, rather naively in retrospect, had greeted with applause, embraces, banners and balloons the first wave of migrant arrivals. Ordinary Germans, who for the best part of a year had borne the brunt of the consequences, all negative, of their establishment's policy of encouraging illegal and uncontrolled Muslim migration, were enraged. Non-

dhimmi women took to the streets holding placards that asked, 'Mrs Merkel, where are you?' Where indeed.

As if co-ordinated migrant sex assaults in seven German cities were not enough embarrassment for Merkel, on January 10 she learned that the Muslim terrorist who attacked a Paris police station on the first anniversary of the *Charlie Hebdo* massacre had, like two of the assassins involved in the Paris massacres of November 2015, passed through Germany posing as an asylum seeker *en route* to his suicide mission, having previously stayed in a refugee centre in western Germany. The worst blow all to Merkel's illegal migrant policy however fell the next day, when after a week of dissemblement, prevarication, leaks to the press and frantic back-peddling, the Interior Ministry finally came clean on those responsible for the attacks of December 31: 'Based on testimony from witnesses, the report [presumably a revised and more truthful one] from the Cologne police and descriptions by the Federal police, it looks [sic] as if people with a migration background were almost exclusively [sic] responsible for the criminal acts.'

However, 'improper' Merkel believed it was to say the sex assaults were the work of migrants, finally the truth was out…they were, 'almost exclusively'. Even so, the devoutly Lutheran and politically conservative Merkel found what was on the face of it, highly improbable support for her resistance to acknowledging migrant, and therefore her own responsibility for the events of December 31. It came, again almost exclusively, from women, mainly *dhimmi* feminists, who were far more concerned with protesting against what they claimed was the greater threat of racism than denouncing gang rape, demanding justice for its victims and better police protection for women. Whereas a number of male politicians and government officials had been prepared to unequivocally condemn the attackers and, equally to the point, to say who they were, with one exception, this was not the case with women politicians and social activists. Cologne's ultra Islamophile Mayor, the aptly named Henrietta Wreker, like Merkel, warned against 'jumping to conclusions' about the identity of their attackers, even though both their victims and the police were certain as to what that identity was. Echoing Merkel's disclaimer almost word for word she said 'It's completely improper [sic] to link a group that appeared [sic] to come from north Africa with the refugees'. 'Improper'…. but not untrue, as her police, belatedly, confirmed. One of the sex attackers, when later questioned by police, said 'I am a Syrian. You have to treat me kindly. [sic] Mrs Merkel invited me'…which she did. And yes, a leaked police report did indeed say said that 'some of the Cologne sex attackers claimed to be Syrian refugees.' One police officer told a Cologne newspaper, 'we arrested 15 people. These people have been in Germany for only a few days or weeks'. As tourists? No. 14 were from Syria and one from Afghanistan. The officer continued: 'This is the truth, even if it hurts. I had young women standing next to me crying because they no longer had any underwear after the mob had spat them out.' Police found sheets of paper with Germany translations of Arabic phrases to facilitate their amorous approaches to German women, such as 'Busty I want to kiss you', 'I will kill you' and 'I want to fuck'. Shades of the Arabian Nights.

If Wreker was justified in expressing her doubts about about the identity of the attackers, she needed to explain how it was that before the arrival in 2015 of one million mainly young male Muslims, no such events even remotely resembling these had ever occurred before in post-war Germany. Instead of denouncing as barbarians the (Muslim) men who organised and carried out the assaults, she placed the responsibility for preventing them in future on their potential victims. Her solution, justly treated with derision (by men but not feminists) was to propose that women should 'stick together in groups' and 'keep at a certain distance of more than an arm's length' from men 'with whom they do not have a trusting relationship'. (A group of young women did in fact adopt this very tactic but succumbed to vastly superior numbers of migrant attackers.) What could be easily inferred from Wreker's anti-rape precautions is that if women failed to follow this advice by continuing to behave normally, potential sexual predators could assume they were 'asking for it', a presumption shared by most Muslim men. So although the problem was presented as of one male behaviour in general (and not men of a certain religious persuasion, culture and age) it was women, the potential victims, and not men, their potential assailants, who had to change their behaviour. And this from a woman who doubtless regards herself as a full-on feminist.

As, thanks to Merkel, the Muslim rape rate soared in Germany during 2016, public officials offered women advice on how best to protect themselves. One suggested that they should stay indoors, another that they should stop wearing high heels so that they could make good their escape from a potential attacker. Anything rather than confront the issue…Muslim misogyny. The idea that women had to change their public behaviour now that Merkel's Muslim guests were on the prowl had already been proposed in a much more extreme form by the Norwegian anthropologist and Sharia apologist Unna Wikan back in 2014. Norwegian woman had been 'inviting rapes' (sic) by 'acting [sic] like Norwegian women' instead of 'internalising that we live in a multicultural society and accommodating that fact. In most Muslim countries, it is assumed that the woman is at fault for being raped, and it is only fair [sic] that Muslims bring these kinds of opinions with them when they move to Norway.' Will the reader please read this again, several times, before continuing, and, as they do so, keep reminding themselves that this was written by a highly-educated European woman.

Following this prescription, what Wikan called 'multiculturalism' becomes in reality the imposition of a misogynistic Islamic monoculturalism, one which requires the adoption by the host nation of the culture and mores of the Muslim male migrant. Hence her demand that Norwegian women should cease thinking and acting like (emancipated) Norwegian woman and start thinking and acting like (subjugated) Muslim women. If they don't, they will only have themselves to blame if they are raped ('fairly') by Muslim men. Another Norwegian academic, the historian of religion Hanne Herland, also placed the blame for Norway's spectacular increase in rape squarely on the culture of the victims. 'Africans rape when they come to Norway', she explained, because they 'discover what a low value Western culture places on a woman's sexuality', presumably, because unlike where they come from, it outlaws rape and wife-beating. Once again, it is 'our fault'.

Canadian Sharia feminists have already begun to move in the direction proposed by Wikan. At their instigation, on February 25, 2016, Ottawa officially celebrated 'Hijab Solidarity Day' with the city's *kuffar* women being urged to sport the Muslim symbol of female oppression by 'walking with our Muslim sisters'. There was a time long ago when feminists would have not have demonstrated their approval of this cowl of servitude, but their solidarity with the brave and genuine feminists in Iran who refuse to conform to dress codes imposed by misogynist Muslim men. Now the solidarity is with the dress code and, necessarily, with the men and the draconian laws which enforce it. Perhaps on future such occasions, Ottawa's *dhimmi* feminists can shift up a gear by holding a Burka Solidarity Day, shuffling around town, heads down and peering through the eye slits of their brand-new burkas. The day's festivities could then be rounded off in Ottawa's central square with an exemplary simulated stoning of an Islamophobic sister who refused to celebrate her subjugation in the approved manner. Lowered down to her waist in a personhole cover, she could be bombarded with papier maché replica Iranian regulation size stones by enthusiastic male Muslim volunteers from the local diaspora.

Token hijab days are all very well, but Canada's feminists still have a long way to go before than can truly claim to have fully embraced the enriching life of a Muslim woman. The ultimate test of their sisterly solidarity would be to take regular thrashings from their male partners…and enjoy it. In Toronto, one the of texts distributed free of charge by the York University Muslim Students Association at its 2015 Annual Islamic Awareness Week (sic) in a section entitled 'Wife Disciplining' says the following: 'Submissive or subdued women may even enjoy being beaten at times as a sign of love or concern', while a Montreal imam, Hussein Amer, has defined wife beating as 'a type of education'. If any of Canada's playacting *dhimmi* feminists intend to go the whole hog and convert, as indeed some inadequate, desperate, naïve or just plain stupid women do, then before embarking on this one-way path, listen first to Calgary imam Abdi Hersy advising Muslim husbands of their rights:

> The husband has many rights on his wife. First and foremost, she has to obey you. He comes with the orders. You come with the orders and she has to obey you. She cannot leave the house without your permission.' [He then addresses himself to their wives] You have to choose either Allah or your country. Canada is a feminine [he means feminist] country. So, ladies, the other thing I want to quit from your life is feminism.

Not to be outdone by their transatlantic *dhimmi* sisters, British Sharia feminists acted out a no less ludicrous scene than in Ottawa when, on August 25, 2016, to the certain delight of any Muslim misogynist who may have passed by, they proudly sported their shrouds of submission outside the French embassy in London to protest against the French ban on the Islamic swimwear. Their slogan 'wear what you want' presupposed that Muslim women who cover up their entire bodies in public have in every case freely chosen to do so, something they surely must have known was not the case. If the demonstrators really believed what their slogan said, why then had they not mounted similar protests outside the embassies of the many Islamic countries, in the first place Saudi Arabia and Iran, that not only deny precisely this choice to their Muslim sisters, but inflict on those brave few who do exercise it the cruellest punishments? I think I know the answer. Any such action would be deemed 'Islamophobic'. A matter of days later, a poll found that the UK favoured the banning of the burka by a majority of two to one, while in the Syrian city of Manbij, Muslim women celebrated their liberation by a Kurdish army from Islamic State Sharia tyranny by burning their sartorial symbols of female enslavement.

Another variation on the theme of embracing the Islamic life-style was offered by the former UK race relations industry supremo Trevor Phillips, in comments made after the Cologne events, to the Policy Change 'think tank'. It showed the 'deepest lack of respect' towards Muslims to ask or expect them to change their ways, because 'they see the world differently from us'. But what if these 'ways' include those that were demonstrated in Rotherham for more than thirty years, and Cologne on New Year's Eve, when in both cities they displayed their 'deepest lack of respect' towards *kuffar* girls and women? Coming from another angle, but homing in on the same target, Labour MP Jess Philips claimed on BBC TV's Question Time that in Birmingham's Broad Street, there was 'every week' a 'very similar situation' to what took place in Cologne, only the culprits were not Muslims. So the problem was men in general, not young male Muslims. Like Rotherham perhaps? If her claim is true, there must be hordes of up to a thousand or so drunken non-Muslim young men gang-raping and robbing young women and girls 'every week' in her Birmingham constituency. Well, not exactly. What she described as 'violence against girls' turned out to be women being 'baited and heckled'. Unpleasant, to say the least, and in certain given cases, quite possibly illegal. But not organised mass physical sexual assault and rape. And local women were quick to deny that Broad Street in any way resembled Cologne on New Year's Eve. Some of her constituents, disgusted by what amounted to a belittling of the Cologne assaults, demanded her resignation.

Finally, there are those who not because of political correctness, but just plain stupidity or even worse, exhibit the symptoms of the Sharia Stockholm Syndrome without themselves having been victims of Muslim sex crime. The classic case is that of Deborah Green, aged 47, a juror in the 2014 trial of the Sheffield Muslim child rapists. After their conviction and sentencing, it transpired that during the trial, she had been writing to one of the rapists, Shakeal Rehman, encouraging him to 'keep you chin up, sexy' and letting him know that in the jury room she was arguing for his acquittal. In the event, her efforts proved in vain. Her 'sexy' child rapist was given a jail term of twelve years. Signing herself 'Dee', other letters offered money to the accused men. When subsequently appearing herself in court on a charge of contempt of court, she explained that she felt sorry for the rapists, and just wanted to make sure they were alright. Could it be that she was hankering after the treatment Rehman had been dealing out to his 13-year-old 'spoil of war'? Because here for sure we have the kind of sad loser who writes to the Yorkshire Ripper with proposals of marriage, or converts to Islam as a last desperate attempt to get a bloke.

To return to Cologne and its Stockholm Syndrome Mayor. With the money-spinning Cologne carnival due in a month, and fears that thousands would keep away for their own safety, Mayor Wreker made the following suggestion, which I assume she expected to be taken seriously: 'We will explain our Carnival much better to people who come from other cultures [sic] so there won't be any confusion [sic] about what constitutes celebratory [sic] behaviour in Cologne, which has nothing to do with sexual frankness [sic!]'. What? Rape is *'sexual frankness'?* And those engaged in it were simply 'celebrating' in their own multicultural fashion a festival that their own religion's calendar does not recognise? The Mayor of Cologne evidently believed in all seriousness that all that was required to avoid any repetition of the New Year's Eve events was to explain to 'confused' Muslim migrants that whatever it might mean in Islamic countries, in Germany, 'celebration' is not another word for rape, or rather, 'sexual frankness'. In line with this policy, in the run-up to the carnival, leaflets (presumably not in German) were distributed explaining to migrants the does and don'ts of celebratory behaviour, among which were not urinating in public and requesting permission for kissing

German women. Not everyone appeared to have got the message, because just on the first day of the carnival, despite a massive security presence double that of previous years, police reported 190 arrests, with 22 sexual attacks, including, rape, 143 bodily assaults and 30 thefts. Eleven police were injured defending themselves from assaults, and a women TV reporting covering the event was groped while on camera. A case of Muslim 'sexual frankness', or just another migrant 'misunderstanding'? As in the wake of the New Year's Eve assaults, police declined to provide details as to the background of the culprits. And as in other German cities, women continued to be targeted by Muslim men, especially at swimming baths. On March 6, six migrants were arrested by Cologne police after a sexual assault on a 12-year-old girl in a swimming pool.

Handing out leaflets cannot eradicate literally overnight beliefs and patterns of behaviour that have been ingrained in a culture and sanctioned by a religion over centuries. The delusion that it is simply a matter of rectifying a 'misunderstanding', akin perhaps to Brits being reminded to drive on the right-hand side of the road when arriving on the continent, is the result when Sharia feminism meets political correctness. Perhaps the Wrekers of this world feel guilty about what must surely be their initial instinctive revulsion at gang rape, and so feel compelled to demonstrate to all and sundry that they are neither racist nor Islamophobic by devising the most preposterous and self-demeaning arguments to prove it. Though Muslim men were the culprits, it was their intended victims who had to learn to modify their public behaviour or face the consequences. No wonder sales to women of self-defence devices boomed in Germany.

There was however one woman who had the civic courage and honesty to draw the correct conclusions from outrages that are unprecedented in the history of post-Nazi Germany and, save for the Balkans in the 1990s, of the entire western world. Mina Ahdi, who headed the German Council of ex-Muslims, is an Iranian apostate from Islam who has been under a death sentence imposed by the Religion of Peace, Love and Tolerance since 1981. Like many others in her predicament, she is under constant police protection from the attentions of this same Religion of Peace, Love and Tolerance. So understandably, she did not mince her words: 'For them [the Muslim gropers and rapists] women are dirty. They are sex objects to be enjoyed in the home and allowed outside only in a burka in the company of a man.' There spoke the voice of bitter experience, and not *dhimmi* delusion and wishful thinking.

Sharia feminists can always be relied upon on when Muslim men behave badly to deny, divert attention from or excuse Islamic misogyny, and so it proved again in the aftermath of the Cologne sexual assaults. For Wreker, the problem was not Islam, but 'misunderstandings' and men. For others, there was the ever-present danger of racism, German racism. One woman demonstrator held aloft a banner with the slogan 'Against Sexism [is rape just 'sexism'?], against Racism', while young leftist women displayed a large banner demanding a 'Nazi Free Zone' in Cologne *but saying nothing about a rape-free zone.* Had Nazis, German ones that is, been doing the raping, perhaps disguised as migrants to stir up racial tensions? Apparently not. Neither were the young ladies, posing as 'Young Socialist German Workers', alluding to anti-Semitic Muslims who carried out the sex attacks on December 31, because this slogan, was in fact aimed at those 'Nazis', among whom we must we must include Mina Ahdi, who had the temerity to protest against them. As for 'sexism', this term is traditionally reserved by feminists to denote gender-based discrimination against women. However, the issue on this occasion was not one of gender bias, but something much worse, namely one of massive sexual violence against women, *including rape.* So why not a banner that simply said: *Gegen Vergewaltigung* - Against Rape? And why racism? The only racism on display in Cologne, Dusseldorf, Stuttgart, Frankfurt, Berlin, Bremen, Bielefeld and Hamburg on New Year's Eve had been that of Muslims treating white *kuffar* German women as mere objects for sexual gratification. But I have a sneaking suspicion that Muslim racism was not the one that the woman holding the banner had in mind.

Another line of approach was to canvas the idea there were as bad or even worse things that could happen to a German woman than being gang raped (that is, when the rapists are Muslim migrants). In the considered opinion of the (male) Interior Minister of North Rhine-Westphalia, 'what happens on right wing platforms and in chat rooms is at least as awful as the acts of those assaulting the women'. *At least*! Whatever might take place on 'right wing platforms' and in 'chat rooms', it is not gang rape by rampaging mobs of drunken Muslim migrants and, given the choice, with the possible exception of lobotomized Sharia feminists, no woman would think twice before deciding which experience to undergo. There was a time, and it seems so long ago now, when if an official charged with upholding the law were to publicly trivialise the crime of rape, in this case *gang rape*, it would have been regarded as grounds for automatic dismissal, No longer. Today such views, endorsed of course by feminists, are judged to be the acme of enlightened, progressive thinking, and those that dissent from them run the risk of being accused of racism.

While some public figures frantically rummaged around for the most improbable explanations and excuses for Muslim sexual predators, another male commentator distinguished himself by dispensing with excuses altogether. Mass sexual assault by Muslims, including we must always remember, gang rape, must not be seen as a crime, *but as a form of social rebellion.* But let us begin at the beginning. The initial response of the inventor of this theory was to deny that there had been any sexual assaults, and only subsequently, when it was impossible to sustain this lie, did he then find it necessary to celebrate them. Ridiculing reports that Muslim migrants could have been responsible for sex attacks in Cologne on New Year's Eve, *Der Speigel* columnist Jakob Augstein wrote on his Facebook page: 'We are so racist. Everyone immediately wanted to believe that 1,000 North Africans were committing mischief.' Rape was in his book, not 'frankness' but simply 'mischief'. In fact, we have seen that there were others in positions of authority and influence who like Augstein, also refused to believe it. He continues: 'One thousand. This is a fairy tale figure. Just like the three golden hairs of the devil. Or the seven dwarfs. Or the thirteenth fairy.'

Once the scale and nature of the attack, and the number and identity of their perpetrators became impossible to deny, Augstein decided that only option left was to transform his fairy tale mischief-makers into real-life warriors for social justice. Armed with this new truth, he returned to his Facebook page on February 23:

> The victims of Cologne were inferior to their perpetrators only [sic] in the immediate moment of the attacks. These women were powerless and helpless at the moment they were assaulted and robbed [by 'seven dwarfs' perhaps?]. But before the attacks and after, they were their [presumably social] superiors.

Now Augstein drew the threads together, leading to the conclusion that the rape of German women by Muslim men is, in its way a kind of (admittedly rough) social justice:

> The lawbreaking [sic] in Cologne brought a brief rupture in the social hierarchy, a reversal of the true balance of power. The reason is that in this moment the relationship between victim and perpetrator [that is to say, the raped and the rapist] was reduced to physical strength [i.e., a gang of thirty men overpower and rape one woman]. In all other respects, the victims of Cologne are superior to their perpetrators [to save his Sharia left blushes, Augstein never once uses the words 'rapists' and 'rape']; language, nationality, education, social status, wealth, legal certainty, self-confidence.

Now we had three more definitions of rape to add that of Mayor Wrecker's 'sexual frankness'; namely, 'mischief', a 'brief rupture in the social hierarchy' and 'a reversal in the true balance of power'. Perhaps that is also what it was in Rotherham, Sheffield, Oxford, Rochdale, Aylesbury, Keighley, etc etc… We await comment by our Sharia feminists.

In the wake of the attacks, *dhimmi* feminists queued up to denounce the public outcry, such as it was, against the Cologne assaults, one claiming that 'the debate [sic] about Muslim immigrants [surely she means 'refugees'] has reached its recent hysterical [sic] climax'. What she found 'disgusting' was not the rapes, but 'the debate' about the identity of the rapists. She complained of 'lurid descriptions of tattered underwear and fingers to body orifices', oblivious perhaps to the fact that these were accounts of the victims themselves. As to the identity of the perpetrators, which was her sole interest, their 'origin was not clear'. So there is rape and rape, depending on the 'origin' of the rapist. Another from the same stable confessed that 'on New Year's Eve, something happened that I don't really want to talk about'. A feminist who 'doesn't walk to talk about' the premeditated and organised sexual assault of women? This is because in the arcane pecking order of 'intersectional', 'identity'- driven 'Third Wave' feminism, Muslim men, rapists or no, rank above white non-Muslim women, even when the former are raping the later. Yet another feminist piled in, arguing that the Cologne attacks had been 'set upon enthusiastically by those who wish to turn emotions against the new arrivals [sic]' and who had in fact 'little respect for women'…who knows, perhaps even less than those who had been sexually assaulting them. Concerned to conform to the already referred to pecking order, she continues: Feminists 'are finding it difficult to speak up about the event [sic]' because 'it might be used to encourage aggression against refugees. I can't say I blame them.' So, better keep *shtum* about organised sexual aggression against her sisters. Now that really is showing respect for women.

Finally, inevitably, we had the Pope, as always in times of stress and tragedy ready to offer kind words of solace, understanding and hope. He urged angry Germans, presumably also those hundreds of fathers, husbands, brothers and boyfriends of as well as the actual victims of sexual assault and rape, 'not to lose the values of humanity however much they prove in some moments of history, a difficult burden to bear'. Such words come all too easily from someone who so far as I am aware, has neither suffered the trauma of being raped (unlike so many sexual victims his clergy) nor offered sanctuary to a single refugee, and is the head of a State which has as a matter of policy, consistently concealed and protected those of its clergy guilty of sexual abuse of their charges, and at the time of the Holocaust, not only turned a blind eye to the extermination of six million Jews, but did all it could to help those responsible for their murder evade justice by aiding their escape via the Vatican's infamous 'rate line' to sanctuary in Catholic South America and a Muslim Middle East.

But the Pope's exercise in clerical hogwash was not done. Instead of condemning those who, lacking any 'values of humanity', were responsible for the outrages, and advising Germany's Muslim guests to be in future on their very best behaviour, he drew a picture of Germany's migrants that with the best will in the world, few, especially women, who had unwillingly encountered them sexually at first hand, would not easily recognise: 'Many migrants from Africa and Asia see Europe as a beacon for principles such as equality before the law and values inherent in human nature'. But as the 1990 Cairo declaration of the Organisation of the Islamic Conference made very clear, Islam utterly repudiates the idea of human values. All values, all rights, such as they are, come only from Allah (just as for the Pope they come from god) as does the Islamic system of justice, the Sharia, which in its treatment women and infidels likewise rejects the idea of 'equality before the law'.

As for Europe as a 'beacon', judging by their choice of country, the only beacon most migrants are drawn towards is that of a free ride on the welfare states of Germany, the UK and Scandinavia. And data released in January 2016 showed that despite talk of tighter controls, an ever-increasing proportion of migrants arriving in Germany were from countries that in no way can be described as war zones. In just one month, December 2015, 2,300 Algerians and 3,000 Moroccans applied for asylum, compared with 4,000 from the two countries in the whole of 2014. The two questions that have to be asked and answered are, firstly, given that their nationality was known, why were they not refused asylum and returned to their country of origin on arrival in the EU; and, secondly, why were they allowed to travel north from Italy, their country of entry in the EU, through Austria to be illegally admitted by Germany? As of January 2016, only 53 had been returned to their country of origin. This massive official encouragement of the abuse of asylum will for certain lead to its discrediting in the eyes of the public not only in Germany but right across Europe for the foreseeable future, which will be a tragedy for those whose need for it is genuine…exactly what the xenophobic right wants. Well done Merkel, well done Sharia left, well done *dhimmi* Stockholm Syndrome feminists.

Addenda

i

1) In a belated attempt to curb the surge in sex assaults committed by Muslim migrants, on July 7, 2016, the German Bundestag unanimously approved an amendment to the existing law relating to sexual assault, including rape. Hitherto, the relevant law followed the Old Testament principle that a woman had to provide proof that she had physically resisted her assailment. This is now no longer necessary. Sharia law requires the unanimous testimony of four reliable male witnesses that the woman (or girl) had resisted her rapist, while Deuteronomy Chapter 22 requires that in a city, a married woman must cry out and presumably

be heard, otherwise she will be stoned to death together with her rapist. If the victim is an unmarried virgin, the rapist is obliged to marry her, and pay 50 silver shekels to her father. However, Jews and Christians today neither approve of nor apply their rape laws, but many Muslims do theirs.

2) According to statistics released by Germany's Federal Criminal Police Office, migrants committed 142,500 crimes in the first six months of 2016, an increase of 40% over the whole of 2015, and at rate of 380 crimes per day.

3) According to former MI6 head of counter-terrorism Richard Barrrett, as of December 2016, there were in Germany 'hundreds of really extreme terrorists on the books. In addition to that, if you include all the Lander [states] in Germany, they have about 7,000 cases.'

ii

Unlike Germany, France is habituated to Muslim gang rapes, known in the trade as *tournantes*, or 'pass-arounds', which average between 5,000 and 7,000 per year. Even so, one case attracted much outrage, not only for the crime itself, but the leniency shown by the court to its perpetrators. In October 2012, two girls reported to police being repeatedly gang-raped between 1999 and 2005 by on one occasion as many as 50 young males in a Muslim suburb on the outskirts of Paris. When the case came to court, ten men were acquitted, and four found guilty, three receiving suspended sentences, and the fourth, one year in prison that he had already served on remand. All 14 walked from the court free men. In 2002, French and Arab feminists founded the movement *Ni Putes Ni Soumises* – neither whores not doormats - to campaign against Muslim gang rape, only to be promptly denounced, as in the UK after protests against Muslim gang rape in Rotherham, as Islamophobic by *dhimmi* feminists, male Muslims and leftists

iii

The 'night of the Muslim rapes' broke the spell of collective denial imposed on Germany by its political establishment in the wake of Merkel's illegal decision to invite into her country an unlimited number of Muslim migrants, irrespective of their countries of origin, status and motives. After nearly a week of self-imposed censorship, the press began to report the events and politicians confront the issues that millions of ordinary Germans had been only too well aware of since Merkel opened her door back in the summer of 2015, but about which they had often been afraid to publicly voice their concerns lest they be accused of racism or worse. For obvious reasons, when it came to silencing critics of Merkel's migrant policy, nothing worked better in Germany than the charge that it is Nazi to doubt the wisdom of unlimited Muslim immigration. Starting on January 1, 2016, that tactic no longer worked. A series of opinion polls charted an ever-growing majority of Germans who judged Merkel's open-door policy to have been mistake, and even amongst her own party's voters, a sizable minority who believed she should resign. What follows is a summary of some of the incidents in the month after the Cologne events that continued to force the question of unlimited Muslim migration out into the open, and public comments and official statements that reflected this radical change of mood.

January 1: The International Monetary Fund estimates that 2.6 million more migrants will enter the European Union in the next two years.

January 2: Fighting that breaks out among children as young as 11 at a refugee shelter in Stockach in south Germany is joined by parents. Seven people are injured before police restore order

January 3: The Chairman of the Bremen, north Germany, Police Union, Jochen Kopelke, says that migrants are attacking police with increasing frequency: 'The tone has become extremely aggressive; sometimes the police must apply massive force to get a situation under control.' Bremen Senator Ulrich Maurer says 'the excesses of violence against police officers show that these people have no respect for our constitutional order and its representatives.'

January 3: In one of many similar incidents, more than 50 migrants are involved in a mass brawl at a refugee shelter in Ellwangen, near Stuttgart. Migrants attack each other with fire extinguishers, metal pipes, rocks and stones. January 3: A leading German economist cites estimates that German taxpayers could pay up to 450 billion euros for the upkeep of the million migrants who arrived in 2015. If as expected a similar number arrive in 2016, in total, the bill would be in the region of one trillion euros.

January 4: *Der Spiegel* and *Bild* both publish a leaked report by a senior police officer that in the centre of Cologne on New Year's Eve, women were forced to 'run a gauntlet' of drunken men 'of a migrant background' to enter or leave the main train station. 'Even the appearance of the police officers and their initial measures did not stop the masses from their actions.'

January 5: Cologne Mayor Henriette Wrecker says: 'There is no [sic] reason to believe that those involved in the sexual assaults in Cologne were refugees'. Cologne Police Chief Wolfgang Albers says: 'At this time we have no information about the offenders.'

January 6: Former Interior Minister Hans-Peter Friedrich says: 'It is scandalous that it took the mainstream media several days to report on the sexual assaults in Cologne.' He adds that the public media were a 'cartel of silence' that exercised censorship to protect migrants from accusations of wrongdoing.

January 7: The charity Refugees Welcome Bonn which organised a Rhine cruise to welcome migrants to Bonn apologises to German female guests who were sexually assaulted by migrants on the boat.

January 10: Three teenage migrants from north Africa try to stone to death two transsexuals in Dortmund. After being rescued by police, one of the victims says: 'I never could have imagined that something like this could happen in Germany.'

January 11: A 35 five-year-old migrant from Pakistan (sic) sexually assaults a three-year-old girl at a refugee shelter in the Ruhr town of Kamen.

January 12: Following an interview with *Bild,* Christian Democratic Party politician Frank Oesterhelweg is met with outrage from political correctors when he demands that police should be prepared to use force to protect women from sexual assaults by migrants: 'These criminals deserve no tolerance, they have to be stopped by the police. By force if necessary and, yes, you read correctly, even with firearms. An armed police officer has a duty to help a desperate woman. One must, if necessary, protect the victims by means of force: with truncheons, water cannon or firearms.'

January 12: A YouGov poll finds that 62% of Germans believe the number of refugees is too high, up from 53% in November. Most of those opposed are women.

January 13: A 20-year-old Somali migrant is sentenced to four (sic) years in prison for raping an 88-year-old woman in the Rhineland town of Herford. In Gelsenkirchen, also in the Rhineland, four migrants attack a 45-year-old man when he tries to prevent them from raping a 13-year-old girl.

January 14: A Bavarian politician sends a bus load of 31 migrants on a seven-hour journey to Chancellor Markel's office in Berlin as a protest against her open-door policy. Merkel sends them back to Bavaria.

January 14: Unable to guarantee the safety of women revellers, city officials in Rheinberg cancel the annual carnival.

January 15: A 36-year-old migrant sexually assaults an 8-year-old girl in a park in the Rhineland town of Hilden. A 31-year-old Moroccan migrant is arrested after attempting to rape a woman in Dresden. Two women are sexually assaulted by migrants in separate attacks in Mainz. An African migrant sexually assaults a 55-year-old woman in Mannheim.

January 16: A 19-year-old migrant from Afghanistan sexually assaults four (sic) girls between the ages of 11 and 13 at an indoor swimming pool in Dresden. The migrant is arrested and then released. A migrant from Syria sexually assaults 12-year-old girl in the Rhineland town of Mudersbach. A 36-year-old migrant sexually assaults an 8-year-old-girl in Mettmann, near Dusseldorf.

January 16: A group of between 6 and 8 African migrants are ejected from a discotheque in Offenburg after sexually molesting women clients. They then ambush three people leaving the discotheque with metal rods, street signs and garbage cans.

January 17: Holger Munch, President of the federal Criminal Police, tells *Bild am Sonntag* that the number of crimes in migrant shelters has increased 'significantly' since 2015. Those most responsible are from the Balkans (sic!!) and north Africa, especially Algerians (!), Tunisians (!) and Moroccans (!). Most offences involve physical assaults, with a growing number of homicides and sexual crimes.

January 17: Berlin clergyman Gottfried Martens accuses politicians and church leaders (but of course) of ignoring the persecution of Christians by Muslims in refugee shelters. Christian refugees are facing 'verbal threats, threats with knives, blows to the face, ripped crucifixes, torn bibles, insults of being an infidel, and denial of access to kitchens because of their alleged uncleanness'.

January 18: A migrant from the Sudan who receives 300 euros a month in welfare payments drops his trousers in a Hanover street and exposes himself, shouting, 'Who are you? You cannot do anything to me. What I cannot get from the state I will steal.' Held for questioning by the police, he is then released.

January 19: A 28-year-old migrant from Iran (sic) pushes a 20-year old under an oncoming train in Berlin. The woman dies.

January 20: Male migrants invade female changing rooms and showers at two swimming baths in Leipzig. They then jump into the pools in their street clothes. City official try to supress reports of the incidents, but the story is leaked to the media.

January 22: A report is leaked to *Bild* that migrants are defecating in public swimming pools in the Saxon city of Zwickau. Security cameras film migrants harassing women in a public sauna and storming the female dressing room.

January 22: In Stuttgart, a migrant attempt to rape a 16-year-old girl, and four migrants sexually assault a 23-year-old woman.

January 23: Two migrants sexually assault an 18-year-old woman in Weisbaden, and a 35-year-old migrant sexually assaults a woman in a toilet on a train in Dusseldorf.

January 26: In an interview with the public radio station Deutschlandfunk, retired public media personality Wolfgang Herles reveals that public broadcasters receive 'instructions from above' concerning the reporting of certain topics:

> We have the problem that we are too close to the government. The topics that we cover are determined by the government. But many of the topics the government wants to prevent us from reporting about are more important than the topics they want us to cover. We must report in such a way that serves the European Union and the common good, as it pleases Mrs. Merkel. There are written instructions. Today we are not allowed to say anything negative about the refugees. This is government journalism, and this leads to a situation in which the public loses their trust in us. This is scandalous.

January 26: The Mayor of Freiberg, Dieter Salomon, orders police to crack down on migrants snatching purses and assaulting women in the city's clubs. Migrants are robbing women on the dance floor and raping them in cloakrooms. Club owners say the migrants 'know that nothing will happen to them'.

January 28: *Bild* reports that politicians in Kiel have ordered police to ignore crimes committed by migrants. Similar instructions have been given to police in North Rhine-Westphalia, where Cologne is situated, and Lower Saxony.

January 29: A vocational school in Hamburg cancelled classes for migrants after they sexually harassed dozens of female students.

January 30: A gang of Afghan migrants on a Munich subway train are filmed attacking two elderly men who try to stop them groping a woman.

January 31: Migrants deface more than 40 gravestones at a cemetery in Konstanz with slogans, among them 'Germans out of Syria [sic]', 'Christ is dead' and 'Islamic State'.

On January 1, the Minister President of North Rhine-Westphalia asked what he clearly intended to be understood as a rhetorical question, 'how could Muslims, who represent a minority, Islamise our society?' The events and facts listed above suggest an answer.

F 9 or 19?

References to Mohammed's sexual prowess are legion in the *hadith,* as are those describing his sexual relations with his last wife, Aisha, whom he married when he was 51 and she was six. As to the first, Bukhari 5: 268 records the following superhuman display of sexual stamina: 'The prophet used to visit all his wives in round, during the day and the night and there were eleven in number. I asked Anas, "has the prophet strength for it?" Anas replied, "we used to say the Prophet had the strength of thirty men".' We must assume that the need for relief from the burdens of leadership entitled the Prophet to exceed by seven the number of wives he permitted to his followers. Bukhari, regarded by all schools of Islam as the most reliable of all the *hadith* collections, says this of his sexual relations with Aisha: 'Narrated Aisha, that the Prophet married her when she was six years old and he consummated his marriage when she was nine years old, and then she remained with him for nine years [until his death]'. (Bukhari: *Book of Wedlock, hadith* Number 64)

With numerous other *hadith* collections telling the same story of a middle-aged man having his holy way with a nine old child, this was a challenge the Sharia left could not afford to ignore. So on September 17, 2012, the Islamophile *Guardian* carried a feature by the *dhimmi* feminist Miriam Franceois-Cerrah, the purpose of which was to combat 'Islamophobic' criticisms of Mohammed's sexual conduct by situating it in what she regarded as its proper historical and cultural context. Consequently, calling the Prophet a paedophile was a 'slander'. 'Aisha may [sic] have been young, but she was not young for the time.' Well, that's all right then. Slavery, torture, capital punishment, child labour and a lot else we, or at least most of us, now abhor was also the norm 'for the time'. See how post-modernist cultural relativism sits so easily with, and re-enforces, moral relativism or, as in this case, moral nihilism. This extraordinary article can be accessed on line, so I will cite only its conclusion. Having argued, without citing any alternative sources, that all *hadith* accounts of Aisha's age are unreliable, and that the consummation of her marriage could have occurred when she was as old as 19 (sic!!!), Francois-Cerrah nevertheless was prepared to claim that these very same unreliable sources mysteriously became totally reliable when they described their 'loving and egalitarian relationship, which set the standard for reciprocity, tenderness [sic] and respect enjoined by the *Koran.*' How naïve can one get? Since Islam teaches that Mohammed was perfect in all things, including the matrimonial, what else did she expect them to say? 'Egalitarian'? Could she be alluding to the verse (Chapter 4: 34) which says 'men are guardians over women because Allah has made some of them excel others'? 'Tenderness' and 'reciprocity', when the same verse advocates wife beating and Chapter 2, Verse 223, marital rape? Yes...they were normal 'for the time' too. And for many Muslim men, they still are.

G Under the Ayatollahs

'Those who know nothing of Islam pretend that Islam counsels against war. Those who say this are witless...I spit on the foolish souls that make such a claim.' Ayatollah Khomeini, *Islam is not a Religion of Pacifists.*

I

The Iranian theocracy is not only admired by the Sharia left for its resolute stand against the American 'Great Satan', and of course the 'Zionist entity' that it says it will one day 'wipe off the map'. Some of the Sharia left's most prominent representatives have gone beyond praise by actually serving as its paid broadcasters on Iran's English language channel 'Press TV'. Amongst those so honoured are, as of writing, the current Labour Party Leader Jeremy Corby who, in the year 2012, as an MP, registered four payments totalling £20,000, as remunerations for appearances on the State-funded channel. When these payments from the murderous theocracy came to light, Corbyn's cynical response was to quip that '£20,000 is not a lot of money'. Well, that all depends on one's personal circumstances. Corbyn is a multi-millionaire currently drawing an annual salary of £79,458 as an MP, £49,191 as Leader of Her Majesty's Opposition, sundry sums for extra-parliamentary engagements and activities, and an undisclosed income from two pensions. Being paid £5,000 a time for a four hour appearance on an Islamic TV chat show in a comfortable studio in west London, which works out at £1,250.00 per hour is, all but devotees of the Corbyn cult would surely agree, a different proposition to the pittance - at a rate of no more than 50p an hour, 2,252 times less than Corbyn's - paid to those workers who in the non-union sweat shops of Haiti, Bangladesh and Nicaragua, manufactured the Corbyn T shirts that selling at £10.00 a time, raised £100,000 to fund Corbyn's election campaign for the Labour leadership.

Interviewed on BBC TV by Andrew Marr on January 28, 2018, and asked about his employment by Press TV, inveterate liar that he is, Corbyn claimed that he had worked for the station 'a very long time ago', whereas his last appearance had been on August 12, 2012, even though he falsely claimed that he stopped working for Press TV when his employers violently supressed Iran's green movement (10,000 arrests and over a hundred killed) which arose in response to the rigging of the Presidential elections of 2009, the year Corbyn made his *first*, not last appearance on Press TV. (This is confirmed by his declaration in the House of Common Register of MPs financial interests) What was worse, Corbyn continued to work for the station even though in December 2011 it had been fined £100,000 and banned from broadcasting in the UK by Ofcom for screening a forced confession, extracted under torture, of an Iranian political prisoner. Useful idiot Corbyn's last appearance on the channel came *nine months later*, on August 12, 2012, and can be seen on YouTube. And what an appearance it was, shared with Muslim convert Lauren Booth, Islamophile Cherie Blair's sister. One of the topics discussed was a Jihadi attack in Egypt's Sinai that left sixteen police officers dead. Corbyn, in denial mode about Muslim involvement in an act of terrorism, predictably pinned the blame on

Israel: '...you have to look at the big picture [Always the 'big picture']. In whose interests is it to destabilise the new government in Egypt? In whose interest is it to kill Egyptians, other than Israel, concerned at the growing closeness between Palestine and the new Egyptian government?'

As we have seen, this kind of pseudo-reasoning proliferates on a number of Corbynista websites, where the hand of Mossad is detected behind every act of terrorism, beginning with 9/11, carried out in the name of Islam. Booth naturally endorsed the Jewish conspiracy theory advocated by Corbyn. The evidence which she presented for it was laughable: 'Would a Muslim go against his Egyptian brother?' To which Corbyn, warming to the idea, replied 'It seems a bit unlikely that would happen during Ramadan, to put it mildly, and I suspect *the hand of Israel* in this whole process of destabilisation.' (emphasis added)

Also to put it mildly, both Booth and Corbyn were talking bollocks, specifically, anti-Semitic, *Protocols* conspiracy theory bollocks. First, Booth's ludicrous claim that Muslims do not kill their Muslim brothers. In Egypt alone, in the upheavals which followed the so-called 'Arab Spring' that began in 2012, nearly 5,500 Egyptians were killed by their Muslims brothers. Taking a wider view, in the war between two Islamic states, Iraq and Iran, which began in 1980 and ended in 1988, the number of deaths...all, *pace* Booth, the result of Muslims killing their Muslim brothers...was in excess of half a million. Thousands have died in Afghanistan as a result of terrorist operations by the Taliban and clashes between the Taliban and government forces. In Yemen, a proxy war rages between Houthi rebels, sponsored by Iran, and government forces backed by Saudi Arabia. In Syria and Iraq, the death toll generated by the emergence of the Islamic State and clashes between a range of Islamic factions that have been at each other's throats for centuries runs into the tens, possibly even hundreds of thousands. The University of Maryland's Global Terrorism data base has recorded 167,221 terrorist fatalities between 2001 and 2015, 75% of which occurred in 25 Muslim majority countries. And so on. Yet Booth tells us that Muslims do not kill each other. As for Corbyn's claim that Muslims do not wage war in Ramadan, an Islamic website, *Muslimink*, proudly lists six battles that Muslims have fought in Ramadan, the first being the battle of Badr, fought by Mohammed on the 17th of Ramadan, (March 24) in the year AD 624, with the permission of a verse, so says his biographer, conveniently sent down by Allah on the eve of battle. Thus a precedent had been set and, being sanctioned by Allah, it is one which operates until the end of time. The practise has therefore continued into the modern era without any censure on the part of Muslims versed, unlike Corbyn, in Islamic law. For example, there were no Ramadan cease-fires in the eight-year war between Iran and Iran. But, Booth and Corbyn still insisted, without a shred of evidence to support their accusation, it had to be the Jews wot did it.

Was it for services such as this, telling lies about Islam and disseminating conspiracy theories about the Jews, that Corbyn, instead of being paid the normal rate of £500.00 per appearance, received *eight times* that amount? In the four years of his employment, 2009 to 2012, there were 2,204 executions in Iran, which works out at just over £9.00 per execution, probably more than paid to those doing the actual hanging. Nice work if you can get it, and the Parliamentary register of MP's financial interests, which I have checked personally, proves that Corbyn, avowed opponent of capital punishment, certainly did. (Corbyn asserted on Press TV in 2011 that he 'profoundly disagreed with the death penalty in any circumstances for anybody', but this was said in response, not to any one of the thousands carried out by his employers, but the US 'execution' of Osama Bin Laden, architect of 9/11.) Others hiring themselves out for their theocratic pimps include, as one would expect, the seasoned Sharia leftists Ken Livingstone and George Galloway, but also from the far right, Holocaust denier Kevin Barret, Jewish conspiracy theorist James Thring, the German neo-Nazi Manuel Ochsenrieter and Corbyn associate, Palestine Solidarity Campaign activist and Jewish conspiracy theorist the Rev. Stephen Sizer.

Corbyn's final appearance on Press TV in August 2012, did not bring to end his association with the Holy hangmen of Tehran. From January 6 to 10, 2014, he and his wife, together with a 'research worker', enjoyed the hospitality of the 'Iran-UK Parliamentary Friendship Group of the Iranian Parliament', jointly funded by the Iranian Parliament and the UK-based Iranian billionaire Ardeshir Nagashineh. A month later, on February 9, Corbyn addressed what was billed as a 'seminar marking the 35th anniversary of the Islamic revolution in Iran' at the Maida Vale Islamic Centre of England. Corbyn chose as the title of his address, 'The Case for Iran'. (see below for excerpts) As of 2009, the year Corbyn began his employment by Press TV, the official number of children awaiting execution in Iran was 137. A kinder politics.

The governing principles of the regime Corbyn was being paid to promote were clearly set out by its founder and, after the crushing of the Iranian left, undisputed ruler, Ayatollah Khomeini, in his *Green Book*, relevant excerpts of which are reproduced here:

> The leaders of our country [this text dates from the time of the Shah] have been so deeply influenced by the West that they have regulated the standard time of their country upon that of Europe...Greenwich Mean Time. What a nightmare! In the past century, during which European medicine and surgery have been introduced into Iran, our leaders have forgotten our traditional medicine and encouraged a handful of inexperienced young men to study this cursed European medicine. Today we realise that illnesses such as typhus, typhoid fever and the like are curable only by traditional remedies. [Like the quack homeopathic potions recommended by Corbyn...and the no less gullible Prince Charles.]
>
> The clergy must undertake no functions other than religious ones which serve monotheism, virtue, the teaching of divine laws, and the upholding of public morals. The army must also be under the control of the clergy in order to be efficacious and useful. We clergy forcefully affirm that refusal to wear the veil is against the law of Allah and the Prophet, and a material and moral affront to the entire country. We affirm that the ludicrous use of the Western hat [sic] stands in the way of our independence and is contrary to the will of Allah. We affirm that co-educational schools are an obstacle to a wholesome life; they are a material and moral affront to the country and contrary to the divine will. We affirm that Music engenders immorality, lust and licentiousness, and stifles courage, valour and the chivalrous spirit; it is forbidden by Koranic law and must not be taught in the schools. Radio Tehran, by broadcasting Western music, Oriental and Iranian music, plays a nefarious role by introducing immorality and licentiousness into respectable families...
>
> We see today that Jews - may Allah bring them down! - have manipulated the editions of the *Koran* published in their occupied zones. We have to protest, to make everyone understand that these Jews are bent upon the destruction of Islam and the establishment of a universal Jewish government. [like the Hamas Charter, lifted straight from the *Protocols*] And since they are a cunning and active people, I fear - may Allah protect us from it - that sooner or later they may succeed in attaining this

goal, that through the weakness of some among us we may one day find ourselves under Jewish rule - Allah preserve us from it!

An Islamic government cannot be totalitarian or despotic but is conditional and democratic. In this democracy, however, the laws are not made by the will of the people, but only by the *Koran* and the *Sunnah* [the traditions, e.g., the *hadith*] of the Prophet. The constitution, the civil code and the criminal code should be inspired only by Islamic laws contained in the *Koran* and transcribed by the Prophet. Islamic government is the government of divine right, and its laws cannot be changed, modified or contested. The Islamic government is subject to the law of Islam, which comes neither from the people nor from its representatives, but directly from Allah and his divine will [And this is 'democracy'?]...The Prophet, the Caliphs and the people owe absolute obedience to these eternal laws of the Almighty, transmitted to mortals through the *Koran* and the Prophet, which remain immutable until the end of time...the imam and the clergy have the duty to use the political apparatus to apply the laws of Allah to bring about a system of equality for the benefit of the people. Governing for them means nothing but pain and duty, but what else can they do? The rule of the clergy is an obligation they must fulfil.'

II

Iranian Nights

'Oh, Allah's Apostle! We get female captives as our share of booty, and we are interested in their prices, what is your opinion about *coitus interruptus*?" The Prophet said, "Do you really do that? It is better for you not to do it. No soul that which Allah has destined to exists but will surely come into existence".' Bukhari *Hadith*, Volume 3, Book 34, Number 432

'I drove them [captured female slaves] along until I brought them to Abu Bakr, who bestowed that girl upon me as a prize, So we arrived in Medina. I had not yet disrobed her when the Messenger of Allah met me in the street and said, "Give me that girl".' Salih Muslim *Hadith*, Book 19, Number 4345.

Both major branches of Islam, the Shi'a and the Sunni, seek, through the enforcement of Sharia law, total control over the lives of Muslims. This is nowhere more obvious and explicit than in the sexual act, the human activity that is in its very nature the most personal and private, or at least should be. That is of course why Islam goes to the most inordinate and extraordinary lengths to regulate it, and it must be conceded that Ayatollah Khomeini's *Green Book* admirably and appropriately rises to the challenge. What follows is a representative sample of the rules that the leading modern authority of Shi'a Islam believed were necessary to regulate human sexual activity in accordance with the will of Allah. Some the reader may find hard to credit. If so, then the full text is readily accessible on line in several English language translations. On a technical point: Sharia law divides human behaviour, all human behaviour, into five categories: that which is: Forbidden, Disapproved, Permitted, Approved and Obligatory:

If a man has had sexual relations with his wife during periods of prescribed abstinence, such as the fast of Ramadan, he must avoid saying his prayers so long as he still has upon him the traces of post-coital sweat...Sperm is always impure, whether it results from actual coitus or from an emission while one is either conscious or asleep, whether it is abundant or not, whether or not it results from sexual pleasure, whether emission is intentional or not....During sexual intercourse if the penis enters the woman's vagina or a man's anus [sic] fully, or only as far as the circumcision ring, both partners become impure, even if they have not reached puberty [nb re Islamic paedophilia]; they must consequently perform their ablutions. If the man thinks he has not entered the woman's vagina beyond the circumcision ring, ablution is not required. If a man - Allah protect him from it – fornicates with an animal [sic], ablution is necessary. If a sperm moves inside the penis, but does not come out, or if there was doubt about whether it was actually emitted, ablution is not required... [While defecating or urinating] it is not sufficient to turn one's sex organs away while facing or turning one's back on Mecca; and one's privates must never be exposed either facing Mecca or facing directly way from Mecca...It is recommended to urinate before prayers, before going to bed, before having sexual intercourse, and after ejaculating.

[Eating] the meat of horses, mules and donkeys is not recommended. It is strictly forbidden if the animal was sodomised while alive by a man. [sic] If one commits an act of sodomy with a cow, a ewe or a camel [as one does] their urine and their excrements become impure and even their milk may not be consumed. The animal must then be killed as quickly as possible, and the price of it paid to its owner by him who sodomised it... If one performs his ablutions after having ejaculated and one has a verse of the *Koran* or the name of Allah written or tattooed on his body, one's hand must not touch that part of the body during the ablution, but that part must be washed without being touched...If a man [it is always a man] becomes aroused by a woman other than his wife but then has intercourse with his own wife, it is preferable for him to pray if he has sweated; but if he first has intercourse with his spouse and then with another woman, he may say his prayers even though he be in a sweat. A man who has ejaculated as a result of intercourse with a woman other than his wife and who ejaculates again while having coitus with his legal wife, does not have the right to say his prayers while still sweating, but if he had intercourse with his wife first and then with a woman not his wife, he may say his prayers even though still sweating... [Obviously...anyone could have worked that out. Now it gets highly technical]

Sexual intercourse is a breaking of the fast, even if the penis enters only as far as the circumcision ring, and even if no ejaculation results. If the penis enters less deeply into the vagina, the fast has not been broken. If the man cannot determine with certainty what length of his penis entered the vagina, and if he has gone on beyond the circumcision ring [and only Allah would know this] his fast has not been broken. If a man has intercourse because he has forgotten he is in a fasting period, or someone forces him to have intercourse [sic!] his fast has not been broken. But if he remembers the fast while the sex act is taking place [hold it...I've just remembered...it's Ramadan!] or if he is no longer forcibly constrained [?] to complete the coitus, he must interrupt it immediately. [Sharia *coitus interruptus*] If a man during a fasting period masturbates and brings himself to ejaculation, his fast has been broken. During the time a woman is menstruating, it is preferable for a man to avoid coitus, even if it does not involve full penetration...it is also highly inadvisable to avoid sodomising her during this time...If a man sodomises the son, brother or father of his wife after their marriage [again, as one does] the marriage remains valid...A woman who has contracted a continuing marriage [Shi'a Islam in Iran permits 'marriages' as brief as a few minutes for the purposes of prostitution] does not have the right to go out of the house without her husband's permission; she must remain at his disposal for the fulfilment of any one of his desires, and may not refuse herself to him except for a religiously valid reason.

III

Filling the Vacuum

In the February 2009 number of the Socialist Workers Party journal *Socialist Review*, in line with the party's orientation towards Jihadi movements and the most resolutely anti-western Islamic regimes, it was argued that in the Middle East generally, and specifically Iran, 'Islam has filled the vacuum left by the bankruptcy of Stalinism and [secular] nationalism'. It therefore followed, the article continued, that 'any Left in Iran or the region must now relate to this reality if it is not to make the same mistakes'. I reproduce below the nature of this 'reality' the Sharia left now relates to, as described by one of its countless victims. Let the three doyens of Sharia leftism, Corbyn, Galloway and Livingstone, who have over the years served as propagandists and apologists for Islamic terrorism and theocracy, answer this question: *What has been the fate of the Left under Islam*?

> I have lived thousands of days in Iran when Islam has shed its blood. In the name of Allah, a hundred thousand have been executed in Iran since 1979. I have lived days when I, along with thousands of men and women throughout the country, looked for the names of our lovers, husbands, wives, friends, daughters, sons, colleagues, and students in the papers that announced the names of the executed on a daily basis. Days when the soldiers of Allah attacked bookstores and publishing house and burned books. Days or armed attacks on universities and the killing of innocent students all over the country. Weeks and months of bloody attacks on workers' strikes and demonstrations [nb]. Years of brutal murder and suppression of atheists, freethinkers, socialists [nb], Marxists [nb], Baha'is, women who resisted the misery of *hijab* and the rule of sexual apartheid, and many others who were none of these, those who were arrested in the streets and then executed simply because of their innocent non-Islamic appearance. Years of mass killing of youth that kept the keys to heaven in their fists during the Iran-Iraq war. Years of brutal assassination of opponents inside and outside of Iran.
>
> I, along with thousands of political prisoners, was tortured by order of the representative of Allah and *Shar'ia*. Tortured, while the verses of the *Koran* were played in the torture chambers. The mechanical voice reading the *Koran* was mixed with our cries of pain from the lashes and other forms of brutal torture. Thousands were shot by execution squads who recited koranic verses while conducting the killings, regarding as blasphemous those who were simply political opponents of the regime, the death of blasphemers is required by the *Koran*. They prayed before raping female political prisoners for the sake of Allah and in order to enter heaven. Those who were in prisons and not yet executed were awakened every day at dawn only to hear more gunshots aimed at their friends and cellmates. From the numbers of gunshots, you could find out how many were murdered on that day. The killing machine did not stop for a minute. Then, fathers and mothers, husbands and wives who received the bloody clothes of their loved ones had to pay for the bullets. [The Nazis also billed relatives for the cost of executions] Islamic Auschwitz was created. Many of best, the most passionate and progressive people were massacred. The dimension was and is beyond imagination.

Excerpted from: Azam Kamguian: *Leaving Islam and Living Islam*

III

Jeremy in Ayatollahland

'The Zionists are crooks. A small handful of Zionists, with a very intricate organisation, have taken over the power centres of the world'. (President Mahmoud Ahmadinejad of Iran, September 18, 2008)

Hundreds of celebrity pilgrims to Stalinist Russia, after being taken on the same conducted tour of Potemkin showpiece prisons, collective farms, industrial projects and other wonders of the Five-Year Plan, returned to their homes in the capitalist west convinced, in the words of one dupe, the American journalist Lincoln Steffens, that 'they had seen the future, and it worked.' For some two decades now, Islam in its most militant manifestations has replaced Soviet-style communism as the longed-for alternative sought by western radicals to what they perceive as the failings of western liberal democracy. And perhaps the prime example of our later-day political pilgrims is Labour Party Leader Jeremey Corbyn, whose admiration for the theocracy that rules Iran is such that he has over the years taken up paid employment, together with fellow Sharia leftists Livingstone and Galloway, along with a team of far-right anti-Semites, as a propagandist for the Ayatollahs on the London-based Iranian Press TV channel. As revealed in the *Daily Telegraph* of July 18, 2015, Corbyn's travelling and other expenses incurred in his trips to Iran have met in part at least by an extremely wealthy British-Iranian businessman (see below). This is in addition to payments Corbyn has received from organisations linked to the Iran-sponsored anti-Semitic terrorist movement Hamas which, as everybody by now should know, the Labour leader chose to call his 'friends'. He is also on record as claiming, ludicrously, that this same Jew-killing, homophobic, misogynist, genocidal, *Protocols*-citing collection of theocratic thugs 'is an organisation that is dedicated towards bringing about long-term peace and social justice in the whole region.' If the infinitely gullible Corbyn had taken the trouble to read the Hamas Charter, perhaps even he might have noticed that is dedicated not to peace, but to the destruction of the state of Israel and the extermination of the world's Jews.

In addition to numerous public speeches, articles in the Communist Party's *Morning Star* and statements in the House of Commons in support of the Iranian theocracy, the nature of the services Corbyn has performed over the years for the Ayatollahs is captured in one appearance on Press TV, screened in 2010. Corbyn could be seen responding to phone-ins by viewers. One complains that the BBC are 'Zionist liars' to which Corbyn replies that the caller had a 'good point' and suggests that the caller complain directly to the BBC. Another describes Israel as 'a disease' that the Arabs must 'get rid of'. Assuming, perhaps too charitably, that he may have wanted to dissent from such an opinion but feared that doing so could well have endangered his continued employment, because the destruction of Israel is the declared aim of Iran's Supreme Leader, Corbyn instead replies, 'OK. Thank you for your call'.

As it was for those millions whose misery, and even slavery Stalin's so easily bamboozled guests were never allowed to see, actually living, and dying, in Iran can be a very different experience compared to that of the likes of Corbyn, who on their fleeting visits to confer with and promote to the world the regime of their clerical pimps, only see what they are allowed, or want to see. They are unconcerned, because it is hard to credit that they do not know, that for every day they spend as propagandists for or guests of the Ayatollahs, it can happen that a dozen or more Iranians will die at the hands of the executioner, among whom there will be, as the account above and the reports below tell us, those whose only crime is their beliefs, their writings, their sexual orientation, their desire for the rights of labour, individual liberty and justice. It is not as if Corbyn is unaware of these abuses. However, his response has always been, as he explained to MPs in the House of Commons on January 11, 2012, that 'any change within Iran is more likely to come from internal opposition and internal organisation than from anything done from the outside or any outside pressure.' But that precisely is the point! As Corbyn knew only too well, the Iranian theocracy does not allow 'internal opposition' and anyone who attempts to create one is likely to be arrested, and possibly tortured and then executed. (For details, see the UN Secretary-General's report below.)

Yet on another occasion, he tried to convince sceptical MPs that 'a lively, if [sic] robust and sometimes very dangerous [!!!] debate is going on in Iran'. How can a debate be at the same time 'lively', 'robust' and yet 'very dangerous'? Let us recall that Iran ranks 150 in the world democratic index, and has by far the world's highest per capita execution rate. When it comes to Israel, which ranks 120 places higher, and executes no one, not even terrorists who kill its civilians, Corbyn tactics are reversed. Even though Israel's pluralist multi-party-political system does allow 'lively debates' that are not 'very dangerous', a free press and a legal 'internal opposition', including that of parties representing Palestinian voters, Corbyn has for decades been actively involved in numerous campaigns and with movements that apply 'outside pressure' on including not only boycotts (never demanded by Corbyn for any Islamic state, or any other for that matter, no matter how repressive) but the indiscriminate murder of its civilians, including children, whose aim is not not to bring about reforms within Israel, but its total destruction and the extermination of its entire Jewish population. Yet it is Corbyn who accuses the west of having 'double standards' on human rights issues.

Do not, then, expect those like Corbyn who make their subsidised pilgrimages to Iran to apply any 'outside pressure' on their hosts, as we were once invited to, and rightly, to Apartheid South Africa and the Chilean Junta. They see only the official Iran, and only meet with its official representatives. But the other Iran, the real Iran of Kurds denied their national freedom, of the torture chamber and the gallows, of the public hanging from cranes, of the compulsory hijab and the stoning to death of women who stray from the path of Sharia, of mobs chanting death to the Jews, of Iran's Supreme leader boasting of his intention to wipe Israel off the map within twenty five years, and who in 2016 on International Holocaust Day released a video in which he questioned whether the Holocaust was 'reality or not', of anti-Semitic cartoon competitions…righting these wrongs (if indeed wrongs they be), even though a 'very dangerous' task, is best left to Iran's 'internal opposition'. Neither should we expect Corbyn, when he mounts the rostrum to address Jew-baiting al-Quds Day rallies in honour of Ayatollah Khomeini, to speak of the Iran of the *pays real,* but only of the fake *pays legal* Iran of the political tourist and the hired propagandist, the Iran insulated from any criticism of its abysmal human rights record by the mutual protection mafia of its Muslim and other Third World partners in crime, who sit by rotation on the United Nations Human Rights Council, directing all their diversionary venom at only one state...Israel.

In February 2014, Corbyn was a guest of honour at a function at the London Islamic Centre of England celebrating the 35th anniversary of the murderous theocracy that today goes by the name of the Islamic Republic of Iran, and whose guiding principles, and some of their consequences, are contained in the previous three items and the two following. These are excerpts, with interpolations, from his sycophantic speech, entitled, *The Case for Iran'*:

> When the Director spoke in opening this conference, I thought it was a very interesting address, and it is one that I wish a much larger number of people in this country could have heard, because he was describing the history and traditions of Islam, but he was also describing the inclusivity, the tolerance and the acceptance of other faiths and other traditions and other ethnic groupings within Iran. I think that is something that most people in the West simply do not understand [If so, it is because they do not exist] ... Iran is a member of the United Nations Human Rights Council, which I also attend. Iran, like every other country, must undergo its universal periodic review, and I raised these [human rights?] questions with the [Iranian] Foreign Minister during our visit and the assurance was given that the full response will be given at the UN Human Rights Council in June [2014] as is required.
>
> [This is a pack of lies. The clerics who rule Iran have never in the past co-operated with UN in any investigation into its their abuses of human rights, and the Human Rights Council session of December 22, 2014, and UN Secretary-General's report of March 3, 2016, excerpts of which are reproduced below, make it clear even to regime stooges like Corbyn that they have no intention of doing so now or in the future. Corbyn surely also must have known when he made this speech that his Iranian friends would be given a clean bill of health by its partners in human rights violations sitting on the Council. (Examples of this practice are also reproduced below) The UN General Assembly and its General Secretary are however not quite such a soft touch. See below for details]
>
> The message I got from my visit was that Iran is a country that is strong, a country with the most amazing history and a country that has suffered very grievously during the Iran-Iraq war. [Initiated, as I recall, by fellow Press TV broadcaster Galloway's 'indefatigable' anti-imperialist hero and paymaster, Saddam Hussein] ...Are we to go down [the road of] yet more wars? [Jihad excluded of course] Or are we to bring up our children to understand our history, to understand the principles of Islam as one would the principles of every other faith? There is a commonality [between them] of humanity, of understanding, of acceptance.
>
> [Here I must interrupt Corbyn's homage to the Religion of Peace to remind readers not only of Islam's doctrine of Jihad and aim of world conquest, but of the well-advertised pledge made by Iran's current Supreme Leader' Ayatollah Ali Khamenei, that within twenty-five years, 'there will be no more Israel'. And it is indeed ironic that the anti-American Corbyn shares US President Obama's delusion that Islam embraces with the infidel or, to use the Arabic vernacular, the *kuffar* a 'commonalty of humanity' when the *Koran* not only says exactly the opposite, (16: 93, 49: 10, 32: 3, 3: 38) but on no fewer than six occasions, instructs Muslims 'not to take Jews and Christians as your friends'. There must have been many in his Muslim audience who knew that Corbyn was either lying about or totally ignorant of the faith he was extolling.]
>
> I respect Iran's history. I respect what brought about the revolution in 1979. ['understand' surely?] And I hope I understand the need and wish of the people of

Iran to have a peaceful relationship with the rest of the world.

[But that is not the wish of its rulers, who in addition to their long-standing support for the anti-Semitic terrorist movements Hamas and Hezbollah and intervention in the wars in Syria and Yemen, to complement their nuclear programme, are with Putin's help busily constructing long range ballistic missiles than will be able to reach the 'Zionist entity' and even the 'Great Satan', the United States.]

It was my pleasure [sic] to go to Iran and I am very much looking forward to returning, and I have been invited to go again to talk about British politics and all that sort of thing [sic]...Thank you very much for the honour of inviting me today.' [Applause]

Corbyn speaks of Iran's 'amazing history', though what he has to say about it is confined to those times and events in which the west, principally the UK and USA, were to their shame, ranged on the side of the Shah and the western oil companies against its people. Since Corbyn is a veteran leftist who writes for the Stalinist *Morning Star,* some, though not myself, might find it strange that in his entire speech of some fifteen minutes' duration, he had nothing at all to say about the 'amazing history' of what was once Iran's major left-wing party, the Tudeh, which in all but its name, was also communist. He could, for example, have made the telling point that it was his leftist comrades, not the Islamic clergy, that bore the brunt of the repression under the Shah's police regime, and that the clergy had collaborated with the CIA-sponsored overthrow of the leftist and secular Mosaddegh government in 1953, which it rightly saw as a threat to its power and immense wealth.

After the Shah's coup, again with the technical assistance of the CIA and the support of the clergy, the Shah's secret police, SAVAK, rounded up no fewer than 4,121 Tudeh Party militants. Massive protests in the west succeeded in saving the most prominent Tudeh leaders from execution, though the party was viciously persecuted and driven underground until the overthrow of the Shah in 1979. Naively applying the classic Stalinist strategy of the 'popular front', the Tudeh Party then sought an accommodation with the Islamic forces mobilised under the leadership of the returned Ayatollah Khomeini. The party was following the Kremlin line, now taken up by all the Sharia left, that by overthrowing the pro-western Shah, the 'Islamic Revolution' had ranged Iran in the camp of the progressive anti-imperialist forces. Be that as it may, along with the national minorities and other secular and western-oriented groupings, the Tudeh Party very quickly found itself under attack by the Khomeinists, whose objective was not the replacement of the Sha's police regime by a genuine democracy, but the establishment of a fully-blown totalitarian theocracy, one that by its ruthless suppression of all political opposition, rapidly proved itself to be far more repressive than the worst the Shah's regime had to offer.

Yet it is at this point, the post-1979 crushing of Corbyn's leftist comrades, that his 'amazing history' with the omissions I have outlined, stops, and it cannot be because he does not know it, but rather because of the audience he was addressing. If he was not such a wretched, craven opportunist, always telling audiences what they want to hear rather than what they needed to be told, Corbyn could have and should have related to his all-Muslim audience how their hero, the Supreme Leader Ayatollah Khomeini, presided over the arrest of at least 10,000 members of the Tudeh Party, followed in many cases by Stalinist-style show trials, tortures, forced false confessions of collusion with Zionism and the CIA, forced conversions to Islam and of course executions. The number of all leftist victims is known to run into the tens of thousands. None of this mattered to Corbyn, who was instead 'looking forward' to meeting again representatives of the regime that murdered them, and is still murdering them today.

But events have a way of exposing such dupes, if that, to be charitable, is what they are. First came one of Corbyn's other loves, the authoritarian regime of Venezuelan President Maduro, whose repression of demonstrators in the summer of 2017 protesting against the corruption, economic bankruptcy and electoral frauds he has inflicted on his people resulted in over a hundred dead and many more wounded and imprisoned. Then at the end of the year came the turn of Iran, with mass protests against the identical abuses of power by the clerical regime, with the same result, dead bodies on the streets, and mass arrests, followed in the Spring of 2018 by the killing of more than 200 demonstrators protesting against the bankrupt authoritarian regime of Nicaraguan President Daniel Ortega and his wife, Vice President Rosario Zambrano. And also, just with Venezuela and Iran, no protest from Corbyn. In the case of Iran, fronting for her boss, his Shadow Foreign Secretary, Emily Thornberry declared that the Labour Party could not condemn the killings or support the demonstrators because it was not clear who was wearing the 'white hats' (sic). And anyway, her master's voice argued in the classic cultural relativist manner, 'we can't simply impose our views on other countries'.

Yet the left once supported boycotts of South Africa to impose an end to apartheid did it not? No one would expect the Labour Party to 'impose' anything on Iran's theocratic rulers - how could it? - but simply to condemn their killing of unarmed demonstrators. But she knew she couldn't, because Jeremy was a friend and former employee of the regime doing the killing. Then on June 25, 2018, thousands took to the streets of Tehran to protest against the cripplingly costly foreign involvements of the Ayatollahs, chanting, not the state-sponsored 'death to Israel', but death to *Palestine*, and 'no to Gaza, no to Lebanon, leave Syria'. Corbyn must have been mortified, because here for once was a genuine 'stop the war', or rather wars, protest, directed against his former theocratic employers and terrorist 'friends'. Five weeks later, they were back on the streets again in cities and towns across Iran, again chanting 'death', not to America or Israel, but to 'the Dictator', Corbyn's former employer 'Supreme Leader' Ayatollah Ali Khamenei, and one of the targets of their anger not the US embassy, but a religious school near Tehran. Millions of young Iranians have had more than their fill of a clergy and religion that has nothing to offer them except repression and economic decline at home, and abroad, proxy wars with Saudi Arabia, hatred for the West in general and for the Jews in particular.

IV

I want a kinder politics

So said Jeremy Corbyn to the 2015 Labour Party Conference. However, his friends Hamas and Hezbollah would make an exception when it comes to the Jews, whom they are both sworn to exterminate. But what of his former theocratic employers? The answer is to be found in what follows, beginning with an article from the *Daily Telegraph* of January 4, 2001, entitled, 'Khomeini fatwa "led to killing of 30,0000 in Iran"':

> Children as young as 13 were hanged from cranes, six at a time, in a barbaric two-month purge of Iran's prisons on the direct orders of Ayatollah Khomeini, according to a new book by his former deputy. More than 30,000 political prisoners were executed in the 1988 massacre - a far larger number than previously suspected. Secret documents smuggled out of Iran reveal that, because of the large numbers of necks to be broken, prisoners were loaded onto forklift trucks in groups of six and hanged from cranes in half-hourly intervals. Gruesome details are contained in the memoirs of Grand Ayatollah Hossein-Ali-Montazeri, one of the founders of the Islamic regime. He was once considered Khomeini's anointed successor, but was disposed of for his outspokenness, and is now under house arrest in the holy city of Qom. Published privately last month after regime attempts to suppress it, the revelations have prompted demands from Iranian exiles for those involved to be tried from crimes against humanity.
>
> The most damning of the letters and documents published in the book is Khomeini's fatwa decree calling for all Mojahedin (as opponents of the Iranian regime are called) to be killed. Issues shortly after the end of the Iran-Iraq war in July 1988 and an incursion into western Iran by the Iranian resistance, the fatwah reads: "It is decreed that those who are in prisons throughout the country and remain steadfast in their support for the Mojahedin are waging war on God and are condemned to execution." It goes on to entrust the decision to "death committees" - three-member panels consisting of an Islamic judge, a representative of the Ministry of Intelligence [sic] and a state prosecutor. Prisoners were to be asked if they had changed their loyalties, and if not, were to be executed. Montazeri, who states that 3,800 people had been killed by the end of the first fortnight of executions, includes his own correspondence with Khomeini, saying that the killings would be seen as a "a vendetta" and would spark opposition to the regime. He wrote: "The execution of several thousand prisoners in a few days will not have positive repercussions and will not be mistake-free." The massacre, which came just before the Lockerbie bombing, were seen as a sop to the hardliners at a time when Khomeini was already in failing health and the battle for the succession had begun between fundamentalists and moderates. He died the following year.
>
> According to testimony from prison officials - including Kamal Afkami Ardekani, who formerly worked at Evin prison, - recently given to United Nations human rights rapporteurs: "They would line up prisoners in a 14-by-five-metre hall in the central office building and ask them one simple question, 'what is your political affiliation?' Those who said the Mojahedin would be hanged from cranes in position in the car park behind the building. He went on to describe how, every half hour from 7.30am to 5pm, 33 people were lifted onto three fork lift trucks to six cranes, each of which had five or six ropes. He said: "The process went on and on without interruption". In two weeks, 8,000 people were hanged. Similar carnage took place across the country. Many of those in the ruling council at the time of the 1988

massacre are still in power, including President Mohammed Khatami, who was the Director of Ideological and Cultural [sic] Affairs.

"The massacre may have happened 12 years ago, but the relevance is that these atrocities are still happening" said Mohammed Mohaddesin, the Chairman of the Foreign Affairs Committee of the Iranian Council of National Resistance, (NCR) the main opposition group, who was in London last week to present evidence to MPs. The NCR has prepared files on 21 senior members of the regime whom it alleges were "principal protagonists of the massacre" including Mr Khatami and Ayatollah Ali Khamenei, Iran's 'Supreme Leader', Mr Mohaddesin will travel to New York to present the files to the UN and call for a tribunal to try them for crimes against humanity. Mr Mohaddesin said human rights abuses were continuing in Iran despite the election of Mr Khatami, who "presents himself as a reformist".

V

Allah Rules OK

As we have seen, Islamic states such Iran, together with many other member states of the United Nations no less guilty of human rights violations, have managed to frustrate any effective indictment of or action against their crimes by participation in a mutual protection cartel operating within the UN Human Rights Council. However, this strategy does not work quite so well at the level of the General Assembly, where representation is more diverse and, with a large number of western states committed to liberal democracy, not so easily either intimidated or manipulated. Even so, just in 2015, Israel was condemned 20 times, all but five in matters relating to the Palestinian issue, and nearly always by huge majorities averaging around 150. In the same year, the General Assembly recorded only *three* other votes critical of member states: Iran, where the voting was 81 for, 37 against and 67 abstentions, Syria, 104, for, 13 against and 47 abstentions, and North Korea, 119 for, against 19 (sic!!!) and 48 abstentions. If all we had to go on were these results, we would have to conclude that the Jews of Israel are by far the biggest criminals on this planet, being responsible for nearly 90% of all its human rights abuses, twenty time worse even than North Korea where human rights are non-existent, and the regime of Syria's Bashar al-Assad, which in 2015 killed 200,000 of its own people and drove out millions of others as refugees. And even here, 61 members found themselves unable to condemn these unprecedented crimes. As for other states where rights are abused as a matter of course on a daily basis, such as Saudi Arabia, China, Russia and its client states, and by a host of other similarly repressive regimes...nothing. In fact, they are the ones setting the pace for the onslaught on Israel.

However, because the UN General Assembly ranks above the Human Rights Council, and its Secretary-General therefore not only acts and speaks on behalf of the higher body, but is also empowered to ensure that the subordinate Human Rights Council carries out its duties objectively, and has the right to take to task any member state of the UN that fails to respond positively to demands for information or action in connection with human rights issues, this has resulted in Iran finding itself in the unaccustomed situation for an Islamic regime of being held to account for its notorious human rights abuses, even if only by a minority vote. Contrary to the lie told by Corbyn that Iran honours its duty to comply with UN Human Rights investigations and recommendations, this is of course what its clerical rulers, safe in the knowledge that no punitive measures will ensue, has consistently failed to do, as the report cited below proves beyond all doubt. On December 7, 1984 Iran's representative to the UN General Assembly, Rajaie-Khorassani, explained why:

> Iran recognises no authority or power but that of Almighty God and no legal tradition apart from Islamic law…declarations and resolutions or decisions of international organisations which are contrary to Islam have no validity in the Islamic Republic of Iran…The Universal Declaration of Human Rights, which represents a secular understanding of the Judeo-Christian tradition, cannot be implemented by Muslims and does not accord with the system of values recognised by the Islamic Republic of Iran. Iran will therefore not hesitate [nb] to violate [nb] its provisions, since it has to choose between violating the divine law and violating secular conventions.

One of the tragic consequences of this quite open flouting of human rights as defined by the United Nations is Iran's legalisation of paedophilia. Even though having signed in 1994 the UN Convention on Rights of the Child, in which a child is defined as 'a human being below the age of eighteen years', Iran's clerical rulers have since the Islamic Revolution of 1979 enforced a law legalising marriage for females at the age of nine, this being the same age that all Islamic sources state Mohammed consummated his marriage to his last wife Aisha, whom he married when she was six years of age. Child marriages in Iran are on the rise, in 2016 accounting for 24% of all marriages, more than double the rate of a few years previously.

The following excerpts are taken from a lengthy report by the UN Secretary General on the human rights situation in Iran, submitted to the Human Rights Council after Iran's failure, *pace* Corbyn, to comply with repeated requests by the General Assembly to cease a large number of human rights abuses. Dated March 3, 2016, the Report followed on from *non-binding* resolutions adopted by the UNs' so-called Third Committee, 'on the human rights situation in Iran', which were adopted as far back as October 27, 2011. They called on Iran 'to positively avail itself of the opportunity to co-operate fully with the Special Rapporteur and other human rights mechanisms, including by allowing the Special Rapporteur unfettered access to the country to carry out his mandate' so that 'credible and independent investigations of all human rights violations can be conducted'. This access was of course denied. What a farce! Sharia leftist pilgrims and propagandists are made welcome and financially rewarded by those who perpetrate and then lie about these crimes, while the denial of UN access to their victims goes unpunished. It is indicative of the reluctance of many UN member states to investigate Iran's notorious human rights abuses that when put to the vote at the General Assembly in 2011, the resolution, which bear in mind was anyway 'non-binding', secured the support of considerably less than half of the UN's total membership, 86 votes, with 32 (the Islamic bloc) voting against and 75 either abstaining or not voting at all. Six year on, and with still no reply from the Ayatollahs, the UN Secretary General felt it was time to give Corbyn's torturer friends a gentle tap on the wrist.

Report of the Secretary-General on the situation of human rights in Iran. (Excerpts)

I. Introduction

3. Since the submission of the report of the Secretary-General to the 70th session of the General Assembly [September 2015] the application of the death penalty persisted at an alarmingly high rate, including in relation to drug-related crimes, and with regard to juveniles. Corporal punishment, including amputation, flogging and forced blinding [sic!!!], was applied against individuals in detention.

4. The crackdown on journalists, human rights defenders, in particular women human rights offenders, intensified, with a large number of individuals arrested, detained and persecuted for the mere and peaceful exercise of their profession or their legitimate rights to freedom of expression and association. No improvement was observed regarding the situation of religious and ethnic minorities, who remain subjected to restrictions. [Contrary to the claim Corbyn made in his Address] Women and girls continue to face discrimination in the areas of marriage, employment and political participation.

II. Overview of the human rights situation in the Islamic Republic of Iran

A. The death penalty. [Corbyn is on record as saying 'I profoundly disagree with the death penalty in any circumstances for anybody' but, so far as I am aware, has never publicly protested its use in Iran.]
 6. The Secretary-General remains alarmed at the staggering rate of executions carried out in Iran. At least 900 executions including women [only when they are flogged, stoned or on the gallows are they equal to men] and children [but surely only Jews kill children?] were reportedly recorded in 2015, with some sources suggesting the figure to be as high as over 1,000, confirming a consistent pattern since 2005...On 26 June 2015 alone, 25 individuals were executed in Rajai Shahr prison.
 8. Executions for drug-related offences, which amount to a violation of international law [but remember that in Iran as in other Islamic states, Allah's law trumps all others] account for over 60% of all executions in Iran. These executions are often carried after trials that do not meet international fair trial standards.
 10. In 2015, at least eight political prisoners were executed for charges such as taking up arms for terrorism and disruption of public safety [sic] and several others were handed down the death penalty for politically motivated charges. On 4 March 2015, six individuals including Hamed Ahmadi, Kamal Malaee, Jahngir Dehghani and Jamshed Dehghani, all members of the Kurdish community, were executed on charges of *Moharebeh* and *Mofsid fil Arz,* corruption on earth. [That is, on theological grounds]
 11. Furthermore, on 5 August, the High Commissioner and a group of Special Procedures mandate holders separately expressed serious concern at the imposition of the death penalty on Mohammed Ali Taheri, the founder of a spiritual movement, writer and practitioner of alternative medicine theories used in Iran and abroad...Shahram Ahmadi, a religious activist promoting Sunni belief [there's the rub] by distributing books and leaflets, was arrested on 26 April 2009 and sentenced to death in early 2015...He was held in solitary confinement for 33 months and

subjected to beatings, psychological attacks, and exposure to extreme cold. Mr Ahmadi was forced to sign a blank paper on which revolutionary guards later reportedly composed a confession. [Is this what Corbyn had in mind when in his address he praised Islam's 'inclusivity, tolerance and the acceptance of other faiths'?]

12. The Secretary-General notes with concern that the practice of public executions continued despite their dehumanising, cruel, inhuman and degrading nature on the victims and on observers. At least 47 individuals were publicly executed in 2015. Despite statements to the contrary by the Government, photos taken at the scene demonstrate that children are often present at these events.

13. On 16 December 2015, several Special Procedures mandate holders expressed outrage at the executions, on 6 and 13 October, of two juvenile offenders. The Special Rapporteur on summary executions described these executions as unlawful killings by the State, comparing them with murders performed by individuals. Underlining that executing a juvenile offender, especially after a questionable trial, directly contravenes international human rights law, the Special Rapporteur urged the Government of Iran to immediately stop killing children…On 25 November, according to a semi-official Iranian news outlet, Mr Alireza, a juvenile offender was sentenced to death for the murder of his friend on 30 October 2008, these cases bring to four the number of confirmed juvenile executions in Iran in 2015.

B: Torture, inhuman or degrading treatment and punishment

16 The Secretary-General remains concerned about the persistent practice of corporal punishment, such as amputation of limbs, blinding and flogging. The Islamic Penal Code, which came into force in June 2013, recognises corporal punishment, including limb amputations, flogging and stoning.

17. At least 21 cases of corporal punishment were reported in 2015, including three cases of forceful blinding, five cases of amputation of limbs, one stoning to death and 12 cases of flogging in public. On 13 December 2015, Iranian media reported that a woman convicted of adultery was sentenced to death by stoning in Gilan province.

18. The Secretary General regrets [sic] the Government' refusal to accept all the recommendations concerning torture and other cruel, inhuman or degrading punishment. [It has rejected] recommendations to outlaw inhuman corporal punishments, revoke all laws that allow corporal punishment of children, and investigate and prosecute all those responsible for ill-treatments or abuse of detainees. The Government also rejected recommendations to ratify the Convention against Torture and Other Cruel, Inhuman or Degrading Punishment and its Optional Protocol.

19. The persistence of torture and other cruel, inhuman or degrading punishment in various places of detention and prisons also remains of serious concern. Beatings, stress positions, denial of medical attention and prolonged solitary confinement are among commonly applied methods of ill-treatment. Such treatment appears to mainly affect human rights defenders, journalists, social activists, political activists, members of some religious groups and individuals associated with some minority groups.

20. Between January and November 2015, several procedures transmitted 14

communications to the Government of Iran concerning prolonged solitary confinements, forced confessions, flogging, amputations, blindings, virginity tests (also referred to as virginity examinations), pregnancy tests and lack of medical attention to prisoners. For instance, on 13 September 2015, Shahrokh Zamani, a labour rights activist, reportedly died of a stroke in Rajai Shahr prison…The denial of health care, along with severely overcrowded and unsanitary conditions and deficient food, are believed to have caused his death. [How fitting that in the same week that Corbyn the internationalist is elected Leader of the UK's Labour Party, his pimps in Tehran preside over the death of an Iranian labour activist. Three years later, on the eve of another Labour Party Conference, an Iranian court sentenced to 74 lashes and ten years in prison the trade union activist Mohammed Habibi for taking part in a peaceful anti-government protest.]

21. On 10 January 2015, Atena Farghdani a peaceful activist and artist, was arrested and beaten in front of her parents and later in front of a court judge. In June 2015, she received a sentence of 12 years and 6 months' imprisonment. While in prison, she was reportedly subject to torture, sexual harassment and degrading detention conditions…On 14 October 2015, Fatemeh Ekhtesari, a prominent poet, was sentenced to nine years and 6 months of imprisonment on charges of 'insulting the sacred', 'publishing unauthorized content in cyberspace' and 'propaganda against the state' for the publication of a collection of poetry online entitled 'A Feminist Discussion before Boiling the Potatoes'.

C. Restrictions to freedom of opinion and expression.

[Readers will recall that in 2006, Corbyn was a *kuffar* useful idiot speaker at a Muslim rally held in Trafalgar Square to protest against the publication of the Danish cartoons. In the course of his speech he called in effect for the censoring of adverse comments on religion, with his declaration, 'we demand that respect be shown for all faiths' Such calls are redundant in Iran, where the theocracy ruthlessly controls not only comment on religion, but on just about everything else.]

24. The Secretary-General is particularly concerned about the crackdown on journalists and social media activists ahead of the parliamentary elections scheduled for 26 February 2016. [In which to be allowed to run for office, as in all other elections, all candidates require the approval of the Guardian Council, whose members are in turn selected by the Supreme Spiritual Leader, Ayatollah Ali Khamenei.] On 2 November 2014, five journalists were reportedly arrested by Revolutionary Guards in Tehran on suspicion of taking part in an 'infiltration network' 'seeking to influence public opinion' [something Corbyn is paid to do with impunity in the imperialist west] and undermine the Islamic Republic on behalf of western governments.

25. Iran has one the highest number of journalists and social media activists in detention, with at least 45 being held for their peaceful activities.

26. On 14 October 2015, the Revolutionary Court in Tehran sentenced Mehdi Mousasi, a poet, to 11 years of imprisonment and 99 lashes on charges of 'insulting the sacred' due to the social criticism expressed in his poetry. The convictions were reportedly based on forced confessions…He refuted the charges against him during his trial.

27. The authorities continued to filter and block social media websites, such as

Facebook [used by Corbyn], YouTube, [ditto] Twitter, [ditto] Viber, Tango, WhatsApp [ditto] and Instagram [ditto]…On 20 October, 2015, the Chief Executive Officer of the instant messaging service Telegram, Mr. Pavel Durov, affirmed publicly that the Government [of Iran] has asked the company to spy on its users in Iran. On 15 November 2015, the administrators of more than 20 groups on Telegram were arrested for spreading 'immoral content'…In September 2015, 11 individuals were also arrested in relation to jokes circulated on social media that were deemed offensive to the former Supreme Leader, Ayatollah Khomeini. [A sure indicator of totalitarianism, as it was under Hitler and Stalin.]

D. Rights to freedoms of association and peaceful assembly

28. The Secretary-General deplores the Government's refusal to accept the recommendations that it received during the second cycle of Iran's UPR to 'repeal all legal provisions that infringe the freedoms of peaceful assembly and association.

['UPR' refers to a series of recommendations made to the Iranian government in relation to its failure to respect the above and other human rights. Given that the state under review was Iran, as one would expect, the recommendations only had the endorsement of western, liberal democratic states, including Belgium, Canada, the Czech Republic, Finland, Germany, Netherlands, the UK, Norway and the Great Satan, the USA. The minutes of the session of the UN Human Rights Council which convened on December 22, 2014, to debate the recommendations, illustrates how the Muslim Mafia goes about protecting its own. Rather like judges at the Eurovision Song Contest, where voting is mainly by religious and ethnic blocs, the Muslim Mafia, supported as is the norm by infidel regimes no less unsavoury, speaks with one voice, usually by pre-arrangement, with each delegation focusing on issues designed to distract attention away from the subject under review, which in this case, was Iran's stubborn and long-standing refusal to comply with repeated requests to end, or at the very least, reduce those practices that are in conflict with the UN Universal Declaration of Hunan Rights of 1948.

Reading the report, it is as if the rival camps of democracy and Islam are speaking about two totally different countries. While the Spanish delegate voiced concerns about the 'continued use of cruel punishment' (as specified above), Switzerland's about the 'increasing number of death penalty cases' and that of the USA about the 'harassment of religious minorities and the detention of journalists', the Syrian delegation (closely allied with fellow Shi'ite Iran) 'cautioned against basing human rights reviews on 'confrontation, politicisation and double standards', while Yemen's 'commended the enactment [by Iran] of a number of laws aimed at supporting human rights'. Kuwait 'welcomed the measures taken on behalf of persons with disabilities' but had nothing to say about those caused by physical and mental torture in Iran's prisons. In all apparent seriousness, Qatar, whose own human rights record is not without the occasional blemish, 'commended the inclusion of human rights in school curricula and the organisation of human rights training for Government officials', without making it clear that like all other signatories to the 1990 OIC Cairo declaration, Iran's concept of human rights is defined by Sharia law.

It would be tedious to cite all the many statements made by the Muslim Mafia in support of Iran, since they all followed the same tactic of either diverting attention away from the subject under review, or re-cycling Iranian regime claims that there was no case to answer. Far more interesting is the support Iran received from the lands of the normally despised *kuffar*. Let us begin, appropriately in the circumstances, with Corbyn's Chavista comrades from Venezuela, who declared that 'unilateral sanctions violated the fundamental rights of the Iranian people', even though the proceedings had no bearing whatsoever upon the sanctions then being imposed on the Iranian government in connection with its nuclear programme. (BDS sanctions against Israel are another matter entirely.) Comrade Mugabe's delegation, like Qatar's, commended Iran for its 'organisation of human rights training courses for Government officials, the judiciary and law enforcement officers'. Putin's delegation 'noted the new laws to protect children', such as those that still permit their execution, while his neo-Stalinist colony, Belarus, faithfully echoing its master, 'noted the development of national institutions to protect the most vulnerable.' Yet another prolific human rights abuser, China, called for the UN to 'examine human rights in the country objectively,' that is, to believe what the Iranian government says, while one-party Cuba, another Corbyn favourite, 'noted the progress made by the country in areas such as health and education' but, like the rest of the Ayatollahs' infidel allies of convenience, had nothing whatsoever critical to say about the subject that had necessitated the review in the first place, namely, Iran's proven abuse of human rights.

Finally, we have two contributions to the debate issuing from countries that in almost every way imaginable, are diametrically opposed to each other. First, North Korea, which is officially an atheist state, the only one in the world, and where practising any form of worship other than of its Supreme Leader can have unpleasant consequences. Since North Korea shared with Iran the same principal enemy, the USA, or 'Great Satan', it was only to be expected that following the strategy 'the enemy of my enemy is my friend', the atheists of Pyongyang would follow the example set by other infidel human rights abusers by closing ranks with the theocrats of Tehran, commending Iran's 'achievements regarding economic, social and cultural rights'. But pride of place must go to *Dhimmi* Sweden. In 2014, on the eve of a mass Muslim migration that would find its Islamophiliac establishment in denial at its consequences, and the country's population finally roused from its politically correct stupor, few media outlets or anyone on the public stage would have dared to breath so much as a critical word against the Religion of Peace, Torture, Child Murder, Censorship, Public Executions, Floggings, Stonings, Blindings, Amputations and the rest. And so Sweden's delegation cast its lot with the defenders of the faith along with Mugabe, Putin, the Chavistas and Emperor Kim Jong-un in 'welcoming the President's commitment to reduce [sic] media censorship and promote a less [sic] security-oriented atmosphere'. This, from *Sweden*? Picking up where we left off, the Secretary-General's report continues]:

Between January and November 2015, the Special Procedures transmitted five communications to the Government concerning freedom of assembly and association, drawing attention to its international obligation to respect and full protect the rights of all individuals to associate freely, including individuals adhering to minority views of beliefs, and human rights defenders

29. Article 498 of the Penal Code imposes a punishment of two to 10 years of imprisonment for any individual who 'establishes or directs a group, society or

branch, with aims to perturb the security of the country'. [A catch-all clause if ever there was one. So much for Corbyn's 'lively' and 'robust' debate.]

30. The Secretary-General remains concerned about the large number of political prisoners, including members of political parties [mostly of the left be it noted] who continue to serve sentences for charges that are believed to be linked to the exercise of their freedom of association and peaceful assembly…In particular, the house arrest, since February 2011, of the two former presidential candidates and leaders of the 'Green Movement', Mir Hossein Mousavi and Mehdi Karoubi, remains of concern.

[In view of Corbyn's pronouncement, after two decades and more of opposition to UK membership the EU, that leaving the European Union would result in a 'bonfire of workers' rights', and his close relations of late with a number of left trade union officials who sit on the Labour Party's National Executive Committee, the following item is of special interest.]

31. The Secretary-General remains concerned about the ongoing ban on the activities of the Workers' Union and Teachers Association, whose members continue to face judicial harassment, arrest and prosecution for legitimately and peacefully exercising their right to freely associate and assemble. Teachers' unions were targeted in recent months for protesting against inequality, poor living standards and overdue wages. Some of their leaders have been arrested and prosecuted. [A list of such cases then follows]

F. The situation of women

[Islam is notorious amongst civilised people for its subjugation of women, and Iran lacks no zeal in that respect, as the following cases illustrate.]

35. [Iran] is not party to the Convention on the Elimination of All Forms of discrimination against Women.

36. The Secretary-General remains concerned about violations of the human rights of women including in relation to the freedom of movement, the right to health and in work. Following the adoption of the April 2015 Plan to Promote Virtue and Prevent Vice, [here as always since the time of Eve, blamed on women] strict and discriminatory rules on women's and girls' dress are being enforced across the country. On 15 November 2015, police announced that cars driven by women not observing the Hijab will be impounded for a week and fines will be imposed…On December 15 2015, the head of Tehran's traffic police was quoted by media stating that during the previous eight months, Traffic police had dealt with 40,000 cases of 'bad Hijabs, with vehicles seized and their owners brought before courts…The authorities stressed that wearing the Hijab was a moral matter and its imposition in public places is to maintain security. [sic]

37. There has been no progress in efforts to end child marriages. According to the Global Gender Gap Report 2015, 21 percent of Iranian women aged between 15 and 19 married as children…the legal age of marriage for girls is still 13 years old, as established by the Civil Code. The same Civil Code allows girls below the legal age to be married with the consent of their father or the permission of a court. In their comments on this report, the authorities acknowledged occurrences of

underage marriage in rural areas and noted that it is legitimate in some regions due to geography [sic] and sexual maturity. [sic]

38. Article 1117 of the Civil Code allows men to prevent their wives from being employed in the public and private sector if they consider it to be 'incompatible with the interests of the family or with his or his wife's dignity'. The Code also requires women to be submissive to men *and specifies that they may lose their rights, including to maintenance, if they fail to respond to the sexual needs of their husband.* [Emphasis added. Forget the pathetic Sharia stooge Corbyn for a moment, and ask yet again: Where are the feminist protests in the west on behalf of their Iranian sisters against a law that effectively upholds the Koranically-sanctioned right of a husband *to rape his wife*?]

39. The report ranks Iran 106 out of 145 countries in terms of educational achievement…In this context, the gender gap among out of school children of primary age is particularly alarming, with 63.3 percent of girls not enrolled in primary education compared to 35 percent boys.

40. Iran was ranked 141 out of 143 countries in terms of women's economic participation and opportunity, with unemployment for women reaching 19.8 percent compared with 8.6 percent for men. [As with item 39, these are of course official Government statistics]

VI

Equal…Under the Lash

In the religion so admired by western *dhimmi* feminists, when it comes to the law, in all respects save one, women are deemed to be only half as worthy as men. In the penal code of Jeremy Corbyn's former Iranian pimps, women achieve full equality with men only when they come under the lash, hanged or stoned to death. For example, while Article 75 specifies that 'if adultery is punishable by flogging it may be provable by the testimony of two just men or four just women', when it comes to the infliction of punishment for this crime, Article 88 states that 'the punishment for an unmarried adulterer or adulteress shall be 100 lashes'…exactly the same. The only gender variation allowed for in the execution of this punishment is in posture and state of attire:

> The flogging of an adulterer shall be carried out while the adulterer is standing upright and his body is bare except for his genitals. The lashes shall strike all parts of his body except his face, head and genitals and with full force. The adulteress shall be flogged while she is seated and her clothing tightly bound to her body. (Article 100)

When it comes to stoning, the same commendable concern for the modesty of the female victim is observed:

> The stoning of an adulterer or an adulteress shall be carried out when each is placed in a hole and covered up with soil, he up his waist, and she up to a line above her breasts.' (Article 102) Another variation arises due to biology: 'If an ailing woman or a woman in menstruation has been condemned to death or stoning, the punishment

shall be carried out. If, however, she has been condemned to flogging, the punishment shall be delayed until she has recovered or her menstruation period is over.' (Article 93)

The same equation of one man = two women applies even in the case of murder, which is not regarded as nearly so serious a crime as adultery or homosexuality, which carries an automatic death penalty: 'The blood money for second or first-degree murder of a Muslim woman is half that of a Muslim man.' (Article 300)

Likewise, for abortion:

Blood money for the aborted foetus which has taken in the human spirit shall be paid in full if it is male, one half if it is female and three quarters if its gender is in doubt.' (Article 487) According to Article 297, the blood money, or fine, for killing a man is set at the value of 100 camels, this being the same penalty incurred for irreparably damaging a man's testicles. Since according to the Sharia, a man's left testicle carries the seed for males, and the right for females (another testimony to the superiority of Islamic science over the inferior *kuffar* version) the separate fine for damage to just the left testicle is 66.6 camels, and the right, 33.3.

H Return of the Caliphate?

The fostering by successive UK Governments of a proliferation of faith schools has probably contributed more than any other single external factor to the increased segregation of Muslims from the rest of British society, ensuring as it must do that the children of Muslim parents will have ever fewer opportunities to encounter children from other cultural backgrounds. Ironically, this policy is one of the fruits of what goes by the name of multi-culturalism and promoting diversity. Let us be for once charitable and allow that that those who engage in this act of cultural suicide simply do not know or lack the capacity to imagine what it means to be ruled by Islam. Spain, which only finally liberated itself from nearly eight centuries of Muslim rule in 1492, has no such excuse. And just in case anyone had forgotten what Islamic Jihad is about, they were given a reminder when in March 2004, with a series of bomb explosions, Muslim terrorists killed 192 and wounded another 2,000 at Madrid's main railway station. In 2010, Spain's Muslims numbered just over one million, 2.3% of the country's total population. Even after discounting the impact of the surge of Muslim migrants into Europe since 2014, by the year 2030, the number of Spain's Muslims is projected to reach nearly two million, 3.7% of the total population.

As elsewhere in Europe, the vast majority of Spain's Muslims have shown no desire to integrate themselves into the host society, highlighted by their vast over-representation in crime statistics. Though comprising only, a little over 2% of the country's population, Muslims make up 70% of Spain's prison inmates, the highest percentage in Europe. Put another way, a Muslim is at least *thirty times* more likely to end up in jail than any other Spaniard. As of 2010, 42% of Moroccans, the largest Muslim group resident in Spain, were unemployed, double the national jobless rate. And of course, self-ghettoisation has proceeded apace, just as it has in all other European states with a substantial and growing Muslim population. In Salt, a township north of Barcelona, the Muslim population has reached 40% and is heading for a majority any time soon. Until it was exposed, a secret deal, agreed by a Socialist council blatantly bidding for the Muslim vote, would have allowed the construction of Europe's largest Salafist mosque, funded like so many others across Europe by Saudi oil money. Here in Spain as elsewhere, leftist politicians, unabashed to be riding on the backs of a brutal feudal monarchy, are likewise unperturbed by Salafist preachers publicly advocating the adoption, or rather in this case, the restoration of Sharia law.

Pending Sharia law's formal introduction, Muslims are enforcing it piecemeal. After failing to persuade Lleida city authorities to ban dogs from all public places as Islam requires, local Muslims took the (Sharia) law into their hands. In just one day, 14 dogs were found dead, believed to have been poisoned. In Tarragona, the local Salafi imam was arrested after forcing a 31-year-old woman to wear a hijab. He had threatened to burn the woman's house down for being an infidel. In order to avoid what the court called 'social conflict' (to be precise, Muslim rioting) the imam was cleared of any wrongdoing. In Barcelona, following the ban on bull fighting in Catalonia, Muslim leaders demanded the right to build a mega-mosque on the now disused Coliseum Bull Ring even though Spain already has well over 100 Wahhabi mosques with more, we can be sure, on the way. Wahhabi Islam is the warrior version dominant in Saudi Arabia and promoted worldwide by its mosque and *madrassah* building programmes. It should therefore come as no surprise to learn that when polled on the subject, 7 out of ten Muslims ranked their allegiance to Islam higher than their loyalty, if any, to their host country.

In the light of the above, one would expect public policy, in so far as it relates to the Muslim population, to be one of encouraging, especially amongst the young, a more positive attitude towards the society and culture of their host nation. One might reasonably think so, but one would be wrong. The entire thrust of Spain's conservative government educational strategy was in the opposite direction, one of using the school system to re-enforce what they already have drilled into them at home and in their 'communities', a policy that can only result in accentuating the already deep divisions that exist in Spain between Muslims and non-Muslims. As in the UK with its Muslim faith schools, but more systematically, the solution to the problem of Jihadi terrorism was to ensure that the young are force-fed with Islam 24/7.

In April 2016, Spain's Ministry of Education announced plans to spend vast amounts of mainly non-Muslim tax payer's money on a programme of Islamic instruction aimed at the children of Muslim parents. According to the Education Ministry, this programme would seek to stimulate 'interest in religious and cultural texts' and what it called 'curiosity' for the *Koran* in oral and written language. Pupils would be encouraged to memorise 'Islamic recitations, narration and descriptions', just as they do in Saudi-funded and pupil-beating *madrassahs* across the Muslim diaspora. So instead of special courses designed to acquaint Muslim pupils with the classic texts of western liberal and democratic thought, in the first place those of Salvador Maradiaga, an eloquent and tireless opponent of Franco's fascism, they will chant in Arabic hour after hour verses from a book that preaches contempt for women, hatred of the Jews, and the duty to wage Jihad against their infidel hosts. And it is this policy, claims Spain's Ministry of Education, that will ensure the defeat of Islamic 'extremism'! Perhaps in their eagerness to appease Islam, those who devised this policy forgot the stark warning of George Santayana that 'he who does not learn from history is condemned to repeat it'.

While in the UK, the Department of Education goes through the motions of checking up on what is taught in schools run by Islamic organisations, in Spain, even this pretence of supervision is to be dispensed with. Those who teach the curriculum of Islamic indoctrination, *in state schools, at state expense,* are nevertheless to be chosen by local 'Muslim communities', which in practice will mean their mainly Salafist clerics. The content of the courses, and the textbooks to be used, will also selected in the same way, and will need final approval, not by the Ministry of Education, *but by a Muslim body*, the Islamic Commission of Spain. Let me repeat, for this could well be the music of the near future elsewhere, here we have the scandal of public money, collected almost entirely from non-Muslims, being spent exclusively on Muslims, with private, Muslim, control over how it will be spent. And this is how: Pupils between the ages of 3 (sic) and 18 who undergo this course will be expected to 'emulate the values of Mohammed', many of which have been the subject of a critical evaluation in this work and should require no repetition here. Suffice it to say that should the project achieve this particular goal, it will have trained yet more generations of wife-beaters, thieves, liars, parasites, rapists, paedophiles, anti-Semites and Jihadis. Instead of being encouraged to learn about and appreciate the achievements of the country and continent in which they will grow up, without which there can be no prospect of integration, pupils will be studying the 'achievements of Islamic civilisation', specifically including the 1990 Cairo declaration of the Organisation of the Islamic Conference, which counterposed to the United Nations' secular definition of natural Universal Human Rights the theocratic notion that all human freedoms are defined by and subjected to Sharia law; exactly what Spain's Salafist clerics are demanding. As the old proverb has it, 'those whom the gods would destroy, they first make mad'.

I A Voice in the Desert

On two occasions, in 1991 and 2003, with scarcely a dissenting voice, throughout the West, the far Left mobilised to defend the fascist, genocidal regime of Saddam Hussein against invasions led by the United States. In a political re-alignment redolent of the Stalin-Hitler pact of August 23, 1939, leftists who up until the very eve of Saddam's invasion and annexation of Kuwait in August 1991 had denounced and demonstrated against the Ba'athist dictatorship's relentless persecution of leftists, Kurds and Shi'as, literally overnight began to hail this same regime as a resolute foe of western imperialism. Saddam's useful idiot George Galloway captured perfectly this slavish submission to the butcher of Baghdad when in the presence of his puppet and pay master, he was caught on camera saluting his 'courage, strength and indefatigability'.

As I have tried to demonstrate with many examples, the Sharia left's version of international solidarity almost invariably results in supporting any regime, no matter how reactionary or despotic, that finds itself at odds with the west. And this, as we have seen, is the official policy of the Stop the War Coalition, founded, and from 2011 to 2015, chaired by as of October 20019, the Leader of the Labour Party and Her Majesty's Opposition, Comrade Corbyn. As we have seen also seen, the same principle extends to Jihadist movements, especially those dedicated to the destruction of Israel and the extermination of the Jews. A necessary corollary of this orientation is that there can be no international solidarity of the traditional kind in support of internal oppositions to such 'anti-imperialist' regimes, for example, the Kurds, ('western pawns') secularists, cultural figures, leftists, labour and human rights activists and feminists. In the judgment of Sharia leftists, no less than that of rulers of these states, they are all, consciously or otherwise, by opposing the enemy at home and failing to see the 'bigger picture', simply serving the goals of western imperialism.

What follows is a broadcast on Lebanese TV that puts to shame those on the left who now and in the past have betrayed the cause of democracy and freedom for the Arab peoples by siding with their domestic oppressors. The date is July 31, 2005, at the height of the combined Ba'athist and al-Qaeda terrorist campaign to overthrow the democratically-elected government of post-Saddam Iraq, a war that despite its catalogue of appalling atrocities inflicted on the Iraqi people, the Sharia left falsely depicted and supported as a legitimate 'resistance' to western imperialism. The speaker is Sayyed Ayad Jamal Aldin, an Iraqi Shi'a cleric, secularist intellectual, member of the Iraqi parliament and anti-corruption campaigner.

> First of all, no-one can accuse me of sectarianism, because I support a secular regime which will fully separate religion and state. I believe that my freedom as a Shiite and a religious person will never be complete unless I preserve the freedom of the Sunni, the Christian, the Jew, the Sabai [related to Hinduism] and the Yazidi. We will not be able to preserve the freedom of the mosque unless we preserve the freedom of the entertainment clubs. The curricula, both the modern ones in some Arab and Islamic countries, and the books of jurisprudence and heritage, have many flaws that must be fixed once and for all. There are the rulings about *Ahl Al-Dhimma,* [rules governing the treatment of non-Muslims in an Islamic state] even if Allah be praised, no modern

regime can enforce these rulings. However, just for the sake of amusement and diversion, I recommend that the viewer read the books of jurisprudence and see how *Ahl Al-Dhimma* are treated. I especially recommend this to a people with a lust for Arab and Islamic history who claim that our history is a source of pride and that others were treated with kindness and love, especially Christians and Jews. [this is a very different appraisal, made from the inside so to speak, from Obama's "proud tradition of tolerance".] Among these rulings, a *Dhimmi* must wear a belt so he would be identifiable [like the yellow star worn by Jews under the Nazis]. Moreover, it is recommended that he be forced to the narrowest paths, and there are even jurisprudents who say that it is recommended to slap a Christian on the back of his neck so he would feel humiliated and degraded. This is how we harass him and then invite him to join Islam.

I can swear that the Prophet Mohammed is innocent of such inhuman jurisprudence. I challenge anyone among our people with a lust for history, to talk candidly to the west, to the advocates of human rights, and tell them that our heritage has such evils and flaws. We are a nation of blackout and darkness. [Not according to the anti-Orientalist Professor Edward Said] We cannot live in the light of day. We do not hold ourselves accountable. This is why America came to demand that the Arabs be accountable. We must have more self-confidence and be accountable before others hold us accountable. We must discipline ourselves before the Americans and the English discipline us. We must maintain human rights that we have neglected for 1,300 or 1,400 years, to this day [that is, throughout the entire history of Islam] until the arrival of the Americans, the Christians, the English, the Zionists, the Crusaders - call them what you will. They came to teach you, the followers of Mohammed how to respect human rights.

The Arab governments should support the Iraqi government, which was legally elected. I think this is the only government in our Arab region that was formed following free and fair elections. The Arabs must stop meddling in Iraq's affairs and stop inciting hatred, violence and terrorism. *They should not call these terrorist attacks resistance.* [emphasis added] There isn't any kind of resistance in Iraq, these are terrorist attacks under the guise of patriotism and of claims about defeating the occupation. They have nothing to do with the Americans or others. *They are scum, remnants of the previous corrupt regime.* [emphasis added] They attracted all the Arab terrorists, this riffraff, which entered Iraq in order to kill according to ethnicity. [Not according to Corbyn, who from the safety of London proclaimed his support for what he described as 'the resistance', 'engaged in a titanic struggle to rid their country of occupying forces'.

They kill the Shiites in public. We have not heard a single Arab jurisprudent condemn the terrorist attacks that target Shiites [nor a Sharia leftist]. We are killed because of our identity. They kill Shiites became of their identity and the killers are the dirtiest riffraff among the Arabs. Nevertheless, we have heard no condemnation of Al Zaqawi [Al-Qaeda terrorist leader in Iraq] and his followers. If we were English or Americans, you would see the court jurisprudents of the Arab regimes and all the Arab governments that stand behind them convene thousands of summits to condemn terrorism, but they remain silent about what happens in Iraq. [again, like the Sharia left] Moreover, we saw the President of a large Arab state say: "We call for national reconciliation", as though there is a real problem among the Iraqi people. There is no problem. There is the tyrannical Saddam Hussein regime, which is the only legitimate heir to the Arab and Islamic civilisation. [sic…what would the late Professor say to *that*?] This corrupt regime, which has been toppled, and on whose ruins a modern and democratic state will be established, this is not what the Arabs like. The Arabs want tyrannical regimes, in line with their backward culture. If we were English or Americans, you would see how the Arabs would raise an outcry over every [civilian] casualty. Today, dozens of people and children queuing in front of bakeries are killed and we hear no condemnation from any jurisprudent, quasi jurisprudent or any government.

What is happening in Iraq is a real massacre and a real war between truth and falsehood, between a democratic government that relies on the public, and the remnants of the Umayyad, Abbasid [early Sunni caliphates] and Ottoman tyranny. Iraq will be a cemetery for them and those behind them. The terrified and self-defeated Arab states who fear the establishment of a democratic regime in Iraq would prefer a stupid and reckless dictator like Saddam to a democratic regime in Iraq because the epidemic of democracy and the winds of freedom will reach them whether they like it or not.

J Back Channel to Allah?

In 2016, while several western powers, including the USA, France and the UK, conducted military operations against the Islamic State, two contestants for the leadership of the Labour Party advocated an entirely different approach. As someone who, when it is a matter of combatting Islamic terrorism, is invariably devoted to the cause of peace, the incumbent, Jeremy Corbyn, felt obliged to seek what he called a 'political solution' to the rise of ISIS, one that, in an BBC TV interview on January 17, he described as a 'back channel' approach to the Islamic State, leading to what he termed on another occasion as a 'peace process', analogous presumably to that negotiated between the IRA and the British government in the 1990s. His opponent, Owen Smith, favoured exactly the same policy, announcing in a televised husting on August 16 that the aim should be to get 'all of the actors' (sic) 'around the table'. In both cases, the assumption was that the Islamic State could be negotiated with, and would sooner or later be prepared, perhaps even obliged, to sit at the same table with those who are currently at war with it. This assumption in turn rested upon another, that the Islamic State was, for all its religious nomenclature, rhetoric and claims, essentially a secular political entity, and that its leaders were therefore driven primarily by worldly concerns.

As a corrective to this widely shared and dangerous delusion, and as proof that the Islamic State Caliphate was exactly what its leaders said it was, the instrument of Allah's will on earth, I have reproduced below an item from number 15 of the Islamic State's official journal, *Dabiq*, entitled, appropriately, *Why We Hate You, and Why We Fight You*. What they hated about 'us', that is, the infidel west, was not our foreign policy. As the article makes clear, this was the very least of our sins. The Islamic State hated and fought us because we infidels had refused to worship Allah and because we denied the teachings of his prophet. What our clerics, Corbyns, Smiths, Camerons, Clintons, Obamas, Merkels and Hollandes simply could not accept was that *this war was about theology, that and nothing else*. Of this issue's 80 odd pages, well over half are devoted purely to theology, the bulk of the remainder comprising accounts of various terrorist operations (a term they gladly embrace since it is in the *Koran*) against the enemies of Allah. There is also the by now familiar graphic depiction of a beheading, captioned, 'The Sword is Part of Allah's Law'.

No amount of searching for 'back channels' or tables to sit around was going to convince the rulers of the Islamic state, and those who had left Europe to kill and be killed for its cause, that they were in error in matters theological, and that Islam is a faith of peace, love and tolerance. And the same applies to all other Jihadi movements that fight for the same cause, Corbyn's Hamas and Hezbollah friends included. What they do is in accordance with commands inscribed in a thirteen-hundred-year old book they believe was transmitted from an all-powerful god to his last prophet, Mohammed, a god to whom his Muslim slaves are alone answerable. The mandate of the Caliphate that ruled the Islamic State did not come from those it governs, but from heaven. The terms that we in the west employ to conduct our political discourse, like freedom, democracy, accountability, either have a totally different meaning, or mean nothing at all. Instead, the reader will see that at every step, what the Islamic State did, and why, is purely religious in content and purpose, and justified and buttressed with citations from Islam's highest authority, the *Koran*. It therefore follows, as indeed the article states, that any negotiations with the Islamic State would have had to have been conducted on these terms, and these alone. What in the end defeated it was not Corbyn's 'back channel', but Kurdish bullets and Western bombs.

Why We Hate You and Why We Fight You

Shortly following the blessed attack on a sodomite Crusader night club by the mujahid Omar Mateen, American politicians were quick to jump into the spotlight and denounce the shooting, declaring it a hate crime, an act of terrorism, of senseless violence. A hate crime? Yes. Muslims undoubtedly hate liberalist sodomites, as does anyone else with any shred of their fitrah, (their inborn human nature) still intact. An act of terror? Most definitely. Muslims have been commanded to terrorise the disbelieving enemies of Allah. [The author of this text missed a trick here. He (it is safe to assume it must be a 'he') should have quoted at this point the *Koran,* Chapter 8, Verse 12: 'I will strike terror into the hearts of those that disbelieve'.] But an act of senseless violence? One would think that the average Westerner by now would have abandoned the tired claim that the actions of the mujahidin - who have repeatedly stated their goals, intentions and motivations - don't make sense. Unless you truly - and naively - believe that the crimes of the West against Islam and the Muslims, whether insulting the prophet or burning the *Koran* or waging war against the Caliphate, won't prompt brutal retaliation from the mujahidin, you know full well that the likes of the attacks carried out by Omar Mateen, Larossi Aballa and many others before and after them in revenge for Islam and the Muslims make complete sense. The only senseless thing would be for there to be no fierce, violent retaliation in the first place.

Many Westerners however are already aware that claiming the attacks of the mujahidin to be senseless and questioning incessantly as to why we hate the West and why we fight them is nothing more than a political act and a propaganda tool. The politicians will say it regardless of how much it stands in opposition to facts and common sense just to garner votes for the next election cycle. The analysts and journalists will say it order to keep themselves from becoming a target for saying something that the masses deem to be politically incorrect. [This is wrong. In fact, the reverse is the case. Living as they do in daily contact with, and now fear of Islam, the 'masses', who care nothing for political correctness, have a pretty clear idea of what the Jihadis are about. It is the politically correct establishment that has tried to persuade them, with diminishing success, that the real Islam has nothing to do with terrorism.]

The apostate 'imams' in the West will adhere to the same tired cliché in order to avoid a backlash from the disbelieving societies in which they've chosen to reside. The point is, people know that it's foolish, but they keep repeating it regardless because they're afraid of the consequences of deviating from the script. There are exceptions among the disbelievers, no doubt, people who will unabashedly declare that jihad and the laws of the Sharia - as well as everything else deemed taboo by the Islam-is-a-peaceful-religion crowd - are in fact completely Islamic [those we in the west condemn as Islamophobes] but they tend to be people with far less credibility who are painted as a social fringe, so their voices are dismissed and a large segment of the ignorant masses continues believing the false narrative. As such, it becomes important for us to clarify to the West in unequivocal terms - yet again - why we hate you and why you fight you.

1. We hate you, first and foremost, because you are disbelievers [so, not because we are imperialists]; you reject the oneness of Allah - whether you realise it or not - by making partners for Him in worship, you blaspheme against Him, claiming He has a son, you fabricate lies against His prophets and messengers, and you indulge in all manner of devilish practices. It is for this reason that we were commanded to openly declare our hatred for you and our enmity towards you. There has already been for you an excellent example in Abraham and those with him, when they said to their people, "indeed, we are disassociated from you and from whatever you worship other than Allah. We have rejected you, and there has arisen, between us and you, enmity and hatred forever until you believe in Allah alone." (*Koran,* Chapter 60, Verse 4)

Furthermore, just as your disbelief is the primary [sic] reason we hate you, as we have been commanded to fight the disbelievers until they submit to the authority of Islam, either by becoming Muslims, or by paying jizyah [the tax on non-believing monotheists] - for those afford this option - and living in humiliation under the rule of the Muslims. Thus, even if you were to stop fighting us, your best-case scenario in a state of war would be that we would suspend our attacks against you - if we deemed it necessary - in order to focus on the closer and more immediate threats before eventually resuming our campaigns against you. Apart from the option of a temporary truce, this is the only likely scenario that would bring you fleeting respite from our attacks. So in the end, you cannot bring an indefinite halt to our war against you. At most, you could only delay it temporarily. 'And fight the until there is no fitnah [paganism] and [until] the religion, all of it, is for Allah.' (*Koran,* Chapter 2, Verse 193)

2. We hate you because your secular, liberal societies permit the very things that Allah has prohibited while banning many of things He has permitted [such as slavery, wife beating marital rape, female genital mutilation and paedophilia], a matter that doesn't concern you because you separate between religion and state, thereby granting supreme authority to your whims and desires via the legislators you vote into power. In doing so, you desire to rob Allah of His right to be obeyed and you wish to usurp that right for yourselves. 'Legislation is not but for Allah'. (*Koran,* Chapter, 12, Verse 40) Your secular liberalism has led to tolerate and even support 'gay rights', to allow alcohol, drugs, fornication, gambling and usury to become widespread [but not slavery, marital rape, wife beating, paedophilia and female genital mutilation] and to encourage the people to mock those who denounce these filthy sins and vices. As such, we wage war against you to stop you from spreading your disbelief and debauchery – your secularism and nationalism, your perverted liberal values, your Christianity and atheism - and all the depravity and corruption they entail. You've made it your mission to 'liberate' Muslim societies; we've made it our mission to fight off your influence and protect mankind from your misguided concepts and your deviant way of life.

3. In the case of the atheist fringe. We hate you and wage war against you because you disbelieve in the existence of your Lord and Creator. You witness the extraordinarily complex makeup of created beings, and the astonishing and inexplicably precise physical laws that govern the entire universe [not 'precise', but unvarying], but insist that they all came about through randomness [not so] and that

one should be faulted, mocked and ostracised for recognising that the astonishing signs we witness day after day are the creation of the Wise, All-Known Creator and not the result of accidental occurrence [not 'accidental', but natural]. 'Or were they created by nothing, or were they the creators of themselves?' (*Koran,* Chapter 14, Verse 35) Your disbelief in your Creator further leads you to deny the day of judgement, claiming that 'you only live once': 'Those who disbelieve have claimed that they will never be resurrected. Say, "yes, by my Lord, you will surely be resurrected; then you will surely be informed of what you did." And that, for Allah, is easy.' (*Koran,* Chapter 14, Verse 7)

4. We hate you for your crimes against Islam and wage war against you to punish you for your transgressions against our religion. As long as your subjects [sic] continue to mock our faith, insult the prophets of Allah - including Noah, Abraham, Moses and Muhammad - burn the Quran, and openly vilify the laws of the Shari'ah, we will continue to retaliate, not with slogans and placards, but with bullets and knives.

5. We hate you for your crimes against the Muslims; your drones and fighter jets bomb, kill, and maim our people around the world, and your puppets in the usurped lands and the Muslims oppress, torture, and wage war against anyone who calls to the truth. As such, we fight to stop you from killing, our men, women, and children, to liberate them those of them whom you imprison and torture, and to take revenge for the countless Muslims who've suffered as result of your deeds.

6. We hate you for invading our lands and fight you to repel you and drive you out. As long as there is an inch of territory left for us to reclaim, jihad will continue to be a personal obligation on every single Muslim. [Here too, a Koranic citation would have been appropriate: 'Fighting is prescribed for you, and ye dislike it. But it is possible that ye dislike a thing which is good for you, and that ye love a thing that is bad for you. But Allah knoweth, and ye know not.' (Chapter 2, Verse 216)]

What's so important to understand here is that although some might argue that your foreign policies are the extent of what drives out hatred, this particular reason for hating you is secondary, hence the reasons we addressed it at the end of the above list. The fact is, even if you were to stop bombing us, imprisoning us, vilifying us, and usurping our lands, *we would continue to hate you because our primary reason for hating will not cease until you embrace Islam.* [emphasis added] Even if you were to pay jizyah and live under the authority of Islam in humiliation, we would continue to hate you.

No doubt, we would stop fighting you then as we would stop fighting any disbelievers who enter into a covenant with us, but we would not stop hating you. What's equally if not more important to understand is that we fight you, not simply to punish and deter you, but to bring you true freedom in this life and salvation in the Hereafter, freedom from being enslaved to your whims and desires as well as those of your clergy and legislatures, and salvation by worshipping your Creator alone and following His messenger. We fight you in order to bring you out from the darkness of disbelief and into the light of Islam, and to liberate you from the constraints of living for the sake of the worldly life alone so that you may enjoy both the blessings of the worldly life and the bliss of the Hereafter. [Again, one notes the total absence of any concern for what the Sharia left would describe as the 'struggle against Western imperialism'. The war is against our godlessness, which the Sharia left, for all its simulated enthusiasm for Islam, is guiltier of than most.]

The gist of the matter is that there is indeed a rhyme to our terrorism, [sic] warfare, ruthlessness, and brutality [sic]. As much as some liberal journalist would like you to believe that we do what we do because we're simply monsters with no logic to our action [and which therefore has no connection with the 'real' Islam], the fact is that we continue to wage - and escalate - a calculated war that the West thought it had ended several years ago. We continue dragging you further and further into a swamp you thought you'd already escaped only to realise that you're stuck even deeper within its murky waters…And we do so while offering you a way out on our terms. So you can continue to believe that those 'despicable terrorists hate you because of your lattes and Timberlands, and continue spending ridiculous amounts of money to try to prevail in an unwinnable war, or you can accept reality and recognise that we will never stop hating you *until you embrace Islam*, and will never stop fighting you until you're ready to leave the swamp of warfare and terrorism through the exits we provide, the very exits put forth by our Lord for the People of the Scripture: Islam, jizyah, or – as a last means of fleeting respite - a temporary truce. (emphasis added)

[Corbyn seeks a 'back channel' to the Islamic State, Owen Smith a place with it at the same table. My advice to them both is, mind you head.]

K Volunteers for Genocide?

For obvious reasons, estimates of the number of Arabs who have illegally migrated into Israel, excluding the 'occupied territories', since 1967, vary. All however agree that the number is at least in the tens of thousands, and probably higher. In addition, there are the approximately 70,000 Arabs who have returned legally since 1948 in accordance with Israel's policy of re-uniting families lies torn apart by the Arab invasion and ensuing war of that year, and those many thousands more who have in recent years taken up legal employment in Israel. There has also been a much larger movement of Palestinian Arabs from Jordan into the West Bank since it came under Israeli administration following the June of war of 1967. Again, accurate figures are hard to come by, since this migration is also mainly illegal, but the number is in the region of half a million.

All this must seem inexplicable to anyone who is gullible or prejudiced enough to take seriously the often-repeated allegation emanating from all quarters of the political spectrum that the Jews of Israel are set on a course of exterminating the Palestinians. Why risk the hazards and endure the upheaval involved in illegal migration only then to knowingly put you head in the Zionist noose? I say knowingly, because as we have seen, around the clock, 24/7, the Palestinian Authority and Hamas media, clergy and public institutions, in the first place, naturally, their partly UN-funded schools, from infancy drum into the brains of every Palestinian that the Zionists seek their deaths.

And yet they still come, while virtually no Arabs move in the opposite direction, fleeing to escape what their political and clerical leaders assure them is, according to the two versions, either an impending or actual genocide. (Arabs comprise barely 5% of those annually migrating from Israel.) It is as if millions of Jews, in the full knowledge that they faced near certain death in the gas chambers of Hitler's Final Solution, chose nevertheless to migrate into Germany at the height of the Holocaust. So why do so many Palestinians apparently prefer to risk an early death in an Israeli Auschwitz rather than continue to savour the many joys and blessings of life in the West Bank and the Gaza Strip? Let us attempt to answer that question with a number of facts.

Just in one year, 2015, 180,000 Palestinians crossed the border into Israel, not as illegal immigrants (or suicide bombers) but for treatment in an Israeli medical facility. In addition, there are many who also prefer to work for their Zionist enemies rather than their fellow Palestinians. Speaking on Palestinian Authority TV on March 16, 2016, the Palestinian labour lawyer Khaled Fukhi said the following:

> The Palestinians female workers in the Israeli agricultural sector enjoy many rights, like any Israeli worker in the agricultural sector. The salary is higher than the minimum wage, fourteen vacation days a year in the first four years, 2,000 shekels convalescence pay yearly, payment for holidays, whether Islamic or Jewish. But in reality, Palestinian workers - and especially the female workers - do not receive these things….The Palestinian middleman takes 50%, 60% and even 70% of her salary. If her daily salary is 180 shekels, in the end she receives 60 shekels…. Excuse the word steals, but that is the exact word.

On February 4, 2016, speaking on the same TV channel, Qassem Abu Hadwah, a labourer from Hebron said the following:

> The lack of monitoring of Palestinian owners or companies and factories and their exploitation of workers is what has forced people to Israel…If only the salary in the Palestinian Authority was at least half of the salary in Israel, no one would work in Israel. However, workers have to go to Israel, because no one in the PA gives them what they deserve for their work.

According to the official PA daily, *Al-Hayat Al-Jadida*, of February 26, 2016, 'the average daily wage for employees in the West Bank was 94.1 shekels, and 61.9 shekels in the Gaza Strip, while the average wage for employees in Israel and the [Jewish] settlements is 198.9 shekels' and 'the number of [Palestinian] workers from the West Bank who work in Israel and the [Jewish] settlements reached 112,300.' As of 2018, the unemployment rate in the West Bank was 18%, Gaza 52%, and Israel, 3.6%.

L Jihad

There is an historic precedent for the failure of western politicians, academics, journalists and other opinion formers to fully comprehend, and therefore to effectively resist the gathering threat to modern civilisation posed by Islam. Whether it was the extermination of the Jews, crushing the left, war in the East for *Lebensraum*, or reversing the Treaty of Versailles, Hitler never made any secret of his strategic aims, which were first set out systematically and at some length in 1925 in his *Mein Kampf* and subsequently in innumerable public speeches. On the sixth anniversary of Hitler's appointment as Chancellor on January 30, 1933, he announced to the world what his plan was for the Jews:

> If the Jewish financiers in and outside Europe should succeed once in plunging the nations once more into a world war, the result will not be the Bolshevisation of the earth, and thus the victory of Jewry, but the annihilation of the Jewish race in Europe.

On January 30, 1941, Hitler repeated this threat, but minus the reference to the 'Bolshevisation of the earth,' out of deference to his Bolshevik colleagues in the Kremlin, together with whom he, and not 'Jewish financiers' had launched the Second World by conquering and partitioning Poland. In these speeches, Hitler could not have made his intention to go to war and exterminate European Jewry any clearer. Yet hardly anyone took him seriously, least of all those whom he threatened, in the first place the Jews, or those who had to the power to prevent him carrying out his programme. In the latter case, this was due not so much to stupidity or gullibility, though there was that in plenty, but a lack of imagination or, if you will, to wishful thinking, the false assumption that modern politics would always be played according to the same set of rules by all its participants - hence, for example the Geneva Convention and the League of Nations.

Today, exactly the same mind set is preventing the West, with its declarations, conventions and courts of Human Rights,(each of which are rejected by all 57 Islamic states) from properly comprehending, and therefore combatting, the Jihad being waged against the liberal democracies by Islam, even though, just like Hitler's speeches, its founding text, readily available in all the world's major languages, makes no attempt conceal its objective of world conquest. For example, the genocidal intentions of Hamas and Hezbollah towards the Jews are no less specific than were those of Hitler, but this has not prevented Corbyn from emulating Chamberlain by praising them as movements dedicated to the cause of 'peace', 'understanding' and' dialogue'. Likewise, the faith that inspires these two terrorist organisations is not only assumed to be a religion just like any other, but even depicted, in defiance of its declared aims and methods to achieve them, as 'a (sometimes even 'the') religion of peace'. But then did not Neville Chamberlain, after handing over to him a chunk of Czechoslovakia, come to the same conclusion about the pacific intentions of Hitler?

After each terrorist atrocity committed by Muslims in the name of Islam and, more often than not, accompanied by exultant cries of *'Allahu Akbar'*, 'God is Great', comes the refrain from all and sundry, be they politician, cleric, academic or journalist, 'Nothing to do with Islam', though what it is to do with is a matter of some confusion and no little disagreement. Anyone who dares say it is to do with Islam (and, as we have seen, there are Muslims who do) will invariably be branded by all right-thinking people as racist, Islamophobic and far rightist, by so doing even running the risk in some countries of prosecution for 'hate speech'. What we have here is, to use an expression now much in vogue, a state of denial, one no less monumental or fraught with tragic consequences than that concerning Hitler's declared intentions and his ability to come perilously close to achieving them.

This paralysis of minds steeped to varying degrees in the traditions of the Enlightenment and principles of secular liberal democracy, minds that cannot conceive of a degree and nature of evil so utterly alien to their own culture, is well-described in Walter Laqueur's *The Terrible Secret*, which meticulously documents the failure to either believe or comprehend, and in some cases, even more reprehensibly, when accepted as true, to make public the scale of the Nazi Holocaust of European Jewry. In the passage I cite below, nearly every word applies with equal force to the same lack of imagination that is preventing the West, with the exception of the Jews, from understanding the nature and objectives of Islam's global Jihad against the infidel:

> Democratic societies demonstrated on this occasion as on many others, before and after, that they are incapable of understanding regimes of a different character. Not every modern dictatorship is Hitlerian in character and engages in genocide but every one has the potential to do so. Democratic societies are accustomed to think in liberal, pragmatic categories; conflicts are believed to be based on misunderstandings and can be solved with a modicum of goodwill; extremism is a temporary aberration, so is irrational behaviour in general, such as intolerance, cruelty etc. The effect to overcome such basic psychological handicaps is immense. It will be undertaken only in the light of immediate (and painful) experience. Each new generation faces this challenge again for experience cannot be inherited.

David Hume, the 18th century Scottish sceptic, came to exactly the same sobering conclusion: 'There is a universal tendency among mankind to conceive all beings like themselves and to transfer to every object those qualities with which they familiarly acquitted, and of which they are intimately conscious.' Exactly. This insight explains why, for example, Prime Minister David Cameron sincerely believed that young Muslim men could be weaned from terrorism by enabling them to climb the property ladder. And so it is that like the opponents of and refugees from the tyranny of Hitler and Stalin, only the apostates from Islam, because they have endured and rejected it, can truly comprehend its totalitarian nature and barbaric methods. The unwelcome message the apostates from Islam bring of a religion dedicated to the overthrow of western civilisation is dismissed as 'horror stories, 'Islamophobia' and even criminalised as 'hate speech', even though is there for all to read in the faith's holiest texts as it was in the writings and speeches of Hitler, Lenin and Stalin

Readers by now should be familiar with some of the many pronouncements by liars or ignoramuses (and in some cases by those who are both) that Islam is a religion of peace. Earlier in this work, I made what I assumed was the correct observation that one of the few places in the UK where it is possible to speak the truth about Islam without reprimand or fear of prosecution is a court of law, together with Parliament a place where free speech is privileged. Now I am not so sure. Justice Haddon-Cave, the judge presiding over the case of the Parsons Green bomber Ahmed Hassan, when sentencing Hassan to life imprisonment, in the opinion of the National Secular Society, went beyond his brief by extoling what he saw as the peaceful nature of Islam. The Judicial Conduct Investigation Office to which the NSS made its case did not agree, ruling that that the judge's reference to the *Koran* as 'a book of peace' was 'founded on case law', and that there was a 'legitimate public interest' in making such statements to 'address Islamophobia', presumably even if such statements might not necessarily be true. This is what Judge Haddon-Cave actually said to Hassan: 'You will have plenty of time to study the *Koran* in prison. The *Koran* is a book of peace…Islam is a religion of peace…the *Koran* and Islam forbid terror'. Only the first of these statements is true. The rest are outright falsehoods, all the more despicable because they have been made by a judge in his capacity as a custodian of English justice. The *Koran* does not 'forbid terror', it explicitly prescribes it, as in Chapter 8, Verses 13: 'I will cast terror into the hearts of the disbelievers. Smite them above their necks [i.e., decapitate them] and cut off their fingertips.'

This ruling may well have profound implications. Are we know to understand that, based upon case law, it is now part of Common Law that that *Koran* and Islam are a book and religion of peace, and that to say otherwise in a court is inadmissible evidence and/or to be in contempt of court, and outside of court, can constitute an indicatable offence? We shall see.

While not always agreeing on the exact total, scholars of Islam, whether they be themselves Muslims or infidels, agree that the number of Koranic verses advocating Jihad exceeds one hundred. Jihad, strictly speaking, does not mean 'holy war', as some infidels believe, just as Islam does not mean peace, as some Muslims duplicitously claim and infidel dupes, including, so it would seem, Justice Haddon-Cave, believe. The Arabic for peace is *salaam*. Islam means 'submission' and Jihad means 'struggle', of which it is claimed by some, falsely, there are two kinds; what is sometimes referred as the 'greater' Jihad, the 'internal' struggle of a Muslim within him or herself to become a good Muslim, and the 'lesser' Jihad, an 'external' struggle against the enemies of Islam. This 'inner Jihad' against oneself has no Koranic foundation whatsoever, first appearing in what most Muslim scholars have always regarded as a spurious *hadith* dating from the 12th century, that is, at the end of a 'chain' five centuries long. Even if authentic, the so-called 'greater' Jihad does not concern us here, except inasmuch as it should lead to the better pursuing of the 'lesser', the 'struggle' or 'striving' against the enemies of Islam that is incumbent on all those Muslims who are in a position to wage it. Generally speaking, Jihad is translated into English as 'strive' or 'struggle' and their various derivatives. It has not escaped the notice of some critics of Islam that the German equivalent of Jihad is *Kampf,* as in in Hitler's work of that name.

The following selection of 61 citations from the *Koran* include some that are not complete verses, but only those passages which invoke Jihad. Since many of such verses are similar, near-duplicates have in some cases been omitted. The reader will easily detect a common theme to many of them, one that in addition to the 'spoils of war' - human and otherwise - also promises rewards in the afterlife in return for the sacrifice of oneself in the cause of Islam in this. The numbering of the verses might not always exactly tally with some English translations of the *Koran*.

Chapter 2

And say not of those who are slain in the way of Allah that they are dead; nay, they are living, only you perceive it not. (155

And fight in the way of Allah against those who fight against you, but do not transgress. Surely, Allah loves not the transgressors. (191)

And slay these transgressors wherever you meet them and drive them out from where they have driven you out, for persecution is worse than slaying. (192)

And fight them until there is no persecution, and religion is professed only for Allah. (194)

Fighting is ordained for you though it is repugnant to you. (217)

Persecution is worse than killing. (218)

Those who believe and those who emigrate and strive Hard in the cause of Allah, it is these who hope for Allah's mercy, and Allah is Most Forgiving, Merciful. (219)

Hast thou not heard of those who went forward from their homes, and they were thousands, fearing death? And Allah said to them, 'Die, and then He brought them back to life.' (244)

And fight in the cause of Allah and know that Allah is all-hearing and all-knowing. (245)

Chapter 3

And remember when thou didst go forth early in the morning from thy household, assigning to the believers their positions for battle. (122)

Yes, and if you be steadfast and righteous, and they come upon you immediately in hot haste, your Lord will help you with five thousand angels, attacking vehemently. (126)

Do you suppose that you will enter Heaven while Allah has not yet caused to be distinguished those of you that strive in the cause of Allah and has yet caused to be distinguished this steadfast? (143)

And you used to wish for such a death before you met it, now you have seen it face to face, then why do some of you seek to avoid it? (144)

And if you are slain in the cause of Allah or you die, surely forgiveness from Allah and mercy are better than what they hoard. (158)

And if you die or be slain, surely unto Allah shall you all be gathered together. (159)

Think not of those who have been slain in the cause of Allah, as dead. Nay, they are living, and are granted gifts from him. (170)

Those who answered the call of Allah and the Messenger after they have received an injury – such of them as do good and act righteously shall have a great reward. (173)

So they returned with a mighty bounty from Allah and a great bounty, while no evil had touched them; and they followed the pleasure of Allah; and Allah is the Lord of great bounty. (175)

Those, therefore, who have emigrated and have been driven out from their homes, and have been persecuted for My cause, and have fought and been slain, I will surely remit from them their evil deeds and will cause them to enter gardens through which streams flow- a reward from Allah, and with Allah is the best of rewards. (196)

Chapter 4

O ye who believe! Take your precautions for security, then go forth in separate parties, or go forth all together. (72)

Let those who fight in the cause of Allah who would sell the present life for the Hereafter. And those whoso fights in the cause of Allah, be he slain or be he victorious, We shall soon give him a great reward. (75)

Those who believe fight in the cause of Allah, and those who disbelieve fight in the cause of the Evil One. Fight ye, therefore, against the friends of Satan; surely, Satan's strategy is weak. (77)

And when fighting, behold! A section of them fear men as they should fear Allah, or with great fear; and they say, "Our Lord, why hast Thou prescribed fighting for us? Wouldst thou not grant us respite yet a while?" Say, "The benefit of this world is little and the Hereafter will be better for him who fears Allah; and you shall not be wronged a whit." (78)

Fight therefore in the way of Allah - thou art not made responsible except for thyself – and urge on the believers to fight. (85)

Those of the believers who sit at home, excepting the disabled ones, and those who strive in the cause of Allah with their wealth and their persons, are not equal. Allah has exalted in rank those who strive with their wealth and their persons above those who it at home (96)

And whoso goes forth from his home, emigrating in the cause of Allah and His Messenger, and death overtakes him, his regard lies on Allah. (101)

Chapter 5

The only reward of those who wage war against Allah and His Messenger and strive to create disorder in the land, is that they be slain or crucified or their hands and feet be cut off on account of their enmity, or they be expelled from the land. (34)

Chapter 8

They ask thee concerning the spoils. Say, the 'the spoils of war are for Allah and the Messenger'. (2)

I will cast terror into the hearts of the disbelievers. Smite them above the necks and smite off all finger-tips. (13)

O ye who believe! When you meet those who disbelieve, advancing in force, turn not your back to them. And those who turn his back to them on such a day, unless manoeuvring for battle or turning to join another company, he indeed draws upon himself the wrath of Allah and Hell shall be his abode. (16-17)

And fight until there is no more persecution and religion is wholly for Allah. (40)

And know that whatever you take as spoils of war, a fifth is for Allah and for the Messenger and the kindred and the orphans and the needy and the wayfarer. (42)

So, if thou overcomest them in war, then thereby strike fear in those that are behind them, that they be mindful. (58)

And make ready for them who fight you whatever you can of armed force and of mounted pickets whereby you may frighten the enemy of Allah and your enemy and others beside them who you know not, but Allah knows them. (61)

O Prophet, urge the believers to fight. If there be of you twenty who are steadfast, they shall overcome two hundred; and if there be a hundred of you, they shall overcome a thousand of those who disbelieve because they are people who do not understand. (66)

So, eat of that which you have won in war as lawful and good and fear Allah. Surely, Allah is Most Forgiving, Merciful. (70)

Chapter 9

And when the forbidden months [the four months of pilgrimage] have passed, slay idolaters wherever you find them and take them captive and beleaguer them and lie in wait for them at every place of ambush. (5)

And if they break their oaths after their covenant and attack your religion, then fight these leaders of disbelief. (12)

Fight them, that Allah may punish them at your hands, and humiliate them, and help you to victory over them, and relieve the minds of a people who believe. (14)

Those who believed and left their homes for the sake of Allah and strove in the cause of Allah with their wealth and their lives have the highest rank in the sight of Allah. (20)

Surely, Allah has helped you on many a battlefield. (25)

Fight those from among the People of the Book, who believe not in Allah…until they pay the tax considering it a favour and acknowledge their subjection. (29)

And fight the idolaters all together as they fight you altogether; and know that Allah is with those who fear Him. (36)

If you will not go forth to fight, in the cause of Allah, He will punish you with a painful punishment and will choose in your stead a people other than you. (39)

Go forth, light or heavy, and strive with your wealth and your lives in the cause of Allah. That is best for you, if only you knew. (41)

O Prophet! Strive hard against the disbelievers and the Hypocrites. And be firm against them. Their abode is Hell, and an evil destination it is. (73)

But the Messenger and those who believe with him strive in the cause of Allah with their wealth and their persons, and it is they who shall have good things, and it is they who shall prosper. (88)

Surely, Allah has purchased of the believers their persons and their property in return for the heavenly Garden they shall have; they fight in the cause of Allah, and they slay and are slain. (111)

O ye who believe! Fight such of the disbelievers as are near to you and let them find hardness in you; and know that Allah is with the righteous. (123)

Chapter 17

And when We intend to destroy a township, we command its people who live in comfort to adopt the way of righteousness but they transgress therein, so the sentence of punishment becomes due against it, so We destroy it with utter destruction. (17)

Chapter 22

Permission to take up arms is given to those against whom war is made, because they have been wronged, and Allah, indeed has power to help them. (40)

Those who leave their homes for the cause of Allah, and are then slain or die, Allah will, surely, provide for them a goodly provision. And, surely, Allah is the best of providers. (59)

And strive in the cause of Allah as it behoves you to strive for it. (79)

Chapter 33

Say, 'Flight shall not avail you if you flee from death or slaughter; and even then you will not be allowed to enjoy yourselves but little.' (17)

Verily, Allah knows well those among you who hinder others from fighting and those who say to their brethren, 'come and be with us', and they themselves come not to the fight but little. (19)

And He brought those of the People of the Book who aided them ['the disbelievers'] down from their fortress and cast terror into their hearts. Some you slew, and some you took captive. And He made you inherit their land and their houses and their wealth, and also a land on which you have not yet set foot. And Allah has power over all things. (27-28)

Chapter 47

And when you meet in regular battle those who disbelieve, smite their necks; and when you have overcome them, by causing a great slaughter among them, bind fast the fetters – then afterwards release them as a favour or by taking ransom - until the war lays down its burdens. (5)

And those who believe say 'Why is not a Surah [a chapter in the *Koran*] revealed?' But when a decisive Surah is revealed and fighting is mentioned therein, thou seest those in whose hearts is a disease, looking towards thee like the look of one who is fainting on account of approaching death. So woe to them! (21)

So be not slack and sue not for peace, for you will certainly have the upper hand. And Allah is with you, and He will not deprive you of the rewards of your actions. (36)

Chapter 48

Those, who contrived to be left behind, will say, when you go forth to the spoils to take them, 'Let us follow you.' They seek to change the decree of Allah. Say, 'You shall not follow us'. (16)

Allah has promised you great spoils that you will take and He has given you this in advance. (21)

And if those who disbelieve should fight you, they would, certainly turn their backs; then they would find neither protector nor helper. (23)

Chapter 49

The believers are only those who truly believe in Allah and His Messenger, and doubt not, but strive with their possessions and their persons in the cause of Allah. (16)

Chapter 50

The believers are only those who truly believe in Allah and his Messenger, and then doubt not, but strive with their possessions and their persons in the cause of Allah. It is they who are truthful. (16)

Chapter 59

But Allah came upon them whence they did not expect, and cast terror into their hearts, so that they demolished their houses with their own hands and with the hands of the believers. So take a lesson, O ye who have eyes. (3)
    And whatever Allah has given to the Messenger as spoils from them is of Allah's grace. (7)

Chapter 100

In the name of Allah, the Gracious and the Merciful, by the snorting chargers which strike sparks of fire with their hoofs, making raids at dawn and rising clouds of dust thereby and thus penetrate into the centre of the enemy ranks. (1-7)

The book of *peace*, Judge Haddon-Cave?

Addendum

'Verily, you have in the Prophet an excellent model'. *Koran*, Chapter 33, Verse 21

So far as its believers are concerned, and in the first place, its theologians and clerics, the sources of Islamic doctrine are, in order of precedence of authority, the *Koran*, conveyed by Allah via the angel Gabril to his prophet, and the *Sunnah*, the saying and deeds of Mohammed as recorded in the *Hadith*, and as related by his biographer Ibn Ishaq, born in Medina in 702 AD, 70 years after the death of the prophet in 632, and died in Baghdad in 768. This last is regarded by Muslim scholars as the most trustworthy account because, as with the equally respected Buhkari *Hadith*, it has the shortest 'chain' connecting it with Mohammed and his immediate contemporaries. A reading of this work undoubtedly helps to further round out the picture that we already have of the founder of the religion of peace as a war-lord, mass murderer, plunderer, slave-holder, Jew-killer, liar and rapist. Here I focus only on his role as military leader. An overview of this aspect of his activities in the service of Allah can be partly at least gleaned from some of the book's chapter headings:

    Jewish opponents
    Jews joined by hypocrites among the Helpers
    The chapter [of the *Koran*] of The Cow and Jewish opposition
    The first raid on Waddin
    Raid on Buwat

Raid on al-'Ushayra
Raid on al-Kharrar
Raid on Safawan
Fighting in the sacred month [re Corbyn's assertion on Press TV to contrary]
The chapter [of the *Koran*] of The Spoils [of war]
Names of the Emigrants who fought at Badr
Names of the Helpers who fought at Badr
Names of the [Jewish tribe of] Quraysh prisoners
Verses on the battle [20 pages]
Raid on B. Salaym
Raid on Dhu Amarr
Raid on al-Furu
Killing of Ka'b b. al-Ashraf
Battle of Uhud
Names of Muslims slain at Uhud
Names of polytheists slain at Uhud
Verses on Uhud [23 pages]
Raid of Dharu'l-Riua
Last expedition to Badr
Raid on Dumatu'l-Jandal
Battle of the Ditch
Attack on B. Qurayza
Poetry thereon [six pages]
Killing of Sallam
Attack on B. Libyan
Attack on Dhu Qarad
Attack on B. al-Mustaliq
Expedition to Khaybar
Division of the spoils of Khaybar
Raid on Mu'ta
The occupation of Mecca
Battle of Hunayn
Verses thereon [15 pages]
Capture of al-T'a'if
Division of the spoils of Hawazin
Raid on Tabuk
Those who hung back from the raid on Tabuk
Destruction of al-Lat
Hassan's odes on the campaigns [3 pages]
A summary of Muhammed's raids and expeditions.

Of these last, Ibn Ishaq says: 'The apostle took party personally in twenty-seven' and that 'he actually fought in nine engagements' ...peacefully, naturally.

Mohammed only gets into his stride in the ways that by now should be familiar when he and his small band of proselytising followers are unceremoniously bum-rushed out of Mecca by the pagan Quaraysh tribe and head north to Medina. Here too his message falls on largely stony ground, rejected by the Jews, who 'became insolent towards God and rejected His gracious purpose,' that is, to convert to Islam.

This time, however Mohammed does not intend to undergo a second humiliation. Allah 'gave permission to His apostle to fight and to protect himself against those who wronged them and treated them badly'. Conveniently, as on so many other occasions when Mohammed was in a tight spot, Allah sent down a new verse, instructing him to 'fight them so that there be no more seduction…and the religion is God's, until God alone is worshipped.' And so was born Islam Mark Two, which would now involve the cancelling out, or 'abrogation' of all earlier verses that spoke of peaceful and tolerant relations between Mohammed's followers and those who rejected his message.

One of the prophet's early encounters with the Jews of Medina involved a battle of wits with a delegation of rabbis, who put four questions to him. If he answered them correctly, they would convert to Islam. One is worth repeating as perhaps the first example of 'Islamic science': To the question, 'Why does a boy resemble its mother when the semen comes from the man?' Mohammed replied: 'Do you not know that a man's semen is white and thick while a woman's is yellow and thin and the likeness goes with that which is on top?' On another occasion, a married man had committed adultery with a married woman, and Mohammed was asked to provide the appropriate punishment. 'The apostle ordered them to be stoned, and they were stoned at the door of his mosque. And when the Jew felt the first stone, he crouched over the woman to protect her from the stones until both of them were killed This is what God did for the apostle in exacting the penalty for adultery for the pair.' Mohammed had passed the test with flying colours, and in doing so, had proved himself truer to the *Torah* than the Jewish elders, who had advocated a less harsh punishment. 'Woe to you Jews! What has induced you to abandon the judgment of God which you hold in your hands?' Evidently tiring of these fruitless contests, Mohammed moved up several gears, because we soon find him plotting the first of what would be a string of caravan raids: '…when the apostle heard about Abu Sufyan coming from Syria, he summoned the Muslims and said: "This is the Quaraysh caravan containing their property. Go out and attack it, perhaps God will give us a prey."'.

Sure enough, Allah came through for his apostle, just as he always would in future. *En route* to Mecca, the caravan was ambushed by Mohammed's followers at Badr, the first battle of the religion of peace. It was also the prophet's first opportunity to savour the 'spoils of war'. As we shall see, here too Allah was more than a little helpful, 'abrogating' one of his hitherto immutable laws concerning the distribution of the spoils. The battle of Badr looms large in the life story of Mohammed, because here for the first time, he was operating as military leader and not, as previously, a peaceful advocate of a new religion. (Hence the need for Koranic textual 'abrogation'.) The prominence awarded the engagement and its aftermath by Ibn Ishaq is quite extraordinary. Of the 463 pages describing Mohammed's life following his *Hijra*, that is from the time he left Mecca for Medina in 622, no fewer than 71 are devoted to this one single battle. In view of its historical significance, some of its features are worth relating. one of them being that his biographer tells us it began 'on Friday morning on the 17th of Ramadan', even though on an Islamic website, *My mercy embraces all things*, Farhana Qazi expressed his astonishment that 'religious extremists choose to kill during one of Islam's holiest months'.(Recalling his claim on Press TV, so would have Corbyn.) The founder of Islam an *extremist*? Another feature worthy of note was its being a purely offensive undertaking which, according to legend, was contrary to the rules for Jihad. A third gives us a revealing glimpse of the prophet's sexual proclivities. While at Badr, he saw a certain Ummu'l-Fadl 'when she was a baby and crawling before him. Said Allah's apostle, if she grows up and I am still alive I will marry her.' Fortunately for Ummu'l-Fadl, in view of his consummation of his last marriage to Aisha when she was 'grown up' at nine, he died before he could have his holy way with her.

Badr was a desert watering hole, and it was there Mohammed's forces ambushed the Quaraysh as they watered themselves and their camels: 'And when Quaraysh encamped, some of them went to the cistern of the apostle to drink. "Let them be", he [Mohammed] said; and every man that drank of it on that that day was killed'. We are not spared the gory details of the slaughter. One Quaraysh had his 'foot and half his shank sent flying' and lay by the cistern, 'blood streaming from his foot', while another had his leg cut off, with 'marrow oozing from it'. It was at Badr that the prophet first sanctioned an Islamic practice we have become all too familiar with...decapitation. One of his warriors, Ibn Mas'ud, related that he brought him the head of a Quaraysh: "This the head of the enemy of God, Abu Jahl." He [Mohammed] said, "By God than Whom there is no other, is it?" "Yes" I said and threw his head before the apostle and he [the prophet] gave thanks to God.'

Here too for the first time we encounter the prophet enunciating the doctrine of Muslim martyrdom: '70,000 of my people shall enter Paradise like the full moon'. Rather like the three robbers in Chaucer's *Pardoner's Tale,* no sooner was the battle won than Allah's warriors fell out over the proceeds of their victory. So, 'when Badr was over, God sent down the whole *Sura* [chapter] *Anfal* about it. ['The Spoils of War'] With regard to their quarrelling about the spoils there came down [via Gabril to Mohammed, who unlike his trusting followers, claimed to have a direct line to heaven]: "They will ask you about the spoils, say, the spoils belong to God and [of course] the apostle, so fear God and be at peace with one another, and obey God and His apostle if you are believers".' This evidently did not go down too well with those who done the fighting and the plundering, so down came another verse: 'He [Allah] taught them how to divide the spoil', only now, they were to have four fifths, while of 'what you take, a fifth belongs to God and his apostle and the next of kin and orphans the poor and the and wayfarer.' Nice one, Allah. Or should I say, Mohammed?

Supported by a growing band of followers eager for booty, human and otherwise, all that was now needed was a verse from above conferring upon Mohammed the right and in fact duty to wage war against the unbelievers. And down it came, as always, bang on time: 'And then He [Allah] said, "Fight them so that there is no more persecution [sic] and religion, all of it, shall belong to God".' And so, in the midst of plunder, rape, beheadings, blood, gore and marrow, was born the religion of peace. Having, at least temporarily, squared accounts with the Quaraysh, it was the turn of the Jews of Medina, the tribe of B. Qaynuqa, to feel the wrath of Allah. Bang on cue, down came a verse authorising another punitive military action against the infidel: 'Say to those who disbelieve, you will be vanquished and gathered to Hell, and evil resting place.' Said one participant in the ensuing battle, 'our attack upon God's enemy cast terror among the Jews, and there was no Jew in Medina who did not fear for his life.' 'And the apostle said, "*Kill any Jew that falls into your power*".' This is the language of Nazi-style genocide and it is back today in the manifestos of Corbyn's 'friends' Hamas and Hezbollah. But those who attribute Muslim anti-Semitism to the sins of Zionism need to take note:

the Jews were despised as the prime enemy of Islam and the Arabs more than thirteen centuries before the birth of Israel.

Terror and conversion went hand in hand. One Jewish captive asked of his captor,' By God, if Mohammed had ordered you to kill me would you have killed me?' His captor answered, 'Yes, by God, had he ordered me to cut off your head I would have done so.' The captive Jew then replied, '"By God, a religion which can bring you to this is marvellous!", and he became a Muslim.' Could this be the first recorded instance of the Stockholm Syndrome? Having twice tasted victory and the fruits thereof, the prophet now began a series of military campaigns that he waged to the end of his life, and which his successors have continued until the present day. Returning home after one such engagement, the battle of Uhud, a return match against the Quaraysh, 'he handed his sword to his daughter Fatima, saying, "Wash the blood from this, daughter, for by God it has served me well today".'

It served him even better after his victory over the Jews of B. Qurayza. Their men having surrendered, 'the apostle confined them in Medina the quarter of al-Harith, a woman of B. al-Najjar. Then the apostle went out to the market of Medina and dug trenches in it. Then he sent for them [the Jewish prisoners] and struck off their heads in those trenches as they were brought to him in batches…There were 600 or 700 in all, though some put the figure as high as 800 or 900'. Those familiar with the Holocaust of the Jews will, save for the use of a sword rather than firearms, recognise at once the identical method employed by the Nazi murder squads, the *Einsatzgruppen*, on the Eastern front during the Second World War, filling up trenches with massacred Jews. 'Then the apostle divided the property, wives and children of B. Qurayza among the Muslims.' For his own sexual needs, 'the apostle had chosen one of their women', a wife of a Jew he had just beheaded. In his infinite wisdom, god chose this very moment to send down another verse, one that to this day provides a *carte blanche* for every Muslim man to rape, plunder and murder in the name of Allah: 'In God's apostle you have a fine example'. Now see what follows.

M Anything You Can Do…

For decades now, western liberals and leftists have allowed their thinking on serious matters to be warped by what is commonly known as post-colonial guilt. Starting with the Crusades, then Christian slavery, and ending with the era of empire (while by-passing Islamic slavery and the vast empires of Allah), the western radical intelligentsia has taken upon itself the guilt of their forebears to such a degree of self-abasement that it has blinded its members to the failings and misdeeds of any culture other than their own. The high priest of this latter-day flagellant cult is of course Noam Chomsky. Islamic imperialism, with its avowed goal of world conquest in the name of and for Allah, is not now, and never has been troubled by such qualms of conscience. Its cause is noble, therefore its means are justified, even if they exceed in brutality and savagery those of the despised infidel West. Reproduced below is a text from the same issue number 15 of the Islamic State journal, being part of an article entitled *By the Sword.* To drive home its message, as if that were necessary, the article is accompanied by a photograph of an Islamic State executioner caught in the act of slicing off the head of a sinner against the laws of Allah, a spectacle watched by an audience of men, male youths and young male children.

By the Sword

The clear difference between Muslims and the corrupt and deviant Jews and Christians is that Muslims are not ashamed of abiding by the rules sent down from their Lord regarding war and the enforcement of divine law. So if it were the Muslims, instead of the Crusaders [by which is meant the infidel West] who had fought the Japanese and Vietnamese or invaded the lands of the native Americans, there would have been no regrets in killing and enslaving [sic!] those therein. And since those mujahidin would have done so bound by the Law, they would have been thorough and without some 'politically correct' need to apologise years later. The Japanese, for example, would have forcefully converted to Islam from their pagan ways - and if they stubbornly declined, perhaps another nuke [sic!!!] would have changed their mind. The Vietnamese would likewise be offered Islam or beds of napalm [sic!!!]. As for the Native Americans - after the slaughter of their men, those who would favour small-pox to surrendering to the Lord – then the Muslims would have taken their surviving women and children as slaves [sic!], raising the children as model Muslims and impregnating [by rape] their women to produce a new generation of mujahidin. As for the treacherous Jews of Europe and elsewhere - those who would betray their covenant – then their post-pubescent males would face a slaughter that would make the Holocaust sound like a bedtime story, as their women would be made to serve their husbands' and fathers' killers. Furthermore, the lucrative African slave trade would have continued [sic!], supporting a strong economy. The Islamic leadership would not have bye-passed Allah's permission to sell captured pagan humans, to teach them, and to convert them, as they worked hard for their masters in building a beautiful country.

N Goodbye to All That

I first conceived of this work five years ago, at the time when anti-Zionists ranging from the infidel far left to the Islamic and Neo-Nazi far right were storming through the streets of western Europe in support of the anti-Semitic Hamas regime in Gaza. Little did I or anyone else for that matter then suspect that a year later an identical combination of forces would succeed in securing the election of one of their own to the leadership of the UK's major leftist party. The letter below is my response to this succession of events:

September 24, 2016

To whom it may concern:

The purpose of this communication is to formally inform you of my resignation from the Labour Party, effective as from the date of this email. I owe it both to you and myself to provide the reasons for this decision, which I can assure I have not taken lightly. I joined the Labour Party forty-two years ago, believing that it was the only political organisation that could represent and advance the interests of working people. The re-election of Jeremy Corbyn as party leader has convinced me, and I have good reasons to believe many others, that this is no longer the case. The party has allowed itself to be hi-jacked by infiltrators, many of whom have been proved to have either belonged to or voted for parties other than Labour, or to members of organisations whose ethos and methods are totally opposed to those of the Labour Party and are incompatible with its rules of membership.

Since the election of Corbyn and the emergence of Momentum as the dominant force in the party, electoral support has been in catastrophic decline in those very areas of the country that are its traditional strongholds, not least because the party has become the vehicle for the ambitions of self-indulgent political play-boys who care nothing for those the party was founded to represent. However, important though they are, these are not my main reasons for leaving the Labour Party.

As a life-long opponent of anti-Semitism, I cannot remain in a party led by someone who throughout his career as an MP, has collaborated with individuals and movements who make no secret their enmity towards the Jews, and in the cases of his 'friends' Hamas and Hezbollah, have as their avowed goal not only the destruction of Israel but the murder of its entire Jewish population. Corbyn has also taken paid employment with the state-run Iranian Press TV channel, that is, with a regime whose Supreme Leader proclaims that it is his aim to 'wipe Israel off the map' and which amongst its many victims that include poets, secularists and Kurds, publicly hangs homosexuals from cranes.

I do not believe that it was by coincidence that Corbyn's election as leader was accompanied by an upsurge of quite open hostility towards the Jews, to such a degree that he was with some reluctance compelled to commission what predictably proved to be a toothless inquiry into Labour party anti-Semitism. What sort of a party has Labour become that a Jewish MP critical of Corbyn's leadership, after receiving 25,000 abusive messages, some of them death threats and many of them anti-Semitic, has found it necessary to attend the party conference accompanied by a body guard?

Robin Blick, membership number A314906

Swansea East CLP.

O When Did You Last Beat Your Wife?

We have seen how some Muslim clerics based in the west have tied themselves in semantic knots in their attempts to present Islam as a humane faith, especially so with regard to its treatment of women. We have also seen that in this endeavour, they have been able to enlist the invaluable support of quisling western feminists engaged in the same enterprise. In the Middle East, where the whole filthy business began, no such subterfuges are called for. There, Islam is served up to the faithful hot and strong, and in no subject more so than the noble task sanctified by Allah of keeping Muslim wives in line. What follows is a verbatim transcript of a Friday sermon preached on Qatar TV on August 27, 2004. It is readily accessible on YouTube. But first, the Koranic verse which the preacher invokes as the authority for this barbaric practice. It occurs in Sura (Chapter) 4, *An Nisa*, meaning 'The Women'. The number of the verse varies, being either usually 34 or, less often, 35. The translations from the Arabic that I have consulted translate the Arabic word '*daraba*' as either 'beat', 'chastise' or 'scourge'. So far as the wife on the receiving end of the operation is concerned, it makes no difference. The source I have used for Verse 34 is from the Islamic website Ayyid Ahul Ala Maududi - Tafhim al - Qur'an: The Meaning of the Koran. It reads:

> Men are the managers of the affairs of women because Allah has made one superior to the others and because men spend of their wealth on women. Virtuous women are, therefore, obedient. They guard their rights carefully in their absences under the care and watch of Allah. As for those women, whose defiance you have cause to fear, admonish them and keep them apart from your beds and beat them.

Now the Sermon:

> We must know that wife beating is a punishment in Islamic religious law. No one should deny this because this was permitted by the Creator of Man, and because when you purchase an electrical appliance or a car, you get a manual, a catalogue, explaining how to use it. The creator of man has sent down this book, the *Koran*, in order to show man which ways he must choose. We shouldn't be ashamed before the nations of the world who are still in their days of ignorance to admit that these beatings are part of our religious law. We must remind the ignorant from among the Islamic nation who followed the West that those Westerners acknowledge the wondrous nature of this verse. There are three types of women with whom life is impossible without beatings. The *Koran* says 'and beat them'. This verse is of a wondrous nature. There are three types of women with whom a man cannot live unless he carries a rod on his shoulder. The first type is a woman who was brought up this way. Her parents ask her to go school and she doesn't – [so] they beat her. 'Eat' – 'I don't want to' – so they beat her. So she becomes accustomed to beatings, she was brought up that way. We pray Allah will help her husband later. He will only get along with her if he practices wife beating. The second type is a woman who is condescending towards her husband and ignores him. With her, too, only a rod will help. The third type is a twisted woman who will not obey her husband unless her oppresses her, beats her, uses force against her, and overpowers her with his voice.

Here we have another Muslim cleric, Sa'id Arafat, expounding on what he calls 'the etiquette' of wife-beating:

Allah honoured [sic] wives by installing the punishment of beatings...The Prophet Mohammad said, 'don't beat her in the face and do not make her ugly.' See how she is honoured...Even when he beats her, he must not curse her...He beats her in order to discipline her. In addition, there must not be more than ten beatings and he must not break her bones, injure her, break her teeth, or poke her in the eye. There is a beating etiquette. If he beats to discipline her, he must not raise his hand high. He must beat her from chest level. All these things honour a woman. [sic] She is in need of discipline...He can beat her with a short rod...The honouring of the wife is also evident in the fact that the punishment of beating is permissible in one case only: when she refuses to sleep with him.

P Dutch Cowardice

Of all Europe's peoples, it is the Dutch who over the centuries have arguably given more proof than any other of their commitment to liberty, both of their nation, and of the individuals who have lived within its borders. Beginning with their revolt against the tyranny of Spanish rule in the sixteenth century, which after their victory, made Holland a haven for those persecuted for their beliefs, through to their resistance to Nazi occupation, when the workers of Amsterdam staged a general strike against the deportation of the Jews to the gas chambers of the Third Reich, the Dutch have deservedly won for their country a global reputation for their respect for personal freedom and acceptance of the widest variety of life styles and beliefs. But tragically, that reputation is now in tatters. Holland is no longer a land of the free, but one ruled by politicians who rather than resist the assault of Islam on their hard-won freedoms, have chosen to capitulate to it, and persecute with all legal means at their disposal those who fight back.

The alarm was first raised by Pim Fortuyn. Being by profession a sociologist, and by sexual orientation a homosexual, Fortuyn was more attuned than most to the impact of large-scale Islam on a society that shared little, if any of the life-style and beliefs of the large numbers of Muslim migrants their hosts had naively assumed would in time exchange for Dutch ones. Based on his observations of the failure, in fact refusal, of Muslim immigrants to integrate into liberal Dutch society, in 1997, Fortuyn published his book, *The Islamisation of Our Culture.* His next step was to enter politics as the leader of his Livable Netherlands party to defend the traditional Dutch commitment to individual freedom, in particular freedoms fanatically opposed by Muslims; those of sexual equality and orientation, and of expression. While he made it clear in an interview that he believed Islam to be 'an extraordinary threat, a hostile religion' to Dutch values, he also insisted, contrary to the lies of his opponents, 'I want to live together with the Muslim people', adding, correctly, 'but it takes two to tango'. In an allusion to his own sexuality, and to the vicious persecution and even murder of gays in Islamic countries, Fortuyn made a point that any leftist would be only too willing to endorse had it made by one of their own: 'Look at the Netherlands. In what country, an electoral leader of such a large movement as mine be openly homosexual? How wonderful that that is possible. That's something that one can be proud of. And I would like to keep it that way, thank you very much.'

But for some, especially those on the left, such statements constituted proof, along with his unconditional support for free speech above all other rights, that that he was fascist. And as anyone conversant with its history knows, fascism has always been foremost in upholding the rights of gays and the protection of free speech. It rapidly become obvious however that despite all the slanders, Fortuyn had struck a chord with millions of Dutch citizens who shared his concern about the failure of Holland's political elite to defend their country's liberal values and way of life, either out of fear of Muslim backlash or because their brains had been addled by the new fads of political correctness and multi-culturalism. Sensing that Fortuyn now had a powerful wind in his sails, the establishment almost to a man launched a campaign of vilification, denouncing him as a fascist, a slander echoed by the *New York Times* with its headline that Fortuyn was 'marching the Dutch to the Right', seemingly oblivious to the fact that it was Islam that was marching Holland to the right, and Fortuyn, by defending his country's secular democratic values and institutions, who was resisting it.

On May 6, 2002, only a matter of days before a general election that would have resulted (and fact did result) in his party making sweeping gains, Fortuyn was assassinated by a far leftist, Vokert Van der Graaf, because, so he said at his trial, of his views on the impact of Muslim migration on Dutch society. Even after his murder, the slanders continued: 'Dutch Len Pen Assassinated' proclaimed the UK's pro-Labour *Daily Mirror*. The mould had been set: he or she who criticises Islam, no matter from what standpoint, is, necessarily, by that fact alone, a far rightist, possibly even a fascist. Fortuyn had been slain, but the cause he represented was taken up by three courageous critics of Islam, each of whom we have already encountered: the film-maker Theo van Gogh, murdered by a Muslim in revenge for his film *Submission* (in Arabic, *Islam*) depicting the plight of Muslim women; his Somali-born collaborator on the film, the atheist ex-Muslim writer Ayaan Hirsi Ali, no-platformed by Brandies University for her outspoken attacks on the Islamic oppression of women, and the MP Gert Wilders, denied entry to the UK to show his anti-Islam film *Fitna* to MPs at Westminster.

Van Gogh's assassination on November 2, 2004 triggered identical reactions to those that would eleven years later be displayed in response to the *Charlie Hebdo* massacre. He had been 'insensitive' to 'Muslim feelings', and if not in so many words, 'had it coming'. Naturally the *Guardian* hastened to advertise its 'understanding' for the motives of Van Gogh's killer. Belying without any sense of shame its own title, *Index on Censorship* denigrated Van Gogh as a 'free speech fundamentalist' (sic) who had been 'on a martyrdom operation, roaring his Muslim critics into silence' with his 'abuse of the right to free speech'. Indeed, so lacking was there any solidarity with the victim or the cause for which he had been slain that Peter Whitehead of the New Culture Forum felt obliged to complain that the film-maker's murder had elicited 'no significant expressions of outrage from Britain's creative figures and institutions', a sure indicator that amongst the literati, Sharia leftism was already well and truly on the march. So was Sharia self-censorship.

A showing of *Submission* at a Dutch festival of censored films was cancelled because of a fear of Muslim reprisals. The film's producer, Gijs van de Westelaken, frankly admitted that he was 'yielding to terror'. What Fortuyn had feared had now come to pass. The pattern had been set. It now became *de rigueur* to counterpose to free expression the sensitivities of Muslims, invariably to the advantage of the latter. Where they did not already exist, laws would be enacted to ensure that those who chose to act otherwise would be punished. Such would the fate of Geert Wilders. In November 2007, Associated Press reported that the Dutch MP was planning to make a film highly critical of Islam; a brave, some would say foolhardy venture in view of the fate that befell van Gogh. The same report revealed that Dutch 'Interior and Justice Ministers said they were concerned but believed they had no authority to prevent Wilders from screening his film'. Bear in mind that even though the two ministers could have had only the haziest idea of what the film might contain, they were already seeking ways to prevent its being shown. And this was not China, Iran, Saudi Arabia or North Korea, but once liberal Holland, the land of the free. And all to protect Muslim 'sensitivities'.

No wiser than the two ministers to the film's actual contents, but now alerted as to its imminent showing and galvanised by the prospect of yet more Muslim violence, the forces of political correctness mobilised. Doekle Terpstra, chairman of the Netherlands Association of Universities of Applied Science, charged Wilders with 'abusing his position and freedom of speech' to divide Dutch society, as if the Dutch, always a quarrelsome people, should all be of the one mind sought by totalitarian dictators. With this end in view, Terpstra assembled an anti-Wilders popular front comprised of Christian and Muslim clerics, politicians from various parties, business leaders and assorted establishment personalities, and led them into battle to the cry 'Wilders is the evil'…all because the MP had announced his intention to make film about Islam, a film, I repeat, that none of Terpstra's army of the great and the good had seen. The Islamic component of the alliance immediately began to flex its muscles, with the Dutch Muslim Council warning that if Wilder's film was screened, 'the youths on the street will have the last word. We can't stop them'. As if they wanted to.

Though no part of his brief, Foreign Minister Maxime Verhagen intoned what has now become a familiar *non-sequitur*, that 'freedom of expression does not mean the right to offend'. Whoever said it does? It simply recognises the possibility, in fact probability, that expressing an opinion freely on a matter of substance can give offence, even if not intentionally so, to someone, somewhere who thinks differently, and that such a possibility should be no grounds for curtailing the right to free expression. If it was allowed to do so, no-one would be allowed to say anything for fear of giving offence to someone, somehow, somewhere. Of course, in this instance, the whole object of the exercise was the suppression of the right to criticise Islam, and the specific target, the film *Fitna,* still as yet to be viewed by its legions of outraged critics

The day of reckoning arrived on March 27, 2008, when the film was released on-line (naturally no cinema would dare screen it). Would it live up to its advanced billing of seeking to 'polarise Dutch society' and the 'stigmatising of entire population groups' (code for Muslims)? Would it be 'hate-inciting or blasphemous' or, as the London *Observer* confidently predicted, define Wilders as a 'new brand of right-wing populist'? For the record, I do not like some of the political company Wilders chooses to keep, but that should not invalidate his right to free speech, and to make and show a film. In the event *Fitna* did none of the things its opponents warned of. Just over sixteen minutes long, to a soundtrack of classical music, the film consisted largely of quotations from the *Koran* on Jihad (also cited in my text) and sermons by Muslim preachers, together with footage of the deaths and destruction caused by Muslims who acted upon them. Excepting the cries of terror victims, all the words spoken were by Muslims.

Wrong footed by the absence of a content they had so confidently predicted, the film's release was accompanied not only in Holland but globally by a surge of simulated *kuffar* outrage. Leading the pack was UN Secretary-General Ban Ki-moon, with his charge that *Fitna* constituted 'hate speech', even though the film's only 'hate speech' were Muslim sermons and citations from the *Koran*. CNN reported that the Bush administration feared 'the film could spark protests and riots'. Jorge Sampaio, the UN Representative for the Alliance of Civilisation (sic), found *Fitna* 'an insulting film on the Holy *Koran'*, again begging the same question…how can quoting from a book insult it? In accordance with what had by now become the required norm, Sampaio spelled out the UN's new stance on free expression, one that implicitly repudiated Article 19 of its own founding Universal Declaration of Human Rights, that 'it does not preclude the protection of people from discriminatory and xenophobic language'. To repeat yet again: the only 'language' in *Fitna* was that either inspired by or to be found in the *Koran*. Are we to assume then, as some *dhimmi* law makers have indeed successfully insisted, that only Muslims should be allowed to quote from it?

Dutch courage is no more. Not only in Holland, but across the western world, publishers will not publish books and TV and internet channels will not screen programmes critical of Islam and of Muslims who commit crimes inspired by its teachings, even when their authors and makers are highly respected academic authorities on the subject. Bookshops will not sell such books. Journals and newspapers will not review them, but they will invariably slander their authors as 'far right' for opposing in the name of individual freedom a doctrine that is itself analgous to fascism. But, unfortunately for Allah's *Kuffar* Thought Police and his army of terrorist enforcers, in the era of the internet, the self-publishing of such books is booming.

Q Sweated Labour

In the darkest days of the Second World war, George Orwell took comfort from his conviction that the British, for all their faults, and he was never slow to criticise them, were by tradition resistant to the appeals of the totalitarianism and leader cultism that had extinguished democracy on the European continent. 'No party rallies, no Youth Movements, no coloured shirts, no Jew-baiting, or spontaneous demonstrations.' That was then. Following his election as Labour Party Leader in September 2015, in addition to Nuremberg-style chanting of his name at pop festivals, we had a Jeremy chant and pop song, an oil painting, T-shirts and umpteen memorabilia, including life-size cardboard cut-outs of the Dear Leader, Jeremy underpants, Lego, garden gnomes, shopping bags, pillow cases, colouring-in books, teddy bears and fake tattoos.

Helping to fund Corbyn's campaign for the Labour leadership, the T-shirts were priced in the UK at £10.00, while being produced at minimal cost by third world sweated labour. In Nicaragua, where workers were paid under £6.00 for a 12-hour day to make T-shirts for Corbyn, they toiled under a regime headed by the husband and wife team of President Daniel Ortega and his wife, Vice President Rosario, one that in the spring of 2018, emulating the example of Corbyn's Chavista comrades in Venezuela, unleashed a repression of street protests against poverty and cuts in welfare that led to the killing at least 170 demonstrators by security forces. A kinder politics. Among items advertised on the Nicaraguan Solidarity (with the regime, naturally) website are Jeremy mugs (sic) and Jeremy magnets.

In Bangladesh, the going rate for Jeremy shirt-makers was even lower, at £3.00 for a ten-hour day. One worker commented, 'I feel angry that a politician is using T-shirts created with our back-breaking work to make a statement about workers' rights when he clearly doesn't care about our rights at all.' Corbyn T-shirts were also made in Haiti, where the rate was £20.00 for a six-day week. In all, proceeds from the sale of Corbyn T-shirts netted £100,000. Corbyn had pledged to raise the minimum wage for British workers to £10.00 an hour, more than twenty times the rate paid to those workers who helped to finance his leadership campaign. When working for Iran's Press TV channel, Corbyn was paid £1,250.00 an hour. He also received a payment of £5,000 for a single appearance on Al-jazeera TV. His combined annual income as MP and Leader of the Opposition is £128,559. According to the magazine *Spears,* multi-millionaire Corbyn's private fortune stood at £3,000,000. On his retirement as MP, he will receive a pension of another £1,600,000.

As I scrolled through Corbyn's numerous entries on the register of MP's financial interests, I came across one item that in view of his pecuniary and political relationship with the hangmen of the Iranian theocracy, merited closer scrutiny. It concerned Corbyn's visit to Tehran (accompanied by his wife and a 'research worker') from January 6 to 10, 2014, on behalf of the 'All-Party [UK] Parliamentary Group on Iran at the invitation of the Iran-UK Parliamentary Friendship Group of the Iranian Parliament'. The junket was funded by two donors, again quoting Corbyn's register entry, 'the Parliament of the Islamic Republic of Iran' and 'Ardeshir Nagashineh, Chairman of Targetfellow Group Ltd', based in Norwich. Just as has been the case with Jew-killing Jihadis, there is nothing out of the ordinary in Corbyn's 'friendship'(or as he likes to say, 'solidarity') with regimes, which as matter of course, murder their opponents and rig elections to rubber-stamp 'parliaments'. What is of special interest is the profile of Mr Nagashineh. A little digging uncovered the following: Listed as a billionaire, Corbyn's benefactor is an Iranian-born property tycoon, as of September 2019 holding directorships in *sixty-five* companies, out of total of 227 in his entire business career. Undeniably an exemplary case of 'For the very Few' and, as such, unless considerations of a political nature come into play, surely a prime candidate for expropriation under a Corbyn regime.

.

R Dialogue?

After meeting Hitler in Berlin in April 1937, George Lansbury, the pacifist Leader of the Labour Party from 1932 to 1935, returned to England convinced that 'history will regard Hitler as one of the great men of our time…with no love for pomp and show, Christianity in its purest form might stand a chance with him.' One can still see on-line a YouTube video where Corbyn is uttering no less delusional platitudes about his anti-Semitic terrorist 'friends' Hamas and Hezbollah:

> It will be my pleasure and my honour to host an event in Parliament where our friends from Hezbollah will be speaking. I have also invited friends from Hamas to come and speak as well…so we can promote that peace, that understanding and that dialogue. The idea that an organisation that is dedicated towards the good of the Palestinian people and bringing back long-term peace in the whole region should be labelled as terrorist organisations by the British government is really a big, big, historical mistake. [Corbyn's customary hapless syntax has the 'idea' making the mistake, not the government.]

Like his predecessor in his estimation of Hitler as a man of peace, it was Corbyn who was making a 'really big, big, historical mistake'. The only difference was the religion. The way Corbyn described Hamas and Hezbollah, they could easily be taken for the Middle Eastern equivalents of a European social democratic party rather than terrorist movements dedicated to the elimination of a member state of the United Nations. In fact, both Hamas and Hezbollah are religiously-driven anti-Semitic war machines pure and simple, awash with the most advanced conventional weaponry that money can buy, and they make no secret of it. The Shia militia, Hezbollah, does not attempt to disguise that it is little more than an Irian proxy, and its sponsors have seen to it that it is better equipped for war than the armed forces of its Lebanese hosts. Both movements' genocidal intentions towards the Jews and Israel, defined with total clarity in their respective charters and numerous public statements by their leaders, those whom Corbyn described as his 'friends', are no different in intention and no less transparent than were those of Hitler towards the Jews. Given his close relationship with his Hamas and Hezbollah 'friends' and the Iranian theocracy, Corbyn must be fully aware of this.

Just one example of many of Hezbollah's dedication to peace is the tenfold increase in its stock of missiles, a purely offensive weapon, in the period between 2006 and 2015, giving it the capacity to launch 1,000 missiles *per day* into Israeli territory for a period of two months. Yet although equipped for and pledged to a war of aggression and elimination against the 'Zionist entity', in true Orwellian fashion, Hezbollah invariably refers to itself in its *Manifesto* as a 'resistance' movement…just like Hitler's Waffen SS. And how does Corbyn reconcile his description of Hamas as a movement dedicated to 'bringing back long-term peace' with its suicide attacks on Israeli restaurants, cafes, markets and school buses, its tunnelling into Israel's territory, the kidnapping and murder of its civilians and the bombarding of civilian targets with thousands of rockets, and the round-the-clock pumping out of genocidal hatred towards the Jews on its TV channels? Just between January 2000 and August 2005, during the so-called 'Second Intifada', Hamas was responsible for more than 40% of all suicide attacks carried out in that period, nearly all of them on civilian targets, such as the Tel Aviv Dolphinarium discothèque of June 1, 2001, with 21 victims, the Haifa bus bombing of December 2 of the same year, with 15 victims, and on March 31, 2002, the Mazta Restaurant bombing, also in Haifa, with another 15 killed. The list goes on. According to Wikipedia, in the twelve years between 1993, the year of the adoption of the Oslo Accords, and 2005, the end of the second 'Intifada', there were 171 suicide attacks, nearly all aimed at civilian targets. Of these attacks, 87 were carried out by Hamas, including one against a school and another against a school bus. Hamas subsequently claimed responsibility for nearly all of these attacks. In the same period, as a result of these 'martyrdom operations', 805 Israelis were killed, 503 by those of Hamas. Of the 964 wounded, 388 were caused by Hamas suicide bombers. And this is not terrorism? Corbyn speaks of 'dialogue', knowing full well that both Hezbollah and Hamas have always on principle rejected any negotiations with Israel on the grounds that the Jewish state has no right to exist. Article 13 of the Hamas Charter says 'there is no solution to the Palestinian problem except by Jihad'. Section Three of Chapter Three of *The New Hezbollah Manifesto* (2009) reads as follows:

> Our stance on the negotiations and compromises made by the Madrid conference, the 'Araba Valley retrospect', the 'Oslo Accords', is a total refusal to any kind of compromise with the Zionist entity, which is based on admitting its legitimate presence and giving in [sic] what it occupied from the Palestinian and Islamic land. This stance is predetermined and permanent [n.b.] and isn't set for any compromise, even if the whole world admits to 'Israel'.

Hezbollah leader Sheikh Hassan Nasrallah goes much further; it is not just Israel, but the Jews, *all the Jews*, who must disappear: 'If Jews all gather in Israel it will save us the trouble of going after them worldwide.' Is this what Corbyn means by 'dialogue'?

S For the Attention of Mr K. Livingstone

Minute of the meeting between Reich Chancellor Adolf Hitler and Grand Mufti Haj Amin al-Husseini; Berlin, November 28, 1941, in the presence of Reich Foreign Minister Joachim von Ribbentrop and Minister Fritz Grobba, Head of the Reich Foreign Ministry Middle East Desk.

The Grand Mufti began by thanking the Fuhrer for the great honour he had bestowed by receiving him. He wished to seize the opportunity to convey to the Fuehrer of the Greater German Reich, admired by the entire Arab world, his thanks of [sic] the sympathy which he had always shown for the Arab and especially the Palestinian cause, and to which he had given clear expression in his public speeches. The Arab countries were firmly convinced that Germany would win the war and that the Arab cause would then prosper. The Arabs were Germany's natural friends because they had the same enemies as had Germany, namely the English, the Jews, and the Communists. Therefore, they were prepared to cooperate with Germany with all their hearts and stood ready to participate in the war, not only negatively but positively by the formation of an Arab Legion. The Arabs could be more useful to Germany as allies than might be apparent at first glance, both for geographical reasons and because of the suffering inflicted upon them by the English and the Jews. Furthermore, they had close relations with all Muslim nations, of which they could make use in behalf of the common cause. The Arab Legion would be quite easy to raise. An appeal by the Mufti to the Arab countries and the prisoners of Arab, Algerian, Tunisian and Moroccan nationality in Germany would produce a great number of volunteers eager to fight. Of Germany's victory, the Arab world was firmly convinced, not only because the Reich possessed a large army, brave soldiers, and military leaders of genius, but also because the Almighty could never award the victory to an unjust cause. In this struggle, the Arabs were striving for the independence and unity of Palestine, Syria and Iraq. They had the fullest confidence in the Fuehrer and looked to his hand for the balm on their wounds, which had been inflicted upon them by the enemies of Germany.

The Mufti then mentioned the letter he had received from Germany, which stated that Germany was holding no Arab territories and understood and recognized the aspirations to impendence and freedom of the Arabs, just as she supported the elimination of the Jewish national home. A public declaration in this sense would be very useful for its propagandistic effects on the Arab peoples at this moment. It would rouse the Arabs from their momentary lethargy and give them new courage. It would also ease the Mufti's work of secretly organising the Arabs against [sic] the moment when they could strike. At the same time, he could give the assurance that the Arabs would in strict discipline patiently wait for the right moment and only strike upon an order from Berlin.

With regard to the events in Iraq [the failed pro-Nazi coup of April 1941], the Mufti observed that the Arabs in that country certainly had by no means been incited by Germany to attack England, but solely had reacted in reaction to a direct English assault upon their honour. The Turks, he believed, would welcome the establishment of an Arab government in the neighbouring territories because they would prefer weaker Arab to strong European governments in the neighbouring countries, and being themselves a nation of 7 million, they had moreover nothing to fear from the 1,700,000 Arabs inhabiting Syria, Transjordan, Iraq and Palestine.

France likewise would have no objections to the unification plan [sic: Palestine was thus not considered by Husseini to be a nation distinct from its Arab neighbours] because she had conceded independence to Syria as early as 1936 and had given her approval to the unification of Iraq and Syria under King Faisal as early as 1933. In these circumstances, he was renewing his request that the Fuehrer make a public declaration so that the Arabs would not lose hope, which is so powerful a force in the life of nations., With such hope in their hearts the Arabs, as he had said, we willing to wait. They were not pressing for immediate realization for [sic] their aspirations; they could easily wait half a year or a whole year. But if they were not inspired with such a hope by a declaration of this sort, it could be expected that the English would be the gainers from it.

The Fuehrer replied that Germany's fundamental attitude on these questions, as the Mufti himself had already stated, was clear. Germany stood for uncompromising war against the Jews. That naturally included active opposition to the Jewish national home in Palestine, which was nothing other than a centre, in the form of a state, for the exercise of destructive influence by Jewish interests. Germany was also aware that the assertion that the Jews were carrying out the functions of economic pioneers in Palestine was a lie. The work there that was done only by the Arabs, not by the Jews. Germany was resolved, step by step, to ask one European nation after the other to solve its Jewish problem, and at the proper time to direct a similar appeal to non-European nations as well.

Germany was at the present time engaged in a life and death struggle with two citadels of Jewish power: Great Britain and Soviet Russia. Theoretically there was a difference between English capitalism and Soviet Russia's communism; actually, however, the Jews in both countries were pursuing a common goal. This was the decisive struggle; on the political plane, it presented itself in the main as a conflict between Germany and England, but ideologically it was between National Socialism and the Jews. It went without saying that Germany would furnish positive and practical aid to the Arabs involved in the same struggle, because platonic promises were useless in a war for survival or destruction in which the Jews were able to mobilize all of England's power for their ends.,

The aid to the Arabs would have to be material aid. Of how little sympathies alone were in such a battle had been demonstrated plainly by the operation in Iraq [the failed coup of April 1941], where circumstances had not permitted the rendering of really effective, practical aid. In spite of all the sympathies, German aid had not been sufficient and Iraq was overcome by the power of Britain, that is, the guardian of the Jews.

The Mufti could not but be aware however, that the outcome of the struggle going on at present would also decide the fate of the Arab world. The Fuehrer therefore had to think and speak coolly and deliberately, as a rational man and primarily as a soldier, as the leader of the German and allied armies. Everything of a nature to help this titanic battle for the common cause, and thus also for the Arabs, would have to be done. Anything however, that might contribute to weakening the military situation must be put aside, no matter how unpopular this move might be.

Germany was now engaged in very severe battles to force the gateway to the northern Caucasus region. The difficulties were mainly with regard to maintaining the supply, which was most difficult as a result of the destruction of railroads and highways as well as the oncoming winter. If at such a moment, the Fuehrer were to raise the problem of Syria in a declaration, those elements in France which were under de Gaulle's influence would receive new strength. They would interpret the Fuehrer's declaration as an intention to break up France's colonial empire and appeal to their fellow countrymen that they should rather make common cause with the English to try to save what could be saved. A German declaration regarding Syria would in France be understood to refer to the French colonies in general, and that would at the present time create new troubles in western Europe, which means that a portion of the German armed forces would be immobilised in the west, and no longer available for the campaign in the east.

The Fuehrer then made the following statement to the Mufti, enjoining him to lock in the utmost depths of his heart:

1. He, (the Fuehrer) would carry on the battle to the total destruction of the Judeo-Communist empire in Europe.

2. At some moment which was impossible to set exactly today but which in any event was not distant, the German armies would in the course of this struggle reach the southern exit from Caucasia.

3. As soon as this had happened, the Fuehrer would on his own give the Arab world the assurance that its hour of liberation had arrived. Germany's objective would then be solely the destruction of the Jewish element residing in the Arab sphere under the protection of British power. In that hour, the Mufti would be the most authoritative spokesman for the Arab world. It would then be his task to set off the Arab operations, which he had secretly prepared. When that time had come, Germany could also be indifferent to French reaction to such a declaration

Once Germany had forced open the road to Iran and Iraq through Rostov, it would also be the beginning of the end of the British World Empire. He (the Fuehrer) hoped that the coming year would make it possible for Germany to thrust open the Caucasian gates to the Middle East. For the good of the common cause, it would be better if the Arab proclamation were put off for a few more months than if Germany were to create difficulties for herself without thereby being able to help the Arabs.

He (the Fuehrer) fully appreciated the eagerness of the Arabs for a public declaration of the sort requested by the Grand Mufti. But he would beg him to consider that he (the Fuehrer) himself was the Chief of State of the German Reich for five long years during which he was unable to make to his own homeland the announcement of its liberation. He had to wait with that [sic] until the announcement could be made on the basis of a situation brought about by the force of arms that the Anschluss had been carried out [sic].The moment that Germany's tank divisions and air squadrons had made their appearance south of the Caucasus, the public appeal requested by the Grand Mufti could go out to the Arab world.

The Grand Mufti replied that it was his view that everything would come to pass just as the Fuhrer had indicated. He was fully reassured and satisfied by the words which he had heard from the Chief of the German State. He asked, however, whether it would not be possible, secretly at least, to enter into an agreement with Germany of the kind he had just outlined for the Fuehrer. The Fuehrer replied that he had just now given the grand Mufti precisely that confidential deceleration. The Grand Mufti thanked him for it and stated in conclusion that he was taking his leave from the Fuehrer in full confidence and with reiterated thanks for the interest shown in the Arab cause.'

From the Memoirs of Haj Amin al-Husseini:

> I did not expect that my reception at the famous chancellery would be an official one, but a private meeting with the Fuhrer. I had just arrived at the wide square in front of the chancellery and stepped out of the car in front of the entrance of the great building, when I was startled by the sound of a military band and guards of honour composed of around two hundred German soldiers who gathered in the square. My escorts from the Foreign Office invited me to inspect the guards, which I did. Then we entered the chancellery and passed through its long colonnades and impressive portals until we reached the large reception hall. There, the head of state protocols greeted me, and after a short while led me to the Fuhrer's special room. Hitler greeted me warmly with a cheerful face, expressive eyes, and clear joy...
>
> Our fundamental condition for cooperating with Germany was a free hand to eradicate every last Jew from Palestine and the Arab world. I asked Hitler for an explicit undertaking to allow us to solve the Jewish problem in a manner befitting our national and racial aspirations and according to the scientific methods innovated by Germany [i.e., gassing] in the handling of the Jews. The answer I got was: 'The Jews are all yours.'

Not according to Ken Livingstone and the Secretary-General of the Organisation of the Islamic Conference.

Addendum

Some months before the Mufti's arrival in Berlin, the path of his collaboration with the Third Reich in the extermination of the Jews had been smoothed by Nazi academics specialising in matters racial. At a conference convened at Alfred Rosenberg's Frankfurt 'Institute for Research into the Jewish Question' (sic) in March 1941, speakers were at pains to make a clear-cut racial distinction between their sought-for allies, the Arabs, and their mutual enemies, the Jews. As one explained, 'it would be well for the sake of clarity if the European world in its struggle against the Jews always remained aware of this context and did not call the struggle, as hitherto, anti-Semitism, because it is directed not against peoples of Semitic tongue, but against the unharmonious Near Eastern-Oriental-Mediterranean Jew-people which is being so passionately rejected also by the purely Oriental, Semitic tribes and peoples.' (i.e., the Arabs) When in October 1942 Rashid Ali, the former pro-Nazi Prime Ministry of Iraq, now like the Mufti an exile in Berlin after being ousted by the British, inquired as to the attitude of Germany's racial experts towards the Arabs, one replied that

> the Semitic-Arab peoples, languages and cultures always were the object of affectionate interest on the part of German scholarship. No responsible person or institution in Germany ever said that the Arabs were racially inferior or stood on an unfavourable place in the rank order of human races. On the contrary, National Socialist racial theory considers the Arabs [to be] members of a high-value race that looks back upon a glorious and heroic history. That is why, too, the struggle of the Arabs for political liberation against the Jewish usurpation of Palestine has always been observed and supported by Germany with particular sympathy.

T Labour's Black-Shirts: Jeremy and the Jew-Baiters

'He who toucheth pitch shall be defiled therewith'. Ecclesiasticus 13:1

'[Jeremy]'s been steeped in anti-Semitism.' Shadow Leader of the House Valerie Vaz, Radio Four, March 25, 2018

Jeremy Corbyn and his apologists have always insisted that his long-standing political collaboration, declared friendship and even brotherhood with Jew-killers, anti-Semites and Holocaust and 9/11 deniers does not constitute proof of the Labour Leader's alleged prejudices against the Jews. There are facts that suggest otherwise, and his repeated claim that they do not carries no more weight than a not-guilty plea in a criminal trial. For more three decades, at least since his launching, with the anti-Semite Ken Livingstone, of the forerunner of the Palestinian Solidarity Campaign in 1982. Corbyn's political career has been dominated and his thinking shaped by his obsession with Israel. Of the 834 Early Day Motions sponsored by Corbyn in the 20 years since 1989, 63 criticised Israel. The next highest number concerning a country is 26, on Morocco. As his Press Officer, Seumas Milne puts it, anti-Zionism is 'the great international issue of our time'. And so far as Muslim Jihadis, and much of the Neo-Nazi right and the neo-Leninist left are concerned, this is indubitably true. Like Corbyn's, their anti-Zionism is a Manichean struggle of absolute good, embodied in the Palestinians (or rather those genocidal terrorists who claim to represent them) against absolute evil, personified by the Jewish state of Israel, a mental and moral world not far removed from that inhabited by the Russian clerics who at beginning of the 20th century, conjured up the fabrications of that notorious text commended not only by Hitler and Hamas but as we shall see, websites associated with and visited by none other Corbyn himself...*The Protocols of the Learned Elders of Zion.* This utterly depraved world has become by his choice Corbyn's natural habitat, one where a virulent hatred of Israel has repeatedly slipped its mask to reveal what it truly is... a loathing of Jews...all Jews.

Corbyn has frequently been accused, and with good reason, of sharing platforms or associating with individuals who before Zionist-baiting became the fashion, would have never been given house-room by the vast majority of the left. Let two instances suffice here, since I have cited many others in the main body of this work. Speaking on the same platform with Corbyn at an event he hosted in Parliament in 2009, was Dyab Abou Jahjah, a Hezbollah supporter. The day before, addressing a meeting of the Stop the War Coalition, Corbyn, in the course of advertising his meeting the next day, famously or infamously, described Hezbollah and Hamas, two terrorist movements dedicated to the destruction of Israel and the extermination of the Jews, as his 'friends'. One of them, his guest speaker at Westminster, in the wake of 9/11 had hailed the atrocity as 'sweet revenge', and in 2004, told a Flemish magazine, 'I consider every dead American, British and Dutch soldier a victory'. 'Stop the War?' Nor was this all. Prior to the meeting, Jahjah had posted Holocaust-denial cartoons on his website, for which he was convicted by a Dutch court. Appraised of his posting, and the subsequent conviction, the Board of Deputies of British Jews wrote to the Home Security objecting to his presence in the UK to attend the Westminster meeting.

Some six years later, when Corbyn emerged as the leading contender for the Labour Leadership, he was criticised for sharing a platform with a convicted Holocaust denier and apologist for terrorism. Corbyn initially claimed in a BBC Radio 4 interview that he had never heard of or met Jahjah, let alone shared a platform with him: 'I saw the name this morning and asked somebody, "Who is he?" ...I'm sorry, I don't know who this person is.' In a matter of hours, Corbyn's lie was exposed when a photo was produced showing Corbyn and Jahjah siting side by side at their Westminster meeting. Jahjah then confirmed that not only did he know Corbyn, but that 'we worked together closely...we had two lunches or breakfast together...He is a political friend. I am very sympathetic to his political ideas...I am hopeful he will win the leadership of Labour and help build a better future for the British people.' Yet a few hours earlier, Corbyn had said, 'I don't know who this person is'. At the meeting in question, responding to criticism his of sharing a platform with a Holocaust denier and advocate of terrorist attacks on civilians, Corbyn was unrepentant. 'I refuse to be dragged into this stuff [sic] that somehow or other because we're pro-Palestinian we're anti-Semitic. It's a nonsense.' Holocaust denial not anti-Semitic?

Two years after sharing a platform with Jahjah, Corbyn became the subject of another controversy involving a relationship with an anti-Semite who advocated terrorism against Israeli politicians. In 2002, the Polish journalist Ewa Jasciewicz, who writes regularly for the fanatically anti-Israel on-line *Electronic Intifada,* (sic) called, on a pro-Palestinian website, for the assassination of members of the Israeli parliament, the Knesset, saying they should be 'bumped off', preferably while it was in session. Active on behalf of *Kampania Palystina*, the Polish equivalent of BDS and Corbyn's PSC, she has brushed aside accusations of its collaboration with movements that were only too willing, as is the way in Poland, to further their own anti-Semitic agendas. It should have come as no surprise then that in 2010, together with another anti-Zionist activist, she scribbled anti-Israeli graffiti on a wall of the Warsaw Ghetto, where in April 1943, Jews destined for the gas chambers of Hitler's Final Solution staged an uprising against the Nazis. Some of the survivors of the uprising made their way at the end of the war to what in 1948 became the new state of Israel, where they founded a kibbutz that is today run by their descendants. They rose against the Nazis at a time when the Palestinian leader, the Grand Mufti of Jerusalem, together with other prominent Muslim politicians, was collaborating with Hitler in the extermination of the Jews. What Ms Jasciewicz claimed was a protest against what she saw as Israel's exploitation of the Holocaust to justify the 'colonisation and repression' of the Palestinians was in fact a desecration of the memory of the Jews' struggle for their liberation from centuries of persecution, pogroms and finally, genocide. Israel's Yad Vashem Holocaust museum condemned her action as 'tainted with anti-Semitism', while the Community Security Trust described it as an 'act of arrogance and callousness'.

Not everyone shared that view of Ms Jasciewicz. Speaking at a pro-Gaza, or more accurately, pro-Hamas rally in 2009, Corbyn referred to her as a 'good friend', and her notorious exploit in Warsaw the next year did nothing to harm that friendship. In 2011, the Palestine Solidarity Campaign, of which Corbyn is both a founder and a patron, staged what it called a 'Literary Festival' (sic) in Tottenham, North London. Children from eight local primary schools, that is, those under the age of 12, had been invited to attend the event, where they would be addressed by amongst other speakers, none other than Corbyn's 'good friend', Ms Jasciewicz. As in the case of the Hezbollah Holocaust denier Dyab Abou Jahjah, the Board of Deputies of British Jews understanbly found itself at odds with the organisers of the event. Dismissing their objection to what was obviously his choice of speaker, Corbyn announced he would be attending the event, adding, 'it's great opportunity for children to understand the wealth and joy of Palestinian literature and a little [sic] of the history of the region.' He insisted that the festival would 'not in any way be biased.' 'In any way'? In which case, why invite a notorious anti-Israeli activist? With her track record, which Corbyn must surely have been aware of, what kind of 'unbiased' history of the Middle East would she be instilling into her charges? This one can guess from her comments on the Gaza conflict of 2014 on behalf of 'London Palestine Action', when she defined Israel's polices towards the Palestinians as those of 'massacre', 'apartheid' and 'genocide'. She surfaced again when she was due to share a Momentum platform with Corbyn and his Shadow Chancellor John McDonnell at the September 2018 Labour Party conference. She and Jeremy were obviously still 'good friends'. As Aesop puts it, 'a man is known by the company he keeps'. But such was the outcry, that that she withdrew at the last moment.

From the PSC's inception in 1982, Corbyn has been has been amongst, if not the most frequent and prominent of the campaign's public speakers. Also numbered among its patrons are film director and one-time WRP sympathiser Ken Loach, who is in favour of a re-examination of whether the Holocaust happened, and former Liberal (sic) Democratic Peer Baroness Tonge, who in 2010 retailed the accusation Israel relief workers had harvested body organs from victims of the Haiti earthquake, and who in 2016, resigned from the Liberal Democratic Party after being suspended for hosting a meeting at Westminster where claims were made that Zionists encouraged the Nazis to carry out the Holocaust to gain sympathy for a Jewish state in Palestine, as if they needed any such inducement. She resigned from her sponsorship of the PSC following an uproar when she implied that that the massacre of 11 Jews at prayer in a Pittsburgh synagogue by a Neo-Nazi was caused by Israel's ill-treatment of the Palestinians. With patrons such as these, little wonder that irrefutable evidence has been found of the dissemination within the campaign of the most extreme manifestations of anti-Semitism, giving the lie to the PSC's statement that it is 'opposed to all form of racism, including anti-Jewish prejudice'.

The attacks on the Jews go far beyond the routine denunciations of Zionism that are the stock in trade of the Sharia left and the Neo-Nazi fringe. The target of the invective, with items on Jewish conspiracies and Holocaust denial being the most frequently posted and re-cycled, is not just Israel, but the Jews, *all Jews*. Yet Patron Corbyn has not only failed to denounce and demand the expulsion of these Jew-baiters from the PSC. He is on the most cordial of terms with some of them and can be seen in photos taken with three of these purveyors of the myths of the *Protocols*. And even more to the point, he shares the views of the most extreme of them, to the extent of signing the Cairo Declaration of December 2002, which twice accused Israel of perpetrating, quote, 'genocidal crimes against the Palestinian people', that is to say, actively attempting to exterminate an entire people. The main purpose of the declaration was to rally support for a regime that *was* guilty of genocide, the fascist regime of Saddam Hussein, faced with the imminent prospect of overthrow by a coalition of forces led by the USA. As someone so passionately committed to the defence of human rights, as in Iran for example, he must have been better informed than most about Sandam's gassing of the Kurds in 1988. But yet he still signed. One must see the bigger picture…an Arab regime that commits genocide must at all costs be defended, while a Jewish state that is the intended victim of Palestinian genocidists must be treated as an enemy, and those who would if they could murder its entire Jewish population, as his friends. One of the proposals endorsed by Corbyn was 'to prepare for sending human shields to Iraq', and another 'the boycott of US and Israeli commodities'. Corbyn's name heads the list of signatories to this lying Declaration, followed by a cavalcade of veteran Zionists-baiters…Andrew Murray, George Galloway, Ken Loach, Tariq Ali, Paul Foot, Alex Callinicos and Lindsey (Shibboleth) German.

Before exploring the nether regions of this fetid world inhabited by Corbyn, let us first look at two examples of the beliefs that led him there, which have him subscribing to two classic Jewish stereotypes, as conspirators and exploiters. They are related by Tom Bowyer in his biography of the Labour Leader, *Dangerous Hero*. In 2003, with Jewish bankers in New York in mind, Corbyn told a meeting of Hamas supporters that in the USA, 'the power of the Israel lobby is truly phenomenal'. 62 two years previously, another anti-Semitic politician, announcing to the German Reichstag his declaration of war on the USA, described the USA as a country ruled by a 'Jewish clique which surrounds Roosevelt and exploits the American people'. Racialist minds think…and speak… alike, as also in this next case. In 2015, recalling his time as an assistant researcher for the National Union of Taylor and Garment Workers in the early 1970s, Corbyn called the mainly Jewish employers of the union's members 'scumbags' and 'crooks' for using devious methods to defraud their workers of their wages. This story, like others of Corbyn's about the Jews, proved to be a lie. The union's archives have no record of such exploitative malpractices, and a colleague of Corbyn's assured Bowyer that Corbyn 'never had any contact with our members. He just sat in meetings and passed me information.'

What follows are samples of mainly on-line Jew-baiting by those on the left whose guiding principle, judging by their content, could, with the change of just one letter, easily be a paraphrase of the Corbynite mantra, 'For the Many, not the Few'. They have been selected from a wide range of sources, the most comprehensive being by David Collier, of postings by the Palestine Solidarity Campaign, the Boycott, Disinvestment and Sanctions campaign backed by Corbyn, the Facebook site *Palestine Live*, one of whose secret members was Jeremy Corbyn, and by individual, mainly pro-Corbyn Labour Party members.

Over a period of two years, Collier investigated the on-line activity of members of 31 branches of the Palestine Solidarity Campaign in England and Wales, samples of 17 of which are featured in his 80-page report. (The photos of the saintly Jeremy with his Jew-baiting comrades can be seen on pages 12 and 51) Collier had very strict criteria for what could be included as examples of PSC anti-Semitism: 'If the worst I found was an activist saying that Israel should be destroyed, is committing genocide, and Zionists are all Nazis, that activist would not have made the grade for this research. Let that fact sink in.'

Now for samples.

Bristol:

'The USA is controlled by Zionists. Israel controls US government and media... Record number of Jews in US government.'
'Did you know that the only people to be arrested on September 11 in connection to [sic] the attacks were 5 Israeli Mossad agents?'
'Report in *Veteran Today* that ISIS is Israeli.'
'Suspicions are growing that Paris shootings are a false flag operation.'
'The genocide of 15 million+ Germans by the Jews.'
'The France attacks. What better excuse to get the France [sic] Jews to move to Israel.'
[This is patently a variant on the oft-repeated claim that the Zionists collaborated with the Nazis in the Holocaust in order to generate sympathy and support for a Jewish state in the British Mandate.]
'ISIS leader Al-Baghdadi is a Jewish Mossad agent.'
'Settler Rabbi publishes *The Complete Guide to Killing Non-Jews.*'
On page 12, Saint Jeremy is posing with each arm around a Bristol Jewish conspiracy theorist, Edward Clarke on his right, and Rita Tiziana to his left. Clarke is the expert on the motive for the *Charlie Hebdo* massacre, Tiziana on Mossad and settler Rabbis.

Cardiff

'Mossad is busy in Paris again.'
'Israel executing Palestinians, harvesting their organs.'
'Bibi [Netanyahu] a suspect in *Charlie Hebdo* massacre.'
'The greatest lie ever told - The Holocaust - 2015 documentary HD.'
'Critical discussion of the Holocaust is dangerous.'
'Auschwitz Museum is a fraudulent enterprise.'
'ISIS is working on a Mossad/CIA plan to make a Greater Israel.'

Durham

'25000 Ukrainian children organs harvested in Israel.'

Jersey

'Israelis - not Muslims - cheered in Jersey City on 9/11.'

Merton, London

'Israelis stealing organs from living people - including testicles and ovaries.'
[This myth has bled into the political mainstream, with PSC Patron Baroness Tonge's insinuation that Israeli relief workers harvested the organs of victims of the Haiti earthquake of 2010, and Rutgers University Professor and former Syrian diplomat Mazen Adi's allegation at the United Nations in April 2012 that

'international gangs led by some Israeli religious figures are now trafficking children's organs.']

'French journalist arrested after exposing Israel link to Paris attacks.'

'CIA and Mossad are behind Boko Haram and ISIS, says Sudan President.'

'9/11 Tel Aviv-based outside job.'

'The "Zionist Power Configuration" (ZPC) operates at both a global and local level as was indicated on 9/11.'

'Ukrainian General: "Ukraine is under Zionist occupation".'

Richmond, London

'Zionist Broadcasting Corporation forthcoming events: BBC to broadcast Holocaust Memorial Day.'

'There was no Holocaust. It's a pack of lies…Fuck Zionism and fuck its Holy Holocash.'

'The Zionist tentacles on our Parliament almost complete.'

'Jewish donors to the Labour Party run it.'

'The attack by the pro-Israel lobby on the Labour Party 7 days before the election is not just an attack on Jeremy Corbyn…what we are witnessing is an attack on British democracy by a foreign power.'

'The only individuals arrested on 9/11 in connection with the attacks were Israeli nationals.'

Luton

'The belief that the Jews were responsible for the Holocaust is common to orthodox Jews.'

'What is it with Zionists and children, killing children and stealing children to sell them on the black market. And yet we are always told Israel has a right to exist.'

Medway

Advertising a video: 'New world Order as planned in the elders of Zion.'

In a posting advertising a 'Stand up to Racism' public meeting featuring Momentum Vice Chairperson Jackie Walker, twice suspended and eventually expelled from the Labour Party (but not Momentum) for anti-Semitism, we read the following]

"No to Islamophobia, no to anti-Semitism."

[while in another posting *on the same page*]

'Literally a bus load of Zionist Jews arrested for organ smuggling.'

Norwich

'We no longer have a democracy when the Jewish lobby can tell what we can and cannot discuss.'

'Of course, we are used to being [a Freudian slip, or does she mean accused of being?] anti-Semitic all of the time. I can live with it now, knowing that it isn't true.'

[but in another of hers]

'Bodies of murdered Palestinians are being returned with organs missing.'
[and yet another]:
'Have questions on the Holocaust? Tony Blair wants you arrested.'

Peterborough

(Where in June 2019, Labour's conspiracy theorist candidate Liz Forbes [see below] was possibly elected with fraudulent votes.)
A posting promoting the video entitled: 'The Covenant of the Jew Illuminati.'
'Israeli Jews admit they run America.'

Reading

It is here on page 51 we see Reading PSC's Tony Gratrex, sporting a PSC T-shirt, posing in a photo with a grinning Jeremy Corbyn, who has his right arm around Gratrex's shoulder. They are clearly on more than nodding terms with each other, because Gratrex was also snapped in an identical pose with Corbyn at another PSC function. How does a quite open anti-Semite, Holocaust denier, and Nazi apologist come to enjoy the patronage of the Labour Party's Leader? Another link with Corbyn is Gratrex's membership of the congregation of the anti-Semitic Rev. Stephen Sizer's Anglican Church in nearby Virginia Water. Sizer is a high-profile PSC member, sharing its platforms with Corbyn, while Corbyn, it will be remembered, came to the Reverend's defence when he was reprimanded by his Bishop for claiming that the Jews were responsible for 9/11. Like Sizer and so many other members of the PSC, Corbyn, as we have seen, also does not accept the 'official version' of what happened on that day.
These are some of Comrade Gratrex's postings:
'There is still not a shred of evidence in the public domain that a single "terrorist" was involved in any part of 9/11' [Corbyn also believes that 9/11 was 'manipulated']
'Paris attacks. Another false flag?'
'Jewish power for you…The Daily Telegraph and other press outlets list the sex abuse allegations against Lord Janner, a 27-year Labour MP. But there is one thing The Telegraph and other British press outlets fail to mention. They omit the fact that at the time Lord Janner was allegedly sexually abusing young British [sic] orphans…he was head of the British Jewish community.'
'A century of deceit: Iraq, the World Wars, Holocaust, Zionist militarism…In an effort to whitewash their own egregious war crimes, the Allied powers went along with the Zionists' pre-mediated fictional account of six million dead Jews. At the post-war Nuremberg Trials, an Allied-run kangaroo court staffed to the brim by Zionist Jews and their Allied lackeys, the truth was buried ['drowned' surely] under a tidal wave of falsehoods. The Zionist motives for the war itself were purposefully obscured and a cartoonish propaganda narrative of "Nazi evil" was foisted upon the world to advance the victors' post-war aims for Europe and accelerate the Zionists' ambitions for a Jewish ethno-state in Palestine.'
A posting advertising The *Protocols of the Learned Elders of Labour*:
'Jewish power is no longer a vague and mysterious concept. We should listen to the words of a few of the prime Elder Jewish oligarchs and learn from them about the future of the Labour Party and its political role.'

Inevitably, Gratrex detected the hand of the Jews in the anti-Semitic crisis that beset Labour after Corbyn's election as party leader: 'If Jewish power is the power to silence opposition to Jewish power, then the scandal over the alleged anti-Semitism within the Labour Party is a perfect example of that power.'

West Midlands

'The Babylonian Jewish Talmud advocates sex with a child of three years, saying with every tear, the virginity is renewed.'

'Essential reading: Many claims around the Holocaust were debunked long ago, yet they are still regurgitated to this day…Evidence collected by scientists, engineers, historians, scholars and others, some of which [sic] are Jewish, strongly support the conclusion that the facilities alleged to have been homicidal gas chambers could not possibly have been used to exterminate human beings for a number of fundamental reasons.'

'Did you know that just months before 9/11, the World Trade Centre's lease was privatised and sold to Larry Silverstein. Silverstein took out an insurance plan that "fortuitously" covered terrorism.'

Next, PSC Scotland

Posted by some guests at the SPSC Christmas Dinner, 2015, with Scotland's First Minister Nicola Sturgeon in attendance:

'The real Holocaust of World War Two - the genocide of 15 + million Germans.'

'Why does extreme Muslim state ISIS attack Muslim state after Muslim state but never fire a shot at Israel?'

'It is the ghastly truth of the Jewish-orchestrated plundering, mass rape, mass murder, and subjugation of the German people in the latter days of the and aftermath of World War Two, which continues to this day.'

'These were the real death camps of World War Two, not the slave labour and internment camps run by the Germans in the alleged Jewish "Holocaust", which is a Jewish fraud and lie.'

'The biggest single source of Holohoax in modern times is Jewish Hollywood. Most people's views of the Second World War are formed by watching movies and the Jewish propaganda documentaries on Jewish owned or run channels such as the history Channel National Geographic of the BBC.'

West Dunbartonshire

'ISIS leader "Al-Baghdadi" is Jewish Mossad agent Simon Elliot.'

'Mossad agent accidentally admits they did 7/7 London bombings.'

'…Princess Diana was assassinated by Mossad…'

'25,000 Ukrainian children organs harvested in [sic] Israel.'

'Fake Muslim preacher Omar Bakri busted as Mossad Mole - tied to Woolwich'. [i.e., murder of Lee Rigby]

'The fall of the Holocaust lie and the rise of truth and reason.'

Posting promoting 'The Protocols of the Learned Elders of Zion. Zionist plan for world conquest through Jewish world government.'

'Israel murdered 3,000 Americans on 9/11 2001.'

Glasgow

'Nazis and Zionist Jews made a deal behind the real Jewish people's backs and that is how the state of Israel was created with the help of Adolf Hitler.'

'ISIS is a Zionist creation being used to achieve a "greater Israel".'

Posting of speech by Hitler: 'Adolf Hitler talks about the Jews and the Allies.' 'Never mind the alleged Holocaust, just listen to his opening lines and tell me its not happening now.'

'American gas chamber export [sic] Dr. Leuchter visited all sites and testified that supposed gas chambers "incapable" of supporting gas executions.'

'Press TV [Corbyn's former employer]: "9/11 was Zionist coup d'état."'

'How is France under attack? Jewish owners recently sold Paris's Bataclan theatre where ISIS killed dozens.'

'Did Mossad do Charlie Hebdo?'

'David Icke [sic]: The Rothschild Zionist Agenda. New World Order and the Third World War.'

Dundee

'So we have France voting to give Palestine statehood and then all of a sudden they get attacked by ISIS.'

'Paris admits Nice attack was false flag operation.'

'Israel linked to Istanbul Airport terror attack.'

'96% of world's media is controlled by Jews.'

'Israel did 9/11 to destroy "7 countries in 5 years". Trump's Muslim ban targets almost [sic] exactly [sic] the same seven countries.'

Fife

'International Red Cross report confirms the Holocaust of six million Jews is a hoax.'

Aberdeen

'Israel kills its own teenagers. Zionist money owns the mainstream media. Kennedy was assassinated because he wanted to take on the Rothschilds.'

'ISIS belongs to Jew Zionism.'

'Israel injects Palestinian prisoners with dangerous viruses.'

Here are some postings by BDS activists:

'Some Israelis/Jews worked at WTC were tipped off to absent on that day, and those who did die in the attacks ignored or missed the tip.'

'All Zionists must die.'

'ISIS is Israel.'

'Because Israel OWNS the USA, all American taxpayers are slaves to the Zionists. Without the US support Israel will collapse.'

'Edward Snowden: Top ISIS leader Abu Bakr Al Baghdadi was trained by Israeli Mossad.'

'ISIS is working on Mossad/CIA plan to create Greater Israel.'

'Complete list of banks owned by Illuminati Rothschild family.'

'Former Italian President says 9/11 solved. It's common knowledge, Mossad, CIA behind 9/11 terror attacks.'

'The "Six Million" Holocaust lie.'

'International Red Cross report confirms the Holocaust of six million Jews is a hoax.'

'They [the Jews] are ALL terribly ugly because of the evil inside them. And they all look alike.'

'A Century of Deceit: Iraq, the World Wars, Holocaust Mythology and Zionist Militarism.'

Video: 'Israeli terrorism against America. By Dr. David Duke.' [Duke is the former KKK Grand Wizard and white supremacist who admires Corbyn and is admired by Green Party members.]

Now the Campaign Against Anti-Semitism's report, based on a month-long monitoring of the PSC's Facebook page during November 2016:

'Sure the Jews own America what do you expect?'

'The Rothschilds run every country in the world except 5. That's why Israel can do this.'

'…the Zionist mafia run the planet.'

'I hate my government. Weak puppets for the Zionists NWO [New World Order] their bankers and their puppet governments and regimes.'

'Pretty much most right-wing organisations around the world including those that claim to be Islamic are actually Zionist funded.'

'They are bloody thirsty. They want to kill entire humanity except America. God will punish them soon.'

'Filthy jew dirtbags.'

'What Jewish Zionist mother*****zzzzz. Inshallah [Allah willing] they will rot in hell for their messed-up actions.'

'Israel is a syndicate crime country. It should be destroyed in the world for ever.'

'Allah will destroy Israel soon.'

Another website devoted to the same subject, Stand for Peace, reports a posting by former PSC West Midlands branch chairperson Sammi Ibrahim. Like Gratrex, he deplores the Nuremberg Trials; 'I bow my head to those who were judicially murdered at Nuremberg. They were the world's martyrs, not villains. Not one of them would have been condemned to death in a fair trial - not one! They sacrificed an entire nation, and in the end, themselves, to save western civilisation. They were defeated by thugs in robes and gangster in uniform - and conspiracies hatched by shysters from the ghettoes of Eastern Europe.'

To see if PSC Facebook pages were being monitored for racists comments, the Campaign Against Anti-Semitism posted three about a fictitious 'Bangalla people' identical in sentiment to those that had been made about the Jews. *All were removed within six hours.* Those about the Jews remained. As a personal spot check, I scrolled down the PSC national website, and in no time, came across this posting by a Marty Chamberlain, dated December 2, 2017: 'Israel is like a disease on this planet...can we get a vaccine for that?' I toyed with and then rejected the idea of answering: 'Yes, Zyklon B.' (the gas used to exterminate the Jews in the Nazi gas chambers.) Immediately below this posting, blatantly anti-Semitic by any standards other than those of Corbyn's PSC, there was another, which stated, in all seriousness:

'Please help raise money for a legal challenge to the Independent Press Standards Organisation to prevent Palestinian events being smeared [sic] as anti-Semitic.'

From his two-year study of the postings and public activities of the Palestinian Solidarity Campaign, Collier concluded that around 40% of its activists qualified as anti-Semites, attracted to the Campaign like iron filings to a magnet, just as is Corbyn to movements and regimes that propagate the lies they subscribe to. The evidence presented by Collier reveals an on-line culture of festering Jew-hatred, one awash with fake news, 'alternative facts' and demented conspiracy theories that within the PSC are its *lingua franca*. It is a culture which those who inhabit it not only make no attempt to hide but advertise to all and sundry. It is obvious from numerous postings reproduced by Collier that for many PSC activists, the Palestinian issue serves merely as a pretext to spew their venom on the Jews. It was just their kind who back in the 1930s, motivated by the same vile prejudice, would have been activists in LINK, like the PSC infested with anti-Semites and pro-Nazis, which campaigned for what it euphemistically called 'Anglo-German understanding'. Anyone reading their postings and not *au fait* with the PSC's un-hidden agenda would surely ask themselves, what have harvesting body organs, the Nuremberg Trials, and the causes of world wars one and two got do with the Palestine question? The simple answer is, nothing.

In addition to Gratrex, Corbyn appears in numerous other photos in Collier's report with PSC anti-Semites during the course of his political engagements with the PSC and the Labour Party. They include one with to Corbyn's right, Edward Clarke, one of whose postings refers to an 'ugly Israel species', and another which reads, 'can I tell you how much I hate Israel and its rich western backers'; and another with on his left, Rita Roberta Tiziana, who believes, like many other PSC members, that the Islamic State is a creation of Mossad. She also posted on-line her claim that the Islamic State terror attacks in France were part of a Zionist plot to provide an 'excuse to get the France [sic] Jews [to] move to Israel. They want the Jews out of Europe to populate the stolen land'. Another snap shows Corbyn posing with Dr. Swee Ang, who shared on line a video made by David Duke alleging the existence of a world Jewish conspiracy.

As well as being a patron of the PSC, Corbyn has been a highly visible supporter of Unite Against Fascism from its founding in 2003. The human rights campaigner Peter Tatchell has criticised UAF for being 'silent about Islamic fascists who promote anti-Semitism', and with good reason. We have seen that the 'anti-fascist' Corbyn has no problem in sharing platforms with notorious Muslim anti-Semites, and to be photographed with a neo-Nazi (twice), two Jewish conspiracy theorists and two Holocaust deniers. Just how he conceives of the struggle against fascism is graphically depicted in another photo, this time on a UAF website, where he can be seen holding a UAF poster, inscribed in large letters, NEVER AGAIN. This is an exclusively Jewish slogan, especially popular with Zionists, and it conveys the resolve of the Jews never again to be subject to another Holocaust, such as Corbyn's friends Hamas and Hezbollah have in mind. It is also the title of a book by the founder of the Jewish Defence League, Meir Kahane. But the UAF purloined these two words to give them an entirely different, and in fact opposite meaning, because below them, on the poster held up by Corbyn, there is no reference to anti-Semitism, but instead, 'No to racist Pediga, no to Islamophobia'.

Corbyn also plays a prominent role in Labour Friends of Palestine which, despite its membership being restricted to MPs, is not immune from the kind of Nazi-style thinking that infests the PSC. On September 25, 2017, there appeared on the LFP website a tweet that blatantly alluded to the Holocaust and implied that the final objective was the total elimination of Israel, with the comment that a 'two-state solution will end the occupation - our solution will be the final solution.'(sic) Only two weeks previously, anti-Zionists had demanded at the Labour Party conference that the affiliated Jewish Labour Movement should be expelled from the Labour Party, a demand first raised by Corbyn and Livingstone back in 1984. Then on December 11, in Committee Room 1 of the House of Commons, Corbyn, his Shadow Chancellor John McDonnell, who is on record as being opposed to very existence of Israel, and Bradford West MP Naz(i) Shah, suspended for anti-Semitic remarks about Israel, launched the Labour Muslim Network. This is an organisation based purely on a religion, and not, like the Jewish Labour Movement, on ethnicity, and a religion, moreover, that preaches hatred against the Jews. The Network is headed by Ali Milani, who doubles up as Vice-President of the *dhimmi* National Union of Students, and who in that capacity has made a series of anti-Semitic comments that he was subsequently required to apologise for. He has also declared like McDonnell that 'Israel has no right to exist.' Posing with Milani, Corbyn once again used the occasion to have himself photographed with an anti-Semite. Among other MPs present was Afzal Khan, who during the 2014 Gaza conflict, accused Israel of 'acting like Nazis'. This, from someone whose own religion is saturated with anti-Semitism. Representing the clerical interest was Mohammed Kozbar, who just happens to be Chairman of Corbyn's local Finsbury Park Mosque, where on the first anniversary of 9/11, a packed to overflowing congregation celebrated the attack on the World Trade Centre.

Next, Corbyn as art critic. The following item, titled *There is only one word for Jeremy Corbyn*, appeared in the *Jewish Chronicle* on March 24, 2018:

> The word is overused in politics. Politicians rarely lie, if for no other reason than the risk of being caught out. But sometimes it is the only appropriate word when a politician is guilty of a deliberate attempt at distorting the truth wilfully and shamelessly. That time is now, and the politician is Jeremy Corbyn. In November 21015, the *JC* reported that back in 2012, Jeremy Corbyn had defended the existence of a mural which had been widely condemned as being anti-Semitic. The work, *Freedom for Humanity*, was painted near Brick Lane in London's East End by 'graffiti artist' Kalen Ockerman, he goes by the name of Mear One. Its intent was obvious. It showed businessmen and bankers sitting counting their money. Not only did they look like obvious caricatures of Jews - in a style reminiscent of Nazi propaganda in the 1930s - the artist himself confirmed they were intended as such, writing: 'Some of the older white Jewish folk in the local community had an issue with me portraying their beloved Rothschild or Warburg etc as the demons they are.'
>
> Anyone with even a basic knowledge of politics, history and the world would see that the [20 foot-high] work was caricaturing Jews. And, to be blunt, anyone denying that is indulging in the sophistry of the most pathetically unconvincing kind. Indeed, the then Mayor of Tower Hamlets, Lutfar Rahman [certainly no friend of the Jews]

himself ordered council officials to 'do everything possible' to remove the mural, agreeing that 'the images of the bankers perpetuate anti-Semitic propaganda about conspiratorial Jewish domination of financial institutions'. But when Mr Ockerman wrote on Facebook that his mural was to be removed, a then insignificant Labour MP expressed his support for the piece, writing in response: 'Why? You are in good company. [Yes, that of the Nazi's *Die Sturmer*] Rockefeller destroyed Diego Viera's [sic]. mural because it included a picture of Lenin.' Mr Corbyn was referring to the removal in 1934 of a work by the Mexican artist Diego Rivera from the Rockefeller Centre in New York. When we unearthed Mr Corbyn's 2012 comment in 2015, we contacted his office for a response, asking about his support for a clearly [and expressly] anti-Semitic mural remaining on display.

No response was forthcoming then or, indeed, for over two years - until yesterday, when the Labour MP Luciana Berger came across the story and asked Mr Corbyn's office for a response. That response was perhaps the most appalling single comment by any mainstream party leader of my lifetime. A spokesman for the Labour leader said [why can't leaders speak for themselves?]: 'In 2012, Jeremy was responding to concerns about the removal of public art on grounds of freedom of speech [which Corbyn does not believe in]. However, the mural was offensive [when did he say this?], used anti-Semitic imagery, which has no place in our society [but it does on websites frequented by Corbyn], and it is right that it was removed.' [which Corbyn at the time said it should not be] The more one thinks about this, the more shocking it is. The statement acknowledges what it could hardly deny, that the mural was anti-Semitic. But it also says that Mr Corbyn was defending it on 'grounds of free speech'. [something Corbyn has made it clear that when it comes to criticising Islam, he does not believe in].

In other words, we are expected to accept that it was perfectly fine for the leader of the Labour Party to support the existence of a large public anti-Semitic mural. The free speech argument is of course risible. Few politicians have been less committed to upholding free speech principles than Mr Corbyn. In February 2006, for example, he did not merely attend but spoke at a rally in London against the Danish cartoons of Mohammed published in the *Jyllands-Posten*. The obvious truth of the matter is that he liked the mural and saw it as wrong that it should be destroyed. There is almost no room for ambiguity over this, despite his spokesman's attempt yesterday to create some. But deplorable as this was, it was not even the worst aspect of this affair. The spokesman's comment prompted outrage on social media and from some Labour MPs. Ian Austin, who has consistently stood up to Mr Corbyn and taken him to task over anti-Semitism, tweeted: 'Luciana won't be alone. I think lots of Labour members will want an explanation for this.' [I am not so sure. As we have seen, anti-Semitism runs deep nowadays on the left.] Gavin Shuker, MP for Luton South, said that the statement from Mr Corbyn's spokesman 'isn't even an apology. I know this is like screaming into the wind, it'll make zero difference, but I want to say that this is just so wrong. It's impossible to confront anti-Semitism in our party if this is the response from the very top.' And Mrs Berger said the response was 'wholly inadequate'. Even Mr Corbyn's office could see that its explanation made things worse. So a few hours later, a statement from Mr Corbyn himself was issued:

'In 2012 I made a general [sic] comment about the removal of public art on the grounds of freedom of speech. My comment referred to the destruction of the mural *Man at the Crossroads* by Diego Rivera on the Rockefeller Centre. That is no way comparable with the mural in the original post. I sincerely regret that I did not look more closely at the image I was commenting on, the contents of which are deeply disturbing [so deeply, he did not notice them] and anti-Semitic. I wholeheartedly support its removal. [But at the time, you *opposed* it.] I am opposed to the production of anti-Semitic material of any kind, and the defence of free speech cannot be used as a justification for promotion of anti-Semitism in any form. That is a view I have always held.' [Then, just to give one example of many, why has Corbyn not condemned the genocidal anti-Semitism of the 1988 Hamas Charter?]

As I wrote at the start, the word 'lie' is overused in politics. But it impossible not to regard this statement as a lie. Mr Corbyn saw the image. He went out of his way to comment on it in Facebook. He knew what the mural depicted; it is not possible not to see that after a moments glance. The Jewish caricatures were the entire point of the mural. This incident must be judged on its own terms and those terms show that Jeremy Corbyn a) defended an anti-Semitic mural b) refused to answer questions on that defence for over two years c) when pushed for an explanation by a Labour MP argued that it was a free speech issue and then d) said that he hadn't really looked at it. But there is a pattern here. Only last week Mr Corbyn was revealed as having been an active member of a private [in fact 'secret'] Facebook group that was suffused with anti-Semitism. His excuse then was the same as his latest excuse yesterday: that he hadn't noticed it. This newspaper has spent the two years and six months since Mr Corbyn's election as Labour leader exposing anti-Semitism within the Labour Party. Barely a day has gone by in that time when another incident has not emerged. During his first leadership campaign in 2015 we posed seven questions to Mr Corbyn on the front page of the *JC* over what we knew already knew back then about his unsavoury associations with anti-Semites. To date, no serious response has been given even to those original questions. Now this, and last week's Facebook story. Mr Corbyn protests that he cares about anti-Semitism 'and all forms of racism', in the formulation he insists on using. Mr Corbyn is a liar.

Corbyn was also caught down-playing the closeness of his relationship with Palestine Live Administrator Elleanne Green, who in one of her many anti-Semitic postings, quoted approvingly from Hitler's *Mein Kampf* a passage attacking Zionism. The Campaign Against Anti-Semitism published on March 27, 2018, the following refutation of Corbyn's claim, reported in the *Guardian*, that she was merely an 'acquittance'.

Last week, Jeremy Corbyn was exposed as being a member of a deeply anti-Semitic Facebook group in which he participated for two years. Now, damning new evidence made available to Campaign Against Anti-Semitism proves that Mr Corbyn or his team were demonstrably lying when, as was reported in The *Guardian* they had said that his relationship with the founder and key administrator of the Facebook group 'Palestine Live' was that of a mere 'acquaintance'. Research and documents in our possession indicate that he had an intimate relationship with Elleanne Green, a woman who has expressed anti-Semitic beliefs and who has prolifically disseminated extreme anti-Semitic material, including neo-Nazi articles. They shared a love of the same poetry and of various common causes even before he joined the Facebook group, almost certainly at her invitation, despite Mr Corbyn implying that he was added against his wishes. [in which case, why did he remain a member for more than two years?] They organised events together, and she proudly noted the two years he spent in the group with her.

Those familiar with Mr Corbyn know well that he was not - before becoming Party Leader - someone who posted frequently on social media, so when he bothers to pay attention to someone publicly, it is noticeable. Mr Corbyn has paid Ms Green a lot of attention, and that attention has been returned. In fact, Mr Corbyn and Ms Green could be described as sharing a personal bond. As early as January 2014, he approved when she spoke of Caroline Kennedy's poetry; when she publicly posted a favourite poem by Rose Milligan, he confessed to her that it contains a sentiment meaningful to him; when she professed her fears for the future of the rhinoceros, he agreed; similarly when she backed an African water charity they shared a little joke together online; and when she was off on her travels to Cuba [together with another anti-Semite, Ken Livingstone, Corbyn is a leading member of the Castroite Cuban Solidarity Campaign] he wished her a 'wonderful time'.

In short, there is not much about Ms Green's tastes and opinions that Mr Corbyn does not seem to know or approve of, and he singles her out to use when he wishes to thank others. She is clearly not just an acquaintance or friend, she is 'special'. However, this is all without their mutually shared passion, even above poetry and rhinos; namely; the Palestinians. So it is no surprise that Ms Green signed Mr Corbyn up to her 'Palestine Live' group, of which, at that time, it appears that she was the only administrator, and Mr Corbyn can be seen, for example, approving of her Palestine-themed posts in August 2014, and again in October 2014. There is evidence that Mr Corbyn joined in late 2013, participated in online conversations, and remained a member for two years.

With regard to 'Palestine Live' and other so-called 'pro-Palestinian forums', Ms Green and Mr Corbyn don't just interact online, but in person (she is also on chatting terms with MPs such as Chris Williamson [praised by Corbyn as a 'very good MP', only to be then suspended, despite Corbyn's attempt to prevent it, for one of a number anti-Semitic outbursts] and John McDonnell [opposed to the existence of the state of Israel] when she sees them.) Finally, her involvement with him is deep enough that at one point they jointly organised a talk to be given by the controversial Max Blumenthal at Mr Corbyn's own office, using Mr Corbyn's staff, as chronicled in detail by David Collier in his report into the 'Palestine Live' Facebook group. Again, the talk having taken place this venue, Mr Corbyn thanked those who attended on the 'Palestine Live' Facebook group in a thread with Ms Green. But what of Ms Green's views? Ms Green is a prolific and obsessive poster of conspiracy theories. A list of those to which she subscribes constitutes an A to Z of the genre: on more than one occasion she promoted the theory that Israeli intelligence services were secretly behind the 9/11 terrorist atrocities, as well as the terrorist massacres in Paris, able to boast when the celebrated conspiracy theorist who has written the article became a member of the group. She shared a post that suggested that a wife of a witness to 9/11 was deliberately killed six days after meeting President Obama; shared a post suggesting that the BBC is deliberately employing 'obnoxious Jews' in order to encourage anti-Semitism and suggests it 'could even be true'; claimed that Israel bombed its own embassy in a 'false flag' operation; shared a link to an article claiming that ISIS leaders were trained by Israel; supported the idea that London Bridge terrorist attacks may have been a stunt to throw the general election off track; and posted a claim that the BBC is 'completely controlled' by Rothschild influence.

Similarly, the people she supports, and has invited to be members in the group, are a Who's Who of Britain's most infamous anti-Semites. She participates in conversations with Holocaust denier Paul Eisen (a friend of Mr Corbyn's whose work he used to help fund, but with whom he claims no longer to associate) in one of which, Mr Eisen says to Baroness Tonge [together with Corbyn a Patron of the Palestine Solidarity Campaign] and Ms Green: 'You'll continue feeling depressed, dismal and let down until you start standing up to Jews - not the Israelis, not the Zionists, the Jews', to which Ms Green responds, asking: 'What do you suggest?' Mr Eisen asked of another member, 'but what do you find so unsavoury about Dr Duke?' (Dr Duke is the former Grand Wizard of the Ku Klux Klan). She defended disgraced Baroness Tonge, who resigned from her [Liberal Democratic] party over anti-Semitism allegations, claiming that the notion of her remarks might be anti-semitic is 'appalling'. She shared posts by David Icke. [!!!] She is personally friendly with and supports Gilad Atzmon, who has allegedly said that 'the burning down of a synagogue is a rational act', whose ideas are better described as far-right than far-left [when it comes to anti-Semitism, this distinction no longer applies anyway], and whose book *The Wandering Jew* has been described as 'probably the most anti-Semitic book published in this country in recent years'. She posts his work on the group, and praises his 'truth' when, ironically, Gilad Atzmon is considered so anti-Semitic that 'anti-Zionist' Palestinian groups and activists have taken care to distance themselves from him. Ms Green also appears to be friendly with and supportive of Jackie Walker [of Momentum] who is touring the country describing how she was 'lunched' for claiming that Jews were the 'chief financiers of the slave trade'.

It is difficult to give an account of every example of anti-Semitic discourse in which Ms Green has participated. She has shared a post claiming 'Zionists' are 'killing children to sell them on the black market'. She promotes the London Forum, described as 'a secret Neo-Nazi society'. She has posted an article by an author convicted in a Canadian court for promoting hatred against Jews, a piece that appeared on the Radical Press website that promotes the Protocols of the Elders of Zion and Adolf Hitler's book, *Mein Kampf*. Bearing in mind that the overwhelming majority of British Jews are Zionists, her assertion that 'the time must surely come' when no "friend of Israel" can stand as an MP is chilling. She adored Gerald Kaufman, who claimed that 'Jewish money…biase[es] the Tory Party'. She likes social media posts that suggest Jewish influence in Britain is 'dangerously close to being treasonable'. She shared a post and endorses the author of a raw anti-Semitic diatribe describing Jewish values as 'massacre, rape…torture, sex trafficking and child abuse', describing the author as a "great man". [Possibly a mistake here…could the author in question be referring to the 'values' of certain Muslims?] She refers to 'zios', which even Labour's Baroness Chakrabarti accepts is an unacceptable term of abuse. She was proud to be among those who yelled and intimidated when Haringey Council adopted the International Definition of Anti-Semitism.

So much of what she posts is simply raw Jew-hatred that she seems to have forgotten that she is supposed to be maintaining the fiction of being a mere critic of Israeli policy. However, at one point in the Palestine Live Facebook group she admits that the ideas behind Holocaust denial are 'true and clearly the questions are legitimate…but not HERE' - a cynical admission that while she has sympathies with Holocaust deniers she is, on the group at least, trying to draw a virtuous skein over the views aired. In the end, by commenting positively on a link to the neo-Nazi *Daily Stormer*, all pretence disappears. Elleanne Green is a member of the Labour Party [yes…the *Labour* Party] in the Cities of London and Westminster, who enthusiastically backs the Reverend Steven Saxby - also a member of Palestine Live - as a future Parliamentary candidate; is a representative of Momentum, and a member of the so-called Jewish Voice for Labour. Evidence held by Campaign Against Anti-Semitism shows that she was reported to the Labour Party on 4th September 2017 yet clearly no action has been taken. Instead she is on friendly personal terms with Mr Corbyn, Chris Williamson MP, John McDonnell MP, Clive Lewis MP (who even blows her virtual kisses) journalist Paul Mason and others. Elleanne Green is not the only individual propagating extreme anti-Semitism on Palestine Live.

As David Collier's research demonstrates, using a sample period to analyse posters and their postings from 1st to 15th February 2018, anti-Semitic postings on the site were ubiquitous and unmissable. Furthermore, witness reports bear testimony to the level of anti-Semitism a member would have to be subjected to during the summer of 2014, when Mr Corbyn was an actively posting member of the group. Members of Palestine Live comprise a roll call of the UK's leading so-called "anti-Zionists" either posting or tolerating nakedly anti-Semitic material that hardly requires the International Definition of Anti-Semitism to assist in its identification. The naked truth laid bare by Mr Collier's report is that the in the current culture of the UK's far-left, anti-Zionism and anti-Semitism are indistinguishable. The very notion that anti-Zionism on the British left is, in practice an historical debating point that honourably takes up a political position regarding the State of Israel, is now shattered.

For Mr Corbyn to suggest that Ms Green is a mere 'acquaintance' [and even if this were true, what an acquaintance!], as he or Labour's press officers have communicated, is demonstrably a lie. Given both their intimacy and the fact that she prolifically posts hardcore anti-Semitic material, to say that he had no knowledge of her anti-Semitism stretches credulity. [as it does with many other of his anti-Semitic 'acquaintances'] Further, to claim that in two years as a member and close friend of Ms Green's he saw no- anti-Semitism posted by her or others on the site itself would be like standing in an open field in a rainstorm and claiming that the raindrops missed you. Perhaps another explanation lies in two posts in which Ms Green says: 'Am disgusted [to be under investigation] but suppose it is inevitable if one speaks up for justice for the Palestinians' and 'I am NOT anti-Semitic'. [that is what they all say - even David Irving.] Ultimately, people like Ms Green are perhaps blinded to their own racism, however extreme., by cloaking it with the virtue of a 'pro-Palestinian' position, both externally for others, but also for themselves. If Mr Corbyn is similarly blind, it is perhaps because he is so similar to his friend, Ms Green.

Joseph D. Glassman, Head of Political and Government Investigations at Campaign Against Anti-Semitism, said 'Jeremy Corbyn said he did not see anti-Semitism in the Palestine Live Facebook group but he wrote comments on anti-Semitic posts during his two-year membership of the group. He said he was added to the group by an 'acquaintance' but in fact it was his intimate friend Elleanne Green, a prolific disseminator of extreme anti-Semitic material. By lying about their relationship and pretending that he saw no anti-Semitism on Palestine Live, he takes the British public for fools, drags the Labour Party into further disrepute and causes yet more fear and anguish for British Jews. But what is most frightening is the lack of public outrage. [Dead right!!!] Where are the cries of 'Not in my name'? Through their silence these past weeks, British politicians are allowing our society to descend deeper into a dark place where anti-Semitism is tolerated, and history shows as where that path leads.' Ms Green did not respond to a request for comment.

Hard on the heels of the mural scandal came the revelation by the *Guido Fawkes* website that Corbyn was a member of two other anti-Semitic Facebook groups, *Labour Party Supporter* (sic) and *History* of *Palestine*. They feature the same genre of postings as the others he frequents…body organs…Rothschilds…the Illuminati…Again, he saw nothing untoward, and only when outed did Corbyn announce he had left them.

Now, David Collier's report on the cesspit that calls itself *Palestine Live*, where there are featured some of the notorious anti-Semites, we have already observed fraternising with Corbyn in other settings. Founded on August 2, 2013, as of February 20, 2018, Palestine Live has 3,279 members. Previously listed as 'closed', Palestine Live has been listed as 'secret' since November 2014, meaning it cannot be accessed by using Facebook search functions. New users have to be invited to join by someone already a member of the group who has been granted permission to add new members. Corbyn interacted with this website at least 30 times.

Introducing his report, Collier says

> It would be easy to start this blog with Jeremy Corbyn. After all, it seems as if he was part of a rabidly anti-Semitic Facebook Group, along with Paul Eisen, Gilad Atzmon, numerous other Holocaust Deniers, hard-core anti-Semites, white supremacists, and all the other wretched political ideologues that gather together to pretend it is about

Palestine and not the Jews...I have been engaged in an exercise to analyse a secret [nb] Facebook Group called 'Palestine Live' Immersed deeply in an anti-Semitic soup was disturbing enough but seeing names there that simply should not ever have stepped foot inside, gave an entirely new, and far darker feel to the entire exercise. Corbyn was there in late 2014, he may have joined a year earlier, and every indication is, that he stayed in the group until shortly after he became leader of the Labour Party. Jenny [body organs] Tonge is still a member. David Ward too. Clive Lewis? Go figure. It just shows how blind everyone is to anti-Jewish racism. I quantified the level of anti-Semitism within the group by analysing all those who shared posts over a two-week period during February 2018. The level was 64% When I extracted the Jewish anti-Zionists, the level rose to 73%. Nobody should be able to spend any time at all in that group, without understanding the twisted anti-Semitism that drives so much of the activity.

The founder of the group, the Jew-baiting, *Mein Kamp*-quoting anti-Israeli activist Elleanne Green, is one of its three administrators, the other two being the ubiquitous photo-op companion of Jeremy Corbyn, the Neo-Nazi Tony Gratrex, and Carol Foster of the obsessively anti-Zionist Socialist Fight. Recruitment is tightly controlled, as is evident from this exchange between Green and Jacquie Walker of Momentum, twice suspended and then eventually expelled from the Labour party for anti-Semitism:

'Walker: 'How safe is this group?' [Safe from *what*?]
'Green: 'Very. No one allowed in who is not trusted. I am very careful...and it is a Secret Group...so it really is as safe as you will be able to find anywhere...anyone here will be your friend and admirer.' [So, Jeremy was 'trusted'.]

Group Founder and Administrator Green's stance on the 'Jewish question' is reflected in her posting of a lengthy quote from *Mein Kampf* where Hitler engages in an exposure of the aims of Zionism, which are to create in Palestine 'a haven for convicted scoundrels and a university for budding crooks'. Now a sample of the postings by some of Corbyn's fellow members of this 'secret group':

First, Administrator Foster:

'The Jewish lobby it's plain to see
Is full of people unlike me
They're bigoted and full of bile
Their talk is cheap and rather vile
From what they say it's really clear
They are everything that they most fear
So it's really clear now is the hour
To rob these demons of their power.'

Here is Corbyn's twice photo partner Administrator Gratrex, riding his favourite hobby-horse:
'Revisionist scholarship has determined that somewhere between 100-150 thousand people perished in Auschwitz mainly as a result of disease and starvation, which was not a deliberate act on the part of the Germans, but rather outcome of Allied carpet bombing of Germany's infrastructure. In an effort to whitewash their own egregious war-crimes, the Allies went along with the Zionists' premeditated

fictional account of six million dead Jews.'

Pam Arnold: '...we just do not recognise this barbarian part of that tribe that is lording it over every single government in the world and using their untold wealth to control the agenda for all of us in order to further their nefarious aims for the Jewish state and to wipe out the Palestinians in the process.'

'Am reading Mein Kampf...everybody should be forced [sic!!!] to read it, especially jews who have their own agenda as to why they are not liked.'

Andy Hopkins: 'Perhaps if one asked some very basic questions, they might learn the truth about the HOLOCAUST. Most people have accepted the story given out by a group of people who in reality have EVERYTHING TO HIDE. They were talking about 6,000,000 (6 million) dead for at least 50yrs before Hitler came to power in 1933.'

Hopkins then recommends 'a video about one person awakening to the truth', *A Holocaust Inquiry,* by Corbyn enthusiast David Duke.

Elleanne Green: 'Ex-MI5 Agent knows that Israeli Mossad was behind 9/11.'

'Mossad's fingerprints on Paris attacks.'

'Former CIA Agent: The ISIS leader Abu Bakr Al Baghdadi was trained by the Israeli Mossad.'

Two boosts for Jeremy:

June Tobin: 'We must remember too who owns most of the media [i.e. the Jews] and why Jeremy Corbyn would not be a good appointment for them.'

George Garside: 'The Jewish minority have far too much to say in this country, they are pandered to and over represented in the corridors of power and their influence is dangerously close to treasonable...The people of this country know right from wrong, they are choosing truth, justice and transparency. Jeremy Corbyn will see they get it.'

Tony Gratrex, again: '...a cursory glance using the internet will show that a majority of the media is Jewish owned or controlled'.

'JFK was the last American President who wasn't chosen by the [Jewish] Cabal... [His assassination] was a really a Cabal job...All American elections have been arranged by the Cabal ever since, based on the two principles of Cabal politics, bribery and blackmail. Trump won because he wouldn't succumb to either. These principles are used in the UK as well. We've seen how Jeremy Corbyn has been treated by the Cabal.'

Baroness Tonge (she of the body parts slander) is featured praising fellow Palestine Solidarity Campaign Patron Ken Loach for a 'useful article' rebutting accusations that the Labour Party has an anti-Semitism problem.

Neville Thomas: 'Jews thrown out of 100 countries. Why?'

Michael Summer posts a reproduction of an anti-Semitic cartoon from the Nazi journal *Der Sturmer* of October 1938, the editor of which, Julius Streicher, was hanged at Nuremberg. He archly asks the question: 'Agree he should have been hanged or disagree?'

Benefactor of Corbyn's generosity, Paul Eisen: 'And you'll continue feeling depressed, dismal and let down until you start standing up to the Jews - not the Israelis, not the Zionists, the Jews.'

Eisen again: 'I see anti-Semitism as a legitimate opposition to appalling Jewish behaviour so I accept the label with pride.' (along with Corbyn's donation)

Next, a posting of a page from a Neo-Nazi website, *The Daily Archive,* promoting Nazi memorabilia:

Tony Murphy: 'The Jews are like a cancer, when they enter the host nation, e.g., US and EU, they spread their rotten virus until they take control of all the host nations arteries, media, government, banking etc.'

'I just heard on the radio that Jews do not donate their organs after death. This, in my opinion, lends credence to the theories that is why they murder Palestinians and not inclined to return their bodies to their families so they can harvest their organs.'

A sizable section of Collier's report is devoted to the role played in Palestine Live by Corbyn, both as participant and as source of inspiration for many of its members. As Collier comments, 'Wherever you look in Palestine Live, you find people that shouldn't be there, and endless images of Jeremy Corbyn.' PL Founder and *Mein Kampf* quoter Elleanne Green posted:

'Jenny [body organs] Tonge and Jeremy Corbyn are inspirational here in the UK. I commend them to anyone anywhere who wants to know who the brave and articulate [sic!!!] politicians in my country are.'

And again;

'I do know how much Jeremy Corbyn opposes all these evils though – he is quite astonishing in his energy and efforts.'

And again:

'Jeremy is so active - he cares about Palestine.'

And yet again:

'Gratitude to Jeremy Corbyn.'

Corbyn's services and staff proved invaluable in setting up a meeting at Westminster on October 2, 2014, where the keynote speaker would be the US anti-Zionist campaigner Max Blumenthal:

Elleanne Green: 'Would Jenny Tonge or Jeremy Corbyn know if is possible to organise something in a room at Portcullis House?'

Never one to miss out on a good Zionist bashing, Jeremy is indeed up for it:

Green: 'Have a reply from Jeremy's office. V[ery] helpful indeed.'

Sadly, Jeremy couldn't make the meeting, as 'is away next week…conference on'…guess what? 'Palestine.'

But still, 'kudos and thanks to the office of Jeremy Corbyn MP'.

According to Corbyn, he could not attend because 'Sadly, I was at the funeral of a very old friend, Ron Blanchard, so missed event.'

This posting is proof of his membership of the secret Palestine Live group, and that he has read other posts on its website. Green cannot resist advertising to PL's (secret) members the name of their far and away biggest catch:

'Jeremy Corbyn is even a member of this group' and

'Jeremy was a member of this group for several years ['several years'…and he saw nothing untoward?] until a few weeks after his election as Labour leader…such a friend to Palestine.'

And enemy of Israel. Here is Green again: 'Jeremy Corbyn sparks row by turning down dinner with Israeli MP.'

Rivalling Corbyn in cult status is veteran conspiracy nutter David Icke:

Sandra Wafta: 'British author and lecturer [!!!] David Icke has written 20 books and travelled to over 55 countries since 1990.'

Derek Hands, promoting the video *Israel's Fake History*: *The Cruellest Hoax* by David Icke: 'The David Icke video can be delivered to your email every Sunday.'

Lynn Faulkner, promoting Icke's video, *Rothschild Zionism*: 'His books reveal how a hidden hand is behind world-changing events like the attacks of 9/11 and the manufactured wars in the Middle East'. In the book refereed to, Icke says 'Israel is not the home of the Jewish people, it is the fiefdom of the Rothschild dynast that also controls the American administration, the British administration.'

George Garside posts a photo of Jeremy with the caption, 'Join the Labour Party', followed by a promo for Icke's *The Rothschild Zionist Agenda* and the comment:

'He's on the money on this one and there's no lizards in it.'

And this: 'Why are murdering Jews exempt from criticism and immune from prosecution? By their actions are they not inviting a new Holocaust on themselves?'

Two PL members who joined Labour to vote for Jeremy:

Pam Arnold: 'Once I see what these right-wing fascists [left-wing ones OK?] do to Jeremy I will rescind my labour party membership which I only took up to vote for Jeremy.'

Felix Allen: 'As I haven't received my membership card yet (I allowed my membership lapse) does this mean I cannot vote for Corbyn?'

And we see a posting by Corbynista Allen promoting the video, *Holocaust: The Greatest Lie Ever Told.*

Now yet another Corbynista, Rosemary Henke. First a photo of Jeremy on ITV news, followed by a photo of 9/11, with the caption, 'on 9/11/2001, the laws of physics took the day off, along with NORAD, security cameras, and 4000 Israelis'.

And another: 'The Realist Report: How the "Holocaust" was faked.' According to this Corbynista's posting the Jewish inmates of Nazis camps were 'well-fed, well-provided for, and given medical treatment and entertainment. They were allowed to attend concerts, organise plays, make music and play sports. If the Germans were hell bent on murdering these people, why would they provide medical care for them and allow them to entertain themselves?'

Sarah Scott is an anti-Semite, posting a cartoon of a Jew with a huge hooked nose, with the caption, 'I don't deny the Holocaust…do you?'

Sarah Scott is a big fan of David Icke, posting a clip from his *Rothschild Zionism* video. She is also a big fan of Corbyn: In huge letters: 'I just voted for Jeremy Corbyn', and 'The quicker he is elected as PM the sooner we can rid the Party of Blair for ever.'

Camilla George posted a fake map of the Middle East entirely under Israeli rule, with the caption, 'Greater Israel'.

She also posted 'We support Jeremy Corbyn'.

So does David Birkett.: '…join the Labour Party and stand by the man who looks out for the interests that serve us all.' Birkett is also an anti-Semite: 'Holocaust: Not even one body, of thousands autopsied by US medical examiners across ALL camps after World War II exhibited any signs of dying from ANY type of "|Gas poisoning. Nor evidence of any viable gas chambers for the purpose of killing humans.'

David Carter posted a photo of the entrance to Auschwitz, with its legend, *Arbeit Macht Frei* and the caption, 'Why the Holocaust Story was invented'. He also made another posting:

'Thank God for a politician who sticks to his principles and beliefs and won't be swayed to abandon them, just to curry with the political elite and their financial backers.' (who might these be I wonder?)

To cut a long anti-Semitic posting short, Aleksandra Davies believes the Jews 'are beyond evil.' But with Saint Jeremy, the opposite is true: 'That's precisely why we urgently need Jeremy Corbyn to take the lead of this country.'

Simon Massey is yet another Ikista/Corbynista, who believes that 'the Israelis had something to do with the 7/7 attacks in London'.

So is Simon Fox, who posts more Ikisms on the Rothschilds, and then this:

'Last chance for a labour leader that supports Palestine. £3 to join as a supporter and get to vote – come on!'

Palestine Live has proved an irresistible attraction for anti-Semitic and Neo-Nazi crackpots, for whom the group is more about applauding Jeremy and baiting Jews than it is supporting the Palestinians. Yet although the website is awash with their ravings, and despite the fact that Corbyn was a member of the group for more than two years, and as the record shows, worked closely with its leading officials to help further its objectives, he claims he knew nothing about what went on in Palestine Live. Like, for example:

Chaz Labrock: 'International Red Cross report confirms the Holocaust of six million Jews is a Hoax.'

Corbyn's anti-Semitic Vicar friend from the PSC, the 9/11 conspiracy theorist Stephen Sizer:

'Why would the Jews make up the 'holocaust'? Jews want you to feel sorry for them…why? Because any group of people viewed as "victims" tend to be allowed much more leeway within society.'

One of the consequences of Corbyn's election as Leader has been the enrolment of anti-Semites and even Nazis into the Labour Party. Here is a posting by Jake Moose, which carries two images, one of a Labour Poster: 'We're now over 380,000 members strong. Are you one of them yet? Join.labour.org.uk' and another, of white supremacist provenance, *Renegade Tribune*, which has three guards standing outside a prison cage which has a prisoner inside. The guards are sporting the star of David, and the cage has a sign above it which reads: 'Asked for Proof of 6 Million Gassed During Holocaust'.

Here is Patricia Sheerin-Richman: 'Mossad officer leading ISIS as mosque Imam arrested in Libya', and

'Ukrainian General: "Ukraine is under Zionist occupation"', followed by: 'I'm still confident in Jeremy Corbyn. Do you still have confidence in Jeremy Corbyn? Over the last two days, we have seen a huge swell of support for Jeremy Corbyn from amongst Labour members and Labour voters. We've had hundreds of thousands of people contacting us with messages of support, signing petitions…' [Clearly someone of standing in the Labour Party…and a Corbynista anti-Semite.]

Finally, Dave Christopher: 'Israeli forces bury Palestinian kids alive –-The 41 News', and 'The Jews and the Concentration Camps: No evidence of genocide.'

Dave is yet another anti-Semitic Corbynista. He posts a photo of the Dear Leader, and the comment, on the 2017 general election, which Corbyn claimed he had won,

'Jeremy was 2,227 votes away from becoming Prime Minister. So, to all of the fekin dipshits who didn't bother to vote, see what you could have done if you did?'

Collier's breakdown by content of all the postings scrutinised, 794 in total, was 53% anti-Semitic, and at that with the bar raised very high for what constituted anti-Semitism. One of the recurring themes of the postings reproduced above is their concern to solve the mystery posed by the political establishment's parroting of 'nothing to do with Islam' after every Jihadi atrocity. If not Muslims, then whom? The Corbynista websites provide the answer: 9/11, 7/7, Paris, Islamic State, Boko Harem, Al Shabaab...all are manifestations and proof of the world Jewish conspiracy, hell-bent on depicting the religion of peace as the one of terror. To paraphrase Voltaire, if the Jews, the all-purpose scapegoat, did not exist, they would have to be invented.

The following item appeared in the *Jewish Chronicle* of October 8, 2017. It throws light on Corbyn's dealings with yet another notorious anti-Semite, this time one who is a member of both the Palestine Solidarity Campaign, Patron, Jeremy Corbyn, and the Labour Party, Leader, Jeremy Corbyn:

> A Labour Party member who is reported to have shared anti-Semitic conspiracy theories was manning the Palestine Solidarity Campaign stall at this year's Labour Party conference - and previously enjoyed a guided tour of the Houses of Parliament with Jeremy Corbyn. [Corbyn really has a thing about inviting anti-Semites to be his guests at Parliament] Tapash Abu Shaim, who is now understood to be under investigation by Labour, shared articles on social media claiming that Israel was behind the *Charlie Hebdo* killings and the ISIS terror group, as well as promoting the anti-Semitic conspiracy theory that Israel was behind the 9/11 terror attacks. According to the *Guido Fawkes* political blog, the Labour Party was notified about Mr Shaim's social media activity back in August [2017], with articles earlier in the year noting Mr Shaim's presence at the 2016 Labour Party conference despite his social media posts. However, no action appeared to be taken at the time. In 2012, Mr Shaim shared an article on social media from the far-right anti-Semitic *Veterans Today* website, the title of which was '9/11 Truth Could be the Answer to the Palestine/Israel Conflict'.
>
> Three months later, Mr Shaim was a member of a PSC delegation which enjoyed a guided tour around Parliament, courtesy of Jeremy Corbyn. Mr Shaim later praised Mr Corbyn on Twitter as being 'the best tour guide...your knowledge of history is so deep and clear'. [Maybe even as deep and clear as that of his anti-Semitic comrade, Ken Livingstone.] Mr Corbyn responded by saying, 'it was a pleasure showing PSC supporters around the vagaries [?] of Parliament and British history'.
>
> In a statement given to Guido, Jennifer Gerba, Director of Labour Friends of Israel, said it was 'disgusting that a Labour Party and Palestine Solidarity Campaign activist promotes conspiracy theories about the Jewish state being behind Islamist terror attacks. Given that the Labour Party and the PSC were made aware of Mr Shaim's posts earlier this year, questions must be asked about how this individual was allowed into conference. The Labour Party should expel Mr Shaim immediately and the Palestine Solidarity Campaign, should cease all relations with him.

In view of his prominent role in the PSC, I find it impossible to accept that this orgy of quite open and widely distributed Jew-baiting by PSC members and supporters goes unnoticed by the patron saint of British anti-Zionism and Leader of Her Majesty's Opposition. And it certainly cannot be by those who are responsible for monitoring the PSC's postings, as the test cited above proved. Given that he has never expressed any public disquiet with this scandalous state of affairs but has even chosen to be photographed with a number of the campaign's most notorious Jew-baiters, this is compelling evidence that at best, Corbyn is prepared to turn a blind eye to PSC anti-Semitism, and at worst, does not even see it for what it is, since he shares their prejudices. The un-deleted postings cited above make a mockery of the PSC's claim that 'anti-Semitism has no place anywhere [n.b.] in our campaign for Palestinian human rights'.

What follows next is a report by the *Daily Mail* of September 26, 2017, on manifestations of anti-Semitism at the 2017 Labour Party conference, with interpolations by myself:

> Labour was branded as the 'new nasty party' last night after an outbreak of intimidation and anti-Semitism as its annual conference. Jeremy Corbyn was urged to act after activists applauded panellists at a fringe meeting who likened supporters of Israel to Nazis. One speaker even suggested Labour should be free to debate whether the Holocaust had happened. [Of course, anyone should be free to say what they like about the Holocaust. But why should whether it happened be a subject for debate in the Labour party?] Mr Corbyn was also facing a row about intimidation of Laura Kuenssberg. The BBC political editor had been given a bodyguard following threats from left-wingers [sic] at the conference. [Almost certainly because of her name it was wrongly assumed she was Jewish] A Labour shadow minister yesterday claimed using an ex-soldier for protection was a 'ploy' to demonise hardliners. [This was not the first time the BBC had been accused of conspiring, on behalf of whom we are left to guess, against the Dear Leader.] Chris Williamson, who is a close ally of Mr Corbyn, refused to say whether party members who abused Miss Kuenssberg should be expelled. And he questioned whether anyone in Labour was involved, saying, 'People join the Labour Party because they are caring individuals. [Like the Luton Labour Councillor who admired 'my man Hitler'] They are not the sort of people that indulge in intimidation and violence.' But Andrew Percy, a former Tory minister who has also been the target of anti-Semitic abuse, last night described Labour as the 'new nasty party'. He said Labour appeared to be in the grip of a 'frightening cult'. 'What we are seeing is really dangerous', he added. 'The idea that the political editor of the BBC would need a bodyguard to attend the conference of the official opposition should appal all decent people in politics. The kind of anti-Semitic abuse we are seeing is also something that has not been part of our political system until the past couple of years.' [That is, if one discounts the Neo-Nazi fringe]
>
> There is a cult of personality around Jeremy Corbyn that will not allow questioning him or his views. It is deeply sinister, nasty and quite frightening. These people are genuinely extreme. Sheryll Murray, a Tory MP who has had swastikas daubed on her general election posters, said: 'From what we've seen today at the Labour conference, it feels like things are getting worse [in relation to anti-Semitism she must mean] rather than better. I worry it's putting good people off from working in politics. It's hardly the kinder, gentler politics that Jeremy Corbyn promised.' Yesterday's events horrified moderate Labour MPs. Former deputy leader Harriet Harman urged Mr Corbyn to condemn the abuse of Miss Kuenssberg. In a message on Twitter, she said: 'Is this from the left? If it is, it's even worse as the Left is supposed to be for equality and women's rights and online trolls is about silencing women.' Fellow Labour MP Jess Philips said: 'Let's clean up our act please. Women's safety is the reason we champion the Uber action for example Let's walk the walk.' Senior Labour MPs last night urged Mr Corbyn to act against anti-Semitism in the party. John Cryer, who is chairman of the Parliamentary Labour Party, said some social media postings were 'redolent of the 1930s' and 'made you hair stand on end'.
>
> Labour denies building a personality cult around Mr Corbyn. [Stalinists also denied there was one of Stalin] But criticism of the party leader is so frowned upon that senior figures yesterday refused to accept he had even lost the election. Len McCluskey, general secretary of the Unite trade union, yesterday rounded on 'traitors' in the party, telling cheering activists at the Brighton conference: 'Let me

say this to those merchants of doom, the whingers and the whiners who say we should have done better, we didn't win. I say we did win.' In which case, why is Theresa May in Number 10, and not Corbyn? Cat Smith, a member of the Shadow Cabinet and close ally of Mr Corbyn, said: 'We didn't win the general election, but we didn't lose the general election either.' A Labour spokesman last night said Mr Corbyn was now tightening up [sic] on the rules on those who make anti-Semitic comments. He said the party 'condemns anti-Semitism in the strongest possible terms' and 'will not tolerate Holocaust denial'. [And yet] Corbyn activists applauded speakers who delivered vile anti-Semitic rants at the Labour conference yesterday. Delegates at a fringe event demanded the expulsion of the Jewish Labour Movement from the party for supporting the state of Israel. One compared 'Zionists' to the Nazis and [yet] claimed it was part of free speech to ask the question, 'Holocaust yes or no.' The event, which took place outside the main conference venue but was listed in its official handbook, was titled, 'Free speech on Israel [where alone in the Middle East, there is free speech]: why we oppose the witch hunt.' Several attendees said claims of anti-Semitism in the Labour Party were part of a plot [why not say conspiracy and have done with it] by the pro-Israeli lobby and the Labour right to stop Jeremy Corbyn from becoming Prime Minister. [Actually, it was voters who did that] And some spoke up in favour of former London mayor Ken Livingstone who remains suspended from the party for claiming that Hitler supported Zionism. The statements exposed that anti-Semitism is still a big problem in Mr Corbyn's party more than a year after he pledged to get to grips with the issue. It came as: A leaflet was circulated at the conference from 'Labour Party Marxists' discussing the 'commonality between Zionists and Nazis' and quoting Reinhard Heydrich, the architect of the Final Solution [who in that capacity chaired the Wannsee conference of January 1942, which planned and authorised the extermination of European Jewry] saying, 'National Socialists had no intention of attacking Jewish people'. [If so, how come the Holocaust? Or perhaps it never happened after all.]

The chairman of the Parliamentary Labour Party, John Cryer, said he has seen tweets from party members which 'made his hair stand on end' and were 'redolent of the 1930s'. Another Labour MP, Wes Streeting, criticised Mr Corbyn, saying there was 'too many people in our party, including at the top of the party, who have adopted an ostrich strategy' on anti-Semitism. ['Too many'? One is one too many] Fellow MP John Mann said 200 Labour members had forwarded him links to a US white supremacist site to back up Mr Livingstone's claims about Zionism. The Holocaust Educational Trust suggested that in the two years since Mr Corbyn was elected there was a 'fertile ground' for people to express such views. Analysis released last night by the Campaign Against Anti-Semitism found the problem is worse in Labour than any other party. The group looked at 4 million social media posts of 2000 parliamentary candidates and found that 61 per cent of anti-Semitic posts were written by Labour candidates – eight times higher than any other party.

The controversial meeting on Free Speech on Israel was chaired by Naomi Wimborne-Idrisi, who said that there was a 'vicious campaign that's been directed at the Palestinian cause, misusing anti-Semitic allegations.' Although described as a free speech event, audience members were told not to record it. Miko Peled, an Israeli-American who sat on the panel, said 'they' - an apparent reference to Israel or the pro-Israeli lobby - did not want Mr Corbyn to enter Number 10. 'This is about free speech, the freedom to criticise and to discuss every issue, whether it's the Holocaust yes or no, Palestine, the liberation the whole spectrum. [It is a rather narrow spectrum that only encompasses things Jewish.] There should be no limits on the discussion.' [But who was saying there should be?] He adds: 'It's about the limits of tolerance: we don't invite the Nazis and give them an hour to explain why they are right; we do not invite apartheid South Africa racists to explain why apartheid was good for the blacks, and in the same way we do not invite Zionists - it's the same kind of thing.' [One moment there are 'no limits', not even for Holocaust deniers, and the next, there are, and they exclude amongst others, 'Zionists'.] Michael Kalmanovitz, from the International Jewish Anti-Zionist Network, was applauded for calling from the audience for the expulsion from Labour of the Jewish Labour Movement and the Labour Friends of Israel. A Labour spokesman said: 'Labour condemns anti-Semitism in the strongest terms. We will not tolerate anti-Semitism or Holocaust denial.'

And now an excerpt from an article from the *Jewish Chronicle* of August 26, 2015, by Louise Mensch, entitled *Corbyn supporters post vile racism and he says nothing*. All that needs to said by way of an introduction is that in the same year that this article was written, a survey revealed that around 40% of the UK electorate was anti-Semitic, and in another, that the Muslim vote could determine which party wins in as many as a quarter of all Parliamentary seats. The votes of Jews, only one tenth that of Muslims, do not determine any. But then, Corbynistas of the kind described below would say that they don't need to, as they already control Britain anyway:

> Twitter has given voice and focus to a loud, dedicated minority among Mr Corbyn's wider support; those who dislike, hate or even loath Jews. It is through social media that Mr Corbyn's links to the anti-Semite Paul Eisen were exposed. It was through Twitter that I discovered Jeremy Corbyn's 'friend', the racist and homophobe Abou Jahjah, whom he invited to Parliament. Abou Jahjah has said 'every dead British soldier I consider a victory'. Twitter pointed me to CEC [Citizens Electoral Council], a tiny Australian party, followers of the La Rouche anti-Semitic cultists whom Corbyn brought to Parliament to interview him just this spring. So it was, in that sense, useful. But the more Mr Corbyn's embrace of Eisen, Raed Salah, Hamas and Hezbollah are exposed, the better he did in the swollen electorate that has swamped real Labour members two to one (600,000 now vs 200,000 at the start of the race). And instead of decrying his links to anti-Semites, the left broadly shrugged their shoulders - or rejoiced that Mr Corbyn had given them comfort. The majority of Jeremy Corbyn's supporters are not anti-Semites but hundreds, maybe even thousands of them are. Anti-Semites form a significant minority of Corbynites and they are among the loudest online.
>
> Abuse and Jew-hatred is rife. First you have the open loathers of Jews like Alison Chabloz, a performer at the Edinburgh Fringe who tweeted a quenelle [the much-emulated disguised Nazi salute pioneered by the Holocaust-denying French Muslim comedian Dieudonne M'bala M'bala] then said that Jewish people brought pogroms on themselves. You have those who said Liz Kendall was a 'servile Jewish cow'. You have Fred Litten, who tweeted 'Hitler was right and we were wrong'. You have the commenter on my blog reporting on Mr Corbyn's meetings with anti-Semites who said that the Holocaust was fake but added wistfully: 'I wish there were six million less of them'. Next you have people who are anti-Semitic but do not know they are. Perhaps these are more worrying. 'What, are you saying that all Jews, not just the business owning rich ones, hate Corbyn?' one man asked me. 'Nothing wrong with denying the Holocaust, history is written by the victors', said another. 'Zyklon B was used for delousing'. Another, a Scottish nationalist who likes Mr Corbyn, replied to a tweet saying that he had called for an inquiry into 'Jewish donors to the Conservative party' with 'About time!'. (In fact, Mr Corbyn has supported an inquiry into 'Zionist' donors to the Conservatives, but every name mentioned at the event where he endorsed this was Jewish.)
>
> The anti-Semites are drawn to Mr Corbyn like a moth to a flame. 'The Nuremberg Trials were for show', says Mathew Lees. Susan John Richards, a deselected Tory councillor in 2010, now supports him because of her anti-Semitism. 'All Jews are

intermarried anyway' she says'. 'Jews and Zionists own the whole world.' She also believes in the blood libel [Jews murdering Christian children for their blood] and that '9/11 was an inside job'. Respect Party supporters of George Galloway have flocked to back Corbyn. Adnan Sadiq, for example, [previously] condemned by the Corbyn [Labour Leadership] campaign in the Sunday Times for his tweeting, worked for Mr Galloway in Bradford. Joanne Stowell, formerly a staunch Respect supporter, is now a huge Corbyn fan. 'We've had the Holocaust rammed down our throat by the Zionists forever ensuring only Jewish suffering counts', she said. 'Holocaust "denying" is research and fact-finding', she insists. Is Mr Corbyn complicit? He must answer for the known anti-Semites he invited to Parliament and donated to. But he is not responsible for the tweets of his supporters. [I disagree, to the extent that he has not accounted for why these and many other anti-Semites are so taken with him] Yet he is responsible for the shabby silence which greeted this tsunami. All he says is 'no rudeness'. Holocaust denial is not 'rudeness'. '#F**kjews' as Peter Farquhar, a Corbyn supporter, tweeted, isn't rudeness: 'f**kisrael and f**kjews they are the c**ts ruining the planet #F**kJews', he said helpfully. This is hatred, not rudeness.

If Mr Corbyn hates racism and has fought it all his life as he tells us, then he is failing to keep that up at the moment. The Corbyn campaign [for the Labour leadership] has called unearthing these facts a smear. Yet Mr Corbyn is a hypocrite, for he himself said of Nick Griffin of the BNP: 'No one should share a platform with an avowed racist'. That is his standard response. We are simply holding him to it. Mr Corbyn has shared platform with racists countless times. In 2005 he attended a Deir Yassin Remembered celebration with the anti-Semites Eisen and Gilad Atzmon. Now Atzmon is tweeting that Jeremy Corbyn should be voted in because Jews fear him. He wrote a blog post to that effect; anti-Semites who support Mr Corbyn are now re-tweeting it again and again. What can we say of Mr Corbyn's silence? It is not good enough. Were his parents silent at Cable Street?

Mr Corbyn can at best say in the face of the evidence that he never knew his collaborators were racists. But what does that tell us? It says he does not think that the Jewish people are worth even a basic check - that his tax-funded staff should have Googled his guests. In spring of this year [2015] he gave an interview in Parliament to the anti-semitic La Rouche cultist group CEC. Now his campaign says it is 'concerned' to hear of the La Rouche links. But the name La Rouche is in bold letters on the group's front page. If Mr Corbyn says he didn't know, then that in itself shows no regard for British Jews, because he is an MP with an office, with a staff, with plenty of resources to check. He has not defended his fellow MP Liz Kendall in the face of tweets like 'Kendal would serve Israel before you or your family'. He has done nothing, said nothing - other than a vague platitude or two. Where is his thundering speech in defence of the Jewish community? Nowhere. Nothing. It is pathetic. This is no smear This is Mr Corbyn's record in meeting anti-Semites; and it is the record of anti-Semitism or a large, vocal minority of his supporters.

The next survey by David Collier cited here is of 56 Labour Party members who have posted on line their endorsement of Jewish conspiracy theories, many of whom make it clear they have joined the party after and because of Corbyn's election as party Leader in September 2015. Collier categorises their postings under a number of headings: Mossad, Jews, Zionists, Israel and the Rothschilds variously control or are responsible for: 9/11, London 7/7, *Charlie Hebdo*. Nice and Munich, July 2016, Manchester May 2017, London Bridge June 2017, Paris November 2015, Brussels, March 2016, the assassination of President Kennedy, the death of Princess Diana, both World Wars, the Iraq war, the slave trade, child trafficking, paedophile rings, the attacks on oil tankers in the Gulf, ISIS, the Arab Spring, Grenfell Tower, six mass shootings in the USA, blackmailing MPs, MI5, Wahhabism (sic) the media, the myth of the Holocaust, the world's banks, the internet, the Labour Party, the USA, the UK, the royal family, the trade in children's body organs, the poisoning of Sergei and Yulia Skripal, the shooting down over the Ukraine of Malaysia Flight MH1 and sinking the Titanic (sic). These are the delusional ravings of the deranged and the psychopathic. Their natural home would be either be an institution that cares for the mentally ill or a viable leftist-tinged Nazi movement, but since none exists, they have gravitated to Corbynised Labour. The websites featuring these blatant and unashamed anti-Semitic postings, all by self-declared Labour Party members, include:

> We Support Jeremy Corbyn
> Register to vote for Jeremy Corbyn
> @Jeremy Corbyn
> Join Labour Org UK
> On the Left with Jeremy Corbyn
> #JC4PM
> #keepCorbyn
> Supporters Labour Org UK
> YourLabourNec.Co.UK
> Debating Zionism

And now some of their comments:

> Feeling great. Just voted for Jeremy Corbyn.
> Jeremy Corbyn for Labour Leader.
> These [NEC candidates] are the six to put your cross against for Jeremy Corbyn. Spread the word.
> I wouldn't have done this [joined Labour] for anyone else…only Jeremy Corbyn. [This we can believe. She is Elleanne Green, the *Mein Kampf*-quoting Administrator of the secret Palestine Live group.]
> I joined the Labour Party to support the wonderful gentleman Jeremy Corbyn.
> If they oust Jeremy as Leader, then I will be cancelling my direct debit and terminating my membership tonight.
> For the first time in my life (58) I have just registered to vote. Will be voting for Corbyn [not Labour].
> I've just joined the Labour Party so I can vote for Jeremy Corbyn.
> Corbynites are go! What a privilege to know him. [Which indeed he does. This is the neo-Nazi Palestine Live Administrator Tony Gratrex, pictured, twice, with fellow group member Corbyn.]

Perhaps the most telling evidence of the role played by Corbyn in the rise of Labour anti-Semitism are Collier's surveys of two groups of Corbynistas, one comprised of those who joined the Labour Party expressly to vote for and support Corbyn and who were already posting anti-Semitic materials, and another, whose on-line activity initially displayed no interest in let alone animosity towards either Israel or the Jews but who, after joining Labour, were rapidly sucked into the same Corbynista bubble and became venomous opponents of both. Each group vented their Jew-hatred in a spate of on-line postings, in some cases numbering hundreds, that relied mainly on the recycling of material from white supremacist and neo-Nazi websites, (the mainstream media being rejected as controlled by the Jews) consisting of the usual Jewish conspiracy theories' (the Rothschilds, ISIS, the media) and allegations (Israeli genocide of the Palestinians, collusion with or being Nazis) and, as a bonus, the French Yellow Vest accusation that President Macron is a 'Zionist gangster'.

One of the many bizarre features of the postings on websites with a Corbyn connection is the harmony that prevails between those whose anti-Semitism is clearly and, in some cases, explicitly inspired by Nazi propaganda, and those which liken Jews to Nazis and Israel to the Third Reich. There is also a similar perverse division of labour between Holocaust deniers and approvers, just as among Muslims there are those who attribute to Mossad both 9/11 and ISIS, and those who in their thousands celebrated the attack on the World Trade Centre and have volunteered to fight as Jihadis for what other Muslims claim is the Mossad-controlled Islamic State.

Following their mentor's election as Party Leader, rank and file Corbynista Jew-baiters judged the times propitious to advance their careers by selection as local councillors. When Alison Grove Humphries was selected as Labour council candidate in Birmingham's Hall Green Constituency, postings by her came to light that included a claim that 'the Israel lobby manufactured UK Labour's anti-Semitic crisis', and the recycling of another that Israel was the 'key link in the exporting of ISIS oil'. Although deselected by her local party as an anti-Semite, she was nevertheless allowed to attend the 2017 Brighton Labour Party conference, where she could be seen on her website enjoying herself in Corbynista company at a Momentum event in a photo taken by its founder (and owner) Jon Lansman. Mike Sivier, former editor the *Brecon and Radnor Express*, adopted as a Labour candidate to stand for a seat in the 2017 Powys County Council elections, had among his postings endorsements of Livingstone's claim that Hitler 'supported Zionism' and of former Labour MP Tam Dalyell's that Tony Blair had been 'unduly influenced by cabal of Jewish advisers'. Sivier also endorsed the anti-Semitic postings of the Corbynista MP Naz(i) Shah and defended the exclusion of the Jews from the notorious SWP leaflet listing the victims of the Nazis as 'politically [if not historically] correct'. The media were 'Zionist led', further proof that, at least to comrade Sivier's satisfaction, there was 'no doubt' there was a Jewish conspiracy. When these and other similar postings came to light, Sivier, who claimed he was being accused of 'guilt by association' was not deselected by his local party, though he did fail to get elected.

What follows are some, by no means all, such cases of alleged anti-Semitism by Labour Party members. They are at every level of the party, from constituency activists and local councillors up to MPs and even members of Corbyn's Shadow Cabinet. As of July 2019, of all the several thousand cases of alleged anti-Semitism by Labour Party members, only fifteen had resulted in expulsions.

Former Witham Labour Councillor John Clarke, suspended after posting a comment on a Neo-Nazi website which claimed the Rothschilds used Israel to 'take over the world', saying it 'contained a great deal of truth'.

Zafar Iqbal, a Labour Councillor in Birmingham, shared a video by the Neo-Nazi, Corbyn admirer and former KKK Grand Wizard David Duke. No action was taken after he claimed he had no recollection of the video.

Two Jewish Labour Councillors in Haringey, London (a Corbynista stronghold), resigned after experiencing anti-Semitic abuse by fellow party members - 'Jews have big noses' and 'control the world'.

Chesterfield Labour Councillor Andrew Slack, suspended after sharing an anti-Semitic meme of a blood-stained, hooked-nosed Israeli soldier with the comment that 'Israel was created by the Rothschilds, not God. And what they are doing to the Palestinian people now is EXACTLY what they intend for the whole world.'

Teesside Labour Party member and Momentum activist Bob Campbell shared an image of a rat marked with the Star of David which claimed Israel controlled ISIS. No action taken.

Labour Councillor and former Mayor of Blackburn Salim Mulla called Jews a 'disgrace to humanity', endorsed a video which blamed Jews for the school shootings in the USA (at least this was original) and claimed Israel was behind ISIS (which most definitely was not). After being suspended, reinstated.

Tayyib Nawaz, Chairperson of Manchester Labour Students, resigned after tweeting that 'Hitler was Jewish'. (full marks for out-Livingstoning Livingstone)

Former Chairperson of Spitalfields and Banglatown (sic) Labour Party Musabbir Ali, suspended after tweeting a Neo-Nazi 'Timeline of the Jewish Genocide of the British People'

Sean McCallum, suspended after being chosen as Labour candidate for mayor of Mansfield. when a posting came to light claiming Nazism and Zionism were 'equally foul'.

Renfrewshire Labour Councillor Terry Kelly claimed that the 'American Jewish lobby is extremely powerful and it has its boot on Obama's neck', and that the film *The Kings Speech* might not win an Oscar because 'there is a powerful Jewish lobby campaigning against the film because of its historical inaccuracy about Hitler and the anti-Semitism.' Reinstated after a month's suspension.

Josh Simons, former policy advisor to Corbyn, said that one member of the Labour Leader's team referred to a 'Jewish conspiracy' in an office discussion and that Corbyn's chief spokesperson, Seumas Milne, subjected him to an 'inquisition' concerning his Jewishness, his family and his attitude to Israel.

Billy Wells, dropped as a council candidate in Great Yarmouth after writing on Facebook 'It's the super-rich families of the Zionist lobby that control the world. Our world leaders sell their souls for greed and do the bidding of Israel.'

Deputy Leader of Kirklees Council David Sheed tweeted that 'Jewish organisations run a concerted campaign against JC [Jeremy Corbyn]'.

Eleanor Tristam was adopted as a Council candidate for Labour after sharing on Facebook one posting that Jewish MP Ruth Smeeth was funded by the 'Israel lobby' and another claiming that 'the current anti-Semitism witch-hunt' was 'a fraud' and 'a cover for sabotage'.

Mick Bone, adopted as Labour candidate for Middlesbrough Council after sharing an image implying that the BBC is control by the Israeli embassy and a posting demanding that Israeli diplomats should be expelled from the UK. (Corbyn has made the same claim regarding the BBC.)

Anti-Zionist zealot Labour MP for Easington Grahame Morris in 2014 posted a picture of the Israeli flag, with the comment, 'Nazis in my village, do you see the flag they fly'. Later the same year, he compared Israeli soldiers to ISIS. Like other Corbynistas, Morris is always on the look-out for any stick with which to beat the Zionists, no matter how dubious its provenance (he has visited a website that features myths about the Rothschilds conspiracy). More recently, he shared a video which purported to show to show Israeli soldiers beating a child when in fact the soldiers were Guatemalan. No action taken.

Labour MP for Blyth Valley Ronald Campbell told the BBC that 'the Jewish issue' is being used 'as a big stick to beat Corbyn and get rid of him'. No action taken.

Corbynista NEC member Peter Willsman was suspended for alleging that accusations of Labour anti-Semitism were 'all lies' and had been instigated by the Israeli embassy.

Labour activist Frances Naggs authored an open letter endorsed by thousands of party members claiming that Jewish protests against the party's anti-Semitism were the work of 'a very special interest group' that could 'employ the full might of the BBC'. Subsequently adopted as a Staffordshire Council candidate.

Former Labour NEC member Martin Mayer was adopted as a candidate for the EU election of May 2019 after sending an email titled 'How Israel manufactured UK Labour anti-Semitism crisis', in which he claimed that the 'smear of anti-Semitism' was being used 'to undermine Jeremy Corbyn's leadership'.

Momentum activist Marlene Ellis was suspended after saying in an open letter in defence of the suspended Ken Livingstone that Zionists were 'involved with the Nazis and that the Labour Party sought to 'curry favour with the pro-Zionist lobby in and beyond the media'. (This last was indeed actionable. Surely not under Corbyn.)

In December 21016, Corbyn attended the book launch of, and posed for photos with, Hatem Bazian, organised by the Iranian Human Rights Commission. (This is not a spoof. There is such an organisation, and like Corbyn's former employer Press TV, it is sponsored by the human rights-respecting Ayatollahs). Bazian later apologised for anti-Semitic tweets where he shared a picture of an ultra-orthodox Jew with the message: 'Mom, look! I is chosen! I can now kill, rape, smuggle organs [yes…again] and steal the land of the Palestinians. Yay #Ashke-Nazi.' What charming friends Jeremy has.

Former Labour Parliamentary candidate for Woking Vicki Kirby was suspended and then reinstated after tweeting that Hitler might be a 'Zionist God' and Jews have 'big noses'.

Luke Creswell, suspended, reinstated, and then adopted to stand as a Labour Councillor in Suffolk after tweeting an image of a blood-stained Israeli flag with the caption 'Moses must be proud of you'.

North Wales Labour Councillor Max Tasker posted YouTube videos to his Facebook page entitled: 'Is ISIS good for the Jews?', 'The whole story of Zionist conspiracy', 'The filthy history of paedophilia, murder and bigotry. Not for the immature!', 'Zionist Antichrist will rule the New World order' and 'Ukraine's anti-Russian stance is a Zionist master plan.' (Here too, a welcome spark of originality)

Nottingham Labour Councillor Ilyas Aziz, was suspended and then reinstated after sharing anti-Semitic posts from the conspiracy theorist crackpot David Icke and one called 'Israel - Rothschilds' Frankenstein Monster.'

Brighton Council candidate Alexandria Braithwaite was suspended for tweeting that the Rothschilds were 'Satanists', 'responsible for every war on earth' and linked to the Illuminati. Brighton has an active branch of the Palestine Solidarity Campaign.

Brighton Labour activist Amanda Bishop, suspended when as a protest against Braithwaite's suspension, she posted that party members 'need to march about this to the Synagogue in Brighton' adding, 'why are we continuing to accept this bullshit? Why aren't we defending ourselves?' There are three synagogues in Brighton. One of them was defaced with pro-Hamas graffiti during the Gaza conflict of 2014. What Bishop did have in mind this time? A Labour version of the Crystal Night?

Manchester Council candidate Jade Doswell posted that seeing the Israeli flag 'made her feel sick'.

Sara Conway stood down as Labour's Parliamentary candidate for Finchley and Golders Green after protests for her claim that Labour's anti-Semitism scandal had been 'drummed up' and 'weaponised by certain media commentators'.

Bradford Labour Councillor Mohammed Shabbir tweeted that Israel was behind ISIS and that the BBC was run by a 'hasbar media cartel'.

Mary Bain, a Labour Councillor for Lochgelly, Cardenden and Benarty, Scotland, speculated that Jewish accusations of anti-Semitism in the Corbyn wing of the Labour Party could be a 'Mossad assisted campaign to get rid of Jeremy Corbyn as Labour Leader' and 'prevent the election of a Labour government pledged to recognise Palestine as a State.'

Bognor Regis Labour Councillor Damien Enticott, suspended after sharing a video entitled *Jewish Ritual* with a subtitle claiming Jews 'drink blood and suck baby's dick.'

Labour activist and Corbynista Ash Small, re-instated after being suspended, not expelled, for a series of anti-Semitic postings. One proposed that pro-Israel party Jews should be 'taken out one at a time' and another asked, 'can someone please explain where the figure of 6 million Holocaust victims came from? 'He shared an article which objected to what it claimed was 'Jewish and Zionist influence at the BBC', a complaint also voiced by Corbyn on Iran's Press TV, and another which claimed that the USA and the UK were 'slaves of Israel'. One of the Jews scheduled to be 'taken out', Luke Akehurst, Director of We Believe in Israel, said he was 'left wondering what anyone has to say to have disciplinary action taken against them in the Labour Party.'

Angela Ormerod, one of the Corbyn intake joining the Labour Party after his election as Leader, suspended for claiming that 'Jews control the media'.

Pastor (sic) Liam Moore, Labour candidate for Liverpool's Norris Green Ward, tweeted: 'People, understand that Rothschilds Zionists run Israel and world government, don't give a toss about ordinary Jews, Jesus is coming back his people'; and 'Zionism is not healthy for children and other living things.' Another referred to a 'Zionist coup' by pro-Israel MPs 'infiltrating' the Labour Party and, like Judas, 'selling out for thirty pieces of silver'.

Nottingham Councillor Ilyas Aziz, suspended then re-instated after urging Jews to 'stop drinking Gaza's blood' and comparing Israel to Nazi Germany.

Mohammed Yasin, Labour Party West Midlands Organiser, suspended, not expelled, for a series of anti-Semitic postings on social media, including: 'Jews are responsible for the all the wars in world' and another of a picture of a Rabbi with the caption 'Goyim were born only to serve us'.

Miqdad al-Nuaimi, Labour Councillor for Newport, suspended then re-instated after tweeting that Israel was 'increasingly assuming the arrogance and genocide character of the Nazis.'

Kasey Carver, adopted as Labour Candidate for High Peak Council after posting on the website 'Semitic Controversies', 'just looked at the potential Zionist influences of the BBC'.

Kate Linnegar, adopted as both a Parliamentary candidate for North Swindon and for Swindon Council after sharing an article that alleged anti-Semitism was being 'weaponised' to discredit Corbyn.

Sian Bloor, Secretary of the Trafford branch of the National Education Union, suspended, then re-instated after claiming that Corbyn has 'the 'full force of the Rothschild Zionist agenda drawing down on him', and that 'Jewish Israelis' were behind 9/11.

Council candidate for Kingston-upon-Thames Simon Attwood tweeted that a world Jewish conspiracy controls UK politics and the media, and that anti-Corbyn Labour MP John Mann, who chairs the all- party Parliamentary Group against anti-Semitism, is a paid agent of Israel.

Ex Labour MP for Paisley and Renfrewshire North Jim Sheridan had his membership restored after being suspended for writing that he had 'lost respect and empathy for the Jewish community and their historic suffering due to what they and their Blairite plotters have done to my party.'

Tina McKay, prospective Parliamentary Candidate for Colchester, posted on Facebook that 'there have been individuals who have said that it [anti-Semitism] has been used as a plot, there is evidence of what they said being true.'

Mike Amesbury, Shadow Minister for Employment, after initially denying it, admitted tweeting an-anti-Semitic cartoon from the website 'IlluminatiAgenda.com'. (sic). It displayed an archetypically hooked-nosed 'Father Christmas' Jew with the caption, 'remember to support the banks and corporations this Christmas in their continued efforts to enslave mankind, by spending money you haven't got on things you don't need'.

Shadow Immigration Minister Afzal Khan, selected Labour candidate for the 2017 by-election in Gorton after being investigated and then and cleared for endorsing a tweet that compared Israel to Nazi Germany.

Naz(i) Shah, MP for West Bradford and Private Secretary to Shadow Chancellor John McDonnell, suspended in April 2016 for tweeting a map which showed Israeli Jews re-located to the United States. In an allusion to US aid to Israel, she added the comment that the move 'saved them some pocket money'. She also tweeted that 'everything that Hitler did in Germany was legal'. Really? So what were the Nuremberg Trials about? After being restored to membership, no action was taken in August 2017 when she endorsed in good faith a spoof tweet which said that 'for the good of diversity', 'those abused girls in Rotherham and elsewhere just need to shut their mouths', and when, following the death of Winnie Mandela in April 2018, she tweeted her image with the quote, 'together, hand in hand, with our matches and our necklaces [sic] we shall liberate this country', a reference to the ANC leader's notorious practice of burning alive her political opponents. A kinder politics.

In March 2019, disgraced former Rotherham Deputy Council Leader Jahangir Akhtar, suspected of but never charged with having sexual relations with an under-age gang-rape victim, posted two viciously anti-Semitic cartoons, one with a hooked-nosed Jew. He has reportedly combined with Momentum in a bid to de-select Rotherham Labour MP Sarah Champion, who resigned from the shadow cabinet after coming under fire from Corbyn loyalists for writing in the *Sun* about the gang rape industry in her constituency.

Lancashire Labour Councillor Pam Bromley posted links to an article entitled, 'World War 3: Trump Begins Paying His Homage to Rothschilds. As in all other similar samples, 'Rothschilds' serves as code for 'the Jews'. Here for example Bromley added the comment that the Rothschilds 'represent capitalism and big businesses. She also claimed the Manchester Arena terror attack was not the work of a Muslim terrorist but a 'false flag' operation carried out on Prime Minister Theresa May's orders as 'a handy excuse to squash Jeremy Corbyn's growing support'. How this would work was not explained, but Corbyn, obviously out of the loop on this one, unwittingly helped things along by insisting that the massacre was a protest against British foreign policy. But that is so like Saint Jeremy, always trying to see the good in people, so long as they are not Zionists, even when they massacre children at a pop concert.

Hampstead and Kilburn CLP member Terrance Flanagan compared a Jewish Councillor to Josef Goebbels. Suspended, and then re-admitted after a warning.

Former Labour prospective Parliamentary candidate John Clarke shared a neo-Nazi meme saying that the Rothschilds used money lending and Israel to 'take over the world'. The meme, he said, 'contained a great deal of truth'. Suspended, not expelled.

Maureen Madden, Labour Councillor in North Tyneside, shared an image of banker Jacob Rothschild captioned: 'The people who invisibly control the world.' No action taken, re-elected in 2018.

Alex Scott-Samuel, Chair of Liverpool Wavertree CLP, in one of his regular appearances on the David Icke-sponsored Richie Allen Show, claimed that 'the Rothschild family are behind a lot of the neo-liberal influence in the UK and the US. You only have to Google them to look at this.' It was Scott-Samuel who moved the vote of confidence in Jewish MP Luciana Berger, that led to her resignation from the Labour Party.

Luton Councillor Aysegal Gurbuz tweeted that Hitler was 'the greatest man in history and that if it was not for Hitler, 'these Jews would've wiped Palestine years ago.' After first denying then admitting she was the author (she initially blamed her sister) Gurbuz resigned from the Labour Party.

George McManus of Labour's National Policy Forum, suspended after posting on Facebook; 'Apparently [Deputy Labour Leader Tom] Watson received £50,000 from Jewish donors. At least Judas only got 30 pieces of silver.' His suspension was lifted after the usual ritual apology and appointed Labour Spokesman for the East Riding of Yorkshire.

Chesterfield Labour Councillor Andrew Slack, suspended after sharing a meme of a blood-smeared hook-nosed Israeli soldier. The caption said 'Israel was created by the Rothschilds. Slack was re-instated and remains a Councillor. Slack indeed.

Former chair of Spitalfields and Banglatown [sic] CLP Musabbir Ali tweeted a neo-Nazi 'Timeline of the Jewish genocide of the British People' claiming that 'Jews control Britain and are committing genocide on us.' Suspended, not expelled. Makes a change from the Palestinians.

Paul Ashworth of Tameside tweeted to his 30,000 on-line followers that 'most of top movers at BBC are Jewish. Their head of news is married to a Jew from a well-known banking dynasty. (Could it just be the Rothschilds?)

Kensington Labour Councillor Beinazir Lasharie, suspended and then reinstated after sharing a video on Facebook claiming that ISIS is run by Mossad. She commented, 'Many people know about who was behind 9/11 and also who is behind ISIS. I've nothing against Jews…just sharing it.' (sic)

Enfield Labour Councillor Ayfer Orhan had the whip withdrawn after retweeting the same claim.

Lambeth Labour Councillor Irfan Mohammed shared a post that said 'Jews working in the World Trade centre received a text message before the incident "Do not come to work in [sic] September 11."'

Dorian Bartley, a 'Diversity' officer of Lambeth CLP, posted images comparing Israel to the Nazis. He also shared a post defending the anti-Semitic mural approved by Corbyn and an image of Hitler giving the Nazi salute with the caption, 'we are the master race', next to an image of Israel Premier Netanyahu.

Luke Cresswell tweeted an image of a blood-soaked Israeli flag and captioned the image, 'Moses must be proud of you.' Suspended, then re-instated and elected as Suffolk Labour Councillor.

Wiltshire Labour Council candidate Terry Couchman, suspended, then expelled for using social media to attack 'ZioNazi storm troopers of IsraelHell'.

In an interview in the *Radio Times*, Corbynista actress Miriam Margoleyes claimed there was not 'the extent of anti-Semitism in the Labour Party that people seem to imply. It is to do with trying to stop Corbyn from becoming Prime Minister.' On previous occasions, she claimed 'Jews and blacks are stingy', that 'nobody likes Jews', and 'people understandably and correctly associate Israel with Jews and Jews are killing innocent people.'

Rachel Abbotts, elected Labour Councillor in High Peak after posting on Facebook the claim that 'the Jews declared war on Germany' and another which asked, 'is Israel's hand behind the attacks on Jeremy Corbyn?'

Fylde council candidate Harry Verco, suspended after tweeting 'Israel is turning itself into a Neo-Nazi state' and sharing an article with the comment:' Disgusting pair Murdoch/Rothschilds Israel exposed secretly paying Syria rebels to protect Rothschild Murdoch oil'.

Rebecca Massey of Hove tweeted that 'Israel has Tory and Labour Parties under control, and that Labour's anti-Semitism crisis had been 'manufactured'. No action. Instead, she was appointed Treasurer of Hove and Portslade CLP.

Redditch Labour Party Branch Secretary Alan Mason resigned from the party when there came to light a posting which claimed that Jewish Labour MP Ruth Smeeth was funded by an 'Israeli Lobby', that the Rothschilds funded Hitler, that Hilary Clinton's 'Zio strillionaire [sic] friends in London are sucking America and 99% of Americans dry', and that Jewish real estate developer Larry Silverstein profited from 9/11.

Paul Merron, Ealing Labour Party member, and video-maker for PSC and Stop the War Coalition. shared one post saying that 'a 15-year-old girl learns the truth about the Holohoax', and another which claimed that '6 Jewish companies control 96% of the world's media.' Merron says that he 'joined the Labour Party to support Jeremy Corbyn'.

Tony Greenstein, the archetypical 'self-hating Jew', suspended after comments such as 'Zio idiots', 'Zionist scum', that Jewish MP Loise Ellman 'supported Israeli child abuse' and 'gay Zionists make me want to puke'.

Essex Councillor John Clarke and Labour Parliamentary candidate in 2015 tweeted that the Rothschilds have 'used usury as an imperial instrument to take over the world and all its resources, include you and I.'

Former Labour MP Michelle Harris shared a Facebook post from David Icke (sic) entitled 'Rothschild Zionist Israel an International Pariah' and others comparing Israel to Nazi Germany. No action taken.

Corbynista MPs Chris Williamson and Dan Carden were present at a Momentum rally where a member of Liverpool Sefton CLP, to a standing ovation, declared, 'What could be greater threat to our democracy than a foreign government who [sic]is trying to veto the person we want for Prime Minister? Of course, I'm talking about the Israelis with their foot soldiers in Labour, the Labour Friends of Israel, the Jewish Labour Movement. They are trying to take out democracy away from us.' Neither Williamson nor Carden challenged this exposition of the World Jewish Conspiracy.

In the same vein, Fife Labour Councillor Mary Lockhart suggested on Facebook that there could be a 'Mossad-assisted campaign to prevent the election of a Labour Government.' Suspended, then reinstated.

Dipu Ahad, a Labour Councillor for Newcastle, posted that he didn't vote for a new mega Marks and Spencer store in Gosforth 'as a matter of principle' because the company was 'directly killing innocent Palestinian people by directly funding the Zionist regime'. In another posting, he claimed western countries went to war in Iraq, Afghanistan and Libya to 'achieve the Zionist goal…to have each country in the debt of the Rothschilds.' Again, a ritual apology for saying something he obviously believed to be true (otherwise, why advertise it?) and no further action. Adopted to stand again as candidate for the Elswick ward.

When Steve Cooke, Secretary of Stockton CLP moved a resolution condemning the Pittsburgh synagogue massacre in which 11 Jews died, objections were made it did not condemn all forms of racism, only anti-Semitism. A previous resolution, condemning 'Islamophobia 'was not subjected to the same criticism.

Invited to address a Momentum fringe meeting at a Labour Party conference, Ewa Jasiewicz withdrew when it was revealed that she had daubed 'Free Gaza and Palestine' on the Warsaw Ghetto wall in 2010, and had called for Palestinian 'activists' (sic) to 'do' the Israeli Parliament or 'bump off' a 'sophisticated politician' rather than target Israeli civilians.

Addressing a party meeting in 2014, Labour MP for Leeds East and Corbyn's Shadow Justice Secretary Richard Burgon said that that 'Zionism is the enemy of peace' and that all Labour MP's who are members of Labour Friends of Israel should resign their seats. In a subsequent TV interview with Andrew Neil, he denied using these words: 'I didn't say that. It's not my view'. When a video of the meeting proved that he did, he issued the usual pro-forma apology, claiming that he was only criticising the Israeli government, not Jews who identified themselves as Zionists because, as nearly all Jews do, they support the right of Israel to exist. No action was taken.

Rupa Huq, MP for Ealing Central and Acton, accused of a number of anti-Semitic comments and actions by two of her employees. One was repeatedly asked, 'why do you have the flag of Israel on your bag? 'even after being told it was nothing of the sort. A briefing he wrote on the Middle East conflict was criticised for being too pro-Israel. He was subsequently banned from writing any more. For one potential Jewish employee, Huq 'devised a whole separate list of questioning based on Judaism and loyalty to Israel'. The other employee claims Huq regaled an employee with stories about Jewish conspiracies and in her office tore down a 'No tolerance for anti-Semitism' poster, saying that it was not needed any more. No action taken.

Labour's council candidate for Tonbridge Wells Roy Smart, suspended after sharing a series of links on a Holocaust denial website and posting that 'people being allowed to question if the Holocaust happened is not the same as being a Holocaust denier, any more than protesting about the Israeli government's treatment of the Palestinians is anti-Semitic'.

Margaret Tyson of Liverpool Wavertree CLP accused local Jewish Labour MP Luciana Berger of supporting the 'Zionist Israeli government' whose 'Nazi masters [sic] taught them well'. In another posting, she wrote, 'Is it any wonder the Zionest [sic] are hated and despised throughout the world?' No action taken. Berger has been the target for abuse on Corbynista websites that even by their standards are especially vicious: 'She is a vile Zionist'; 'Get rid of this cancer'; 'Deselect the cunt'. A kinder politics.

Former Shadow Fire and Emergency Services Minister Chris Williamson, Labour MP for North Derby, described by his leader Jeremy Corbyn as 'a very great friend', dismissed accusations of Labour Party anti-Semitism, as 'proxy wars' [waged on behalf of whom?], 'bullshit' and 'smears', for which, after an outcry by anti-Corbynistas, despite his very great friend's attempt to save him, he was suspended from party membership. Williamson was speaking at a meeting called to protest at the expulsion and suspension of party members on charges of anti-Semitism, referring to 'dark forces' at work in the media and elsewhere to undermine Corbyn. Nothing deterred, the suspended and unrepentant Williamson provoked more outrage when he 'liked' a Jewish conspiracy posting by expelled Momentum activist Nadeem Ahmed claiming that 'Israel have [sic] offered a £1m bounty for Labour insiders to undermine Jeremy Corbyn.' One of these 'insiders' was said to be Labour Friends of Israel Chair Joan Ryan who, according to Ahmed, had been 'filmed asking Shai Masot [an official at the Israeli embassy] about a list of names that were sent to the Israeli embassy.' Williamson's suspension was lifted in June 2019 by a panel of three NEC members/ by a vote of two to one. Those voting to lift the suspension were Keith Vaz, a close friend of Corbyn's of more than thirty years standing and like his Leader, an Islamophile, leading a demonstration of Muslims in his Leicester constituency in 1989 demanding the banning of Salman Rushdie's *Satanic Verses*, and Huda Elmi of the Palestine Solidarity Campaign and Momentum. Like her Leader, she is a supporter of Venezuelan dictator Nicolas Maduro and an enemy of Israel, posting on *The Electronic Intifada* the warning that 'Israel's [sic] definition of anti-Semitism will unleash havoc in Labour', and at a public meeting, describing Israel as a 'settler-colonial state' and Corbyn as a 'pro-Palestinian leader'. She has called the Human Equality and Human Rights Commission, currently investigating her party's anti-Semitism, a 'failed experiment' (in what she did not say), and demanded that it should be wound up. 120 Labour MPs and peers and 70 staffers protested Williamson's re-instatement, resulting in the withholding of the Labour whip.

In March 2018, actor and Labour Council candidate for Stratford-on Avon Chris Jury posted on-line the allegation that the Israeli embassy had 'aided and abetted' the 'right wing of the of the Labour Party' in its 'cynical abuse' of the Holocaust to undermine the Corbyn leadership. In April, likening Israel to Nazi Germany, Jury said its 'racist, colonial, Eurocentric [sic] moral; degeneracy' was 'still playing out in the Middle East'. Again, in August, Jury claimed that British politics were being 'subverted' and anti-Semitism 'weaponised' by Labour's right wing. In a statement to the online *Daily Mail,* Jury stood by all these and other similar comments. No action taken.

In Peterborough, one of growing number of Labour's rotten Muslim boroughs, a by-election triggered by the resignation of Fiona (Jesus Christ) Onasanya following her conviction and jailing for perverting the course of justice, Labour replaced a crook by an exponent of Jewish conspiracy theory, namely Corbyn loyalist Liz Forbes She had endorsed a posting accusing Theresa May of following a 'Zionist slave masters agenda' and another, one that she 'enjoyed reading so much', claiming that that ISIS was created by Mossad and the CIA. As a PSC activist and supporter of BDS, Forbes also rejected one of the 11 articles in the International Holocaust Remembrance Association's definition of anti-Semitism, adopted with a caveat, and after prolonged resistance, by the party's NEC and opposed personally by Corbyn. She insisted that Labour Party members should be free to criticise Israel's 'system [sic] of apartheid and ongoing ethnic cleansing'. Like other Corbynistas exposed as Jew-baiters, Forbes agreed to undergo 'anti-Semitism awareness training', presumably because like many of her ilk, her racism is so deeply ingrained that it can only be eradicated by a course of intensive re-programming in elementary human decency. Forbes was elected on the lowest-ever percentage vote for a winning candidate...30.9%, compared with Jesus Christ's 48.1% at the 2017 General Election, and the highest percentage of postal votes. Despite what impartial observers described as flagrant fraud, Labour's vote fell from 22,950 to10,844. Rejecting demands that she be denied the Labour whip, Corbyn insisted Forbes was a 'good woman, not a racist in any way whatsoever'. Jewish conspiracy theories not racist? Not for Corbyn, because he shares them. Corbyn and Forbes were frequently photographed posing and canvassing with convicted and jailed vote-rigger and former Peterborough party secretary Tariq Mahmood, who also featured in a Labour election video. Corbyn was also seen visiting local mosques, again accompanied by election fraudster Mahmood. And why not? Corbyn is, after all, a supporter and in the case of Iran, even the former employee, of regimes that when they deign to hold elections, rig them as a matter of course. Mahmood, expelled from the party after his conviction, describes his services to it as those of a 'freelance Labour campaigner'.

Jo Bird, a Wirral Councillor, in a meeting called to defend party members accused of anti-Semitism complained, to laughter and applause, of what she called 'Jew process'. This, and other similar remarks, led to her suspension, which days later, was lifted.

Conspiracy (again, explicitly Jewish) was the central theme of a meeting convened on March 11 2019, by the far left to rally support for a Comrade Corbyn besieged by false accusations of anti-Semitism. The audience included 60s student protestor and Brexit campaigner Tariq Ali, Glyn Secker, columnist for the Stalinist *Morning Star* and suspended from Labour Party membership for 'comments on social media that may be anti-Semitic', and Gerry Downing, expelled from the Labour Party for *supporting* 9/11, and who publishes *Protocols*-style diatribes against the sinister role of a 'world Jewish bourgeoisie'. Addressing the meeting, Corbyn's old comrade from the Stop the War Coalition Lindsey German, after reading out a letter of greetings to the event by Comrade Corbyn, denounced accusations of anti-Semitism against the Labour Party and its Leader as a 'huge lie'. 'There is one dominant racism that is going on [sic] and that is Islamophobia.' (Yet again, Islam becomes a race when circumstances require it.) Corbyn's leadership was being undermined by a 'wrecking operation' organised by the Jewish MP Margaret Hodge: 'We are here tonight to say we are not going to allow that wrecking operation to continue'. Two weeks later, hard-core Corbynistas gathered again, this time under the auspices of 'Labour Against the Witch-hunt', to listen to Livingstone intone the same tune, that Labour's anti-Semitic crisis was the product of 'lies and smears' peddled by 'ghastly old Blairites'. He said that his own fall from grace as Corbyn's adviser on matters military (sic), which after more than two years of suspension, was climaxed by his resignation, had been engineered by a 'Labour machine staffed by 'Blairites'. Corbyn's own office, he revealed 'did not want it to happen'. That at least we can believe. Unrepentant as ever, he insisted 'it's not anti-Semitic to hate the Jews of Israel'.

The reader will no doubt have noticed several recurring themes in the above citings, two of the most frequent being that ISIS is a Mossad creation and that Labour's anti-Semitic crisis has been artificially fomented and then exploited by Jews in the party and/or Israeli intelligence to undermine Corbyn's leadership. No surprises here, since identical allegations proliferate on numerous websites associated with the Corbynista and Palestinian causes. Then there is the claim that *opposition* to anti-Semitism was being 'weaponised' to undertime Corbyn's leadership, an inversion of the traditional left-wing thesis that *anti-Semitism itself*, not opposition to it, was whipped up by the far right to divert the masses from the struggle against capitalism. But the one that merits the most interest because of its provenance are the repeated allusions to the existence of a world Jewish conspiracy, almost invariably personified by the Rothschilds family. Here we have, in its purest and most explicit form, the thesis of *The Protocols of the Learned Elders* of *Zion*, one that found full favour both with the Nazis and has more recently in the Muslim world and on the left, that Jews, largely by stealth, control the entire world's banking system and, by doing so, virtually everything else on our planet. It was Hitler's ruling obsession, one he returned to it again and again in his *Mien Kampf*, and one which led directly to the gas chambers of the Holocaust. *It is also an obsession shared by members of the Labour Party.*

In the cited cases of anti-Semitism listed above, no fewer than 23 contain direct references by Labour Party members to the Rothschilds. A search online quickly brought up a dozen or more websites that could have been the source of these references, all overtly anti-Semitic and in some case, also Nazi. One, titled *Real Jew News,* listed no fewer than 13 articles on the alleged conspiratorial activities of the Rothschilds, with titles such as 'Greek Riots and the Rothschild Bankers', 'The Rothschilds' Secret Operations', 'George Soros: An Evil Rothschild Agent', 'England's Jews Control Europe', 'The Rothschild-Israeli Occult Connection' and 'How the Rothschild Dynasty Operates'. So much information…and yet strange, because all this and much more is supposed to be a closely-guarded secret. Another revealed 'how the Rothschilds own Israel and direct its genocidal policy', like all the others I surveyed, more grist to the mill of gullible Jew-baiting Corbynites, as at the London anti-Trump rally addressed by Corbyn on June 9. 2019, where one of the audience displayed a large poster with the legend: 'They All [underlined] Work for Rothschild'.

In the normal run of things, these are the kinds of opinions that one would expect to find being voiced by members of a fully-fledged Nazi movement. But today, those that advertise them are quite at home in the Corbynista wing of the Labour Party, with many of them being protected from disciplinary action by their Dear Leader's personal staff. This is only to be expected when, as we have already seen, Corbyn himself is no stranger to Jewish conspiracy theory. Another example, devastating in the extreme, came to light in April 2019 when the *Sunday Times* carried a story concerning a 3,500-word Foreword Corbyn had written in 2010 for a new edition by Spokesman Books of John Hobson's *Imperialism*, first published in 1902. One passage of the work (which Lenin used as source material for his own book on same subject some 14 years later) advances the same claim that features prominently on Corbynista websites and postings by his Labour Party supporters, namely, that the Jews, usually personified by the Rothschilds, control the world economy through their monopoly of the banking system…precisely Bebel's 'socialism of fools'. Hobson confined himself to Europe, but the thesis is essentially the same, even down to the Rothchilds as the main villains of the piece:

> United by the strongest bonds of organisation, always in closest and quickest touch with one another, situated in the very heart of the business capital of every state, controlled, so far as Europe is concerned, by men of a single and peculiar race, who

have behind them many centuries of financial experience, they are in a unique position to control the policy of nations.

He continues in the same vein:

'Does anyone seriously suppose that any great war could be undertaken by any European state if the House of Rothschild [sic] and their connections set their face against it?' He goes even further, anticipating the claim made by Hitler in *Mein Kampf*, which he derived from the *Protocols*, that the Jews not only control the world of finance, but its ostensible enemy, the revolutionary left: 'There is not a war, a revolution, an anarchist assassination or any other public shock' from which these 'harpies' cannot 'suck their gains'. The *Protocols* has it thus: 'We [that is, the mythical "Learned Elders of Zion"] shall create by all secret subterranean methods open to us with the aid of gold, which is in all our hands, a universal economic crisis whereby we shall throw upon the streets whole mobs of workers simultaneously in all the countries of Europe.' And likewise, according to Hitler, the German economy had 'fallen victim to the united attack of [Jewish] finance capital, which carried on its fight with the special help of its faithful comrade, the [no less Jewish] Marxist movement'.

The core of Hobson's economic argument, one that was endorsed by Lenin, minus the anti-Semitism, was that in order to boost its profits, capitalism is compelled to find new markets, sources of raw materials and fresh outlets for investment. by means of colonial conquest and exploitation, which in turn leads to rivalry and eventually war between the competing imperial powers. And, masterminding the entire process, is an international conspiracy of Jewish bankers. Even though one of the central messages of Hobson's book is therefore that rich Jews conspire to conquer and suck dry the riches of the world, just as in the scandal of the anti-Semitic Tower Hamlets mural which he initially praised, Corbyn found his study exemplary in its exposure of the evils of capitalism: 'brilliant', 'correct and prescient [sic], a 'great tome' no less. As for its diatribes against the Jews…not a word. Instead, he titles his Forward 'Internationalist at Work'! If it is the case, as a Labour Party statement claimed, that 'Jeremy completely rejects the anti-Semitic elements of his [i.e., Hobson's] analysis', given that Hobson the 'internationalist' is known to have harboured and advertised in other writings his prejudices against the Jews, and that they formed a central component of his 'analysis' in *Imperialism*, why didn't Corbyn, the dedicated anti-racist, immediately spot them, and then take the opportunity to condemn them in his Foreword, and when he spoke at the launching of the book on January 12, 2011? Far from condemning Hobson's 'analysis', this is how Corbyn responded to it:

For someone who was revered by Marxists, and quoted by Lenin, for his analysis of the pressures to extend empire, his analysis of the then current empire and its future, was not very revolutionary What is brilliant, and very controversial at the time, is his analysis of the pressures that were hard at work in pushing for a vast national effort in grabbing new outposts of empire on distant lands and shores.

But who was doing the 'pushing' and 'grabbing'? Hobson says, Jewish finance, which 'control[s] the policy of nations'. Corbyn must had read those passages where this central element of Hobson's 'brilliant' analysis is developed. But he passes them over without comment. Instead, he declares Hobson's anti-Semitic book to a work that 'deserves enormous credit and recognition'. How did Corbyn reply to the well-founded accusation that once again, he had uncritically praised a work with an undisguised anti-Semitic theme?

> This accusation is the latest in a series of equally ill-founded accusations of anti-Jewish racism that Labour's political opponents have made against me. [In fact, as Corbyn was only too well aware, most of them have come from within his own party.] I note that the Foreword story was written by a Conservative Party peer [as if that *ipso facto* renders it untrue] in a newspaper whose editorial policy and owner [Rupert Murdoch - more *ad hominem*] have long been hostile to Labour. At a time when Jewish communities in the UK and indeed, across Europe feel [sic] under attack, it is a matter of great regret that the issue of anti-Semitism is often politicised in this way.

Corbyn cannot even bring himself to acknowledge that Jews actually *are* 'under attack', including by his supporters in the Labour Party, only that they 'feel' they are. It's all in the mind. And yet, as he must have known that in France Jews were leaving in their thousands because of anti-Semitic violence, including murder, and that Jewish MPs of his own party were being subjected to death and even rape threats. On the same day that the Campaign Against Anti-Semitism website carried Corbyn's defence of his uncritical treatment of Hobson's book, Corbyn's Hamas 'friends' fired more than 600 rockets supplied by his former Iranian employers into Israeli territory, killing four civilians and wounding more than 100. Again, on that day, the same source reported two expressions of viciously anti-Jewish attitudes in the UK. Omar Choudhury, 'Black and [?] Minority Ethnic Officer' of Bristol University Students Union, told a Jewish student that he should be like Israel and 'cease to exit'. So much for 'minorities'. Despite a petition calling for his removal being signed by more than a thousand students, and his employers agreeing that his comment was anti-Semitic, Choudhury was not even given a formal warning, but merely required to apologise to the student he had insulted. The second case concerned Kamran Ishtiaq, President of the British Pakistani Youth Council since 2009. In 2014, he posted a picture of Hitler on his Facebook page. When another Facebook user objected that 'Hitler was a racist bro', Ishtiaq, obviously unaware that Hitler had allied himself with Muslim leaders in the Second World War, replied, 'I know that and to be honest he would have killed Muslims too if he got the chance'. But then he continued, 'But do you know what, I would salute him still if he killed 90 Muslims and 92 Jews.' Hitler was his hero 'cuz he just killed Jews, didn't get a chance to kill Muslims.' All in the mind? When these comments came to light five years later, he told the *Birmingham Post* that he stood by them, adding that the number of Jews killed in the Holocaust had been 'exaggerated' in order to justify what he called Jewish 'revenge'.

Should Jews be concerned about such cases of flagrant anti-Semitism exhibited by individuals who hold offices of influence within British society including, as we have seen, in one of the UK's two largest political parties? Or is it the case, as Corbyn implies, that Jewish concerns are unfounded, that the issue has been stirred up by his party's enemies, that opposition to anti-Semitism is being 'weaponised', in his case by the Tory peer in question, the Jewish Lord Finkelstein, and a Tory press magnate? Not that Corbyn has any objection *per se* to Tory peers, only those who expose his indulgence of anti-Semitism. He accompanied a Muslim one, Lord Sheikh, on two freebees to the lands of Arabia, the first as guest of President Assad of Syria (who later played host to the Neo-Nazi Nick Griffin), the second to attend a Hamas council of war against Israel in Tunisia, where he laid a wreath at the graveside of Fatah operatives involved in the planning of the hostage-taking operation that led to the massacre of the Israeli team at the 1972 Munch Olympics.

Ad hominem arguments avail Corbyn nothing. The plain fact, one that Corbyn takes care to avoid, is that the book he had unreservedly and fulsomely praised (I have read his *Foreword*) was flagrantly and deeply flawed by its anti-Semitism, and that fact is true irrespective of who reports it, even when the reporter is a Jewish Tory. Is it any wonder then that with a track record such as his on the 'Jewish question', a poll conducted in April 2019, revealed that 55% of voters agreed with the statement that 'Jeremy Corbyn's failure to tackle anti-Semitism within his own party shows he is unfit to be Prime Minister'?

How the Labour Leadership responded, or as many have claimed, failed to respond, to this extraordinary surge of Jew-hatred, became a subject of adverse comment both by anti-Corbyn MPs and sections of the media, being partly informed by leaks of documents officially privy only to Corbyn's central staff. In March, 2019, the *Sunday Times* acquired access to confidential information held at Labour Party HQ which revealed that of 863 Labour Party members reported to have made anti-Semitic comments, 249 had not been investigated, and another 454 remained unresolved. Of the 409 cases resolved, 191 required no further action, 145 received a formal warning, and 15 were expelled. One party member, on Corbyn's staff, said Israel was excused being an 'apartheid state' 'because of the Holocaust'. No action was taken...hardly a surprise, since this is a routine Corbynista accusation against Israel. Also restored to full membership were Labour Councillor Ben Lloyd-Shogbesan, who had compared Israel to Nazi Germany, and Council candidate Alan Myers, who had posted a comment about 'Zionist leaders and their billionaire masters'. (Who might they be, one wonders?) A Lancashire Councillor who was expelled for posting claims that the media were controlled by the Jews, was re-admitted after explaining she used 'Jewish' as 'a blanket term of description without any racist connotations'. A blanket term for whom? She gave a clue when she also attacked the Rothschilds in the same posting. Make of this arcane excuse what you like, the fact is that prominent party members were being licensed to say virtually anything derogatory about the Jews. For example, in another case, a member who described Labour's Jewish MPs as 'Zionist infiltrators' was let off because he was a council candidate. Incredibly, even a member who posted on-line 'Heil Hitler, fuck the Jews' escaped expulsion, while Thomas Gardiner, a close ally of Corbyn, blocked the fast-track expulsion of a party member who described two Jewish Labour MPs, obviously both women, as 'shit-stirring cunt buckets'. What a nice bunch these Corbynistas are.

The same report revealed that in violation of the required procedure, cases involving members whom Corbyn's Chief of Staff, Karie Murphy defined as 'elected politicians or candidates', were being referred to Corbyn's office, resulting in the blocking or delaying of 101 complaints, refuting the assurance Corbyn gave to Margaret Hodge that 'I do not involve myself in a complaint at all.' Understandably, in view of this assurance, MPs were outraged when they learned that both Andrew Murray and his daughter Laura, described as 'Stakeholder Manager' on Corbyn's staff, (tying things up nicely, Corbyn's son Seb, also 'appointed on merit', is on McDonnell's) had for at least a year been blocking and reversing disciplinary actions against members charged with anti-Semitism, usurping the role ascribed to Labour's disputes committee. Murray junior's role as Corbyn's overseer was regularised when she was appointed Head of Complaints in April 2019. Responding to accusations of political favouritism and nepotism, a party source said she was 'the best person for the job'…just like Corbyn junior.

One case binned by Murray senior was a claim by a party member that ISIS was a creation of Mossad, while Murray junior cleared a member who, like Corbyn, had approved of the Tower Hamlets anti-Semitic mural. In March of 2018, she had also reversed, *but only after consulting Corbyn*, the suspension of Patricia Sheerin: 'LTO [Leader of the Opposition] recommendations are that you investigate but without suspension as although her tweets are drawing upon conspiracy theories, they are about Israel and no mention [sic] of Jews or Jewishness etc'. Conspiracy theories about the Jewish state of Israel are OK, as long as there is no actual mention of the Jews. Just a nod and wink will do, as with Corbyn when on Press TV in August 2012, he referred to the 'hand of Israel' but not the Jews. A year later, Sheerin was one of three party members arrested by police on charges of inciting racial hatred against Jews. Another member who had recycled a cartoon on a Nazi website (sic!) was cleared by Corbyn himself, on the grounds that it was not anti-Jew but anti-Israel.

Days later, the *Sunday Times* revealed that Murray senior and yet another Corbyn insider, his 'Director of Strategy and Communications', fellow Stalin apologist Seumas Milne, had intervened to lift the suspension of Glyn Secker, a member of the viciously anti-Zionist and frequently no less anti-Semitic secret website Palestine Live that Corbyn, its highest profile member, visited at least 30 times, until withdrawing after being elected Labour leader in September 2015. After Secker had been suspended for postings on its website, including one which said 'Jew=Zionist=Israel=Jew', Murray and Milne sprang to his defence, emailing the party's Disputes Committee that 'none of the posts can be identified as anti-Semitic in the terms we have adopted as a party,' adding, as a clincher, that Corbyn 'was interested in this one'. The suspension was promptly lifted, as it was for Momentum activist Marlene Ellis, suspended in 2016 for declaring in an Open Letter to Corbyn that by suspending Livingstone for claiming that Zionists collaborated with the Nazis (a claim she endorsed) the party had 'played right into the hands of the Zionist criminals' by 'seeking to curry favour with the pro-Zionist lobby in and beyond the media.' Commenting on these revelations, Labour MP Wes Streeting said he did not understand 'how anyone on the left can even try and defend Labour's handling of anti-Semitism - or continued to deny the problem.' He had 'absolutely no confidence in the Labour Party's approach to tackling anti-Semitism and will discuss next steps with colleagues.' In a secretly taped interview with Margaret Hodge, Corbyn can be heard admitting that evidence of anti-Semitism was 'either being mislaid, ignored or not used'.

Interviewed by Andrew Marr on BBC TV on February 23, 2019, Deputy Leader Tom Watson revealed that he had a file of 50 cases still waiting to be processed, while MP Margaret Hodge said she had personally submitted another 200. Watson's included: an accusation that Jews were guilty of 'double-dealing, back stabbing, cheating'; that Jews were 'pervert[ing] democracy in the UK'; that 'Jews murder people and children'; the claim that Hitler was an 'illegitimate Rothschild'(sic!), that the numbers of Jews said to be have been killed in the Holocaust 'don't add up'; and that Jewish MPs Ruth Smeeth and Louise Ellman 'don't know what runs through their veins, not human blood'. Yes, these are the expressed views of *Labour Party members*, the same 'socialism of fools' ridiculed by Bebel and Engels, views which, before the election of Corbyn as Leader, no-one would have dared to voice so brazenly. Now, Labour's anti-Semites wanted to tell the world what they think of the Jews, and those who defend them. In the on-line *Daily Mirror* story covering the Watson interview, there were the following comments: 'You [Watson] need to join the right-wing Blairites. Good riddance.' 'With deputy leaders like Watson who needs a Tory party.' 'Always follow the money. Who's paying them…Israel.'

Labour's anti-Semitism crisis deepened still further when on July 10, 2019, it was the subject of a Panorama investigation on BBC1. Corbyn had been invited to appear on the programme to answer the charges made against him by former members of his staff, but he declined the offer. Instead, Panorama screened a series of statements issued by the party in answer to the charges made against it. Anticipating that the programme will remain accessible on line, I simply draw attention to one damning fact of many that emerged from it, namely that out of the thousands of cases processed, and thanks largely to the efforts of Milne and the Murrays, as of July 2019, only 15 had resulted in expulsions. After turning down the invitation to state his case, following the programme's screening, Corbyn claimed it had 'many, many inaccuracies,' though he did not say what they were, merely that it had a 'pre-determined position'…again unspecified. A predictable response, not least in that on Iran's Press TV, Corbyn had accused the BBC of a pro-Israel bias emanating from the country's London embassy. His dismissal of the programme's findings proved too much for one-time loyalist Emily Thornberry, who said it was mistake to 'attack the messengers' when it was so obvious that the party had an 'ongoing problem with anti-Semitism'. This was confirmed when, only a matter of days later, fully a third of Labour Peers - 67 - signed an Open Letter to their party leader entitled, 'This is your Legacy, Mr Corbyn', protesting at his continued failure (at best) to weed out the party's anti-Semites. It concluded: 'You have failed to defend our party's anti-racist values. You have therefore failed the test of leadership.' (Acting with an alacrity and severity rarely if ever in evidence even in cases of proven anti-Semitism, within the week, the Sunderland Labour Party expelled Hilary Armstrong for signing the Open Letter to Corbyn.)

The peers' devasting letter followed the resignation from the party of three other Labour peers, not by accident two Jews and one of Armenian origin. Then, days later, came a revolt of the plebs, as all the staff at Labour's Newcastle-based Membership Department walked out when, on first her first day as Corbyn's new appointment as the Department's Head, it was discovered that Jules Rutherford had previously tweeted that allegations of anti-Semitism were 'smears against the Party Leader'. Not for the first time, a Labour spokesman refused to comment and, following the example of her Leader, that the tweet was quickly consigned to the memory hole.

Three conclusions arising from facts presented in this work are undeniable. One, that despite repeated claims to the contrary, Labour's anti-Semitism has been on the rise only since the election of Corbyn as leader; Two, those who promote it get more often than not an easy ride from the top party leadership. Three, with the election of a party leader widely celebrated in the 'Muslim community' as a champion of Islam and the enemy of Israel, it was now considered safe for some Labour Party Muslims to voice openly views about the Jews which hitherto had been, as one Muslim commentator has described it, their 'dirty little secret'.

Symptomatic of the tolerant attitude towards Labour Party Jew-baiting is the scandal that led in March 2018 to the resignation of Corbyn loyalist Christine Shawcross from both the Labour Party National Executive Committee and as head the Labour Party's Disputes Panel. Her duties in the latter office included investigating accusations of anti-Semitism made against party members. One such charge was made against Allan Bull, who was due to stand as a Labour candidate in that hot-bed of anti-Zionism and dubious voting practices, Peterborough, in the local elections due in May 2018. Bull had been suspended from his local party after posting on Facebook an article saying the Holocaust was a 'hoax'. Shawcross, also a Director of the Corbynista Momentum, lifted his suspension and then, after an outcry, resigned. Reversing the old adage by appointing a thief to protect many others, Corbyn proposed as her replacement another loyalist, Claudia Webbe, a councillor in Corbyn's Islington North constituency and former Mayoral adviser to and election agent of the disgraced Livingstone. Webbe defended him when in 2005, as Mayor of London, he was suspended for a month for likening a Jewish journalist to a Nazi concentration camp guard.

Aside from the Islington connection, it is easy to see why Webbe was Corbyn's choice. She did not even believe Labour had an anti-Semitism problem, having previously tweeted that it was a plot engineered by the 'combined machinery of state, political and mainstream elite' to undermine Corbyn's leadership. Not only this. Webbe had also shared platforms with three Labour Party members who had been suspended on charges of anti-Semitism. Webbe was assisted by yet another Corbyn loyalist, party General Secretary Jennie Formby, who then, in her turn, found herself usurped by the super loyalists Milne and the Murray dynasty. Labour Peer Lord Falconer, appointed to bring some sort of order to a disciplinary process that had escaped control, when questioned about the interventions of Milne and the Murrays on Radio 4, asked 'what on earth is going on?... how can we ask people to vote for a party that is anti-Semitic?' How indeed. Days later, there came a truly surrealist moment when a MP who likens herself to Jesus entered the chamber of the Commons wearing an electronic leg tag after her early release from prison.

Of the cases of alleged or proven anti-Semitism I have culled from various sources, no fewer than five involved members of Corbyn's Shadow cabinet, seven were back-bench MPs, five were Parliamentary candidates, one a candidate for the EU Parliament, 38 were councillors, 16 were council candidates, and 16 had Muslim names. Nevertheless, her master's (often very confused) voice Diane Abbott, who is herself an anti-white racist, is quoted as saying on May 1, 2016, that 'it is a smear to say that Labour has a problem with anti-Semitism', a position that in the wake of the 'Corbyn mural' scandal, finally became indefensible. Comments that occasioned accusations of anti-Semitism ran the usual gamut from Jews are no better than Nazis to praise for Hitler as 'the greatest man in history' who 'killed six million Zionists', and from denying the Holocaust to applauding it. And yet again we have the Rothschilds, Jews kidnapping Palestinian children (whether for their body organs or their blood was left unsaid), a Jewish Holocaust of the Palestinians, a Jewish world conspiracy, ISIS created by Mossad, 'ZioNazi vermin', a Mossad conspiracy against Corbyn, a David Duke video, praise for David Icke, 'Jews have big noses and slaughter the oppressed', 'Israel has Tory and Labour parties under [its] control', Hamas justified in killing Israeli civilians, 'Zionist Jews' a 'disgrace to humanity', '150,000 Jewish SS personally involved in the Holocaust', BBC and press controlled by Zionists, 'apartheid' Israel, Jews the chief financiers of the slave trade and the 'Zionist conspiracy', the 'the filthy history of paedophilia, murder and bigotry', and inevitably, much praise for Jew-baiter number one, Ken Livingstone.

These are beliefs quite openly promoted and recycled by members, not of Hamas or of a Nazi movement but *of the Labour Party*, many of them having been elected or chosen to represent the party in the UK's democratic institutions up to the very highest level. They have served in Corbyn's Shadow Cabinet and in Livingstone's case, as his adviser on defence policy. The *Sunday Times* of April 1, 2018, revealed that twelve of Corbyn's and McDonnell's staff, and McDonnell himself, were members of 20 social media groups which featured more than 2,000 violently abusive and anti-Semitic postings, among them, the Corbyn cultist 'We Support Jeremy Corbyn', 'Jeremy Corbyn leads us to victory' and 'Let's help make Jeremy Prime Minister'. Another, 'Supporting Jeremy Corbyn and John McDonnell', carried a posting which read; 'Adolph, [sic] you should have finished the job.' The same day, Corbyn announced that he had consigned his own personal Facebook account to the same Orwellian memory hole that swallowed up his adulatory postings on Venezuela.

On April 12, 2018, the *Jewish News* reported that at a screening of his film *I, Daniel Blake* at the Kingswood Constituency Labour Party, Corbynista film director, one-time Healyite and Patron of the Palestine Solidarity Campaign Ken Loach called for 30 Labour MPs who attended a demonstration outside Parliament against Labour anti-Semitism to be de-selected. At the same event, he recommended to the audience a series of programmes on Al-jazeera TV entitled *The Lobby*: 'It explains the role of the Israeli government in infiltrating and undermining the Labour left.' He followed this up by posting online the prediction that 'it will get worse because if the Labour Party gets into power and if they stick with their manifesto and go even further you will have the full range of international capital [sic] against us.' In other words, the Israeli government is undermining Labour by supporting the campaign against anti-Semitism on behalf of 'international capital', or what the Nazis called 'international Jewish finance'. This excursion into classic Jewish conspiracy theory evidently proved an embarrassment to a Corbyn leadership already deeply mired in the party's anti-Semitic scandal, because Loach's services as producer of Labour's TV local election broadcasts were promptly dispensed with. So why not offer them to Al-jazeera or better still, Hamas TV?

A survey of Labour Party anti-Semitism would not be complete without recognition of the pioneering contributions of that doyen of leftist Jew-baiters, Ken Livingstone, who after more than two years of suspension for making remarks concerning Hitler and Zionism that were considered to be anti-Semitic, resigned in May 2018. (The reader will recall that Livingstone does not regard anti-Semitism as racism.) The first was that Hitler 'supported Zionism' an assertion on a par in its mendacity with professional Holocaust denier David Irving's claim that Hitler was 'probably the biggest friend the Jews had in the Third Reich'. Another no less Holocaust revisionist, was that the SS 'set up training camps so that German Jews that were going to go [to Palestine] could be trained to cope with a very different sort of country when then got there.' As any *bona fide* historian of the Holocaust will tell Livingstone, the 'different sort of country' the SS dispatched the Jews to was not Palestine, then under the British Mandate, and therefore rendering such an operation impossible, but the six death camps in Poland: Treblinka, Sobibor, Belzec, Maidenek, Auschwitz and Chelmno. (Could it be that Livingstone is confusing his imaginary Jewish SS division with the all-too-real Muslim Handschar Division trained by the Waffen SS to hunt down and murder Jews and communist partisans in Yugoslavia?)

This was not the first time Livingstone has been suspended for anti-Semitism. When Leader of the Greater London Council, he was suspended from office for four weeks for likening a Jewish journalist to a Nazi concentration camp guard. The friendship and political collaboration of Livingstone and Corbyn goes back a long way, at least as far as 1982, when they jointly founded the forerunner of that proven stamping-ground for anti-Semites, the Palestinian Solidarity Campaign. Corbyn was first elected as a Labour MP the next year, while Livingstone had been Leader of the Greater London Council since 1981, with Corbyn's current Shadow Chancellor John McDonnell as his Deputy. While Corbyn moved in the orbit of what was to become the Stalinist British Communist Party, contributing frequently, as we have seen, to its daily paper, the *Morning Star*, Livingstone was co-editing the *Labour Herald*, a weekly journal that began publication in September 1981, printed by Astmoor Litho, the same printers that printed both the publications of the *soi-disant* Trotskyist Workers Revolutionary Party led by Gerry Healy and the English language version of the Gaddafi regime's weekly bulletin, *The Green March*. (Corbyn however shared Livingstone's admiration for the *Herald's* paymaster. Addressing a meeting called to protest at western involvement in the dictator's overthrow, his gushing praise for Gaddafi's 'achievements' was met by groans from what was an overwhelmingly far left audience.)

Those conversant with the history of communism might indeed find it odd that Corbyn, a fellow-traveller of the ultra-Stalinists, and Livingstone, not only an editor of a journal closely aligned with an avowedly Trotskyist party, but a prominently featured guest speaker at its public meetings and an interviewee in its daily paper, *News Line*, could collaborate so harmoniously for more than two decades. Even with their limited knowledge of history, they both must have been aware that Stalin not only had Trotsky assassinated in Mexico in August 1940 but ordered the murder of thousands of his followers in the Soviet Union in the terror purges of the 1930s. The key to solving this riddle is to be found in the issue that first brought them together…anti-Zionism. When the common enemy is the Jewish state, other issues that may divide must be put to one side. Here Livingstone, at least initially, led the way, by virtue of his intimate relationship with the WRP, beginning in 1981.

An internal WRP document acquired from a former member by the *Sunday Times* revealed that the party began to receive funding from Libya following a secret agreement between the WRP and Gaddafi, concluded in April 1976 in Tripoli by Corrine Redgrave and a representative of the Libyan regime. In addition to promoting Gaddafi's politics in its press, the WRP undertook to supply information to Libya's anti-Semitic dictator on the 'activities, names and positions held in finance, politics, business, the communications, media and elsewhere' of 'Zionists', the standard code word for Jews. The same document itemised WRP funding between the years 1977 and 1983 by no fewer than five Arab states and the PLO. The five states were Libya (£542,267) with smaller sums from Iraq, Kuwait, (invaded by Iraq in 1990) Qatar, and Abu Dhabi, in toto, around £813,000. These sums might not have been the whole picture. An Arab journalist was told by an employee of the Libyan news agency in London that the agency was in receipt annually of £1.5 million, part of which was then used to pay far above cost for printing work done by Astmoor Litho, the WRP's printers, thus providing in effect a hidden subsidy.

These publications included the Libyan embassy's *Green March*, an English language propaganda journal, and no fewer than 250,000 copies of an English edition of Gaddafi's *Green Book,* launched in 1980 in London by Vanessa Redgrave. The WRP's 1981 manifesto's enthusiasm for the Libyan dictator's at best semi-coherent ramblings knew no bounds: 'The WRP salutes the courageous struggle of Colonel Gaddafi, whose Green Book has guided the struggle to introduce workers' control of factories, government offices and the diplomatic service, and in opposing the reactionary maneuverers of [Egypt's] Sadat, [Israel's] Begin and Washington.' Gadhafi's excursion into high theory found equal favour with another anti-Zionist organisation: 'This vital book cannot be obtained from any other book suppliers in Britain. Read the ideas which the Zionists and capitalists want to suppress. Only £3.00 p&p.' This puff appeared in the journal of the Neo-Nazi National Front, *NF News*, and it raised a number of intriguing questions. If the NF's claim to have a monopoly on sales of the *Green Book* in the UK was true, where did they get their supplies of the book from? Did there operate a novel division labour, with Healy's Gaddafi-subsidised printing press printing the book, and the National Front selling it?

The WRP's financial dependency on Gaddafi was immediately reflected in the party's almost daily reporting in its press of the Libyan dictator's sayings and deeds, and vituperative attacks not only on Israel but exposures of what were claimed to be the sinister Zionist manipulation of British political organisations. For example, an editorial in the *News Line* of December 8, 1980, claimed to have detected a 'deep Zionist influence' in the Anti-Nazi League, the proof being that its Secretary, Paul Holborow, had said that 'the main fight is now against anti-Semitism'. 'The sudden switch to anti-Semitic issues', claimed *News Line,* was to 'facilitate the participation of another pro-Zionist Mr Anthony Wedgwood Benn, whose attempts to groom himself for the Labour leadership have become positively offensive'. Having unearthed yet another Zionist conspiracy, this being a hijacking of the Labour Party, the Editorial then offered its own version of a now-fashionable left-wing Holocaust revisionism, the purpose of which was to deny its uniquely anti-Jewish nature and genocidal objective, and to down play the need to combat anti-Semitism: 'No one will forget that the gas chambers of the Third Reich did not discriminate. They were used to exterminate Jews, Christians, gypsies, Russians, Poles, Czechs, socialists and communists.' No-one can forget it, for the simple reason, as I have said before in relation to three other identical leftist subterfuges, it did not happen. This statement is blatantly false and whoever wrote it, unless they were as ignorant of the history of the Holocaust as Livingstone, must have known it. The gas chambers *did* discriminate, on the grounds of race. Of this list, only Jews and Gypsies were gassed, though unlike the Jews, the Nazis had no plans to exterminate all the Gypsies. Those deemed to be of 'pure gypsy blood', whom the Nazis believed were 'Aryan' in origin, were exempted. Of Europe's roughly one million gypsies, some 220,000 are believed to have died at the hands of the Nazis during the war compared with six million of Europe's ten million Jews.

Corbyn has deployed exactly this particular version of Holocaust revisionism as part of his campaign to de-Judaize Holocaust Memorial Day, to this end, sponsoring a motion in the House of Commons proposed by fellow anti-Zionist zealot John McDonnell on January 27, 2011, to change its name to 'Genocide Memorial Day' on the same specious grounds that 'Nazis targeted not only Jewish people.' but the 'disabled', 'working class activists and trade unionists', 'Roma, Jehovahs Witnesses, lesbian, gay and bisexual people and others they considered undesirable.' How historically and semantically illiterate can you get? To repeat, save for Roma, none of these categories is a race, and therefore, could not have been a victim of 'genocide', which means the killing, or the attempt to kill, an entire race. Neither were they, unlike the Jews, targeted for total extermination, and that includes the 'disabled', because the aborted Nazi euthanasia programme put to death not all the 'disabled', for example victims of accidents and war injuries, but only those specifically deemed genetically unfit to procreate or live a useful life. But what do such piffling details matter when the objective of the exercise is to deJudaify the Holocaust?

By the time Livingstone had been attracted into the magnetic field of the WRP, and this would have been no later than 1981, the party was operating as little more than a propaganda vehicle for not only Gaddafi, but Saddam Hussein and the PLO, while pumping out daily doses of venom against Israel and its supporters in the British labour movement. With Livingstone as one of its three editors, this role was now also taken on by the *Labour Herald*, like the WRP's *News Line*, printed by Astmoor Litho and sold at well below cost price. Livingstone was obviously in his element, the viciousness of the journal's tone exceeding even that of what was in effect its parent publication, the WRP's *News Line*, with one issue of June 25, 1982 featuring a cartoon of a huge and hook-nosed Israel Prime Menachem Begin in a Nazi uniform, standing on a heap of corpses oozing with blood and giving a Nazi salute, with the caption, *The Final Solution*; and another, a favourable review of a book which claimed Zionists collaborated with the Nazis in the Holocaust.

In letters to *Tribune*, the socialist weekly, of October 22, 1982 both Livingstone for the *Labour Herald* and Alex Mitchell of *News Line* naturally and lyingly denied the allegation made in a letter the previous week that their respective publications were in any way connected with, or dependent on the Libyan regime. 'We completely reject these insinuations' said Livingstone. True to form, Mitchell sniffed out the nature of the conspiracy at work:

> The Zionists were comprehensively thrashed at the TUC in Brighton and the Labour Party conference in Blackpool. It ended their *35-year grip* on the Middle East policies of the Labour and trade union movement. For the first time, the leadership of the Palestinian Liberation Organisation and the national rights of the Palestinian people were unequivocally recognised. Is it any wonder that a policy of retaliation should be put in motion and that the Workers Revolutionary Party and its daily newspaper, the *News Line*, are prime targets?... The Zionists work on the "big lie" theory that if you tell the 'Libyan gold' story often enough, then some people are bound to believe it. (emphasis added)

As the WRP internal documents proved, it was Mitchell and Livingstone who were doing the lying, big time. A year on, the *Daily Express* of December 21 carried an amusing and revealing item by 'William Hickey'. Livingstone had been spotted in the exclusive five-star West End restaurant *L'Ecu De France* dining with two officials from the Libyan embassy. In reply to enquiries at County Hall, Hickey was told the two Libyans 'wanted to talk to Ken about a programme they want to do for Libya. It's supposed to be [sic] about left-wing politics in Britain. They wanted him to advise on the planning of it as well as taking part.' There are reasonable grounds for suspecting that this too was another 'big lie' or as his one time-mentor Healy used to say, a 'class truth'.

While Leader of the GLC, Livingstone made a number of public comments about the Jews which attracted considerable criticism, the gist of some being that British Jews were going fascist. Following the 1981 election victory in Israel of Menachem Begin's rightist Likud, British Jews 'suddenly became reactionary, turned right, nearly to fascists.' In London and elsewhere, 'extremist Jews' were organising 'para-military groups, which resemble fascist organisations' - though presumably not, as in Nazi Germany, under SS supervision. As for the Holocaust, while careful not to deny it happened, Livingstone insisted there were far worse crimes than those committed by the Nazis, another claim that has recently gained currency on the left, in many cases motivated by a concern not to provide ammunition to justify the creation of the state of Israel. 'Every year [sic] the international finance system kills more people than World War Two. But at least Hitler was mad.' Yet again, Livingstone was talking nonsense, and even he must have known it. Something in the region of 70 million people were killed in World War Two, more than 80% by the Nazis and their allies. As for Livingstone's claim that Hitler was mad (which he repeated in the remarks that led to his suspension) the implication is that his unbalanced state of mind exonerated him from any legal or moral responsibility for the Holocaust. Hitler was not 'mad'. He was an anti-Semite…like Livingstone, who is also not mad and who, again like Hitler, subscribes to the belief that Jews conspire to gain political power. Back in 1982, in his *Labour Herald*, Livingstone made a scarcely veiled allusion to the existence of an undue Jewish influence in the Labour Party: 'There is a distortion [sic!] running right the way through British politics…a majority of Jews in this country supported the Labour Party and elected a number of Labour MPs.' We can be sure that if Jews had been equally prominent in the Tory party, that too would have been seized on (and with a modicum of plausibility) as even stronger proof of the same conspiracy.

Faced with the prospect of unemployment when the Thatcher government announced its intention to close down the GLC, Livingstone made a bid to become selected as a candidate in the safe but not vacant Labour seat of Brent East, whose current occupant was the Jewish Reginald Freeson. Freeson was also a prominent supporter of Israel, and Chairman of Poale Zion, a Jewish socialist group affiliated to the Labour Party, now called the Jewish Labour Movement, which, at this very time, Livingstone, together with Corbyn, was campaigning to have expelled from the Labour Party. Freeson was on the Labour left, having opposed the US military involvement in Vietnam, marched with CND against British possession of nuclear weapons, and supported a united Ireland. Impeccable socialist credentials, one might have thought. However, things were not so simple, because Freeson was also a Jew and a Zionist. Only Livingstone knows for certain what his motives were in choosing this particular seat to launch his Parliamentary career. But one is entitled to guess.

The constituency had a large first and second-generation Irish population, many of whom were possibly influenced in their attitude towards the Jews by their church's historical antipathy towards those its good book and up to 1959, its Good Friday liturgy ('the perfidious Jews') say betrayed the (no less Jewish) son of God. How much this favoured Livingstone's bid for the seat it is impossible to say, but certainly, a remark made by Livingstone on Irish radio on August 6, 1983 would have done him no harm in what was to become his battleground with Freeson for the Brent East seat in 1985. In the interview, Livingstone presented his own version of Holocaust revisionism, like the WRP's in that it minimised the uniqueness and scale of the Nazi genocide of the Jews, and similar to Corbyn's insistence that any refence to the Holocaust must always be accompanied by one 'in the same breath' to slavery: 'What Britain has done for [sic] the Irish nation is, although it is spread over 800 years, worse than what Hitler did to the Jews.' And remember, unlike the British, at least Hitler had the excuse that he was mad.

Comments like these were bound to, and maybe designed to produce a response from prominent Jews. Replying to the claim that British Jews were going fascist, in a letter to the *Jewish Chronicle,* Freeson said Livingstone should stop being 'his master's voice' to the WRP. After Livingstone ousted him from the Brent East seat in 1985, Freeson said his support, albeit at times critical, for Israel, had resulted in him being branded as 'that bloody Jew'. In his capacity as Chairman of Poale Zion, Freeson wrote to the Labour's Party's National Executive Committee to warn of the likely consequences of Livingstone's unrelenting attacks on Jews:

> This letter is by way of a friendly warning about a situation that I fear could deteriorate soon if the Party does not dissociate itself from the crude populism which Mr Livingston's anti-zionism and anti-Jewish remarks represent. It could permanently alienate the Jewish community collectively from the very Party to which so many members of our community have looked for support and their own political involvement.

Proof that the Brent East Constituency Labour Party had been de-Zionised' was forthcoming when in October 1985 the Chief Rabbi, Emmanuel Jakobovits, declined an invitation to attend a lunch at which Livingstone would be present. He was attacked in a letter to the *North West London Press* as 'rude, bigoted and narrow minded' by Livingstone acolyte Emma Tait, Chairperson of Brent East Labour Party. She in turn received a stinging response from Dr Jacob Gewirtz of the Board of Deputies of British Jews:

> As a close colleague of Mr Ken Livingstone, she is well aware of the reasons why no self-respecting Jewish personality would wish to appear on a public platform with the GLC leader. Mr Livingstone has hardly missed an opportunity to take a swipe at the Jewish community, referring to its leading members as 'near-fascists' and to Israel as 'a racist state not entitled to secure borders'… Instead of vilification by Ms Tait, the Chief Rabbi is deserving of the highest praise for his principled refusal to lunch with Mr Livingstone.

Elected MP for Brent East in the 1987 General Election Labour, Livingstone returned to big-time London politics in 2000 when, after narrowly losing the Labour Party nomination for mayor, he ran and won as an independent, resulting in his expulsion from the party. From his new vantage point, following 9/11, he became deeply involved in a number of anti-Zionist campaigns with Corbyn, along the way taking time out, as we have already seen, to raise the profile in the UK of the Hitler-admiring Muslim cleric Yusuf al-Qaradawi. Here are just two typical examples of the preacher's message so admired by Livingstone:

> Throughout history, Allah has imposed upon the Jews people who would punish them for their corruption…The last punishment was carried out by

Hitler...He put them in their place. [sic] This was divine punishment for them. Allah willing, the next time [sic] will be at the hands of the believers. [i.e., Muslims]. (Al Jazeera TV, January 28, 2009)

and:

Oh Allah, take the treacherous Jews. Oh Allah, take this profligate, cunning arrogant band of people. Oh Allah, they have spread much corruption and tyranny in the land. Pour your wrath upon them Oh our God. Lie in wait from them... Oh Allah, take this oppressive Jewish, Zionist band of people. Oh Allah, do not spare a single one of them. Oh Allah, count their numbers, and kill them, down to the very last one. (Sermon on Al-Jazeera TV, January 9, 2009)

In the *Muslim News* of September 2010, that is, *after* his *protégé* had made these statements extolling Hitler and advocating the extermination of the Jews, Livingstone praised their author as 'one of the leading progressive voices in the Islamic world'. Following his election as Leader of the Labour Party in September 2015, Corbyn appointed his comrade of more than thirty years standing as his adviser on defence, or rather disarmament policy.

As a consequence of the upsurge of anti-Semitism in the Labour Party after the election of Jeremy Corbyn as its Leader in September 2015, on April 10, 2018, Avi Gabbay, Chairperson of the Israel Labour party, sent the following letter.

Dear Mr Corbyn: The Labour Party of Israel and the Labour Party of Israel have a long history of friendship We remember fondly the warm relations that Prime Ministers Wilson, Blair and Brown had with Israel's Labour Party and the State of Israel and the Jewish community in the UK, along with the ongoing visits and friendship with many Labour Party UK MPs and Labour Israel MPs. And yet, it is my responsibility to acknowledge the hostility you have shown to the Jewish community and the anti-Semitic statements and actions you have allowed as Leader of the Labour Party UK. This is in addition to your very public hatred of the polices of the government of the State of Israel, many of which regard the security of our citizens and the actions of our soldiers - policies where the coalition and the opposition in Israel are aligned. As Israel approaches Holocaust and Heroism Remembrance Day this week, we are reminded of the horrors of anti-Semitism in Europe and our commitment to combatting anti-Semitism in all forms and in all places. As such, I write to you to inform you of the temporary suspension of all formal relations between the Israel Labour Party and the Leader of the Labour Party UK. While there are many areas where our respective parties can and will cooperate, we cannot maintain relations with you, Leader of the Labour Party UK, while you fail to address adequately the anti-Semitism within Labour Party UK. I have informed all Labour Israel staff, Members of Knesset, and elected Leaders of the Labour Party Israel of the suspension of ties with your office. I have asked the International Secretary of the Labour Party Israel to update me quarterly on this situation, and should this suspension change, you will be updated accordingly.

On the same day, Jennifer Gerber, Director of (UK) Labour Friends of Israel, said:

We fully understand why the Israeli Labour Party has decided to suspend relations with Jeremy Corbyn. He has failed to respond to their repeated offers of dialogue, including offers to host him at Yad Vashem, Israel's National Holocaust Museum.

LFI's relations with the Israeli Labour Party remains unaffected and we will continue our close cooperation.

Also on the same day, Joan Ryan MP, Chair of the Labour Friends of Israel sent the following letter:

> As you will be aware, the leader of the Israeli Labour Party, Avi Gabby, announced today that he is suspending relations with you due to your failure to deal with anti-Semitism in the Labour Party and your hostility to the state of Israel. I fully understand why Mr Gabby has taken this course of action and I am ashamed that one of sister parties has no option but to take this unprecedented step. [This is correct. Founded in 1889, never before in the entire history of the Socialist International, of which the UK and the Israeli Labour Party are fraternal members, has one of its parties felt obliged to break off all relations with the leader of another. Neither, prior to the election of Corbyn in 2015, had of its party leaders in entire history been accused by its own members of anti-Semitism.] As you know, in 2016, the leader of the [Israeli Knesset] Opposition, Isaac Herzog, invited you to visit Israel and offered to take you to Yad Vashem. I remain perplexed as to why you were happy to sit down with Hamas and Hezbollah but could not find the time to meet with those who are working to advance the cause of peace, reconciliation and a two-state solution. I would now urge you to consider why it is that Israeli Labour feels it cannot have a relationship with you. Leadership is about taking responsibility and it is yours to urgently heal this breach and take action to reassure our comrades in Israel.

And yet again on the same day, April 10, 2018, Holocaust-denying Nick Griffin (he once referred to it as the 'Holohoax') and former *Fuehrer* of the British National Party, announced that he would vote Labour if Corbyn opposed British military action against the regime of Syria's President Assad:

> If he sticks to his guns then for the 1st time in my life I will vote Labour - right now nothing is more important to me than resisting the psychotic rush to #WW3 of Boris [Johnson] and the #neocons. Corbyn refuses to blame Assad for chemical attack in #Syria…

True to form, just as he did when he opposed the removal of a Saddam Hussein guilty of the same war crime, Chemical Corbyn did indeed 'stick to his guns'. Quite a day for Jeremy…Israeli Labour out, Nick Griffin in. Some would say, more than a fair swap. This was not the first occasion on which Griffin had aligned himself with the far left. He had previously claimed the western military interventions in Afghanistan and Iraq were 'illegal' and accused the British military of committing war crimes by participating in them. In June 2013, Griffin visited Syria at the invitation of President Assad's Ba'ath Party. He was there again in November 2014 as a guest of the Syrian Justice (sic) Ministry, following in the footsteps of Corbyn, who made the same pilgrimage in 2011, accompanied by Tory Peer Lord Sheikh and Baroness 'body parts' Tonge.

In October 2016, Corbyn wrote an account in the Communist Party's *Morning Star* of his Syria trip, funded to the tune of £1,300 by the Hamas-affiliated UK-based Palestine Return Centre. (By accepting President Assad's hospitality, Corbyn was evidently prepared to overlook the fact that unlike Israel, his Ba'athist host did not recognise the existence of a distinct Palestinian nation.) During that visit, from

October 31 to November 2, 2011, Corbyn recalled, Assad had provided him with evidence that 'the Israeli tail wags the US dog', a notion revisited by the *New York Times* when on April 25, 2019, it published a cartoon worthy of the Nazi *Der Sturmer*, with Trump wearing opaque dark classes and Jewish skull cap being pulled along on a leash by a hooked-nosed dog with a star of David collar and the face of Netanyahu. (This is the world-famous journal which, despite its being protected by the First Amendment, along with the entire US media, lacked the courage shown by many of its European counterparts to reproduce as an act of solidarity with the Danish journal which published the cartoons that triggered riots across the Muslim world. What was the mind set of those who sanctioned the publishing of this filth, safe in the knowledge that unlike those of the Muslim rioters, the inevitable protests would be peaceful and dignified?)

As for Griffin, he must have felt very much at home in Damascus as the guest of a regime that elevates to its summits Jew-baiters such as Defence Minister Mustafa Tlass, author of *The Matzah of Zion*, a work which dredges up from the sewers the Islamo-Christian legend of the Jewish blood libel and gives them contemporary political twist with the assertion that 'the Jew can kill you and take your blood to make his Zionist [sic] bread.' So yes, Griffin we can understand…but what was Corbyn doing in the same company?

With relations suspended between Corbyn and the Israeli Labour Party, Shadow Foreign Secretary Emily Thornberry was a matter of days later dispatched to the West Bank, where she was among an audience that was addressed for three hours by Palestinian Authority President Mahmood Abbas. Abbas is the proud possessor of a Doctorate from Moscow University in Holocaust revisionism, entitled, 'The Other Side: The Secret Relationship between Nazism and Zionism', a subject that would have all too familiar to Thornberry, as it was saying Hitler supported Zionism that had led to the suspension of Corbyn intimate Ken Livingstone. In the course of his address, Abbas gave the assembled delegates the benefit of his grasp of this highly demanding subject. The misfortunes of the Jews, he explained, were their own fault, brought on by their 'social behaviour, usury, charging interest and financial matters'. An old refrain sung by anti-Semites down the ages, as for example by the UK's most notorious Nazi, Sir Oswald Mosley: 'The Jew himself has created anti-Semitism - created as he has always done, by letting people see him and his methods. Even Hitler was not an anti-Semite before he saw a Jew.'

Thornberry's Facebook comment on the speech, far from condemning these outrageous slanders on the Jews, said that it had been a 'privilege' to represent her party at the Palestinian National Council. Only when challenged by journalists did she issue a subsequent statement deploring the PA President's 'anti-Semitic remarks'. One has to ask…what was an official delegate of the Labour Party doing at a gathering where the featured speaker hurled insults at the Jews that would not have been out of place at a Nuremberg Rally…or for that matter, on websites frequented by her Leader?

Perhaps the ultimate humiliation for Corbyn came in the House of Commons on April 17, 2018. Only once before had anti-Semitism been a matter formally brought before the House. This was on December 17, 1942, when MPs stood for one minute in silence in remembrance of the millions of Jews being murdered in Hitler's Holocaust. Now anti-Semitism was back, only with Corbyn in the firing line, not Hitler, in a formal three-hour debate on Labour Party Jew-baiting. Two years previously, Corbyn had been summoned to appear before the House of Commons

Home Affairs Select Committee to answer charges that he had failed to combat anti-Semitism in his party following his election as its Leader in September 2015. Now the issue was back again at Westminster...with a vengeance. Even though he was its prime target, Corbyn chose to absent himself for most of the debate, and while present in the chamber, remained silent. The debate was opened by Sajid Javid, Secretary of State for Communities and Local Government:

> We cannot and must not ignore the particular [anti-Semitic] elements within the Labour Party, and nor can we ignore the fact that this particular concern is currently corelating with the Leader of the Opposition and the waves of activists that have come with him...Is there a culture that attracts them and is allowed to fester? Unfortunately, when it comes to the Leader of the Opposition, there are simply too many of his apparently accidental [sic] associations to list. As the Board of Deputies of British Jews put it in a letter to the Leader of the Opposition, 'Rightly or wrongly, those who push this offensive material regard Jeremy Corbyn as their figurehead'. [At this point, an outraged Corbynista loyalist intervened, asking, 'is that allowed in the Chamber - such shameless personal abuse?'. The Deputy Speaker explained that the Secretary of State was quoting from a letter.]

When Andrew Gwynne, Javid's Shadow, replying on behalf of the opposition, made the ringing declaration that 'there is no place for anti-Semitism in the Labour Party', Tory MP Simon Hoare retorted that 'actions speak louder than words', and pointed out that 'Mr Livingstone remains a member of the hon. Gentleman's party'. Gwynne lamely replied that 'due process was going on' - one that had taken over two years, with Jew-baiter Livingstone still not expelled, and threatening legal action if he was. This laid-back attitude was too much for Labour's Ian Austin:

> Let me be clear about this. Ken Livingstone claimed that Hitler was a Zionist. That is anti-Semitism pure and simple. It happened more than two years ago, and there has been ample time to deal with it. It is a disgrace that it has not been dealt with. Kick him out immediately... My hon. Friend should stand at the dispatch box and tell the leader of the Labour Party that Livingstone must be booted out. Boot him out!

A Jewish Tory MP, Robert Halfon, went for the Corbynista jugular:

> I genuinely believe that the current Labour leadership is, at best, turning a blind eye to the problem and, at worst condoning anti-Semitism...I see the membership of dubious Facebook groups, the defence of anti-Semitic murals and the phoney reports produced by the now Baroness Chakrabarti and they indicate three unwise monkeys: see no anti-Semitism, hear no anti-Semitism, and do not speak out against anti-Semitism.

He then went off-piste by demanding his own government 'must go further in stamping out all extremist terror groups, including proscribing Hezbollah's political arm. People should not be allowed to march down Trafalgar Square and Whitehall waving Hezbollah flags.' He could have added, neither should the Leader of the Opposition be a featured speaker at such rallies, where banners and posters are displayed demanding the destruction of the state of Israel and likening it to Nazi Germany. Labour's Luciana Berger, who is also Jewish, spoke of anti-Semitic insults directed at herself from the Corbynista wing of her own party:

It pains me to say this as the proud parliamentary chair of the Jewish Labour Movement that in 2018, anti-Semitism is now more commonplace, more conspicuous and more corrosive within the Labour Party. That is why I have no words for the people have purporting to be both members and supporters of our party and using the hashtag JCforPM who have attacked me in recent weeks for my comments, for speaking at the rally against anti-Semitism, and for questioning the remarks of those endorsing the anti-Semitic mural...There are people who have accused me of having two masters. They have said that I am Tel Aviv's servant, and called me a paid-up Israeli operative...They have called me Judas, a Zionazi and an absolute parasite, and they have told me to get out of this country and go back to Israel...My party urgently needs to address this issue publicly and consistently, and we need to expel from our ranks those people who hold these views, including Ken Livingstone.

Berger was followed by another Jewish MP, Tory Andrew Percy. He related how in a recent visit to the Jewish community in Brussels, he saw 'people living in genuine fear not just behind security guards in their schools, but behind 10-foot or 15-foot gates with military personnel and tanks [!!!] outside.' Blunt-speaking Percy evidently has no time for the Corbyn/Clinton/Cameron/Blair/Papal 'nothing to with Islam']: A recent study undertaken by the Institute for Jewish Policy Research found that certain communities in this country, particularly the Muslim communities, are twice as likely to hold deeply anti-Semitic views. As for Labour Party anti-Semitism, the topic under debate, he noted that Corbynista Andrew Gwynne's contribution had focused on anti-Semitism that came from the far right. 'What I did not hear him talk about quite so much, however, are the Labour members who have been defended by some of the people sitting beside him [on Labour's front Bench]. One Labour member, who said that the Jews were responsible for the slave trade [Momentum activist Jackie Walker, then suspended, for the second time, on charges of anti-Semitism] was defended by a [Corbynista] Member who sits behind him'. [Percy was now getting into his stride, homing in on the main target]:

> What I saw throughout this debate was the Leader of the Opposition chuntering repeatedly when anyone stood up and tried to hold him to account for some of the things that people have said and done in his name., This a leader of the Labour Party who found himself not in one, but in four or five racist anti-Semitic Facebook groups by accident. He did not look at the material. He did not read the material. He did not know the material was there. He did not understand the material. He looked at the mural and made a comment on the mural, but he did not know about it. How are we supposed to believe any of this?

At this point, another Tory MP, Alec Shelbrooke, recalled that while campaigning at the 2016 General Election, after shaking Percy's hand, a Labour Party member had said, 'I now have to go and wash my hands'. Percy then continued]:

> I am sorry the Leader of the Opposition has left his place., because he needs to be held to account. The question I would like to ask him is why he has still not taken the opportunity to respond to the invite from the Labour Party in Israel to visit Israel and to visit Yad Vashem [the Holocaust Museum] ... Labour member after Labour

member has made all sorts of disgusting comments about Jews...Laura Stuart felt the need to post a picture on Facebook of a photograph from the Holocaust Educational Trust that had been changed to include the words 'Zionist fairy tales' and 'Fat Zionist conference'. A Labour Party member did this. There are countless other examples. I have to say to the leadership of the Labour Party: this is in your name by people who are being motivated by the actions of the Labour Leader. [Here the Deputy Speaker asked Percy to moderate his tone, to which he replied]: How can one possibly be moderate in one's language when we are dealing with a leader of a political party in this country who has stood up and described people who want to wipe Jews off the planet as his friends?...I have spent several years campaigning in politics. The last general election was the first time anybody stood up and told me I was Israeli scum and did so having named the Leader of the Opposition as a motivation for saying it.

Next up was Labour's John Mann, for thirteen years the outspoken Chair of the all-party group against anti-Semitism, who for this very reason, had been singled out by Corbynistas for special treatment:

When I took this voluntary cross-party role, I did not expect today, when Labour members [of Parliament] stand in solidarity with our Jewish colleagues and with the Jewish community, to be targeted by an organisation called Momentum, which has happened to all of us which stood in solidarity. But worse than that, explicitly targeting Jewish members of the Parliamentary Labour Party because they are Jewish. That is what is going on at the moment. I did not expect, when I took on this cross-party role, my wife to be sent, by a Labour Marxist anti-Semite, a dead bird through the post. I did not expect my son, after an Islamist death threat, to open the door to the bomb squad. I did not expect my wife, in the last few weeks, from a leftist anti-Semite in response to the demonstration, to be threatened with rape...We identified 13 years ago the three forms of anti-Semitism: Islamist anti-Semitism, traditional right anti-Semitism, and the anti-Semitism of the new left...Those who say it is a smear in raising this issue need to publicly apologise...Where this stuff ends is what happened in Copenhagen, is what happened in Brussels, it's what happened in France repeatedly...people murdered because they are Jewish, that's where this ends...This week-end in my constituency...it's constant, explicit anti-Semitism. And then the bigger group, the excusers of anti-Semitism, who say it is something to do with challenging the Leader of the Labour Party. No, it isn't. What Jewish people say to me now is different to what they said thirteen years ago. I'm stopped in the street by Jewish people who say to me very discreetly, 'I am scared'...People - young Jewish members - are scared to go to Labour Party meetings with me, because they are fearful they will be intimidated and threatened and that their identity will be challenged...Any Jewish person, as the vast majority do, has the right to say, 'I am a Zionist', and I have no right to deny him that right, and those that do are racists. And just that change in language, by making the word Zionist as a pejorative insult by the Labour Party, just that change, would alter the dialogue in this country in a very big way.

The other highlight of the session, one which exposed the vile, concerted Jew-baiting by Corbynistas, was Labour's Ruth Smeeth reading out milder examples of emails sent to her that she described as 'the poison of anti-Semitism that is engulfing parts of my own party and wider political discourse']:

Hang yourself you vile treacherous Zionist Tory filth. You are a cancer of humanity.
    Smeeth is a Zionist; she has no shame and trades on the murder of Jews by Hitler whom the Zionists betrayed.

Ruth Smeeth must surely be travelling 1st class to Tel Aviv with all that slush. After all, she's complicit in trying to bring Corbyn down.

First job for Jeremy Corbyn tomorrow: expel the Zionist BICOM smear hag bitch Ruth Smeeth from the Party.

This Ruth Smeeth bitch is Britanophobic, we need to cleanse out nation of these types.

#JC4PM Deselect Ruth Smeeth ASAP. Poke the pig – get all Zionist child killer scum out of Labour.

You are a spy! You are evil, satanic! Leave! #Labour #Corbyn.

Ruth you are a Zionist plant. I am ashamed you in Labour. Better suited to the murderous Knesset! #I Support Ken.

Your fellow traitor Tony Blair abolished hanging for treason. Your kind need to leave before we bring it back. #Smeeth Is Filth.

The gallows would be fine and fitting place for this dyke piece of Yid shit to swing from.

Two that she did not read out were: 'Yid cunt' and 'Fucking traitor.' As the mantra has it, a kinder politics…As if on cue, Labour's Stephen Doughty then rose to inform the House that he had 'just seen a tweet from someone claiming to be a member of Momentum suggesting that those of us who have spoken out about anti-Semitism have taken a bounty of £1 million from Israel to undermine the leader of the Labour Party.' Tory MP Simon Clarke returned to Corbyn's role in furthering the rise of Labour anti-Semitism:

The leadership of the Labour Party has been captured by a man who, more than any other, embodies the selective blindness of his political beliefs in regard to anti-Semitism. It is worth noticing that, after defending the despicable mural in Tower Hamlets, the Leader of the Opposition condemned himself in his own excuses. He said, I didn't notice the anti-Semitism. I believe him, for failing to notice blatant anti-Semitism is precisely the problem. Perhaps he has become immune. The problem is that he sets the tone…The former Member for Sunderland South, Chris Mullin, tweeted on 26 March: 'Sorry to see Jewish leaders ganging up on Corbyn…' [Clarke put the question to Corbyn]: Will he now utterly disassociate himself from Hamas and Hezbollah? Is he proud that Salim Mulla, who said that Israel was responsible for the Sandy Hook massacre and ISIS, is still representing his party as a councillor in Blackburn?

But answer came there none, because Corbyn was not in the Chamber to answer it. Ian Austin, Labour, related an embarrassing encounter with a Holocaust survivor he had recently met in Poland:

The first words he said to me when he learned I was a Labour MP were: 'Are you not ashamed to be in the Labour Party, with all the anti-Semitism?' [Austin admitted that he was indeed 'deeply ashamed'.] We have witnessed appalling anti-Semitic claims. We have seen Labour candidates denying the Holocaust. At last year's conference, one speaker said, 'The Holocaust, yes or no?' What does he mean by 'yes or no'? Was it right? Did it happen? [Austin then broke off to comment with biting irony that he was] pleased that the leader of the Labour Party has returned, because the current crisis was triggered by the shocking discovery that he had defended a grotesque racist caricature. For three days he issued excuses. Only on the fourth day, with that unprecedented protest planned, did he manage to say sorry. Labour Party members, all of us, have to ask ourselves what we would be saying - what he would be saying -

if a senior member of the Conservative Party had defended a racist caricature of anybody else. I am afraid - I want to say this very directly to him - that he spent decades defending these people. Hamas's charter is avowedly anti-Semitic, Hezbollah too, yet our leader describes them as 'friends' and invites them to Parliament. Raed Salah, found guilty in court of the blood libel, was described as a 'very honoured citizen' and invited here too. Stephen Sizer, a Church of England vicar, was disciplined by his own church when he spread ideas that were 'clearly anti-Semitic', yet our leader defended him and claimed he was 'under attack' by a pro-Israeli smear campaign.

In answer to these charges, Corbyn said not a word. He did not need to, because he knew that while most Labour MPs were revolted by his pandering to anti-Semitism, those whose opinions counted in the Labour Party, and a sufficient number of its rank and file activists, believed that their Dear Leader had been the victim of a Zionist plot.

Rounding off this easily the most sordid episode in the entire history of the Labour Party came the adoption on July 17, 2018 by the Labour Party National Executive Committee, of its new definition of anti-Semitism, one that was supposedly intended to create a 'more thorough and detailed code for members which can actually be put into practice' to combat anti-Semitism. To their credit, and at last showing some moral backbone, the previous day, Labour MPs, with only four votes against, supported a resolution rejecting the Corbyn code. By deleting four classic examples of anti-Semitism that did the rounds in the Corbynista wing of the party from the almost universally recognised definition of anti-Semitism advanced by the Intentional Holocaust Remembrance Alliance, the NEC had given official approval to some of the very views that triggered the Labour Party anti-Semitic scandal in the first place. Under the proposed new, Corbynista, code it would *not* be anti-Semitic to:

Accuse British Jews of being more loyal to Israel than the UK;
Describe the policies of Israel as racist and comparable to those of Nazi Germany;
Argue that Israel should not exist;
Hold Israel to standards of conduct not demanded of any other country.

Let me anticipate what I hope will be the incredulous reactions of the reader: Accusing Jews of treason or Israel of being a Nazi state are *not* examples of anti-Semitism, but of opinions that are perfectly compatible with membership of a thoroughly Corbynised and de-Zionised Labour Party. Corbyn loyalists objected to the four examples on the grounds that including them would stifle 'legitimate criticism of Israel'. It is as if for them the prime task of the Labour Party is combatting Zionism, even at the risk of splitting the party, thereby possibly facilitating its exclusion from government for the next decade or more, as the Social Democratic split did in the Thatcher years. (I wrote this some months before the split did occur on February 18, 2019) Furthermore, in order to prove that a statement vilifying Israel is anti-Semitic, it would be necessary to have 'evidence of anti-Semitic intent.'. Unless the person making the statement, admitted that it was deliberately intended to be anti-Semitic (and none had done), how did one prove such intent? It is as if the party's definition of anti-Semitism had been tailored to accommodate the fanatical anti-Zionism of the Corbynistas and the anti-Semitism of many of Labour's increasing number of Muslim members. This included Corbyn himself with regard to all four excluded examples.

Not only this. With his reference on Press TV to the 'hand of Israel', Corbyn has dabbled in Jewish conspiracy theory, which contravened even his own faction's proposed code He has also implied that the same 'hand' at work on the domestic UK scene. In 2013, during a speech made to the Palestine Return Centre, he demanded, without giving any proof that they were not, that schools 'should start teaching a lot of people [sic] the history of the Middle East in a more accurate and balanced way'. Corbyn then outlined his 'accurate' and 'balanced' version of the history of the Middle East, in which the policies of Israel were likened to those of Nazis Germany: 'The West Bank is under occupation of the very sort [sic] that is recognisable by many people in Europe who suffered occupation during the Second World War'. Interviewed by Iran's Press TV in 2012 on the subject of what he believed was BBC bias towards Israel, an accusation repeated *ad nauseum* by anti-Semites on pro-Palestinian and Corbynista websites, Corbyn said:

> There seems to be [so again, he has no proof] a great deal of pressure on the BBC from the Israeli government and the Israeli embassy and they are very assertive toward all [sic] journalists and the BBC itself. They challenge every single thing [sic] on the reporting all the time [sic]. I think there is a bias towards saying that Israel is a democracy in the Middle East, *that Israel has a right to exist, that Israel has its security concerns.* [Emphasis added]

The previous year, Corbyn had claimed in the *Morning Star* that Israel exerted 'unbelievably [sic] high levels of influence' over 'upper echelons of parts of the media'... more conspiracy theory, in contravention of his own party's already watered-down definition of anti-Semitism. Here we have the key to understanding why throughout his political career, Corbyn has aligned himself with movements that were or still are opposed to the existence of a Jewish state in the Middle East. Shortly before being first elected as Labour MP for Islington North in 1983, Corbyn became one of the founders, and a sponsor, of the Labour Movement Campaign for Palestine, the predecessor to the current movement also founded and patronised by Corbyn, the Palestine Solidarity Campaign. The central demand of the LMCP was the replacement of Israel by a secular state of Palestine with equal rights for all its Jewish and Arab citizens, one that by including the West Bank and the Gaza Strip, would have a Palestinian majority, with consequences for its Jewish minority that need no elucidation here. This was also the stated policy of the PLO until its acceptance of the Oslo Accords of 1993, which embraced the goal of the so-called 'two-state solution'. In its 'mission statement,', the LMCP pledged itself to 'eradicate Zionism' within the Labour party and the broader labour movement; that is to say, 'eradicate' support, no matter how critical of its polices and actions, for the existence of Israel.

Shortly joined by Livingstone, Corbyn became a high profile and active member of the LCMP through the 1980s, speaking at and chairing its meetings. Even at this early stage in his career as an MP, it was evident that opposing Zionism was not only for him one his most pressing concerns. He believed it should also be for every Labour Party member: 'The Labour Movement Campaign is the only campaign rooted in the Labour Movement whose platform really tackles the important issues in relation to this question. Its activities ought to be supported by every [sic] Labour Party member'- including, presumably, its Jewish ones, nearly all of whom would have counted themselves as supporters of the state of Israel. In this already obsessional fight against Zionism, Corbyn's initial allegiance was to the PLO, with its goal of a secular Palestine 'from the river to the sea'. With the PLO's and Fatah's acceptance of a 'two state solution' in 1993, followed by the rise of a Jihadi, theocratic terrorist Islam that repudiated it, Corbyn turned his back on the PLO and found new allies in Hamas and Hezbollah, with their goal of a Palestine founded on the ruins of Israel and the corpses of its Jewish population. First Fatah and the PLO, then Hamas and Hezbollah.... Why the switch of allegiance by Corbyn? Because in each case, the shared objective was unchanging...the elimination of the 'Zionist entity', which the PLO, at least on paper, had repudiated in 1993. The only substantial distinction to be made between Corbyn and the anti-Zionist movements he has associated with over the years are not their objectives, but their division of labour. For Corbyn it has been a matter of meetings, conferences and speeches, while his Jihadi partners get on with the other end of the business...killing Jews.

If the elimination of Israel is not his goal, why then does Corbyn imply the BBC should be constantly emphasising, when covering Middle Eastern events, that Israel is *not* a democratic country, has *no* right to exist, and has *no* security concerns? As in the case of the teaching of Middle Eastern history in British schools, because the BBC does not do what Corbyn wants, this for him is conclusive proof, as it is for many Jewish conspiracy theorists who frequent Corbynista websites, of the BBC's pro-Zionist bias. Corbyn perhaps forgets that the BBC has a different remit from the channel on which he made his accusation, one which obliges it to be neutral and objective in its news reporting. There can be only one possible construction to put on these remarks. Israel *is* conspiring in various ways to subvert British institutions, is *not* a democracy (though it is indisputably in the Middle East), has *no* right to exist, and despite its being the target of attacks by Corbyn's terrorist 'friends' that have killed more than a thousand Jewish civilians and three attempts by Arab armies to 'wipe it off the map', Israel has *no* legitimate security concerns, and is to boot carrying out Nazi policies. Remarks such as these reveal Corbyn as someone who believes that when things are not as he would like, it is because a 'hand' is at work, whether it is directed against the Palestinians, staging 'false flag' terrorist attacks in the Middle East, controlling the BBC and schools, or undermining his leadership of the Labour Party. I invite the reader to surmise whose hand that might be.

Just how deeply runs anti-Semitism in the Corbynista wing of the Labour Party was confirmed by two on-line outbursts in August 2018. When Party Chairman Tom Watson, hitherto mute on the issue, demanded that Corbyn support the adoption of the international definition of anti-Semitism, George McManus, Chairman of the Labour Party's National Policy Forum, tweeted that 'Watson received £50,000+ from Jewish donors. At least Judas only got 30 pieces of silver.' Days previously, after making yet another *pro-forma* commitment to combat anti-Semitism in his party, there appeared on Corbyn's website the following postings, none of which was deleted:

'This is such a distraction issue. Where exactly is the anti-Semitism in the UK? This is all about the Friends of Israel being the biggest lobby group in Parliament.'

'Notice how and when this started. When the polls started putting Labour ahead of the Conservatives. I support you JC.'

'Perhaps the issue should be the murderous brutality and active Apartheid of the

Israeli Zionists. Worse than the Nazis.'

'But Jeremy Corbyn these Jewish people are very violent people. They are the 21st century terrorists.'

'Why is it that jews are so established in this country of ours. They control the media and have a powerful influence on the political stage now that should be looked into ASAP.'

'Giving way to a cabal [again!] of Zionists, Tories and right-wing Labour MPs and letting them set the agenda is a serious mistake.'

Still the skeletons continued to float to the surface of the latrine. On August 23, 2018 the *Daily Mail* released a video of Corbyn addressing in 2013 a London conference sponsored by the Qassem Brigades, the military wing of Hamas, the clerical Nazi movement dedicated to the destruction of the state of Israel and the extermination of the world's Jews. Another speaker was the Reverend Stephen Sizer, whom Corbyn had defended when suspended by his bishop for claiming that 9/11 was the work of the Jews. In the course of a making number of derogatory remarks about a particular group of Zionists, Corbyn said the following: 'One is, they don't want to study history, and secondly, they don't understand English irony either, having lived in this country for a very long time, probably all their lives, they don't understand English irony either [sic]. I think they need two lessons we [sic!!!] can help them with.' Had these remarks been made about British Muslims, Corbyn would have been the first to condemn them as racial stereotyping. But since they were made about British Jews at a gathering promoted by a movement that seeks their extermination, it is reasonable to assume that no-one objected.

Less than two weeks later, it became clear that Hamas was not alone in its genocidal designs on the Jews. On September 4, the day that the Labour Party National Executive Committee met to either adopt or amend the party's proposed definition of anti-Semitism, the media reported that the Metropolitan Police had received from the London radio station LBC a leaked dossier of more than 80 pages on 45 cases of anti-Semitic conduct by Labour Party members currently being investigated by the party's disciplinary disputes panel. Of these, at least 17 were considered serious enough to be investigated as race-hate crimes. One party member called the Jews 'devils', adding, 'We shall be rid of the Jews who are a cancer on us all', and suggesting that the Red Sea would be an 'ideal destination' for them. 'No need for gas chambers anyway as gas is so expensive and we need it in England.' Another posting by a Labour MP no less called for a woman Jewish Labour MP to 'get a good kicking'. A third member posted, 'One cannot understand the state of the world without understanding Jewish power, and one cannot understand the nature of Jewish power until one understands the nature of Jewish thinking'.

These are the thoughts and words of Nazis, and judging by their tone, they would, if given the opportunity, act upon them. Yet they are those of paid-up members of the *Labour Party*, one of them an MP. The body supposedly investigating these cases, the party's Disputes Panel, was headed by Corbyn's appointee, Claudia Webbe, despite (or could it because of?) her previous public defence of Ken Livingstone against well-founded charges of anti-Semitism. Incredibly, she retained this strategic position even after tweeting on August 13, 2018, that the 'combined machinery of state, political and mainstream elite' had 'join[ed] together' to 'make false allegations and pretended [sic] claims' of anti-Semitism. A mole with a conscience ensured that the file, which included evidence of death threats against Jewish Labour MPs, evidence which had been withheld by Claudia Webbe, ended up in the hands of the one branch of the 'combined machinery of state' empowered by law to act on what it contained. On November 2, the Metropolitan Police announced that (contrary to Webbe's claim) the file contained evidence that criminal offences had been committed, and that it had begun legal proceedings against those Labour Party members deemed responsible. A kinder politics.

On September 13, 2018, for the third time in two years, Parliament addressed itself to the virus of anti-Semitism in the Labour party. The occasion was a 90-minute debate in the House of Lords. Following the example of her Leader, absent from the proceedings was Baroness Chakrabarti, Corbyn 's appointment to the chamber as her reward for whitewashing Labour Party anti-Semitism. Extracts from some of the speeches follow.

> Lord Popot (Con): Jews have long felt safe in this country. Regardless of what was happening elsewhere in the world, here in the UK - like us - they felt at home…So when my Jewish friends say they fear for their children's safety in schools, in synagogues and universities; when they are afraid of openly identifying as Jewish, and when they start to question their future in this country, the rest of us have a duty first to listen and then to ask: How has it come to this? Why has it come to this? Unlike the anti-Semitism of the past, which was rooted in religious and racial hatred of the Jews, modern anti-Semitism is expressed through the anti-Israel and anti-Zionist movements. How many times have we heard that the problem today is not with the Jews but with Zionists? Yet the connection between anti-Zionism and anti-Semitism is not always understood. Zionism is the proposition that the Jews have a right to their own state in their ancient homeland. Anti-Zionism advocates the opposite.
>
> Present-day anti-Zionists also believe that the Jewish state is not only illegitimate but should be dismantled. They argue that they are simply standing up to colonial oppression and for human rights and that it has nothing to do with anti-Semitism. But would they also, on anti-colonial and humanitarian grounds, question the legitimacy of the USA, Pakistan, Bangladesh, Australia and most modern states in the Middle East-countries created through colonial intervention? Would they question the legality of practically the whole of Europe, the borders of which were shaped, destroyed and redrawn through centuries of war? There are many Hindu, Christian and Muslim countries across the world, but just one Jewish state. Why is Israel–this tiny strip of land the size of Wales–singled out for criticism with so much intensity and loathing?... Look up Israel on social media and you will be shocked to see the level of hate directed against Jews There are phrases such as 'Zionists controlling the media, financial institutions and foreign policy'. It is not long before you find yourself in Holocaust denial or blood-libel territory…These age-old anti-Semitic tropes have found a new audience in both the far right and the far left of the political spectrum. Whether it comes from the left or the right, make no mistake: today the word 'Zionist' is code for Jews. Jews have long suspected it. Anti-Zionists have always known it. Recent events have exposed it.

> Lord Mendelsohn (Lab): How did things get so far that recent polls have shown that nearly 40% of Jews in Britain feel so uncomfortable that they are thinking of leaving the country? Close to 90% are convinced that the leader of a main political party is an-anti-Semite, as does a staggering 39% of the general public How is it that a part of the UK no longer feels that a party which has always stood up for justice, liberty and progress is the one to which they can entrust their lives and those of their

children? They feel this so intensely that many are considering emigration?... In 1984, an anti-Zionist Jew, Steve Cohen, wrote a book calling out the far left for its anti-Semitism, called *That's Funny, You Don't Look Anti-Semitic.* I commend it to everyone It is as relevant today as it was then. Far too few of the non-Labour Party left were prepared to accept it then. But it illustrates a direct line the politics of which have entered the Labour Party en masse and are now causing this current crisis. That crisis has never been gripped since the start of Jeremy Corbyn's leadership and it has, over the summer, placed his position - his record, his views and his conduct - at the heart of it. It astounds me that it is a revelation no longer worthy of questioning that I too believe that the leader of my party, Jeremy Corbyn, has been a perpetrator of anti-Semitism.

Lord Sugar (Ex Labour, now Cross Bencher): The real question should be put to the leader of the Opposition. The Labour leader allowed the issue of alleged anti-Semitism in the Labour Party to ramble on for months. What kind of leader is it he not to take his party by the scruff of the neck, making it see sense and kill the matter off once and for all? He should terminate the obsession of the hard left with Israel and Palestine on far more pressing matters, such as Brexit and jobs [The trouble was, it was Corbyn's own obsession too] Labour eventually adopted the IHRA but, from what I hear, Mr Corbyn tried to add an 11th-hour rider [permitting members to call Israel a racist state] which resulted in hours of debate among his own people; people such as Peter Willsman who once accused Jewish 'Trump fanatics' of fabricating allegations of anti-Semitism. What a complete and utter clown; everyone knows that no Jew in the UK| in their right mind would be a Trump fanatic. Mr Corbyn allowed matters to rumble on because, frankly, he does not give two hoots about what Jews in the UK think. He simply does not care. Of some 250,000 Jews in the UK, let us say 220,000 may be eligible to vote. If it comes to an election, 220,000 votes are a drop in the ocean. We mean nothing to him.

Lord Pannick (Cross-Bencher): There have always been anti-Semites and I am afraid there always will be. But what is so alarming is that in this great country - a country that gave refuge to my great-grandparents when they were fleeing pogroms at the end of the 19th century - the leadership of one of our major political parties is incubating anti-Semitism. When the leader of the Labour Party calls representatives of Hamas his friends, despite the fact that their policy is to kill as many Jews - I emphasise Jews - as possible, when he applauds graffiti that shows the working man oppressed by Jewish bankers, when he expresses support for a vicar who suggests that Mossad was responsible for 9/11 outage, and when he contends that British citizens who are Zionists do not really understand this country, it is not surprising that his shameful conduct encourages the release into the political atmosphere of a poison that is polluting our civil society. No politician who tolerates, far less encourages, such a virus is fit for public office. [This was not a view shared by Robin Rowles, a Church of England lay preacher. On the website of the Friends of Jeremy Corbyn Facebook group, he claimed that the Jews would 'vote Corbyn out as leader so that they would lose the next elections [sic], which is what the Jews want']"

On June 20, 2019, the Lords returned to the subject of anti-Semitism. For the third time, Corbyn was in the dock, under attack yet again not only from the Tories, but from his own party. And for the second time, nothing was heard from his specialist on the topic, Baroness Chakrabarti. Lord Harris (Labour), after acknowledging the rise of Jew-hatred across continental Europe, and barely concealing, because he made little or no attempt to do so, his contempt for Corbyn, then continued:

However, I want to focus nearer to home, on this country; with a deep sense of shame, I want to talk about the party I have been a member of for almost 50 years. Labour has a proud history of combatting racism and discrimination, and of opposing fascism and anti-Semitism. It is therefore profoundly shocking for those of us brought up on that tradition to find our party now the subject of a formal investigation by the Equality and Human Rights Commission. This is nothing short of humiliating for those of us on these benches. It is causing dismay among party members outside this House, and is deeply alienating for those we might hope would vote for us, whether they are from the Jewish community or not. It undermines the Labour Party's whole ethos, the values of equality, decency and solidarity that brought so many of us here on these benches into the Labour Party in the first place. Over three months ago, I wrote as chair of the Labour Peers' group to Jeremy Corbyn, the leader of the party. That letter expressed our dismay - no, worse than that, our alarm - at the continuing failure to remove anti-Semites from our party. I have not had the courtesy of a reply. Last week, I met two women who had been verbally and physically harassed at a meeting of their local Labour Party because they were Jewish.

I wish I could say this was an isolated instance but, alas it was not. [How times had changed from before Corbyn, when just one such 'isolated instance' would have been unthinkable.] The process of dealing with complaints of anti-Semitic behaviours within the party has been slow, tortuous and frequently inconclusive. Too often individuals are suspended [and as often as not, then quietly re-instated by Corbyn's vetting team] only when their cases receive external publicity. Action was taken against one member of the party's National Executive Committee only after a second anti-Semitic rant was recorded and publicised; he had been let off with a warning after the first one. Too often those who have complained about anti-Semitism have been dismissed as apologist for, or even in the pay of, the Israeli government or Mossad, or we are told that the cases are few and far between. Any anti-Semite in the Labour Party is one too many. The party's abject failure to deal effectively with anti-Semitism over the last three years cannot be ascribed to inadequate resourcing of the complaints and compliance function in the Labour Party head office, or blamed on an inadequate or outdated process. The failure is a political one; it is a failure of leadership. Those of your Lordships who have been responsible for major organisations know that that the tone, style and ethos of such organisations are set at the top. That is what leadership means. Leadership is not about hiding behind procedure by blaming more junior officials or allowing you acolytes to dismiss legitimate complaints to spite those who disagree with your political approach. We on these benches must take the task of cleansing our party of anti-Semitism and those who condone and foster it.

Lord Pickles (Conservative) witnessed leftist anti-semites in action at his party's annual conference in Manchester in 2017:

> A young man wearing a kippah was abused by s very sell-dressed middle-class left-wing crowd the Y[id] word, the c[unt] word and the f[uck] word was used. There were references to the smoking chimneys of Auschwitz. He was spat upon and to their eternal shame, the police stood by and did nothing,

Corbyn had two defenders, but their apologias were of such a nature that he could have best done without them. The debate, officially listed on Hansard as one about anti-Semitism, was for them simply one more opportunity to put the boot into Israel. First Lord Campbell-Savours, who sought to attribute the rise of anti-Semitism to the policies of the Israeli government. He began by denying that his party was 'institutionally racist' and that while Labour did have what he called 'a problem' so did all the other parties. Having put his party's critics in their place, this zealous Corbynista homed in on the real villain of the piece - Israel:

> What is happening is that many in my party are deeply concerned and confused by Netanyahu's attitude to the settlements and calls for annexations. There is a particular problem in Labour-supporting ethnic minority communities [only one, actually, the Muslim] who join with Palestinians in feeling targeted as fellow Muslims, and a small minority of whom are clearly anti-Semitic. The treatment of the Palestinians is being used by racists across Europe to foster prejudice against Jews. It is all very frightening, *and Israel needs to reflect.* (Emphasis added)

What does he mean, '*and Israel needs to reflect*'? That the Jews of Israel have brought this hatred upon their fellow Jews in Europe? And who precisely are those supposedly 'targeting' UK Muslims? Certainly not his own party, unless we are talking about their votes, legally or otherwise, nor the various public agencies. including Labour Councils, that it is now acknowdged, either connived at or at best, ignored what one official report described as 'industrial scale' Muslim sexual 'targeting', grooming, trafficking and gang rape of non-Muslim under - age girls, nor the media, which while aware of the rape gangs scandal, decided to say nothing about it. Neither, finally, can he mean successive governments, Labour and Tory alike who, in the name of multi-culturalism and promoting 'diversity', have gone far beyond what is either reasonable or necessary in accommodating aspects of their religion and culture which are incompatible with the norms and even in some cases, as with FGM and Sharia courts, laws of British society. Since he associates this 'targeting' of Muslims with that supposedly inflicted on their co-religionists in Palestine, the only inference one can draw is that those 'targeting' British Muslims are British Jews. And so what was supposed to be a speech against anti-Semitism morphed seamlessly into an attack on Zionism and the Jews, and an apologia for the anti-Semitism of Muslims. As for his Dear Leader]:

> I do not believe that Corbyn is prejudiced. [What are we then to make of his allegations that Israel controls the BBC and US foreign policy, and influences the curricula of UK schools?] Caught in the headlamps of public outrage, he is agonising [poor Jeremy] over how to respond...People simply do not understand what Corbyn is all about. He is obsessed with human rights and sometimes he gets the nuances [!!!!] wrong.

We are asked to believe that the Leader of the Labour Party and of her Majesty's Opposition, the life-long campaigner against racism, with his two E grade A levels and an uncompleted course in 'trade union studies', cannot explain himself coherently in such a straightforward matter as anti-Semitism? It is akin to non-*dhimmi* feminist finding herself being repeatedly accused of defending rape or wife-beating. One would assume, surely, that as in all other intellectual and artistic endeavours, here too an obsession would be an aid to focus and clarity, not its complete opposite. That aside, there are no 'nuances' to human rights. You are either for them, for everybody, everywhere, or you are not. Corbyn is most definitely not. As we have seen in his highly selective attitude towards human rights, such as his support for repressive regimes in Iran, Syria, Russia, Cuba, Nicaragua and Venezuela, and movements that murder Jewish civilians, 'nuance' is in effect a euphemism for his rejection of that principle.

The other defence, for want of a better word, came from a fellow anti-Semite, Baroness Tonge. As someone who has re-cycled the accusation that an Israeli relief team harvested body organs from dead victims of the 2010 Haiti earthquake; resigned from the Liberal Democrats as a result of her involvement in an anti-Semitic scandal; as one its Patrons, also resigned from the Palestine Solidarity Campaign after associating the massacre on October 27, 2018, by a Neo-Nazi, of eleven Jews at their Pittsburgh synagogue with the polices of the Israeli government and, in 2011, accompanied Corbyn on a junket to Syria funded by Hamas-related Palestine Return, as the guest of an anti-Semitic President who, like Corbyn, has a highly nuanced approach to human right; after all this and more, not surprisingly, most of her speech was devoted to an unrestrained attack on Israel. Her defence of Corbyn replicated that of Campbell-Savours: 'He is not an anti-Semite; he is a man who feels passionately about human rights and, like me does not always express it in the right sort of way.' No wonder he is misunderstood when these 'ways' include associating with avowed Holocaust deniers and Jewish conspiracy theorists, and describing as his 'friends' and even 'brothers' terrorists who murder Jewish civilians. As one Tory Lord put succinctly: 'I understand what Jeremy Corbyn is about and I do not approve of it. It is as near to anti-Semitic as one can get'.

Sharing with most religions their Manichean view of the world as one of a struggle to the death between the forces of absolute good and absolute evil, every totalitarian movement and ideology needs an 'other', a mortal enemy which fulfils two functions; one that personifies the absolute evil and, no less essential, by conspiring to bring about the defeat of the absolute good embodied in the movement and, above all, in its beloved Leader, is the sole cause of all the set-backs and betrayals that befall the sacred cause. Such was role ascribed by Islam, the Catholic Church and the Nazis to the Jews, and by the anti-Semitic Stalin to the Jewish Trotsky. Not by co-incidence, the Corbynista 'other' is also, like those of Mohammed, the Vatican, Hitler and Stalin, Jewish, in this case principally personified by the state of Israel and its various agencies and supporters, the 'hand' behind terrorist acts blamed on Muslims and which controls ISIS, the BBC, the UK's school history syllabus, the media, the Conservative Party and US foreign policy, which suborns Jewish Labour MPs and is responsible for the 'weaponising' of a spurious anti-Semitism against the Dear Leader, that rules the state which is the seat of the world dominance of the Rothschilds and responsible for the apartheid and genocide of the Palestinians, whose operatives harvest body organs and variously exploits, invents and facilitates the Holocaust to further the aims of Zionism etc etc…Small wonder then that after enduring more than three years under a Leader who throughout his political career has bootlicked and hobnobbed with dictators, associated intimately with Stalinists, terrorists, anti-Semites, Jew-killers and Holocaust deniers, and whose cultic supporters accuse his Jewish critics of working for Israeli intelligence and threaten them with death and their female ones with rape; that on the morning of Monday, February 18, 2019, seven Labour MPs announced their resignation from the Labour Party and their formation of the centrist and pro-European Union Independent Group. One of their number, Mike Gates, MP for Ilford South, 52 years a Labour Party member, gave some of their reasons for doing so:

> I am sickened that the Labour Party is now a racist, anti-Semitic party. I am furious that the Labour leadership is complicit in facilitating Brexit which will cause great

economic political and social damage to our country. Jeremy Corbyn and those around him are on the wrong side in so many international issues from Russia to Syria to Venezuela. A Corbyn government would threaten our national security and international alliances.

The same day, a YouGov poll revealed that 34% of voters thought Corbyn was an anti-Semite, while nearly 40% of potential Labour voters said that anti-Semitism made them less likely to vote Labour. This was in vivid contrast to a majority of party members, 77% of whom when polled by YouGov in March 2108, said they believed claims of anti-Semitism had been deliberately exaggerated to undermine Corbyn's leadership.

The next day, Corbynista loyalist MP Ruth George demonstrated yet again why the break had occurred, claiming on Facebook that 'support [for the new Group] from the state of Israel' was 'possible', because one of the seven, the Jewish MP Luciana Berger, whom zealous Corbynista activists had called 'a dirty little Zionist rat', was a former Chair of the PLP Labour friends of Israel. Also the same day, it was reported that at a meeting of the Wimbledon Labour Party, Sir Duncan Michael, knighted in 2001 for services to engineering, claimed the anti-Semitism controversy had been contrived, that it was 'a storm that had started after we elected Jeremy', and had been directed at him by a 'very undemocratic elite from within our party', because Corbyn was 'kindly [sic] to Palestine and others [sic]'. 'Attacking Corbyn', he continued, had failed. He passed three democratic tests, so the Jewish community [sic] plans to attack our party'. This clear accusation that there is a collective conspiracy by the 'Jewish community' to unseat Corbyn was ruled by party officials not to be anti-Semitic.

The eighth MP to resign, the non-Jewish Joan Ryan, Chair of Labour Friends of Israel, went for Corbyn's jugular: 'Until Corbyn became its leader in September 2015, Labour did not have a problem with anti-Jewish racism…Having spent so long in the company of Holocaust deniers, anti-Semites and terrorists who murder Jews, he is simply blind to the problem.' Corbyn, she said, had surrounded himself with a 'Stalinist clique.' In reply, the party's *Corybynjugend*, Young Labour, tweeted, 'Joan Ryan gone - Palestine lives', yet more evidence Corbyn is a rallying point for all those who see Labour chiefly as vehicle for promoting their hatred of Israel and the Jews. Meanwhile, two unsavoury blasts from the past who fit this description to perfection, the Saddamista George Galloway, who claimed that accusations of Labour anti-Semitism were 'pure Goebbelsian propaganda', and Derek Liverpool redundancy notices by taxi Hatton, sought readmission to the party. Galloway was turned down, but Hatton was admitted on the Monday, only for him two days later to be suspended (surely a record) after a tweet dating from 2012 came to light saying 'Jewish people with any sense of humanity need to start speaking out publicly against the ruthless murdering being carried out by Israel.' A bemused Hatton claimed his tweet was 'innocuous', which by normal Corbynista standards, it was. But then these were not normal times. With the suspension of Williamson, no fewer than 16 Labour MPs elected in 2017 were for various reasons no longer taking the party whip, a state of affairs unprecedented in the history of Parliament. Also unprecedented in the history of major UK political parties was the announcement on March 7, 2019, by the Equality and Human Rights Commission, established the Blair administration in 2008, that it was to investigate whether the Labour Party under Corbyn's leadership had 'unlawfully discriminated against people because of their ethnicity and religious beliefs'. The only other party to have been investigated on the basis of the same charge is the neo-Nazi British National Party. Let us hope Corbyn and his Stalinist clique receive the 'Jew process' they so richly deserve.

Addendum

Labour's nomination of candidates for the UK General Election of December 12, 2019 called forth a new batch of anti-Semites in addition to those listed above. Pride of place must surely go to Maria Carroll, Corbynista candidate for Carmarthen East. Carroll was the organiser of a secret Facebook group which advised Labour Party members on how to beat charges of anti-Semitism. Amongst those so advised was Peterborough Labour Councillor Alan Bull who, in June 2015, posted a link on Facebook claiming 'the murder of six million Jews is a hoax', shared posts asserting that Labour under Tony Blair had been a 'Mossad front' and that the same Israeli intelligence agency had murdered Princess Diana. When investigated by Labour's Compliance Unit, Bull was advised by Carroll's secret group, which goes by the very official-sounding name of 'Labour Party Compliance: Suspensions, Expulsions, Rejections Co-Op [sic]'. In addition to being given legal advice, which in previous cases had led to investigators 'backing off', Bull was told the postings were 'anti-Zionist but not anti-Semitic'. The 'Co-Op' also advised former Weymouth Labour Councillor Mollie Collins who, in January 2016, posted a link on Facebook to a web site which claimed to know 'how the Holocaust was faked', and another in 2015 that the Rothschilds 'took down' the missing Malaysian MH370 airliner, and that the BBC was a 'mouthpiece for Israel'. Another 'client' of the group, Exeter party activist Sue Grant, shared a Facebook post accusing the Israeli Jews of being as bad as the Nazis and, a tad inconsistently, a link to a film which claimed the Nazi extermination camps were 'not DEATH CAMPS!

Running her close is Dan Greef, Labour's candidate for South Cambridgeshire. Greef posted on Facebook in 2013 that he 'had great day out at a concentration camp' and that he had voted for the BNP. I will repeat that, that he had voted for the BNP. In another posting, he declared, 'Bloody Israel, I sometimes want to rip it all up.' He can be seen in a photo op with a smiling Corbyn.

Next, we have Alana Bates, Labour's candidate for St Ives. She plays bass in a group called The Tribunes, which describes itself as a 'radical-political alternative rock four-piece band. One of its 'radical' songs is entitled 'From the River to the Sea', which also happens to be the anthem of the anti-Israel Boycott, Disinvestment and Sanctions campaign endorsed by her party Leader, the river being the Jordan and the sea, the Mediterranean, and in between, a Palestinian state and no Israel. A quatrain in the song, which she can be seen and heard singing on YouTube, goes like this:

> 'Justice should not have to wait
> Israel's an apartheid state
> Justice should not have to wait
> Israel is a racist state.'
> And a promo couplet goes:
> 'Ethnic cleansing and the rest [sic]
> Support BDS.'

Bates claimed the song did not call for the destruction of Israel.

Gideon Bull, Labour's candidate for Clacton, stood down after it was revealed that he had called a Jewish fellow Labour councillor in Haringey a 'Shylock'. Laura McAlpine, Labour's candidate for Harlow, stood by her chief campaigner Brett Hawksbee after a 2018 blog came to light in which he claimed that some Israelis would be happy to see a 'pogrom in Gaza and the West Bank, a Jewish final solution to the Palestine problem'. Kate Ramsden, Labour's candidate for Gordon in Scotland, stood down after it emerged she had compared Israel's policies to the actions of a child abuser. (She can be seen on a demo proudly displaying the front page of the Stalinist *Morning Star*) Zara Sultana, Labour's Corbynista candidate for Coventry South, refused to stand down when it was revealed that she had declared in a posting that she would 'celebrate' the deaths of two Prime Ministers; her own party's Tony Blair, and Israel's Benjamin Netanyahu. Jane Aitchison, Labour's candidate for Pudsey, came to her defence, saying that 'some people celebrated the death of Hitler'. Ali Malini, Labour's Momentum-backed candidate for Uxbridge, promoted 9/11 conspiracy theories on line, and used the tag '#jew' and the word 'Zionist' as forms of insult in messages. Corbynista Kate Linnegar, Labour's candidate for North Swindon, posted messages about 'Holocaust mongers' and liked a post entitled 'How Israel lobby manufactured UK Labour party's anti-Semitism crisis'. She also likened Israel to Nazi Germany, described Livingstone as a 'decent' man', and liked another post calling Israel a 'so-called country'. Salma Yaqoob, Labour's Mayoral candidate for the West Midlands, was formerly Leader and Vice-Chair of George Galloway's Muslim based-Respect, and is a Patron of the Corbynista Stop the War Coalition. She appeared on a YouTube video speaking at an anti-Israel rally where in the course of an anti-Zionist diatribe, she described Jews as pigs (*a la Koran*).

In the General Election of July 5, 1945, which under the leadership of Clement Atlee, Labour won with 47.7% of the total vote and a majority over all other parties of 145 seats, 18 Jews were newly-elected to Parliament. Of these 18, 17 were Labour and one, a communist. As I write these lines, Labour goes into the General Election of December 12, 2019, as a party in which 13 MPs and three peers, five of them Jews, have resigned in disgust at their party's failure to rid itself of its Jew-baiters, a party the overwhelming majority of British Jews not only believe is led by an anti-Semite, but one that the prospect of it winning that election has led to nearly half of Britain's Jews seriously considering leaving the UK. The findings of a survey conducted by YouGov and devised and analysed by Dr Daniel Allington of Kings College London were published by the Campaign Against Anti-Semitism on December 1, 2019. They confirm what I have argued in this work, that non-Islamic anti-Semitism has migrated from the far right to the far left, to the extent that Corbyn and his party is seen by anti-Semites and Jews alike as far and away the most hostile to the Jews, and that judged by their responses to a wide range of questions relating to the Jews, two thirds of self-identifying Corbynistas are anti-Semitic.

Consistent with these findings is the following: Among the many examples of anti-Semitism submitted by the Jewish Labour Movement to the Equalities and Human Rights Commission investigation into Labour Party anti-Semitism were:

One Jewish party member at his local branch was called a 'Tory Jew', a 'child killer, 'Zio scum' and told 'Hitler was right'.

MP Margaret Hodge received Facebook messages calling her a' Zionist Bitch' and 'Zionist remedial cancer'. Two others accused her of 'damaging Labour in the interests of Israel' and being 'under the orders of her paymaster in Israel'.

A Jewish 2017 General Election candidate was told on social media, 'You and your Zionist cult are not welcome. This is London, not Tel Aviv.'

A party member was defended by other members for saying at a branch meeting that it was 'the over-representation of Jews in the capitalist ruling class that gives the Isaeli-Zonist lobby its power.'

Likewise consistent is the Labour Party General Election video promoting its concern for the UK's religious and ethnic minorities. Two are missing from the 20 or so listed…the Jews, and Judaism.

On December 8, 2019, the *Sunday Times* published a selection of comments made by Labour Party members about the Jews. One of several with explicit genocidal intent read: 'I call for the complete annihilation and extermination of every Jew on the planet.' In the General Election that followed four days later, it was the author's party that was annihilated, recording its worst performance since the General Election of 1935.

U The Corbynistas Strike Back

In the main body of this work, I posed the question, if, after being elected Labour Leader, he was faced with the choice of remaining true to his anti-Zionist convictions and commitments, or yielding to those who favoured a slightly more politic course in the party's attitude towards Israel and the Jews, would Corbyn re-enact the role of a Prince Hal now crowned king, and say to his boon Jew-baiting and killing companions of yesteryear, 'Anti-Semites and Holocaust deniers, I know you not'? The answer came in the extraordinary events surrounding the meeting of the Labour Party National Executive Committee on September 4, 20018, convened to make a final decision on whether to adopt *in toto* the International Holocaust Remembrance Alliance definition of anti-Semitism, or retain the existing version known to be favoured by Corbyn, which excluded four of the IHRA's eleven examples of what constitutes anti-Semitism. As within Labour Party HQ, the NEC deliberated, outside, unprecedented scenes unfolded. Demonstrating Momentum storm troopers demanded a firm stand against any revision of their favoured draft, which permitted members to say that Jews are disloyal to Britain, and that Israel is a racist state that should not exist, while Jews and their supporters called for the full IRHA version. Could this really be London in the year 2018, and not Berlin in 1933? After three hours of heated debate and despite a personal intervention by Corbyn with a 500-word amendment in support of a minority who wanted to stand firm on the original draft, the overwhelmingly Corbynista NEC announced its decision. It had adopted the full IRHA definition, but with a caveat that rendered it ineffective: 'The NEC has today adopted all of the IHRA examples of anti-Semitism in addition to the IRHA which Labour adopted in 2016, alongside a statement which ensures that this will not *in any way* undermine freedom of expression on Israel or the rights of the Palestinians.' (emphasis added)

In other words, anti-Semitic party members could exercise their unlimited freedom of expression (one which their Leader would deny to critics of Islam) by continuing to liken Israel to Nazi Germany or deny its right to exist. But would it have been legitimate to question whether by the same token members would be free to advocate denying the right of Palestinians to their own state, or for that matter, as Corbyn's Syrian hosts have done, that there is even such an entity as a Palestinian people? To ask is to answer. The reference to 'freedom of expression' is therefore selective, hypocritical and a red herring. Hypocritical because beginning with their leader, the politically correct Corbynistas do not believe in free speech, the proof being that in addition to Corbyn's outspoken views on the subject at a pro-censorship rally in Trafalgar Square in 2006, nowhere in Labour's policies can there be found proposals to repeal any of the accumulation of laws dating back to the Thatcher and Blairite scum eras that criminalise making statements that could have (not necessarily have) given offence; and a red herring because, while anyone should be free to say what they like about Israel or any other subject as members of society, once they freely choose to join a party that finds some of what they advocate incompatible with its principles and rules, different rules necessarily apply. Would the current Labour Party NEC for example uphold in the name of free expression the right of members to claim that all Muslims are terrorist and rapists? It would not, and rightly so. Why, then, make an exception for insulting lies about

Israel and its Jewish inhabitants and diaspora supporters? There are, however a number of organisations that will gladly accept those who wish to vent such feelings about Israel, and provide them with every opportunity to do so. In the event, the NEC's patent subversion of the intent of the IRHA code was for Corbyn insufficient. With the full support of his Shadow Chancellor John McDonnell, who is on record as being opposed to the very existence of the state of Israel, he had submitted to the NEC at its meeting a clause which said openly what the NEC wanted to permit by a nod and a wink, namely that it should not be regarded as racist to 'describe Israel, its policies or the circumstances around its foundation as racist because of their discriminatory impact.'

These 'circumstances' that Corbyn alluded to but failed to elucidate were firstly a resolution passed by the United Nations on November 29, 1947 establishing two states west of the River Jordan in the former British Palestinian Mandate, one Jewish, the other Palestinian; thereby in fact if not in name, establishing what is now called the 'two state solution' agreed between Israel and the PLO at Oslo in 1993. The Zionists unconditionally accepted the resolution, while all the Arab states voted against and unconditionally rejected it, and then proceeded to invade Israel on the first day of its independence on May 14, 1948. Defeated by tiny Israel, Jordan and Egypt cut their losses by annexing respectively the West Bank and the Gaza Strip, *the two territories designated by the UN for the proposed Palestinian state*. So much for Arab and Muslim brotherhood. If they had instead of making war on Israel, accepted the UN resolution, there would be no 'refugee' issue today or 'occupied territories', but a predominantly Jewish and a Palestinian state living, one hopes, peacefully as neighbours, as was the UN's intention and that of the Zionist leadership. Those Palestinians, far from all, who fled Israel in 1948 did so as a result of the Arab invasion, not, as Corbyn appears to be implying, as result of any policy or actions by the Israeli authorities, who pleaded with them to stay.

So much for Corbyn's accusation that British schools do not teach the true, anti-Zionist version of Middle Eastern history. And history was also made when for the first time, the Dear Leader was rebuffed by his devotees, who in rejecting his clause, made it clear that they had gone as far as they dare in accommodating his fanatical anti-Zionism. Their leader publicly defeated, and indeed humiliated by the lukewarm, the hard-core Corbynistas of London Palestine Action struck back the next day, when posters illegally displayed on bus stops informed Londoners that 'Israel is a racist endeavour'. Corbyn's fixation on Israel had already divided the Labour Party. Now it was threating to tear apart his own faction. The same day, the *Jewish Chronicle* reported that a survey of British Jews indicated that around 40% would consider leaving the UK if Corbyn became Prime Minister. The day after that, September 6, *The Times of Israel* carried a report of a UK school teacher who had been cleared of charges of anti-Semitic conduct. He had posted on Facebook the following comments:

> Every sane human is anti-Semitic. Because you bastards have made Zionism synonymous with the mistreatment of Palestinians. Billions are anti-Semitic and proud of it...Of course we hate Jews. Israel is the evillest regime on the planet. Supported by Jews from within, and around the world...Israel should be wiped off the planet. [Could this last be a crib from Corbyn's former employer, Iran's Supreme leader Ayatollah Khamenei?]

The same day, the Corbynista counter-attack shifted up a gear with Joan Ryan, Labour MP for Enfield North and more to the point, Chair of the Labour Friends of Israel, losing a vote of confidence in her local party by 94 to 92 after being accused by what she described as an alliance of 'Trots, Stalinists and communists and asserted hard lefts' of 'smearing' Corbyn and 'fuelling and indeed inflaming' his 'trial by media'. One posting on the 'Corbyn True Socialism' website said she should be 'shoved right back in the gas ovens'. The proceedings were illegally filmed by Corbyn's former employers, Press TN, banned from the UK since 2011 for screening a forced confession by an Iranian journalist. Dismiss the thought that targeting in this way the one Labour MP who more than any other is most closely identified with the Israeli cause was a co-incidence. A party founded by the trade unions to represent the working class was being transformed into one whose prime purpose, no matter with whose support, or at what cost, was to wage war on Zionism. The next day, two more anti-Corbyn MPs lost votes of confidence. All this in less than a week.

At the Labour Party Conference in Liverpool the next month, proceedings began with the now ritual Nuremberg chanting of the Dear Leader's name and his signing a life-size cardboard cut-out of himself. As for his own responsibility for the explosion of anti-Semitism in the Labour Party after his election as its Leader, his only regret, he told reporters, was 'the stuff I've had thrown at me and the ill-informed nature of it.'

Ignoring all the human rights abuses rampant in the world, from Venezuela, Nicaragua, Turkey, Syria, Russia, Iran and the entire Islamic world to China and Myanmar, where Muslims were being interned, persecuted and murdered in their thousands, and doubtless buoyed by the knowledge that in the name of a free speech neither they nor their leader believes in, they could continue to say exactly what they liked about Israel, delegates waving Hamas Palestinian flags passed just one foreign policy resolution, condemning Israel for its response to the attempted illegal incursions into its territory by Hamas. Can this really be the UK in 2018 and not Germany in 1933? No wonder British Jews are seriously considering packing their bags.

V Nightmare in Tunisia (with apologies to Dizzy Gillespie)

On August 11, 2018, the *Daily Mail* published a story refuting Corbyn's claim that the wreath-laying ceremony he attended in Tunisia in 2014 had only been for the victims of an air attack in 1986 by Israel on a PLO camp in the same country. Photos published by the *Mail* clearly showed Corbyn praying (Islamic fashion) and standing, massive wreath in hand, in front of the graves of leading members of the PLO involved in the planning and execution of the failed Black September hostage operation at the 1972 Munich Olympics, all of whom, it is generally believed, had been hunted down and killed by Mossad. Pressed to explain what he was doing there, Corbyn told the *Independent,* using the passive, that 'a wreath was laid by some of those who attended the conference [sic] for those who were killed in Paris in 1992. I was present when it was laid. I don't think [sic] I was actually involved in it.' This proved to be a lie, contradicted by his later admission that he did lay a wreath. In a photo published by the *Mail*, he is seen actually holding the wreath as he stands, prominently, among a group in front of the graves. On August 13 during a visit to Walsall, Corbyn now confirmed that the wreath in question had been 'laid to those who were killed in Paris in 1992', that is, the Black September Munich operatives, not the victims of the Israeli air attack in 1986. On the same day, he told Channel Four News, 'I laid one wreath along with many other people'. However, in the several photos of the ceremony, only one person is carrying a wreath, Comrade Corbyn. But then on the 14th, back in London, there came a denial from Labour HQ, with a statement claiming that the PLO operativities in question were not even buried in the Tunisia cemetery, and therefore there was no ceremony for them, with or without Corbyn. If so, for whom was Corbyn praying and holding a wreath in the photos? Yet the Facebook page of Fatah, the organisation behind the Munich massacre, carries a tribute to Atel Belson, who it says 'joined in the planning of the Munich operation' and who after being killed in the Meridian Hotel in Paris in 1992, was buried in the Tunisian cemetery.

> As I was going up the stair
> I met a man who wasn't there!
> He wasn't there again today
> Oh how I wish he'd go away!

The 'conference' which Corbyn refers to in the *Independent* (which he addressed and is pictured by the *Mail* seated at the speaker's table) he described as one for 'peace'. But then everything Jeremy does is for peace, even though what he was participating in was in fact a council of war against Israel. One of Corbyn's 'friends', top Hamas commander Oussama Hamdan, outlined, quote, a 'four-point vision to fight against Israel', in the course of which he praised his movement's, quote, 'great success on the military and national levels.' 'Violence' he said, was, quote, 'magnificent' albeit to be sure in the interests of what Corbyn invariably describes as 'peace and dialogue'. Hamdan is not only, as he says, a successful military commander. He is also something of an authority on the so-called 'Jewish blood libel' in which Jews are supposed to drink the blood of Christian children.

Interviewed on Lebanon TV, he assured viewers (many of whom would not have needed reassuring) that 'it is not a figment of imagination or taken from a film. It is a fact.' The reader will recall the no less virulently anti-Semitic Hamas preacher, Sheikh Raed Salah, who recycled the same myth, and of whom Corbyn subsequently said, 'I look forward to giving you tea on the [House of Commons] terrace because you deserve it', and praised as an 'honoured citizen' with a 'voice that must be heard'. What nice people Corbyn chooses to associate with and call his friends. Also in attendance at the 'peace conference', though not at the wreath-laying, was a Tory Peer, Lord Sheikh. Questioned as to his presence at such a gathering, he said, 'there may have been [sic] Hamas. I did not meet any Hamas people. I am very careful, obviously'. Unlike Corbyn, who just can't keep way from the action.

But this also proved not to be the whole story. The Tory Peer had protested too much, because the *Daily Mail* then carried a feature which showed the 'ever careful' Lord Sheikh, again in the company of Corbyn (never one to miss out on a freebee, no matter how vile his host)) shaking hands with the blood-drenched President of Syria, Bashar al-Assad, having arrived with Corbyn and Baroness 'body parts' Tonge on the same road to Damascus as later travelled twice by the Neo-Nazi Nick Griffin. This convergence demonstrates yet again how politicians from widely-separated segments of the political spectrum can put aside their petty party squabbles when the common enemy is the J... sorry, I meant Zionism.

And still the Jeremy stories kept coming, as is the way when the press senses it has struck a particularly rich vein. The *Daily Telegraph* carried a photo of Corbyn, taken at 'his' notorious Finsbury Park mosque in February 2016, a year and half after he became Labour Leader, giving the four-finger salute of the Muslim Brotherhood, sponsor of Corbyn's 'friends' Hamas and, during the Second World War, deeply involved in collaboration with the Nazis in north Africa. Then the *Times* published a photo of Corbyn at the wreath-laying ceremony standing next to Maher el-Taher, whose Popular Front for the Liberation of Palestine one month later murdered four rabbis in a Jerusalem synagogue, hacking them to death with an axe while they prayed. All no doubt in the interests of peace and dialogue.

The 'Black September wreath' story broke after the *Mail* had dispatched a photographer to Tunisia to check out and photograph the relative positions of the two groups of graves. They are 15 yards apart, and the photos of Corbyn beyond any doubt show him standing close to and facing those of the Black September operatives. The Corbyn spin machine went into over-drive. As ever-more damning evidence of his involvement in the ceremony accumulated almost by the hour, so Corbyn's story was recalibrated accordingly. Beginning with an official Labour Party no comment, by the end of the day, Corbyn had been compelled to confess all. He had no choice. The evidence was visual, unambiguous and overwhelming. But no matter. He had his reasons. His now active role in a ceremony commemorating a Jew-killing terrorist was in the interests of... yes, 'peace': 'You cannot pursue peace by a cycle of violence. The only way you can pursue peace is by dialogue.' And, it seems, by honouring those who, far from conducting a 'dialogue' in the 'pursuit of peace', were leading members of a terrorist organisation, Fatah, dedicated to the destruction of Israel, and themselves, personally responsible for the slaughter of the entire Israeli team in Munich in 1972.

Corbyn's lies caught up with him yet again when the Howie's Corner website reproduced an article by Corbyn for the British Communist Party's *Morning Star* dated October 5, 2014, with the headline, *Palestine United*, and subtitled: 'Unity was in evidence during a major meeting [sic] in Tunisia, writes Jeremy Corbyn'. The fifth paragraph of Corbyn's article related that after 'wreaths were laid on the graves of those who died on that day [that of the Israel air attack] and *on the graves of others [sic] killed by Mossad agents in Paris in 1991*, we [n.b.] moved on to the poignant statue in the main avenue of the coastal town of Ben Arous.' (emphasis added) Three years later, in an interview on Sky TV, Corbyn contradicted this account, which proved to be the true one, claiming he had only attended the ceremony commemorating those killed in the Israeli air attack. How easily lies trip off his tongue.

Rounding off what had been a lively week for Corbyn came a report in the Jewish online *Forward* that in his last appearance on Press TV in August 2012, Corbyn had described Hamas terrorists released in a prisoner swap with Israel, who had been convicted of killing seven Jews in Jerusalem in 2003, as his 'brothers', a step up from just being his 'friends'. For Corbynista loyalists, as on all previous occasions when their Dear Leader's anti-Semitism had been exposed, there could be only one possible explanation for these latest revelations. Union chief Len McCluskey could be relied upon to provide it. Disingenuously claiming he was 'at a loss to understand the motives of the leadership of the Jewish community', he then proceeded to specify what they in fact were. He accused those Labour MPs who had spoken out against anti-Semitism of being involved in a conspiracy 'embracing capitalism, the free market and the alliance with Trump's America'. It reads just like the *Protocols*, as did another union chief's explanation of why the Labour Party was being wracked by accusation of anti-Semitism. Speaking at a Palestine Solidarity Campaign event at the 2018 Trades Union Congress, far leftist Mark Serwolka, General Secretary of the Public and Commercial Service Union claimed that accusations of Labour Party anti-Semitism had been invented to divert attention from the killing of 'dozens of Palestinians...unarmed innocent civilians' by Israeli troops. Having assured his audience that he was 'not a conspiracy theorist', though had he told them that he was, that would not have worried them in the least, he then went on to prove the exact opposite:

> ...but I'll tell you what - one of the best forms of trying to hide from [sic] the atrocities that you are committing [the Hamas-instigated clashes on the Israel border were screened on TV and fully reported in all the media.... How else did Serwolka know about them?] is to go one the offensive and to create a story that does not actually exist [sic] for people on this platform, the trade union movement or, I have to say, for the Leader of the Labour Party.

How does Serwolka know the minds of Britain's 6.23 million trade unionists, some of whom will be Jews, and others will be like Unite's Assistant General Secretary, Steve Turner, who reject the Left's double standards on human rights. Addressing an anti-racist event at the same TUC, Turner acknowdged that because of the left's refusal to speak the truth about Islamic terrorism, traditional working-class Labour supporters were looking elsewhere for those that did. They were saying,

> You're protesting austerity. I see you advertising the protest against Trump. I see you protesting against the Israeli government, against this and that. But where were you

protesting when someone used a car as a weapon to mow people down on Waterloo Bridge? Where was the left? Where were we? Where were we when the Manchester bomb went off? [like Shamima Begum, the would-be returnee Jihadi bride from the Islamic State, State, Corbyn was blaming it on British foreign policy.] Where were we on Westminster Bridge? Where was the left? Where's the left criticisms of the state of Iran for instance, who whipped trade unionists for taking strike action, who denies women human rights, who runs an obscene regime. [Surely a thrust at Corbyn] Saudi Arabia, where we welcome the head of state of Saudi Arabia to the UK. Did we protest? No, we didn't. Why not? What's so sensitive in the left about having discussions about these issues that leaves a vacuum that the right, for no reasons, are only too willing to fill.... They are filling a vacuum that in part in being left by us. We need to talk to those people who are attracted by it and stop talking to ourselves. And we don't do it. And it's uncomfortable.

That says it all. To return to Corbyn's escapade in Tunisia, which epitomises what Turner was objecting to. What on earth was a Labour MP, soon to be elected Leader of the Labour Party, doing in Tunisia on an undeclared freebee, hobnobbing with terrorists and praying and laying a wreath at the graves of Jew-killers, and when caught out, resorting to torturous evasions of the truth more fitting for a career criminal caught in the act on CCTV than the Leader of Her Majesty's Opposition?

W Stalin's Final Solution of the Zionist Question

'The Jews are a spying nation.' J. V Stalin, December 1, 1952

'I knew all too well my father's obsession with "Zionist" plots around every corner.' Stalin's daughter, Svetlana Allilueva.

The accusation that the first loyalty of the Jews is to Israel, which we have seen has featured prominently in the Corbynista abuse heaped on Jewish Labour MPs, (one being referred to by Corbyn as 'the Honourable member for Tel Aviv') and excluded, one suspects for that very reason, from the Labour Party's first definition, later amended, of anti-Semitism, has an intriguing pedigree, antedating by decades the actual creation of the Jewish state in 1948. For all his alleged (by Ken Livingstone) pro-Zionism, Hitler asserts this claim in his *Mein Kampf*, in the same passage cited with approval by Corbyn *confidante* Elleanne Green on her secret *Palestine Live* website ninety years later. Following the Second World War, it resurfaced, this time on the left, with Stalin's state-sponsored pogrom of Soviet Jewry who, after the creation of the state of Israel, were accused, under the rubric of being 'cosmopolitans without kith and kin', of 'subservience towards things foreign', in effect, to be guilty of treason to the Soviet State.

Even during the war, anti-Semitism in the USSR was never far below the surface. There was no official acknowledgment, either then or up to end of the Soviet Union in 1991, of the extermination by Nazi death squads of more than two million Jews in territories occupied by the German invaders, or that 142,000 Jews died fighting in the Soviet armed forces against the *Wehrmacht*. As Jewish Red Army men battled the Nazis in the outskirts of Moscow, Stalin told a Polish delegation in the Kremlin on December 3, 1941, that 'Jews are bad soldiers'. A diary found on a dead German soldier which chronicled his role in the Holocaust, when published in *Pravda*, was doctored to erase all references to his killing of Jews. In 1944, the Tsarist *'numerus clausus'* was revived to limit Jewish students to 10% of the total in higher education …a Stalinist version of 'affirmative action', on behalf of Russian dunces. As Lenin used to say, 'if you meet a clever Russian, the chances are he's a Jew, an opinion evidently not shared by Stalin, who claimed in 1945 that it was Russians who were especially endowed with 'a clear mind'. These were straws in the wind of the hurricane to come. Stalin's anti-Zionist campaign only really began in earnest in 1948, the year of the birth of the Jewish state. As one of Stalin's top intelligence operatives, Pavel Sudoplatov, later related in his memoirs, *Special Tasks*, 'Israel's victory in its war of independence greatly strengthened awareness among Soviet Jews of their cultural identity. Israel presented a new magnet for emigration. The anti-cosmopolitan campaign quickly turned anti-Semitic. Now the battle was against "rootless cosmopolitanism", meaning Jews who had Western ties or ideas and might not hold the Soviet Union first in their hearts.'

To generate the pogrom atmosphere conducive to the planned onslaught on Soviet Jewry, Stalin's secret police put into circulation rumours that in any civilised country would have been dismissed as the ravings of lunatics. One that went the rounds was that of a tunnel being dug by actors from the soon to be closed Jewish Theatre to the Kremlin a full two kilometres away, with the intention of blowing it up, together with all its occupants. Jews were purged from leading positions in the armed forces and party apparatus. Previously overrepresented by a sizable margin, by 1951, there was only one Jew out of more than 1,000 party secretaries. There then followed the arrest, torture and on August 12, 1952, execution as US and Israeli spies of all the members of the Soviet Jewish Anti-Fascist Committee. Miron Vorsi, a cousin of the moving spirit of the Committee, the world-famous actor Solomon Mikheols, whom the secret police had murdered on Stalin's orders in 1948, was made to confess that he was the leader of a 'terrorist group' consisting of Jewish doctors and 'a number of Jewish nationalists', which, 'by means of criminal methods of treatment', would attempt to 'destroy the health of leading [government] workers'. According to Vorsi's scripted confession, his cousin was the mastermind of a classic *Protocols* international Jewish conspiracy:

> Mikheols said that for us Jews, it was necessary at all times to maintain key positions in science, art, literature and in pedagogical institutions, and only then would we be able to unite the uncoordinated strengths and preserve the unity of the Jewish population…In this way, it was already clear to me that the name Jewish Ant-fascist Committee was only a smokescreen under which Jewish nationalists realised their anti-Soviet, nationalist goals; and this fact that the Committee directed to the USA various kinds of information about the Soviet Union, directly shows that he essentially served the interests of Zionists circles in the USA.

This and other similarly scripted confessions, followed by the purging of all leading Soviet institutions of Jews, climaxed in late 1952 in the fabrication and then 'unmasking' of the so-called 'Doctors Plot', in which the cream of the Soviet medical profession, many of them Jews, were accused of planning to poison the entire Soviet party and state leadership on behalf of their US and Zionist paymasters. It was not only Jewish doctors who were targeted. There was an *in-camera* trial of Jewish poets and their associates, 13 of whom were convicted of treason and shot on August 12, 1952. Jewish managers of the Stalin (sic) car plant were charged with Zionism after sending a telegram to the world-famous (but soon to be murdered on Stalin's instructions) Jewish actor Solomon Mikheols celebrating the founding of Israel. Learning of this case, Stalin response was to say to Khrushchev, 'the good workers at the factor should be given clubs so they can beat the hell out of those Jews at the end of the working day.' More executions of Jews followed. Sensing that not all his immediate entourage shared his conviction that all Jews were born traitors, he lectured a meeting of the Party's ruling Presidium of December 1, 1952, on the threat they posed to the security of the Soviet Union: 'Every Jew-nationalist is an agent of American intelligence'. Amongst Stalin's inner circle, it was an open secret that he enjoyed 'anti-Semitic anecdotes', on one occasion being convulsed with mirth when his bodyguard viciously parodied the last moments of the executed Jewish Bolshevik leader Zinoviev, on his knees crying out: 'Hear Israel, our God is the only God'.

Stalin's war on the Jews was accompanied by the erasing, *a la* Third Reich, of all visible manifestations of Jewish contributions to world and Soviet culture. Even the portrait of Mendelsohn at the Moscow Conservatoire was removed, just as for the same reason his statue in Leipzig had been demolished by the Nazis a decade previously. But the portrait of the anti-Semite Wagner, Hitler's favourite composer, remained on display. As was the intention, public manifestations of anti-Semitism boiled over as Jews were assaulted in the street, while men accused of being Jewish had to prove their gentile credentials by exposing their genitals. Male party members divorced their Jewish wives, who were then either imprisoned or executed, to be quickly replaced by new gentile partners provided by the party. Molotov, Stalin's most devoted stalwart, duly obeyed an order by his master to divorce his Jewish wife, Polina, who was charged with 'links with Zionism' and 'betrayal of the motherland' and despatched to a labour camp in Kazakhstan.

On Stalin's specific instructions - 'beat, beat and beat again' - Jews accused of treason were tortured remorselessly until they signed pre-fabricated confessions, one of which declared: 'enveloped by nationalist poison, we agreed to the blind conviction that Jews, by virtue of their alleged special qualities of intelligence, were called by history itself to rule the world'… a fair precis of the version of the myth of the world Jewish conspiracy first expounded in 1905 by a Russian priest, Sergei Nilus, in the *Protocols of the Learned Elders of Zion*, a text that has found favour right across political and religious spectra from Nazis to Corbynistas and from Muslims to Christians.

Some of the 'confessions' extracted under torture were even absurd by Soviet standards, at least in one case deliberately so, as related by Sudoplatov. Colonel Naum Schwartzman, before his turn came, had himself been employed to edit the confessions of previous victims. When interrogated for his role in a Jewish plot to overthrow the Soviet regime, in order to prove himself insane, he elaborated on the main charge by confessing to have had 'homosexual relations with [the now arrested previous police chief] Abakumov, his son, and the British Ambassador'. Piling on the lunacy, 'he invented unbelievable stories, like being inspired in his terrorist activities by drinking Zionist soup [sic] by his Jewish aunt, or sleeping with his step daughter, or having homosexual relations with his son.' Just when he seemed to have succeeded in convincing his interrogators that he was indeed mad, Stalin intervened. 'That scoundrel is playing for time. No need for any [medical] expert. Arrest the whole group immediately.' Then 'Stalin ordered the arrest of all Jewish colonels and generals in the Ministry of Security. A total of some fifty senor officers and generals were arrested'. Stalin instructed his investigators to 'put them in handcuffs and beat them until they confess'. One surviving victim of Stalin's pogrom recalled many years later the atmosphere of menace of that time:

> Events were mounting to a climax. Horrible news was passed by word of mouth. The MGB [successor to the NKVD, and predecessor of the KGB] had disclosed a Jewish conspiracy at the Moscow automobile plant. Mass arrests had been made, wreaking havoc on the leading engineering and technical personnel…More Jewish plots were unearthed - in the Moscow metro and elsewhere…the medical world was not simply deflated, it was crushed…everyone who was still at large expected arrest that night…Every physician was regarded as a potential murderer. I shall never forget the face of my laboratory assistant, distorted with fury and hatred, as she hissed through clenched teeth 'Damn intellectuals [code for too clever by half Jews R.B.], they all deserve to be cudgelled.' Meetings were held at all factories and offices, some organised, some spontaneous, and almost all openly anti-Semitic. Speakers would vehemently demand that all criminals should be put to a terrible death. Many went so far as to offer their services in carrying out the actual executions.

On December 1, 1952, Stalin addressed the Soviets Union's ruling body, the Presidium of the Party Central Committee: His subject was the political meaning of the Doctors' Plot:

> Every Jew-nationalist [i.e., Zionist] is an agent of America intelligence. The Jew-nationalists think the USA has saved their nation, where they hope may become rich men, bourgeois. They consider themselves obligated to the Americans. Among the doctors are many Jewish nationalists.

On January 13, 1953, *Pravda* [Russian for 'truth'] carried an article drafted by Stalin:

> The unmasking of the band of doctor poisoners dealt a shattering blow to the American-English instigators of war...the whole world can now see once again the true face of the slave-master cannibals from the USA and England ...The bosses of the USA and their English "junior partners" know that success in ruling another country cannot be achieved by peaceful means. Feverishly preparing for a new world war, they urgently sent their spies into the rear of the USSR and into the countries of the People's Democracies [a reference to the series of show trials of alleged agents of Tito] they attempted to implement what had been destroyed among the Hitlerites - to create in the USSR their own subversive 'fifth column.'

Given the context, the message was unambiguous. The capitalist West's Jewish 'fifth column' was resuming Hitler's lost war against the Soviet Union. 58 prominent Jewish intellectuals, writers and artists, fearful with good reason that their turn could be next, sent a letter to *Pravda* denouncing Israel with a venom and themes that are common coin today among leftist anti-Semites. Zionists were' the helpers of the Jewish rich' and Israel 'a kingdom [sic] of exploiters...a kingdom of profit for a small bunch of rich people...a vanguard outpost of war provocateures...a bridgehead for USA aggression...a war is necessary to Jewish millionaires and billionaires' because 'it is for them a source of great profit.' 'Jewish industrialists and bank magnates' were conspiring to 'unleash a new world war', while Israel itself was ruled by 'a small bunch of rich people' who served the interests of 'Jewish and American capitalism'. What the Zionists claimed to be the homeland of the Jews was in reality the 'homeland of America', a weapon for the development of a new war...a bridgehead for US aggression against the Soviet Union and all peace-loving peoples'. The Soviet people were expected to believe, and assuredly many did, that Israel, one of the smallest countries in the world, with less than one hundredth of the Soviet Union's population and a miniscule and poorly equipped army comprised then as now largely of reservists, was threatening with annihilation a country covering one sixth of the land surface of the globe, possessed of nuclear weapons and the largest army in the world. Even so, it was 'impossible to be an authentic fighter for the affairs of peace and freedom of nations without conducting a struggle against Jewish billionaires and millionaires and their Zionist agents'.

Self-abasement could sink no lower. Yet the letter was not published. Instead *Pravda* carried a story on the 'plot' with the headline, 'Murderers in White Gowns'. Clearly more was required than just attacks on Israel. Denunciations of fellow Jews were now the order of the day.

Once armed with the 'evidence', extracted by torture, that all Jews were either potential or actual traitors, in the last weeks before his death, Stalin set in motion his Bolshevik version of the final solution of the Jewish question. With all existing slave camps already bursting at the seams, he ordered the construction of four new camps in the East to house the first *tranche* of arrested Jews. Convoys of cattle trucks to transport them, Nazi style, to their early deaths were being assembled in the railway marshalling yards of Moscow and other major Soviet cities, while the Soviet press whipped the public into a frenzy of hatred against 'rootless cosmopolitans without kith and kin'…not a difficult task given Russia's appalling history of pogroms and Jew-baiting. As the campaign escalated, so 'spontaneous' mass meetings, no more so than the pogrom set in motion by the Nazis on the 'Night of the Crystals' of November 9-10, 1938, voted unanimously for the planned deportation of Soviet Jewry to the Far East. After interrogating one of the suspects in the 'Doctor's Plot', security chief Mikhail Ryumin included in his report the following comment: 'In Moscow there live more than a million and a half Jews. They have seized the medical posts, the legal profession, the union of composers and the union of writers. I'm not even speaking of the trade networks. Meanwhile, of these Jews, only a handful are useful to us. All the rest are potential enemies of the state' In his biography of the Soviet composer Dimitri Shostakovich, who despite being himself at this time out of favour for failing to conform to the dictates of 'socialist realism', courageously set Jewish texts to music, Ian MacDonald set the scene for this return to medieval barbarism:

> In January 1953, two ominous themes appeared in the Soviet press: a campaign for 'greater vigilance', accompanied by slogans contending that there was no nobler act than denouncing your best friend; and what amounted to a call for a national pogrom of the Jews. The key element was the so called Doctors' Plot', announced by an article in *Pravda* by Stalin himself. According to this, the Jews were literally poisoning Soviet society: Jewish doctors by injecting their patients with carcinogens or syphilis, Jewish pharmacists by serving their customers with pills made of dried fleas.

In their *The Unknown Stalin*, the historians Zhores and Roy Medvedev tell the same story:

> These entirely absurd accusations provided the basis for an unrestrained and increasingly hysterical crusade in the press, particularly in *Pravda*. Every day the major papers published some item or other exposing subversive activity in the USSR by American, British, Israeli and various other secret services. The evident signs of an incipient pogrom aroused anxiety throughout the world.

Sergo Beria, the son of Stalin's last but two police chiefs, provides an insider's view of the then prevailing mood:

> The entire intelligentsia took part in that shameless campaign against the Jews, whatever they may say nowadays…I say nothing of the masses, who had no need for encouragement. We came close to pogroms. The hounds were unleashed. I saw apparently normal people transformed into mad dogs. The most fantastic stories were spread. The Jews were said to have deliberately inoculated children with diphtheria, to have poisoned vaccines, to have killed new-born babies in the maternity hospitals so as to annihilate the Russian people and so on ['Baby killers']. The human vileness and baseness described so complacently by Dostoyevsky burst forth in every journal. This was the first time that I experienced evil in a purely unreasoned form. It was

unbearable, worse than the Nazis' murders. An entire people was being conditioned to kill.

Stalin died on March 5, 1953, so the last act of his 'final solution', the Kremlin's version of Hitler's Crystal Night pogrom of November 1938, was never staged, but if it had been, this is what it would have entailed. True to the tradition of the autocracy's Black Hundreds, with their war cry of 'Beat the Yids and Save Russia', not the state, but the outraged popular masses were to have delivered the *coup de grace*. Gallows to hang those prominent Jews convicted of treason, 'beasts in human form' as *Pravda* Koranically described them, were to be erected in Red Square, but before the sentences could be carried out, gangs would exact lynch law justice, while other mobs, pure-blooded sons of holy mother Russia, would hunt down and kill Jews at addresses provided by the security police. Supposedly to rescue them from the same fate, the remainder would be deported in cattle trucks to the Soviet far east, there to be left to waste away. These facts have been established by a number of writers on Stalin's last years, most notably the Russian investigative journalist Arkady Vaksberg in his *Stalin Against the Jews*, who had access to previously unseen documents relevant to the case and security officials involved in the operation.

This story has a sequel. In October 1956, the British Communist Party, rocked by revelations of Stalin's crimes in Khrushchev's 'secret speech' earlier that year, sent a delegation to the USSR to investigate the fate of Soviet Jewry under the idol of Corbyn's election strategist and, taking turns with Corbyn, Chairman of the Sharia left Stop the War Coalition. What they learned horrified even these case-hardened loyalists:

> Jewish writers, artists and intellectuals had been tortured and physically destroyed [why not say it, *murdered?*], particularly during the period 1948-52, and this included the whole of the Jewish Anti-fascist Committee...deliberate efforts had been made to repress all expressions of Jewish culture...the Moscow Jewish State Theatre had been shut down, Jewish papers had ceased publication and the Yiddish Publishing House had been closed...The *Soviet Encyclopaedia*, which in its 1932 edition devoted about 160 columns to the Jews, reduced this in the 1952 edition to four columns. The biographies of many eminent Jews have been removed. Marx was no longer referred to as a Jew...the years 1948-52 were known [among Soviet Jews] as 'The Black Years', the period during which many Jews were dismissed and charged with treason and executed...Those arrested and charged in secret were prominent political or cultural workers. Shortly after his arrest, the immediate relatives of the arrested man would be deported to some distant place and there set to work, and often at low wages. Finally, the husband would be shot, perhaps after torture to try to force him to confess or to incriminate others.

One decade on, little had changed. A symphony by Shostakovich was banned because it commemorated the massacre in September 1941 of 40,000 Jews by the Nazis at the Babi Yar ravine outside Kiev. Two decades on, when, on the hundredth anniversary of Lenin's birth in 1870, western scholars referred to the Bolshevik leader's maternal Jewish ancestry, the Kremlin responded with outraged denials, as if Lenin had been falsely accused of some unspeakable crime. Five years later, taken to task by the Israeli delegation for having engineered the United Nations resolution defining Zionism as a racist ideology, Soviet diplomat Yakov Malik retorted, 'do not poke you long [sic] noses into our Soviet garden. Anyone. who pokes his long [sic] nose into out garden will find himself without a nose. You had better carve this on your long [sic] noses, Zionists.'

Five decades and more on, anti-Semitism was and is still the norm amongst Russia's post-Bolshevik political class. More than 150 anti-Semitic newspapers pump out the same bile as *Pravda* did in Stalin's day. Very much in the spirit and letter of Hamas, the manifesto of the anti-Semitic *Pamyat* (memory) movement demands a 'German-Russian alliance [sic…again!] that will finally put an end to Zionism', for which read, the Jews. In December 1998, Chairman of the Russia Duma Security Committee Viktor Ilyukhin accused President Yeltsin's 'Jewish entourage' of committing 'genocide' against the Russian people. (at least it made a change from the Palestinians), while Duma member General Albert Makashov blamed 'the Yids' for Russia's problems and threatened to 'send them to the other world': 'We will remain anti-Semites, and we must triumph.'

Seven decades on, Jewish migration from Europe to Israel has reached record levels, 55,000 from France alone since 2000, fuelled not only by the traditional anti-Semitism of the far right, but the vicious anti-Zionism of the left, and most of all, by the illegal mass immigration of anti-Semitic Muslims orchestrated by German Chancellor Angel Merkel. For the first time since the expulsion of the Jews from England by Edward the First in 1290, British Jews have joined this modern exodus, fearful of the consequences of a government headed by a politician who has counted genocidal Islamic terrorists among his friends, and has presided over a party many of whose members have quite openly and with impunity paraded their hatred of the Jews.

On the very day I wrote these lines, *The Times of Israel* of November 27, 2018, carried a report of a CNN survey of attitudes towards the Jews in seven European countries; the UK, Germany, Poland, Hungary, Austria, France and Sweden, which revealed the following: 20% of Europeans think the Jews have 'too much influence world-wide'; 28% too much influence in business and finance, 25% in wars and conflicts and 32% that they exploit the Holocaust 'to advance their position or achieve certain goals', (predictably, in Poland this was 50%). 34% said they either knew nothing or 'very little' about the Holocaust while 31% said that commemorating the Holocaust distracts attention from other atrocities around the world... all allegations featured prominently on Corbynista websites. On December 11, the same journal reported that the European Union Agency for Fundamental Rights had conducted a survey of Jewish experiences of anti-Semitic attitudes and incidents in 12 EU member states, again including the UK. A third of the 16,395 Jews interviewed said they were considering emigrating as result of a recent sudden increase of hostility towards, them, which included physical attacks as well as verbal abuse, mainly, so it would seem, by Muslim migrants. A final thought. With something like a quarter of Europeans subscribing to a belief in a Jewish world conspiracy, is it any wonder that European Jews feel *persona non grata*?

Addendum: Stalin's Pogrom in Prague

Given Stalin's obsession with the 'Jewish Question', it was only to expected that when Yugoslavia's break from the Kremlin in the spring of 1948 precipitated a series of show trails of suspected Titoites in Eastern Europe, the role of Zionism should be placed at the centre of this imaged conspiracy. Nowhere was this more so than in the trial of prominent Czech state and party leaders conducted in Prague in November 1952. On his way to total power, Stalin had made short work of his leading Jewish opponents in the Soviet communist party...Trotsky, Zinoviev, Kamenev and Radek. Now it was the turn of the Czechoslovaks. Of the 14 defendants, no fewer than 11 were listed in the indictment as Jews, and of these 11, eight were sentenced to death and executed after confessing to and being convicted of treason (all these verdicts were posthumously quashed in 1963). According to the indictment prepared by a team of Soviet advisers known affectionately by their Czech subordinates as 'The Teachers', the accused had organised a 'Trotskyist, Titoist, Zionist, bourgeois nationalist' anti-state conspiracy on behalf of US imperialism. Just as in the 'Doctors Plot', a special role in this mythical operation had been allotted by the prosecutors to Jews, hence their blatant preponderance in the dock. The remaining three non-Jews were obviously included to counter the inevitable accusations from anti-Stalinists that the trial was in reality a judicial pogrom.

The pre-scripted testimonies of the accused Jews made it all too clear that the central theme of the trial was indeed anti-Semitism, disguised not always, and when it, was, thinly, as anti-Zionism. One defendant typically confessed that 'in trade negotiations with capitalist states I concluded commercial agreements that were favourable to capitalist, above all Jewish merchants, but disadvantageous to the Republic'. The highest profile defendant, former Vice Premier and party General Secretary Rudolf Slansky, confessed to 'placing Zionists [that is, Jews] in important posts' because, as Slansky explained:

> Zionists [again, obviously, Jews] were conducting activity aimed at the liquidation of the popular [sic] democratic [sic] regime in Czechoslovakia. These Zionists [Jews] in turn placed other Zionists [Jews] in various posts in the administration and economic offices and through them I was linked with the Zionist [Jewish] organisations. The significance of this lay in the fact that Zionist [Jewish] organisations in Czechoslovakia were in turn connected with similar Zionist [Jewish] organisations in the capitalist countries. The whole world-wide [sic] Zionist [Jewish] movement was in in fact led by the imperialists, in particular the US imperialists, by means of US Zionists. [i.e., the 'Israel lobby' Corbyn and his cohorts assert still control US foreign policy 60 years and more later.]

There we have it…. the world Zionist, i.e., Jewish conspiracy. Once again, it could be the *Protocols*…or for that matter, just as easily, a Corbynista website. As Slansky was the star defendant at the trial, establishing his intrinsic 'Jewishness' - treachery - was integral to the prosecution's case against not only him but his Jewish co-conspirators:

> The witness Oskar Langer, an international Zionist agent, also confirmed that Slansky was the patron all Jewish bourgeois nationalists, and that he had expressly said that it was necessary to fill important positions in economic, political and public life with

Zionists and Jewish bourgeois nationalists....His closest associates from the days of his youth were Germnder, Frejka and Sling [Jewish co-defendants] – all Zionist agents.' [Then came the punch line, line, dictated by the trial's architect in the Kremlin]: '*Slansky cannot deny his Jewish bourgeois character.* (emphasis added)

The message was clear: Ignore the *pro forma* 'bourgeois. Conspirator-in-chief Slansky was a Jew and Jews have a certain 'character', which impels them to treason. Just as Stalin said, they were a' spying nation'.

Another aspect of the trial that also features prominently in today's anti-Zionism was the prosecution's associating defendants with both the Nazis and Israel. Two defendants had been inmates of Nazi concentration camps, so this provided the prosecution with the opportunity to accuse them of collaboration with their captors. One admitted that he had 'cooperated with the Nazis and been promoted to foreman. As a Nazi henchman, he had helped the Nazis maintain order by torturing his fellow prisoners and by stealing their food'. Although not a Jew, he nevertheless confessed to his involvement in Zionist plottings. Asked why, he replied:

> Slansky, who led the conspiratorial Centre, is himself a Jewish bourgeois nationalist, and a whole number of other members of our centre are also Jewish bourgeois nationalists or even directly Zionists [why the distinction?] The main reason for our [the non-Jewish conspirators'] support, however, was that the Zionists were the most reliable imperialist agency, which gave Slansky the best opportunity for maintaining his link with the imperialist West.

Another former Nazi camp inmate, this time Jewish, was described by the prosecution as 'a bourgeois [i.e., Jewish] nationalist, son of a rich merchant and collaborator of the Nazis', and as if this was not enough to ensure his conviction, he also admitted taking part in 'actions which were organised by the Anglo-US imperialists and their agents in Israel aimed at enriching the Jewish bourgeoisie.' The purpose becomes clear when one notices the linkage between Nazis, the 'Jewish bourgeoisie' and the state of Israel. Asked why he had betrayed his country, the same defendant replied that it was because 'I am a Jewish bourgeois nationalist'...in other words, a Zionist, whose only loyalty is to Israel. Where have we heard that before?

Several other themes will be familiar to those who follow the fortunes of Corbynism. As already noted, the prosecution made great play with the role played by 'Jewish billionaires' in the mythical conspiracies concocted by Stalin's 'teachers. Among those listed were the banking scions of Morgenthau, Baruch, Mandel and...yes. that favourite Corbynista whipping-boy, the Rothschilds. Then there was Slansky's confession that in order to protect his Jewish co-conspirators from exposure, to use the current Corbynista term, he 'weaponised' anti-Semitism:

> I deliberately shielded them by abusing the campaign against so-called [sic!!!] anti-Semitism. By proposing that a big campaign be waged against anti-Semitism, by magnifying the danger of anti-Semitism and by proposing various measures against anti-Semitism – such as the writing of articles, the publication of pamphlets, the holding of lectures - I criminally [sic] prevented the waging of a campaign against Zionism...I deliberately shielded Zionists by publicly speaking out against the people who pointed to the hostile activities of Zionists and by describing these peoples as anti-Semites...

No, this is not Corbyn's Labour Party, *circa* 2019, but Stalinist Prague, 1952. The absurdity and inconsistencies of the charges and the scripted confessions echoed those of Stalin's pre-war frame up trials and purges, as result of which, millions were either executed or dispatched to an early death in remote slave camps, accused, in every case falsely, of having conspired with the Soviet Union's enemies to subvert Bolshevik, or to be more precise, Stalin's rule. For example, in the first of the three Moscow trials, defendants confessed to having begun their collaboration with the Gestapo no later than the Autumn of 1932, several months before Hitler's appointment as German Chancellor on January 30, 1933 and a full half a year before the Gestapo was founded by Herman Goering on April 26, 1933.

The relentless anti-Semitism pervading the Prague trial can be measured by the frequency of the use of certain key words and terms as reported by the far from complete public record of its proceedings. Among these were: Israel: 43; Cosmopolitan: 7; Zionist or Zionism: 124; Jew: 60. Nothing daunted, the British Communist Party loyally rebutted accusations that the Prague trial was in any way anti-Semitic. The party's *Daily Worker* (predecessor to Corbyn's favourite newspaper the *Morning Star*), in insisting that 'Gentiles and Jews stood in the dock together accused of hostile acts against the people's democracy of Czechoslovakia', understandably neglected to add that while Jews, due to the ravages of the Holocaust, comprised only a minuscule fraction of the country's population, they outnumbered the 'gentiles' in the dock by a ratio of 11 to 3. (A precedent for this device had been set in the first of the three Moscow trials of Bolshevik leaders of 1936, 37 and 38. In the dock were no fewer than ten Jews out of out of a total of 16 defendants, all accused of and convicted and executed for collaborating with Nazi Germany…as Jewish communists do. And in August 1939, Stalin did just that, signing his pact with Hitler to partition Poland between them.)

Defiantly, the *Worker* continued: 'The [unspecified] number of Jews involved was decided by the number who participated in the anti-State conspiracy and not by the authorities at all.'. But the truth was, and there surely must have been even loyal Stalinists who secretly entertained the thought, as some certainly did over Moscow show trials (Stalin admitted to his cronies, strictly off the record, that all their accused were innocent) there was no 'anti-State conspiracy' and therefore those Jews selected for trial had been chosen by the 'authorities', not on the basis of an equally non-existent guilt, but for no other reason than they were Jews.

X Money for Old Rope

Of Livingstone's famous *bon mot*, which later served as title of his autobiography, 'if voting changed anything, they'd ban it', if anyone can be said to have devoted their adult life to chasing after votes, it is Livingstone, from Lambeth Council and Leader of the GLC to MP for Brent East and finally, his crowning glory, in the footsteps of Dick Wittington, to be elected, if only twice, Mayor of London. Simultaneously with this electoral ascent, Livingstone very publicly associated himself with regimes and movements that have indeed banned, rigged or opposed free elections precisely because they could bring about political change...Cuba, Syria, Nicaragua, Venezuela, Iran, the PLO, Hamas, Hezbollah...Then there is Livingstone the anti-racist, a profile he is no doubt able to reconcile with his praise for Yusuf al- Qaradawi as 'one of the leading progressive voices in the Islamic world', a cleric who on Al-Jazeera TV, praised Hitler for visiting Allah's just punishment on six million Jews, and his own insistence that 'anti-Semitism is not the same thing as racism', and in the same vein, that 'it's not anti-Semitic to hate the Jews of Israel,' presumably, all six million of them. Finally, we have gay rights. Throughout his political career, and especially when Leader of the GLC and then Mayor of London, Livingstone acquired a deserved reputation as a promotor of the rights of sexual minorities...at least in the UK. But here too, he was able to reconcile this stance with taking up paid employment as a host for Iran's Press TV, owned by a regime that puts gays, including children, to death by throwing them from tall buildings and publicly hanging them from cranes.

I have previously referred to the unmatched capacity of Livingstone to adjust his stated opinions to what he regards as the needs and milieu of the moment. His old Sharia comrade Jeremy Corbyn is a no less seasoned exponent of the same tactic. They make a fine duo. This is nowhere better demonstrated in their duplicitous attitude towards the death penalty. First, Livingstone: 'I have been opposed to the death penalty throughout my life.' (Sangat Television, March 25, 2012, reporting a speech by Livingstone to a Sikh protest in London against the death sentence imposed by an Indian court on Balwant Singh Rajoana, convicted of the murder of former chief Minister Beant Singh.) But then: 'One of the things [Venezuelan President] Chavez did when he came to power, he didn't kill all the oligarchs...he allowed them to live, to carry on.' (Livingstone on Talk Radio, as reported by *HuffPost*, August 3, 2017.) One cannot but notice a certain discrepancy between these two statements.

Now Corbyn, with reference to the US killing of Osama Bin Laden, the architect of 9/11: 'I profoundly disagree with the death penalty for anybody.' (Iranian Press TV, August 2011) Next, a letter from Corbyn to Prime Minister David Cameron concerning the impending execution by the Saudis of Ali al Nimr on charges of anti-government activities, as reported on the BBC News website, September 26, 2015: 'As you may be aware, Ali has exhausted all his appeals, and could be executed any day - in a particularly horrific manner, which involves beheading and the public display or "crucifixion" of the body.' Now consider this. In that same year, 2015, Iran carried out 997 recorded executions without any public protest that I have been able to trace from its former Press TV employee, Jeremy Corbyn, or for that matter fellow employee Ken Livingstone. According to Amnesty

International, Iran, with a population of 80 million, is responsible for half of all executions carried out *in the entire world*, with its population of 7.5 billion. The evidence is indisputable that Corbyn and others with double standards identical to his own have been prepared to take up highly-paid employment with a regime drenched in the blood of tens of thousands of victims of its theocratic tyranny.

There was a repeat performance of Corbyn's selective opposition to the death penalty when in October 2018, the Saudi *Washington Post* journalist Kamal Jashoggi was reported missing, presumed murdered (which proved to be the case) after visiting the Saudi Consulate in Istanbul, Corbyn's Shadow Foreign Secretary Emily Thornberry criticised the Conservative government's response as being 'too little, too late'. In Iran that same week, despite a campaign by Amnesty International to save her from the gallows, Zeinab Sekaanvand Lokran, accused of killing her brute of a husband, for which if true, she deserved a medal, in the name of Allah the Merciful and the Compassionate was hanged in Iran three days after giving birth to her baby, which died. But there were no protests, either too little or too late, from Ms. Thornberry. Why the difference? Could it be because Corbyn regards the Sunni Saudis as fair game, being allegedly allies of the west in the 'war on terror'; that is, though nobody who is supposed to be waging it dares say so, on Jihadi Islam, while he has proved himself a true friend of both Jihadi Islam and the hangmen of Shi'a Iran?

Let me repeat: The evidence is incontestable that together with Saddam useful idiot George Galloway from the far left, and from the far right James Thring, Kevin Barrett, and Manuel Ochsenrieter, editor of the Neo-Nazi monthly *Zuerst*!, Corbyn and Livingstone have taken paid employment from the Iranian Press TV Chanel, in Livingstone's case as a programme presenter. Launched in January 2007, Press TV is funded by the Iranian state, and is a division of Islamic Republic of Iran Broadcasting, the sole legal broadcaster in Iran. Its head is appointed by the Iranian theocracy's Supreme Leader, currently Ayatollah Ali Khamenei. Normal payment per appearance on a programme is around £500. However, as recorded in the House of Commons Register of MPs interests, Corbyn received ten times that amount for four hours work. Concerning Livingstone, the following excerpted item appeared in the London *Evening Standard* on January 11, 2009:

> Ken Livingstone was today accused of 'showing a lack of judgment' after it emerged, he had been paid thousands of pounds to front a programme on Iranian state television. He has presented seven shows on the English-language Press TV channel, three of which have been broadcast since he became Labour's London mayoral candidate in September. The government-funded international news network was launched by Iranian President Mahmoud Ahmadinejad in 2007 and is run by the Islamic Republic of Iran Broadcasting. The broadcaster was investigated last year by Ofcom after interviewing a Jailed *Newsweek* journalist who was allegedly under extreme duress at the time in an interrogation room.
>
> Mr Livingstone's appearances, reviewing books on the channel, put him at odds with senior Labour figures including party leader Ed Miliband, who called last month for the release of an Iranian woman sentenced to death by stoning after her alleged confession to her part in her husband's murder was shown on Press TV. [Remember, Livingstone has been 'opposed to the death penalty' throughout his life.]
>
> Human rights campaigners condemned the channel after its report on Sakineh Mohammadi Ashtiani. In a report on its website, Press TV said she had accompanied a film crew to her house 'to recount details of the killing of her husband at the crime

scene.' Activists, however, claim her apparent confession was coerced. The criticism of Mr Livingstone follows calls for his expulsion from Labour in October, after he campaigned openly alongside Tower Hamlets mayor Lutfur Rahman, who had been deselected by the party over alleged links to [Islamic] extremism. [Rahman was subsequently found by a judge to have been corruptly elected and was removed from office.]
Mr Livingstone first appeared on Press TV in March 2009, standing in for former Respect MP George Galloway. Previous presenters on the channel have been paid about £500 per show. [Now we get an insight into Livingstone's literary tastes] Books reviewed on his Epilogue programme include *Zionist Israel and Apartheid South Africa*, *The Invention of the Jewish People* [sic], and *Israel and The Clash of Civilisations: Iraq, Iran, And The Plan To Remake The Middle East*.

As we have seen, like Livingstone's, Corbyn's opposition to the death penalty is highly selective. Let us first note that its repeated prescribing in both the *Koran* and Sharia law are overwhelmingly for acts and totally for thoughts that in the civilised world are nowhere treated as crimes, and that the Saudi, Ali al Nimr, had been condemned and was to be punished in accordance with the very same laws that are used to the same effect in Iran. Yet as we have seen, despite voicing his opposition to the death penalty on of all TV channels, one controlled by the state with the highest per capita execution rate in the world, Corbyn wants, in fact, demands, that everybody should show their respect for the faith that has gifted to the world the system of justice which had led to the sentence passed on Ali al Nimr. And why did Corbyn feel free to protest about this particular execution, while he has remained silent in his acquiescence of thousands of others carried out in Iran, including the more than two thousand that took place while he was in the employ of the executioners?

Here we have again a case of 'the enemy of my friend is also my enemy'. As I have already said, it is because those who were about to carry it out in Saudi Arabia were, officially at least, allies of the West, principally the USA, in the so-called war on terror, which Corbyn vehemently opposes, and because Saudi Arabia, in its role as the leader of the Sunni branch of Islam, is the sworn enemy of Corbyn's former employers, the Ayatollahs of Iran, rulers of the Islamic world's premier Shi'a power, fighting proxy wars against the Saudis in Yemen and on behalf of President Assad of Syria, and dedicated to 'wiping Israel off the map'. Finally, Iran is the patron and quartermaster of Corbyn's 'friends' Hezbollah.

Though he lied on BBC TV about the dates of his appearances, Corbyn has himself acknowledged receiving the sum the sum of £20,000 in payment for his services to Press TV, earned between 2009 and 2012. The normal payment is £500 a session, but since Corbyn made only four appearances, he was, for some unspecified reason, being paid £5,000 a time, *ten times the normal rate*. Why? Meanwhile, back in Iran, his theocratic pimps were conducting executions at a rate of sometimes more than three a day, including, in that term of service, three of alleged homosexuals. A kinder politics.

Now some facts about the use of the death penalty by the former employers of Livingstone and Corbyn. The offences for which it can be imposed by Iran's legal code, which just like Saudi Arabia's, is based exclusively on Sharia and Koranic law, number more than 300, and include: 'Waging war on God' (a catch-all rubric covering umpteen crimes, including those of violence, political opposition, trade unionism, and corruption); Adultery, Rape, Sodomy, Apostasy from Islam,

Blasphemy and Consumption of Alcohol. *These offences are almost identical to those that carry the death penalty in Saudi Arabia*. Since the Ayatollahs came to power in 1979, all executions have by law to be in public, and take place at 4.00 AM, just before the call to morning prayer. Virgin females sentenced to death are raped by guards just before being hanged, because the law says that virgins cannot be executed. Most of those executed are hanged, frequently simultaneously in batches, either from cranes or gallows, the rest, are either stoned or shot by firing squad, except for homosexuals, who are thrown from cliff tops or tall buildings, as prescribed by Sharia law.

As to the frequency of executions, with its highest rate per capita, Iran has not only led Saudi Arabia but the entire world in this abominable competition, without so much as a murmur of protest from either Livingstone or Corbyn as I have been able to locate. As we have seen, just in one year, 1988, more than 30,000 political prisoners were executed on the basis of a *fatwah* issued by Ayatollah Khomeini. According to an Amnesty International report, in 2015, the former employers of Livingstone, Galloway and Corbyn carried out 694 executions in the six months between January 1 and July 15; that is, at a rate of more than three per *day*. In just one day, September 25, 2017, the Ayatollahs hanged 42 alleged 'terrorists', a blanket term that covers a multitude of alleged sins, and on December 14, 24, another 38. But as Livingstone says, he has been opposed to capital punishment throughout his life. Or, to be more precise, just like Corbyn, only when it suits him.

The same double standards were in evidence again when, following the adoption of the Sharia law punishment of death by stoning by the Sultan of Brunei, in March 2019, Corbyn's Shadow Foreign Secretary Emily Thornberry, joined protesters outside the Brunei-owned Dorchester hotel in London. This is the same Thornberry who when called upon to condemn the killing of demonstrators by the Iranian police, refused to do so because it was not clear who was wearing 'the white hats'.

Corbyn excelled even his own exemplary standards of selective outrage when on April 7, 2018, he called on western leaders to condemn the killing of demonstrating Gaza civilians by the Israel Defence Force. (As we have seen, he has failed to do so when the killed civilians have been Israeli Jews, Venezuelans, Syrians, Nicaraguans or Iranians.) As with the conflict of 2014, which began when Hamas kidnaped and killed three Jewish youths, and tunnelled and fired rockets into Israeli territory, the IDF response was also claimed on this occasion to be 'disproportionate', since neither the security of Israel nor its civilian lives were endangered by the Hamas demonstrations while they remained within the border of the Gaza Strip. However, urged on by armed Hamas fighters, who as revealed by a Hamas official, accounted for the bulk of those killed by the IDF, some demonstrators, who included numerous children, a mother with her baby and an invalid in a wheelchair, did succeed in breaking into Israeli territory.

As in the Hamas acts of aggression which began the conflict of 2014, this so-called 'March of Return' was also an act of aggression, as defined by the United Nations General Assembly at its session of 1974, specifically, in Article 1, 'the use of armed force against the sovereignty, territorial integrity or political independence of another state'. To qualify as such, acts of aggression need not be carried by regular armies. Article 3, clause G is quite specific on this point, which covers exactly the incursions into Israel launched by Hamas in April and May 2018: 'The sending by or on behalf of a state armed bands, groups, irregulars, which carry out acts of armed force against another state of such gravity as amount to those listed above, or its substantial involvement therein.'

Hamas claimed that these acts of aggression were in fact simply the asserting the right of the Palestinians of the Gaza Strip to return to their homeland in Israel. Even if this lie were true, and their claimed right to abandon Gaza and settle in Israel justified, these acts are nevertheless described by the UN resolution to be ones of aggression: Article 5, clause 1: 'No consideration of whatever nature, whether political, economic, military or otherwise, may serve as justification for aggression.' As in 2014, Israel exercised the right to defend itself from such acts of aggression, as defined by the UN Charter, Article 51: 'Nothing in the present Charter shall impair the right of individual or collective self-defence if an armed attack occurs against a member of the United Nations, until the Security Council has taken measures necessary to maintain international peace and security.'

Yet once again, Israel, not Hamas, found itself pilloried for exercising its legal right to self-defence, while the cannon fodder manipulated by Hamas were glorified as the heroic victims of Zionist brutality, even though it was obviously the intention of Hamas, virtually friendless in the Arab world (but not in the leadership of the Labour Party), to provide their movement with martyrs and by so doing, win the sympathy of the ever-gullible west. Hamas's tactic of exploiting what, in the Middle East of today, is an entirely bogus refugee problem, has a long tradition in the Arab world.

The real purpose is not 'return', but invasion and conquest, which as far back as 1949, in the aftermath of Israel's defeat of five invading Arab armies, the Egyptian Foreign Minister made very clear when he declared that 'in demanding the return of the refugees to Palestine [by which was meant, the new state of Israel] the Arabs mean their return as masters of their country and not as slaves'. One of the stated aims of BDS is 'promoting the rights of Palestinian refugees to return to their homes and properties.' Only those Palestinians who left Israel as result the Arab invasion of 1948 can be classed as genuine 'refugees', and of those, the vast majority are no longer alive. Their descendants are not refugees, and therefore their 'home" is not Israel, any more than Russia was the 'home' of the American descendants of the Jews who fled the pogroms of the tsars. The fact that they are treated in most cases as outcasts in the Arab countries where they live is not the responsibility of Israel but of the regimes that refuse, for political reasons, to accord them rights of full citizens in the land of their birth. 'Open Borders? For Muslims arriving in Europe? Of course. But not for Palestinians in the Middle East…unless that is the borders are Israel's.

As in the Hamas-Israel of conflict of 2014, the question that should have been asked, but never was by those whose job it was to do so was: what would any government have done, faced with repeated illegal, violent incursions into its territory by tens of thousands of people, some of them armed, and all reared from early childhood to hate and want to kill its citizens, who were attempting to enforce by an invasion a spurious right to settle in a land they were not born in? All those who genuinely support the goal of a two-state solution to the Palestinian issue have a both a right and duty to protest at any killings by Israeli forces if they can be proved to have been caused by the deliberate targeting of unarmed civilians. I will be one of them. But neither Hamas, which stands for the destruction of Israel and the extermination of all its Jews and, by staging a series of violent provocations at the Israeli border, seeks to bring about the killing of Palestinian civilians that could then, with the always compliant assistance of the world's media, be blamed on the

Israelis, nor Corbyn, who has never condemned the cynical tactics and genocidal goal of Hamas, have any moral right to do so. In Corbyn's case, his hypocrisy over the Gaza killings was compounded by his refusal, when challenged, to condemn the killing of over a hundred Venezuelan demonstrators protesting against the corrupt, bankrupt and election-rigging regime of President Maduro in the summer of 2017, the thousands of civilians killed by the regime of President Assad in Syria with the massive military assistance of President Putin of Russia, including chemical weapons, and the tens of thousands murdered by his former paymasters, the Ayatollahs of Iran. The day after Corbyn issued his statement condemning the deaths at the Gaza border, at least 90 civilians were killed in a chemical attack on the town of Douma near Damascus. A report in the *Guardian* said 'videos showed bodies of dead children and other family members, some foaming at the mouth.' On this occasion, from Corbyn's duplicitous mouth, not a word, proving that sometimes silence can indeed speak louder than words.

Then there are for Corbyn the not inconsequential matters of the atrocious persecution of the Rohingya Muslims of Myanmar (formerly Burma) by the country's Buddhist military, and the incarceration in concentration camps in Sin-Kiang province of more than a million of their co-religionists by China, neither of which has been the occasion for protests outside the London embassies of the regimes responsible for these outrages, because although the victims in both cases are followers of what the Sharia left describes as the religion of the oppressed, their oppressors were not Jews or the USA, but governments hostile to the West. One must always see the 'bigger picture'. Applying the same tactical device, 'the enemy of my enemy is my friend' (with respect to Hamas and Hezbollah, literally so) led Corbyn to support the Kremlin-backed Eastern Orthodox Serbs in their 'ethnic cleansing' campaigns *against* the (belatedly) western-backed Muslims of Bosnia and Kosovo in the early 1990s. Finally, and perhaps most despicable of all, is this self-proclaimed champion of the Palestinian's silence concerning the crimes against their compatriots by the Ba'athist Assad regime which, unlike Israel, neither recognises the existence of a Palestinian people nor its right to nationhood. The website of the Action Group for Palestinians of Syria meticulously documents the persecution of Palestinians by the regime that played host to both Corbyn and the neo-Nazi Nick Griffin. As of May 2019, the number just of those killed stood at 3,946. A kinder politics.

Y Who Dunnit?

According to *Al-Hayat Al-Jadida,* the official daily of the Palestine Authority, the *Charlie Hebdo* massacre of January 7, 2015, was not the work of the Islamic State. It was 'a carefully executed and fully controlled plan', with the aim of creating in France a climate of terror 'to encourage Jews to emigrate to Israel.' 'The entire operation had been 'planned by Mossad'. The 'crime committed against *Charlie Hebdo* and the Jewish story in Paris were not co-incidences. We believe that there is a conspiracy at work, for the US and Israeli intelligence services are the greatest experts at exploiting the organisations that emerge in areas of conflict.'

This is a none too subtle variation on the theme which proliferates on Corbynista websites that the Islamic State has been created and controlled by Mosad. The same journal, dated March 24, 2016, offers an identical explanation for the Brussels massacres two days previously, in the form of a question:

> ...why did the crimes and terrorist massacres of ISIS in France and Brussels coincide with the European Union's first attempt to free itself from the Israeli extortion and of the Jewish persecution complex in Europe, and coincide with European members of parliament's support of the Palestinian right to statehood?

PA Security Forces Spokesman Adnan Al-Damiri repeated and expanded on the question, only to then seemingly struggle for an answer:

> How come Europe has turned into the scene of terror attacks and murder of innocent civilians after the expansion of European boycotts of products made in Israeli settlements? Is it possible that the timing of the targeting of Europe by ISIS and its offshoots is innocent [?] and a coincidence? And why specifically Europe now that the European popular and official support for Palestine is growing? Help me understand and answer.

The answer they were seeking, but not expecting, came in the form of a sermon at Jerusalem's Al-Aqsa mosque on July, 2016, by Sheikh Al-Abu Ahmad:

> Any action carried out, and explosion, and any operation in which a Muslim is killed in Muslim countries, American stands behind it. together with the infidel West that hates Islam and Muslims. It doesn't matter who takes responsibility for the crime and who announces it. We will never believe it. We will never believe it because America is the one that blows up Muslims and is the one that kills Muslims.

Z Orwell on the Corbynistas *(mutatis mutandis)*

There is a minority of intellectual pacifists whose real though unadmitted motive appears to be hatred of western democracy and admiration for totalitarianism. Pacifist propaganda usually boils down to saying that one side is as bad as the other, but if one looks closely at the writings of young intellectual pacifists, one finds that they do not by any means express impartial disapproval, but are directed almost entirely against Britain and the United States [today also, and mainly, Israel]. Moreover, they do not as a rule condemn violence as such, but only violence used in the defence of the Western countries. The Russians, unlike the British, are not blamed for defending themselves [in this instance, attacking others] by warlike means. (*Notes on Nationalism*, October 1945)

Left-wing intellectuals do not think of themselves as nationalist, because as a rule they transfer their loyalty to some foreign country, such as the USSR, [today, Cuba, Venezuela, Iran, Syria, Nicaragua, Russia, North Korea, ISIS, Hamas and Hezbollah] or indulge it in a merely negative form, in hatred of their own country and its rulers...[O]ne expects governments and newspapers to tell lies. What is worse, to me, is the contempt even of intellectuals for objective truth so long as their own brand of nationalism is being boosted. The most intelligent people seem capable of holding schizophrenic beliefs [viz., Corbyn and Livingstone], or disregarding plain facts, of evading serious questions with debating-society repartees, or swallowing baseless rumours [Zionist plots against the Dear Leader] and of looking on indifferently while history is falsified. [viz., re the Holocaust] (*Partisan Review*, Winter 1944)

You are wrong also in thinking that I dislike wholehearted pacifism, though I do think it is mistaken. What I object to is the circumspect kind of pacifism which denounces one kind of violence while endorsing or avoiding mention of another. [viz., of Jihadis, Assad and Putin] (Letter to the pacifist John Middleton Murry, July 21, 1944)

...a message to English left-wing journalists and intellectuals generally: 'Do remember that dishonesty and cowardice have to be paid for. Don't imagine that for years on end you can make yourself the boot-licking propagandists of the Soviet regime, or any other regime, [viz., Cuba, Venezuela, Iran etc] and then suddenly return to mental decency. Once a whore, always a whore.' (*Tribune*, September 1, 1944)

At present we are all but openly applying the double standard of morality. With one side of our mouth we cry out that mass deportations, concentration camps, forced labour and suppression of freedom of speech are appalling crimes, while with the other we proclaim that those things are perfectly all right if done by the USSR or its satellite states [today, Cuba, Venezuela, Iran etc], and where necessary we make this plausible by doctoring the news and cutting out unpleasant facts. (Unpublished letter to *Tribune* June 1945)

Lightning Source UK Ltd.
Milton Keynes UK
UKHW011953230120
357517UK00001B/143